THE TANK CORPS BOOK OF HONOUR

George R.I.
1919.

[Photo by W. & D. Downey, Ltd.

HIS MAJESTY THE KING,
Colonel-in-Chief, the Tank Corps.

PREFACE

THIS book is in no sense a history of the Tank Corps. It aims merely at recording the deeds which won distinction for the Corps in a form which may be more permanent than a passing reference in the Press.

The arrangement of these deeds by battles will enable the reader to trace the growth of the new arm from its first appearance in the field to that final victory in which it bore so proud a part ; extracts from despatches and orders have been added for the same reason. The messages of compliment may well be regarded as among the highest honours of a Corps whose first object is ' to save the lives of the infantry with whom they work.'

Printed and bound by Antony Rowe Ltd, Eastbourne

CONTENTS

ILLUSTRATIONS

THE
TANK CORPS BOOK OF HONOUR

CHAPTER I

EXTRACTS FROM THE DESPATCHES OF FIELD-MARSHAL SIR DOUGLAS HAIG, K.T., G.C.B., G.C.V.O., K.C.I.E., COMMANDER-IN-CHIEF, BRITISH ARMIES IN FRANCE

THE SOMME, 1916

THE general plan of the combined Allied attack which was opened on September 15 was to pivot on the high ground south of the Ancre and north of the Albert-Bapaume road, while the Fourth Army devoted its whole effort to the rearmost of the enemy's original systems of defence between Morval and Le Sars. Should our success in this direction warrant it, I made arrangements to enable me to extend the left of the attack to embrace the villages of Martinpuich and Courcelette. As soon as our advance on this front had reached the Morval line, the time would have arrived to bring forward my left across the Thiepval Ridge. Meanwhile, on my right our Allies arranged to continue the line of advance in close co-operation with me from the Somme to the slopes above Combles ; but directing their main effort northwards against the villages of Rancourt and Frégicourt, so as to complete the isolation of Combles and open the way for their attack upon Sailly-Saillisel.

A methodical bombardment was commenced at 6 A.M.

on September 12 and was continued steadily and uninterruptedly till the moment of attack.

At 6.20 A.M. on September 15 the infantry assault commenced, and at the same moment the bombardment became intense. Our new heavily armoured cars—known as ' Tanks —now brought into action for the first time, successfully co-operated with the infantry, and coming as a surprise to the enemy rank and file gave valuable help in breaking down their resistance.

The advance met with immediate success on almost the whole of the front attacked. At 8.40 A.M. tanks were seen to be entering Flers, followed by large numbers of troops. Fighting continued in Flers for some time, but by 10 A.M. our troops had reached the north side of the village, and by midday had occupied the enemy's trenches for some distance beyond.

.　　.　　.　　.　　.　　.　　.

The result of the fighting of September 15 and following days was a gain more considerable than any which had attended our arms in the course of a single operation since the commencement of the offensive. In the course of one day's fighting we had broken through two of the enemy's main defensive systems and had advanced on a front of over six miles to an average depth of a mile. In the course of this advance we had taken three large villages, each powerfully organised for prolonged resistance. Two of these villages had been carried by assault with short preparation in the course of a few hours' fighting. All this had been accomplished with a small number of casualties in comparison with the troops employed.

.　　.　　.　　.　　.　　.　　.

The total number of prisoners taken by us in these operations since their commencement on the evening of September 14 amounted at this date to over 4,000, including 127 officers.

On the same day Gueudecourt was carried, after the protecting trench to the west had been captured in a somewhat interesting fashion. In the early morning a tank started down the portion of the trench held by the enemy from the north-west, firing its machine-guns and followed by bombers. The enemy could not escape, as we held the trench at the southern end. At the same time an aeroplane flew down the length of the trench, also firing a machine-gun at the enemy holding it. These then waved white handkerchiefs in token of surrender, and when this was reported by the aeroplane the infantry accepted the surrender of the garrison. By 8.30 A.M. the whole trench had been cleared, great numbers of the enemy had been killed, and 8 officers and 362 other ranks made prisoners. Our total casualties amounted to five.

.   .   .   .

At 12.25 P.M. on September 26, before the enemy had been given time to recover from the blow struck by the Fourth Army, a general attack was launched against Thiepval and the Thiepval Ridge. The objective consisted of the whole of the high ground still remaining in enemy hands, extending over a front of some 3,000 yards north and east of Thiepval, and including, in addition to that fortress, the Zollern Redoubt, the Stuff Redoubt, and the Schwaben Redoubt, with the connecting lines of trenches.

The attack was a brilliant success. On the right our troops reached the system of enemy trenches which formed their objectives without great difficulty. In Thiepval and the strong works to the north of it the enemy's resistance was more desperate. Three waves of our attacking troops carried the outer defences of Mouquet Farm, and, pushing on, entered Zollern Redoubt, which they stormed and consolidated. In the strong point formed by the buildings of the farm itself, the enemy garrison, securely posted in deep cellars, held out until 6 P.M., when their last defences were forced by a working party of a Pioneer Battalion acting on its own initiative.

On the left of the attack fierce fighting, in which tanks again gave valuable assistance to our troops, continued in Thiepval during that day and the following night, but by 8.30 A.M. on September 27 the whole of the village of Thiepval was in our hands.

Some 2,300 prisoners were taken in the course of the fighting on the Thiepval Ridge on these and the subsequent days, bringing the total number of prisoners taken in the battle area in the operations of September 14–30 to nearly 10,000. In the same period we had captured 27 guns, over 200 machine-guns, and some 40 trench mortars.

.   .   .   .

The part played by the new armoured cars—known as ' Tanks '—in some of the later fights has been brought to notice by me already in my daily reports. These cars proved of great value on various occasions, and the personnel in charge of them performed many deeds of remarkable valour.

THE SPRING CAMPAIGN, 1917

THE ARRAS BATTLE

Tanks, which on many occasions since their first use in September of last year had done excellent service, were attached to each corps for the assault and again did admirable work in co-operation with our infantry. Their assistance was particularly valuable in the capture of hostile strong points, such as Telegraph Hill and the Harp.

MONCHY-LE-PREUX

Heavy fighting, in which cavalry again took part, continued south of the Scarpe on April 11. Two English infantry brigades, acting in co-operation with cavalry, attacked Monchy-le-Preux at 5 A.M., and, after hard fighting, in which tanks arrived at an opportune moment, carried the position. As our men pushed through the village, the enemy was seen retreating eastwards over the open, and many casualties were inflicted on him by our machine-guns. By 9 A.M. the whole of Monchy-le-Preux was in our hands, with a number of prisoners.

4

EXTRACTS FROM DESPATCHES

THE SUMMER CAMPAIGN, 1917

THE MESSINES BATTLE

June 7

North-east of Messines our infantry were held up for a time by machine-gun fire from a strong point known as Fanny's Farm, but the arrival of a tank enabled our progress to be resumed.

During the night our infantry consolidated the captured positions ; while tanks patrolled the ground east of the Oosttaverne Line, and in the early morning of June 8 assisted in the repulse of an enemy counter-attack up the Wambeke Valley.

Our progress on the right of the battle front made the enemy's positions between the Lys River and St. Yves very dangerous, and he now gradually began to evacuate them. Our patrols kept close touch with the enemy, and by the evening of June 14 the whole of the old German front and support lines north of the Lys had passed into our possession.

THE THIRD BATTLE OF YPRES

After the capture of the German first-line system our troops on this part of our front had advanced in time with the divisions on their left against their second objectives. Great opposition was at once encountered in front of two small woods known as Inverness Copse and Glencorse Wood.

At Inverness Copse and Glencorse Wood a few tanks succeeded in reaching the fighting line, in spite of exceedingly bad ground, and came into action with our infantry.

Over 6,100 prisoners, including 133 officers, were captured by us in this battle. In addition to our gains in prisoners and ground we also captured some twenty-five guns.

Although throughout the major part of the Ypres Battle, and especially in its latter stages, the condition of the ground made the use of tanks difficult or impossible, yet whenever circumstances were in any way favourable, and even when they were not, very gallant and valuable work has been accomplished by tank commanders and crews on a great number of occasions. Long before the conclusion of the Flanders offensive these new instruments had proved their worth and amply justified the labour, material and personnel diverted to their construction and development.

In the course of the various operations in which tanks have taken part, at Arras, Messines and Ypres, officers and men have given frequent examples of high and self-sacrificing courage as well as strong esprit-de-corps.

THE OPERATIONS ON THE CAMBRAI FRONT DURING NOVEMBER AND DECEMBER, 1917

The Cambrai front had been selected as the most suitable for the surprise operation in contemplation. The ground there was, on the whole, favourable for the employment of tanks, which were to play an important part in the enterprise, and facilities existed for the concealment of the necessary preparations for the attack.

The general plan of attack was to dispense with previous artillery preparation, and to depend instead on tanks to smash through the enemy's wire, of which there was a great quantity protecting his trenches.

As soon as the advance of the tanks and infantry, working in close co-operation, began, the artillery was to assist with counter-battery and barrage work ; but no previous registration of guns for this purpose could be permitted, as it would rouse the enemy's suspicions.

The infantry, tanks, and artillery thus working in combination were to endeavour to break through all the enemy's lines of defence on the first day.

THE ENEMY'S DEFENCES

The German defences on this front had been greatly improved and extended since the opening of our offensive in April, and comprised three main systems of resistance. The first of these three trench systems, constituting part of the Hindenburg Line proper, ran in a general north-westerly direction for a distance of six miles from the Canal de l'Escaut at Banteux to Havrincourt. There it turned abruptly north along the line of the Canal du Nord for a distance of four miles to Mœuvres, thus forming a pronounced salient in the German front.

In advance of the Hindenburg Line the enemy had constructed a series of strong forward positions, including La Vacquerie and the north-eastern corner of Havrincourt Wood. Behind it, and at distances respectively varying from a little less to rather more than a mile, and from three and a half to four and a half miles lay the second and third main German systems, known as the Hindenburg Reserve Line, and the Beaurevoir, Masnières, Marquion Lines.

THE ATTACK

All necessary preparations were completed in time and with a secrecy reflecting the greatest credit on all concerned. At 6.20 A.M. on November 20, without any previous artillery bombardment, tanks and infantry attacked on a front of about six miles from east of Gonnelieu to the Canal du Nord opposite Hermies.

At the same hour, demonstrations with gas, smoke and artillery took place on practically the whole of the British front south of the Scarpe, and subsidiary attacks were launched east of Epehy and between Bullecourt and Fontaine-lez-Croisilles.

On the principal front of attack, the tanks moved forward in advance of the infantry, crushing down the enemy's wire and forming great lanes through which our infantry could pass. Protected by smoke barrages from the view of the enemy's artillery, they rolled on across the German trenches, smashing up the enemy's machine-guns and driving his infantry to ground. Close behind our tanks our own infantry followed and, while the tanks patrolled the line of hostile trenches, cleared the German infantry from their dug-outs and shelters.

In this way, both the main system of the Hindenburg Line and its outer defences were rapidly overrun, and tanks and infantry proceeded in accordance with programme to the attack upon the Hindenburg Reserve Line.

In this advance, the 12th (Eastern) Division, moving along the Bonavis Ridge on the right of our attack, encountered obstinate resistance at Lateau Wood, which sheltered a number of German batteries. Fierce fighting, in which infantry and tank crews displayed the greatest gallantry, continued throughout the morning at this point, and ended in the capture of the position, together with the enemy's guns.

Meanwhile the 20th (Light) Division, which had captured La Vacquerie at the opening of its attack, stormed the powerful defences of Welsh Ridge. The 6th Division carried the village of Ribecourt, after sharp fighting among the streets and houses, while the 62nd (West Riding) Division (T.) stormed Havrincourt, where also parties of the enemy held out for a time.

The capture of these two villages secured the flanks of the 51st (Highland) Division (T.), advancing on the left centre of our attack up the slopes of Flesquieres Hill against the German trench lines on the southern side of Flesquieres village. Here very heavy fighting took place. The stout brick wall skirting the Château grounds opposed a formidable obstacle to our advance, while German machine-guns swept the approaches. A number of tanks were knocked out by direct hits from German field batteries in position beyond the crest of the hill. None the less, with the exception of the village itself, our second objectives in this area were gained before midday.

Many of the hits upon our tanks at Flesquieres were obtained by a German artillery officer who, remaining alone at his battery, served a field gun single-handed until killed at his gun. The great bravery of this officer aroused the admiration of all ranks.

On the left of our attack west of the Canal du Nord, the 36th (Ulster) Division captured a German strong point on the spoil bank of the canal and pushed northwards in touch with the West Riding troops, who, as the first stage in a most gallant and remarkably successful advance, had

EXTRACTS FROM DESPATCHES

taken Havrincourt. By 10.30 A.M. the general advance beyond the Hindenburg Reserve Line to our final objectives had begun, and cavalry were moving up behind our infantry.

In this period of the attack, tanks and British infantry battalions of the 29th Division entered Masnières and captured Marcoing and Neuf Wood, securing the passages of the Canal de l'Escaut at both villages.

At Marcoing the tanks arrived at the moment when a party of the enemy were in the act of running out an electrical connection to blow up one of the bridges. This party was fired on by a tank and the bridge secured intact. At Masnières, however, the retreating enemy succeeded in destroying partially the bridge carrying the main road. In consequence the first tank which endeavoured to cross at this point fell through the bridge, completing its destruction.

The advance of a number of our guns had been unavoidably delayed in the sunken roads which served this part of the battlefield, and though our infantry continued their progress beyond Masnières, without the assistance of tanks and artillery, they were not able at first to clear the enemy entirely from the northern portion of the village.

West of Flesquieres the 62nd Division, operating northwards from Havrincourt, made important progress. Having carried the Hindenburg Reserve Line north of that village, it rapidly continued its attack and captured Graincourt, where two anti-tank guns were destroyed by the tanks accompanying our infantry. Before nightfall infantry and cavalry had entered Anneux, though the enemy's resistance in this village does not appear to have been entirely overcome until the following morning.

This attack of the 62nd (West Riding) Division constitutes a brilliant achievement, in which the troops concerned completed an advance of four and a half miles from their original front, overrunning two German systems of defence and gaining possession of three villages.

At the end of the first day of the attack, therefore, three German systems of defence had been broken through to a depth of some four and a half miles on a wide front, and over 5,000 prisoners had already been brought in. But for the wrecking of the bridge at Masnières and the check at Flesquieres still greater results might have been attained.

Throughout these operations the value of the services rendered by the tanks was very great, and the utmost gallantry, enterprise and resolution were displayed by both officers and crews. In combination with the other arms they helped to make possible a remarkable success. Without their aid in opening a way through the German wire, success could only have been attained by methods which would have given the enemy ample warning of our attack, and have allowed him time to mass troops to oppose it. As has been pointed out above, to enable me to undertake such an operation with the troops at my disposal secrecy to the last moment was essential. The tanks alone made it possible to dispense with artillery preparation, and so to conceal our intentions from the enemy up to the actual moment of attack.

The Advance Continued

On the morning of November 21 the attack on Flesquieres was resumed, and by 8 A.M. the village had been turned from the north-west and captured. The obstacle which more than anything else had limited the results of November 20 was thereby removed, and later in the morning the advance once more became general.

Following upon the capture of Flesquieres, the 51st and 62nd Divisions, in co-operation with a number of tanks and squadrons of the 1st Cavalry Division, attacked at 10.30 A.M. in the direction of Fontaine-Notre-Dame and Bourlon.

In this attack the capture of Anneux was completed, and early in the afternoon Cantaing was seized, with some hundreds of prisoners. Progress was made on the outskirts of Bourlon Wood, and late in the afternoon Fontaine-Notre-Dame was taken by troops of the 51st Division and tanks. The attack on Bourlon Wood itself was checked by machine-gun fire, though tanks advanced some distance into the wood.

EXTRACTS FROM DESPATCHES

THE STRUGGLE FOR BOURLON RIDGE

On the morning of November 23 the 51st Division, supported by tanks, attacked Fontaine-Notre-Dame, but was unable to force an entrance. Early in the afternoon this division repeated its attack from the west, and a number of tanks entered Fontaine, where they remained till dusk, inflicting considerable loss on the enemy. We did not succeed, however, in clearing the village, and at the end of the day no progress had been made on this part of our front.

At 10.30 A.M. the 40th Division attacked Bourlon Wood, and after four and a half hours of hard fighting, in which tanks again rendered valuable assistance to our infantry, captured the whole of the wood and entered Bourlon Village. Here hostile counter-attacks prevented our further progress, and though the village was at one time reported to have been taken by us, this proved later to be erroneous. A heavy hostile attack upon our positions in the wood, in which all three battalions of the 9th Grenadier Regiment appear to have been employed, was completely repulsed.

. . . .

With the enemy in possession of the shoulder of the ridge above Fontaine-Notre-Dame, as well as of part of the high ground west of Bourlon Wood, our position in the wood itself was a difficult one, and much of the ground to the south of it was still exposed to the enemy's observation. It was decided, therefore, to make another effort on November 27 to capture Fontaine-Notre-Dame and Bourlon Village, and to gain possession of the whole of the Bourlon Ridge.

In this attack, in which tanks co-operated, British Guards temporarily regained possession of Fontaine-Notre-Dame, taking some hundreds of prisoners, and troops of the 62nd Division once more entered Bourlon Village. Later in the morning, however, heavy counter-attacks developed in both localities and our troops were unable to maintain the ground they had gained.

. . . .

At the end of November the number of prisoners taken in our operations south-west of Cambrai exceeded 10,500. We had also captured 142 guns, some 350 machine-guns, and seventy trench mortars, with great quantities of ammunition, material and stores of all kinds.

The German Attack : Gouzeaucourt

During the afternoon three battalions of tanks, which when they received news of the attack were preparing to move away from the battlefield to refit, arrived at Gouzeaucourt and aided the infantry to hold the recaptured ground. Great credit is due to the officers and men of the Tank Brigade concerned for the speed with which they brought their tanks into action.

The Fighting at Gonnelieu and Masnières

On December 1 fighting continued fiercely on the whole front.

The Guards completed the capture of the St. Quentin Ridge and entered Gonnelieu, where they captured over 350 prisoners and a large number of machine-guns. Tanks took an effective part in the fighting for the ridge. At one point, where our infantry were held up by fire from a hostile trench, a single tank attacked and operated up and down the trench, inflicting heavy losses on the enemy's garrison. Our infantry were then able to advance and secure the trench, which was found full of dead Germans. In it were also found fifteen machine-guns that had been silenced by the tank. In the whole of this fighting splendid targets were obtained by all tank crews, and the German casualties were seen to be very great.

Farther south, a number of tanks co-operated with dismounted Indian cavalry of the 5th Cavalry Division and with the Guards in the attacks upon Villers Guislain and Gauche Wood, and were in great measure responsible for the capture of the wood. Heavy fighting took place for this position, which it is clear that the enemy had decided to hold at all costs. When the infantry and cavalry finally took possession of the wood, great numbers of German dead and smashed machine-guns were found. In one spot four German machine-guns, with dead crews lying round, were discovered within a radius of twenty yards. Three German field guns, complete with teams, were also captured in this wood.

Other tanks proceeded to Villers Guislain, and, in spite of heavy direct artillery fire, three reached the outskirts of the village, but the fire of the enemy's machine-guns prevented our troops advancing from the south from supporting them, and the tanks ultimately withdrew.

The Results of the Battle

The material results of the three weeks' fighting described above can be stated in general terms very shortly.

We had captured and retained in our possession over 12,000 yards of the former German front line from La Vacquerie to a point opposite Boursies, together with between 10,000 and 11,000 yards of the Hindenburg Line and Hindenburg Reserve Line and the villages of Ribecourt, Flesquieres and Havrincourt. A total of 145 German guns were taken or destroyed by us in the course of the operations, and 11,000 German prisoners were captured.

On the other hand, the enemy had occupied an unimportant section of our front line between Vendhuille and Gonnelieu.

There is little doubt that our operations were of considerable indirect assistance to the Allied forces in Italy.

.   .   .   .

In conclusion, I would point out that the sudden breaking through by our troops of an immense system of defence has had a most inspiring moral effect on the Armies I command, and must have a correspondingly depressing influence upon the enemy. The great value of the tanks in the offensive has been conclusively proved. In view of this experience, the enemy may well hesitate to deplete any portion of his front, as he did last summer, in order to set free troops to concentrate for decisive action at some other point.

THE GERMAN OFFENSIVE, 1918

The Retreat Across the Somme Battlefield

On March 24 certain composite battalions composed of all available troops in the Albert area, and including Tanks personnel with Lewis guns, were hurried forward along the north bank of the river to the support of the VII Corps.

.   .   .   .

During the morning of March 26 our troops continued the taking up of the Ancre line without much interference from the enemy, but between Hamel and Puisieux the situation was not yet clear. In the fighting in this area our light tanks came into action for the first time and did valuable service.

The Withdrawal from Bray-sur-Somme

The left flank of the Fifth Army was dangerously uncovered, being protected merely by the natural obstacle of the river and an improvised force of 350 men with Lewis guns and armoured cars which had been sent up to hold the crossings.

The Attack on Villers-Bretonneux

Local attacks, meanwhile, had taken place from time to time on both sides of the Somme battle front, particularly in the vicinity of Hangard, where our line linked up with the French, and about Aveluy Wood. On April 23 a more serious attack, in which four German divisions were employed against the British forces alone and German and British tanks came into conflict for the first time, took place on the Allied front between the Somme and the Avre Valleys.

At about 6.30 A.M., after a heavy bombardment lasting about three hours, the enemy advanced to the assault on the whole British front south of the Somme, under cover of fog. In the ensuing struggle, German tanks broke through our line south-east of Villers-Bretonneux, and turning to north and south, opened the way for their infantry. After heavy fighting, in which great losses were inflicted on his troops both by our infantry fire and by our light tanks, the enemy gained possession of Villers-Bretonneux, but was held up on the edge of the wood just west of that place by a counter-attack by the 8th Division. South of Villers-Bretonneux, some of our heavy tanks came into action and drove back the German tanks, with the result that the enemy's infantry were stopped some distance to the east of Cachy Village, which formed their objective. North of Villers-Bretonneux, all attacks were repulsed.

. . . .

At daybreak Villers-Bretonneux was practically surrounded by our troops. During the morning two battalions of the 8th Division worked their way through the streets and houses, overcoming the resistance of such parties of the enemy as were still holding out. That afternoon Villers-Bretonneux was again completely in our possession. In this well conceived and brilliantly executed operation nearly 1,000 prisoners were captured by our troops. A German tank was left derelict in our lines and was salved subsequently.

. . . .

In the six weeks of almost constant fighting, from March 21 to April 30, a total of fifty-five British infantry divisions and three cavalry divisions was employed on the battle fronts against a force of 109 different German divisions. During this period a total of 141 different German divisions were engaged against the combined British and French forces. The splendid qualities displayed by all ranks and services throughout the Somme and Lys battles make it possible to view with confidence whatever further tests the future may bring.

. . . .

THE TANK CORPS BOOK OF HONOUR

Reference has been made more than once in the body of this report to the very valuable work accomplished by tanks and tank personnel in the course of the Somme battle. Throughout the whole of this fighting tanks took part in numerous successful counter-attacks, many of which were instrumental in checking the enemy's progress at critical points. On these occasions tanks have shown that they possess capabilities in defence little, if at all, less than those which they have already proved in attack. In their first encounter with German tanks, officers and men of the Tank Corps displayed with success under conditions new in warfare the same energy and resource which have always characterised their action.

In this connection, a generous recognition is due to the gallant conduct of the various composite battalions which, on different occasions, took their place in the firing line.

THE BRITISH ADVANCE TO VICTORY

HAMEL

July 4, 1918

A necessary preliminary to any operation to disengage Amiens was the recapture of our old positions east of Hamel and Vaire Wood and the clearing of the Villers-Bretonneux Plateau. This was accomplished on July 4 by the Australian Corps (Lieut.-General Sir S. Monash), with the aid of four companies of the 53rd American Division and sixty tanks.

.　　　.　　　.　　　.　　　.　　　.　　　.

The most striking characteristic of the attack was the close and effective co-operation between tanks and infantry. Moving up and down behind the barrage, the tanks either killed the enemy or forced him to take shelter in dug-outs, where he became an easy prey to the infantry. Hamel was taken by envelopment from the flanks and rear, the enemy was driven from Vaire Wood, and at the end of the day our troops had gained all their objectives and over 1,500 prisoners.

EXTRACTS FROM DESPATCHES

THE ADVANCE ON THE SOMME

Arrangements were made to give the impression that a great concentration of tanks was taking place in the St. Pol area. Training operations, in which infantry and tanks co-operated, were carried out in this neighbourhood on days on which the enemy's long-distance reconnaissance and photographic machines were likely to be at work behind our lines.

The Battle Opened

At 4.20 A.M. on August 8 our massed artillery opened intense fire on the whole front of attack, completely crushing the enemy's batteries, some of which never succeeded in coming into action. Simultaneously British infantry and tanks advanced to the assault. The enemy was taken completely by surprise, and under cover of a very heavy ground mist our first objectives, on the line Demuin, Marcelcave, Cerisy, south of Morlancourt, were gained rapidly.

After a halt of two hours on this line by the leading troops, infantry, cavalry, and tanks passed through and continued the advance, the different arms working in co-operation in the most admirable manner. At the close of the day's operations our troops had completed an advance of between six and seven miles. The Amiens outer defence line, including the villages of Caix, Harbonnieres and Morcourt, had been gained on the whole front of attack, except at Le Quesnel itself. Cavalry and armoured cars were in action well to the east of this line, and before dawn on August 9 Le Quesnel also had been taken.

.   .   .   .

Over 13,000 prisoners, between 300 and 400 guns, and vast quantities of ammunition and stores of all kinds remained in our possession.

.   .   .   .

During the following days our operations continued successfully in close co-operation with the French.

THE RESULTS OF THE BATTLE OF AMIENS

The results of the Battle of Amiens may be summarised as follows. Within the space of five days the town of Amiens and the railway centring upon it had been disengaged. Twenty German divisions had been heavily defeated by thirteen British infantry divisions and three cavalry divisions, assisted by a regiment of the 33rd American Division and supported by 400 tanks. Nearly 22,000 prisoners and over 400 guns had been taken by us, and our line had been pushed forward to a depth of some twelve miles in a vital sector. Further, our deep advance, combined with the attacks of the French Armies on our right, had compelled the enemy to evacuate hurriedly a wide extent of territory to the south of us.

The effect of this victory, following so closely after the Allied victory on the Marne, upon the moral both of the German and British troops was very great. Buoyed up by the hope of immediate and decisive victory, to be followed by an early and favourable peace, constantly assured that the Allied reserves were exhausted, the German soldiery suddenly found themselves attacked on two fronts and thrown back with heavy losses from large and important portions of their earlier gains. The reaction was inevitable and of a deep and lasting character.

On the other hand, our own troops felt that at last their opportunity had come, and that, supported by a superior artillery and numerous tanks, they could now press forward resolutely to reap the reward of their patient, dauntless, and successful defence in March and April. This they were eager to do, and as they moved forward during the ensuing months from one success to another, suffering, danger, and losses were alike forgotten in their desire to beat the enemy, and their confidence that they could do so.

EXTRACTS FROM DESPATCHES

THE BATTLE OF BAPAUME

August 21 to September 1

OPENING ATTACKS : ALBERT

At 4.55 A.M. on August 21 the IV and VI Corps of General Sir Julian Byng's Third Army, under command respectively of Lieut.-General Sir G. M. Harper and Lieut.-General Sir J. A. L. Haldane, attacked on a front of about nine miles north of the Ancre, from Miraumont and Moyenneville.

The opening assault was delivered by the divisions then in line, supported by tanks, and carried the enemy's foremost defences rapidly and without difficulty.

.   .   .   .

As a result of the whole operation, the positions we required from which to launch our principal attack were gained successfully with over 2,000 prisoners.

Early next morning the III Corps of the Fourth Army, assisted by a small number of tanks, attacked with the 47th, 12th, and 18th Divisions, the 3rd Australian Division and the 38th Division co-operating on either flank. By this attack, in which the 18th Division (Major-General R. P. Lee) forced the passage of the River Ancre and captured Albert by a well-executed enveloping movement from the south-east, our line between the Somme and the Ancre was advanced well to the east of the Bray-Albert Road. The left of the Fourth Army was brought forward in conformity with the remainder of our line, and over 2,400 prisoners and a few guns were taken by us.

THE MAIN ATTACK LAUNCHED

These preliminary attacks cleared the way for the main operation. This was opened on August 23 by a series of strong assaults on practically the whole front of thirty-three miles, from our junction with the French north of Lihons to Mercatel, in which neighbourhood the Hindenburg Line from Queant and Bullecourt joined the old Arras-Vimy defence line of 1916. About 100 tanks were employed by us on different parts of this front, and were of great assistance, particularly in overcoming the enemy's machine-gunners. Many of these fought with great determination, continuing to fire until their guns were run over by the tanks.

At 1 A.M. on the night of August 23–24, the Third and Fourth Armies again attacked, and during the early morning the advance was resumed on the whole front from the Somme to Neuville Vitasse.

The 5th Division (Major-General J. Ponsonby) having captured Irles, cleared Loupart Wood in co-operation with the New Zealand Division (Major-General Sir A. H. Russell), tanks rendering valuable assistance to our infantry in both localities.

Several thousand prisoners, many guns, and great quantities of material of every kind were captured by us on this day.

The Storming of the Drocourt-Queant Line

On September 2 the Drocourt-Queant Line was broken, the maze of trenches at the junction of that line and the Hindenburg System was stormed, and the enemy was thrown into precipitate retreat on the whole front to the south of it. This gallant feat of arms was carried out by the Canadian Corps of the First Army employing the 1st and 4th Canadian Divisions and the 4th English Division, and the XVII Corps of the Third Army employing the 52nd, 57th and 63rd Divisions.

The assault of the Canadians was launched at 5 A.M. on a front of about four and half miles south of the Trinquis Brook, our infantry being supported by forty tanks of the 3rd Tank Brigade and assisted by a mobile force of motor machine-gun units, Canadian cavalry and armoured cars. The attack was a complete success, and by noon the whole of the elaborate system of wire, trenches and strong points constituting the Drocourt-Queant Line on the front of our advance was in our hands.

EXTRACTS FROM DESPATCHES

THE BATTLE OF HAVRINCOURT AND EPEHY

September 12 to 18

At 7 A.M. on September 18 the Fourth and Third Armies attacked in heavy rain on a front of about seventeen miles from Holnon to Gouzeaucourt, the First French Army co-operating south of Holnon. A small number of tanks accompanied our infantry, and were of great assistance.

In this operation our troops penetrated to a depth of three miles through the deep, continuous, and well-organised defensive belt formed by the old British and German lines.

On practically the whole front our objectives were gained successfully.

Before nightfall, the last centres of resistance in Epehy were reduced, and both in this area and on our right about Gricourt local actions during the succeeding days secured for us the remainder of the positions required for an attack on the main Hindenburg defences.

At the close of these operations, in which fifteen British divisions defeated twenty German divisions and completed the fourth stage of our offensive, we had captured nearly 12,000 prisoners and 100 guns.

At 5.20 A.M. on September 27 the Third and First British Armies attacked with the IV, VI, XVII, and Canadian Corps in the direction of Cambrai on a front of about thirteen miles from Gouzeaucourt to the neighbourhood of Sauchy Lestree. The success of the northern part of the attack depended upon the ability of our troops to debouch from the neighbourhood of Mœuvres, and to secure the crossings of the Canal du Nord in that locality. The northern portion of the canal was too formidable an obstacle to be crossed in the face of the enemy. It was therefore necessary for the attacking divisions to force a passage on a comparatively narrow front about Mœuvres, and thereafter turn the line of the canal farther north by a divergent attack developed fanwise from the point of the crossing. This difficult manœuvre was carried out successfully, and on the whole front of attack our infantry, assisted by some sixty-five tanks, broke deeply into the enemy's position.

THE HINDENBURG LINE BROKEN

The heavy and continuous bombardment opened on the morning of September 27 had been maintained by the Fourth Army along its whole front without intermission for two days. The intensity of our fire drove the enemy's garrisons to take refuge in their deep dug-outs and tunnels, and made it impossible for his carrying parties to bring up food and ammunition.

At 5.50 A.M. on September 29, under an intense artillery barrage, General Rawlinson's Fourth Army attacked on a front of twelve miles, between Holnon and Vendhuille, with the IX, II, American (General G. W. Read commanding) and III Corps, a strong force of tanks, manned by British and American crews, accompanying the infantry.

During the first week of October the Cambrai battle was completed by a series of successful minor operations, in which the breach driven through the Hindenburg Line, and such prepared defences as lay behind it, was widened.

On October 3 the Fourth Army attacked between Sequehart and Le Catelet and captured those villages and Ramicourt, together with the Beaurevoir-Fonsomme Line on that front. In this operation the 50th Division took Guoy and Le Catelet after heavy and prolonged fighting, in which a number of counter-attacks were driven off.

In the course of the next two days, other local improvements were effected in our line in this sector, and the villages of Montbrehain and Beaurevoir were captured after hard fighting, in which tanks did good service.

The great and critical assaults in which, during these nine days of battle, the First, Third and Fourth Armies stormed the line of the Canal du Nord and broke through the Hindenburg Line, mark the close of the first phase of the British offensive. The enemy's defence in the last and strongest of his prepared positions had been shattered. The whole of the main Hindenburg defences had passed into our possession, and a wide gap had been driven through such rear trench systems as had existed behind them. The effect of the victory upon the subsequent course of the campaign was decisive. In the fighting of these days, in which thirty British and two American infantry divisions and one British cavalry division were engaged against thirty-nine German divisions, over 36,000 prisoners and 380 guns had been captured. Great as were the material losses the enemy had suffered, the effect of so overwhelming a defeat upon a moral already deteriorated was of even larger importance.

SECOND BATTLE OF LE CATEAU

Having completed their arrangements, at 4.30 A.M. and 5.10 A.M. respectively on October 8 the Third and Fourth Armies attacked on a front of over seventeen miles from Sequehart to south of Cambrai. French troops continued the line of attack on our right as far south as St. Quentin. Farther south, French and American troops attacked on this day east of the Meuse and in Champagne, and made important progress.

On the British battle front our infantry and tanks penetrated the enemy's positions to a depth of between three and four miles, passing rapidly over the incomplete trench lines above referred to and gaining the open country beyond. Strong at the outset of our attack, during the later stages opposition weakened. Brancourt and Premont were taken by the 30th American Division, while to the north of them the 66th Division (Major-General H. K. Bethell), attacking beside the 25th Division (Major-General J. R. E. Charles) captured Serain. Villers Outreaux was cleared by the 38th Division, with the assistance of tanks, after heavy fighting, and late in the afternoon Malincourt was captured. The New Zealand Division passed through Lesdain and took Esnes, while on the left of the attack the 3rd, 2nd and 63rd Divisions captured Seranvillers, Forenville and Niergnies after very heavy fighting, in the course of which the enemy counter attacked with tanks. On the extreme left the 57th Division made progress in the southern outskirts of Cambrai.

As a result of this attack the enemy's resistance temporarily gave way. His infantry became disorganised and retired steadily eastwards, while our airmen reported that the roads converging on Le Cateau were blocked with troops and transport. Several thousand prisoners and many guns fell into our hands.

BATTLE OF THE SELLE RIVER

October 17 to 25

By the evening of October 19, after much severe fighting, the enemy had been driven across the Sambre et Oise Canal at practically all points south of Catillon, whence our line followed the valley of the Richemont east and north of Le Cateau.

This success was followed at 2 A.M. on October 20 by an attack upon the line of the Selle River north of Le Cateau.

On this occasion also the enemy's resistance was serious, and he had been able to erect wire entanglements along the greater part of the line. Our advance was strongly contested at every point, frequent counter-attacks being made. Supported by a number of tanks which had successfully crossed the river, our infantry, after severe fighting about Neuvilly, Amerval, Solesmes and Haspres, gained their objectives on the high ground east of the Selle.

The capture of the Selle positions was followed almost immediately by the larger operation for the attainment of the required general line above mentioned, running from the Sambre Canal along the edge of the Mormal Forest to the neighbourhood of Valenciennes.

The assault was opened by the Fourth Army at 1.20 A.M. on October 23.

The unfavourable weather of the preceding days had made it difficult to locate the enemy's batteries, and during the earlier stages of the battle hostile artillery fire was heavy. Despite this, and in spite of determined opposition at many points from the German machine-gunners, in two days our infantry and tanks realised an advance of six miles over difficult country.

EXTRACTS FROM DESPATCHES

In the Selle Battle the twenty-four British and two American divisions engaged had captured a further 20,000 prisoners and 475 guns from the thirty-one German divisions opposed to them, and had advanced to a great depth with certainty and precision.

The great series of victories won by the British forces between August 8 and November 11 is the outstanding feature of the events described in this despatch. At Amiens and Bapaume, in the breaking of the Drocourt-Queant and Hindenburg systems, before Le Cateau and on the Selle, in Flanders and on the Sambre, the enemy was again and again brought to battle and defeated.

In the decisive contests of this period, the strongest and most vital parts of the enemy's front were attacked by the British, his lateral communications were cut, and his best divisions fought to a standstill. On the different battle fronts 187,000 prisoners and 2,850 guns were captured by us, bringing the total of our prisoners for the present year to over 201,000. Immense numbers of machine-guns and trench mortars were taken also, the figures of those actually counted exceeding 29,000 machine-guns and some 3,000 trench mortars. These results were achieved by fifty-nine fighting British divisions, which in the course of three months of battle engaged and defeated ninety-nine separate German divisions.

This record furnishes proof of the skill of our commanders and their staffs, as well as the fine fighting qualities of the British regimental officer and soldier. It is a proof also of the overwhelmingly decisive part played by the British Armies on the Western front in bringing the enemy to his final defeat.

It is an accepted military doctrine that in good defensive positions any given force can hold up an attacking force of considerably greater numbers. This doctrine was proved in the fighting of March and April of this year, when, despite the enormous superiority of force which the enemy was able to concentrate against the right of the British Armies, all his efforts to effect a definite breakthrough were frustrated by our defence. Yet, as has been seen, when the tide of battle turned and the British Armies advanced to the attack, throughout practically the whole of the long succession of battles which ended in the complete destruction of the German powers of resistance, the attacking British troops were numerically inferior to the German forces they defeated.

Since the opening of our offensive on August 8, tanks have been employed in every battle, and the importance of the part played by them in breaking the resistance of the German infantry can scarcely be exaggerated. The whole scheme of the attack of August 8 was dependent upon tanks, and ever since that date on numberless occasions the success of our infantry has been powerfully assisted or confirmed by their timely arrival. So great had been the effect produced upon the German infantry by the appearance of British tanks that in more than one instance, when for various reasons real tanks were not available in sufficient numbers, valuable results have been obtained by the use of dummy tanks painted on frames of wood and canvas.

It is no disparagement of the courage of our infantry or of the skill and devotion of our artillery, to say that the achievements of those essential arms would have fallen short of the full measure of success achieved by our armies had it not been for the very gallant and devoted work of the Tank Corps, under the command of Major-General H. J. Elles.

Note.—The despatches of the Commander-in-Chief, concerned as they are mainly with the narrative of events in the field, refer only in general terms to those units at home who were engaged throughout in raising and training the troops whom he led to victory. In the Tank Corps it must be felt that a fuller acknowledgment is due to the training centre at Bovington Camp, with its branches at Wareham, Lulworth, and Swanage. The demands made upon the training centre may be judged from the facts that, originating with Bovington Camp only, it had successively to expand to the big camps at Lulworth,

Wareham, and Swanage, and even all these were inadequate to meet the demands of the final expansion of the corps just prior to the Armistice without a considerable additional building programme, which was only commenced one month before the expansion took place.

With the exception of the 1st to 4th Battalions, one Salvage Company, and the original formation of the Central Workshops and Central Stores—all of which units were raised in France from trained personnel drafted into the corps—the whole of the remainder of the Tank Corps has been raised, trained, equipped and despatched to France and Egypt, together with some 7,000 reinforcements, from the training centre. And this has been done from almost entirely raw personnel in the space of two years.

The Tank Corps units so raised and despatched to France—many went into action within a few weeks of arrival—include :

5th to 18th Tank Battalions, *i.e.* 14 Battalions.
5 Carrier (or Supply) Companies.
2 Gun Carrier Companies.
1 Salvage Company.
2 Workshop Companies.
Some 7,000 Reinforcements.

Which means a total of twenty-four tank units into the field in two years. Surely a record unsurpassed by any training centre at home ; considering also that the training centre itself had to be organised at the same time.

In addition to the above, all the American heavy tank units were trained at the training centre from absolutely raw material and sent to France, comprising three battalions and two salvage units. A further eight British tank battalions and one Canadian tank battalion had also been raised and were under training at the time of the Armistice.

In all, some thirty-four units had been raised for the Tank Corps within two years—an average of about one unit every six weeks.

As an average, about four months was the limit of time allowed for the raising, equipping and training of a tank battalion, with a shorter period for subsidiary units. The most difficult problem which had to be overcome was the formation of efficient schools of instruction for the many tank specialist subjects concurrently with the raising and training of the tank battalions and other units, and the organisation and erection of workshops to keep training tanks in running order.

The schools of instruction included :—Tank Driving and Maintenance School, Tank Gunnery School (including 6-pdr. machine-gun and revolver), Camouflage School, Gas School, Reconnaissance School, Compass School, Signalling and Pigeon School. The Tank Gunnery School on several occasions sent their instructors to assist in the organisation of the same school in France.

The strain on the workshop personnel was very great, as only a few tanks were allotted for training purposes, owing to all being taken for fighting. The wear and tear was therefore very great.

Yet another institution which should receive our recognition is the 24th Tank Corps (Officers Cadet Battalion). This unit has sent to the Tank Corps large numbers of young officers who have received a very thorough early training in this battalion.

We owe our gratitude, also, to the Naval Gunnery Schools of H.M.S. *Excellent* (Whale Island), and H.M.S. *Pembroke* (Chatham), for training our 6-pdr. gunners before the training centre was able to complete their instruction.

Finally, a tribute is due to the large number of officer and N.C.O. instructors and training centre staff who had to be retained at the training centre to carry out their work there for the ultimate benefit of the Tank Corps, and so were unable to take their places in the field.

Note.—For a full description of the growth of the corps and the stages of its development, readers are referred to the official History of the Tank Corps.—ED.

CHAPTER II

EARLY BATTLES

MESSAGE RECEIVED FROM FIELD-MARSHAL COMMANDING-IN-CHIEF

' My congratulations on the excellent work performed by the Heavy Branch of the Machine-Gun Corps during yesterday's operations. Please convey to those who took part my appreciation of the gallantry and skill shown by them.

' *April* 10, 1917.'

' COLONEL COMMANDING, 1st Brigade, H.B., M.G.C.

' Will you kindly convey to your brigade my high appreciation for, and great satisfaction at, the splendid work they have performed while with this corps.

' Naturally I have but few details regarding all they have done as yet, but it is unquestionable that the capture of the most difficult parts of the several systems of trenches taken on the 9th and 10th, and that of Monchy, is in a very great part due to the gallantry and skill with which the tanks were handled.

' I am really most grateful for all the tanks and their commanders have done, and the great success of this corps is only attributable to the help you have given us.

' This has been my first experience of the co-operation

29

of tanks, and I certainly never again want to be without them when so well commanded and led.

'J. A. HALDANE, *Lieut.-General, VI Corps.*
'*April* 13, 1917.'

'The advance of the six tanks of " C " Battalion, Heavy Branch M.G. Corps, to Feuchy Chapel, and thence to Monchy in time to co-operate with the attack of the 111th and 112th Brigades on the early morning of April 11 was a great achievement, and in itself more than justified their existence. The officers and men concerned deserve the highest credit.

'H. P. WILLIAMS, *Major-General,*
'*Commanding 37th Division.*
'HEADQUARTERS, *April* 14, 1917.'

Following telephone message received from Second Army at 11.40 A.M., June 7 :—
'The Army Commander congratulates the 2nd Brigade Heavy Branch on the action of the tanks.
'Please inform all ranks.'

'FIFTH ARMY.

'The Army Commander wishes to offer his heartiest congratulations to the troops under his command on the success gained by them on July 31.

'For a fortnight prior to the attack the enemy has maintained a heavy and continuous artillery fire, including an unprecedented use of H.V. guns against back areas, and a new form of gas-shell, all of which caused severe casualties. Despite this and the fact that the forward areas were dominated by the enemy at all points, the necessary preparations for the battle were completed and the difficult forward march and assembly of nine divisions successfully carried out and the assault launched. This alone constitutes a performance of which the Army may well be proud.

'As a result of the battle the enemy has once again been driven by the 1st French Army and ourselves from the whole of his front system on a front of about eight miles, and we are now firmly established in or beyond his second line on a front of seven miles.

' We have already captured 5,448 prisoners, including 125 officers. Up to date the capture of eight guns, ten trench mortars and thirty-six machine-guns has been reported.

' In addition we have inflicted extremely heavy casualties on the enemy. Owing to losses during our preliminary bombardment he was forced to bring up six fresh divisions. Since then three more divisions hâve been withdrawn shattered. Thus in a fortnight we have disposed of seven or eight divisions, and severely handled ten more, several of which must shortly be withdrawn.

' The Second Army on our right and the 1st French Army on our left have been as successful as ourselves. The French captures to date number 157 prisoners and three guns. The Second Army have also taken 390 prisoners and several machine-guns.

' Despite the weather on the date of the battle, we shot down five enemy machines and one balloon, losing only one machine ourselves.

' R. T. COLLINS, <i>Lieut.-Colonel</i>,
' <i>for Major-General, G.S.</i>'

' G.H.Q., BRITISH ARMIES IN FRANCE,
' <i>August</i> 1, 1917.

' GENERAL SIR H. GOUGH.

' My warmest congratulations to yourself and to the commanders, staffs and troops under your command on the great success gained yesterday. The severity of the fighting and the very heavy losses suffered by the enemy will force him to expend his remaining reserves rapidly in the effort to stay our advance, and this is even more important than the gain of ground, great as this was.

' You and all ranks under your command may well be proud of, and fully satisfied with, such a splendid day's work.

' D. HAIG, <i>Field-Marshal.</i>'

'XVIII Corps.

' 1ST BRIGADE TANKS.

' The Corps Commander wishes to congratulate " G " Battalion, 1st Brigade Tanks, on its brilliant success in to-day's operations, of which it may be justly proud.

' By its good arrangements, untiring energy and gallantry, it has enabled the infantry to penetrate the enemy's defences on a front of 1,500 yards to a maximum depth of 500 yards with only 15 casualties.

' The Corps Commander feels confident that even greater successes are in store for the 1st Brigade Tanks in the forthcoming operations.

' Please convey to the officers, N.C.O.'s and men of " G " Battalion the Corps Commander's appreciation of their good work.

' S. G. HOLLAND, Brig.-General,
' General Staff, XVIII Corps.

' August 19, 1917.'

' September 7, 1917.

' The Corps Commander desires to thank all ranks of the 2nd Brigade Tank Corps for the fine work they performed during recent operations.

' The weather and ground were as unfavourable as it was possible to meet with for operations by " The Tanks," but thanks to good reconnaissance, careful study of maps and aeroplane photos, and the great gallantry and devotion to duty shown by all ranks, the 2nd Brigade, Tank Corps, was able to render material assistance to the infantry throughout the operations.

' The Corps Commander wishes all ranks of the 2nd Brigade Tank Corps every success, and hopes that when the II Corps again come into the line he may be fortunate enough to have the 2nd Brigade to assist in the operations.

' STANHOPE, Major, for B.-G., G.S.'

' FIFTH ARMY.

' The Army Commander has read the report of the operations of the tanks of the 1st Brigade on October 4 with great interest. He considers that the tanks were of considerable assistance to the infantry, and that the personnel deserve great credit.

'M. MALCOLM, *Major-General, G.S.*'

'The Field-Marshal Commanding-in-Chief to-day paid a personal visit to XVII Corps Headquarters to congratulate all ranks on their splendid victory in the battle of 20th instant. He desired me to convey to you his high appreciation of the successful attacks of the 51st and 58th Divisions. They gained all their objectives, advancing close behind the barrage. They consolidated their gains. They held their ground in spite of several intense bombardments. They were attacked by no less than ten Prussian battalions at different times between 3 P.M. and 8 P.M. These counter-attacks were all repulsed after fighting at close quarters. The rifle and the machine-gun, as well as the artillery, killed great numbers of Germans. Our Heavy and Field Artillery deserve the greatest credit for the accuracy of the barrage and for the rapidity with which their forward observing officers directed the guns on hostile counter-attacks.

'I request that a copy of this letter be sent to each brigade, battalion, and group commander who took part in the action, and desire that all ranks be informed that we have ample evidence to prove that the enemy's losses were heavy and that our own were light.

'IVOR MAXSE, *Lieutenant-General,*
'*Commanding XVII Corps.*
'*September* 22, 1917.'

'*September* 28, 1917.

'The following message has been received by the Army Commander from the Commander-in-Chief, and is circulated for information :—

'"GENERAL SIR H. GOUGH, Commanding the Fifth Army :—

'"I congratulate you and all corps and divisions of the Fifth Army which took part in yesterday's operations on the great results achieved, which reflect the highest credit on the fighting capabilities and determination of all ranks under your command.

'"SIR D. HAIG, *Field-Marshal,*
" *Adv. G.H.Q.*" '

' I have received the following telegram from the Fifth Army Commander :—

'"The Army Commander wishes you to thank all the troops under your command who took part in the battle on October 4. Captured documents make it clear that this was one of the heaviest blows which the enemy has ever received. All arms deserve their share of praise, but particularly the Flying Corps, which did most valuable work on a day in which the German airmen did not dare to leave the ground."

' I have great pleasure in circulating the above telegram, and would add my hearty congratulations to all ranks who took part in our victory of the 4th instant.

' The tanks in Poelcappelle were a decisive factor in our success on the left flank ; the infantry of the 11th and 48th Divisions gained their objectives along the whole front, and the Royal Artillery undoubtedly killed a great number of Germans. We now look forward with confidence to delivering further blows of the same sort.

' A copy of this is sent for every company and battery commander in order that he may read it to his subordinates.

' IVOR MAXSE, *Lieutenant-General,*
' *Commanding XVII Corps.*

' *October* 7, 1917.'

' The Brigadier-General has read your general account of the attack on, and capture of, Poelcappelle on October 4, and has instructed me to inform you that he considers that the work carried out by the 1st Brigade Tanks was a most creditable performance by all concerned.

' J. F. C. FULLER, *Lieut.-Colonel, General Staff.*
' H.Q., TANK CORPS, *October* 10, 1917 '

COMPLIMENTARY MESSAGES

WIRE FROM 20TH DIVISION, *November* 21, 1917 :—

' G.O.C. 20th Div. wishes to convey to you and all ranks under your command his appreciation and thanks for the very gallant and whole-hearted services rendered to his Div. in late attack which were the main factors in obtaining a great success.'

' IV CORPS, *November* 29, 1917.

' DEAR COURAGE,—I am very grateful to you and your brigade for all the help you gave my corps. I am afraid you have lost a lot of men and a lot of tanks, but I hope your brigade will help us again some day.

' Would you kindly let your officers and men know how very grateful the IV Corps are to them for their splendid services.

' Yours sincerely,
' C. L. WOOLLCOMBE.'

CAMBRAI

FROM ACCOUNT OF OPERATIONS BEFORE CAMBRAI, NOVEMBER 20 TO 23, 1917, BY THE 152ND INFANTRY BRIGADE.[1]

' " E " Battalion of the Tank Corps was allotted to this brigade for the battle, and I would here mention that Lieut.-Colonel Burnett, D.S.O., and his battalion staff and company commanders spared no effort in their endeavours to ensure the success of the operations, and I am satisfied that the careful training, thorough reconnaissance and close liaison carried out by the officers of the Tank Corps in conjunction with my battalion, company and platoon commanders were such that, failing any untoward incident, success was assured before the battle commenced.

' The arrangements for the assembly of the tanks, a most difficult task on a dark night, were also carried out exactly as intended.

---

[1] A very large number of messages received at this time were subsequently lost in action.

'While all tank commanders did well, the officer commanding 6th Seaforth Highlanders has brought specially to my notice the good work done by No. 15 Company, " E " Battalion, under Major V. R. Montgomerie. Of the eleven tanks belonging to this company ten reached their objective on the Flesquieres Ridge, and of these only one returned to its rallying point, the remainder being knocked out by direct hits. Lieut.-Colonel McDonald mentions Major Montgomerie as having done specially good work during the action, while his preliminary arrangements left nothing to be desired.'

LEWIS GUN DETACHMENTS

' To THE OFFICER COMMANDING 4th Tank Brigade.

' On my own behalf and that of 49th (West Riding) Division I send you warm thanks for the brave and loyal help which your gallant men have given us during the period April 25 to May 5, with special reference to the fighting on April 29, when the enemy attacked in strength and was bloodily repulsed.

' M. G. CAMERON, *Major-General.*

' From G.O.C 49th (W.R.) Division.'

' *April* 22, 1918.

' From LIEUT.-GENERAL R. HAKING, commanding XI Corps.

' As the Lewis Gun detachments of the 7th and 11th Tank Battalions have been, or are now being, withdrawn, I take the opportunity of expressing my thanks for the valuable assistance given. The work done by the Lewis Gun detachments on the 11th, 12th and 13th, when reinforcements were badly wanted, was of the greatest value, and I am particularly indebted to the detachments which fought so well north of the Lys Canal on April 12.'

' No. 5 TANK BATTALION.

' All ranks in 33rd Division appreciate the great help your officers and men gave in the fighting April 12 to 19.

COMPLIMENTARY MESSAGES

'They are proud to have had you fighting amongst them, and hope to have the good fortune to fight with you again.

'R. J. PINNEY, *Major-General,*
'*Commanding 33rd Division.*

'*April* 19, 1918.'

'Q.C. 5TH TANK BATTALION.

'The G.O.C. 33rd Division has asked me to let you know how much he appreciates the valuable assistance you have given him whilst under his command.

'I would like to add that your presence has given me a great sense of security and that you have fully justified that sense.

'I hope you and your men will enjoy a well-earned rest.

'Many thanks and apologies for making so much use of you.'

'H. H. MAITLAND, *Brigadier-General,*
'*98th Infantry Brigade.*

'*April* 19, 1918.'

'O.C. "G" BATTALION, TANK CORPS.

'I should like to express to you my gratitude for the extremely valuable services rendered by the company of your battalion under Major Crockford, during the period they were attached to my brigade, on their own initiative, in the operations near Bucquoy, March 20 to 31, 1918.

'They on two occasions co-operated with the infantry against Rossignol Wood, and I should like to draw your particular attention to the gallant conduct of Lieut. Symons during the action on night of March 27, when he personally led the tanks up to the wood, and directed their operation on foot. I consider this officer's conduct worthy of recognition, and I shall be very happy to endorse any recommendation for immediate award you may care to put in.

'J. S. BURNETT, *Brigadier-General,*
'*Commanding 166th Infantry Brigade.*

'*April* 7, 1918.'

' 2ND DIVISION, *April* 1, 1918.

' V CORPS.

' I wish to bring to your notice the invaluable assistance given to the 2nd Division by the 8th Battalion Tank Corps, when the division had great difficulty in extricating itself from the Green Line owing to the exposed flanks.

' There is no doubt that the whole-hearted support of the 8th Battalion saved us many casualties, and the 2nd Division are very grateful for their help.

' C. E. PEREIRA, *Major-General*,
' *Commanding 2nd Division.*'

' 2ND BRIGADE TANKS.

' The Corps Commander congratulates the 2nd Brigade Tanks on their magnificent behaviour during the last few days' fighting. Numerous heavy attacks by the enemy have been completely repulsed with heavy loss and the capture of prisoners and machine-guns. He heartily thanks the troops for their courage and endurance, and is confident that they will continue to hold the line against all attacks.

' R. Y. PARKER, *Brigadier-General, G.S.*'

' H.Q.T.C., THIRD ARMY.

' G.O.C. TANK CORPS.

' Throughout the operations of the Third Army from March 21 to April 9 the personnel of the 2nd Tank Brigade have displayed a devotion to duty, a quick appreciation of the battle, and a conspicuous gallantry in helping to save critical situations which I most deeply appreciate.

' I am proud to have them under my command.

' J. BYNG, *General.*

' THIRD ARMY, *April* 11, 1918.'

HAMEL

OPERATIONS OF JULY 4, 1918

Special order by Lieut.-General Sir John Monash, K.C.B., V.D., Commanding Australian Corps :—

COMPLIMENTARY MESSAGES

' Congratulatory.

' The following messages received from the Field-Marshal Commander-in Chief, British Armies in France, and from G.O.C. Fourth Army, are published for information :—

' " Will you please convey to Lieut.-General Sir John Monash, and all ranks under his command, including the Tanks and the detachment of 33rd American Division, my warm congratulations on the success which attended the operation carried out this morning, and on the skill and gallantry with which it was conducted."

' " In forwarding this message the Army Commander desires most heartily to congratulate the Australian Corps, and especially on the way in which the scheme was drawn up and the gallantry with which the operation was carried out. The part played by the tanks and the artillery was a prominent factor in bringing about success, and reflects great credit upon them."

' KEITH, *Officer, Major,*
' *D.A.A.G. Australian Corps.*'

' HEADQUARTERS, 5TH TANK BRIGADE,
' *July* 5, 1918.

'O.C. 8th TANK BATTALION AND O.C. 13TH TANK BATTALION.

' The following messages are published for information of all ranks :—

' FROM FOURTH ARMY.

' " Following received from Sir Douglas Haig :—

' ",Will you please convey to Lieut.-General Sir J. Monash and all ranks under his command, including the Tanks and the detachment of the 33rd American Division, my warm congratulations on the success which attended the operation carried out this morning, and on the skill and gallantry with which it was conducted."

' " In forwarding this message the Army Commander desires most heartily to congratulate the Australian Corps, and especially on the way in which the scheme was drawn up and the gallantry with which the operation was carried out. The part played by the tanks and artillery was a prominent factor in bringing about success, and reflects great credit on them." '

' FROM 4th AUSTRALIAN DIVISION.

" ' Army Commander wishes his congratulations conveyed to you and your men on your excellent work. General Birdwood and Corps Commander both send you and your command best congratulations on your brilliant work. Please add mine."

' FROM G.O.C. TANK CORPS.

' " Very well done." '

' AUSTRALIAN CORPS, *July* 10, 1918.

' Following cable received from Defence, Melbourne :—

' " Commonwealth of Australia desires to congratulate Monash and all ranks in his command on the splendid success attending the recent operations at Hamel and Vaire Wood. That the casualties sustained were light in character is especially pleasing, and adds to the gratification with which the news has been received." '

SOME COMPLIMENTARY MESSAGES RECEIVED BY TANK CORPS UNITS BETWEEN JULY 1918 AND NOVEMBER 1918

' HEADQUARTERS, CANADIAN CORPS,
' *September* 27, 1918.

' DEAR HARDRESS LLOYD,—It gives me much pleasure to forward, herewith, a communication from General Lipsett, formerly in command of our 3rd Division, in which he testifies to the splendid support rendered by the Tank Battalions which operated with our 3rd Division in the recent battles. Such evidence of close harmony and mutual confidence must be very gratifying to all concerned.

' In forwarding this communication to those concerned, will you, at the same time, express to them the appreciation of the whole Canadian Corps for the wonderfully successful part the tanks played in the Battle of Amiens and the Battle of Arras. I am sure a good portion of the success of these operations must be attributed to the tanks.

'It is splendid to see that such a young organization has already developed a very fine *esprit de corps*, and in the final victory over the enemy the tanks will play an ever increasing part.

'Wishing you the best of luck,

'Yours ever,

'A. M. CURRIE.

'BRIG.-GENERAL J. HARDRESS LLOYD, D.S.O.,
'Commanding 3rd Tank Brigade.'

'3RD CANADIAN DIVISION.

'CANADIAN CORPS.

'I would like to place on record my appreciation of the work of the Tank Corps during the recent operations in which this division has been engaged.

'In the battle of Amiens, the part played by Lieut.-Colonel O'Kelly and all ranks of the 5th Battalion Tank Corps was a most essential factor to the ultimate success of the operations. Colonel O'Kelly himself was untiring, and always ready to do anything in his power to assist the infantry attacks, and the zeal and gallantry displayed by his subordinates were the admiration of the infantry with whom they worked. The liaison with the division, brigades and battalions was beyond criticism. The initial assembly before zero in the difficult marshy valley of the Luce River was carried out with the greatest possible skill, and subsequently on the morning of the 8th against the strong points in Dodu and Hamon Woods and other machine-gun nests, the action of the tanks was conspicuous by its promptness and gallantry, operating as they were, in many cases, in the teeth of heavy fire from carefully distributed German anti-tank guns.

'On the 9th again they were of the greatest assistance in cleaning up enemy strong points during their strong rearguard action through the villages of Folle, Bouchoir, and Quesnoy.

'I very much regret the heavy casualties suffered by this battalion, and would wish to express my thanks to Colonel O'Kelly and all ranks of his battalion for the splendid way in which they co-operated with, and assisted us, during the whole battle.

'On August 26 the 11th Battalion Tank Corps were unable to operate during the earlier phases of the attack, owing to the long distance they had to traverse before their arrival on the battlefield. It was, however, owing to the great energy displayed by Colonel Pigot and those under his command that five tanks were able to arrive in time to operate and very materially assist the 7th Canadian Infantry Brigade in their attack later on in the morning.

'G. LIPSETT, *Major-General,*
'*Commanding 3rd Canadian Division.*
'*September* 12, 1918.'

'HEADQUARTERS, 46TH (NORTH MIDLAND) DIVISION,
'*October* 9, 1918.

'DEAR HARDRESS,—Please convey to the 5th and 9th Battalions the gratitude of all ranks of my division for the work they did on September 29 and October 3. The tanks were of the greatest assistance, and accounted for many Germans, especially during the forcing of the Beaurevoir Line and the capture of Romicourt.

'I regret the losses were heavy in personnel, but the enemy losses throughout have been far greater, as the battlefield testified.

'Yours ever,
'GERALD BOYD.'

'*October* 10, 1918.

'MY DEAR HARDRESS LLOYD,—I have not had an opportunity since we were in action of seeing you or any of your officers, but I should be very glad if you would be kind enough to tell all those of the 5th, 6th and 9th Battalions who worked with us how much we all appreciate their efforts. The assistance given by Somers to myself and my staff was invaluable, and though fate decided against our getting the cavalry and Whippets through as quickly as I had at one time hoped, it was, none the less, due to his care and readiness at all times that the Whippets were always prepared for emergencies.

' The tanks that actually worked with us did so with the greatest devotion, and gave us very great help.

' If you get a chance, I hope you will try to let them all know how much we all felt we owed to them,

'Believe me,
'Yours sincerely,
'D. S. LAMBERT, *Major-General,*
'*Commanding 32nd Division.*'

TELEGRAMS

'*September* 27, 1918.
'To 15TH BATTALION.

' Most grateful for splendid assistance given this division by " B " Company's two tanks to-day under Captain Gibson.
'*63rd (R.N.) Division.*'

'*September* 29, 1918.
'To G.O.C. 2ND TANK BRIGADE.

' All ranks 3rd Division are united in their admiration of the work done yesterday by the companies of the 15th Battalion Tank Corps co-operating with this division. They played a great part in the success gained, and their gallantry and determination to assist us to their utmost were much appreciated by all ranks of the division.
'C. J. DEVERALL, *Major-General,*
'*Commanding 3rd Division.*'

' 2ND DIVISION.

' I would like to bring to the notice of the Major-General Commanding the very valuable assistance rendered to this brigade by No. 5 Section, B Company, 15th Battalion Tank Corps, and in particular the help given by the officer commanding section, Captain Foster.

' The crews of the tanks behaved splendidly, and rendered us enormous help. I understand that all the personnel of the four tanks, except four men, were wounded during the course of the fight.

' I would like to bring to notice the gallant action of Captain Foster. I am informed that when one of the tanks was put out of action he himself, with a Lewis gun and one man, took up a position to endeavour to neutralize an enemy machine-gun nest, in order both to assist our advance and to help the tank crew to get their wounded away.

' The whole brigade is loud in its praise of this section of the Tank Corps.

' C. D. HAMILTON MOORE, *Brigadier-General,*
' *Commanding* 157*th Inf. Brigade.*
' *September* 29, 1918.'

' O.C. 10TH TANK BATTALION.

' On the morning of August 21, 1918, at about 9.45 A.M., after the taking of the final objective the enemy launched a strong counter-attack from the N.E. side of Achiet-le-Petit, and at one time it looked as if the village must fall into the hands of the enemy and the battalions cut off. One tank and two armoured cars which had been ordered to proceed down the sunken road in G. 8 realised the situation at once, formed a defensive flank, held on, and held up the enemy and threw them back in disorder, though they themselves were eventually knocked out. I have never seen a more gallantly performed action.

' E. H. RODDY, *Lieut.-Colonel,*
' *Commanding* 1*st Cheshire Regt.*
' *August* 31, 1918.'

' O.C. 10TH TANK BATTALION.

' Will you kindly convey to all the officers and men of your battalion the thanks and high appreciation of all ranks of the 12th Division for the splendid work they did in conjunction with our attacks of the 8th, 9th, and 10th

44

August. It is very largely owing to their gallant co-operation that those attacks were most successful.

' Yours sincerely,
' H. W. HIGGINSON, *Major-General,*
' *12th Division.*

' *August* 13, 1918.'

' 11TH TANK BATTALION.

' I wish to express to all ranks of the company of your battalion that assisted my attack on the 8th instant, my very grateful thanks for their magnificent assistance. As you know, our attack, delivered on a pitch black night, was completely held up on the enemy belt of wire 150 yards deep. The arrival of your tanks, however, enabled my troops to follow them through the wire and eventually to capture Villers-Outreaux.

' Every officer and man I have spoken to are loud in their praise of the splendid advance of your tanks.

' I am convinced that without them we should never have achieved the success that was ultimately gained.

' Further, had we attacked primarily with tanks at dawn, I am persuaded that we should have suffered 800 less casualties and have taken 800 more prisoners.

' A. ASHLEY CUBITT, *Major-General,*
' *Commanding 38th (Welsh) Division.*

' *October* 14, 1918.'

' 12TH TANK BATTALION.

' Please convey to all ranks the Corps Commander's best congratulations on the success of their day's work to-day.

' *IV Corps.*

' *October* 8, 1918.'

' FROM G.O.C. V CORPS THROUGH 1st TANK BRIGADE.

' The 11th Tank Battalion has taken part in the following operations with the troops of the V Corps :—

' The attack on Villers-Guislain, Gouzeaucourt and Gonne-lieu ; the operations against Villers-Outreaux, Wallincourt and Marlincourt, followed by the rapid advance to the River Selle ; the fights for the crossings of the Selle, the capture of Amerval, and the subsequent advance through Forest and Ovillers.

'The assistance afforded by the tanks has been of the greatest value throughout, and the energy and resource which enabled them to move forward and remain in action under trying and difficult circumstances deserve the highest praise.

'Will you please convey my thanks to all ranks of the 11th Tank Battalion for the gallant assistance they have afforded the infantry while attached to this corps ?

'C. D. SHUTE, *Lieut.-General,*
'*Commanding V Corps.*'

'12th TANK BATTALION.

The Divisional Commander 63rd (R.N.) Division wishes to record his appreciation of the gallant manner in which the tanks of " A " Company, 12th Tank Battalion, assisted the infantry of the Royal Naval Division during the operations October 7 to 8. The splendid way in which the tank counter-attack was met, and the able manner in which the commander of the Female Tank met the situation, are greatly appreciated by all ranks.

'J. W. MACKENZIE, *Lieut.-Colonel, General Staff.*
'*October* 9, 1918.'

'I have pleasure in drawing your attention to the following reports on the excellent and gallant work of the tanks attached to this brigade for the attack on Niergnies on October 8 :—

'" FROM THE 2nd ROYAL IRISH REGIMENT.

'" The tank operating with our battalion started off in the centre of our front, right up behind the barrage, and moved forward, steering a zig-zag course, right up beyond the battalion objective, firing right and left as he advanced. When just beyond our trench he turned towards the south end of the village and engaged machine-guns firing from that point, when he returned and remained about 200 yards in front of our trench at G.6.d.5.5. At about 0830 hours the tank was knocked out, some of the personnel getting away all right and making for the N.W. edge of the village of Niergnies. This tank did magnificent work, and was a great help to the battalion. Company commanders speak in the highest terms of the splendid work done by 2nd Lieutenant Delamere, who drove the tank ' Lokiel ' and rendered the greatest assistance to the battalion in getting to, and taking their, objective, and was largely instrumental in keeping down our casualties."

' " From 1st R.M. Battalion.

' " During operations on October 8 a tank—' The Lion '— went forward on the right flank of the 1st R.M.L.I. at 0640 hours, from the first objective. The officer commanding ' Lion ' was asked to deal with a machine-gun which was giving considerable trouble from a shrine S.E. of Niergnies. This he successfully did and enabled the infantry to advance. He was afterwards invaluable in clearing the cemetery of machine-gun nests. The tanks working on the left of the 1st R.M.L.I. (names unknown) were extremely useful in dealing with enemy machine-guns, thus preventing serious flanking fire being brought to bear on the advancing infantry.

' " The tanks were invaluable, and all ranks are enthusiastic regarding the splendid way in which they carried out their tasks." '

' C. A. Harman, *Lieut.-Colonel,*
' *Commanding* 188th *Infantry Brigade.*
' *October* 13, 1918.'

' From Major-General T. S. Lambert, C.B., C.M.G., Commanding 32nd Division, to G.O.C., 4th Tank Brigade.

' *August* 15, 1918.
' I want you, if you will, to convey to all the officers and men of the 4th and 5th Battalions the thanks of my division for the work they did to help us during the two

days we were in action. Their gallantry and readiness to do all they could to help us earned the admiration of us all. I am afraid they suffered severe losses, as we did, up against Parvillers and Damery, but, as you know, war demands sacrifices at times, and your men behaved splendidly. Perhaps the 5th Battalion were able to help us most, but I know what an effort was required from both battalions after all they had already undergone, and I should like you to know that we appreciate it.'

'From MAJOR-GENERAL H. BURSTALL, K.C.B., C.M.G., A.D.C., Commanding 2nd Division, to O.C. 14th Battalion.

'*August* 15, 1918.

' I wish to thank you personally, and on behalf of all the members of the 2nd Canadian Division, for the splendid work you have done and for the very great assistance which you have given us during the recent operations.

' I fully appreciate the difficulties under which you have been working. The very low visibility on the early morning of August 8, the limited assembly positions on the same date, the long distances which you have had to travel and fight over, the short notice at which you have been called on to take part in operations, and the extremely limited extent to which we have been able to help you with barrages or smoke screens, have all been obstacles which could only have been overcome by men of great determination.

' I deeply regret that you should have suffered such severe casualties, and, since your help has so materially reduced our losses, I feel that in any future operations it is distinctly up to us to do our best to assist you as you have assisted us.

' From my own observation, from the enthusiastic statements of all ranks who have benefited by your work, and from the very large number of requests that I have received for tanks, I know the value of your co-operation, and I can only say that in any future engagements I could wish for nothing better than the support of the 14th Battalion Tank Corps.'

COMPLIMENTARY MESSAGES

'From GENERAL SIR H. RAWLINSON, G.C.V.O., K.C.B., K.C.M.G., Commanding Fourth Army, to G.O.C. Tank Corps.

'August 16, 1918.

'The success of the operations of August 8 and succeeding days was largely due to the conspicuous part played by the 3rd, 4th, and 5th Brigades of the Tank Corps, and I desire to place on record my sincere appreciation of the invaluable services rendered both by the Mark V, the Mark V Star, and the Whippets.

'The task of secretly assembling so large a number of tanks entailed very hard and continuous work by all concerned for four or five nights previous to the battle.

'The tactical handling of the tanks in action made calls on the skill and physical endurance of the detachments, which were met with a gallantry and devotion beyond all praise.

'I desire to place on record my appreciation of the splendid success that they achieved, and to heartily congratulate the Tank Corps as a whole on the completeness of their arrangements and the admirable prowess exhibited by all ranks actually engaged on this occasion.

'There are many vitally important lessons to be learned from their experiences. These will, I trust, be taken to heart by all concerned and made full use of when next the Tank Corps is called upon to go into battle.

'The part played by the tanks and whippets in the battle of August 8 was in all respects a very fine performance.'

'From LIEUT.-GENERAL A. GODLEY, K.C.M.G., Commanding III Corps, to G.O.C. Tank Corps.

'August 23, 1918.

'On the departure of the tanks from the zone of operations of the III Corps, I wish to express my thanks, and those of the troops of the III Corps, to the commanders, officers and men of the Tank Corps for their valuable assistance and co-operation during our recent attacks.

' The 4th Tank Brigade, allotted to the Corps . . . lived up to its high traditions, and were of the greatest assistance on August 22 and 23. In especial, the crossing of the River Ancre was much facilitated by a section of the tanks of this brigade, and the co-operation of tanks in the attack on Tara Hill was particularly valuable.

.   .   .   .

' The tanks allotted to the carrying of supplies for the infantry were of the greatest service, and were much appreciated by the troops for whom they worked.'

' From BRIGADIER-GENERAL J. V. CAMPBELL, V.C., C.M.G., D.S.O., Commanding 46th Division.

October 25, 1918.

' During the battle of Regnicourt on October 17 the section of tanks from the 16th Battalion allotted to this division did excellent work, and very materially assisted the operation.

' Tank No. 9146 has been specially brought to my notice. This tank, commanded by a N.C.O. (it is believed the officer was wounded early in the fight), appears to have lost direction somewhat in the fog. On the fog lifting, the N.C.O. in charge found himself opposite Regnicourt, where the infantry were held up by very heavy machine-gun fire.

' Regardless of an enemy 77mm. gun, which was firing at point-blank range, this N.C.O. advanced his tank and, the infantry following, the very strong position of Regnicourt was captured without further difficulty.

' The tank then turned to carry out its mission in the direction of Andigny, but was knocked out by a field gun, already named, before it had gone far.

' It is feared that the tank crew suffered severe casualties, as the following members have been buried alongside it :

307433 Cpl. C. C. DREWITT.
307041 Pte. E. DANIELS.
308059 Pte. J. F. DOIG.
307015 Pte. W. FENSOME.

COMPLIMENTARY MESSAGES

' The very gallant action of this tank crew undoubtedly materially assisted towards the success of the day, and saved many lives.'

Extract from Fourth Army Situation Wire dated November 7, 1918 :—

' The 17th Armoured Car Battalion rendered valuable services on November 6 and 7, dispersing many hostile demolition parties.'

Extract from letter received from G.O.C. 6th French Cavalry Division by O.C. 17th Armoured Car Battalion, dated August 3, 1918 :—

' I do not wish to let you go without expressing the pleasure it has been to me to have you under my orders during these few days, and without thanking you for the services you have rendered me by your reconnaissance. . . . I hope that the future will bring us together again. On the day that the cavalry advance I shall be happy to have at my disposal your powerful cars, handled by officers and men whose valour I have learned to appreciate from my intimate contact with the British Army.'

' GENERAL STAFF,
' 3RD DIVISION.

' G.O.C. 2ND TANK BRIGADE.

' All ranks 3rd Division are united in their admiration of the work done yesterday by the two companies (" A " and " C ") of the 15th Battalion Tank Corps co-operating with the division.

' They played a great part in the success gained, and their gallantry and determination to assist us to their utmost were much appreciated by all ranks of the division.

' C. J. DEVERALL, *Major-General,*
' *Commanding 3rd Division.*

' *September* 28, 1918.'

51

' VI CORPS.

' I wish to express my appreciation of the great assistance given to the 2nd Division during the recent operations —August 21 to 25—by the 2nd Tank Brigade. The tanks responded most gallantly to all calls made upon them by the infantry.

' C. E. PEREIRA, Major-General,
' Commanding 2nd Division.

' *August* 24, 1918.'

' 2ND TANK BRIGADE.

' Your 9th Battalion tanks did splendid work to-day, successfully fulfilling all their tasks. Many thanks from 50th Division.'

' H.Q., TANK CORPS.

' The Commander-in-Chief desires that the following telegram received from General Debeney, Commanding First French Army, should be communicated to Lieut.-Colonel Woods and the officers and men of the 9th Battalion, Tank Corps, whom he congratulates on the high honour given them :—

' " I am happy to convey to you the following telegram which I have just received from the General Commanding the French Armies in response to my request. The collective mention in the Orders of the Army of the 9th Battalion of British Tanks is approved in the following terms :—

' " In the fighting of July 23, under the skilled and capable command of Lieut.-Colonel Woods, they have given the most effective assistance to a French Division, and by their courage, energy, cohesion, and military training have won the enthusiastic admiration of their French comrades. The recommendations for the Legion of Honour and Military Medals are forwarded to the Minister, and strongly recommended."

ENLARGEMENT OF BADGE OF
"LA GRENADIÈRE" DIVISION

COMPLIMENTARY MESSAGES

' The Commander-in-Chief has sent the following reply to General Debeney :—

' " I have received your telegram of August 12 with the greatest pleasure, and have communicated to the 9th Battalion of Tanks the high honour for which they have been recommended."

' H. RUGGLES BRISE,
' *M.G. M.S. to C.-in-C.*'

GENERAL ORDER NO. 248.

' 3RD DIVISION STAFF, H.Q., *July* 24, 1918.

' The 9th Battalion of British Tanks fought yesterday with the 3rd French Division known as " La Grenadiere."

' Commanded by an experienced and skilful leader, Lieut.-Colonel Woods, the tanks again enriched their harvest of laurels, which this new arm has not ceased to gather since its first appearance in August 1916.

' They have given the division the finest example of bravery, energy, of comradeship in action, and of war training carried to the highest degree of perfection.

' Their assistance enabled the infantry to gain a brilliant victory, which they themselves largely shared.

' If sacrifices to be deplored were the price of this success, the officers and men who fell gave an example of how a British soldier can die for his King and Country.

' " La Grenadiere " hereby addresses to its British comrades the touching expression of its gratitude and admiration.

' *Le Général Cdt. la 3ᵉ Division d'Infanterie,*
' NAYAL DE BOURGON.
' *August* 12, 1918.'

' O.C. TANKS.

' All ranks 6th Buffs tender their thanks and great appreciation for the magnificent work of the 10th Battalion at the taking of Morlancourt on August 9. Their help was

53

inestimable, and the success of the operation was due to their close co-operation.

'A. MERTHYR, *Lieut.-Colonel,*
'*6th Buffs.*'

'HEADQUARTERS, 10TH CDN. INF. BATTN.,
'*September*, 6, 1918.

'OFFICER COMMANDING 14th TANK BATTALION.

'I wish to bring to your attention the gallantry and initiative displayed by the tank commanders of your unit while working with this battalion during the operations of September 2 in front of Villers-lez-Cagnicourt. Although, unfortunately, they were knocked out in the early stages of the fighting, the work of the officers and men is worthy of especial mention. To the west of Villers-lez-Cagnicourt it was necessary to pass a most difficult piece of sky-line, during which time they were under direct fire of German machine and field guns, and realising their danger as they did, made no hesitation in any instance.

'They proceeded to their task gallantly and well, and the fact that they were unable to render more assistance was certainly not due to any fault of theirs, rather to the unfortunate situation of the approaches and the accuracy of the German field guns.

'One of your officers, whose name I regret I am unable to state, deserves special recognition. His tank was knocked out in the early part of the attack, in advance of our men, and as a result he fell into the enemy's hands. We had the pleasure, later, of driving the enemy from that sector and releasing this officer and some of his men. Although badly shaken up and painfully wounded in the foot, his coolness and cheerfulness were a splendid example to all ranks who came in contact with him.

'I should be pleased if you would convey my thanks, and the thanks of the 10th Canadian Infantry Battalion, to all of the officers and men who took part with us in this operation.

'E. W. McDONALD, *Lieut.-Colonel,*
'*Commanding 10th Canadian Infantry Battalion.*'

COMPLIMENTARY MESSAGES

' FROM 4th AUSTRALIAN DIVISION.

' Army Commander wishes his congratulations conveyed to you and your men on your excellent work. General Birdwood and Corps Commander both send you and your command best congratulations on your brilliant work. Please add mine.'

' HEADQUARTERS, 4TH AUSTRALIAN DIVISION,
' *August* 21, 1918.
' G.O.C. 5th TANK BRIGADE.

' I wish to express to you and your command associated with us on August 8 and following days, on behalf of the 4th Australian Division, our deep appreciation of the most gallant service rendered during our offensive operations by the Tank Corps. The consistent skill and gallantry with which the tanks, individually and collectively, were handled during the battle were the admiration of all ranks of the infantry with whom they were so intimately associated, and our success was due in very large measure to your efforts.

' We hope sincerely that in future offensive operations in which we may take part we shall have the honour to be associated with the same units of the Tank Corps as during the operations of August 8 and following days.

' E. G. SINCLAIR MACLAGAN, *Major-General,*
' *Commanding 4th Australian Division.*

' *August* 23, 1918.
' 13th TANK BATTALION.

' G.O.C. and all ranks 1st Australian Division desire to place on record their keen appreciation of what the tanks, officers and crews, have done for them to-day. To-day's success is very largely owing to what the tanks have done. Confidence borne of this will make it a great pleasure for the 1st Australian Division to fight with them again at any time.

' FROM 1st AUSTRALIAN DIVISION.'

'O.C. 13th Tank Battalion.

'The following wire, dated 23rd instant, has been sent to the G.O.C., 5th Tank Brigade, by the G.O.C., 1st Australian Division :—

'"G.O.C. and all ranks 1st Australian Division wish to thank the officers and crews of the 5th Tank Brigade for their splendid assistance rendered to-day. They will only be too honoured to serve with them again whenever the opportunity occurs."

'J. C. Jinks, *Captain*,
for Brigade-Major.

'H.Q., 5th Tank Brigade,
'*August* 24, 1918.'

COPY OF WIRE FROM AUSTRALIAN CORPS COMMANDER

'The Corps Commander desires to thank all ranks for their excellent work during yesterday's successful battle. The work by the tanks was admirably and gallantly carried out in the face of great difficulties, and is very highly appreciated. Addressed 2nd Tank Battalion, repeated 5th Tank Brigade.

'AUSTRALIAN CORPS.'

'*August* 12, 1918.

'O.C. 13th Tank Battalion.

'DEAR SIR,—On behalf of the officers, N.C.O.'s and men of "A" Company, 31st Battalion, A.I.F., I want to thank the officers (Capt. Bromley) and crews of the tanks "Mephistophiles," "Mosquito," and "Masterpiece" for the valuable assistance they gave us during the engagement of the 8th instant.

'We all honestly think that, had the tanks not been up to time at the Green Line, the damnably accurate point-blank shooting of the 77's in the neighbourhood would have seriously hindered our advance.

'I have never felt more grateful than I did at 8.20 A.M., when the three tanks waddled over the hill and calmly proceeded to deal with the guns—thereby enabling us to advance.

' I am afraid some members of the crews were badly knocked about, but we all hope that nobody was killed.

' If at any time in the future we are doing a show and tanks are required, we all trust that they will be manned by the 13th Battalion (by " A " Company if possible), and then the stunt will be a success.

' Sincerely yours,
' L. ROUNSON, Captain,
' O.C. " A " Company.'

The tank commanders referred to are :—

> 2nd Lieut. A. Chandley, ' Mephistophiles.'
> 2nd Lieut. H. F. Parker, ' Mosquito.'
> 2nd Lieut. A. King, ' Masterpiece.'

' August 12, 1918.

' MY DEAR MAJOR,—I am writing this note to you to offer yourself and your Tank Company our thanks for your most valuable co-operation with my battalion in the operations of the 7-8 instant.

' If I could only tell you all the flattering things that are said of your tanks I would need a newspaper to record them. I can safely say that if it had not been for the tanks our advance would not have been so rapid, and certainly our casualties would have been ever so much greater than they were. I don't know your tank commanders personally, but I wish you to convey to them and their crews my thanks for their good work.

' We also wish to express our sympathy with the losses sustained by your personnel.

' In conclusion, if we are engaged in any future operation we will be very pleased to have you with us.

' Yours sincerely,
' F. STREET, Major,
' C.O., 30th Battalion, A.I.F.

' MAJOR H. R. PAPE,
' " A " Coy., 13th Tank Battn.'

February 11, 1919.

' FROM 301ST AMERICAN TANK BATTALION.

' MY DEAR GENERAL,—Please accept eight hundred and twelve thanks from officers and other ranks for your recent gift of miniature tanks to this battalion. I know of no single act which has given more pleasure or elation to the command since arrival in Europe.

I thank you and all ranks of the British Tank Corps for your kindness and patience with our unit. During our period of service under five Tank Brigades, we have always met with a never failing courtesy, which has increased our desire to be worthy of serving with you. I regard our relationship as one of the practical examples of Anglo-American friendship with high ideals. We believe in the British Tank Corps.

' My very best regards,

' Cordially,

' R. I. SASSE.'

CHAPTER III

SPECIAL ORDER NO. I

1. (*a*) The following telegram has been received from the Commander-in-Chief :—

April 10.

'GENERAL OFFICER COMMANDING,
    ' Heavy Branch, Machine-Gun Corps.

' My congratulations on the excellent work done by the Heavy Branch of the Machine-Gun Corps during yesterday's operations. Please convey to those who took part my appreciation of the gallantry and skill shown by them.

                                     ' CHIEF.'

(*b*) The following reply was sent :—

April 10.

' ASSISTANT MILITARY SECRETARY,
    ' Commander-in-Chief,
        ' General Headquarters.

' All ranks Heavy Branch greatly inspired by the Chief's message. Please convey our thanks.

                ' *General Officer Commanding,*
                        ' *Heavy Branch.*'

2. In publishing the above telegram the Brigadier-General Commanding desires to add his appreciation of the

fine work done by central workshops and of the loyal co-operation of the 2nd Brigade and the training centre, Wool.
April 11, 1917.

SPECIAL ORDER NO. II

1. The following telegram has been received from the Second Army Commander by the General Commanding 2nd Brigade, Heavy Branch :—

' The Army Commander wishes to convey his sincere congratulations and thanks to the commander and all ranks of the 2nd Brigade for their excellent work in to-day's operations, which has been of the utmost value in assisting the troops of the Second Army to achieve the success they have gained. The Army Commander is very glad to hear that their losses have not been heavy.'

2. In publishing the above, the Brigadier-General commanding desires to express his appreciation of the success attained by the 2nd Brigade in the Messines Battle in spite of great difficulties of ground.

It was due to the admirable staff arrangements made by the brigade and battalions, and the determination displayed by all ranks to get through difficulties and into the enemy.

SPECIAL ORDER NO. III

The following is published for information :—

' *September* 7, 1917.

' 2nd BRIGADE, TANK CORPS.

' The Corps Commander desires to thank all ranks of the 2nd Brigade, Tank Corps, for the fine work they performed during recent operations.

' The weather and the ground were as unfavourable as it was possible to meet with for operations by " The Tanks," but thanks to good reconnaissance, careful study of maps and aeroplane photos, and the great gallantry and devotion

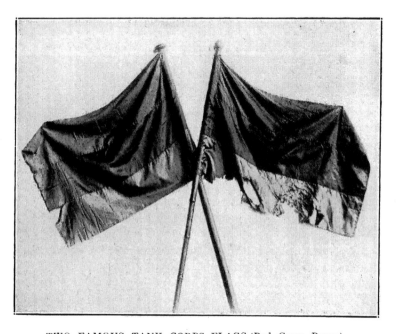

TWO FAMOUS TANK CORPS FLAGS (Red, Green, Brown).

On right, flag borne by Brig.-General H. J. Elles in the van of the attack, battle of Cambrai, November 20, 1917.

On left, flag carried across the Rhine by the 17th A. C. Battalion, the first British troops to enter Cologne.

SPECIAL ORDERS

to duty shown by all ranks, the 2nd Brigade, Tank Corps, was able to render material assistance to the infantry throughout the operations.

'The Corps Commander wishes all ranks of the 2nd Brigade, Tank Corps, every success, and hopes that when the II Corps again comes into the line he may be fortunate enough to have the 2nd Brigade to assist in the operations.

'STANHOPE, *Major*,
'*for B.-G., G.S.*'

SPECIAL ORDER NO. IV

SEPTEMBER 25, 1917

As the result of reports submitted to him by Commanders of Divisions and Brigades with which tanks have worked, the Army Commander was good enough yesterday to express his appreciation of the work done by all ranks in the recent operations and the gallantry displayed by crews.

While realizing the great difficulties we are faced with as regards ground, guns, and weather, he expressed the hope that we would be able to continue to help on our comrades of the infantry in the progress of the battle.

In the circumstances in which we are called upon to fight, this demands a high standard of determination and gallantry. I am confident that the demand will be met, and I so informed the Army Commander.

SPECIAL ORDER NO. V

BEFORE CAMBRAI

To-morrow the Tank Corps will have the chance for which they have been waiting for many months—to operate on good going in the van of the fight.

All that hard work and ingenuity can achieve has been done in the way of preparation.

It remains for unit commanders and tank crews to

complete the work by judgment and pluck in the battle itself.

In the light of past experiences, I leave the good name of the corps with great confidence in their hands.

I propose leading the attack of the centre division.

November 19, 1917.

SPECIAL ORDER NO. VI

AFTER CAMBRAI

The following memorandum from Major-General Sir J. E. Capper, K.C.B., Director-General, Tank Corps, has been received, and is published for the information of all ranks :—

'G.O.C. TANK CORPS, FRANCE.

' As representing the Tank Corps as a whole, I desire, in the name of the corps, to congratulate you and the officers and men under your command on the great success attained by the corps during the recent operations.

' The hard and constant work cheerfully endured during training and preparations, combined with the stout heart, courage and skill shown by all ranks in action, have resulted in one of the most important successes of the British Army in this campaign.

' The conduct of yourself, your staff, and all those under you have brought great honour to the corps.

' To me personally it is a source of great pride to be the representative of such a corps.

' J. E. CAPPER, *Major-General,*
' *Director-General, Tank Corps.*

' *November 28, 1917.*'

SPECIAL ORDER NO. VII

The following letter, which has been received from the Military Secretary, G.H.Q., is published for the information of all ranks :—

SPECIAL ORDERS

'G.O.C. Tank Corps.

' The Commander-in-Chief has read with interest and appreciation the report on the action of the 2nd Brigade, Tank Corps, on November 30 and December 1. He wishes his thanks and congratulations conveyed to Colonel Courage and all ranks of the brigade for their gallant and skilful conduct on this occasion.

' The rapid assembly of the brigade to meet a sudden emergency, and their effective disposal and gallant behaviour, afforded material assistance in a critical situation.

' W. E. Payton, Major-General,
' M.S. to C.-in-C.

'G.H.Q., December 11, 1917.'

SPECIAL ORDER NO. VIII

The following telegrams are published for information of all ranks :—

' To Brigadier-General Elles, Tank Corps, from Dudley Docker, Esq., Chairman Metropolitan Carriage Co., Birmingham.

' A resolution has been passed unanimously by the works people of the Metropolitan Carriage Co. to forego any holidays and do their utmost to expedite delivery of tanks to assist their comrades in the field.'

.   .   .   .

' To Dudley Docker, Esq., Metropolitan Carriage Co., Birmingham, from Brigadier-General Elles, Tank Corps.

' Please thank the men and tell them all ranks much appreciate at this moment the message from their comrades in the works.'

SPECIAL ORDER NO. IX

The value of tank stores (including 256 complete tanks) salved by Nos. 1 and 2 Tank Field Companies since their formation has been assessed at approximately one million three hundred thousand pounds.

The whole of this work has been carried out in conditions of great difficulty and discomfort, much of it under fire.

The result obtained reflects the highest credit on the officers and men of those units, and represents a continuous effort of which the Tank Corps may well be proud.

April 19, 1918.

SPECIAL ORDER NO. X

AFTER THE GERMAN ATTACK ON VILLERS-BRETONNEUX

1. The first engagement between British and German tanks has taken place.

Such actions will occur.

2. It is of importance that our moral and material ascendancy over hostile tanks should be established both early and decisively.

3. All ranks will therefore continue to engage them relentlessly.

4. The honour of the Tank Corps is involved.

HEADQUARTERS, TANK CORPS,
April 24, 1918.

SPECIAL ORDER NO. XI

1. The following telegram was sent on July 3, 1918, to Colonel Rockenback, Chief of Tank Service, G.H.Q., American Expeditionary Force :—

' British Tank Corps sends greetings to American Comrades.'

2. The following reply has been received :—

' American Tanks thank you and British Tank Corps for kind greetings. Hope soon to be charging by your side.'

July 7, 1918.

SPECIAL ORDER NO. XII

AFTER THE SUCCESS ON THE SOMME

At the close of the first phase of the present battle I wish to thank all ranks upon the success which has rewarded the energy, forethought, and devotion to duty which they have displayed.

The fighting reputation of the Tank Corps has been fully maintained.

Many thousand lives have been saved by the gallant way in which tanks have been fought.

Further calls will be made upon us.

We must meet them.

SPECIAL ORDER NO. XIII

The attached memorandum is published for the information of all ranks :—

' TANK CORPS.

' The success of the operations of August 8 and succeeding days was largely due to the conspicuous part played by the 3rd, 4th and 5th Brigades of the Tank Corps, and I desire to place on record my sincere appreciation of the services rendered both by the Mark V, the Mark V star, and the Whippets.

' The task of secretly assembling so large a number of tanks entailed very hard work by all concerned for four or five nights previous to the battle.

' The tactical handling of the tanks in action made calls on the skill and physical endurance of the detachments, which were met with a gallantry and devotion beyond all praise.

' I desire to place on record my appreciation of the splendid success that they achieved, and to heartily congratulate the Tank Corps as a whole on the completeness of their arrangements and the admirable prowess exhibited by all ranks actually engaged on this occasion.

' There are many vitally important lessons to be learned from their experiences. These will, I trust, be taken to heart by all concerned and made full use of when the Tank Corps is called upon to go into battle.

' The part played by the tanks and whippets in the battle of August 8 was in all respects a very fine performance.

'H. RAWLINSON, *General,*
' *Commanding Fourth Army.*'

SPECIAL ORDER NO. XIV

October 13, 1918.

1. Rumours are rife regarding the possibility of an early peace.

2. To spread such rumours by discussion and conjecture is to help forward propaganda initiated by the enemy for his own ends.

3. I place all ranks of the Tank Corps upon honour to refrain from discussion of this subject either directly or indirectly.

4. Our energies must be directed upon War.

(*To be read upon Parade by all Units.*)

SPECIAL ORDER NO. XV

October 18, 1918.

1. His Majesty the King was graciously pleased to become Colonel-in-Chief of the Tank Corps on the 17th instant.

2. The following telegram was sent on behalf of the Tank Corps :—

'To H.M. THE KING.

' The news that your Majesty has graciously consented to become Colonel-in-Chief of the Tank Corps has just been received here. All ranks are deeply sensible of this signal honour conferred upon the corps, and are determined to continue worthy of it.

' GENERAL ELLES.

' ADVANCED H.Q., TANK CORPS,
' In the Field, *October* 17.'

SPECIAL ORDERS

3. The following reply has been received :—
' To Major-General H. J. Elles,
   ' H.Q., Tank Corps,
     ' In the Field.

' I sincerely thank you for the message which you have conveyed to me in the name of all ranks of the Tank Corps.

' I am indeed proud to be Colonel-in-Chief of this great British organisation invented by us, which has played so prominent a part in our recent victories.

' I wish you all every possible good luck.

' George R.I., Colonel-in-Chief.

' Buckingham Palace, London,
   ' October 18.'

SPECIAL ORDER NO. XVI

November 20, 1918.

1. To-day is the anniversary of the Cambrai Battle.

2. During the memorable twelve months just elapsed, the Tank Corps, whilst undergoing laborious measures of expansion and organisation, has taken an honourable part in the great defensive and offensive battles of the year.

3. At Cambrai, which marked the beginning of a definite era in method of attack, and again in the defensive actions of the Spring Campaign, the Tank Corps was fought practically to a standstill.

The first counter-offensive on the Western Front was led by our units on July 4, and since that date we have had the privilege of fighting at the head of the Armies in eleven [1] pitched battles and twenty-six lesser engagements.

4. I take this occasion to express the sincerest thanks to all ranks for this long-sustained and successful effort, which has made high calls not only upon the skill of commanders and staffs and the tried courage of fighting

---

[1] July 23, August 8–11, August 21–25, September 2, September 27, September 29, October 3, October 8, October 17, October 23, November 4.

personnel, but in an especial degree upon the unobtrusive labours and devotion to duty of engineer, training, and administrative units.

5. The period before us will demand from all qualities of patience, steadiness, and good feeling. I am confident that these demands will be met with the same spirit by which past difficulties have been overcome.

SPECIAL ORDER NO. XVII

February 15, 1919.

1. On the departure of the 301st American Tank Battalion, I wish to place on record my appreciation of the services it has rendered.

2. The battalion has practically formed part of the British Tank Corps since April 1918, and while fully maintaining its national identity, has co-operated with British troops and adapted itself to British methods with a spirit that deserves fullest recognition.

3. In the field, the 301st Battalion, after experiencing heavy casualties in its first engagement at Bony, which might have deterred less determined troops, volunteered for the next action, in which, as in subsequent ones, it inflicted heavy casualties upon the enemy at Brancourt, the Selle, and Catillon.

4. I feel I am voicing the opinion of all commanders and troops who have been associated with them, in expressing sincere regret at the departure of our American comrades, and in wishing them all good fortune in the future.

HONOURS AWARDED TO TANK CORPS

List of Awards Gained by the Tank Corps 1916–18.

Officers

Unit.	V.C.	C.B.	C.M.G.	C.B.E.	O.B.E.	M.B.E.	Bar to D.S.O.	D.S.O.	Bar to M.C.	M.C.	Brevet Prom.	Legion d'Honneur.	Croix de Guerre.	Silver Medal of Italy.	Chevalier Leopold.	Belgian Croix de Guerre.	Star of Roumania.	Rising Sun of Japan.
1st Battn.	2							1	9	39			1					
2nd Battn.							2	5	3	37				1				
3rd Battn.	1		1					5	3	31			1	1	1	1		
4th Battn.								3	1	32			1			1		
5th Battn.								5	4	18		2	2				1	
6th Battn.	1						3	7	3	31			1			1		
7th Battn.								7	3	22	2							
8th Battn.							1	7	1	29								
9th Battn.								5	4	26		5	16					
10th Battn.								2	2	25								
11th Battn.								2	1	15			1					
12th Battn.			1					2		13	1							
13th Battn.								1	1	27			1					
14th Battn.									2	13								
15th Battn.									2	27	1							
16th Battn.										1								
17th Battn.										4	1						1	
Staff, H.-Q., Groups and Bdes.		1	3	2	5	1	3	9	1	15	8	1	1				2	1
Works					4			4		2								
Stores					1					1								
Field Coys.								2	1	2			1					
G. C. Coys.										6								
Supply Coys.								1		9								
Signals								1	1	1								
Depot & Schools					4			1		2								
Attached other units					5			3		15								
Home Est.			1		4			1		3	1							
Palestine								1		3								

Summary—Officers.

Total	V.C.	C.B.	C.M.G.	C.B.E.	O.B.E.	M.B.E.	Bar to D.S.O.	D.S.O.	Bar to M.C.	M.C.	Brevet Prom.	Legion d'Honneur.	Croix de Guerre.	Silver Medal of Italy.	Chevalier Leopold.	Belgian Croix de Guerre.	Star of Roumania.	Rising Sun of Japan.
	4	1	6	2	23	1	9	73	42	446	14	8	26	2	1	3	4	1

SUMMARY FOR TANK CORPS

British.

	V.C.	C.B.	C.M.G.	C.B.E.	O.B.E.	M.B.E.	Bar to D.S.O.	D.S.O.	Bar to M.C.	M.C.	Brevet Prom.	Bar to D.C.M.	D.C.M.	Bar to M.M.	M.M.	M.S.M.
Total	4	1	6	2	23	1	9	73	42	447	14	1	144	23	604	106

List of Awards Gained by the Tanks Corps, 1916–18

Other Ranks

Unit	M.C.	Bar to D.C.M.	D.C.M.	Bar to M.M.	M.M.	M.S.M.	Croix de Guerre	Médaille Militaire	Médaille d'Honneur	Ordre de Leopold II	Belg. Croix de Guerre	Decoration Militaire	Bronze Medal of Italy	Croix de V.M. Roumania
1st Battn.			21	1	60	5	2		1		3		2	
2nd Battn.			13	3	44	4	1	1			4			
3rd Battn.			15	7	64	4	1	1		2	3			
4th Battn.			15	1	52	3	5	3	1		2	1		1
5th Battn.			4		29	3		1			2			
6th Battn.			8	1	41	5	1	1			1		1	
7th Battn.			5	1	28	3	3				4		2	1
8th Battn.			9		39	2	2	2			1			
9th Battn.			4	3	47	5	20	12						
10th Battn.			5	2	36	2						1		
11th Battn.			5	1	12	1		1				1		
12th Battn.			2		8	3		2				1		
13th Battn.			4	3	38	3						1		
14th Battn.			4		12	3								
15th Battn.			3		34	2								
16th Battn.			2		5	1								
17th Battn.			2		12									
Staff, Bdes. & H.-Q.			1		2	13						2		
Works						16					2			
Stores						5								
T. Field Coys.	1		7		6	2			2				1	
Supply Coys.			4		11									
G. C. Coys.		1	1		2	2		1	1					
Signals			3		4	2			1					
Attached, other units			3		17	12								
Depot and Schools						1			3					
Home Est.						4								
Palestine			4		1									

Summary—Other Ranks.

Total	1	1	144	23	604	106	35	25	10	2	22	6	6	2

Summary¹ for Tank Corps

	French				Belgian.				Italian.		Roumanian.		Japan.
	Legion d'Honneur.	Croix de Guerre.	Médaille Militaire.	Médaille d'Honneur.	Chevalier Order of Leopold.	Order of Leopold II.	Croix de Guerre.	Decoration Militaire.	Silver Medal.	Bronze Medal.	Star.	Croix de V.M.	Rising Sun.
Total	8	61	25	10	1	2	25	6	2	6	4	2	1

¹ Exclusive of honours in *Peace Gazette*.

CHAPTER IV

DEEDS WHICH WON THE VICTORIA CROSS

Capt. **ROBERTSON, CLEMENT.** 1st Battn.

For conspicuous gallantry and devotion to duty in the Third Battle of Ypres.

From September 30 to October 4 this officer worked without a break under heavy fire preparing a route for his tanks to go into action against Reutel. He finished late on the night of October 3, and at once led his tanks up to the starting point for the attack. He brought them safely up by 3 A.M. on October 4, and at 6 A.M. led them into action. The ground was very bad and heavily broken by shell fire and the road demolished for 500 yards. Captain Robertson, knowing the risk of the tanks missing the way, continued to lead them on foot. In addition to the heavy shell fire, an intense machine-gun and rifle fire was directed at the tanks. Although knowing that his action would almost inevitably cost him his life, Captain Robertson deliberately continued to lead the tanks when well ahead of our own infantry, guiding them carefully and patiently towards their objective. Just as they reached the road he was killed by a bullet through the head ; but his objective had been reached, and the tanks in consequence were enabled to fight a very successful action.

By his very gallant devotion Captain Robertson deliberately sacrificed his life to make certain the success of his tanks.

T. Lieut. (A./Capt.) **WAIN, RICHARD WILLIAM LESLIE.** 1st Battn.

For most conspicuous gallantry in action near Marcoing on November 20, 1917, while in command of a section of tanks.

During the attack, the tank in which he was became disabled by a direct hit near a German strong point in the Hindenburg Support Line, and at L.34.a.3.6, which was holding up the attack, Captain Wain and one man were the only survivors, and they were both seriously wounded. While the infantry were held up there, this officer, in spite of his wounds, rushed from behind the tank in front of the enemy strong point with a Lewis gun and captured the strong point, taking about half the garrison prisoners. Although his wounds were very serious, Captain Wain picked up a rifle and continued to fire at the retiring enemy until he received a fatal wound in the head. Though bleeding profusely from wounds, this gallant officer refused attention of stretcher-bearers in order to carry on clearing the enemy out of the strong point.

It was due to this most gallant act by this officer that the infantry were able to advance.

Lieut. SEWELL, CECIL HAROLD. 3rd Battn.

When in command of a section of whippet (light) tanks in action in front of Fremicourt on the afternoon of August 29, 1918, this officer displayed the greatest gallantry and initiative in getting out of his own tank and crossing open ground under heavy shell and machine-gun fire to rescue the crew of another whippet of his section, which had side-slipped into a large shell-hole, overturned, and taken fire. The door of the tank having become jammed against the side of the shell-hole, Lieut. Sewell, by his own unaided efforts, dug away the entrance to the door and released the crew. In doing so he undoubtedly saved the lives of the officers and men inside the tank, as they could not have got out without his assistance.

After having extricated this crew, seeing one of his own crew lying wounded behind his tank, he again dashed across the open ground to his assistance. He was hit while doing so, but succeeded in reaching the tank, when a few minutes later he was again hit fatally, in the act of dressing his wounded driver.

During the whole of this period he was in full view and short range of enemy machine-guns and rifle pits, and throughout, by his prompt and heroic action, showed an utter disregard for his own personal safety.

Capt. (A/Lieut.-Col.) WEST, RICHARD ANNESLEY. 6th Battn.

For most conspicuous bravery and brilliant leadership on August 21 at Courcelles, and again for amazing self-sacrifice near Vaulx-Vraucourt on September 2, 1918.

On August 21, during the attack on Courcelles, the infantry having lost their bearings in the dense fog, this officer at once took charge of any men he could find. He reorganised them and led them on horseback through the village on to their objective in face of heavy machine-gun fire. He had two horses shot from under him during the morning. Throughout the whole action he displayed the most utter disregard of danger, and the capture of the village was in a great part due to his initiative and gallantry.

On September 2 it was intended that a battalion of light tanks under the command of this officer should exploit the initial infantry and heavy tank attack. He therefore rode forward on horseback to our front infantry line in order to keep in touch with the progress of the battle and to be in a position to launch his tanks at the right moment. He arrived at the front line when the enemy were in process of delivering a local counter-attack. The infantry battalion had suffered heavy officer casualties, and its flanks were exposed. Realising that there was a danger of the battalion giving way, he at once rode out in front of them under extremely heavy machine-gun and rifle fire and rallied the men. In spite of the fact that the enemy were close upon him, he took charge of the situation and detailed N.C.O.'s to replace officer casualties. He then rode up and down in front of them in face of certain death, encouraging the men and calling to them, ' Stick it, men : show them fight, and for God's sake put up a good fight.' He fell riddled by machine-gun bullets.

The magnificent bravery of this very gallant officer at the critical moment inspired the infantry to redoubled efforts, and undoubtedly saved the situation. The hostile attack was defeated.

HONOURS, OTHER THAN IMMEDIATE AWARDS, WON BY THE TANK CORPS

1917

Col. HARDRESS-LLOYD, J., D.S.O., 3rd Brigade, Bar to D.S.O.
Col. COURAGE, A., M.C., 2nd Brigade, D.S.O.
Major DICK, T. S., 'C' Battn. Workshops, D.S.O.
Major JOHNSON, P. H., 'D' Battn. Workshops, D.S.O.
Capt. MARTEL, G. Le Q., D.S.O., M.C., Tank Corps H.Q., Brevet Major.
Capt. BROOME, R. H., M.C., Depot, Brevet Major.
Capt. CARTER, E. J., 'C' Battn., Brevet Major.
Lieut. MURRAY-MENZIES, D. I., 'C.' Battn., M.C.
Capt. WOODS, A. G., 2nd Brigade, M.C.
Capt. VERMALL, J. H., M.C.

JANUARY 1918

Brig.-Gen. ELLES, H. J., D.S.O., Commanding Tank Corps, C.B.
Col. BAKER-CARR, C. D'A., D.S.O., 1st Brigade, C.M.G.
Col. COURAGE, A., D.S.O., M.C., 2nd Brigade, Bt. Lieut.-Col.
Lieut.-Col. FULLER, J. F. C., D.S.O., Headquarters, Bt. Lieut.-Col.
Lieut.-Col. E. B. MATHEW-LANNOWE, D.S.O., Home Est., Bt. Lieut.-Col.
Lieut.-Col. SEARLE, F., Headquarters, D.S.O.
Lieut.-Col. HILL, R. C. R., 'B' Battn., D.S.O.
Lieut.-Col. HANKEY, E. B., 'G' Battn., D.S.O.
Lieut.-Col. KYNGDON, W. F. R., 'D' Battn., D.S.O.
Major BUTLER, Hon. R. T. R. P., M.C., 1st Salvage Coy., D.S.O.
Major HASLAM, P. L. C., 'C' Battn., D.S.O.
Major FERNIE, F. H., 'G' Battn., D.S.O.
Capt. FOOT, S. H., 2nd Brigade, D.S.O.
Major TILLY, J. C., 'A' Battn., M.C.
Capt. WILLIAMS-ELLIS, C., 1st Brigade, M.C.

HONOURS, OTHER THAN IMMEDIATE AWARDS

Capt. COX, L. H., 3rd Brigade, M.C.

Capt. HATTON-HALL, H. C., ' G ' Battn., M.C.

Capt. CAZALET, R. de B., 2nd Brigade, M.C.

Capt. ALLEN, G. W. G., ' A ' Battn., M.C.

Capt. THORP, B. L., Central Workshops, M.C.

Capt. LOWN, F. W., ' B ' Battn., M.C.

Lieut. LEWIS, G. C., ' C ' Battn., M.C.

2nd Lieut. LENNARD, E. S., ' F ' Battn., M.C.

2nd Lieut. BAYNHAM, A. G., ' C ' Battn., M.C.

Lieut.-Col. FULLER, J. F. C., D.S.O., Tank Corps Headquarters, Chevalier Legion d'Honneur.

Lieut.-Col. CHARRINGTON, S. H., D.S.O., 3rd Battn., Croix de Guerre.

Capt. HENRIQUES, B. L. Q., 7th Battn., Italian Silver Medal.

200507 A/R.S.M. BENNETT, G. F., ' C ' Battn., D.C.M.

32554 A/M.S.M. WHITTAKER, F., 1st Salvage Coy., D.C.M.

200940 A/C.S.M. ROBINSON, F., 1st Bde. Workshops, D.C.M.

77474 Sergt. WATT, F. W., ' A ' Battn., D.C.M.

40313 Sergt. WHITE, H. A., ' G ' Battn., D.C.M.

200773 Sergt. ROBERTSON, D., ' D ' Battn., D.C.M.

91977 A/L/Corpl. BURDEN, L. J., ' F ' Battn., D.C.M.

69647 Gunner BREAKEY, W., ' F ' Battn., D.C.M.

40068 A/R.S.M. SMOOTHEY, J., ' B ' Battn., M.S.M.

77426 Sergt. GARDNER, J. E., ' A ' Battn., M.S.M.

77130 A/Sergt. GARRETT, J., Central Workshops, M.S.M.

JUNE 1918

Lieut.-Col. CHARRINGTON, S. H., D.S.O., 3rd Tank Battn., C.M.G.

Capt. (A/Major) ROSSI-ASHTON, C. G., 7th Tank Battn., Brevet Major.

Capt. THORPE, C. R. T., M.C., 1st Tank Battn., Brevet Major.

Major HAMOND, P., D.S.O., M.C., 6th Tank Battn., Bar to D.S.O.

Lieut.-Col. SPROT, A. W. R., T. and R. Depot, D.S.O.

Lieut.-Col. BROCKBANK, J. G., Central Workshops, D.S.O.

Major ATKIN-BERRY, H. C., M.C., Headquarters, D.S.O.

Major HAWKINS, C. F., M.C., 6th Tank Battn., D.S.O.

Major POE, W. S., 9th Tank Battn., D.S.O.

Major RADCLYFFE, C. R., Central Stores, D.S.O.
Capt. PIGOTT, J. G., R.A.M.C., O.B.E.
Capt. KNIGHT, R. C., M.C., 2nd Tank Bde., Bar to M.C.
Capt. JACKSON, W. F., M.C. (R.E.), 2nd Bde. Sig. Coy., Bar to M.C.
Capt. LOVERIDGE, J. L., M.C., 1st Tank Battn., Bar to M.C.
2nd Lieut. CARTER, B. S., M.C., 5th Tank Battn., Bar to M.C.
Major BOYD-ROCHFORT, H., D.S.O., Headquarters, M.C.
Major DUNDAS, R. W., Headquarters, M.C.
Major GREEN, G. A., C. of. W., M.C.
Major LASKEY, F. S., 2nd Tank Battn., M.C.
Capt. ALLDAY, F. C. A., 4th Tank Battn., M.C.
Capt. BROWN, J. C., 1st Tank Battn., M.C.
Capt. HILL, A. C., Central Workshops, M.C.
Capt. HORSLEY, W., 6th Tank Battn., M.C.
Capt. NIXON, G., 4th Tank Battn., M.C.
Capt. PARTINGTON, W., 1st G. C. Coy., M.C.
Capt. SMITH, S. A., 7th Tank Battn., M.C.
Capt. SPRAY, A., 8th Tank Battn., M.C.
Capt. SANDERS, E. R., 3rd Tank Battn., M.C.
Capt. TAPPER, M., 1st Tank Battn., M.C.
Capt. THURSTON, J. S., 6th Tank Battn., M.C.
Capt. WILLIAMS, R. E., 3rd Tank Battn., M.C.
Capt. SPENCER, R., 3rd Tank Battn., M.C.
Lieut. ARNAUD, A. L., Mech. School, M.C.
Lieut. HOPKINS, W. S., Mech. School, M.C.
Lieut. JACKSON, G. J., 8th Tank Battn., M.C.
2nd Lieut. BUDGE, H. P., 5th Tank Battn., M.C.
2nd Lieut. BAKER, A. H., 1st Tank Fd. Coy., M.C.
2nd Lieut. BEECROFT, J. E., 2nd Tank Fd. Coy., M.C
2nd Lieut. LENARD, F. R., 5th Tank Battn., M.C.
2nd Lieut. BENSTEAD, C. G., 1st Tank Battn., M.C.
95393 M.S.S.M. RUTTER, J. F., 2nd Tank Fd. Coy., M.C.
69715 A/Sergt. CUTHBERT, F. W., 6th Tank Battn., D.C.M.
95531 C.S.M. DICK, T., 7th Tank Battn., D.C.M.
75036 Pte. ELLIOTT, S. A., 4th Tank Battn., D.C.M.
96474 Sergt. FOWLER, W., 2nd Tank Fd. Battn., D.C.M.
MS/1585 Sergt. HOOKLEY (R.A.S.C.), 3rd Tank Battn., D.C.M.

HONOURS, OTHER THAN IMMEDIATE AWARDS

200226 **C.S.M. STIRTON, G. C.**, 2nd Tank Battn., D.C.M.

92836 **Sergt. STRANG, J.**, 1st G. C. Coy., D.C.M.

S/14179 **1st Class S.S.M. BOXALL, A. E.** (R.A.S.C.), Headquarters, M.S.M.

200028 **Sergt. ANDERSON, D.**, 1st Tank Battn., M.S.M.

16756 **Sergt. BENNETT, A.** (R.A.S.C.), 2nd Tank Bde., M.S.M.

200124 **Pte. BURGESS, R. J.**, 1st Tank Battn., M.S.M.

92348 **L/Corpl. COLTON, J.**, 9th Tank Battn., M.S.M.

76783 **Sergt. DEVEREUX, A. E.**, 3rd Tank Battn., M.S.M.

202042 **Corpl. DUNN, J. E.**, 8th Tank Battn., M.S.M.

201626 **Sergt. ERRICKER, E. M.**, Central Workshops, M.S.M.

201926 **Sergt. FAULKNER, E. L.**, Mech. School, M.S.M.

77295 **A/M/S. Sergt. FOX, S. J.**, Central Workshops, M.S.M.

75305 **S/Sergt. FILER, L. B.**, 2nd Tank Battn., M.S.M.

81874 **Corpl. HAWORTH, F.**, (R.E.), Headquarters, M.S.M.

201632 **Sergt. HOLLAND, A.**, Central Workshops, M.S.M.

76697 **Corpl. HANDFORTH, J.**, 2nd Tank Battn., M.S.M.

201984 **Sergt. HARRIES, D. G.**, 8th Tank Battn., M.S.M.

91952 **Pte. HAWKINS, F. H.**, 9th Tank Battn., M.S.M.

95533 **Sergt. PEATTIE, W.**, 5th Tank Battn., M.S.M.

77174 **C.S.M. RAWNSLEY, H.**, 1st Tank Battn., M.S.M.

77203 **Corpl. ROACH, J. J.**, Central Workshops, M.S.M.

201624 **A/Sergt. ROURKE, P.**, Central Stores, M.S.M.

201363 **A/C.Q.M.S. ROBERTS, O. W.**, 7th Tank Battn., M.S.M.

201134 **Gnr. REID, W. H.**, 8th Tank Battn., M.S.M.

78798 **A/Sergt. SHIED, O. J.**, 5th Tank Battn., M.S.M.

201077 **A/Corpl. STOKES, E. H.**, 6th Tank Battn., M.S.M.

78425 **Sergt. TUGWELL, C. B.**, 5th Tank Battn., M.S.M.

201331 **L/Corpl. WALLER, R. W.**, 7th Tank Battn., M.S.M.

200436 **L/Corpl. WIENCKE, H. J.**, 3rd Tank Battn., M.S.M.

JANUARY 1919

Brig.-Gen. HANKEY, E. B., D.S.O., 3rd Tank Group, Bt. Col.

Brig.-Gen. PIGOT, R., D.S.O., M.C., 6th Tank Brigade, Bt. Lieut.-Col.

Col. UZIELLI, T. J., D.S.O., M.C., Headquarters, Tank Corps, Bt. Lieut.-Col.

Lieut.-Col. CARTER, E. J., 17th (A.C.) Tank Battn., Bt. Lieut.-Col.

THE TANK CORPS BOOK OF HONOUR

Brig.-Gen. E. B. MATHEW LANNOWE, D.S.O., Training Centre, C.M.G.

Brig.-Gen. RAMSAY-FAIRFAX, W. G. A., D.S.O., 3rd Tank Brigade, C.M.G.

Lieut.-Col. BELFIELD, W., A. D. of T. Tank Corps, C.M.G.

Major LAUGHTON, J. V., T. and R. Depot, C.B.E.

Capt. MOKE-NORRIE, C. W., M.C., 2nd Tank Group, D.S.O.

Major WOODS, A. G., M.C., 1st Tank Group, D.S.O.

Capt. KNIGHT, R. C., Bde. Major, 5th Bde., D.S.O.

Major LESLIE, J., M.C., 6th Tank Battn., D.S.O.

Major BENNEWITH, J. A., 8th Tank Battn., D.S.O.

Lieut.-Col. BUTLER, W. M., 9th Tank Battn., D.S.O.

Major CLARK, C. W., M.C., C.M.E. Estab., D.S.O.

Major CARR, A. E., M.C., Tank Field Battn., D.S.O.

Major LEIGH-MALLORY, T., 8th Squadron, R.A.F., D.S.O.

Major BOXALL, R. W., E. Officer, 3rd Group, M.C.

Capt. ALKER, F., 1st Tank Group, M.C.

Capt. FITZMAURICE, F. G., 1st Tank Group, M.C.

Capt. ROBERTS, A. B. P., 4th Tank Brigade, M.C.

2nd Lieut. CHARTER, C. W., 1st Tank Battn., M.C.

Capt. HOYLAND, W. L., 2nd Tank Battn., M.C.

Capt. WHYTE, A. M., 2nd Tank Battn., M.C.

Capt COZENS, F., 4th Tank Battn., M.C.

Capt. CHAPMAN, A. R., 6th Tank Battn., M.C.

Capt. CHAMBERLEN, Rev. L. G., 8th Tank Battn., M.C.

Capt. DEMUTH, W. E., 3rd Tank Brigade, M.C.

Major CROXFORD, L. J., 10th Tank Battn., M.C.

Major FREEMAN, R. A. F., 11th Tank Battn., M.C.

Capt. COCKSHUT, E. S., 12th Tank Battn., M.C.

Capt. HARLAND, L. S., 4th Tank Carrier Coy., M.C.

Lieut. WOOD, T., No. 1 Tank Stores, M.C.

Capt. CHURCHILL, E. F., 2nd Tank Group, M.C.

Lieut. MILLAR, R. M., 6th Tank Battn., M.C.

Major MARKS, E. S., O.B.E.

Major QUILTER, E. C., Headquarters, Tank Corps, O.B.E.

Major RENOUF, C. P., C.M.E. Estab., O.B.E.

Major WILKS, J. E., C.M.E. Estab., O.B.E.

Capt. HORNIDGE, E. S., R.A.S.C., 1st Group, O.B.E.

Major BRAYBROOK, H. G., R.A.O.C. (Central Ordnance Workshops), O.B.E.

Capt. SHAW, P., School of Gunnery, O.B.E.

Major PALMER, A. J., O.B.E.

HONOURS, OTHER THAN IMMEDIATE AWARDS

Capt. **BRAND, E. B.**, R.A.S.C., 2nd Group, M.B.E.

200043 **C.S.M. ROBERTSON, D.**, 1st Tank Battn., D.C.M.

75013 **Pte. CLEMENTS, G.**, 1st Tank Battn., D.C.M.

75964 **Corpl. KAY, E.**, 1st Tank Battn., D.C.M.

75922 **M/S/Sergt. REES, J.**, 2nd Tank Battn., D.C.M.

75480 **C.Q.M.S. HUNT, J.**, 2nd Tank Battn., D.C.M.

92659 **Sergt. CLEMENTS, A. E.**, 5th Tank Battn., D.C.M.

40274 **Sergt. CALLAGHAN, J.**, 8th Tank Battn., D.C.M.

75700 **Sergt. GOULD, F.**, 11th Tank Battn., D.C.M.

112286, **Pte. SANDFORD, R.**, 11th Tank Battn., D.C.M.

538400 **Corpl. HORWOOD, A. A.**, 3rd Tank Bde. Sig. Company (R.E.), D.C.M.

309081 **Sergt. PARSONS, R. T. G.**, 24th Battn., M.M.

309289 **Corpl. EDMUNDS, F. G.**, 24th Battn., M.M.

302953 **Sergt.-Major GLEESON, A. J.**, Headquarters, Tank Corps, M.S.M.

302972 **Sergt.-Major ROBERTS, W.**, Headquarters, Tank Corps, M.S.M.

120708 **Sergt. HARFIELD, A. G.**, R.E. Headquarters, Tank Corps, M.S.M.

S/5344 **T/Sub/Condr. CAROLAN, W.**, R.A.O.C., Headquarters, Tank Corps, M.S.M.

303008 **L/Corpl. BINNIE, T. G.**, 3rd Tank Brigade, M.S.M.

75161 **S/Sergt. RUTHERFORD, G. B.**, 3rd Tank Battn., M.S.M.

75158 **S/Sergt. WATSON, W.**, 3rd Tank Battn., M.S.M.

200697 **R.S.M. TURNER, A. E.**, 4th Tank Battn., M.S.M.

75429 **C.Q.M.S. STEVENS, S. J.**, 4th Tank Battn., M.S.M.

69723 **L/Corpl. WEATHERALL, C. G. O.**, 6th Tank Battn., M.S.M.

201531 **R.Q.M.S. DEEMING, C.**, 9th Tank Battn., M.S.M.

109845 **M.S/Sergt. GREENHILL, F. J.**, 12th Tank Battn., M.S.M.

205109 **T.M/Sergt. CURTIS, S. B.**, 12th Tank Battn., M.S.M.

301254 **C.S.M. FOLEY, S.**, 13th Tank Battn., M.S.M.

94828 **C.S.M. BANBURY, H. H.**, 13th Tank Battn., M.S.M.

205223 **T.Q.M.S. HILL, A. W.**, 14th Tank Battn., M.S.M.

97200 **T.M.S/Sergt. HITCHCOCK, P. W.**, 14th Tank Battn., M.S.M.

111349 **T.M.S/Sergt. BROWN, J. E.**, 15th Tank Battn., M.S.M.

111231 S/Sergt. **POMEROY, L. E.**, 2nd Tank Carrier Coy., M.S.M.

92451 **C.S.M. BANNISTER, P. F.**, 1st G. C. Company, M.S.M.

111221 Sergt.-Major **MARSH, A.**, Chief Mech. Engineer, M.S.M.

75090 Sergt. **LOW, F. C.**, Tank Field Battn., M.S.M.

76205 Sergt. **MARGETTS, W. P.**, Central Workshops, M.S.M.

93112 L/Corpl. **CARGILL, W. R.**, Central Workshops, M.S.M.

77164 Sergt. **WARD, E.**, Central Workshops, M.S.M.

94841 Pte. **JEFFERIES, H.**, Central Workshops, M.S.M.

77534 Sergt. **PULLEN, J.**, Central Workshops, M.S.M.

76956 **C.Q.M.S. TEMPANY, F. R.**, No. 2 Tank Stores, M.S.M.

75199 Sergt. **HIGSON, B. C.**, No. 2 Tank Stores, M.S.M.

200721 S/Sergt. **ROBINSON, W. E.**, No. 1 Tank Stores, M.S.M.

M2/019287 M.S/Sergt. **BAILEY,W.**, 711 (M.T.) Coy., R.A.S.C., M.S.M.

M2/153394 M.S/Sergt. **PATERSON, H. G. C.**, 711 (M.T.) Coy., R.A.S.C., M.S.M.

M2/116644 Corpl. **RICHARDS, J. A.**, 711 (M.T.) Coy., R.A.S.C., M.S.M.

35497 **C.S.M. BECKETT, F. F.**, 2nd Bde. Sig. Coy., R.E., M.S.M.

77358 **C.S.M. BOTTOMLEY, E.**, **M.M.**, T. and R. Depot, M.S.M.

302266 Sergt. **ROSE, S.**, School of Gunnery, M.S.M.

JUNE 3, 1919

Capt. (A/Lieut.-Col.) **BINGHAM, Hon. J. D. Y.**, **D.S.O.**, 15th Battn. To be Bt. Lieut.-Col. on promotion.

Capt. (T. Lieut.-Col.) **BOYD-ROCHFORT, H.**, **D.S.O.**, **M.C.**, Headquarters. To be Bt. Lieut.-Col. on promotion.

Capt. (Bt. Major) A/Lieut.-Col. **NEAME, P.**, **V.C.**, **D.S.O.**, R.E., 2nd Group. To be Bt. Lieut.-Col. on promotion.

Capt. (T. Major) **KENCHINGTON, A. G.**, **M.C.**, 7th Battn., Bt. Major.

Capt. (T. Major) **COX, L. H.**, 1st Group, Bt. Major.

Lieut. (A/Capt.) **HAMLET, F. A.**, 2nd Battn., Bt. Major.

HONOURS, OTHER THAN IMMEDIATE AWARDS

Major (T. Lieut.-Col.) SHANNON, W. J., D.S.O., 12th Battn., C.M.G.

Major (T. Lieut.-Col.) LYON, P., 13th Battn., D.S.O.

Major (A/Lieut.-Col.) LLOYD, O. F., 12th Battn., D.S.O.

Major (A/Lieut.-Col.) BELL, W., 3rd Battn., D.S.O.

Capt. (A/Lieut.-Col.) TILLY, J. C., 10th Battn., D.S.O.

T. Capt. (A/Lieut.-Col.) ARNOLD, W., C.M.E.'s Dept., D.S.O.

Capt. (A/Lieut.-Col.) A. H. T. LORD SOMERS, M.C., 6th Battn., D.S.O.

T. Major ALLEN, D. C., 15th Battn., D.S.O.

Capt. (T. Major) McMICKING, N., M.C., 3rd Tank Group, D.S.O.

Capt. (T. Major) LEWIS, J. E., 15th Battn., D.S.O.

T. Major WATSON, W. H. L., D.C.M., 4th Carrier Co., D.S.O.

Lieut. ARNOLD, C. B., 6th Battn., D.S.O.

T. Col. SEARLE, F., D.S.O., Headquarters, C.B.E.

T. Capt. ENOCH, A. J., 4th Battn., M.C.

T. 2nd Lieut. COURT, G. R., 4th Battn., M.C.

T. Capt. HODGES, G. A., R.A.M.C., 5th Battn., M.C.

T. Capt. MACGILL, R., R.A.M.C., 6th Battn., M.C.

T. Lieut. (A/Capt.) BEALE, B. S., 7th Battn., M.C.

T. Lieut. (A/Capt.) HOOPER, E. J., 8th Battn., M.C.

Lieut. (A/Capt.) HIGGITT, F. A., 9th Battn., M.C.

Capt. SHOTT, C. D., 10th Battn., M.C.

T. Capt. HISCOCKS, H. H., 11th Battn., M.C.

Lieut. DIXON, A. C., 11th Battn., M.C.

T. Lieut. (A/Capt.) BEDDOW, H. E., 12th Battn., M.C.

Lieut. (A/Capt.) WARBURTON, R., 12th Battn., M.C.

T. Major MAURICE, R. Fitz G., 13th Battn., M.C.

T. Lieut. (T. Capt.) HILL, B. B., 13th Battn., M.C.

T. Lieut. (A/Capt.) HODGKINSON, P. S., 14th Battn., M.C.

T. Lieut. (A/Major) SMITH, G. A., 15th Battn., M.C.

Capt. ATHERTON, J. S., 16th Battn., M.C.

T. 2nd Lieut. HERD, D. W., 17th Battn., M.C.

Capt. (T. Major) TAWSE, A. B., T. Field Battn., M.C.

T. 2nd Lieut. LYLE, R. R., T. Field Battn., M.C.

A/Capt. BURNS, W. P., 1st Battn., M.C.

Capt. MACMILLAN, J., R.A.M.C., 1st Battn., M.C.

T. Capt. DILLON, N. M., 2nd Battn., M.C.

Lieut. (A/Capt.) RICE, C. E., 2nd Battn., M.C.

Lieut. (A/Capt.) DOYLE, J. E., 2nd Battn., M.C.

T. Lieut. (A/Capt.) HENDERSON, A. M., 3rd Battn., M.C.

T. Lieut. (A/Capt.) BULLPITT, K. D., T. Field Battn., M.C.
Lieut. (A/Capt.) SUTTON, W., 2nd Carrier Coy., M.C.
Capt. RODWELL, H., 3rd Carrier Coy., M.C.
A/Capt. RITCHIE, J. D., 4th Carrier Coy., M.C.
Capt. STANFORD, J. K., 2nd Brigade, M.C.
T. Capt. WILDING, F., R.A.S.C., attached 3rd Group, M.C.
Capt. WEIR, C. M., 2nd Brigade, M.C.
A/Capt. FRASER, H. J., 3rd Group, M.C.
T. Lieut. (A/Capt.) SPEARS, E. F. C., 1st Brigade Signals, M.C.
2nd Lieut. (T. Lieut.) FERGUSON, I. R., 8th Battn., M.C.
T. Capt. (A/Lieut.-Col.) PRICE, C. W., M.C., Headquarters, O.B.E.
T. Lieut. (A/Major) BRICE, A. V., R.E., attached Headquarters, O.B.E.
T. Major HUMPHREYS, H. H., M.C., R.A.S.C., attached Headquarters, O.B.E.
T. Capt. (A/Major) BROSTER, L. R. M.B., R.A.M.C., attached Headquarters, O.B.E.
T. Lieut. (A/Major) HASTIE, S. H., M.C., Schools, O.B.E.
Lieut. (A/Major) MASTERSON, W., Schools, O.B.E.
T. Capt. BLISS, W. E., R.A.S.C., Headquarters, O.B.E.
T. Capt. (A/Major) COLIN-YORKE, W. D., C.M.E.'s Dept., O.B.E.
T. Lieut. (A/Major) HOLMES, D. C., C.M.E.'s Dept., O.B.E.
T. Capt. (A/Major) GIBB, W. M., Central Stores, O.B.E.
T. Major MARKS, E. S., Training Centre, O.B.E.
2nd Lieut. (A/Capt.) TARGETT, H., R.W. Surrey Regt., attached C.M.E.'s Dept., O.B.E.
Capt. (T. Major) EATON, H. R., 3rd Tank Group, O.B.E.
T. Major PALMER, A. J., Training Centre, O.B.E.

LATER FOREIGN DECORATIONS

Lieut.-Col. CARTER, E. J., 17th Battn., Off. Star of Roumania.
T. Lieut. REYNOLDS, L., 5th Battn., Chev. Star of Roumania.
Capt. (A/Major) BODEN, A. P., Headquarter Sigs., Croix de Guerre.
Capt. GARLICK, R. R., 11th Battn., Croix de Guerre.
Major BRUCE, E. M., Special Mission, O. of Rising Sun, Japan.

JUNE 9

Major and Bt. Lieut.-Col. (T. Brig.-Gen.) COURAGE, A.,
D.S.O., M.C., 2nd Group, Bt. Col.
Lieut.-Col. (T. Brig.-Gen.) KARSLAKE, H., C.M.G., D.S.O.,
Headquarters, Bt. Col.
210680 R.Q.M.S. MILES, H. A., Field Battn., D.C.M.
76543 Sergt. FINDLAY, J. A., Field Battn., D.C.M.
95246 Sergt. WATSON, R., Field Battn., D.C.M.
75968 Corpl. JOHNSON, T., 1st Battn., D.C.M.
309352 C.S.M. BOUGH, A., 17th Battn., D.C.M.
301487 S/S/M. WILLS, T., 14th Battn., D.C.M.
110119 Sergt. NUTTALL, J. H., 10th Battn., D.C.M.
77427 C.Q.M.S. JARVIS, H., 1st Battn., D.C.M.
547281 Sergt. TURNBULL, S., R.E., 2nd Brigade Signals,
D.C.M.
200459 Corpl. JACK, A., 3rd Battn., D.C.M.
55109 Mech. S/Sergt. TURNER, S. W., 2nd Battn., D.C.M.
307497 Sergt. COATES, T. H., 3rd Carrier Coy., D.C.M.
200394 C.Q.M.S. SHAW, H. S., 2nd Battn., D.C.M.
110410 S/Sergt. HENSON, A. J., 3rd Carrier Coy., D.C.M.
75097 Mech. S/Sergt. WHEELHOUSE, C. E., 2nd Battn.,
D.C.M.
75657 Sergt. FLOWER, W., 3rd Battn., D.C.M.
78827 L/Corpl. ANDERSON, J. A. C., 8th Battn., D.C.M.
307575 Sergt. SIDDLE, W., 3rd Carrier Coy., D.C.M.
202016 Sergt. STITTLE, E. W., 8th Battn., D.C.M.
78659 Corpl. (A/Sergt.) LOWE, J. J., 26th Battn., D.C.M.
300246 Pte. ROBBINS, H., 13th Battn., D.C.M.
69976 L/Corpl. (A/Sergt.) PEPPER, A., 19th Battn., D.C.M.
69945 Sergt. MOFFAT, J. G., 7th Battn., D.C.M.
313430 Spr. HUTCHESON, J., R.E., 1st Brigade Sigs.,
D.C.M.
200837 Corpl. (A/Sergt.) SHELTON, W. G., 16th Battn.,
D.C.M.
95077 R.S.M. CAVEN, J., 9th Battn., M.S.M.
305259 R.S.M. HEDGES, F., M.C., D.C.M., 16th Battn.,
M.S.M.
75106 R.Q.M.S. CROSS, H., Central Stores, M.S.M.
91710 R.Q.M.S. HARRIS, J. M., 6th Battn., M.S.M.
309005 R.Q.M.S. KING, W. F. W., 15th Battn., M.S.M.
201490 R.Q.M.S. WOOSTER, A. E., C.M.E. Dept.'s, M.S.M.

75427 **C.S.M. SHORTER, H. G.**, 4th Battn., M.S.M.

201700 **C.Q.M.S. BOWYER, G.**, M.M., 2nd Bde., M.S.M.

200898 **C.Q.M.S. CULPAN, J.**, 3rd Group, M.S.M.

76542 **T.Q.M.S. ARCHER, W. H.**, Headquarters, M.S.M.

301307 **Q.M.S. BREWSTER, W. A.**, 14th Battn., M.S.M.

302264 **Q.M.S. CARTER, H.**, Schools, M.S.M.

77528 **S/Sergt. DAVIES, H. E.**, C.M.E.'s Dept., M.S.M.

303073 **S/Sergt. DAY, J. G.**, 1st Group, M.S.M.

201082 **Mech. S/Sergt. KENNETT, S. E.**, 6th Battn., M.S.M.

92064 **Mech. S/Sergt. LOVER, F. E.**, 9th Battn., M.S.M.

201743 **S/Sergt. SPENCER, H.**, Headquarters, M.S.M.

110298 **Sergt. ANDERSON, D. McM.**, 12th Battn., M.S.M.

201275 **Sergt. BIRKBECK, D. M.**, 7th Battn., M.S.M.

200808 **Sergt. HONEY, F.**, M.M., 4th Brigade, M.S.M.

75496 **Mech. Sergt. LANGTON, R.**, 12th Battn., M.S.M.

78321 **Sergt. SATTERTHWAITE, W. A.**, 3rd Group, M.S.M.

75031 **Sergt. STANLEY, D.**, Headquarters, M.S.M.

109615 **Corpl. BINNS, J. A.**, 11th Battn., M.S.M.

77182 **Corpl. CLARK, W.**, C.M.E.'s Dept., M.S.M.

76264 **Corpl. TRAIN, W.**, Field Battn., M.S.M.

205012 **Pte. (A/Q.M.S.) CORE, F.**, 13th Battn., M.S.M.

200944 **Pte. MONK, A. C.**, C.M.E.'s Dept., M.S.M.

75118 **Pte. TERRY, W.**, C.M.E.'s Dept., M.S.M.

T/Sub-Conductor KIRBY, R., R.A.O.C., attached Headquarters, M.S.M.

40210 **A/R.S.M. OWEN, C. V.**, Home Estab., M.S.M.

69794 **R.Q.M.S. WAUGH, C. H.**, Home Estab., M.S.M.

260907 **Sergt. WHITTAKER, J. E.**, Home Estab., M.S.M.

S4/158840 **S.Q.M.S. MACDONALD, F.**, R.A.S.C., attached Tank Corps, M.S.M.

M2/192188 **Sergt. TRIBE, H.**, R.A.S.C., attached Tank Corps, M.S.M.

M2/191475 **Sergt. WALLIS, C. B.**, R.A.S.C., attached Tank Corps, M.S.M.

M/24835 **C.S.M. MCKAY, D.**, R.A.S.C., attached Tank Corps, M.S.M.

426832 **A/R.Q.M.S. YOUNG, H. B.**, 78 Lab. Group, M.S.M.

92251 **A/M.S.S.M.I. LONG, H.W.**, M.S.M.

Sergt. GORDON, J., D.C.M., 4th Battn., Roumanian Croix de Virtute Militare.

Sergt. HARRIS, T. H., 7th Battn., Roumanian Croix de Virtute Militare.

CHAPTER V

IMMEDIATE AWARDS—OFFICERS

1916

2nd Lieut. STOREY, CHARLES ERNEST. ' F ' Battn. Awarded D.S.O.

For gallantry and initiative in command of tank ' D. 14 ' on September 26, when he was called upon by G.O.C. 110th Brigade to clear up certain trenches S.E. of Gueudecourt which were holding up the infantry. Lieut. Storey took his car up and down each trench, working until all his petrol was exhausted and only two of the crew were unwounded. He is reported as having been responsible for the taking of between 200 and 300 prisoners.

I consider this to be the best tank performance up to date.

T. Capt. HOTBLACK, FREDERICK ELLIOTT, M.C., Intelligence Corps, attached Heavy Branch, M.G.C. Awarded D.S.O.

For conspicuous gallantry in action on October 18, 1916. A tank being halted from uncertainty as to the proper direction, this officer went forward on foot through very heavy fire, and guided the tank to its objective by walking in front of it. He displayed great courage and determination throughout.

2nd Lieut. PARTINGTON, WALTER. Awarded Italian Silver Medal.

Commanded isolated tank in action on morning of November 18, 1916. He remained in action for two hours under close fire from machine guns, trench mortars, and bombers, out of touch with our own troops, and inflicted losses on the enemy. He continued to fight his tank after two of his crew were wounded, and only returned to our lines in order to undertake a fresh attack in co-operation with the infantry.

THE TANK CORPS BOOK OF HONOUR

1917

T. Lieut. MOORE, ALBERT. ' C ' Battn. Awarded M.C.

For gallantry and devotion to duty. From March 28 to April 12, 1917, this officer, as workshops officer to his company, worked almost continuously to keep his tanks in fighting order. The work he performed, usually in darkness under heavy shell fire, contributed greatly to the success of the operations. His fearless example has been an example to all his subordinates.

T. 2nd Lieut. NELSON, LOUIS ARCHIBALD. ' D ' Battn. Awarded M.C.

During the action on the Hindenburg Line south of Neuville Vitasse on the 9th instant this officer when fighting his tank found a battalion of infantry held up by wire. He made gaps in the wire and cleared the enemy trench, thus saving the battalion severe casualties. On the 11th instant he gained his objective entirely unsupported and remained in action four hours, clearing trenches and strong points. During this operation he was wounded.

T. Lieut. HUMPHREYS, NOEL FORBES. ' D ' Battn. Awarded M.C.

During the action on the Hindenburg Line at Neuville Vitasse, on April 9, fought his tank with great gallantry, gained his first objective, and was ' bellied.' Though wounded by a sniper whilst digging out his tank, he carried on until he had completed his task, and continued in action the whole day, mopping up strong points, and finally brought his tank out of action to his rallying point.

Capt. EGLESTON, THOMAS BUCHANAN McLEAN. ' D ' Battn. Awarded M.C.

During the attack on the Hindenburg Line and Neuville Vitasse, on April 9, he observed several tanks in difficulties, at once proceeded to the scene, and worked unceasingly in heavy fire in overcoming the difficulties. During this time a tank gunner was wounded, and he at once carried him to safety and rendered first aid. He then proceeded to other tanks, attracted the attention of a mobile one, and directed him to a troublesome sniper's post some 400 yards away. The tank dealt successfully with this post. Later he again assisted a wounded officer to safety. He was under every kind of heavy fire continuously for four or five hours, and worked strenuously throughout for the success of the tanks with no thought for personal safety.

IMMEDIATE AWARDS—OFFICERS

T. 2nd Lieut. WEBER, CHARLES FREDERICK. 'C' Battn.. Awarded M.C.

For conspicuous gallantry and devotion to duty. During the opening of the offensive on April 9, 1917, this officer fought his tank with the greatest skill and gallantry in support of the 15th Division. He was of the greatest assistance to the infantry in the capture of Feuchy Redoubt and Feuchy Chapel. In order to keep on the move in support of the infantry he overcame most difficult circumstances, many mechanical defects, and breakdowns. Although very short of fuel, and on his way back to refill, he returned on the request of the infantry to assist them in difficulties, although he knew his tank would be unable to return.

Lieut. MARTIN, JOHN MULGRAVE. 'D' Battn. Awarded M.C.

During the action on the Hindenburg Line on April 9, 1917, did excellent work with his tank, gaining all his objectives, and again on April 13 cleared up several strong points which were holding the infantry up. On April 23, whilst acting as section commander, he guided his tanks personally under a severe barrage to within a few feet of our front line to ensure their success.

T. 2nd Lieut. NORMAN, SIGURD OSWALD. 'C' Battn. Awarded M.C.

For conspicuous gallantry and devotion to duty. On April 10, 1917, during the attack on Feuchy Chapel, this officer navigated and fought his tank with the greatest gallantry and skill. He overcame many mechanical defects and difficulties of ground. He located and silenced several machine-guns and two snipers who were holding up our infantry. Unsupported by any infantry, he passed through the enemy lines north of Feuchy Chapel and dealt with many targets. After cruising in rear of German lines he returned and spent the remainder of the night close to the German front line. By his gallant work he saved the infantry many casualties.

Lieut. SALTER, GODFREY CHARLES TAYLOR. 'C' Battn. Awarded M.C.

For conspicuous gallantry and devotion to duty. During the attack on Monchy-le-Preux on April 11, 1917, this officer handled his tank with the greatest skill and gallantry although unsupported by infantry and becoming involved in our own artillery barrage, owing to a postponement of 'zero' hour with which he was unacquainted. He nevertheless cleared a trench of the enemy, which he handed over to the infantry.

His tank was eventually blown to pieces by artillery fire, which wounded five and killed one of his crew of seven.

THE TANK CORPS BOOK OF HONOUR

T. 2nd Lieut. AMBROSE, CHARLES FREDERICK NELSON.
'C' Battn. Awarded D.S.O.

For conspicuous gallantry and devotion to duty during the attack on Monchy-le-Preux on April 11, 1917.

After his tank had been bombed, blown in by shell-fire, and pierced by armour-piercing bullets, and all his gunners killed or wounded, he continued to keep up a brisk fire on the enemy, who were surrounding his tank and attacking it with bombs. His conduct throughout this action displayed the greatest courage.

On April 9 this officer, whilst in action, received severe shock from a shell which burst by his side, killing several of his men. In spite of this, although far from recovered, he insisted on taking his tank into action again two days later.

T. Lieut. MAY, CHARLES HENRY. 'C' Battn. Awarded M.C.

For conspicuous gallantry and devotion to duty. During the capture of Monchy-le-Preux on April 11, 1917, as section commander, he accompanied one tank part of the way into action and then transferred to another tank of his section, till it reached its objective.

On this tank becoming unfit to take part in further action he took charge of a mixed party of infantry, and directed consolidation under very heavy machine-gun and artillery fire. He set a fine example of coolness and courage.

T. 2nd Lieut. MORRIS, DAVID ALFRED. 'D' Battn. Awarded Croix de Guerre.

For gallantry and skill in the handling of his tank at Bullecourt on April 11. This officer, under an extremely heavy and accurate fire, entered the German trenches and worked down them for over a thousand yards, destroying the machine-gun emplacements at least. He then reported for further orders. He took his tank into action a second time, carried out his instructions, and finally, with considerable skill, brought his tank out of the battle.

T. 2nd. Lieut. BIRKETT, CUTHBERT EDWIN. 'D' Battn. Awarded M.C.

During the attack on Bullecourt---Riencourt—Hendecourt, April 11, 1917, this officer, although wounded at the beginning of the attack, commanded his tank with greatest gallantry and skill. When his tank had twice been hit by shells, and he and his crew had all been wounded, he brought his tank out of action with cool judgment. He was wounded a second time while getting out of his tank to inspect the damage.

Lieut. SMITH, HAROLD REES. 'D' Battn. Awarded M.C.

During the action on the Hindenburg Line on April 23, worked his tank very successfully, destroying one machine-gun emplacement and several snipers' posts. When our infantry were being pushed back, he went forward with his tank to stem the enemy's advance. This officer stuck to his tank until eventually the tank was struck a sixth time by a direct hit and set on fire.

T. 2nd Lieut. LE-CLAIR, CHARLES MILWARD. 'C' Battn. Awarded M.C.

For conspicuous gallantry and devotion to duty. During the attack on Gavrelle, on April 23, 1917, although his tank was subjected to very heavy shell fire and penetrated by armour-piercing bullets, which wounded five of his crew, he continued to fight his tank, and assisted to clear the village until his tank was disabled.

2nd Lieut. RAYNER, JOHN. 'D' Battn. Awarded M.C.

During the action on the Hindenburg Line on April 23 fought his tank from 'zero' hour, 4.45 A.M., until 12 noon continuously. He patrolled the Hindenburg Line immediately south of the River Sensee for seven hours, destroying machine-gun emplacements and several strong points. It was largely due to this tank's magnificent work that the 98th Brigade reached their objective. He brought his tank back safely.

T. 2nd Lieut. SMITH, VICTOR. 'C' Battn. Awarded M.C.

For conspicuous gallantry and devotion to duty. During the Battle of Arras, on April 23, 1917, this officer took his tank into Mount Pleasant Wood and put out of action several enemy machine-guns, thereby enabling the infantry to gain possession of it. He later gave assistance to the infantry during the attack on Roeux, by driving the enemy out of their houses with his 6-pndr., and then doing great execution with his machine-guns. During the whole action he displayed the greatest coolness and initiative, and carried on in spite of having four of his crew wounded by armour-piercing bullets.

Lieut. WESTBROOK, TOM. 'D' Battn. Awarded M.C.

Bullecourt, May 3, 1917. During the action his tank was riddled with armour-piercing bullets, which wounded himself and four of his crew and knocked out five Lewis guns. Unable to work his tank any longer, he withdrew his crew to shell-holes under heavy fire and himself covered the retirement of these men with the remaining Lewis gun. All the crew got back to the rallying point.

Lieut. SMITH, EDWARD GRANVILLE. 'D' Battn. Awarded M.C.

Bullecourt, May 3, 1917. His tank received a direct hit by shell, being set on fire, and under heavy fire of all kinds he got his crew out to shell-holes, went back to his tank and put out the fire, collected his crew, and returned to his rallying point after being in action six hours.

2nd Lieut. KNIGHT, CHARLES MARTEL. ' D ' Battn. Awarded M.C.

Bullecourt, May 3, 1917. This officer went into Bullecourt and came under heavy continuous fire from armour-piercing bullets. After he and four of his crew were wounded, he returned to starting point, evacuated his wounded, took fresh men on board, and went back into Bullecourt, where he remained in action until so many of his crew were wounded that he could not carry on. He brought back his tank to starting point ; all his crew were wounded. He was in action seven hours.

T. 2nd Lieut. SKINNER, HUGH. ' D ' Battn. Awarded M.C.

This officer penetrated, entirely without support, into the strongly fortified village of Bullecourt, inflicted heavy casualties on the enemy, and, when his tank was disabled, brought back all his crew and valuable parts of his guns and tank under heavy machine-gun and shell fire.

MESSINES, 1917

2nd Lieut. DUNCAN, CHRISTOPHER WILLIAM. ' A ' Battn. Awarded M.C.

When his section commander was wounded on June 7, 1917, near Wytschaete, he took command of the section of tanks and led them on foot throughout the day, showing fine judgment. He kept three tanks in action driving and fighting for thirty-six con-secutive hours, showing a complete disregard for his personal safety. Two counter-attacks were broken by his three tanks in the neigh-bourhood of Joye Farm, where the line had not been consolidated.

2nd Lieut. KEOGH, FREDERICK BERTRAM. ' A ' Battn. Awarded M.C. ·

When his tank was broken down, owing to mechanical trouble, in the vicinity of Joye Farm on June 7, 1917, he kept it in action for twenty-four hours, working all his guns and helping the infantry to repel two counter-attacks before the line was consolidated. When the line was fully consolidated and his crew was exhausted, he with-drew after handing his guns over to the infantry. For some hours the tank was without infantry support.

IMMEDIATE AWARDS—OFFICERS

2nd Lieut. HALLAM, HENRY NEVILLE. ' B ' Battn. Awarded M.C.

On June 7, 1917, this officer's tank got ditched in the enemy's line. He got out and started work unditching. He was wounded in the leg, but refused to leave his tank to have it dressed, and continued his work. He was then severely wounded in the back and arm, and still refused to stop work outside his tank until he was in a fainting condition and had to be carried away.

T. Lieut. (A./Capt.) KNIGHT, REGINALD COLDHAM. ' B ' Battn. Awarded M.C.

This officer has shown great gallantry and devotion to duty as battalion reconnaissance officer.

He did, on numerous occasions, make reconnaissances in front of our lines in order to obtain information useful to tank officers before taking their tanks into action.

During the action on June 7, reconnoitred routes through the enemy system after its capture and led tanks in Army Reserve over them. He also proceeded on foot to the Oosttaverne Line and collected valuable information with a view to future operations.

This officer has shown himself regardless of danger in collecting information, and I consider the success which the tanks had is greatly due to his fine work and gallantry.

2nd Lieut. BAILEY, JOHN MARLEY. ' A ' Battn. Awarded M.C.

For gallantry and devotion to duty as reconnaissance officer. On numerous occasions he made reconnaissances in front of our lines in order to obtain information for his tank officers before going into action. On June 7, 1917, he followed up the tanks during their advance on Wytschaete and brought back most valuable information as to their position and condition. His utter disregard of danger and his devotion to duty contributed very greatly to the success of his company.

Lieut. VANS-AGNEW, FRANK. ' B ' Battn. Awarded M.C.

On June 7, 1917, this officer guided his tank with great coolness and judgment up to the Oosttaverne Line and rendered considerable assistance to the infantry. When the camouflage carried on the tank was set on fire he got out, under heavy machine-gun and rifle fire, to assist in putting it out. He was wounded in doing this, but continued to command his tank and brought it back to its rallying point after the action.

YPRES, 1917

T. Major BRYCE, EDWARD DANIELL. ' B ' Battn. Awarded D.S.O.

Extreme gallantry and devotion to duty on the night of July 28–29, south of Zillebeke. His company, on the way up to its position of deployment, came under a heavy barrage of gas and other shells. Two section commanders and several tank officers and men were wounded and gassed. Major Bryce, although suffering from the effects of gas and being twice knocked over by shells bursting alongside him, continued to take charge, and, walking in front, guided his tanks to their positions.

On the 31st, although still suffering from the effects of gas and partially blinded, he commanded his company in action, and at great personal risk went forward to collect information.

He had previously shown gallantry and devotion to duty when commanding his company at Messines on June 7, 1917.

Capt. KINNISON, CLIVE HASTINGS. ' G ' Battn. Awarded M.C.

July 7, 1917. Operations in the Ypres Salient. For conspicuous gallantry and devotion to duty. He followed the tanks of his section into action and helped to guide them over most difficult ground under heavy shell fire. When the other section commander was wounded, he took over command of that section and rallied all the tanks after the action. Throughout the day he displayed great coolness and excellent judgment.

2nd Lieut. EVANS, CLAUDE MULLINER. ' B ' Battn. Awarded M.C.

This officer showed great gallantry and devotion to duty on the night of July 28–29, south of Zillebeke, when the company came under a heavy barrage of gas and other shell fire while moving up.

On the morning of July 31, finding his tank had a serious mechanical defect, he at once changed his crew and equipment to another tank which had previously been hit by a shell, and had a hole in the roof over his seat. This tank he took into action, and, after unditching twice under heavy fire, proceeded in front of our infantry and engaged the enemy in Glencorse Wood. The tank was there put out of action by a direct hit from a shell. He took his crew and guns into a trench close by and continued to fire on hostile machine-gun emplacements. He held his post, 200 yards in front of the infantry, for two hours, and only retired on being ordered to do so.

2nd Lieut. LOVELL, BERTRAM. ' G ' Battn. Awarded M.C.

July 31, 1917. Operations in the Ypres Salient. For conspicuous gallantry and devotion to duty. He gave very valuable assistance to the infantry. After crossing the Steenebeek and becoming badly ditched, the tank was under heavy shell fire. He formed two strong points with his crew near the tank, and kept them supplied with ammunition himself till he was wounded. He stayed with his men in the strong point, which was dropping many of the enemy, for an hour, when the crew persuaded him to go back to the dressing station. He was very weak from loss of blood.

IMMEDIATE AWARDS—OFFICERS

2nd Lieut. ALLDEN, JOHN. ' G ' Battn. Awarded M.C.

July 31, 1917. Operations in the Ypres Salient. For conspicuous gallantry and devotion to duty. He reached his objective at Alberta in front of the infantry, and, by knocking out several machine-gun nests, assisted the infantry very materially in their advance on that objective. At the end of the day, although his unditching gear had been carried away by a shell, he got his tank back to the rallying point.

Lieut. STAFFORD, ROBERT WILLIAM. ' G ' Battn. Awarded M.C.

July 31, 1917. Operations in the Ypres Salient. For conspicuous gallantry and devotion to duty. He reached all his objectives and rendered most valuable assistance to the infantry in knocking out strong points, which resulted in the capture of about 100 prisoners. He was wounded towards the end of the action whilst assisting in unditching his tank.

Capt. CAREW, HALLEWELL. ' A ' Battn. Awarded M.C.

For conspicuous gallantry and devotion to duty during the operations on July 31, 1917. He personally led his section of tanks on foot to its objective in the vicinity of Westhoek, although they were being subjected the whole time to very heavy shelling and intense machine-gun fire. This officer showed great coolness and courage, going from tank to tank and helping them out of difficulties. It was entirely due to his total disregard for personal danger when leading his tanks that they were enabled to reach the infantry when they were held up on the Westhoek Ridge. Before the action he carried out several good reconnaissances under heavy shell fire.

Capt. DIAMOND, HUGH VICTOR. ' B ' Battn. Awarded M.C.

For great gallantry and devotion to duty near Dumbarton Lakes on July 31, 1917. He led his section of tanks into action through very heavy shelling, got into touch with the infantry and found out where they were held up. He then directed his tanks against enemy strong points and machine guns in woods west of Dumbarton Lakes and proceeded in 2nd Lieut. Gordon Clark's tank. When the tank got ditched, he helped to unditch it under machine-gun and rifle fire. After the tank had engaged targets, he got out to see how the remaining tanks of his section were doing, and then proceeded back on foot under heavy machine-gun fire to communicate with the infantry and explain the situation to them, receiving a slight wound. He found the infantry unable to advance, and returned to 2nd Lieut. Gordon Clark's tank, the only one of his section left in action. Here he found 2nd Lieut. Clark and four of the crew wounded and unfit for further action. He ordered the tank to return, and accompanied it back to the position of deployment. Prior to action, this officer had carried out several reconnaissances under dangerous conditions to ensure getting his tanks into action, and also did good work at Messines.

Capt. BLACKBURN, ERIC DEANE. ' A ' Battn. Awarded M.C.

For conspicuous gallantry and devotion to duty during the operations on July 31, 1917. He personally led his section of tanks on foot to their objective in the vicinity of Westhoek. During the whole time they were advancing the tanks were under heavy shell fire and intense machine-gun fire. That the tanks reached the forward position of deployment under the Westhoek Ridge was entirely due to this officer's complete disregard for personal danger when leading them, and the skill with which he directed them over the badly crumped and marshy ground. He showed the utmost courage and coolness and set a fine example to his section.

Capt. RAIKES, DAVID TAUNTON. 3rd Battn. South Wales Borderers, attached ' A ' Battn. Awarded M.C.

For conspicuous gallantry and devotion to duty during the operations on July 31, 1917. He personally led his tanks to their objective near Surbiton Villa under heavy shell and machine-gun fire. When progress became otherwise impossible, he got into a tank, which soon afterwards received a direct hit, killing the tank commander and wounding most of the crew. He then went forward, on foot, with the remaining tanks and directed them towards enemy machine-gun emplacements and silenced the guns. When three of his four tanks were placed out of action, he organised a party and salved all the Lewis guns, again under heavy fire.

T. 2nd Lieut. FLETCHER, ALEXANDER WILLIAM. ' F ' Battn. Awarded M.C.

At Ypres, on July 31, 1917, this officer displayed the greatest gallantry and skill in getting his tank into action over very difficult ground by leading it on foot to within 100 yards of his objective and putting out of action a machine-gun which was holding up the attack. While patrolling in front of the newly-captured line, his unditching gear was shot away and his tank became ditched. Thereupon he got out of the tank under heavy fire from rifles, grenades, and machine-guns, in search of timber to replace the unditching gear, and while so doing he was wounded.

T. 2nd Lieut. TOLLEY, CYRIL JAMES HASTINGS. ' F ' Battn. Awarded M.C.

At Ypres on July 31, 1917, this officer showed great skill and courage in getting his tank into action over very difficult ground, which necessitated him walking in front of his tank till close to his objective. He then dispersed the crews of, and silenced four, separate German machine-guns, one of which he captured himself, and thus materially assisted the infantry in the capture of Pommern Redoubt, which had held up the attack for a considerable time. At the conclusion of the action he brought his tank safely back to the rallying point.

A. Capt. BATES, LEONARD JOHN. ' C ' Battn. Awarded M.C.

For conspicuous gallantry and devotion to duty. During the Battle of Ypres on July 31, 1917, as section commander, this officer led his tanks into action on his feet. On several occasions he guided them over difficult country, frequently under heavy machine-gun and shell fire. It was greatly due to his exertions that the tanks of his section reached their objectives and rendered valuable assistance to the infantry, notably in the vicinity of Beck House. His conduct throughout was most gallant.

A. Capt. KEPPEL-PALMER, STEWART LESLIE. ' C ' Battn. Awarded M.C.

For conspicuous gallantry and devotion to duty. During the Battle of Ypres on July 31, 1917, as section commander this officer led his section with the greatest gallantry. When his ' Flag Tank ' was out of action he joined another one until it became ' ditched.' Being unable to get it into action again after most strenuous exertions, he joined a third tank of his section ; on each occasion having to pass fully exposed over many hundreds of yards of bullet-swept ground. He directed the very successful operations of his third tank, and eventually brought it safely back to the rallying point.

T. 2nd Lieut. RENWICK, ALLAN EVERETT. ' F ' Battn. Awarded M.C.

At Ypres on July 31, 1917, when his tank became ditched and six of his crew were wounded, he personally carried four of them into a trench under heavy shell fire. He then returned to his tank, and with the aid of a new crew which had been sent up, got his tank out and reached the final objective, eventually bringing his tank back to within a mile of the position of assembly. His fine example and cheerfulness inspired confidence in his crew and enabled them to bring back the tank successfully.

T. Lieut. VOSS, GORDON PHILLIPS, M.C. ' F ' Battn. Bar to M.C.

For most conspicuous gallantry and devotion to duty. During the Battle of Ypres on July 31, 1917, he went over with the infantry at zero, waited for tanks at Blue Line (after F. 38 got a direct hit found some battery firing at F. 13), went across and directed it

95

THE TANK CORPS BOOK OF HONOUR

on its objective. This tank was put out of action. Infantry were stopped, and at request of infantry commander got F. 10 up, but tank stuck in mud, and Lieut. Voss walked in front under heavy machine-gun fire and tried to get him out but failed, so helped to put on unditching gear with Lieut. Seymour and two of the crew, sending the rest to take cover. After this, although a shell had broken his stick and bruised his leg, he went on and directed another tank to Pond Farm. Under heavy fire on the return journey he helped three tanks to get back to rallying point. I am of opinion that his coolness and example under fire had a great effect on the men of the company, most of whom were in action for the first time.

T. Capt. HEDDERWECK, GEREVALD. ' C ' Battn. Awarded M.C.

For conspicuous gallantry and devotion to duty. During the Battle of Ypres on July 31, 1917, this officer as 2nd in command of his company displayed the greatest zeal and gallantry in getting his tanks into action. Throughout the whole day he exposed himself, continuously rendering help to his company and bringing back information of the greatest value, on several occasions passing through heavy enemy barrages. The success of his company in action was greatly due to his great devotion to duty.

T. Lieut. CHALMERS, THOMAS EDWARD BAIN. ' C ' Battn. Awarded M.C.

For conspicuous gallantry during the Third Battle of Ypres After the action on July 31, 1917, this officer displayed the utmost gallantry and resource in salving tanks that had became ditched in the vicinity of the Wilde Wood, and which were under a heavy hostile barrage. He made no less than six attempts to get away one tank, each time under heavy artillery and gas bombardments, and eventually succeeded, overcoming all difficulties by his perseverance and courage.

Capt. HUXTABLE, ARTHUR HEWITT. Chaplains Dept. (attached 1st Bde.). Awarded M.C.

For conspicuous gallantry, zeal and devotion in the Ypres Salient, N.E. of Ypres, on August 15 and 27, and September 29, respectively, in the neighbourhood of Oblong Farm and St. Julien.

On each occasion this officer went up with the tanks (a different battalion in each case) to starting point, remaining with them under heavy shell fire, holding services in the tanks, assisting the men with their meals, and doing all in his power to encourage them and make them comfortable.

On September 20 he went forward with the tanks from Bellevue to St. Julien and thence to Janet Farm. At Janet Farm he was wounded and has since been evacuated. He refused to go back, however, until he was satisfied he could do no more to assist the men.

His complete disregard of self and safety and his untiring devotion under shell fire have, without any doubt, very materially assisted all ranks of this brigade and inspired them with a high morale.

2nd Lieut. COUTTS, HARRY GEORGE. ' G ' Battn. Awarded M.C.

August 19, 1917. Operations in the Ypres Salient. For conspicuous gallantry and devotion to duty. He reached his objective—the Cockcroft—a strong concrete emplacement, and drove the enemy out with fire from his tank. He made good the position by getting out his crew with their guns in shell-holes near by. He went back himself when he found the infantry were not coming on, and eventually led a party of infantry up to the Cockcroft. The infantry, with his assistance, took it over, and he and his crew remained with them till dark, assisting in the consolidation.

This officer's name has already been brought to notice for conspicuous gallantry and devotion to duty (July 31, 1917).

T. 2nd Lieut. BAKER, ALBERT GEORGE. ' G ' Battn. Awarded M.C.

August 19, 1917. Operations in the Ypres Salient. For conspicuous gallantry and devotion to duty. He reached his objective —a strong concrete emplacement—and, by getting behind it and firing his 6-pndr. guns, he was able to drive the enemy out. Although his tank was ditched, he was able to inflict severe casualties on the enemy, who were running away. The remainder of the enemy surrendered to the infantry, who were able to capture and consolidate the position. He and his crew assisted the infantry in consolidating the position by manning shell-holes with the guns from his tank for the rest of the day.

T. Lieut. MORGAN, ESMOND THOMAS. ' G ' Battn. Awarded M.C.

August 19, 1917. Operations in the Ypres Salient. For conspicuous gallantry and devotion to duty. He reached his objective at the Triangle, and drove the enemy out. He inflicted severe losses on them with his Lewis guns. Although his tank was ditched, he materially assisted the infantry in consolidating their position. Although all except one of his crew were wounded with bullet splashes, he was able to get his tank back to the rallying point in the evening.

T. 2nd Lieut. ROLLINGS, ERNEST JAMES. ' C ' Battn. Awarded M.C.

For conspicuous gallantry during the Third Battle of Ypres on the night of August 21-22. 1917. This officer was in command of a

' pioneer ' tank, his duties being to help the fighting tanks of his section into action and across the Steenebeek River. Although in difficult ground, and during most of the period under heavy H.E. and gas bombardment, he carried out his duties with the utmost self-sacrifice, courage and perseverance. At one time or other he helped every one of his tanks out of difficulties. If it had not been for his courage and energy it is doubtful if any of the fighting tanks would have got into action. After he had completed his duties he went back to assist a seriously wounded officer and several men who had been wounded and were still under heavy shell fire.

T. 2nd Lieut. (A/Capt.) REARDON, JOHN. ' B ' Battn. Awarded M.C.

For gallantry and devotion to duty on August 21-22, 1917, east of Ypres, in command of a section of tanks. When taking his section up to the starting-point on the night of August 21, Capt. Reardon injured himself by falling on a bayonet in the dark. In spite of this and the bad going and intense hostile barrage he was successful in launching three tanks out of four on the morning of August 2. As he was by this time unable to walk owing to his wound, he proceeded in one of the tanks himself in order to keep in touch with his tanks in action. This section did very good work in the action. By his determination and pluck this officer was the means of causing heavy casualties to the enemy.

Lieut. (A/Capt.) RICHARDSON, DONALD HICKLING. ' F ' Battn. Awarded M.C.

For conspicuous gallantry and devotion to duty in action between St. Julien and Frezenberg on August 22, 23 and 24.

This officer was section commander, and went into action in tank F. 41. During the action the tank became ditched and completely isolated and surrounded by the enemy. The tank commander, 2nd Lieut. Hill, was wounded early in the action on 22nd. Capt Richardson then took charge, though himself wounded. He attempted to fix unditching gear under heavy machine-gun fire at close range, but was unsuccessful. He then, by his splendid example and determination, fought his tank till the night of 24th (seventy-two hours in all). His crew, with one exception, being killed or wounded, he evacuated the tank and brought his surviving crew back to our lines. By his very gallant action he undoubtedly inflicted severe casualties on the enemy.

T. 2nd Lieut. HILL, GEORGE. ' F ' Battn. Awarded M.C.

For conspicuous gallantry and devotion to duty in action between St. Julien and Frezenberg on August 22, 23 and 24. This officer was in command of tank F. 41. He was wounded early on 22nd, and subsequently fainted several times from loss of blood. Despite this he very ably seconded Capt. Richardson, his section commander, in fighting his tank for seventy-two consecutive hours.

2nd Lieut. WOLF, EDWARD MOSES. ' C ' Battn. Awarded M.C.

For conspicuous gallantry during the Third Battle of Ypres on August 22, 1917. This officer commanded his tank with the greatest skill and gallantry in very difficult ground in the attack on Hill 35. Although his tank became ' bellied ' early in the morning, he held on to his position in front of the infantry and enabled them to consolidate by keeping enemy fire down with his Lewis guns. After he and his crew had been in action nearly twenty-six hours, and were very exhausted, he, with the assistance of his crew, completely broke up the right flank of an enemy counter-attack and thereby saved a critical situation. He displayed throughout the day a magnificent example of courage and endurance.

T. 2nd Lieut. IRELAND, ERNEST PENNOCK. ' F ' Battn. Awarded M.C.

For gallantry and initiative in action on August 22, 1917, between St. Julien and Frezenberg. Fought his tank up to the neighbourhood of Gallipoli, having been detailed in support of 2nd Lieut. Pearson when well ahead of the infantry. Seeing 2nd Lieut. Pearson was ditched he got out of his tank and walked across to him to ascertain the position. He then brought his tank over to 2nd Lieut. Pearson's and attempted to tow it out and got ditched in the attempt. He unditched his own tank and brought safely out of action the whole of 2nd Lieut. Pearson's crew, of whom five were wounded. They returned to near Spree Farm and again became ditched, and while trying to unditch the tank was put out of action by shell fire. He brought all the wounded back, and carried on although wounded himself, and saved all the guns, both of his own and 2nd Lieut. Pearson's tank.

He was, during the whole of the action, under heavy shell and machine-gun fire.

T. Lieut. (A/Capt.) GROVES, HENRY BASIL MOLVIN. ' B ' Battn. Awarded M.C.

On August 23, 1917, at Clapham Junction, this officer displayed the greatest gallantry in guiding his tanks on foot over very difficult ground under heavy shell fire.

After the action, hearing that one of his officers was lying wounded in front of our line, he twice crawled out at great risk to get him in. On both occasions he reached the officer, but failed to get him back owing to hostile machine-gun fire. The night 23–24 he went out again, but found the officer dead.

On August 24, at 4.30 A.M., the enemy counter-attacked. Seeing that parties of our infantry were retiring, Capt. Groves rallied them and materially assisted in repelling the attack.

T. Capt. (A/Major) CARR, ALFRED EDWARD. 1st Bde. Workshops. Awarded M.C.

For conspicuous gallantry and devotion to duty in the Ypres Salient, N.E. of Ypres.

On September 13, 1917, a derelict tank was blocking the St. Julien-Triangle Farm road. This officer undertook to repair it. He did so the same evening under heavy shell fire and with a burning ammunition dump 300 yards away. He drove the tank off and cleared the road, materially assisting operations.

In the same area, on the night of September 22-23, this officer went out to Langemarck and examined two disabled tanks. He returned to them on night of 23-24, and succeeded in repairing one tank in spite of very heavy shell fire. A working party was detailed to join Major Carr to dig out the tank but failed to get through a heavy barrage. Major Carr and his mechanics dug the tank out unaided and got it ready for action.

The action of this officer throughout was a combination of great skill, gallantry and determination.

2nd Lieut. SYMONDS, CHARLES LEONARD. ' D ' Battn. Awarded M.C.

For gallantry and devotion to duty. On September 20, 1917, at Delta House, north of St. Julien, N.E. of Ypres, this officer brought his tank through almost insurmountable obstacles. In his journey he surmounted over thirty trees felled slantwise across the road before reaching his final objective, which until his arrival was holding up the infantry.

His tank was ditched on four separate occasions; but under heavy shell fire, and showing a total disregard to danger he collected material to make ramps, thus enabling his tank to reach firm ground.

After the capture of the objective he covered the consolidation of the position.

The success of the operations in connection with this tank were entirely due to the great perseverance and leadership shown by this officer throughout the action.

2nd Lieut. LYLES, REGINALD WYBERT. The ' Buffs,' E. Kent Regt. (attached ' A ' Battn.). Awarded M.C.

For conspicuous gallantry and devotion to duty. On September 23, 1917, in Inverness Copse, while returning from his objective, the tank which was immediately in front of him received a direct hit, killing and wounding all the crew. This officer immediately ran to it, and although the six-pounder ammunition was exploding, he entered the tank and dragged out the wounded, had them carried to his own tank, and took them to the dressing station.

On September 26, 1917, he remained in the open during several heavy barrages in the neighbourhood of Glencorse Wood encouraging the tank crews. Previous to this he assisted his section commander to tape the route and afterwards lead up the tanks to the starting-point under very heavy shell fire.

This officer interviewed his commanding officer on September 25 to get permission to accompany a section of tanks that were to be put into action on September 26, as he stated he knew the country and considered it most difficult. All the crews report that he was of great assistance and walked from tank to tank showing a total disregard for his personal safety. There was a very heavy hostile barrage at the time.

PALESTINE DETACHMENT, APRIL 19, 1917

Major NUTT, NORMAN. Awarded D.S.O.

For conspicuous gallantry and able leadership while in command of a detachment of tanks operating against Gaza. This officer was present throughout the operations, and his skilful dispositions resulted in the saving of many lives among the infantry engaged.

Lieut. SHORE, M. F. Awarded M.C.

This officer was in command of a tank operating against the Gaza defences. With conspicuous gallantry he attacked El Arish Redoubt and held same for half an hour unsupported by the infantry. Though he himself and all his crew were wounded, he managed to get the tank safely back to our lines under most difficult circumstances after inflicting heavy casualties on the enemy.

Lieut. BRAIME. Awarded M.C.

This officer was in command of a tank operating against the Gaza defences. With conspicuous gallantry he attacked Outpost Hill, clearing it of the enemy and helping our infantry to consolidate ; the tank was later put out of action by a direct hit. This officer then evacuated the tank with all machine-guns, and got his crew safely back to our lines during the night.

Lieut. WINDER. Awarded M.C.

This officer was in command of a tank operating against the Gaza defences. With conspicuous gallantry he attacked the Turkish positions, inflicting heavy casualties, and, rolling down the wire, let our infantry through, and afterwards patrolled the position while the infantry consolidated it.

CAMBRAI, NOVEMBER 1917

T. Capt. FIELD, CHRISTOPHER NORMAN CROMWELL. ' D ' Battn. Awarded M.C.

For gallantry and devotion to duty at Flesquieres on November 20, 1917. He commanded his section from a tank until it ran out of petrol. He then went forward to Flesquieres on foot, and under very heavy machine-gun fire rallied his crews of the tanks that had been hit, and supervised the collection of the wounded. His cheerfulness and contempt of danger had a most encouraging effect on all ranks. This officer has been brought to notice for gallantry on a previous occasion.

T. 2nd Lieut. HEAP, FRANK GUSTAVE, ' D ' Battn. Awarded M.C.

In the Cambrai operations near Flesquieres on November 20, 1917, he fought his tank with great gallantry and skill, leading the infantry on to five objectives. He proceeded through the village and engaged a battery of enemy field guns from which his tank received five direct hits, killing four of his crew. Although then behind the German lines he collected the remainder of his crew, and conducted them in good order back to our own lines in spite of heavy machine-gun and snipers' fire.

T. Lieut. BION, WILLIAM RUPPRECHT. ' E ' Battn. Awarded D.S.O.

Near Flesquieres, on November 20, 1917, while in command of his tank, engaged a great number of German machine-gunners all in strong positions in the wood and buildings on the eastern outskirts of the village, thus assisting our infantry to advance. After receiving a direct hit from a German field howitzer, which put his tank out of action, he evacuated his tank with all undamaged machine-guns and manned a German communication trench and reopened fire on the enemy's machine-guns. He took charge of ten men of the 5th Gordons who had arrived and strengthened his post with them. Finding that one enemy machine-gun, which he could not locate, was giving more trouble than others, he climbed to the top of his tank with a Lewis gun and opened fire on the supposed position from behind his fascine. He left this position of cover under heavy fire in order to give directions to other tanks arriving on the scene.

He and his men opened machine-gun fire on a party of about 200 Germans who tried to counter-attack from the village and caused them to withdraw.

Having used up all his ammunition, he found a German machine-gun and ammunition, which he used against the enemy until the

6th Seaforths arrived; the officer of this company ('A'Company) of Seaforths (Capt. Edwards) was shot through the head while talking to 2nd Lieut. Bion.

2nd Lieut. Bion took command of this company until 2nd Lieut. MacLeod of that regiment arrived. After remaining in the line until 2 P.M., he reported to Colonel Macdonald, commanding this battalion, who told him he had no further need of his services.

Throughout all this period this officer, by his coolness, initiative, and complete disregard of his personal safety, probably prevented the situation from being very much more serious.

2nd Lieut. WINDLE, CHARLES ERNEST. 'E' Battn. Awarded M.C.

For conspicuous gallantry and devotion to duty during the Cambrai operations on November 20–23, 1917. He fought his tank with exceptional endurance and cheerfulness for three days. Although wounded on the first day, he continued to fight until his objectives were gained, and when again wounded on the third day he carried on, materially assisting the infantry to clear Bourlon Wood under exceptionally difficult circumstances.

T. Lieut. (A/Capt.) GRIFFITHS, ARTHUR GEORGE. 'E' Battn. Awarded M.C.

For conspicuous gallantry and devotion to duty during the Cambrai operations on November 20, 21, and 23, 1917. He commanded a section of tanks in action on three out of four consecutive days. His excellent work throughout was beyond praise, and he especially distinguished himself by his splendid leadership. Warned at short notice, he organised and led a successful attack against Bourlon Wood, thereby enabling the infantry to capture this important position. He showed the greatest keenness and resource during the whole action.

2nd Lieut. McELROY, FREDERICK WILLIAM. 'G' Battn. Awarded D.S.O.

For conspicuous gallantry and devotion to duty. On November 20, after driving the enemy into the village of Havrincourt and capturing two strongly held craters, his tank caught fire and had to be evacuated. Nevertheless, in spite of the fumes, he himself remained inside firing his Lewis gun and killing many of the enemy. When his crew, many of whom were wounded, were surrounded in the shell-hole they had occupied, he killed eight of the enemy with his revolver. When the enemy attempted to capture the tank by rushes he held them at bay single-handed. It was owing to his bravery and coolness that the crew escaped certain death and the tank was held against capture. Two days afterwards he again took a tank into action with great success.

THE TANK CORPS BOOK OF HONOUR

Capt. Bt. Major (A/Major) BROOME, RALPH HOWARD, M.C.
' G ' Battn. Awarded D.S.O.

For conspicuous bravery and devotion to duty. He was in command of a composite company of thirty tanks on November 20 —eleven of his tanks were in action on the 21st inst. and ten on the 23rd. The way he rallied his tanks at the various objectives and at the end of the day is most praiseworthy. He set a magnificent example of pluck and dash throughout the operations. He got ten tanks into action on the 23rd inst., which did splendid work, though the crews were well-nigh exhausted and he only had a few hours' warning. These tanks cleared the way for the infantry in Bourlon Wood, and the infantry were able to consolidate the position.

T. Capt. GUY, OSWALD VERNON, M.C. ' G ' Battn. Awarded Bar to M.C.

For conspicuous gallantry and devotion to duty during the operations on November 20, 21, and 23. As section commander he followed his tanks on foot all the time, and set a magnificent example of coolness and resource when rallying his tanks. He was able to get most valuable reports back to his company commander from his own personal observation.

T. 2nd Lieut. BAKER, ALBERT GEORGE, M.C. ' G ' Battn. Awarded Bar to M.C.

For conspicuous gallantry and devotion to duty. He handled his tank with most conspicuous dash on November 20–21. He did specially fine work on November 20. When other tanks of his company received direct hits from an anti-tank gun just west of Graincourt, he manœuvred his tank so that he eventually knocked the gun out. This act enabled the infantry to complete the capture of the village, following after Lieut. Baker's and other tanks.

2nd Lieut. ADNEY, GEORGE HENRY. ' G ' Battn. Awarded M.C.

For conspicuous gallantry and devotion to duty. His tank was in action on November 20, 21, and 23. On the first day he took part in three separate assaults on Graincourt village and twice led parties of infantry forward, and returned a third time to fetch more.

In the attack on Anneux village, the second day, and Bourlon Wood, the third day, he displayed great gallantry.

At Bourlon Wood he had to temporarily leave his tank, which was under direct fire from an enemy field gun. Two of his crew were knocked out. Later he went back and gave the infantry further assistance, and eventually got his tank back to the rallying point.

IMMEDIATE AWARDS—OFFICERS

T. Lieut. (A/Capt.) D'URBAN-RUDD, BEVIL GORDON. 'G Battn. Awarded M.C.

For conspicuous gallantry and devotion to duty. He commanded a section of six tanks on November 20–21, 1917, with exceptional ability. On the first day he led over the first line objective, and in the afternoon, when the advance on the left had been stopped by enemy fire, he organised a batch of tanks and pushed forward beyond the final objective, thereby enabling the infantry to advance and consolidate. He inflicted the heaviest casualties on the enemy, and was instrumental in advancing our line more than 7000 yards.

The following day he succeeded in driving the enemy back several hundreds of yards, causing them exceptionally heavy casualties. By his ingenuity, bravery, and skill he saved a situation which had become critical.

Lieut. (A/Capt.) CHADWICK, FRANK DALE. 'G' Battn. Awarded M.C.

For conspicuous gallantry and devotion to duty On November 20 he commanded a section of tanks. His own tank having caught fire at the first objective, he established a strong point in a shell hole. The enemy thereupon surrounded him and attempted to capture the tank. By his coolness and presence of mind he was able to keep the enemy off, thus saving his crew and his tank. The enemy's repeated rushes at the tank were driven off by revolver fire.

T. Lieut. (A/Capt.) WRIGHT, ERNEST VINCENT. 'G' Battn. Awarded M.C.

For conspicuous gallantry and devotion to duty. On November 20 he commanded a section of tanks with great skill and judgment. When his tank ran out of petrol he went forward on foot with the infantry, and assisted in the capture of the final objective. The tanks under his command were instrumental in pushing our line forward 7000 yards. He displayed conspicuous gallantry under fire.

Lieut. (A/Capt.) INGHAM, GEORGE. 'A' Battn. Awarded M.C.

For conspicuous gallantry and devotion to duty in the operations near Nine Wood and Noyelles on November 20–21, 1917. On November 20, 1917, Captain Ingham was in the leading tank of his section, and led the attack on Nine Wood and Noyelles. His tanks put many enemy machine-guns out of action and inflicted very heavy casualties, thus enabling the infantry with whom he was working to gain their objectives with very few losses and in good time. It was entirely due to his brilliant and gallant leadership that whenever the advance of the infantry was held up a tank appeared and cleared the situation. Particularly was this the case with a machine-gun on the outskirts of Noyelles which was holding up our advance. A tank appeared from behind the machine-gun and with two shots from its 6-pndrs. put the gun out of action. On November 21, 1917, this officer's section again went into action and rendered excellent service to our infantry and inflicted heavy casualties on the enemy. On both days Capt. Ingham led his section with great gallantry and skill, and brought all his tanks successfully out of action.

2nd Lieut. (A/Capt.) RICH, CECIL OLIVER, M.C. ' A ' Battn. Awarded Bar to M.C.

For conspicuous gallantry and devotion to duty in the operations near Marcoing on November 20, 1917. This officer led his section into action with great skill and coolness. After advancing about 2000 yards, a masked field battery opened fire on the tanks at about 100 yards range. In spite of the fact that one tank was almost immediately put out of action and he himself very seriously wounded, Captain Rich carried on and effectively silenced the battery, thus enabling the infantry to continue their advance. This officer set a splendid example to all ranks of his section and paid no regard to his own personal safety.

2nd Lieut. SHAW, THOMAS JOSEPH. ' A ' Battn. Awarded M.C.

For conspicuous gallantry and devotion to duty. In the attack on Marcoing on November 20, 1917, he displayed great skill and determination in getting his tank to its objective. On the way he silenced many enemy machine-guns. Later, in attacking an enemy field battery, his tank received two direct hits. On December 1, 1917, he commanded a tank in a composite section. His tank successfully attacked Gauche Wood and put several enemy machine-guns out of action. He then, unsupported by either infantry or other tanks, proceeded to Villers Guislan. The enemy were concentrated here apparently massing for a counter-attack. Although under very heavy shell and machine-gun fire, he brought a destructive fire from his 6-pndr. guns to bear on the enemy, inflicting very severe casualties. As no support was forthcoming, he returned to fetch reinforcements. None were available, so his section commander ordered him to ' stand by.' This officer's example was a splendid inspiration to all ranks in a most difficult situation.

Lieut. (A./Capt.) MISKIN, MAURICE JAMES. ' A ' Battn. Awarded M.C.

For conspicuous gallantry and devotion to duty in the attack on Marcoing on November 20, 1917. The tanks of this officer's section were in the second wave. During the approach march of his section he had continuous mechanical trouble with all three of his tanks. This he successfully overcame, and his section was the first to arrive at Marcoing. He secured the canal crossings and went forward on foot to clear up the situation. No infantry had then reached Marcoing. He then, under heavy fire, went and reported the situation to the Officer Commanding Border Regiment, who was thus enabled to get his battalion across the canal whilst the enemy were still on the run. Throughout the day he showed a complete disregard of his own personal safety, and set a fine example to all his section.

2nd Lieut. MATTHEWS, GEORGE. ' A ' Battn. Awarded M.C.

For conspicuous gallantry and devotion to duty in the operations near Noyelles on November 20, 1917. Five of the members of his crew had been wounded when his tank caught fire, and although surrounded by the enemy and under very heavy fire he, with the help only of his N.C.O., kept the guns going and inflicted heavy losses on the enemy. On four other occasions his tank caught fire during the action. When all his Lewis guns were put out of action he continued to fight with his 6-pndrs. until all the ammunition had been expended. He then, with the aid of his N.C.O. and first driver, successfully brought his tank out of action. Throughout the whole of the operation he set a fine example to his crew.

T. Lieut. WOOTTON, KENNETH EDWIN. 1/21 Battn. London Regt. (attached ' A ' Battn., Tank Corps). Awarded M.C.

For conspicuous gallantry and devotion to duty in the operations near Marcoing on November 20, 1917. His tank was the leading tank of his section, and he skilfully guided it along its exact route, putting many enemy machine-guns out of action on the way. It was due to his exceptional skill and determination that the infantry working with his section were enabled to obtain their objective with very few casualties. Later he attacked an enemy field gun at very close range. He was finally very badly wounded and his tank put out of action by receiving a direct hit from an enemy field battery which he was engaging.

T. Major (A/Lieut.-Col.) BRYCE, EDWARD DANIEL, D.S.O. ' B ' Battn. Awarded Bar to D.S.O.

Commanded ' B ' Battalion, Tank Corps, in action of November 20. This officer showed great gallantry and determination throughout the battle. Immediately after the capture of the Hindenburg support system Lieutenant-Colonel Bryce moved forward and established his battalion headquarters about three-quarters of a mile beyond the support system, about 600 yards west of Marcoing and in advance of the leading infantry.

The battalion flag was erected in a prominent position, and

sixteen tanks of the battalion were rallied at this spot and prepared to move forward again with the cavalry, while fourteen tanks went ahead and attacked Marcoing.

On the following morning this officer went forward with twelve tanks and personally launched them against Cantaing, which was successfully captured, heavy losses being inflicted on the enemy.

The good judgment and tactical dispositions of Lieut-Col. Bryce were largely responsible for the success of the operations, while his coolness, total disregard of personal safety, and determination were a great inspiration to the officers and men of his battalion.

T. 2nd Lieut. (A/Capt.) HARCOURT, ALEXANDER CLARENCE. 'B' Battn. Awarded D.S.O.

On November 20, while the attack on Cantaing was in progress, the 86th Infantry Brigade in Marcoing asked for tanks to assist in the capture of Noyelles, where their infantry had been held up by heavy machine-gun fire. Captain Harcourt's section had not been detailed for the attack on Cantaing and the crews were resting. He immediately, on his own initiative and without waiting for further instructions, started off with one of his section tanks to Noyelles, leaving orders for another to follow him. On reaching the village these two tanks knocked out all resistance, setting a hostile ammunition dump on fire with 6-pndr. guns, and patrolled the village until the arrival of the infantry half an hour later. The capture of Noyelles was due to this officer's initiative and immediate action, which is deserving of the highest praise.

On November 30, in the attack to recapture Gouzeaucourt, this officer led his section of tanks into action. When one of his section commanders, 2nd Lieut. Tuite, was wounded, this officer borrowed a horse and rode back for a stretcher, which he then took back under shell fire. This officer was previously brought to notice.

T. Lieut. (A/Capt.) CROUCH, THOMAS ALFRED. 'B' Battn. Awarded D.S.O.

On November 20, during the attack on the Hindenburg Line and the attack on Marcoing, this officer showed the clearest judgment and greatest initiative in leading his section.

On arrival of the tanks in Marcoing with no infantry support this officer's conduct was most gallant. He moved in the open, on foot, all alone, under heavy machine-gun fire, and succeeded in getting his tanks through the village.

His tank crews were receiving heavy casualties and the situation looked critical, but realising that this resistance must be overcome, Capt. Crouch went from one tank to another on foot and ordered them to advance, thus knocking out the resistance and opening the way to the bridgeheads. The infantry did not enter Marcoing till about an hour later.

IMMEDIATE AWARDS—OFFICERS

T. Lieut. (A/Capt.) GROVES, HENRY BASIL MOLVIN, M.C. ' B ' Battn. Awarded Bar to M.C.

For conspicuous gallantry in action near Marcoing on November 20, 1917, when in command of a section of tanks. To ensure that all his tanks kept to the right routes and reached their objectives, he directed them on foot in spite of the fact that he was exposed to machine-gun and rifle fire. He showed remarkable coolness and daring, and it was largely due to his skill and devotion to duty that the infantry were able to reach their objectives with slight casualties.

. This officer throughout the action showed a total disregard for his personal safety.

T. Lieut. ASHWELL, GEORGE. ' B ' Battn. Awarded M.C.

This officer was in charge of a company workshop section. During the attack on the Hindenburg Line on November 20 he followed his company tanks on foot as closely as possible. His skill and devotion to duty resulted in all the tanks of this company being again ready for immediate action.

On November 22, the day after the action at Cantaing, he set to work on two tanks of the company which had received direct hits on the previous day. These two tanks were about 300 yards from the village and subjected to enemy artillery and machine-gun fire. He nevertheless completed work on them and brought them back two days later.

During the whole of the operations this officer showed a total disregard for his personal safety and the greatest devotion to duty.

He had previously been brought to notice.

T. Major PRATT, DOUGLAS HENRY, M.C. ' H ' Battn. Awarded D.S.O.

This officer commanded No. 24 Company, ' H ' Battn., Tank Corps, during the attack on Premy Chapel and Nine Wood on November 20, 1917.

It was largely due to his careful preparation and organisation and keen devotion that the tanks of his company were successful in reaching all objectives. He himself directed the operations against Nine Wood on foot, in front of our infantry and in face of considerable opposition, and his leadership, power of command, and great coolness under fire inspired all ranks with great confidence.

This officer never spared himself, and showed utter disregard for his personal safety.

The company which Major Pratt commanded on November 20 captured Premy Chapel and Nine Wood about an hour before the infantry arrived.

2nd Lieut. DAVIS, ROBERT CLEMENT. ' H ' Battn. Awarded M.C.

On November 20, 1917, south of Ribecourt, after having crossed the Hindenburg front system of trenches, this officer's tank caught fire. Four of his crew having been either burnt or overcome by fumes, he, with his driver, subdued the fire, the tank the whole time being under observation and subject to hostile artillery fire. He managed to get the tank restarted, and had reached his rallying point in time to take part in the attack on the Brown Line (Hindenburg support system) when the section was again called upon. After this his tank received three direct hits, 2nd Lieut. R. C. Davis being wounded in two places. The gallantry and determination of this officer set an example which is worthy of the highest praise.

T. Lieut. (A/Capt.) BATTEN, PERCY WOODRUFF. ' H ' Battn. Awarded M.C.

This officer was in command of a section of tanks near Ribecourt on November 20, 1917. He was rallying his section after the capture of the Brown Line, when a party of the enemy was seen coming up on his left. He at once ordered his section to prepare to attack, and, riding in the leading tank, himself led the attack.

His tank received a direct hit which put it out of action and wounded most of the crew. He, however, with great gallantry continued to direct operations, walking about in the open under direct fire from the enemy's battery 200 yards away.

This officer showed a total disregard for his personal safety and set a fine example to his men.

Lieut. PARSONS, EDMUND RICHARD. ' H ' Battn. Awarded M.C.

This officer was in charge of No. 1 Workshop Section, No. 22 Coy., ' H ' Battn., Tank Corps, and followed up his company on foot in the attack on the Hindenburg front system on November 20, 1917.

Seeing that a tank was on fire, he went to its assistance and put out the fire. Four of the crew having been put out of action by gas poisoning from fumes, he himself joined the tank and acted as gearsman, thus enabling the tank to carry on in action. It was later put out of action by three direct hits, which killed and wounded the remainder of the crew with the exception of the driver.

Lieut. Parsons continued to work on the tank, and eventually brought it back to the rallying point.

This officer showed a total disregard for his personal safety and set a fine example.

2nd Lieut. (A/Capt.) YOULL, ROBERT ARNOLD. ' C ' Battn. Awarded M.C.

As section commander, on November 20, 1917, this officer led his tanks into action against Bleak House with conspicuous gallantry and determination. On November 23, 1917, he again displayed the greatest bravery in leading his section into action against La Fontaine. It was due to his fine leadership that numbers of the enemy were killed and many machine-guns put out of action. He has been previously brought to notice for conspicuous gallantry in action at Ypres on July 31, 1917.

T. Lieut. (A/Capt.) JOHNSTON, HENRY WATT. 'C' Battn. Awarded M.C.

During the attack on the Gonnelieu Ridge on November 20, 1917, as section commander, this officer led his tanks into action with the greatest gallantry. When the situation in the neighbourhood of Bleak House became disorganised, he left his tank under heavy machine-gun and snipers' fire and co-ordinated the work of the infantry with his tanks in such a way that the advance was able to be resumed.

T. 2nd Lieut. ARCHIBALD, MUNGO TENNANT. 'C' Battn. Awarded M C.

For conspicuous gallantry and skill as a tank commander in action. During the action on November 20, 1917, at Lateau Wood, he fought his tank with exceptional gallantry and skill. Again, on November 21, he volunteered to try and bring in a tank that was ditched in the enemy's lines. In Fontaine-Notre-Dame, on November 23, 1917, by his courage and coolness, his tank was enabled to do great execution amongst the enemy in the streets of the village. When another tank of his company was set on fire by a direct hit, in spite of being surrounded by the enemy, and under heavy machine-gun and sniping fire, he managed to rescue the whole of the disabled crew and transfer them to his own tank. Whilst manœuvring his tank out of the village, with sixteen persons on board, himself and every one, with one exception, being wounded with armour-piercing bullets, this tank was also set on fire by a direct hit. With complete disregard of his own safety, he got both crews out of the burning tank and back to the rallying point.

Throughout the whole of a long and exhausting operation this officer displayed courage, resource, and endurance of the highest order.

T. 2nd Lieut. WALKER, GODFREY. 'C' Battn. Awarded M.C.

For conspicuous gallantry as a tank commander both in action at Pam Pam Farm on November 20, 1917, and again at Fontaine-Notre-Dame on November 23, 1917. By his gallantry and resource at Pam Pam Farm he saved the situation at a very critical period by putting out of action many enemy machine-guns and snipers, who were doing great execution amongst our infantry. He again did excellent work at Fontaine-Notre-Dame, and by his coolness and initiative caused considerable casualties amongst the enemy in the streets of the village. This officer has been previously brought to notice for gallantry in action on July 31, 1917, at Frezenburg Redoubt.

T. 2nd Lieut. MOORE, WILLIE. ' C ' 'Battn. Awarded M.C.

On November 20 and November 23, 1917, in action at Lateau Wood and at Fontaine-Notre-Dame, this officer fought his tank with conspicuous gallantry and skill. Throughout the whole of the action on November 20 he exposed himself continuously, with complete disregard of his own safety, in order to point out targets to his gunners. On November 23 his tank accounted for numbers of the enemy in Fontaine-Notre-Dame until set on fire in the main street by a direct hit. Under intense fire he transferred all his crew to another tank, and was himself severely wounded during the operation. This officer has been previously brought to notice for gallantry in action at Ypres on July 31, 1917.

Lieut. (A/Capt.) SCUPHAM, WILLIAM ERIC HALSTEAD. ' F ' Battn. Awarded M.C.

For conspicuous gallantry and devotion to duty in the tank operations on November 20. He was the officer responsible for the capture of the bridgehead at Masnières, which he held with two tanks throughout the night of November 20–21 till daylight, when he reorganised his section.

Again, in the operations at Bourlon village on November 27 he personally formed up the infantry behind his four tanks at the position of deployment under heavy shell fire. He then proceeded in the tank which penetrated to the northern edge of the village, and finally reorganised his tanks under heavy fire. He displayed great skill and bravery throughout the operations.

T. 2nd Lieut. BORGER, ALEXANDER HENRY CHARLES. ' F ' Battn. Awarded M.C.

During the tank operations on November 20, 1917, and subsequent days, this officer carried out his duties as reconnaissance officer in a most gallant and devoted manner. On November 20 he followed up the company's tanks, taking messages and instructions from his company commander to his own as well as other companies' tanks, reconnoitring crossings of sunken roads, etc., often under machine-gun fire. His coolness and pluck contributed materially to the success of the company in reaching all objectives. On the 21st he again went into action with the tanks to Marcoing, and on the 27th went with his company C.O. close behind the attack at Bourlon village. The previous night he had guided twenty tanks to their assembly point unaided, as all company section commanders had to remain behind to get orders from their Infantry Brigades during the approach march. He was out from 4 P.M., 26th, until 10 P.M., 27th, and carried on throughout with great coolness and courage though under heavy shell fire during the night and day. He was either in action or on reconnaissance work every day and most nights from the 19th to 27th. Nothing but pluck and endurance could have carried him through the prolonged period.

T. 2nd Lieut. FARRAR, WALTER FREDERICK. ' F ' Battn. Awarded M.C.

For conspicuous gallantry and devotion to duty in action at Masnières on November 20, 1917. During the attack he destroyed a machine-gun position, killing the crew and taking the gun on board. On reaching the bridgehead at Masnières he found the bridge partially destroyed, but in view of his orders, which laid down the urgency of crossing, he did not hesitate to drive his tank over in an effort to span the gap, although the river was reported to be twelve feet deep. His tank sank, but he got his crew out safely, being the last to leave.

2nd Lieut. (T. Capt.) RAIKES, DAVID TAUNTON, M.C. 3/8 S.W. Borderers (seconded ' A ' Battn.). Awarded D.S.O.

For conspicuous gallantry in action at Marcoing on November 20 and 21, while in command of a section of tanks. During the afternoon of November 20 this officer controlled the movement of his section of tanks under heavy machine-gun fire with absolute disregard for his personal safety. He got out of his tank at least a dozen times to give instructions to the tank commanders, in spite of the fact that his tank was on most occasions subjected to machine-gun fire and the intervening space between the tanks was entirely devoid of cover and in full view of the enemy. Again, on November 21, under similar conditions, he directed his own section of tanks and also nine others who were in need of confirmation as to the situation. Throughout the two days' fighting he never rested as long as his services could be of any use, and his utter disregard for danger and his great cheerfulness throughout set a fine example to all ranks.

T. Capt. DALBY, A. A. 2nd Battn., Tank Corps. Awarded M.C.

For conspicuous gallantry and initiative as tank commander on November 20, 1917, near Marcoing. It was of great importance to hold the bridges over the canal, and in face of heavy fire he made straight for the main railway bridge in time to prevent the enemy running out a wire and blowing it up. He shot the man with the wire, and beat off a counter-attack. Later, in the attack on Fontaine, he fought most gallantly against heavy odds until his tank was knocked out and the crew killed or wounded. He did fine work.

THE TANK CORPS BOOK OF HONOUR

T. 2nd Lieut. LATCH, ARTHUR RONALD. 'E' Battn. Awarded D.S.O.

For most conspicuous gallantry and devotion to duty during the Cambrai operations on November 21, 1917. He took his tank into action in the afternoon, and by his great bravery, perseverance, and skill he succeeded in saving an infantry battalion from a desperate position. He drove the enemy from some strong points, which had been threatening the left flank of the infantry, and when darkness came on he was surrounded by the enemy, who climbed on top of the tank and seized hold of the machine-guns. With exceptional presence of mind and courage, he succeeded in driving them off, inflicting very severe casualties upon them. He then dispersed the enemy, who were assembling for a counter-attack, and finally rallied his tank. No praise can be too great for the manner in which he handled his tank under especially trying circumstances, and the material help he rendered was invaluable.

T. Major PEARSON, ALGERNON GEORGE. 'H' Battn. Awarded D.S.O.

From La Justice Farm, on November 21, 1917, this officer, in command of No. 23 Company, 'H' Battn., Tank Corps, launched an attack with his eight tanks on Fontaine village. In spite of the fact that all these tanks had been in action the previous day, this officer, by his energy, initiative, and devotion to duty, succeeded in organising his company for the attack.

As the orders for the attack were received only one hour before zero, close liaison with the infantry was practically impossible. Major A. G. Pearson, therefore, launched the attack himself, clearing the situation west of Cantaing, and his tanks then entered Fontaine, where they held on till the infantry arrived about an hour later and established themselves in the village.

Major Pearson then rallied his company and brought the tanks safely out of action.

Major Pearson also launched his company into action on November 20 with exceptionally good results.

Lieut. (T. Capt.) CARLES, C. W. 4th Battn., E. Kent Regt., T.F. (seconded 6th Battn., Tank Corps). Awarded M.C.

For conspicuous gallantry and devotion to duty near Rumilly on November 21, 1917. He was ordered to proceed with his own and three other tanks to crush the wire in front of the enemy trenches defending Rumilly. He led the way in his tank, inflicted heavy casualties on the enemy in face of intense fire and, when forced by direct hits to evacuate his tank, he formed a Lewis gun post with his crew in a stable, after capturing three prisoners there.

IMMEDIATE AWARDS—OFFICERS

T. Capt. HOTBLACK, FREDERICK ELLIOTT, D.S.O., M.C. Headquarters. Awarded Bar to D.S.O.

For conspicuous gallantry on November 23 during the attack on Fontaine-Notre-Dame. By his personal example and initiative he carried on the attack, re-organising the infantry, whose officers had become casualties, and collecting tanks. He had to pass through a heavy barrage and was continuously under machine-gun fire, but succeeded in launching a fresh attack with tanks and infantry.

This officer has been present throughout the four great battles of the year, except Arras, where he was wounded on the first day. He has shown throughout persistent gallantry and contempt of danger in the pursuance of his duty as a reconnaissance and battle liaison officer which has been an inspiration to all ranks.

2nd Lieut. BLACK, JOHN ARMSTRONG. 'E' Battn. Awarded M.C.

Whilst commanding his tank in action east of Moeuvres on November 23, 1917, the tank received a direct hit when in front of the infantry and within thirty yards of the enemy lines, and caught fire, obliging him and his crew to evacuate ; he took up a position with his guns in the open and remained there without being reinforced for five hours, during which time two of his crew were killed and three wounded. When it got dark he crawled back to our lines to fetch infantry to assist, and with them carried in the three wounded men.

T. Lieut. (A/Capt.) ROBERTS, WALTER EMLYN. 'E' Battn. Awarded M.C.

While commanding his section in action east of Moeuvres on November 23, 1917, he was wounded in a tank ; he continued fighting his tank in the enemy's lines until all ammunition had been expended. He then returned on foot to Company Headquarters, where he made reports and arranged for more ammunition, immediately returning to the scene of action, where he found and approached his second tank under heavy fire. He was the means of directing other tanks to certain objectives where they were most needed. Throughout the whole action he displayed great gallantry and initiative.

2nd Lieut. RITCHIE, GEORGE SOUTHERN. 'G' Battn. Awarded M.C.

For conspicuous gallantry and devotion to duty. On November 23, during the attack on Bourlon Wood, his tank broke down owing to mechanical trouble. He got his crew out of the tank with their machine-guns, and followed another tank well ahead of the infantry, and inflicted very heavy casualties on the enemy at close quarters, which the other tanks unearthed. He remained out with his crew, helping the infantry, who afterwards came up to consolidate, until he was recalled that night.

The initiative he displayed and the clever handling of his crew enabled the infantry to gain ground which they could not have won without his assistance.

2nd Lieut. WAINE, FRANK LEE. ' G ' Battn. Awarded M.C.

For conspicuous gallantry and devotion to duty. On November 23 he got his tank through Bourlon Wood right ahead of the infantry, clearing the enemy out of a large part of the wood. When he reached his final objective the tank broke down and was surrounded by the enemy, who poured very heavy machine-gun fire on it. He held them at bay till every one of his guns had been smashed by fire, and did not leave his tank till it finally burst into flames. The endurance he displayed during the whole action was magnificent.

2nd Lieut. LAW, RALPH MELVILLE. ' B ' Battn. Awarded M.C.

This officer commanded his tank with great gallantry on November 23. He fought his tank in Fontaine against great opposition. He took his tank considerably ahead of our infantry, and continued in action for over four hours until his tank was out of action by armour-piercing bullets perforating the radiator.

To prevent his tank falling into German hands he made a determined effort and succeeded in returning to within 100 yards of our infantry. He then found the tank could not possibly run any further, and at once took his Lewis guns out of the tank and fought with them in the open against the Germans as they were advancing.

Eventually, after two of his crew had been killed and two wounded, he returned to report to his company commander, and although in a state of collapse insisted on going back to his tank after darkness to bring back his wounded driver. He then found his tank in No Man's Land and that his driver had died.

This officer showed a fine fighting spirit and set a splendid example.

2nd Lieut. ROGERSON, ARTHUR. ' H ' Battn. Awarded M.C.

For conspicuous gallantry and devotion to duty while in command of a section of tanks at Fontaine on November 23, 1917. This officer was in the leading tank which entered the village. Finding that the infantry were unable to follow, he took his tanks back and, getting out, sought the O.C. Infantry concerned.

He again advanced into the village, but the infantry were still unable to follow. He dealt with several machine-gun emplacements and strong points in the village and again returned to the infantry.

He walked along the line to see the officer in command and

found that the infantry were about to consolidate the line then held. At this time he found that the tank in which he was riding was short of petrol ; he had some spare tins on the tank and, accompanied by one of the crew who volunteered, they proceeded to fill the petrol tank, which is on the outside of the tank, the whole time being subject to machine-gun and rifle fire.

He again went forward and covered the consolidation of the line.

This officer showed a total disregard for his personal safety and set a fine example to his men.

2nd Lieut. MUSTARD, ANDREW. ' H ' Battn. Awarded M.C.

For conspicuous gallantry during the attack on Fontaine on November 23, 1917.

On reaching the outskirts of the village, his tank experienced engine trouble and stopped. The tank was surrounded by the enemy, who bombed it and fired at point-blank range through the gun mountings and loop-holes, three of his gunners being wounded. He was called upon by the enemy to surrender, but ordering his gunners to keep up Lewis-gun fire, he himself worked at the engine, and after three-quarters of an hour succeeded in starting it.

It was entirely to his gallantry and devotion to duty that the tank was saved from falling into the hands of the enemy and the crew becoming prisoners.

None of the infantry were in Fontaine.

T. Lieut. (A/Capt.) JEFFERY, CHARLES ERNEST. ' H ' Battn. Awarded M.C.

This officer was commanding a composite section of 22 Coy., ' H ' Battn., Tank Corps, in the attack on Fontaine village on November 23, 1917. He led the attack in the foremost tank. Finding that his tank was considerably ahead of the infantry, he returned with the intention of keeping in touch. On the way back he found that a large party of the enemy had come in behind him and was holding up the infantry advance. In spite of heavy machine-gun fire and bombs, he fought his way through and succeeded in rejoining the infantry, killing a large number of the enemy, who were crammed in trenches, by driving over them. Throughout the day he showed conspicuous gallantry and devotion to duty.

T. Lieut. (A/Capt.) GRIMLEY, CECIL WALTER GATSKELL. ' H ' Battn. Awarded M.C.

For gallantry and devotion to duty at Bourlon Wood on November 23, 1917. This officer was rallying his section after having reached all objectives and had covered the infantry consolidation. He saw that the infantry were held up by heavy machine-gun fire in the direction of Fontaine. He at once proceeded with one tank and cleared the situation, inflicting heavy casualties on the enemy, and by his initiative averted what might have been a serious check. He remained with and fought his tank eleven hours, and only withdrew when forced to do so owing to lack of petrol and darkness. This officer showed fine judgment and determination.

T. 2nd Lieut. (A/Capt.) DAVIS, REGINALD GRAHAM. ' H ' Battn. Awarded M.C.

For conspicuous gallantry while in command of No. 9 Section, 24 Company, ' H ' Battn., Tank Corps, in the second attack on Fontaine on November 23, 1917.

This officer was in the leading tank of his section when it experienced engine trouble. The tank was at once surrounded by the enemy; three of the gunners in the tank were wounded. After the enemy had been made to retire he left the tank, and proceeded on foot to secure two gunners from another tank that had been put out of action. He brought these gunners back to replace casualties. After this, seeing that another tank of his section had been hit and put out of action, he started on foot to render assistance, although the tank in question was several hundred yards in front of our advanced line of infantry, and the route was covered by enemy machine-gun and rifle fire.

He was wounded in attempting to carry out his duty. During the whole action he showed a total disregard for his personal safety and keen devotion to duty, setting a fine example to the crews of his section.

T. 2nd Lieut. MORTON, HARRY NEWTON. ' F ' Battn. Awarded M.C.

For conspicuous courage and determination in action at Fontaine on November 27, 1917. His was the foremost tank in the village. After fighting his 6 pndrs. till all his ammunition was expended and one Lewis gun out of action, he found the infantry still required assistance. He therefore drove through the village again, using his remaining two Lewis guns until all his ammunition was expended and all his guns out of action. He then stood by with the infantry till satisfied that he was no longer required.

2nd Lieut. DINGLEY, PHILLIP NEVILLE. ' B ' Battn. Awarded M.C.

On November 30, at Gouzeaucourt, this officer's tank got a direct hit which wounded five out of seven of the crew and rendered the tank useless. The officer in the next tank being wounded, Lieut. Dingley took charge of the latter's tank and crew, and proceeded straight to his objective after leaving the wounded officer and wounded men of his own crew in charge of the two unwounded men. The change of tanks was effected under heavy shell fire. This officer was in action altogether for about seven hours. He showed great initiative and devotion to duty, setting a fine example to the crews.

Lieut. CLARKE, BRICE RICHARD. ' B ' Battn. Awarded M.C.

On November 30 this officer took his tank into action west of Gouzeaucourt, where he took up a position to cover the infantry whilst they were consolidating. He kept his tank in action for about five hours, during the whole time being subjected to a heavy hostile artillery barrage. This officer did not withdraw his tank till the infantry were consolidated.

He set a fine example to his crew and showed a total disregard for danger.

Lieut. B. R. Clarke was in action at Cantaing on November 21, when his tank was put out of action by hostile fire.

This officer salved his tank on November 28 from a position on the outskirts of Cantaing, where it was subjected to heavy hostile artillery fire.

Lieut. B. R. Clarke has been brought to notice for gallantry on two previous occasions.

2nd Lieut. SYMMONDS, PERCIVAL ALEXANDER. ' B ' Battn. Awarded M.C.

During the attack on Gauche Wood, on December 1, 1917, this officer commanded his tank with great skill. The tank was subjected to very heavy machine-gun fire and it was impossible to locate the exact position of the machine-guns. 2nd Lieut. Symmonds, therefore, opened the flap in front of the tank, thereby exposing himself, but this enabled him to detect the guns and direct his gunners where to fire, with the result that four machine-guns were put out of action.

The tank afterwards advanced towards Quentin Ridge and was subjected to hostile artillery fire, fired over open sights at close range. This officer observed the position of the guns and ammunition dump, and at once headed his tank towards the guns, directing his gunners where to fire. The ammunition dump was blown up by 6-pndr. guns and the enemy battery silenced. At this time the tank was completely isolated.

This officer showed great determination and coolness in action and set a fine example to his crew. The whole crew speak in marked terms of the ability this officer showed.

T. Lieut. (A/Capt.) GROUNDS, GEORGE AMBROSE. ' H ' Battn. Awarded D.S.O.

For conspicuous gallantry and devotion to duty while in command of a section of tanks east of Gouzeaucourt on December 1, 1917.

THE TANK CORPS BOOK OF HONOUR

When three of his tanks had been put out of action by direct hits this officer organised the crews into Lewis gun sections and himself led them into action to assist in repelling the attack of the enemy.

Having placed his section to the best advantage, Capt. Grounds went to get in touch with the Welsh Guards, with whom he was operating. While proceeding along a trench he met a party of the enemy. With great presence of mind Capt. Grounds made use of some German bombs he found in the trench, and single-handed succeeded for a while in disorganising and holding up this party of the enemy. Capt. Grounds then brought his one remaining tank and also collected a party of the 3rd Coldstream Guards to act as bombers, and succeeded in capturing about 200 yards of trench, fifteen machine-guns and a large number of prisoners.

This officer throughout the action displayed the greatest gallantry and total disregard for his own safety. His initiative and fine leadership resulted in an advance being possible on this part of the front. This officer was brought to notice for gallantry on November 20 and 23.

T. Lieut. (A/Capt.) GERRARD, WALTER DOUGLAS. ' H ' Battn. Awarded D.S.O.

For conspicuous gallantry and devotion to duty while in command of a section of tanks east of Gouzeaucourt. On December 1, 1917, the leading tank in which this officer was riding became ditched. Capt. Gerrard made every endeavour to unditch his tank, but finding it impossible he withdrew his crew from the tank and formed them into a Lewis gun section, which he himself led into action. Having placed his crew to the best advantage he returned to his other three tanks only to find they had all been put out of action by direct hits. This officer, therefore, organised these crews into Lewis gun sections and took them up into the line to join the first crew.

Finding a German machine-gun and ammunition which had been captured earlier in the day, Captain Gerrard himself used this gun with good effect against the enemy. Captain Gerrard fought his section till only seven officers and men remained out of the original thirty-two which started into action.

2nd Lieut. SCOTT, CECIL EWART. ' H ' Battn. Awarded M.C.

For conspicuous gallantry in action near Gauche Wood on December 1, 1917, while in command of a tank.

His tank received a direct hit and caught fire ; three of the crew were killed and two wounded ; this officer continued in action, firing six drums from his Lewis gun and encouraging the remainder of the crew to keep on firing with the other remaining guns until he was forced to withdraw the crew on account of intense heat. He then re-entered the burning tank at great personal risk and brought out the wounded.

During the whole of this time the tank was several hundred yards in front of our own infantry and under direct observation of the enemy and was subjected to heavy artillery shelling and sniping.

2nd Lieut. Scott showed a total disregard for his own safety.

2nd Lieut. BAILEY, JOHN MORLEY, M.C. 1st Battn. Awarded Croix de Guerre.

For gallantry and devotion to duty as reconnaissance officer.

On numerous occasions during the past twelve months this officer has made reconnaissances in front of our line to obtain information for his tank officers before going into action.

He has also been of great assistance in bringing back valuable information from tanks in action. His disregard of danger and devotion to duty have been most marked.

He has been present throughout the Battle of Messines, Ypres, and Cambrai.

Capt. (A/Major) HENSHALL, LOUIS SYDNEY. ' B ' Battn. Awarded D.S.O.

This officer was given the special mission of capturing Marcoing and the bridgeheads with his company.

He made excellent arrangements, which included the rallying and reorganisation of his company after the capture of the Hindenburg Line. During the attack he followed his company very closely on foot and rallied his tanks just beyond the Hindenburg Line. He then asked for two more tanks, which were procured for him. After this he got into the leading tank and led his company straight to Marcoing. Although none of our cavalry or infantry had then reached the village, and in spite of hostile machine-gun fire and sniping, this officer got out of his tank and proceeded to visit each of his tanks on foot to see that they were in their proper places.

It was entirely due to his excellent arrangements and personal bravery that Marcoing was captured with the bridgeheads intact.

T. Lieut. (A/Capt.) KINNISON, CLIVE HASTINGS, M.C. ' G ' Battn. Awarded Bar to M.C.

For conspicuous gallantry and devotion to duty. He rode inside his tank for three assaults and always rallied his men in a masterly way. He was a section commander on each occasion. As the tanks were starting for their objective he led them on foot for a considerable distance. On ' Z ' night, when a fourth assault on Graincourt was considered necessary and volunteers were called for, he was the first to offer his services.

He laid the tape for the approach march on ' Y ' evening to our outpost line for twenty-two tanks, under very difficult conditions, the enemy at one time putting down a considerable trench mortar barrage.

The coolness he displayed throughout the operations was magnificent.

THE GERMAN OFFENSIVE, 1918

T. Lieut. SCALES, ALBERT WARREN. A.S.C. (attached Headquarters, 2nd Bde., Tank Corps). Awarded M.C.

For conspicuous good work during the operations March 21 to 28 in the capacity of brigade supply officer.

By his energy, initiative and personal courage Lieut. Scales has been largely responsible for the efficient manner in which the tanks of this brigade have been kept supplied in action, often under the most difficult and dangerous circumstances. At Fremicourt, on March 22, Lieut. Scales showed a splendid example to his men when supervising the loading of lorries with supplies, under heavy shell fire. At Albert, on the night March 24–25, while the town was being heavily bombed, Lieut. Scales, at great personal risk, completed the loading of some supply lorries for despatching forward to the tanks ; he then loaded his ration lorries and did not leave the town till he had seen all the staff safely away.

Throughout the whole week's fighting this officer has never spared himself, and has at all times shown a total disregard for his own safety.

Lieut. (A/Capt.) YOUNG, REGINALD CHARLES, M.C. 1st Battn. Awarded Bar to M.C.

For most conspicuous gallantry and devotion to duty throughout the operations from March 21 to 27, 1918. Every day he remained behind with broken-down tanks, and repaired and successfully got away several just as the enemy approached. He only stopped work on two tanks at Maricourt when actually fired on by the enemy. He displayed wonderful energy and resource in producing spare parts under very difficult conditions. Tanks that were considered to be in an almost hopeless condition he repaired and enabled them to be driven away and to fight again. His determination to see tanks repaired has been wonderful.

Capt. ELTON, HERBERT LAUZIER. 2nd City of London Regt. (seconded 1st Battn.). Awarded M.C.

For most conspicuous gallantry and devotion to duty throughout the operations from March 21 to 27, 1918, as battn. reconnaissance officer. On many occasions he was ordered to lead tanks to their starting-points over very difficult ground, and always succeeded.

He also displayed wonderful courage and initiative on the battle-field in obtaining information from neighbouring infantry units and carrying orders to isolated tanks. When the battalion was fighting on foot with Lewis guns he showed an absolute disregard of danger in going from one company to another with orders.

Capt. TELFER, FRANK PHILLIPS GOODMAN. 4th Battn. Awarded M.C.

On March 21–22, 1918, at Epehy and Peiziere, this officer showed marked skill and daring whilst in command of a section of tanks.

On three occasions his tanks counter-attacked the enemy and drove his infantry back. Despite heavy shelling and machine-gun and rifle fire, he continued on foot between his tanks until they were disabled by direct hits from shells.

His coolness greatly inspired all ranks.

T. Lieut. ROBINSON, HAROLD HEATLEY. 4th Battn. Awarded M.C.

At St. Emilie, on March 21, 1918, handled his tank with great gallantry and skill. He was instrumental in breaking up two hostile attacks.

During the morning he drove the enemy from our battery positions about Esclairvillers Wood. He then took his tank into a counter-attack on Ronssoy Wood.

Perceiving that the enemy were endeavouring to outflank our counter-attacking infantry, he proceeded towards Malasise Farm and drove him over the Epehy-Lempire road. He then rejoined our infantry and endeavoured to silence an enemy machine-gun which was causing trouble. In the meantime the tank had received a hit on the rear rollers and had to be very cautiously manœuvred to keep it in action. In spite of this the tank was brought back to St. Emilie after our infantry were established in Ronssoy Wood.

T. Capt. (A/Major) BLACKBURN, ERIC DEAN, M.C. 8th Battn. Awarded D.S.O.

Major Blackburn, in command of a company of tanks at Doignies, on March 21, 1918, launched his company into action in a counter-attack. It was entirely due to this officer's initiative and gallantry that the counter-attack was successfully carried out and was the means of checking the advance of the enemy and causing him heavy casualties. Major Blackburn himself led the company into action on foot under heavy machine-gun and shell fire, and greatly inspired all ranks with confidence. Again, at Colincamps, on March 26, Major Blackburn was in command of a Lewis gun company. Scouts reported to him that the enemy were advancing on the village. Major Blackburn immediately rode forward to reconnoitre and, quickly grasping the situation, he showed great initiative by rushing the Lewis gun company forward in a lorry and disposing this company to such advantage that this village was denied to the enemy; about twenty prisoners were taken and heavy casualties were inflicted. Major Blackburn was responsible for rallying the infantry in his immediate vicinity.

Throughout the whole action this officer has shown the greatest determination and a total disregard for his own safety.

T. Lieut. (A/Capt.) QUILLAUME, ERIC. 8th Battn. Awarded M.C.

Throughout the whole of the recent operations Capt. Quillaume, in the capacity of battalion reconnaissance officer, showed the greatest zeal and keenness. He has been responsible for the reconnaissance of tank routes and areas in which tanks might operate in counter-attacks. Particularly at Doignies, on March 21, this officer showed conspicuous bravery in going forward under heavy machine-gun and shell fire to reconnoitre, and the successful counter-attack on Doignies was greatly due to his work. On March 24, for the counter-attack on Barastre, Bus, and Haplincourt, Capt. Quillaume again carried out excellent reconnaissance work under heavy artillery fire. Capt. Quillaume has never spared himself; he has worked cheerfully under all circumstances, and has shown a total disregard for his own safety and the keenest devotion to duty.

Capt. (T. Major) TILLY, JUSTICE CROSSLAND, M.C. 1st Battn. Awarded Bar to M.C.

For most conspicuous gallantry and devotion to duty during the operations of March 22–27, 1918, when 2nd in command of a battalion. While left in command of the battalion at various intervals he displayed great initiative and determination in organising tanks for action and in leading them to their starting-points. Also, on March 2, when in actual command of Lewis gun teams on foot during a rearguard action on the Bray-Corbie road, he showed great skill in handling the various groups. It was very largely due to his skill that the infantry were able to withdraw successfully to various positions. He has throughout set a wonderful example.

T. 2nd Lieut. VAN ZELLER, THOMAS ARUNDELL. 5th Battn. Awarded M.C.

For conspicuous gallantry near Brie on March 23, 1918, when in command of a tank.

This officer was covering the withdrawal of the infantry across the Somme, and moved with his tank from Cartigny to Brie on the east side of the river, between our infantry and the enemy. During this period he inflicted heavy casualties, and was under heavy and continuous shell fire.

On arrival at Brie in the late afternoon he found that the bridge was about to be blown up, and that his tank could not cross. The tank accordingly had to be destroyed, and 2nd Lieut. T. A. Van Zeller directed his crew to assist in carrying wounded across the bridge, under very heavy shell fire. Finding two men seriously wounded who had been left behind, 2nd Lieut. Van Zeller, with three of his crew, decided to make an effort to get them across at the last moment; when half-way across, the bridge was blown up both in front and behind them.

2nd Lieut. T. A. Zeller succeeded in getting his three men and the two wounded men across the debris under heavy shell fire, and finally brought the entire party back behind our lines on the west side of the river.

Lieut. (A/Capt.) ROBSON, THOMAS KENNETH. 6th Battn. Awarded M.C.

This officer reported to me with two tanks at Judd's Farm, St. Leger, about 6.30 P.M. on March 23. At that time the line was in danger of being broken by a heavy attack on the side of the enemy. Capt. Robson, acting under my instructions, took his two tanks out in front of our line under a heavy barrage of shell and machine-gun fire, and personally conducted their operations. Capt. Robson showed great gallantry and rendered invaluable assistance.

Our line was made good, and Capt. Robson only withdrew his tanks on my orders when the light failed and the situation was normal again.

Capt. COGHLAN, JOHN ALOYSIUS. 4th Battn. Awarded M.C.

On March 24, 1918, this officer led his section into action against the advancing enemy, first near Rancourt and secondly near Combles. On the last occasion he advanced on foot in front of his sole remaining tank to within ten yards of a party of the enemy, and enabled the tank to inflict heavy casualties. Throughout the day he showed excellent leadership and the most utter disregard for his personal safety.

Lieut. OLDHAM, EDMUND AINSWORTH. 1st Battn. Awarded M.C.

For most conspicuous gallantry and devotion to duty in the neighbourhood of Curlu and Hem on March 24–25, 1918. This officer was in charge of one of two tanks detailed to hold up the enemy between the River Somme and the Maricourt-Peronne road. He penetrated into the enemy lines for a distance of approximately one and a half miles, when his tank broke down. Throughout the night Lieut. Oldham worked on his tank and eventually repaired it. The following morning he attacked and dispersed numerous bodies of the enemy, making his dispositions with the greatest skill. When his supply of petrol was almost exhausted, he decided to return. His tank again broke down in ' No Man's Land,' where it had to be abandoned.

By his coolness and daring in a difficult situation he rendered the utmost assistance to our own infantry, and created much dismay and disorganisation behind the enemy's lines.

T. 2nd Lieut. GIBBONS, CHARLES PHILLIP. 8th Battn. Awarded M.C.

For conspicuous gallantry and devotion to duty on March 24, 1918, at Bus.

This officer was in command of a tank in action against Bus and was instrumental in driving back the enemy infantry and cavalry with heavy losses and releasing a number of our infantry who were prisoners. In this action his tank received a direct hit and was set on fire. 2nd Lieut. Gibbons was himself wounded, one gunner was killed, and the tank N.C.O. was wounded. 2nd Lieut. Gibbons gave orders for the tank to be evacuated and as many Lewis guns and boxes of ammunition as possible to be withdrawn from the tank. With these this officer took the remainder of the crew and joined the infantry. This party hung on till all ammunition had been expended and they were forced to withdraw. On his way back 2nd Lieut. Gibbons found that his N.C.O. was not with him, and though he himself was wounded in three places he went in search of his N.C.O. and, eventually finding him, brought him back under very heavy machine-gun and shell fire and saved him from falling into the hands of the enemy.

2nd Lieut. COUPER, JAMES (T.F.). 8th Battn. Awarded M.C.

For most conspicuous gallantry and devotion to duty at Barastre on March 24, 1918, while in command of a tank in action. His tank received three direct hits and most of the crew were wounded. The tank having been put out of action by the last direct hit, 2nd Lieut Couper and those of his crew who could help took out the guns and ammunition from the tank and took up a position in front of it. He kept up machine-gun fire on the advancing enemy until his guns were knocked out and he himself had his hand shattered by shell fire. 2nd Lieut. Couper returned to his tank and, before leaving it to the enemy, completely destroyed it by setting it on fire. He then reported with the crew to the rallying point, and was taken to a dressing station. Throughout the action 2nd Lieut. Couper showed a total disregard for his own personal feelings and safety, and set a splendid example of courage to his crew.

T. 2nd Lieut. LYNESS, ISAAC. 8th Battn. Awarded M.C.

For conspicuous gallantry and devotion to duty at Barastre on March 24, 1918. This officer caused heavy loss to the enemy whilst covering the retirement of our infantry by fighting his tank until it received a direct hit which set it on fire. All his crew became casualties and, although wounded and severely hurt about the face and hands, with an utter disregard to his injuries, he remained with his tank and personally succeeded in rescuing the four survivors of his crew. By this action he prevented them being captured by the advancing enemy. Throughout this, and in previous actions, 2nd Lieut. Lyness showed the greatest devotion to duty and consistently set a splendid example of coolness and courage to those under his command.

Capt. (A/Major) LANE, HAROLD, M.C. 9th Battn. Awarded Bar to M.C.

For gallantry and devotion to duty. On the night March 25–26 this officer, commanding a company of Lewis guns, was ordered to take up a position running east and south from Trones Wood and to hold on at all costs. In the early morning the enemy attacked heavily and the line was driven in. He rallied his guns and the infantry and retook the position. Twice during the day his flanks were driven in and the situation saved by the fire of his guns. The line continued to hold out till the order for a general retirement was received. It was mainly due to his courage and fine example that this important position was maintained.

Lieut. (A/Capt.) ROBINSON, HARRY KEMP. 10th Battn. Awarded M.C.

In the action near Achiet-le-Petit, on March 25, 1918, this officer was in command of a section of tanks. In spite of heavy machine-gun and shell fire, he moved about on foot between his tanks, directing them and pointing out targets. His action was most gallant, and the tanks of his section were instrumental in checking the enemy and causing many casualties to be inflicted. He showed a total disregard for his personal safety and set a splendid example to all ranks.

T. 2nd Lieut. ASKEW, GEOFFREY. 10th Battn. Awarded M.C.

This officer was company tank engineer. Near Achiet-le-Grand on March 25, 1918, he showed conspicuous gallantry and devotion to duty.

The tanks of 10th Battalion had just completed a long trek from Haplincourt and were ordered into action again. Numerous minor defects had developed during the trek, and in spite of the fact that the tanks were on the starting-point and were being subjected to shell fire, 2nd Lieut. Askew continued to go from tank to tank ensuring that all were as mechanically fit as possible before starting.

At zero he was still working on one tank (No. 2097, 2nd Lieut. Champeney), which had mechanical trouble, and not being satisfied with it, he accompanied it into action and completed the repairs.

This tank received several hits which wounded most of the gunners but did not stop the engine. In order to keep up the fire on the enemy, who were then in the open, 2nd Lieut. Askew himself manned one of the 6-pndr. guns and was instrumental in inflicting many casualties.

Later, observing that another tank (No. 8092, 2nd Lieut. Linden) had stopped, 2nd Lieut. Askew at once made his way to it, across the open, on foot, under heavy machine-gun fire. He repaired the mechanical trouble that was the cause of the tank stopping, and carried on with this tank in action.

This tank received a direct hit from a shell and most of the crew became casualties.

2nd Lieut. Askew again worked the guns and carried on until the tank received another direct hit. He and the crew then left the tank to join the infantry with their Lewis guns.

This officer showed a total disregard for his personal safety and set a magnificent example of gallantry to all. Later, when making his way forward to another tank, 2nd Lieut. Askew was wounded and, owing to the rapid advance of the enemy, it was impossible to get him away. He is presumably now a prisoner in the hands of the enemy.

Lieut. (A/Capt.) KEOGH, FREDERICK BERTRAM, M.C. 1st Battn. Awarded Bar to M.C.

For most conspicuous gallantry and devotion to duty in the neighbourhood of the Bray-Albert road near Méaulte on March 26, 1918.

This officer was in charge of eight tanks detailed to assist and cover the withdrawal of the 105th Infantry Brigade. His tanks were posted ready for action by midnight 25-26. Throughout the day (26th) Captain Keogh made repeated attacks upon the advancing enemy, preventing him from enveloping the left flank of the 105th Infantry Brigade, which was totally unprotected, and enabled it to withdraw intact.

Captain Keogh followed his tanks on foot in spite of very heavy shelling and rifle and machine-gun fire.

A group of Lewis gun teams from the 4th Tank Battalion was cut off, when Captain Keogh ordered two of his tanks to go to their relief, himself accompanying them and directing their advance.

Throughout the action, lasting many hours, he displayed the utmost gallantry and coolness and showed utter disregard of personal safety.

Lieut. MANN, DAVID MANN. 1st Battn. Awarded M.C.

For most conspicuous gallantry and devotion to duty on March 26, 1918. This officer commanded one of a section of tanks detailed to assist the withdrawal of the 105th Infantry Brigade on the Bray-

Méaulte road. His tank was in a bad condition and one six-pndr. gun was out of action ; nevertheless, throughout the day Lieut. Mann rendered the most valuable assistance to the infantry, penetrating deeply into the advancing enemy on three occasions and inflicting severe losses on him. About 2 P.M. he observed an enemy field battery coming into action, which he managed to approach unobserved, and opened fire upon it at short range, causing the gunners who were left to abandon their guns. He continued harassing the enemy until his tank finally broke down, when he managed to make good his withdrawal with the remainder of the Lewis guns and ammunition.

This officer's coolness and courage upon this occasion, under very trying circumstances, was an example to all ranks.

2nd Lieut. MACFADYEN, JOHN DENNIS GERALD. 1st Battn. Awarded M.C.

For most conspicuous gallantry and devotion to duty on the Bray-Albert road in the neighbourhood of Méaulte on March 26, 1918.

This officer handled his tank with great determination and coolness. He made four separate attacks on his own initiative against the advancing enemy, each time penetrating deeply among them and inflicting very severe casualties. He was subjected to a heavy bombardment at short range, his tank being twice struck by shells, and disabled. He nevertheless managed to keep it running, and rendered most valuable assistance to the infantry and other tanks with whom he was co-operating.

Capt. (T. Major) LAKIN, MICHAEL LAURENCE, D.S.O. 1st Battn. Awarded M.C.

For most conspicuous gallantry and devotion to duty during the operations near Maricourt and Bray on March 26, 1918, whilst commanding a company of tanks. At Maricourt he led his company into action across very difficult country and successfully rallied several of his tanks which had held up the enemy for ten hours. Again, on March 26, near Bray, when fighting on foot a rearguard action with Lewis guns, he remained behind the infantry, who had withdrawn, and inflicted severe losses on the enemy, and after eight hours' fighting in this fashion he successfully rallied his company. Throughout he has displayed an absolute disregard of danger, and was always cheering on his men. His leadership was excellent.

2nd Lieut. (A/Capt.) HUNNIKIN, FRANCIS SYDNEY. 1st Battn. Awarded M.C.

For most conspicuous gallantry and devotion to duty on March 26, 1918, at the Bois-de-Tailles.

When his company was fighting a rearguard action, covering

the withdrawal of the infantry from Bray, it became partially surrounded, and running short of ammunition Capt. Hunnikin at once volunteered to cover the withdrawal of the remainder of the company with two Lewis guns and crews. He continued using his Lewis guns and inflicting very severe casualties on the enemy, who had worked up very close to within 50 to 60 yards.

When the withdrawal of the company was complete, Capt. Hunnikin remained where he was, inflicting severe losses on the enemy until his ammunition was expended, except for two drums. He was by then completely surrounded, but succeeded in cutting his way out with the two remaining drums. Throughout the day this gallant officer showed the utmost coolness, courage, and determination, and was a splendid example to all ranks.

Lieut. GOODALL, ALEC HARRISON. 2nd Battn. Awarded M.C.

This officer, on March 26, 1918, whilst in charge of Lewis gun detachments, fought with great gallantry and tenacity while covering the retreat of the 6th Brigade when they withdrew from Beaucourt to a new line running approximately 1000 yards S.W. of Beaucourt through Beaumont Hamel.

He then came back and placed himself and his guns, on his own initiative, at the disposal of the commanding officer of the 17th Royal Fusiliers, on March 27, remaining with him until the 30th.

Lieut. Goodall was wounded in the leg on the 30th, but refused to leave his position until ordered to do so by the commanding officer, 17th Royal Fusiliers.

T. 2nd Lieut. CALDER, ARCHIBALD. 5th Battn. Awarded D.S.O.

For conspicuous gallantry (March 27–31, 1918), near Harbonnières, Cayeux, and Demuin.

This officer was in charge of eight Lewis guns placed just east of Harbonnières. About 5.30 P.M. the enemy attacked and drove back our troops. 2nd Lieut. Calder checked this attack with Lewis-gun fire, and assisted in rallying a battalion of our infantry and leading them back to their original position.

On March 20, near Cayeux, 2nd Lieut. Calder collected a party of infantry who had lost their officers, and led this party, with two of his Lewis guns, in a counter-attack, driving the enemy back. 2nd Lieut. Calder with this party took up a position just over the crest of the spur between Cayeux and Guillaucourt. From this point the enemy were seen moving in and about Guillaucourt. 2nd Lieut. Calder, whose party were suffering from heavy enfilade machine-gun fire, sent back a message indicating the position where the enemy were massing, and was ordered to withdraw. The enemy's machine-gun fire was so heavy that the party, on receiving these orders, was compelled to crawl back to its original position.

IMMEDIATE AWARDS—OFFICERS

At 1 P.M. (March 29), near Demuin, the enemy appeared moving towards the wood south of Demuin. 2nd Lieut. Calder fired on them until his ammunition was exhausted, inflicting heavy casualties. A supply of ammunition was procured, and at dawn (March 30), the enemy attacked in force, but were driven off by fire from 2nd Lieut. Calder's guns.

Another attack then developed from the direction of Maison Blanche towards Demuin. 2nd Lieut. Calder's ammunition supply had again run out, but collecting his gun teams under cover, he refilled his magazines from bandoliers which he had previously issued to his men. He returned to his position in time to open fire at 100 yards range, and succeeded in stopping the enemy at about thirty yards short of his position. The survivors of the attacking force then fell back. In stopping this attack 2nd Lieut. Calder expended all his ammunition for the third time in twenty-four hours.

T. Lieut. (A/Capt.) BRADBURY, AUSTEN. 5th Battn. Awarded M.C.

For gallantry and devotion to duty near Chaulnes and Vrely on March 27–28, 1918.

This officer was in command of nine Lewis guns. When our infantry withdrew on March 27, following an attack by the enemy, Capt. Bradbury remained with his Lewis guns and covered their withdrawal, firing on the enemy until his ammunition was exhausted, and inflicting heavy casualties. On rejoining the infantry near Vrely, Capt. A. Bradbury collected a party of infantry who had become detached from their units, and with them manned and held a trench for twenty-four hours until ordered to withdraw.

Lieut. WHITESIDE, ELLIS (T.F.). 10th Battn. Awarded M.C.

At night, on March 27, 1918, in his capacity of company reconnaissance officer, this officer led his company into action in an attack near Gommecourt. The ground was difficult, and wide trenches had to be negotiated in the dark. Knowing these difficulties, Lieut. Whiteside personally guided the tanks into action and, although subjected to heavy shell and machine-gun fire, he continued to lead the tanks and enabled them to successfully engage the enemy, causing heavy casualties to be inflicted. This officer has throughout the operations (March 21–28) performed very valuable services.

T. 2nd Lieut. WHYTE, HARTLEY WADDINGTON. 5th Battn. Awarded M.C.

For conspicuous gallantry near Warfusée-Abancourt on March 28–31, 1918.

This officer took charge of a detachment of seven Lewis guns in the line after the officer in charge (Lieut. T. Pitt) had been wounded. On March 28, at about 10 P.M., the enemy attacked under cover of an intense machine-gun barrage. 2nd Lieut. H. W. Whyte rallied a party of about fifty of our infantry, led them up to the front line across the open, took charge of the sector and beat off the attack.

On the following day (March 29) the enemy again attacked. 2nd Lt. Whyte having posted his guns in order to bring enfilade fire to bear, this attack was completely broken up, and heavy casualties inflicted. The enemy then made a third attack in force, and in spite of very heavy casualties succeeded in occupying the village of Marcelcave. Although his right flank was now exposed, 2nd Lieut. Whyte still held to his position until a cavalry unit, coming up on the right during the night of March 29–30, covered the exposed flank.

During March 29–30 hostile machine-guns and snipers were very active at close range, and two machine-guns and three snipers were put out of action by 2nd Lieut. Whyte's Lewis guns. On March 30 the position was heavily bombarded for three periods of $2\frac{1}{2}$ hours each. 2nd Lieut. Whyte held the position until 10.30 P.M. on March 31, when he was relieved by Australian troops. There is no doubt that, but for the gallantry of this officer, the enemy would have gained possession of this important position, which covered the main road through Villers-Bretonneux to Amiens.

Major (A/Lieut.-Col.) O'KELLY, ANDREW NOLAN. 4th Battn.
Awarded D.S.O.

For conspicuous gallantry and devotion to duty when in command of this battalion.

From March 21 to March 31 his battalion was employed on the Fifth Army front under the XIX Corps. Owing to his excellent foresight, his tanks rendered the most valuable assistance to the infantry in carrying out local counter-attacks and assisting to cover the infantry's withdrawal. When his tanks became derelict and the battalion was organised into Lewis gun groups, his battalion was continuously employed in the line south of the Somme. From April 1 to April 19 his battalion was in the line in the Meteren area, north of Bailleul, under the 33rd Division, employed as Lewis gun groups. The fact that the Lewis gun teams held the line under the most trying circumstances, inflicting on several occasions severe casualties on the enemy, whose attacks were repeatedly pushed with the greatest vigour, was entirely due to this officer's splendid and cheerful example, indefatigable energy, and personal supervision of the sighting and general employment of the guns under his command.

T. Capt. BURTON, CHRISTOPHER ROBINSON. 7th Battn.
Awarded M.C.

For great courage and cool judgment during the battle in and around Merville on April 12, 1918, when, on learning that his commanding officer had been wounded, this young officer assumed command of the detachment of twenty-four Lewis guns of his battalion, operating with the 61st Division, and fought his guns during the rearguard action which ensued with the greatest determination. G.O.C. 61st Division directed me to submit this officer's name for immediate reward.

Lieut. (A/Major) GATEHOUSE, ALEXANDER HUGH. 5th Battn. Awarded M.C.

For gallantry and devotion to duty near Meteren, April 15–19, 1918, inclusive.

Major Gatehouse was in command of a composite company of twenty Lewis guns. His sector was attacked three times by the enemy, and the example of cheerfulness and courage set by this officer had the greatest effect on his men, and it was largely due to his own personal efforts that his sector was held intact during the period in question. When the enemy penetrated our line on the right flank of his company, this officer dealt with the situation with the utmost coolness and promptitude, and his cheerfulness and disregard of personal danger inspired his men to hold on under very trying conditions when a withdrawal would have endangered the whole position. The gallantry and powers of command which he displayed are worthy of the highest praise.

T. 2nd Lieut. CARTER, BERTRAND STANLEY. 5th Battn. Awarded M.C.

For conspicuous gallantry near Meteren, April 16, 1918. This officer was reconnaissance officer of his company and was observing the enemy attack. When the enemy broke through on the right flank some of our trenches became untenable and our infantry began to withdraw in small parties. 2nd Lieut. Carter left his position and came out into the open, rallied and reorganised these parties, and took up a line where the enemy was eventually checked. All this was done under close range machine-gun fire. 2nd Lieut. Carter held this line until relieved. There is no doubt that 2nd Lieut. Carter's gallantry was the means of averting a very serious penetration of our line by the enemy.

T. Lieut. (A/Capt.) GRIFFITHS, ARTHUR GEORGE, M.C. 5th Battn. Awarded Bar to M.C.

Near Meteren on April 16–17, 1918, this officer was in command of a section of four Lewis guns, which were dug in along a front of about 200 yards. On each of the dates in question the enemy attacked. Throughout these attacks this officer went along his line from gun to gun. The trench connecting the gun positions was for the most part only three feet deep and in some places did not exist. Capt. Griffiths was exposed throughout to heavy artillery and machine-gun and rifle fire at close range. There is no doubt that his gallantry had the greatest effect on his men, and the fact that his sector of line was never entered by the enemy was largely due to this officer's bravery and devotion to duty.

T. 2nd Lieut. DAWSON, FRED. 5th Battn. Awarded M.C.

Near Meteren on April 16, 17, 18, 1918, this officer was in charge of two Lewis guns. On the morning of April 16 the enemy attacked and penetrated our line on the right flank. 2nd Lieut. Dawson took his two guns and placed them in shell-holes in the open so as to cover the exposed right flank of his company. During the nights April 16–17 and 17–18, assisted by 2nd Lieut. Bayliss and his men, he dug a trench connecting these posts with our original line. Both officers then posted their guns in this new trench. The enemy then mounted two machine-guns in a hedge about 200 yards in front of the position. Both these guns were knocked out by Lewis gun fire before firing a shot. Later the enemy attempted to assemble behind the same hedge for an attack, but were driven out and heavy casualties inflicted by the four Lewis guns. Throughout these operations 2nd Lieut. Dawson was exposed to heavy fire at short range from his front and left flank. His courage and prompt action undoubtedly saved his company from a flank attack which would have endangered the entire position.

T. Lieut. ELSBURY, ARTHUR. 3rd Battn. Awarded M.C.

During the action near Villers-Bretonneux on April 24, 1918, this officer led his section of light tanks into action with the greatest gallantry and determination. Finding a large body of enemy drawn up ready to attack, he charged right into the midst of them, and by running them down and firing on them at point-blank range inflicted on them exceedingly heavy casualties. There is no doubt that this action completely disorganised two battalions of the enemy and prevented any attack developing in this sector during a very critical period.

Later he rescued the crew of another tank, which had been put out of action, under heavy fire and at great personal risk. On April 25–26, 1918, he assisted in carrying out two valuable reconnaissances, on each occasion under heavy fire. Lieut. Elsbury has been previously brought to notice for fighting his tank with gallantry and initiative, especially at the Battle of Cambrai in November 1917.

Lieut. HORE, LAURENCE BROWNING. 3rd Battn. Awarded M.C.

During the action near Villers-Bretonneux on April 24, 1918, this officer led his section of light tanks into action with the greatest gallantry and determination. Finding a large body of enemy drawn up ready to attack, he charged right into the midst of them, and by running them down and firing on them at point-blank range inflicted on them exceedingly heavy casualties. This action completely disorganised two battalions of the enemy and prevented any attack developing in this sector during a very critical period. On the following evening he assisted in carrying out a valuable reconnaissance under intense machine-gun fire. Although the two remaining members of his crew were wounded and his engine developed mechanical trouble, he completed his reconnaissance and brought his tank back safely. Throughout the two days he displayed the greatest gallantry and initiative.

T. Capt. PRICE, THOMAS REGINALD, D.S.O., M.C. 3rd Battn. Awarded Bar to M.C.

During the action at Villers-Bretonneux on April 24, 1918, this officer displayed the utmost gallantry and initiative. He led his detachment of seven tanks into action, and employed them with such success that they completely broke up two enemy battalions which were formed up ready to attack, and caused over 400 casualties amongst them ; on the same evening he took out his surviving tanks and again engaged the enemy with success.

2nd Lieut. MITCHELL, FRANCIS. 1st Battn. Awarded M.C.

For most conspicuous gallantry and devotion to duty in action against enemy tanks at Cachy on April 24, 1918.

This officer was in command of a male tank in action east of Cachy Switch Line, when the hostile tanks came in action. He fought his tank with great gallantry and manœuvred it with much skill in order to bring the most effective fire on the enemy one, but to avoid offering a greater target than possible.

As a result of his skilful handling of his tank and his control of fire, he was able to register five direct hits on the enemy tank and put it out of action.

Throughout he showed the greatest coolness and initiative.

Lieut. (A/Capt.) BROWN, JOHN CAROLAN, M.C. 1st Battn. Awarded Bar to M.C.

For most conspicuous gallantry and devotion to duty on April 24, 1918. He was in command of a section of tanks operating east of Cachy. On the enemy tanks making their appearance, he took his section forward to engage them. Two of his tanks (females) were knocked out by the enemy tanks, but the third tank (male) succeeded in knocking out one enemy tank, and putting two others to flight. Capt. Brown himself accompanied his tanks on foot and directed their movements, being the whole time exposed to heavy machine-gun fire and the enemy barrage. It was entirely due to this officer's fearless leading that the enemy tanks were successfully dealt with.

2nd Lieut. SMITH, ALFRED CHARLES. 13th Battn. Awarded M.C.

For conspicuous gallantry and devotion to duty near Vandamme Farm on April 25, 1918. After three hours' intense bombardment the enemy attacked in force. This officer, who was in charge of a Lewis gun post in front of our main line of resistance, although surrounded by the enemy and subjected to intense rifle and machine-gun fire, held on to his position and kept his Lewis guns in action, causing heavy casualties to the enemy, until all his gun teams, with the exception of four men, became casualties; all his ammunition was expended, and all his guns, with the exception of one, were knocked out. He then fought his way back through the enemy under heavy rifle and machine-gun fire with the four survivors of his original party of thirty. The officer showed an absolute disregard for personal danger and set a fine example to those under his command.

2nd Lieut. CHRISTIAN, STANLEY BERNARD. 13th Battn. Awarded M.C.

For most conspicuous gallantry and devotion to duty on April 25, 1918, whilst carrying out a reconnaissance from Millekreiss towards Kemmel village. With four men he advanced to within fifty yards of the enemy, and obtained most valuable information under a heavy barrage and machine-gun and rifle fire. Before returning, three of his party had become casualties, and on withdrawing to report the position of the enemy the fourth man was severely wounded, and an officer from another unit, who had joined the party, was killed. In spite of very heavy machine-gun and rifle fire from the advancing enemy, he carried the wounded man to a place of safety in the direction of his company, who had meanwhile advanced. He immediately went forward again under a heavy barrage to rejoin his company. His conduct throughout a very trying situation was a splendid example of determination and contempt of danger.

T. Lieut. (A/Capt.) GROVE, CHARLES FREDERICK SMITH. 1st Battn. Awarded M.C.

For most conspicuous gallantry and devotion to duty at Hangard Wood on April 26, 1918. This officer was in command of a section of tanks operating with the Right Brigade of the Moroccan Division in an attack on Hangard Wood. On April 25 he had been in action all day with his section. At 7 P.M. he was withdrawn and warned to co-operate with the Moroccan Division next morning. He immediately went forward and did a reconnaissance of Hangard Wood in partial darkness, being exposed to heavy enemy machine-gun and shell fire. On April 26 Capt. Grove led his section into action, taking his tanks right forward and pointing out each tank's objective.

Throughout this action he showed great gallantry and leadership.

2nd Lieut. (A/Capt.) LOVERIDGE, JOHN LEONARD. Royal Berks Regt. (seconded Tank Corps, 1st Battn.). Awarded M.C.

For most conspicuous gallantry and devotion to duty in action on April 27–28, 1918, near Hangard Wood. On the 27th Capt. Loveridge received orders to co-operate with the Moroccan Division in the second attack on Hangard Wood. As he was to co-operate in a new area it was necessary to carry out a reconnaissance of the ground. This he did most thoroughly though exposed to an extremely heavy barrage the whole time. The following day this officer led his section to the starting-point in spite of the fact that the tanks had been observed by the enemy and submitted to a very heavy barrage. During the whole operation this officer showed great initiative and absolute disregard for personal safety.

2nd Lieut. MILLIKEN, JOHN. 13th Battn. Awarded M.C.

For conspicuous gallantry and devotion to duty near Rossignol Wood on April 27, 1918.

In a counter-attack on the enemy's position, this officer, who was in charge of a group of Lewis guns, showed the greatest gallantry and initiative. When the infantry he was attached to attained their objective, he pushed forward under heavy shell and machine-gun fire to act as a covering party while they were consolidating. By skilful leading he surrounded a small wood from which concentrated machine-gun and rifle fire was being brought to bear on the infantry consolidating, and by so doing captured thirty prisoners and one machine-gun. On receiving orders to rejoin the infantry he withdrew his gun teams without loss under heavy machine-gun fire, and carried back a wounded officer of the infantry for some distance until that officer was hit again and mortally wounded. This officer exhibited great powers of leadership and set a very fine example to those under his command.

T. 2nd Lieut. JONES, JOHN EDGAR. 1st Tank Battn. Awarded M.C.

For most conspicuous bravery and devotion to duty during operations with the French on Hangard Wood on April 28, 1918. On April 27 this officer made a very thorough reconnaissance, under very heavy shell fire, of the area in which he was to operate. On April 28 he took his tank into action against the enemy machine-gun strong points in the western edge of Hangard Wood, which were harassing the infantry, and successfully dealt with these, inflicting very heavy casualties on the enemy. This gallant officer was severely wounded shortly after going into action, but, with great courage and perseverance, he continued to fight his tank until his task was accomplished. He set a splendid example to his crew throughout the operations.

T. 2nd Lieut. CRONSHAW, LEWIS HAYHURST. 10th Battn. Awarded M.C.

At Bucquoy, on the night of June 22-23, this officer showed the greatest gallantry and devotion to duty when in command of his tank during a raid. At one period during the advance he found his route blocked by trees, but though he was being heavily trench-mortared at the time and the dust and smoke made it almost impossible to see, he succeeded in finding a way round and reached his objective. Though his infantry escort had been held up, he remained on his objective for the prearranged period. On his way home his tank broke down in the middle of the enemy trench mortar barrage, and, though continuously fired on, the tank was repaired after thirty minutes' work, and driven to its rallying point.

T. 2nd Lieut. HARPER, THOMAS. 10th Battn. Awarded M.C.

At Bucquoy, on the night of June 22-23, 1918, this officer showed the greatest gallantry and initiative when in command of his tank during a raid. This officer was detailed for the most distant objective, and though heavily fired on during his passage up the street, he succeeded in keeping to his route. Though his infantry escort was held up at the start, he pushed on to his objective and inflicted considerable casualties on the enemy. On his return journey, realising that the infantry had not secured any identifications, he drove his tank to an enemy dug-out, got out himself and collected a valise and great coat.

HAMEL, JULY 4, 1918

Lieut.-Col. BINGHAM, Hon. JOHN DENNIS YELVERTON. 8th Battn. Awarded D.S.O.

Lt.-Col. Hon. J. D. Y. Bingham was responsible for the successful assembly of tanks on the night of July 3, and by his personal supervision largely contributed to the successful launching of the tanks in their attack on the spur running N.E. from Villers-Bretonneux, E. of Amiens, to the River Somme, including the village of Hamel. Prior to July 4, under all conditions of hostile shelling, and almost daily, this officer personally reconnoitred the ground over which the tanks under his command were to operate. Lt.-Col. Bingham showed the utmost devotion to duty in an operation which was particularly successful.

T. 2nd Lieut. JEFFERIES, RICHARD OLIVER GEARY. 8th Battn. Awarded M.C.

On July 4, 1918, in the attack on Hamel, near Corbie, this officer displayed great skill and courage whilst in command of a tank.

By skilful manœuvring he kept within thirty yards of our barrage, thus keeping down any enemy machine-guns which had survived.

He went to the assistance of the infantry when they were held up by machine-guns and ran over the hostile guns with his tank. At the final objective he captured seventy of the enemy, whom he covered with his guns until the infantry came up. He patrolled in front of the final objective east of Hamel, which the infantry consolidated, thus saving them casualties from machine-gun fire.

Throughout this attack this officer showed great initiative, dash, and gallantry.

T. 2nd Lieut. McCAFFERY, JOHN. 8th Battn. Awarded M.C.

This officer was conspicuous for his dash and gallantry throughout the operation. He was continually outside his tank under heavy fire, directing its action and maintaining the closest personal liaison with the attacking infantry. He rendered valuable service in crushing enemy strong points, particularly in P. 20 b. and P. 15 c. He set a fine example throughout, and his cool daring and complete disregard for his own personal safety earned him the admiration of all ranks.

T. 2nd Lieut. PRENTICE, FRANK WINNOLD. 8th Battn. Awarded M.C.

On July 4, 1918, during the attack on Hamel and Vaire Wood, near Corbie, this officer showed the very greatest initiative and gallantry. After seeing the infantry established on the final objective, he patrolled up and down in his tank in front of them, destroying hostile machine-gun groups : smashing one gun and capturing another which had been firing at our infantry. As hostile machine-guns were still firing from beyond our artillery protective barrage, this officer directed his tank through our barrage in order to subdue the machine-guns which were harassing our infantry.

On one occasion 2nd Lieut. Prentice got out of his tank, followed by a gunner, and captured several enemy out of a trench, pulling one out by his gas mask. During the action this officer showed a total disregard of personal safety. He only withdrew from the battle on account of mechanical trouble caused by a bullet from an anti-tank rifle. By his fine personal example he gave his crew the utmost confidence throughout the action.

T. 2nd Lieut. MAYO, ALFRED HARRISON. 13th Battn. Awarded M.C.

For conspicuous gallantry and devotion to duty as a tank commander near Hamel, near Corbie, on July 4, 1918. This officer showed great initiative and disregard of danger. He found another tank broken down within 300 yards of the enemy, after the infantry had reached their final objective. Although under direct observation by the enemy and under shell fire, he left his tank and personally arranged his tow-rope, taking the disabled tank in tow. He was heavily shelled for a considerable distance, but brought the broken-down tank back to its rallying point, a distance of about 7000 yards.

T. 2nd Lieut. DOWER, THOMAS. 13th Battn. Awarded M.C.

For conspicuous gallantry and devotion to duty near Hamel, near Corbie, on July 4, 1918. He caused great confusion among the enemy and ran over a nest of machine-guns which were holding up the advance of our infantry. Soon after reaching the objective, 2nd Lieut. Dower's tank became ditched, but this officer, although under heavy machine-gun and rifle fire, proceeded to dig his tank out and eventually succeeded in getting it out of action once more. He was also responsible for capturing some fifty prisoners. Throughout the operation this officer showed great resource, and by his courage and coolness gave a splendid example to his crew.

T. 2nd Lieut. KAY, ROBERT BUTTERCASE. 13th Battn. Awarded M.C.

For conspicuous gallantry and devotion to duty as company tank engineer near Hamel, near Corbie, on July 4, 1918. When the tanks were proceeding to their starting point, one had serious mechanical trouble. This officer, although there was gas shelling, which eventually compelled him to put on, and work in, his respirator, managed to repair the damage and get the tank up in time to take part in the operations. Later in the day, hearing that a tank had broken down in an exposed position near our new front line and that the crew were unable to get it away, 2nd Lieut. Kay, accompanied by his tank mechanist (L/Sergeant) went up under heavy shell fire and succeeded, although under heavy shell, machine-gun and rifle fire, in repairing the damage and getting the tank out to a place of safety. This, undoubtedly, saved the tank from getting a direct hit.

This officer showed an utter disregard of danger and a fine example to all ranks.

IMMEDIATE AWARDS—OFFICERS

T. 2nd Lieut. RAWLINSON, JOHN. 13th Battn. Awarded M.C.

For conspicuous gallantry and devotion to duty as a tank commander near Hamel, near Corbie, on July 4, 1918. Having carried out his rôle with conspicuous success, this officer, while he was returning, found another tank which had been disabled by a direct hit. Although under observation of the enemy and under shell fire, he took the tank in tow. Further back he found another tank on its side. This he turned over on to its tracks, which necessitated moving about under fire in the open while arranging the tow-ropes round the tank. Having seen the tank move off under its own power, he led his own tank back to the disabled tank, which he towed back into our lines. Throughout the whole operation this officer showed great initiative and resource.

T. 2nd Lieut. ANDERSON, ROBERT. 13th Battn. Awarded M.C.

For conspicuous gallantry near Hamel Wood, south-east of Corbie, on July 4, 1918. This officer was in command of a tank and dealing with an active and troublesome enemy nest of machine-guns at very close quarters when his tank became ditched and unable to proceed. He at once left his tank and proceeded across the open, under heavy fire from close range, to another tank, which he directed round the rear of the enemy strong point. This tank at once put the guns out of action and allowed the infantry to proceed. His display of initiative, prompt action, and absolute disregard for danger, saved much time and many casualties.

T. 2nd Lieut. EDWARD, GORDON ANDRE. 13th Battn. Awarded M.C.

For conspicuous gallantry and devotion to duty as a tank commander near Hamel, near Corbie, on July 4, 1918. He arrived at the final objective ahead of the infantry and came upon a trench which was too wide for his tank to cross. Seeing that a number of dug-outs on the far side of the trench were full of the enemy, he and one man left the tank, although under heavy fire, and attacked the enemy with revolvers, killing seven of them, after which the remainder surrendered and were handed over to the infantry. Throughout the entire action this officer handled his tank with the greatest coolness and skill and set a splendid example to his crew.

2nd Lieut. BAKER, ARTHUR HAROLD, M.C. No. 1 Field Coy. Awarded Bar to M.C.

2nd Lieut. Baker directed tank salvage operations during the action on the north-east sector at Hamel, near Corbie, on July 4, 1918, during which this officer showed great initiative, promptitude of action, and gallantry.

2nd Lieut. Baker went over the top with the assaulting waves of infantry as far as Hamel village, where he found one tank with one track completely ripped off. He organised a party to assist in the heavy labour of lifting the track into position and rendered the tank fit for action in about four hours.

There was another tank in Hamel village which had received a direct hit, and 2nd Lieut. Baker at once started work on this with a party of the Tank Field Company. He worked continuously between the morning of Thursday, July 4, zero being 3.10 A.M., until nearly midnight on Saturday, July 6, 1918, with only six hours' sleep. During practically the whole time Hamel village was exposed to heavy shelling and saturated with gas intermittently. Work had to be carried out in gas masks, and there were six casualties admitted to hospital. .

I visited Hamel village to inspect the work, and in order to avoid casualties which would have interfered with further salvage operations I ordered the temporary withdrawal of 2nd Lieut. Baker and his party during the afternoon of Friday, July 5, 1918, as the shelling and gassing were so intense. He showed an utter disregard for personal danger and set a splendid example throughout.

T. 2nd Lieut. (A/Capt.) SMITH, JAMES EDWARD. 1st Gun Carrier Coy., 5th Tank Bgde. Awarded M.C.

A/Capt. J. E. Smith was in charge of four infantry supply tanks during the attack on Hamel, near Corbie, July 4, 1918. In order to ensure the tanks taking the best route so that they might deliver stores to the infantry, he led his tanks forward on foot just in rear of the supporting waves of infantry. Though exposed to heavy machine-gun fire, he continued to lead his tanks on foot until within 400 yards of the infantry's final objective, where he unloaded his supplies. On his return journey he collected about seventy wounded men, rendering first aid and bringing them back to a dressing station. A/Capt. Smith, throughout the whole operation, showed an utter disregard for his personal safety and a devotion to duty, setting a splendid example to his tank crews.

MOREUIL, JULY 1918 [1]

T. Capt. ROBINSON, DAVID LUBBOCK. R.M.A. (attached 9th Battn.). Awarded D.S.O.

During the operations south of Moreuil on July 23 Capt. Robinson went forward on foot with two sections of tanks and directed them during the action, leading them on to their objectives and pointing

---

[1] For this action the 9th Battalion was cited in French Army Orders (see Chap. II, p. 53) ; its colours were decorated with the Croix de Guerre, and the badge of ' La Grenadière ' Division conferred upon all ranks of the battalion. Numerous decorations were also awarded by citation.

out targets. He was continuously well ahead of the infantry, exposing himself in the open under heavy artillery and machine-gun fire. Capt. Robinson was utterly regardless of his personal safety, and his conduct, in leading his tanks on foot, was largely instrumental in the tanks reaching their objectives, as there was considerable smoke and mist.

The action of Capt. Robinson's section of tanks undoubtedly saved the infantry many casualties. Capt. Robinson continued to expose himself in the open, directing his tanks until he was wounded. He set a magnificent example to the officers and crews of his section.

T. Major JOHNSON, HARRY HOWARD. 9th Battn. Awarded D.S.O.

During the operations south of Moreuil on July 23 Major Johnson followed his tanks closely on foot during the whole day, during which time he was continually exposed to heavy hostile shelling and machine-gun fire. After the infantry had captured Sauvillers Wood, and the tanks had completed their task, this officer personally rallied his company, running from one tank to another, the whole time exposed to intense machine-gun fire.

As the infantry appeared to be held up, Major Johnson made a personal reconnaissance of the ground forward of the leading infantry posts and, on his own initiative, offered to again assist the infantry to advance towards Harpon Wood, as the wood was holding up the attack. The attack was successful, and the infantry captured Harpon Wood, after which Major Johnson again personally rallied his tanks, running in the open from one tank to another, the whole time being exposed to intense artillery and machine-gun fire.

Earlier in the day Major Johnson saw an enemy machine-gun in action on the flank and personally reconnoitred the exact location, creeping for over 200 yards in the open. He then moved back and directed a tank to the position, thus enabling it to silence the machine-gun and capture the crew.

Throughout the day Major Johnson showed an utter disregard for his personal safety and set a fine example to his company. His conduct was the admiration of all who saw him.

T. 2nd Lieut. RONEY, LESLIE. 9th Battn. Awarded M.C.

During the action south of Moreuil on July 23 2nd Lieut. Roney commanded a section of tanks with conspicuous success. On reaching Sauvillers village, as it was difficult to observe from a tank owing to the smoke, he got out and led his tanks on foot in the face of intense machine-gun fire. It was his bravery in thus leading his tanks on foot that enabled them to silence the machine-guns and to hold the village for fifteen minutes until the arrival of the infantry. 2nd Lieut Roney showed an utter disregard of personal safety, and his gallant conduct undoubtedly saved the infantry heavy casualties. He set a magnificent example to his crews of gallantry and devotion to duty under particularly trying circumstances.

T. 2nd Lieut. (A/Capt.) DALTON, JOHN THOMAS. 9th Battn. Awarded M.C.

During the action south of Moreuil on July 23 Capt. Dalton commanded his section of tanks with conspicuous gallantry and success. When some distance in front of the infantry, owing to the difficulty of observation due to smoke, he repeatedly got out of his tank and proceeded on foot guiding the tanks, although exposed to heavy artillery and machine-gun fire, with the result that all his tanks were able to reach their objectives and silence machine-guns which were holding up the infantry.

Near Harpon Wood Capt. Dalton located an enemy gun and battery near it; obtaining a direct hit on the gun with his 6-pndr. gun, he silenced the battery and drove off the gunners with his machine-guns; he then manœuvred his tank into position to tow back the enemy gun. At this moment his tank received a direct hit, followed shortly after by a second. After directing the evacuation of the tank, Capt. Dalton made every effort to get back to it himself, under intense machine-gun fire and in direct view of the enemy, in order to blow up the tank to prevent it falling into the enemy's hands. Unfortunately, Capt. Dalton was severely wounded in the thigh, but, refusing assistance, he managed to crawl to the French lines, and sent in a clear report of the situation before leaving the aid post.

Capt. Dalton's conduct throughout was magnificent.

T. 2nd Lieut. MECREDY, ERIC JAMES. 9th Battn. Awarded M.C.

During the operations south of Moreuil on July 23 2nd Lieut. Mecredy commanded a section of tanks with the greatest coolness and ability on an exposed flank. When his own tank was put out of action by a direct hit, he at once went with smoke bombs to cover the other tanks from the same danger, an action which was successful and allowed time for the tanks to change their direction.

After this he went back to the tanks under heavy hostile shelling and machine-gun fire, to blow up the tank which had been hit so as to prevent it falling into the enemy's hands. This was successfully accomplished.

He discovered that one of his crew was lying out in a very exposed place, wounded in the leg, so went out under heavy machine-gun fire and carried him to safety. During the action he carried out a very valuable reconnaissance and sent in a clear report.

2nd Lieut. Mecredy showed an utter disregard for his personal safety, and a devotion to duty under very trying circumstances.

T. 2nd Lieut. (A/Capt.) MABB, VICTOR LEOPOLD. 9th Battn. Awarded M.C.

During the operations south of Moreuil on July 23 Capt. Mabb commanded his section with great gallantry and conspicuous success. He was continuously on foot in front of the infantry under hostile shelling and intense machine-gun fire, running from tank to tank and directing them on their objectives.

He showed an utter disregard for his own personal safety and set a very fine example to his section. It was undoubtedly Capt. Mabb's gallant act in going on in front to lead his tank—visibility being very poor at the time owing to mist and smoke—that enabled his tanks to crush many machine-gun nests which would otherwise have been missed, and thus saved the infantry heavy casualties.

T. Lieut. WILKINS, WILLIAM CLIFFORD. 9th Battn. Awarded M.C.

During the action south of Moreuil on July 23 Lieut. Wilkins fought his tank with the utmost gallantry.

Near Sauvillers Wood his tank received a direct hit, making a large hole in the side near the track, which restricted the mobility of the tank; but in spite of this he continued in action, fighting his tank. This action enabled him to reach his final objective close to St. Ribert Wood, where his tank received a second direct hit. Lieut. Wilkins then managed to withdraw his crippled tank back to the lines.

It was due to his determination and fine fighting spirit that the tank was enabled to reach its objective and afterwards to withdraw, otherwise it would have fallen into the enemy's hands. Lieut. Wilkins set a magnificent example to his crew of gallantry and devotion to duty under particularly trying circumstances.

T. Lieut. (A/Capt.) WESTCOTT, JOHN. 9th Battn. Awarded M.C.

During the operations south of Moreuil on July 23 Capt. Westcott, battalion reconnaissance officer, behaved with the greatest gallantry throughout the action. He was utterly regardless of his personal safety, and went on foot with the leading tanks. When some tanks had been knocked out by shell fire, he ran out under heavy hostile shelling and machine-gun fire, warning other tanks of the danger and guiding them to safety. Capt. Westcott made many valuable reconnaissances during the day and showed great devotion to duty under particularly trying circumstances. His conduct was the admiration of all who saw him.

T. Capt. HERBERT, GUY ANDERSON. 9th Battn. Awarded M.C.

During the operations south of Moreuil on July 23 Capt. Herbert behaved throughout the action with the greatest gallantry. He continually went backwards and forwards, taking orders and messages between the tanks and his Company Headquarters through heavy hostile shelling and intense machine-gun fire. Capt. Herbert was utterly regardless of his personal safety, and showed great initiative and judgment in directing tanks on to their objectives. He was continually volunteering to carry out work which he well knew would expose him to machine-gun fire.

T. 2nd Lieut. MALLESON, BERNARD KENNETH. 9th Battn. Awarded M.C.

During the operations south of Moreuil on July 23 2nd Lieut. Malleson fought his tank with great gallantry. In spite of heavy hostile shelling and machine-gun fire, he repeatedly got out of his tank and led it on foot, in order to locate enemy machine-gun nests which were holding up the infantry and which he was successful in dealing with. 2nd Lieut. Malleson was utterly regardless of his own personal safety.

T. 2nd Lieut. BAXTER, JOHN THOMAS LESLIE. 9th Battn. Awarded M.C.

During the operations south of Moreuil on July 23 2nd Lieut. Baxter fought his tank with great gallantry throughout the action. When the tank was under heavy hostile shelling and machine-gun fire, it was his promptitude and skill in manœuvring that saved his tank from being knocked out and enabled him to destroy several enemy machine-gun nests, thereby saving the infantry many casualties.

2nd Lieut. Baxter set a splendid example to his crew.

Lieut.-Col. WOODS, HUGH KENNEDY. 9th Battn. Awarded Chevalier de la Legion d'Honneur.

A su faire de son Bataillon de Tanks un Corps d'élite dont l'ésprit guerrier, le sentiment de solidarité, la perfection de l'instruction militaire, ont soulévé l'admiration unanime dans l'aide puissante qu'il a prêtée sans compter à la 3ᵉ Division Française au combat du 23 juillet, 1918.

Has succeeded in bringing the Tanks Battalion under his command to be a first-rate unit. Its martial spirit, high feelings of comradeship, and the perfect degree of its military instruction raised unanimous admiration by the powerful and unlimited support given to the 3rd French Division in the action of the 23rd July, 1918.

IMMEDIATE AWARDS—OFFICERS

Major JOHNSON, HARRY HOWARD. 9th Battn. Awarded Chevalier de la Legion d'Honneur.

Commandait une Cie. de tanks avec une grand habileté et par sa bravoure personnelle a demasqué un nid de mitrailleuses qui arretait l'infanterie en rampant jusqu'à 50 yards sous un feu violent pour le repérer et a dirigé sur ce nid un Tank qui l'y a anéanti.

Commanded a company of tanks with great skill, and by his gallantry in personally searching for a machine-gun nest which was holding up the infantry—creeping within 50 yards of it under heavy fire before spotting it—he directed a tank on it and crushed it.

Major Lord SOMERS, A. H. T. 9th Battn. Awarded Chevalier de la Legion d'Honneur.

A commandé sa Cie. de tanks avec une grande bravoure au cours du combat.

Commanded his company of tanks with great gallantry in action.

Capt. WESTCOTT, JOHN. 9th Battn. Awarded Chevalier de la Legion d'Honneur.

Comme officier de reconnaissance de Btn. est demeuré continuellement sur le front d'attaque et a rendu des services de grande valeur en repérant les nids de mitrailleuses. Sa conduite au cours du combat a été d'une très grande bravoure.

As battalion reconnaissance officer was always in the front of the attack and invaluable in spotting machine-gun nests. His conduct throughout the action was most gallant.

Capt. MABB, VICTOR LEOPOLD. 9th Battn. Awarded Chevalier de la Legion d'Honneur.

A commandé sa section avec une grande bravoure pendant le combat jusqu'à moment où il a été blessé.

Fought his section with great gallantry until wounded.

THE GREAT BRITISH OFFENSIVE, 1918

2nd Lieut. SMITH, GEORGE HENDERSON. No. 1 Gun Carrier Coy. Awarded M.C.

When a fire was caused by enemy shell fire amongst the seventeen gun carrier tanks on the evening of August 7, 1918, at O. 29 b. (Villers-Bretonneux), 2nd Lieut. G. H. Smith rushed to the scene and collected men to aid him, and so initiated the work of rescuing the tanks. He showed the utmost skill in organising the withdrawal of tanks from the blaze.

Although several of his helpers were men from other units and inexperienced in tank work, this gallant officer succeeded in moving two tanks away from the heart of the fire. This bold action undoubtedly enabled the people on his right to save three tanks. Unfortunately, these two tanks were hit and set on fire by the explosions on other tanks. On each occasion 2nd Lieut. Smith was the last to leave the blazing tank. The tanks were loaded with explosives for the infantry—gun-cotton, bombs, trench mortars, etc., besides two fills of petrol each.

It was undoubtedly due to this officer's skill in organisation and total disregard for his own personal safety, and the splendid example he displayed, that kept his men going the way they did, subjected as they were to the most violent of explosions and heavy shell fire.

Capt. (A/Major) WEST, RICHARD ANNESLEY. 6th Battn. Awarded M.C.

During the advance on August 8 at Guillaucourt, in command of a company of light tanks, he displayed magnificent leadership and personal bravery. He was able to point out many targets to his tanks that they could not otherwise have seen. During the day he had two horses shot under him, while he and his orderly between them killed five of the enemy and took seven of them prisoners. On the 10th he rendered great service to the cavalry by personally reconnoitering the ground in front of Le Quesnoy, and later in the day, under very heavy machine-gun fire, rallied and organised the crews of tanks that had been ditched, withdrawing them after dark.

Major RYCROFT, ARTHUR HUGH. 6th Battn. Awarded D.S.O.

In the attack of August 8 he led his company of light tanks with conspicuous success. During the advance his company was responsible for the capture of several batteries of artillery. He led his company on horseback, and during a cavalry charge near Harbonnieres killed two of the enemy with his revolver. He showed great ability as a leader, and his personal bravery throughout the action ensured the success gained by his company.

T. Lieut. LEES, JAMES LOWRY. 6th Battn. Awarded M.C.

During the operations (August 8 to 11) he made several daring reconnaissances. The success of his company was largely due to his skill and daring. Near Guillaucourt, seeing one of the tank commanders become a casualty, although employed as reconnaissance officer, he took command of the tank, capturing two machine-guns. On another occasion, near Parvillers, he crawled out to a derelict tank in No Man's Land, and though heavily shelled he manned the gun and silenced enemy snipers.

IMMEDIATE AWARDS—OFFICERS

T. 2nd Lieut. MUNRO, JOHN. 6th Battn. Awarded M.C.

On August 8th, near Rosieres, he patrolled some distance beyond our objective, and though he and his crew were wounded he continued to fight his tank, destroying several machine-gun emplacements. This officer's endurance and firm leadership undoubtedly enabled the advance to be continued with little loss and delay.

T. Lieut. WATKINS, AUGUSTUS LUBBOCK. 6th Battn. Awarded M.C.

For dash and coolness when, on August 8, in command of a light tank, he advanced eleven miles to Vauvillers, finding many targets of both guns and infantry, showing great initiative. On August 9 he ran over two machine-gun emplacements which were holding up the infantry, killing the gunners. He then got out of his tank, under heavy fire, to ascertain if he could be of further assistance, and stood on his tank to obtain a better view and locate more machine-gun positions.

Lieut. FITZROY COLE, DEREK ARTHUR STEPHEN. 6th Battn. Awarded M.C.

This officer commanded his section with great dash, conspicuous ability, and success from August 8 to 11. When the situation was obscure he showed great initiative by patrolling personally to Lihons, where he located and silenced a hostile battery.

T. Capt. (A/Major) GRAYSON, HARRY ALFRED. 3rd Battn. Awarded M.C.

Near Le Quesnel, on August 8, 1918, this officer commanded his tank company with the greatest skill and initiative. He continuously exposed himself during the whole afternoon to heavy machine-gun and artillery fire, without any regard to his personal safety, in directing his tanks and finding targets for them. He has on previous occasions commanded his company with conspicuous gallantry and success.

Capt. (S.R.) (A/Major) HANNAY, HUGH. 4th Battn. (seconded from Suffolk Regt.). Awarded M.C.

For marked gallantry and devotion to duty during the actions fought on August 8, 9, and 11, 1918.

On all occasions this officer commanded his company with gallantry and enterprise, and showed total disregard for his own personal safety.

On August 8, under heavy machine-gun fire, he followed his tanks closely into action until their final objectives in the vicinity of Cayeux were captured, afterwards rallying them and immediately preparing them for further action.

Owing to his initiative, he had seven tanks ready for action the following morning, August 9, which he took into action at Warvillers and Rouvroy. During this hurried action he grasped the situation so thoroughly that he was able to be of the greatest assistance to the infantry, and launched his tanks against the enemy as they commenced to counter-attack in the vicinity of Beaufort. This attack was immediately broken by his tanks, which afterwards led the infantry to Warvillers.

On August 11 he commanded a composite company in action at Parvillers and again showed the same gallantry and devotion to duty.

T. Lieut. (A/Capt.) ALLDAY, FREDERICK CECIL ATKIN, M.C.
4th Battn. Awarded Bar to M.C.

This officer throughout five actions fought on August 8, 9, 10, 11, and 22, in the Luce Valley, at Warvillers, Parvillers, and Méaulte, showed marked skill, gallantry, and devotion to duty as battalion tank engineer.

On all occasions, chiefly due to his untiring energies, 100 per cent. of tanks were mechanically fit at their starting-points. Once an action had started he showed total disregard for his own personal safety, and was always up with the tanks in action, rendering most useful assistance.

On August 22, although suffering from the effects of hostile gas shelling, he still insisted upon accompanying on foot the tanks in action through Méaulte.

The gallantry and technical ability of this officer in many instances enabled tanks to reach their objectives which otherwise they would have been unable to do.

T. 2nd Lieut. CHURCHILL, JOHN ABEL VIVYAN. 4th Battn.
Awarded M.C.

During the action along the Luce Valley, on August 8, this officer handled his tank with great gallantry and skill.

He assisted in the capture of Demuin, after which he proceeded along the Luce Valley to Cayeux. He showed great daring in the way he fought hostile machine-guns, and many times cleared the way for the infantry when they were unable to advance against heavy machine-gun fire. Suddenly encountering a hostile battery, he handled his tank so skilfully that he dispersed the personnel of it and enabled the guns to be captured by the infantry.

On August 9 he again took his tank into action at Beaucourt, and again engaged a battery of field guns at a range of 200 yards. This battery obtained direct hits upon his tank, wounding most of the crew; nevertheless, this officer remained at his post and,

IMMEDIATE AWARDS—OFFICERS

with the help of his two unwounded men, continued to fight his tank.

He set a splendid example of cheerfulness under most trying conditions.

T. 2nd Lieut. ANDREWS, ERNEST WILLIAM. 4th Battn. Awarded M.C.

This officer showed great initiative and courage in action on August 8. When near Groates and Corbeau trenches, east of Morgemont Wood, he got out of his tank under heavy machine-gun fire to inquire in what manner he could best assist the infantry. He then proceeded to deal with several hostile machine-guns which were offering great opposition ; when four of his crew had been wounded, he himself alternately manned the 6-pndr. and Hotchkiss guns. After overcoming this opposition his tank advanced to Lemaire Wood, where several machine-guns were dealt with in the standing crops ; it continued in action until it received a direct hit, after which only one member of the crew remained unwounded. Even after his tank was hit this officer continued to fire his 6-pndr. guns.

T. 2nd Lieut. KILLEY, GEORGE CHARLTON. 4th Battn. Awarded M.C.

On August 8 and 9, 1918, at Aubercourt and Beaufort, this officer showed marked skill and daring.

On August 8 he did magnificent work in assisting the infantry by silencing machine-guns and demolishing strong points ; on several occasions, when up against particularly difficult opposition, he personally reconnoitred the ground before taking his tank forward, and undoubtedly saved the lives of many infantrymen by his bravery and initiative, for which he was commended by the infantry.

Again, on August 9, he repeated these daring exploits and inflicted heavy casualties upon the enemy.

T. 2nd Lieut. POGUE, REGINALD THOMAS. 4th Battn. Awarded M.C.

For gallantry and devotion to duty throughout the operations. On August 8 he took his tank into Cayeux in advance of our infantry, who were at this time suffering from sniping and machine-gun fire, and assisted very largely in clearing the village. Proceeding to the Amiens Defence Line, he cleared the way for the infantry and enabled them to advance practically without casualties.

On August 9 he again went into action against Beaufort, inflicting heavy casualties on enemy machine-gunners who were holding up our infantry before his arrival. Later he proceeded ahead of our infantry towards Warvillers and was largely responsible for the capture of prisoners. In one week's operations this officer went into action on four occasions, at all times setting a splendid example to his men and always keeping his tank ready for any emergency.

(Comdr.) 2nd Lieut. BURN, MATTHEW. 15th Battn. Awarded M.C.

For great gallantry and devotion to duty during the operations August 8, 1918. During the advance on Proyart, when six of the tanks allotted to the brigade had already been put out of action, 2nd Lieut. Burn continued to go forward well in front of the final objectives with his tank under very heavy shell fire, one gun in Proyart firing at him over open sights, and he manœuvred his tank amongst the enemy until it was finally hit and caught fire. The work done by this officer undoubtedly saved many casualties and was of the greatest assistance to the troops in capturing the final objective.

During the night of August 8–9, 1918, 2nd Lieut. Burn went out under very heavy machine-gun and rifle fire and made a gallant attempt to get his tank back.

Throughout the whole operation 2nd Lieut. Matthew Burn displayed untiring energy and utter disregard for personal safety, which greatly inspired all troops working with him.

Lieut. ROLLINGS, ERNEST JAMES, M.C. 17th Battn. Awarded Bar to M.C.

On the Villers-Bretonneux road, in the attack on August 8, 1918, this officer was commanding a section of armoured cars. He took his section across the shelled area with great skill and afterwards carried out his orders with thoroughness and gallantry. His cars penetrated a village strongly held by the enemy, killing many of them, including some staff officers, and stampeding a quantity of transport. He sent back reports by pigeon which were of the greatest value, and finally, owing to his coolness and resource, extricated his cars and returned to our lines without a casualty.

Lieut. WOOD, NORMAN CLARK. 17th Battn. Awarded M.C.

On the Villers-Bretonneux road, during the attack on August 8, 1918, this officer's section led the battalion into the enemy's territory, clearing trees and débris from the wood under very heavy fire. It was largely to his efforts and skill that the cars were enabled to get into the enemy's lines. Later, when two cars had their wheels broken by shell fire, this officer, by his resource, determination, and disregard of danger, rendered invaluable assistance in getting them back to our lines. The accurate fire of his cars accounted for many of the enemy.

IMMEDIATE AWARDS—OFFICERS

Lieut. KENYON, ALBERT JOHN. 17th Battn. Awarded M.C.

On the Villers-Bretonneux road, in the attack of August 8, 1918, this officer was commanding a section of armoured cars. He displayed great skill in taking his cars across a heavily shelled area. When one of his cars was hit by a shell and set on fire, he displayed great gallantry in returning to his car and arranging the salving of his guns under fire. Later on, with the second car of his section, he killed numbers of the enemy by his accurate fire. His reconnaissances and resource during the fight were of the greatest value. This officer displayed great gallantry a week previously when operating with the French Army on the River Ourcq.

Lieut. WATERHOUSE, CHARLES. 1st Life Guards (seconded Tank Corps, 6th Battn.). Awarded M.C.

Near Rosieres, on August 8, 1918, this officer showed exceptional coolness and set a magnificent example of bravery. His tank was put out of action on the railway bridge within thirty yards of the enemy lines. He sent back his crew into safety and then assisted a dismounted troop of cavalry to take this bridge, only retiring when he had been twice badly wounded.

T. Capt. LISTER, FREDERICK WILLIAM. 1st Battn. Awarded M.C.

For conspicuous gallantry and devotion to duty at Beaucourt-en-Santerre on August 8, 1918, and again at Méaulte on August 23, 1918, when in command of a company of tanks. On August 8, 1918, Captain Lister led his tanks into action and directed them personally to their objectives up to the moment of their engaging the enemy. On two occasions he rallied his tanks to deal with severe local opposition. Again, on August 23, 1918, at half an hour's notice, Capt. Lister got his tanks into action. Every tank reached its objective. Throughout both actions this officer was on foot with his tanks, and showed an absolute disregard and contempt for personal danger. His initiative and complete control of the various situations were wonderful, and his conduct beyond praise.

Capt. (A/Major) COMBE, HENRY CHARLES CHRISTIAN. R.H.G. (seconded Tank Corps, 5th Battn.). Awarded D.S.O.

For conspicuous gallantry near Domart, August 8, 1918, when in command of a company of fourteen tanks. Owing to the nature of the ground, it was impossible for the tanks of this company to deploy until they had almost reached our front line. The only possible route to the position of deployment was along the main Amiens-Roye road, which had to be followed by the tanks in single file for a distance of 1000 yards, including the crossing of the River Luce by Domart Bridge.

After crossing the bridge it was necessary to proceed along the road for 500 yards to the position of deployment.

Major Combe led his tanks across the bridge just before zero. At zero the last tank was about 150 yards clear of the bridge when the enemy put down a heavy barrage on the road. Major Combe kept his tanks moving along the extreme right-hand side of the road in order that subsequent traffic might not be blocked by tanks knocked out by direct hits. As soon as it was possible he deployed his tanks successfully, supervising the operation under very heavy shell fire. The example of coolness and gallantry under fire which he set the officers and men under his command resulted in this extremely difficult operation being carried out without the slightest confusion, and with the loss of only one tank by a direct hit on the road. It was entirely due to Major Combe's foresight and supervision that this tank formed no obstacle to artillery moving along the road later in the day. Throughout the operations on August 8 Major Combe kept in the closest touch with his tanks, his gallantry and judgment being the direct means of enabling the infantry with whom he was working to reach their objectives with very few casualties.

T. Lieut. EMSLIE, JOHN CALTHORPE. 5th Battn. Awarded M.C.

At Hamon Wood, on August 8, 1918, this officer, who was in command of a section of tanks, showed complete disregard of personal danger and set a splendid example to all under his command. He directed his tanks in their attack on Hamon Wood under very heavy machine-gun fire at close range, enabling them to engage and knock out the machine-guns in the wood before they could hold up the advance of our infantry. As a result, the 116th Canadian Infantry Battalion, with whom Lieut. Emslie's section was co-operating, advanced so rapidly that they were able to capture sixteen field guns and a large number of machine-guns before the enemy could succeed in getting them away.

T. 2nd Lieut. BIRCH, DAVID RAY. 5th Battn. Awarded M.C.

For conspicuous gallantry near Demuin, August 8, 1918.

2nd Lieut. Birch engaged a hostile field battery at close range, and continued to fight it until his tank received two direct hits, three of the crew being killed and the remainder wounded. Before his tank was put out of action, 2nd Lieut. Birch knocked out one gun of the battery and inflicted severe casualties on the crews of the remainder. He then, in full view of the enemy, got the three wounded men out of the tank and succeeded in getting them back to a place of safety.

IMMEDIATE AWARDS—OFFICERS

Lieut. (T. Capt., A/Major) HOOLEY, BASIL TERAH. 7th Sherwood Foresters (seconded Tank Corps, 5th Battn.). Awarded M.C.

For gallantry and devotion to duty when in command of a company of tanks near Domart, August 8, 1918. In order to reach his position of deployment this officer had to take his tanks across the River Luce by Thennes Bridge and move them for a distance of 1700 yards to a flank within 100 yards of the enemy's front line. The bridge at Thennes was in a very precarious condition, and the entire approach march had to be carried out through the area in which the enemy's barrage was known to fall. In carrying out this most difficult operation Major Hooley displayed the greatest coolness and judgment, and succeeded in getting all thirteen tanks to their position of deployment, whence they proceeded into action at zero. Throughout the operations on August 8 Major Hooley kept in close touch with his tanks in spite of heavy artillery and machine-gun fire, and supervised and directed them in their operations with the greatest judgment and decision. His gallantry and capable handling of his command enabled the infantry to reach their objectives at the expense of very few casualties.

Lieut. (T. Capt., A/Major) GATEHOUSE, ARTHUR HUGH, M.C. 5th Battn. Awarded Bar to M.C.

For gallantry and devotion to duty at Demuin and Hangard, August 8, 1918, when in command of a company of fourteen tanks.

Major Gatehouse followed close up behind his tanks as they proceeded into action under heavy artillery and machine-gun fire. He superintended their movements in the clearing of Hangard and Demuin of the enemy, both of which operations were carried out with complete success. During this period he was knocked down by a shell which exploded close beside him.

On August 9 this officer again displayed the greatest gallantry whilst in command of twelve tanks which assisted in the capture of Folies and Bouchoir, and again on August 11, whilst in command of tanks co-operating with the infantry in the capture of Le Quesnoy.

The success of the tanks under his command in all three operations was directly due to this officer's skill, judgment, and absolute disregard of personal danger.

T. 2nd Lieut. ALBINSON, ARTHUR, M.M. 5th Battn. Awarded M.C.

For gallantry near Hamon Wood, August 8, 1918. This officer was in command of a tank working in front of the infantry in the attack. Finding it difficult to locate hostile machine-guns from inside his tank, he got out under heavy close range machine-gun fire, located the machine-guns and directed the fire of his gunners from outside his tank, enabling them to knock these machine-guns out. He dealt with machine-guns in Jean Wood, Valley Wood, and White-house in the same manner. As a direct result of this officer's gallantry, the infantry battalion with whom he was operating was enabled to make a very rapid advance to its final objective, their total casualties only amounting to six.

T. 2nd Lieut. HOLLAND, FREDERICK. 5th Battn. Awarded M.C.

For conspicuous gallantry near Hamon Wood, August 8, 1918. After a direct hit had put one 6-pndr. gun out of action and smashed the Hotchkiss gun-mounting, he continued to fight his tank until a second direct hit put the tank finally out of action. 2nd Lieut. Holland then got out of the tank with a Hotchkiss gun and opened fire on a party of about sixty of the enemy, the survivors of whom surrendered. 2nd Lieut. Holland was exposed throughout to heavy machine-gun fire at close range.

Lieut. FISHER, JAMES. 1st Battn. (attached to 102nd Can. Infy. Battn.). Awarded M.C.

For conspicuous gallantry and devotion to duty during the attack carried out by this battalion on August 8, 1918, in the vicinity of Beaucourt-en-Santerre. This officer was in charge of tank 9842, operating on our right flank, and rendered valuable services by destroying machine-gun nests which were holding up our advance. On several occasions he left the shelter of his tank and stood outside under heavy fire in order the better to direct its movement. His skilful and fearless handling of his tank saved us many casualties and contributed largely to the success of our operation.

Lieut. CARTWRIGHT, ALBERT H. 1st Battn. Awarded M.C.

For conspicuous gallantry and devotion to duty during our attack on August 8, 1918, near Beaucourt. Although three direct hits were made on his tank, he continued to carry on with his work of destroying machine-gun posts, exposing himself with the utmost fearlessness to heavy fire in order to direct the movement of his tank to the best advantage. He rendered very valuable services and saved us many casualties.

Lieut. (T. Capt.) RAIKES, DAVID THOMPSON, D.S.O., M.C. 3rd S.W.B. (seconded Tank Corps, 14th Battn.). Awarded Bar to M.C.

During the advance beyond Villers-Bretonneux on August 8 this officer displayed quite exceptional courage, initiative, and devotion to duty. He closely followed his company on foot, horse-back, and bicycle, as he found the means, re-directing his tanks as the situation demanded.

On August 10, near Fouquescourt, he displayed the same high soldierly qualities in superintending the operations. Throughout the operations from August 8 to 15 this officer has been continually reconnoitring and doing good work in the front area with an utter disregard to danger, and frequently under very heavy machine-gun and shell fire. His example to all has been quite exceptional, and his initiative and untiring energy have rivalled any my recollection.

Capt. (A/Major) TUCKER, FRANK. 14th Battn. Awarded M.C.

For conspicuous gallantry and devotion to duty in the advance beyond Villers-Bretonneux on August 8. This officer followed closely behind his company to their final objective on the Red Line. He kept frequent personal touch with his tanks and the infantry brigades and battalions with whom he was operating, frequently under fire of different descriptions, and was consequently able to re-direct the sections as the situation demanded.

On August 9 he acted in a similar manner in the neighbourhood of Vrely and Warvillers, incidentally making a very daring personal reconnaissance towards Rouvroy to clear up the situation in this quarter, in which he narrowly escaped death or capture, as the village proved to be in enemy hands at the time. Throughout he displayed very high soldierly qualities as a leader, and set the highest example to his men.

Capt. (T. Major) COOPER, RICHARD FRANCIS. R. Fus. (seconded Tank Corps, 14th Battn.). Awarded M.C.

For conspicuous gallantry and devotion to duty. This officer led his company with great skill and judgment, on August 8, to close behind the Red Line south-east of Guillaucourt. He then made a thorough reconnaissance of the situation beyond the blue dotted line with a view to his being called on to operate in this direction.

On August 9 he followed close behind his company in the attack on Vrely and Meharicourt, keeping in close personal touch with his tanks and the infantry under considerable fire of all descriptions. There had been no time whatever for previous reconnaissance, and it was due to his immediate presence, dealing with the successive situations that arose, that the operations were so successful.

On August 11, having rallied his company at Meharicourt in order to operate with the 4th Canadian Division in the direction of Faucourt and Chilly, he made a most important reconnaissance under very heavy shell fire, which would have been invaluable had not the operations been cancelled at the last moment.

Throughout the operations he showed a very high example of courage, skill, initiative, and determination to his company and to the infantry with whom he was co-operating.

T. Lieut. (A/Capt.) MACDONALD, GEORGE RANALD. 2nd Tank Supply Coy. Awarded M.C.

For conspicuous gallantry and devotion to duty.

At Demuin, on August 8, this officer, although wounded in the leg shortly after zero hour, refused to leave his section and continued to supervise the carrying up of supplies to the battalion with which he was working, in one case personally reconnoitring a route to Parvillers under heavy machine-gun fire while the village was still in the hands of the enemy. He refused to be medically treated until his section was withdrawn from the operations.

He showed a fine example of devotion to duty and disregard for personal safety.

Lieut. (A/Capt.) MACKENZIE, GEORGE OGILVIE. 10th Battn. Awarded M.C.

Near Morlancourt, on August 8 and 9, 1918, this officer displayed the greatest gallantry and devotion to duty in leading his section into action on three occasions. No less than three times the tank he was in received a direct hit.

Although twice wounded, he continued to guide his section of tanks under heavy shell fire, and successfully led the attacking infantry to their objectives.

On August 8, when the infantry were disorganised owing to the fog, he assisted to lead them forward and helped to organise the consolidation of the positions captured. On the 9th, when the tank he was in was disabled by shell fire, he joined the attacking infantry and organised and led a party to silence a hostile machine-gun which was in action.

Throughout the action he displayed the highest quality of bravery and leadership.

T. Capt. (A/Major) ROBINSON, FREDERICK ANDREW, M.C. 10th Battn. Awarded Bar to M.C.

Near Mallard Wood, on August 8 and 9, 1918, this officer showed conspicuous gallantry and coolness in directing his tanks under heavy fire. Owing to the heavy mist on the 8th, a large number of tanks and infantry lost direction. Major Robinson, realising the situation, came forward under shell fire and rallied the tanks and sent them forward again to lead the infantry to their objectives.

It was largely owing to this officer's personal gallantry and disregard for danger that his company was successful in the attack.

On August 9, when the tank commanded by 2nd Lieut. Champeney was disabled in front of our infantry, Major Robinson went forward to obtain information regarding 2nd Lieut. Champeney and his crew.

Throughout these actions his great coolness and courage were a splendid example to all ranks serving under him, and inspired the whole company.

Lieut. McGUIRE, JAMES ALEXANDER. 10th Battn. Awarded M.C.

Near Morlancourt, on August 8, 1918. After driving his tank for three hours among enemy lines he became lost in the fog. He then reported to G.O.C. 35th Infantry Brigade, who asked him to operate south of Morlancourt. He at once complied, attacked a trench and captured over 200 prisoners.

On the 9th this officer again drove his tank into Morlancourt in the early afternoon with the object of keeping down hostile machine-gun fire while the infantry were forming up in the open to attack. While in Morlancourt he destroyed a large number of machine-guns and trench mortars, and engaged an active field-gun battery.

Throughout the two days this officer showed conspicuous gallantry and initiative although he was detached from his company, and he undoubtedly assisted the attacks in the neighbourhood of Morlancourt by the very gallant way in which he handled his tank.

2nd Lieut. WALKER, FREDERICK COPELAND. 10th Battn. Awarded M.C.

Near Morlancourt, on the night of August 7–8, this officer was in charge of the party detailed to tape the routes of the tanks of his company to the front line. Although wounded in the head early in the evening, he succeeded in getting all routes taped under very heavy fire. During the subsequent operations this officer performed his duty with conspicuous gallantry, and gave great assistance in guiding tanks under heavy fire on each day.

T. Capt. (A/Major) SARGENT, GEORGE HENRY. 5th Brigade H.Q. Awarded M.C.

For gallantry and devotion to duty during the operations of August 8. Major G. H. Sargent, brigade tank engineer, walked close behind the tanks in the assault as far as the Cerisy Valley, which was the first objective. Here he inspected all the tanks as they rallied, and was instrumental in rendering several fit for action to take part in the further assault on the Morcourt-Harbonnières Line. This officer showed a total disregard for his personal safety when following the tanks, and acted on his own initiative, imbued only by a sense of devotion to duty, in order to assure himself that any technical knowledge he possessed might be placed at the disposal of tank commanders at the earliest moment during the operations.

In the subsequent operations of August 9 and 23 Major Sargent again worked with untiring energy. On August 23 this officer volunteered to accompany the tanks to their starting-points, and afterwards, on his own initiative, followed up the tanks on foot. The hostile shelling on August 23 was severe, and Major Sargent exposed himself the whole day in his efforts to render tanks mechanically fit for action. At the time the brigade received orders for action on August 23 the tanks were all on the stocks, and I consider that the services rendered by Major Sargent before the action and during the action were invaluable, and largely instrumental for the success of the operation. This officer during all the operations has shown a fearless disregard for his personal safety, frequently inspecting tanks under heavy fire, and setting a fine example to all ranks.

T. Lieut.-Col. BRYCE, EDWARD DANIEL, D.S.O. and Bar.
2nd Brigade. Awarded 2nd Bar to D.S.O.

For conspicuous leadership and gallantry when in command of a battalion of tanks in action on August 8, 1918, near Villers-Bretonneux. He followed his tanks into action on foot, under heavy artillery and machine-gun fire, and went on with them to the final objective—Harbonnières. This was a distance of about 10,000 yards. Lieut.-Col. Bryce commanded two companies up to the Cerisy Valley, where he rallied them, and then launched two more companies in the attack. It was owing to his personal direction and leadership that these tank companies were instrumental in capturing all objectives, including the villages of Warfusée, Lamotte, Bayonvillers, Harbonnières.

At Harbonnières, Lieut.-Col. Bryce entered the village with his leading tanks and placed the Australian flag in a conspicuous position. This had a most stimulating effect on everyone.

Lt.-Col. Bryce throughout the day showed an utter disregard for his personal safety and set a splendid example of leadership.

Lieut. CRAIG, WILLIAM ANDREW. 2nd Battn. Awarded M.C.

For conspicuous bravery in action near Warfusée on August 8. After the capture of the first objective he took a tank forward through the barrage and captured an enemy howitzer, towing it back with the tank under fire from other hostile guns.

Later, when his tank had received a direct hit, he continued to patrol the front of the captured position until another direct hit put this tank out of action. He carried a wounded N.C.O. of his crew into safety and bandaged him, and then instructed the neighbouring infantry how to use the machine-guns from the tank.

His conduct throughout was most gallant, and he showed a complete disregard of danger.

T. Lieut. PERCY-EADE, CLARENCE RUPERT REGINALD. 2nd Battn. Awarded M.C.

During the attack on August 8 this officer showed great initiative, skill, and bravery in dealing with unexpected resistance by the enemy.

On being informed by the infantry that Marcelcave was still holding out and was endangering their right flank, he arranged a scheme of attack with the infantry commander and proceeded to quell the opposition. He destroyed at least six machine-guns with their crews, besides taking many prisoners. He then handed over the village to the infantry, from whom he took a receipt. After regaining his position, and during the second phase of the attack, he heard opposition coming from Bayonvillers, so he proceeded towards that village. As he was approaching it from the south-west he discovered a group of three light field guns, two of which were firing at him at short range. These guns had already knocked out several tanks. With great gallantry and determination he manœuvred his tank in their direction, and so directed the fire of his own guns that he dispersed the gunners. After running over one of the field guns he proceeded into the village, where his tank was directly responsible for capturing at least forty of the enemy.

Throughout the whole of the operation this tank commander set his crew a magnificent example of courage and determination.

T. Capt. (A/Major) CROUCH, THOMAS ALFRED, D.S.O. 2nd Battn. Awarded M.C.

For conspicuous gallantry and fine leadership in action on August 8 and 9. On August 8, in action at Bayonvillers, the company under his command not only attained all the objectives laid down for it, but rendered much assistance to neighbouring units, notably at Marcelcave, which was taken by a tank from this company. Major Crouch was in command of the composite company of the 2nd Tank Battalion that went into action east of Harbonnières on August 9. Owing to his skilful arrangements all his tanks arrived on their starting-points in time, although the orders for the operation were only received a very short time before the tanks had to start. The company had to wait at the starting point for half an hour before the infantry came up, but thanks to the admirable manner in which the tanks were deployed and the skill with which their position was chosen, no tank was hit, though the enemy shelled them the whole time.

Major Crouch followed his tanks into action on foot under heavy shell fire, and his gallantry and disregard for his personal safety were an example to all.

THE TANK CORPS BOOK OF HONOUR

Capt. (A/Major) SCRUTTON, ALAN EDWARD. 2nd Battn. Awarded M.C.

This officer showed conspicuous ability and gallantry in action on August 8 at Bayonvillers. In order to make certain that his tanks reached their starting points in good time and went into action ahead of the infantry, he went with them to the starting-point, and went into action on foot with the infantry. He afterwards rallied his tanks at the first objective, reorganised them there, and detailed sections for tasks in the second phase of the operations. In this phase his tanks encountered heavy resistance from enemy field guns firing over open sights, but he nevertheless kept in close touch with them throughout and went on with them to their final objective, which they reached after overcoming very formidable resistance at many points on the way.

This officer has fought with the tanks at Messines, Ypres, Cambrai, Beugny, and the present operations, and has at all times, as tank, section, and company commander, shown marked initiative, powers of leadership, and contempt of danger.

T. 2nd Lieut. HEDGES, WILLIAM ROBERT. 2nd Battn. Awarded M.C.

On August 8 this officer showed very great gallantry in action near Villers-Bretonneux. In order to make sure that his tank was not ditched, owing to the driver being unable to see in the fog, he personally led his tank, keeping up to within about 100 yards of the barrage of high explosive shell.

On the 9th, when attacking in the neighbourhood of Harbonnières, he noticed heavy machine-gun fire coming from his left flank near Vauvillers, which was causing casualties to our infantry. He immediately made in that direction, but in avoiding a collision with another tank, and through no fault of his own, his tank became ditched. He was then about 400 yards from the hostile machine-guns. He immediately got out two of his own crew and formed a strong point in front of the tank to keep up a harassing fire to the front, while he and the remainder of the crew endeavoured to fix the unditching gear. Owing to the severity of the enemy's fire and to the fact that on three separate occasions he was bombed by aeroplanes, this took some little time. This gear was eventually fixed, and he had just got inside his tank with the other members of the crew to start up the engine when the whole tank seemed to burst into flames. He ordered evacuation, but owing to the angle at which the tank was lying this took some few moments. He left the tank last, being burned about the head, face, and left hand. By this time the infantry had proceeded well ahead, and this officer reported with his crew and two Hotchkiss guns to his section commander near by for further orders.

This officer, during both days' operations, showed the greatest determination, and set a wonderful example to his men, notwithstanding the fact that he went into action the second day more or less exhausted, having been trekking, fighting, or working on his tank for the thirty-six hours previous.

Lieut. (A/Capt.) BLACK, DENNIS VICTOR. 2nd Battn. Awarded M.C.

For outstanding courage and ability in action on August 8 and 9.

The section of tanks under his command on each of these days did most useful work and was the means of reducing numerous hostile points of resistance and capturing or destroying many guns and machine-guns.

On August 9, after tanks of his own and other sections had been put out of action near Rosières by direct hits from artillery fire, Capt. Black went round the disabled tanks under fire from hostile field guns, machine-guns, and snipers, seeing that the wounded were evacuated and noting the position and condition of the tanks. He also brought back valuable information as to the situation on the flanks. His conduct throughout the action was magnificent. This officer has taken part in action with the tanks at Messines, Ypres, Cambrai, Albert, and the present operations, and has invariably exhibited a remarkable degree of courage and cheerfulness under the most trying conditions.

2nd Lieut. ROTHERY, ALBERT. 2nd Battn. Awarded M.C.

On August 8, in spite of a thick mist, by personally guiding his tank, this officer maintained his direction and proved of great assistance to the infantry.

He also, when other tanks were out of action, went forward alone and tackled and destroyed machine-gun posts. This took place when he could see other tanks around him being destroyed by shell fire.

Throughout the operations he showed himself to be full of determination and initiative.

A/Capt. HOOPER, DOUGLAS STANLEY. 2nd Battn. Awarded M.C.

On August 8, when in action east of Villers-Bretonneux, this officer commanded his section with great gallantry and skill under heavy machine-gun fire.

On several occasions he co-operated with the infantry on the spot, arranging schemes for the subjection of strong points.

At Bayonvillers, when the village was still holding out, he arranged with the battalion commander certain details of the attack, communicated them to his tanks, and followed them closely.

Later, in Harbonnières, discovering that the infantry were

being held up by machine-guns in a house, he again arranged a scheme of attack with the infantry and succeeded in clearing the obstacle.

During the whole of the operations on August 8 and 9 this officer showed great initiative and set a fine example of courage to his men.

T. 2nd Lieut. BOTTERILL, GEORGE VERNON. 2nd Battn. Awarded M.C.

On the 8th inst., when the cavalry were held up north of Harbonnières by hostile machine-gun fire, this officer went to their assistance, overpowering the enemy.

Later, when the enemy were reported to be making preparations for a counter-attack on the south of Harbonnières, he displayed great gallantry and initiative. Without the assistance of any other tanks or infantry he worked his way to the rear of the enemy and attacked them, killing many, destroying a number of machine-guns, and taking between twenty-five and thirty prisoners. Any chance of counter-attack was stopped entirely by his action. During the whole of this action the tank was under exceedingly heavy machine-gun fire and three of the crew were wounded.

2nd Lieut. BAXTER, ERNEST STUART. 2nd Battn. Awarded M.C.

On August 8, in action near Bayonvillers, this officer was in command of a 6-pndr. tank, and when he saw the other two tanks of the section were knocked out, he showed great initiative in covering their area of ground as well as his own, drawing the enemy fire and screening the advance of our infantry. It was due to his so promptly realising the situation that the infantry were able to advance in this sector.

He engaged successfully many hostile centres of resistance, assisting in the capture of some enemy transport in the village by shooting the transport drivers.

Later his tank was knocked out, and this officer and his driver were the only remaining members of the crew, all the rest being killed or wounded. He displayed great gallantry and coolness in attending to the wounded under heavy fire and evacuating them from the tank, which had caught on fire.

His conduct throughout the operations and his quick grasp of difficult situations undoubtedly were great factors in the success of the operations in his section's area.

T. Lieut. MURRAY, JOHN JOSEPH. 8th Battn. Awarded M.C.

During the attack in the vicinity of Morcourt, on August 8, Lieut. Murray showed exceptional skill and courage and determination when in command of his tank. Owing to the difficult nature of the ground he had to lead his tank from outside. Later, four of his crew fainted from heat and fumes, and he then served the guns himself aided by one other gunner. He continued in action till the Red Line was captured, then proceeded onward to the final objective, capturing fifty prisoners. He then went off to assist some other infantry who were held up, and finally engaged Germans with his revolver, killing ten and driving about thirty back to the infantry. He continued in action beyond the Blue Line until knocked out by two direct hits.

His gallant and determined conduct undoubtedly saved the infantry heavy casualties.

T. Lieut. (A/Capt.) ROGERSON, ARTHUR, M.C. 8th Battn.
Awarded Bar to M.C.

During the operation of August 8, 1918, south of Morcourt, Capt. Rogerson displayed conspicuous courage and skill in maintaining touch with his section of tanks, going on foot, under heavy machine-gun fire, from one to another, directing their operations in front of the infantry until his objective was taken. While the line was being consolidated, all his tanks received direct hits whilst patrolling in front. He calmly rallied the surviving members of the crews and led them back to the infantry line.

Throughout the action Capt. Rogerson showed fine judgment and a complete disregard for personal danger.

T. 2nd Lieut. SUNDERLAND, ALBERT ARTHUR. 8th Battn.
Awarded M.C.

During the attack on August 8, 1918, north of Morcourt, 2nd Lieut. Sunderland was in command of tank H 23, and through his determination and skill was instrumental in inflicting heavy casualties until his tank was knocked out by five direct hits and set on fire. 2nd Lieut. Sunderland gave orders to evacuate the tank, and as many Hotchkiss guns with ammunition to be salved as possible. With these he, with one member of the crew, went forward with the infantry and did excellent work.

Throughout the action he showed a disregard of personal safety and the keenest devotion to duty.

T. 2nd Lieut. WHITTENBURY, HAROLD AUGUSTUS. 8th Battn.
Awarded M.C.

During the battle on August 8, 1918, 2nd Lieut. H. A. Whittenbury displayed great resource and coolness throughout.

In addition to destroying enemy dumps of ammunition, he rendered valuable assistance to our infantry, who were held up by machine-gun fire on the high ground east of Morcourt Valley and concealed guns in an isolated building. At first, failing to subdue the fire from this building, 2nd Lieut. Whittenbury three times rammed it with his tank, which had the desired effect. He fought his tank with great skill and judgment, keeping up such a hot fire on machine-gun nests that the infantry were able to continue the advance. 2nd Lieut. Whittenbury behaved throughout the action with much courage and gallantry, and materially assisted in capturing the Blue Line.

2nd Lieut. CHALLIS, THOMAS ARCHIE. 13th Battn. Awarded M.C.

For conspicuous gallantry and devotion to duty as a tank commander near Bayonvillers on August 8, 1918.

This officer attacked three batteries of field guns and received three direct hits on his tank which wounded some of the crew. In spite of this he continued to advance, and endeavoured to silence the batteries with his guns. His tank having received a fourth hit, which entirely disabled it, 2nd Lieut. Challis got out of the tank and, in spite of heavy artillery and machine-gun fire, went forward with his machine-guns and the remainder of his crew and engaged the enemy. The resistance of the batteries was finally overcome and the tanks were enabled to continue the advance.

It is beyond question that the determination exhibited by this officer was a material factor in breaking the resistance of the enemy at this point. 2nd Lieut. Challis continued to assist the infantry with his machine-guns until the final objective had been gained.

Throughout the action 2nd Lieut. Challis showed the greatest coolness and disregard of danger and greatly influenced all ranks.

Lieut. (A/Capt.) BAKER, WILFRED ERNEST. K.O. Lancaster Regt. (seconded Tank Corps, 13th Battn.). Awarded M.C.

For conspicuous bravery and devotion to duty as a section commander near Morcourt on August 8, 1918.

During the early hours of the action, which took part in a thick mist, Captain Baker accompanied his section on foot and succeeded in getting all the tanks of his section on to the first objective. With his tanks he was instrumental in bringing about the surrender of several enemy machine-gun posts. After the first objective had been gained he successfully led his tanks on to the second objective. Seeing that two other tanks had lost their way, he, in spite of heavy enemy artillery and machine-gun fire, walked across to them and indicated the correct direction. When the infantry were held up at various points by machine-gun fire, this officer, with complete disregard of danger, walked between his tanks and indicated many machine-gun positions, which were then satisfactorily dealt with, making it possible for the infantry to get on.

Throughout the action Captain Baker showed the greatest courage and powers of leadership and contributed greatly to the success of the operations in the sector in which his tanks were working.

IMMEDIATE AWARDS—OFFICERS

2nd Lieut. INNES, ALEX. 13th Battn. Awarded M.C.

For conspicuous gallantry and devotion to duty as a tank commander near Cerisy-Gailly on August 8, 1918.

When the attack had succeeded and the infantry were consolidating, the tank commanded by this officer was engaged in patrolling in front of the objective. Seeing that our infantry were being harassed by machine-gun fire, this officer drove his tank right into a nest of machine-guns. His tank broke down temporarily and was fired on from all sides by machine-guns at point-blank range. In spite of this, 2nd Lieut. Innes encouraged his crew to serve their guns and repair the tank, until every man in the crew was wounded. He eventually succeeded in making temporary repairs, put the enemy machine-guns out of action, and withdrew to the rallying point. Throughout the action this officer gave a splendid example of courage and determination.

2nd Lieut. PLEWS, ARTHUR ERNEST. 13th Battn. Awarded M.C.

For conspicuous gallantry and devotion to duty as a tank commander near Bayonvillers on August 8, 1918.

This officer attacked three batteries of field artillery and received two direct hits on his tank. In spite of this, and that other tanks around him had been put out of action and were on fire, he continued to advance, firing with all his guns. He knocked out at least one enemy field gun. His tank having received a third direct hit which entirely disabled it, 2nd Lieut. Plews with his crew and machine-guns got out of the tank and went forward. He then engaged the enemy with his machine-guns. The batteries were finally overpowered, and other tanks were able to continue the advance. The courage and determination exhibited by this officer were of the greatest value in overcoming enemy resistance at this point.

2nd Lieut. Plews continued to advance with the infantry until the final objective had been gained, and throughout showed the greatest coolness and disregard of danger.

2nd Lieut. GILL, ROBERT HENRY. 13th Battn. Awarded M.C.

For conspicuous gallantry and devotion to duty as a tank commander near Cerisy-Gailly on August 8, 1918.

In an attack on August 8, 1918, this officer succeeded in getting his tank through to the objective, destroying many machine-gun posts on the way. Later, while the infantry were consolidating, he patrolled in front of our new front line, and attacked and destroyed numerous machine-gun posts which were hindering the work of consolidation. He undoubtedly saved the infantry many casualties. Later, after the infantry had consolidated, he came upon another tank which was on fire after being hit by an anti-tank gun. He got out of his tank in the face of considerable artillery and machine-gun fire to see what assistance he could give, and helped to carry the tank commander, who had been wounded, to a shell-hole. 2nd Lieut. Gill was slightly gassed while doing this, but, in accordance with orders, brought his tank back to the rallying point.

This officer throughout, although towards the end of the action he was greatly exhausted, showed high courage and resolution and set an inspiring example to his men.

2nd Lieut FLETCHER, HERBERT HENRY. 13th Battn. Awarded M.C.

For conspicuous gallantry and devotion to duty as a tank engineer near Bayonvillers on August 8, 1918.

During the approach march from the assembly to the starting-point the tanks of the company for which Lieut. Fletcher is tank engineer were heavily shelled with gas and H.E. This officer showed the greatest disregard for danger, and walked from tank to tank in order to be quite certain that all engines were running smoothly, and to adjust such mechanical difficulties as might arise.

Later, he followed close behind the tanks of his company, and in spite of heavy shell fire rendered valuable assistance to certain tanks which had developed mechanical trouble during the action. In consequence, tanks were quickly put in order and made ready for action again. Later, 2nd Lieut. Fletcher advanced to the final objective, and with absolute disregard for personal safety again rendered valuable expert services. His courage and energy gave all ranks the greatest confidence, and his mechanical skill contributed greatly to the success which his company attained.

Capt. BLACK, GEORGE BALFOUR. 13th Battn. Awarded M.C.

For conspicuous gallantry and skilful leadership as a section commander near Warfusée-Abancourt on August 8, 1918.

When the infantry were being held up during the second phase of the attack by very heavy fire from machine-gun nests and field guns, this officer personally led his section forward through a thick fog with great skill and gallantry, enabling them to deal with machine-guns which were causing trouble to the infantry, and enabling the infantry to get to their jumping-off places quickly and without casualties.

Later, when his section attacked the second and third objectives, he followed close behind with the first wave of infantry under very heavy machine-gun and shell fire, until the final objective was reached.

At the final objective he rallied his tanks and directed the towing out of a disabled tank under a heavy bombardment.

Throughout the action he showed the greatest coolness and courage, his conduct being an example to all ranks.

IMMEDIATE AWARDS—OFFICERS

T. Capt. HANKEY, FREDERICK JAMES BERNARD. 15th Battn. Awarded M.C.

On August 8, 1918, on the plateau of Santerre, this officer commanded a group of nine tanks, detailed to operate with the 4th Australian Infantry Brigade. The group was subjected to heavy hostile shelling, principally from the north bank of the River Somme. It was largely due to this officer's tireless energy and gallant and skilful leadership that his group, less three tanks that received direct hits, reached their final objective, which lay some 11,000 yards from the position of assembly. He was wounded early in the afternoon, but refused to leave his command and continued, utterly regardless of personal danger, to direct the movements of the tanks, on foot, to within a few hundred yards of the final objective. His fearless example largely contributed to the success of the operations. He was not persuaded to leave the scene of operations until about 7 P.M.

Lieut. IBBOTSON, LAWRENCE, D.C.M. 15th Battn. Awarded M.C.

This officer commanded a section of tanks during the operations of August 8, 1918, during the attack on Harbonnières. On August 8, by untiring energy and devotion to duty, he succeeded in getting all his tanks to their objective, in safely unloading his machine-gun personnel and guns, and in rallying his section. On August 9 he again got all his tanks into action, himself commanding a tank, owing to the crew commander having become a casualty through exhaustion. This tank was patrolling some distance in front of the objective during consolidation, when it received two direct hits, which killed the N.C.O. and first driver. Lieut. Ibbotson then drove the tank, reaching over the body of the dead driver. The tank shortly afterwards received another direct hit from an anti-tank gun, which wounded two more of the crew, set the tank on fire, and wounded Lieut. Ibbotson in the hand. Together with Pte. Abson he salved maps and papers and two guns, but was unable to do more owing to the tank burning furiously. Throughout the actions he maintained a splendid spirit of coolness and devotion to duty, showing a total disregard to personal danger. He showed great ability to command, and set a great example to his entire section.

2nd Lieut. LUCK, CHARLES WALTER, M.M. 15th Battn. Awarded M.C.

For conspicuous gallantry, good work, and devotion to duty during the operations on August 8 and 9, 1918. On August 8, after attaining his objective and dropping his machine-gun personnel on the Blue Line north of Harbonnières, he went almost a mile ahead of the British Line, clearing the ground for the cavalry, who were held up by machine-gun fire, thus enabling them to advance. On August 9, during the attack on the village of Framerville, he handled his tank in such a masterful way that his men were able to inflict many casualties on the enemy and destroy several hostile machine-guns. His skilful manœuvring and careful watching of enemy shell fire saved his tank from getting hit during the heavy shelling to which he was subjected. On his way back to rallying point, after attaining his objective, on receiving a message that a hostile counter-attack was imminent, he at once returned and patrolled the line for another half hour, engaging the enemy with effect. When 400 yards from our front line on his journey back to rallying point he met a disabled tank. Under direct observation of the enemy and considerable machine-gun and shell fire he got this tank into tow, refilled with petrol, and towed the former back to rallying point. He set a great example to his crew and inspired them with confidence and enthusiasm under very arduous conditions.

A/Capt. WILLIS, ARTHUR STEWART WILLIAM. 15th Battn. Awarded M.C.

This officer commanded the section of five tanks on August 8, 1918, operating on the extreme left of the Australian Corps front on the south bank of the River Somme. During the whole action, in which two of his tanks were knocked out by field-gun fire from the north bank of the River Somme, he kept going on foot in the open between his tanks, directing them and encouraging the crews. The country was difficult to traverse and was subjected to heavy enfilade field-gun and machine-gun fire from the exposed flank, where the attack was held up. He succeeded in getting three of his tanks to objectives, and after consolidation hid them behind a bank fifty yards from the front line, as it was impossible to rally them across the open, under the conditions prevailing, during daylight. At nightfall he endeavoured to salve a derelict tank, and eventually succeeded in getting three tanks to the rallying point by night without being observed by the enemy, where he arrived at 4 A.M., August 9. It was due to his ability to command, presence of mind, untiring energy, and devotion to duty under exceptionally difficult circumstances that the objectives were reached and three tanks rallied, one of which had received three direct hits, but had not caught fire. He set a magnificent example to all his section and the Australian personnel carried in the tank.

2nd Lieut. GIBSON, THOMAS COLQUHOUN. 15th Battn. Awarded M.C.

On August 8, 1918, at Morcourt, this officer commanded his tank with great gallantry and devotion to duty. On the Morcourt-

Mericourt road his tank came under heavy enfilade fire from field guns and machine-guns from the north bank of the River Somme, where the attack was held up. His tank received five direct hits from a field gun, was knocked out, and set on fire, members of the crew and Australian machine-gun personnel being wounded. He worked indefatigably to get the wounded out of the tank, and personally bandaged them in the open, under fire. He carried a badly wounded Australian over 300 yards of open ground under machine-gun and field-gun fire, and was himself slightly gassed in this action Throughout the day he set a splendid example of courage, energy, and devotion to duty to his crew and the Australian machine-gun personnel, and it was due to his coolness and energy that all were brought to safety. He returned to his tank to endeavour to salve material and captured documents, and was again slightly gassed. He remained at duty with the infantry until sent down by them.

T. Capt. (A/Major) GRAYSON, HARRY ALFRED. 3rd Battn. Awarded Chevalier de L'Ordre de Leopold.

Near Le Quesnel, on August 8, 1918, this officer commanded his tank company with the greatest skill and initiative. He continuously exposed himself during the whole afternoon to heavy machine-gun and artillery fire without any regard to his personal safety, in directing his tanks and finding targets for them. He has on previous occasions commanded his company with conspicuous gallantry and success.

T. Lieut. (A/Capt.) BION, WILFRED RUPPRECHT, D.S.O. 5th Battn. Awarded Legion d'Honneur.

When in action with the French on August 8 he skilfully led his tanks and indicated targets under heavy fire. Throughout the day he displayed utter disregard of personal danger, and personally kept in touch with the French infantry commanders, although this often entailed crossing wide belts of open ground which were under very heavy enemy fire. Capt. Bion's section was operating with the division at Verdun.

' *This is a very gallant officer, who on more than one occasion has been brought to notice.—H. J. E.*'

2nd Lieut. MELLOR, G. M. 6th Battn. Awarded Croix de Guerre.

On August 8, 1918, his company reached the Red Line at 10.15 A.M. He saw about 400 of the enemy advancing to counter-attack from the direction of Caix. Together with a Mark V he went forward and broke up the enemy's counter-attack, destroying some enemy machine-guns. During this action one of his crew was severely wounded. He deposited him in a place of safety and continued the action with the one remaining man in his crew. After breaking up the enemy counter-attack this officer reported to the G.O.C., one of the cavalry brigade, and asked if he could be any help. He was sent out on another patrol and cleared up the situation.

This officer was in action for about thirteen hours, for seven of which he fought his tank with one other man.

Lieut.-Col. O'KELLY, ANDREW NOLAN, D.S.O. 5th Battn.
Awarded Legion d'Honneur.

For conspicuous energy and devotion to duty as battalion commander during the operations in the Battle of Amiens from August 8 to August 11.

The energy he displayed before and during the days his tanks were in action, the clearness of the orders he issued for the various operations in which they took part, and the splendid example he set to all ranks under his command were very marked.

Capt. (A/Major) PAPE, HAROLD RANDLESON. 2nd Co. London
Yeomanry (attached 13th Battn. Tank Corps.) Awarded M.C.

Major Pape commanded a company of tanks which operated in conjunction with the 8th Australian Infantry Brigade in the action east of Villers-Bretonneux, near Amiens, on August 8, 1918. He guided his tanks into action through a very dense fog, and it was due to his reconnaissances that this difficult task was successfully accomplished. He accompanied his tanks into action and personally directed them. When, before reaching the Morcourt Valley, five of his tanks were knocked out by anti-tank fire, Major Pape sent the remaining tanks forward and set to work to get the derelicts going again. After strenuous work under heavy enemy artillery and machine-gun fire he succeeded in getting one going and took it forward into the fight again. The gallant action of Major Pape and his tanks materially assisted to gain our objectives and undoubtedly saved many lives.

2nd Lieut. WOOD, ARTHUR CHARLES. 17th (A.C.) Battn.
Awarded M.C.

On the Villers-Bretonneux road in the attack of August 8, 1918, this officer displayed great coolness and courage throughout the battle. He took his armoured cars far into the enemy's position, killing many of them and making valuable reconnaissances. The skill and thoroughness with which he did his work were most marked, and at the end of the day he brought his cars back to our lines without a casualty after entirely upsetting the enemy's plans in the area he entered. This officer was brought to notice for exceptional service in commanding a tank in the Battle of Cambrai.

IMMEDIATE AWARDS—OFFICERS

Capt. BOUCHER, WALTER EDMUND. 17th Battn. Awarded M.C.

On the Villers-Bretonneux road on August 8, 1918, this officer was commanding a company of armoured cars. It was largely due to his energy, skill and determination that the cars were taken across the shelled area under heavy fire into the country held by the enemy. When his cars were raiding the vicinity of Framerville he made valuable reconnaissances of the country in advance of our line and got them back to headquarters. He had raised and trained the company and had been solely responsible for bringing it into a high state of efficiency.

T. Capt. (A/Major) HAMPSON, GEOFFREY. 1st Battn. Awarded D.S.O.

For most conspicuous gallantry and devotion to duty and leadership during the three days' operations—August 8, 9, and 10, 1918—in the vicinity of Beaucourt-en-Santerre. He handled his tanks with the most remarkable skill. During the action of August 8, 1918, his tanks deposited their infantry crews in the blue dotted line, having had several actions on the way. His energy was marvellous. When the cavalry were held up at Cayeux Wood he cleared the wood of the enemy and pushed on. He went from tank to tank to give orders and showed an entire disregard for his personal safety. I cannot speak too highly of this officer.

T. 2nd Lieut. SHAW, THOMAS JAMES, M.C. 1st Battn. Awarded Bar to M.C.

For great devotion to duty in the operations in the vicinity of Beaucourt-en-Santerre on August 8 and 9, 1918, when in command of a tank. He did great damage to the enemy and destroyed many machine-gun posts which were holding up our advance, and greatly assisted the infantry in consolidating their line by the skilful manoeuvring of his tank. During action he was under most intense machine-gun fire and his tank was riddled. By his skill and courage he emerged from action with his crew and tank complete. His coolness under fire was an example to all.

T. Lieut. (A/Capt.) MATTHEWS, GEORGE, M.C. 1st Battn. Awarded Bar to M.C.

For conspicuous gallantry and devotion to duty in the operations on August 8, 1918, near Beaucourt-en-Santerre. He commanded a section of tanks and led them towards their objective under very heavy machine-gun fire. He co-operated successfully with other crews, and to a very great extent was responsible for the splendid work done by his section. Throughout the day he set a very fine example to all ranks by his coolness and bravery under heavy fire.

THE TANK CORPS BOOK OF HONOUR

T. 2nd Lieut. BRADBEER, BENJAMIN FRANK JOHN.   1st Battn.
Awarded M.C.

For gallantry and great devotion to duty in the operations near Beaucourt-en-Santerre on August 8, 1918, when company reconnaissance officer. He led the tanks of his company until the moment they came into action. He rendered invaluable services to his company commander throughout the day, far in excess of his duties as reconnaissance officer. All day he showed an utter disregard for his personal safety, and his devotion to duty was most marked.

T. 2nd Lieut. BURFIELD, WILLIAM ROBERT GEORGE.   1st Battn.
Awarded M.C.

For most conspicuous gallantry and devotion to duty in the operations near Beaucourt-en-Santerre on August 8, 1918, when in command of a tank which was carrying infantry. His tank received three direct hits from an enemy field gun at 700 yards range, which killed the infantry officer. He at once got his crew and the infantry out of the tank and formed several strong points with his machine-guns. He then returned alone to his tank and fired at the hostile battery with his 6-pndr. gun. His tank received six more direct hits. Although wounded, he returned to his machine-gun posts. He finally returned to his tank and blew it up, as it was in danger of falling into enemy hands. His great gallantry was a very fine example to all.

T. Lieut. (A/Capt.) DAWKES, ARTHUR HENRY.   1st Battn.
Awarded M.C.

For most conspicuous gallantry and devotion to duty in the operations near Beaucourt-en-Santerre on August 8, 1918. He commanded a section of tanks, and by skilful handling his tanks reached their final objective. At all times of the day he exposed himself to heavy fire regardless of his own personal safety, and on reaching his objective collected information of the utmost value, causing the dispersion of an enemy concentration. During the action Captain Dawkes showed great initiative and coolness, and was responsible for the great success of his section in the battle.

2nd Lieut. HAWTHORNE, EDWARD.   1st Battn.   Awarded M.C.

For gallantry and devotion to duty in the action near Beaucourt-en-Santerre on August 8, 1918, when in command of a tank carrying infantry. His car received two direct hits which wounded most of his crew. He continued to fight his tank to the end, destroying an anti-tank gun and numerous machine-gun posts. His conduct was an inspiring example to his crew.

IMMEDIATE AWARDS—OFFICERS

T. 2nd Lieut. DINGLE, GUY VICKERS IREHANE. 1st Battn.
Awarded M.C.

For great gallantry and devotion to duty in the operations near
Beaucourt-en-Santerre on August 8, 1918, when in command of
a tank. He showed great skill and courage in dealing with enemy
machine-gun posts, which were holding up and inflicting severe
casualties on the infantry. When he reached his objective he
patrolled in front of the infantry for five hours and ran the greatest
risks in manœuvring his tank to take hostile fire. On August 9,
1918, he was again in action, and although wounded he continued
to fight his tank until it caught fire and he was compelled to evacuate
it. Throughout the operations he showed most splendid courage
and devotion to duty.

T. 2nd Lieut. FRENCH, WILLIAM JESSE. 1st Battn. Awarded
M.C.

For conspicuous gallantry and devotion to duty near Beaucourt-
en-Santerre on August 8, 1918, when in command of a tank. This
officer commanded his tank with the utmost skill, and repeatedly
knocked out enemy machine-guns which were holding up our
advance. He also engaged and destroyed two field guns. The
coolness and initiative of this officer undoubtedly saved many lives,
and he himself set a very fine example.

T. Major BEAUCHAMP, HENRY, C.F. Army Chaplains Dept.
(attached 1st Battn.). Awarded M.C.

For great gallantry and devotion to duty in the operations
near Beaucourt-en-Santerre on August 8, 1918, as chaplain to the
battalion. Apart from his duties as chaplain, which he performed
in a fearless manner under very exposed and dangerous conditions,
he continually brought back information of the utmost value, at
a time when other means of communication were not available.
He was always in the fighting line, and his gallant conduct, especially
in rendering assistance to the wounded, was an inspiration to all.
He won the admiration of all ranks.

T. 2nd Lieut. HARROWING, JAMES. 4th Battn. Awarded M.C.

For gallantry and devotion to duty throughout the operations
August 8-10, 1918. On August 8, when carrying up Stokes
mortars and bombs to the final objective, he passed another
tank similarly engaged, broken down with mechanical trouble.
He at once got out of his own tank and, in spite of enemy
sniping and shell fire, transferred the mortars and bombs of the
broken-down tank to a small cart, which he towed behind him to the
dumping point, near Cayeux. For this he was warmly commended
by the 2nd Canadian Infantry Brigade. On August 9 he again
went into action near Beaufort. On this occasion the infantry

were badly held up by heavy machine-gun and rifle fire. He at once took his tank forward and inflicted very heavy casualties on the enemy and enabled our infantry to advance. Later, spotting an anti-tank gun, he immediately attacked it, completely demoralising the crew, who at once bolted. This officer has on all occasions set a splendid example to his men, showing exceptional keenness and devotion to duty.

T. 2nd Lieut. GROUTAGE, LEONARD CHARLES. 6th Battn. Awarded M.C.

On August 9, near Meharicourt, though under heavy anti-tank gun fire, he worked his way continually up and down a trench strongly held by the enemy infantry and machine-guns. On his tank receiving a direct hit, which jammed the door, he climbed out with his guns through the roof and came into action on the ground, though under heavy machine-gun and anti-tank gun fire.

2nd Lieut. WHYTE, WILLIAM PATRICK. 3rd Battn. Awarded D.S.O.

Near Rouvroy, on August 9, 1918, this officer commanded his section of tanks with the greatest gallantry. Whilst fighting his tank he was hit twice through the shoulder and once in the face by bullets. Shortly after, his tank broke down. In spite of his three wounds he continued to direct the remaining tanks of his section on foot and under intense machine-gun and heavy artillery fire. It was only with the greatest difficulty that he could be persuaded to leave his tanks and go to a dressing station by his company commander. Whilst going there he was badly wounded for the third time.

The gallantry and utter disregard for danger displayed by this officer was most conspicuous, and had the greatest moral effect on his section.

2nd Lieut. ROBINOW, WILLIAM. 3rd Battn. Awarded M.C.

Near Rouvroy, on August 9, 1918, this officer throughout the day continuously exposed himself to heavy machine-gun and artillery fire whenever he saw any chance of assisting at pointing out targets to any of the tanks of his company. He was of the greatest assistance to his company in action, the rôle that he voluntarily undertook being outside his duties as company reconnaissance officer. He has on previous occasions displayed conspicuous gallantry in action.

T. Lieut. (A/Capt.) DAWSON, FRED, M.C. 5th Battn. Awarded D.S.O.

During operations near Bouchoir, August 9, 1918, when in command of a section of four tanks, Capt. Dawson displayed most conspicuous gallantry and initiative in his handling of his command. He accompanied his tanks across two miles of open country in front of Bouchoir under heavy machine-gun fire, and directed operations during the clearing of the village. Observing that the French were held up in front of Arvillers and that our right flank was exposed, he then took one tank and a platoon of infantry and captured the village. Prior to operations on August 9 Capt. Dawson had been in action throughout the operations on August 8, and had spent the night (August 8–9) in getting his four tanks fit for action.

T. 2nd Lieut. ODDY, CLIFFORD GRAYSON. 10th Battn. Awarded M.C.

At Morlancourt, on August 9, 1918, during the attack, the tank operating on the left of this officer's tank was put out of action by enemy fire. Seeing that the infantry were held up by machine-gun fire from the village, and quickly realising the situation, 2nd Lieut. Oddy at once turned and entered the village alone. Although surrounded by the enemy, with the greatest gallantry he engaged three machine-guns and a trench mortar battery, and eventually forced them to surrender with 200 enemy infantry.

The great gallantry, quick appreciation of the situation, and skilful handling of his tank displayed by this officer were the means of enabling the infantry to advance, and saved them being checked and suffering heavy casualties.

2nd Lieut. GARROD, EDGAR SAMUEL, D.C.M. 10th Battn. Awarded M.C.

Near Chipilly, on the 9th, this officer showed conspicuous gallantry and endurance in fighting his tank in the enemy lines for five hours without infantry assistance. He successfully dealt with large parties of the enemy who were holding up the infantry attack on Chipilly road.

He then left his tank and went back, and personally led the infantry to first objective. It was largely due to this officer's very gallant behaviour that the infantry were enabled to reach their objective.

2nd Lieut. TAIT, WILLIAM. 10th Battn. Awarded M.C.

Near Chipilly, on August 9, this officer's tank was burnt out owing to a direct hit. Although a long way ahead of the infantry this officer formed a strong point with his crew, and successfully held off the enemy for six hours. When disorganised parties of the infantry reached him, this officer, with the assistance of his crew, reorganised them and led them to the final objective, where he was wounded. It was largely due to the conspicuous gallantry and good leadership shown by this officer that the infantry reached their objectives at this point.

T. Lieut. (A/Capt.) DE THIERRY, JOHN LAWRENCE. 8th Battn. Awarded M.C.

At Vauvillers, on August 9, Capt. J. L. De Thierry showed great determination and courage.

His section was detailed to operate on the west side of the village. and as no time was given for reconnaissance, he led his tanks into action on foot under heavy machine-gun and rifle fire.

Later in the action, when most of his tanks had been knocked out by shell fire, he visited each one and rescued wounded.

Throughout the action he showed a disregard of personal danger and a devotion to duty, setting a splendid example to all ranks.

2nd Lieut. HARDY, HAROLD DOWKER. 15th Battn. Awarded M.C.

On the afternoon of August 9, 1918, when 1000 yards east of Vauvillers, this officer's tank was held up by an explosion of a dump of enemy gas shells, causing himself and his crew to be gassed. On recovering, this officer rallied his men, three of whom had meantime been wounded, got his tank started again, and carried on with the fight. He went well ahead of his objective in order to crush several enemy machine-gun positions which were causing great trouble to the infantry, thus allowing them to consolidate their position in safety. It was owing to this officer's grit and determination that the objective was gained, and undoubtedly the lives of many infantry were saved. Throughout he has set a fine example of courage and devotion to duty to all ranks.

Lieut. (A/Capt.) HENDERSON, JACK. 10th Battn. Awarded M.C.

Near Chipilly, on August 9, 1918, this officer showed conspicuous gallantry in fighting his tank for four hours in the enemy lines without assistance from the infantry. His tank was eventually set on fire and he and his crew were taken prisoners. They were removed under escort, but managed to capture their escort and eventually returned to our lines bringing in ten prisoners. This officer was wounded early in the action, and it was largely due to his very gallant behaviour that heavy losses were inflicted on the enemy and the crew brought back to our lines.

T. 2nd Lieut. SWALES, JOSEPH. 4th Battn. Awarded M.C.

For great gallantry, coolness, and presence of mind when in action on August 10 near Bois Sud, north-west of Damery.

After knocking out a number of German machine-guns in front of our infantry his tank received three direct hits. After the tank was hit this officer continued to fire his 6-pndr. gun until he was wounded by a piece of shell which struck him in the eye.

Although he and all his crew were wounded by this time, he

directed the putting out of a fire which started in the tank, and insisted upon seeing the whole of his crew to a place of safety before he himself was taken to the nearest dressing station.

Lieut. COWAN, GEORGE MIDDLETON. R.E. (T.F.) (seconded Tank Corps, 14th Battn.) Awarded M.C.

For very conspicuous gallantry and devotion to duty at Fouquescourt on August 10. This officer was the senior tank commander of two tanks operating with the 4th Canadian Division, and displayed exceptional gallantry, devotion to duty, and initiative.

The infantry had been held up for some hours prior to his arrival, and he immediately got into touch with the situation, sent the second tank round the right of the village and led his own tank, regardless of danger, through the village, completely silencing the enemy in this part. Leaving his sergeant in command, he went back to explain the situation to the infantry and to lead them into the village; returning after accomplishing this, he shot with his revolver many Germans who had reappeared. Finding his tanks surrounded by Germans and apparently broken down beyond the village, he made a very gallant effort to force his way through it under close and heavy fire, and while doing so was wounded. Throughout he set a very high example and showed considerable tactical skill.

2nd Lieut. FRASER, ADAM ROBERTSON. 13th Battn. Awarded M.C.

For conspicuous bravery and devotion to duty as a tank commander near Hallu on August 10, 1918. During an attack the tank commanded by this officer became ditched in one of the old Somme trenches. He was at this moment some 600 yards ahead of our infantry. The enemy at once surrounded him and concentrated some twenty machine-guns on the tank, which was pierced many times by armour-piercing bullets. 2nd Lieut. Fraser replied with machine-gun fire from the tank until all his guns were put out of action and all his crew wounded. The enemy then called upon him to surrender, but he succeeded in keeping them off with his revolver until they were forced to retire by our infantry coming up three-quarters of an hour later. This officer remained with his tank under heavy rifle and machine-gun fire until all his wounded were dressed and he received orders from his section commander to withdraw. 2nd Lieut. Fraser exhibited great courage and determination and set a magnificent example to all.

This officer had previously done very gallant work during an attack on August 8, 1918, when, after reaching his objective and after the infantry had consolidated, he, although under heavy shell fire, towed back another disabled tank of this battalion to the rallying point.

T. Lieut. SHARP, FRANK WARREN. 5th T. S. Coy. Awarded M.C.

Near Morlancourt, on the night of August 10–11, 1918, this officer showed conspicuous gallantry and endurance in extricating a broken-down supply tank under heavy shell fire. He, with another officer and one man, remained in the neighbourhood of the tank, which was being heavily shelled with H.E. and gas, for several hours, and eventually succeeded in repairing it, and without other assistance brought it back three and a half miles to its rallying point. It was largely due to his gallantry and endurance that this tank was brought out of action.

T. Capt. (A/Major) GROUNDS, GEORGE AMBROSE, D.S.O. Leinster Regt. (attached Tank Corps, 8th Battn.). Awarded Bar to D.S.O.

On the night of August 10–11, 1918, during the operations near Proyart, Major Grounds had two sections of tanks co-operating with the 10th Australian Infantry Brigade. Owing to the heavy machine-gun fire and darkness, the infantry suffered heavy casualties and considerable confusion was caused. This officer went forward with great personal risk and with a complete disregard for danger, to reorganise the column. This he did, keeping the leading tanks in action for one and a half hours after the infantry had withdrawn. He himself still remained out alone for some considerable time after the last tank had withdrawn to ensure getting accurate touch with the situation.

By his coolness and courage in the face of heavy machine-gun fire he was undoubtedly instrumental in effecting an orderly withdrawal.

2nd Lieut. KERMODE, WILLIAM ARCHER. 13th Battn. Awarded M.C.

For conspicuous gallantry and devotion to duty near Hallu on August 10, 1918.

After an attack had begun, this officer, who is the tank engineer of his company, heard that one of the tanks had broken down through mechanical trouble. 2nd Lieut. Kermode went forward with his staff-sergeant, and in spite of heavy shelling and machine-gun fire concentrated on the tank eventually reached it, repaired the breakdown, and rendered the tank fit for action. The tank then proceeded to its objective. 2nd Lieut. Kermode then proceeded to another tank which had come to a standstill, and made sufficient temporary repairs to enable it to return under its own power to the rallying point.

This officer showed the greatest coolness and an absolute disregard for personal danger, and his expert services contributed greatly to the success of his company.

IMMEDIATE AWARDS—OFFICERS

T. Lieut. BUDGE, HAROLD PERCY, M.C. 5th Battn. Awarded
Bar to M.C.

For conspicuous gallantry near Damery, August 11, 1918. Lieut.
Budge was in command of a tank taking part in the attack on the
village. When close to the enemy's position his tank received
twelve direct hits in quick succession. Lieut. Budge got his crew
out of the tank and sent them back, whilst he himself went to
the assistance of his section commander, who was lying in the open
badly wounded. Lieut. Budge, under heavy close range machine-
gun fire, succeeded in dragging his section commander through
two belts of barbed wire to a place of safety.

There is no doubt that his gallantry on this occasion saved his
section commander's life.

T. 2nd Lieut. BELL, PERCY HERBERT. 15th Battn. Awarded
M.C.

For conspicuous gallantry and devotion to duty during the
attack on the Arras-Albert railway on August 21, 1918. Owing to
the thick mist which prevailed during the early part of the attack
2nd Lieut. Bell decided to lead his tanks on foot. This he did,
walking ahead in spite of the heavy machine-gun fire which was
directed at this tank. He led his tank through Courcelles, and
then on to the railway, where he guided his tank right up to hostile
machine-guns and silenced them, and alone took 150 prisoners,
which he handed over to the infantry. He remained with his tank
until the infantry consolidated, and while returning to rally his
tank it received a direct hit which put it out of action and wounded
five of the crew.

This tank's successful action was largely due to 2nd Lieut. Bell's
powers of leadership and coolness under heavy shell and machine-
gun fire.

T. Lieut. BARTON, GLYN HENRY REGINALD. 15th Battn.
Awarded M.C.

On August 21, 1918, during the attack on the Arras-Albert
railway, this officer displayed conspicuous gallantry and ability in
leading his tank to the railway embankment, and exploiting successfully to a point some 400 to 500 yards beyond it, in spite of the
exhaustion of his crew. Before reaching the railway he had assisted
the infantry through Courcelles by silencing machine-guns. On
reaching the railway he noticed that our infantry appeared to be short
of small-arm ammunition ; he therefore took 3000 rounds from his
tank, and himself distributed this among the infantry, in spite of the
fact that he was the while subjected to machine-gun and rifle fire.

He remained on the railway embankment with the infantry
for a considerable time, but later his tank received a direct hit

and was put out of action. Lieut. Barton thereupon took out his Hotchkiss gun and ammunition, and with his crew joined the infantry and remained with them till they went forward to their first line objective.

Throughout the day he set a fine example, and his leadership, ability, and disregard of his personal safety greatly assisted the work of the infantry, and materially contributed to the success of the operations.

T. Lieut. (A/Capt.) WILLIS, ARTHUR STEWART WILLIAM. 15th Battn. Awarded Bar to M.C.

This officer commanded a section of tanks in the attack on the Arras-Albert railway on August 21, 1918. In order to ensure that all tanks reached their objectives in spite of the thick mist, Capt. Willis led his section on foot, walking in front of the tanks in spite of heavy machine-gun fire which was directed at them. It was in a great measure due to this officer's gallantry, skilful leadership, and untiring energy that all tanks of his section reached their objectives ahead of the infantry, silenced a number of machine-guns, and allowed the infantry to reach the railway with very few casualties. He set a splendid example to the officers and other ranks in his section by his fearlessness and powers of leadership.

T. 2nd Lieut. GIBSON, THOMAS COLQUHOUN. 15th Battn. Awarded M.C.

For conspicuous gallantry. On August 21, 1918, near Courcelles, this officer was in command of a tank at the attack on the Arras-Albert railway. In spite of the added difficulties caused by a thick mist, this officer successfully reached his final objective and rallied. On the request by an infantry battalion commander for a tank to deal with a section of the railway embankment that was holding out a little distance away, 2nd Lieut. Gibson volunteered to go forward again. In spite of the fact that the infantry commander had described the undertaking as ' practically suicidal ' on account of the very heavy shelling and machine-gun fire, 2nd Lieut. Gibson took his tank forward and successfully dealt with the situation and took the infantry to their objective. His gallantry and prompt action undoubtedly saved the infantry many casualties.

T. Capt. UNWIN, JOSEPH DANIEL. 15th Battn. Awarded M.C.

For conspicuous gallantry on August 21, 1918, at the attack on the Arras-Albert railway. This officer was second in command of a company of tanks operating in front of the infantry. Realising that there was a danger of his tanks losing direction owing to the thick mist, Capt. Unwin went ahead on foot in front of the tanks and infantry, under heavy machine-gun and rifle fire, to locate the crossings of the railway which were his objective. He then returned to his tanks, and again walking in the open just ahead of them guided them successfully to their objectives.

Capt. Unwin showed a total disregard for his personal safety, and it was undoubtedly due to his gallantry that the tanks reached their objectives up to time.

T. 2nd Lieut. (A/Capt.) SMEDDLE, HENRY. 15th Battn. Awarded M.C.

For conspicuous gallantry and initiative while in command of a section of tanks on August 21, 1918, during the attack on Courcelles le Comte. In order to ensure all his tanks reaching their objective, he personally led them on foot, walking about in the open under machine-gun fire, going from tank to tank and directing them through the heavy mist to their final objective.

Having seen our infantry to their objective, on his own initiative he asked if he could help them still further, and upon being requested he again led his tanks forward and took the infantry on to the Albert-Arras railway, where he silenced a number of machine-guns and took a number of prisoners whom he handed over to our infantry.

Throughout the operation Capt. Smeddle showed great devotion to duty and a total disregard for his personal safety.

T. 2nd Lieut. WADESON, ARCHIBALD RALPH. 15th Battn. Awarded M.C.

On August 21, 1918, during the attack on the Arras-Albert railway, this officer was in command of a tank which he led on foot in the thick fog prevailing all the way to his objective, in front of the infantry. Despite machine-gun and rifle fire and the thickness of the fog, this officer reached his objective on time, and secured the railway embankment north-east of Logeast Wood, for the infantry, and carried on patrolling on the far side of the embankment, killing a number of machine-gunners and snipers. It was greatly due to this officer's coolness and judgment under very difficult circumstances that this portion of the objective was secured at a very light cost to the infantry. He set a fine example of courage and devotion to duty to his crew, who splendidly responded to his leadership.

T. Capt. HUTTON, ARTHUR NORMAN. 15th Battn. Awarded M.C.

On August 21, 1918, during the attack on the Arras-Albert railway, this officer commanded a section of tanks. Owing to the thick mist that prevailed during the early part of the attack, there was a danger of the tanks losing direction. Realising this,

Capt. Hutton, without hesitation, led his tanks on foot, under heavy machine-gun and rifle fire, through Courcelles and on to the railway embankment. On more than one occasion he personally led his tanks right up to hostile machine-gun nests, which the tanks dealt with. It was almost entirely due to Capt. Hutton's great gallantry, initiative, and devotion to duty, that hostile machine-guns were destroyed and the infantry were taken on to their objectives with few casualties.

T. 2nd Lieut. BRANDLE, SAMUEL. 15th Battn. Awarded M.C.

On August 21, 1918, during the attack on the Arras-Albert railway, near Courcelles, this officer directed his tank on foot to the embankment, and having secured the infantry there, crossed the embankment. The fog was so thick that crossing places were very difficult to locate. This officer, however, went forward on foot, under machine-gun and rifle fire, and guided his tank across the embankment and cleared the path for the whippet tanks. He thus contributed greatly to the success of the operations and exploitations beyond the railway objective. It was entirely due to this officer's total disregard of personal danger and initiative that his tank succeeded so well.

T. Capt. (A/Major) GUY, OSWALD VERNON, M.C. and Bar. 7th Battn. Awarded D.S.O.

For conspicuous gallantry and ability. Continuously in action from August 21 to September 2, 1918. He commanded his company, organising attacks at extremely short notice. On August 21, 1918, in the fog, the infantry were held up owing to an unforeseen situation. He quickly organised his sections and killed or drove the enemy from east of Logeast Wood. On September 1 and 2, 1918, at short notice, he organised attacks east of Bapaume with such complete detail that the success was great and the infantry enabled to enter two villages. His energy and co-operation with the infantry staffs gave them detailed information earlier than from any other source.

T. Capt. and Bt. Major (A/Major) ROSSI-ASHTON, CYRIL GEORGE. 7th Battn. Awarded D.S.O.

For conspicuous gallantry and ability. Continuously in action from August 21 to September 2, 1918. He commanded his company with skill and judgment, reorganising his company and achieving with composite crews results with the Mark IV which gained the appreciation and confidence of the infantry and thereby the combined attainment of his objective on every occasion. Owing to the short notice of attacks previous reconnaissance was impossible.

IMMEDIATE AWARDS—OFFICERS

T. 2nd Lieut. SMITH, EDMUND ALDWYN. 12th Battn. Awarded M.C.

For conspicuous gallantry during the attack on Courcelles on August 21. Owing to his excellent and fearless reconnaissance and his total disregard of danger, all tanks of his company reached their starting points in good time. Late in the evening of August 20 it was decided to employ a tank to clear out some tin hutments on the right flank of the attack. There was no time for the tank commander to reconnoitre this route. The infantry, however, were extremely anxious that these hutments should be cleared. On the morning of August 21, to avoid any possibility of mistake, 2nd Lieut. Smith led this tank for 500 yards over No Man's Land through successive rows of barbed wire up to the enemy lines. At all times he was exposed to heavy artillery and machine-gun fire, and his zeal and determination undoubtedly saved the lives of many infantry, as the tank was enabled to clear the hutments and destroy the garrison.

T. Lieut. DE THIERRY, ROBERT LEWIS HALL. 12th Battn. Awarded M.C.

For skilful reconnaissance and exceptional bravery during the attack on Moyenneville on August 21. On the night of August 20 he taped all tank routes and personally guided tanks to their starting points. On the morning of the 21st there was a heavy mist, making it impossible to see more than five yards away.

Lieut. de Thierry went forward on foot to assist the tanks in reaching their objectives, and personally led one tank into the village of Moyenneville, showing a complete disregard for his own safety and coolness under shell fire that had a very inspiriting effect on all ranks with whom he came in contact. He was of great assistance to tank commanders in locating enemy machine-guns, and by this means a large number were put out of action. Later in the day he again went forward on foot to reconnoitre the ground near the Arras-Albert railway, and particularly the crossings over it. He brought back valuable information as to the line held by the enemy. In all these operations he showed himself to be without fear, never failing to penetrate beyond our outpost line into hostile territory if by that means he could ensure the success of tank operations.

2nd Lieut. DUNCAN, WILLIAM BLAKELEY. 7th Battn. Awarded M.C.

In the action of August 21, 1918, at Bucquoy, this tank commander directed his tank through the thick mist with great skill, and rendered invaluable assistance to a battalion of infantry, guiding them throughout the day and practically paving the way for their successful advance. He remained in action over eleven hours.

Again in action on August 24, 1918, at Loupart Wood, he fought his tank most gallantly, inflicting heavy casualties on the enemy, and at one spot outside a wood taking fifty prisoners. His tank there received five direct hits and five of his crew were wounded ; these he assisted to carry to safety under a heavy fire. His conduct and devotion to duty were conspicuous throughout.

Capt. (A/Lieut.-Col.) WEST, RICHARD ANNESLEY, D.S.O. N.I.H. (seconded Tank Corps, 6th Battn.). Awarded Bar to D.S.O.

For conspicuous gallantry near Courcelles on August 21, 1918.

In consequence of this action being fought in a thick mist, this officer decided to accompany the attack to assist in maintaining direction and cohesion. This he did mounted until his horse was shot under him, then on foot until the final objective was reached. During the advance, in addition to directing his tanks, he rallied and led forward small bodies of infantry lost in the mist, showing throughout a fine example of leadership and a total disregard of personal safety, and materially contributing to the success of the operation.

Major West was in command of the battalion most of the time, his C.O. having been killed early in the action.

Lieut. (A/Capt.) ROBSON, THOMAS KENNETH, M.C. 1st Life Guards (seconded Tank Corps, 6th Battn.). Awarded Bar to M.C.

On August 21, 1918, near Gomiecourt, this officer was in command of a section of light tanks. His orders were to cross the railway, which was supposed at that time to be in our possession, and exploit the situation beyond. On approaching the railway, it was found to be held by guns, machine-guns, and infantry. Selecting a crossing and standing in the open under heavy fire, he directed and super-intended the crossing of the railway, subsequently inflicting heavy casualties on the enemy, causing guns to be abandoned. When in a tank and endeavouring to tow one of the guns back to our lines, he was wounded, but nevertheless succeeded in bringing his tank to the rallying point.

2nd Lieut. LOFTHOUSE, FRANCIS LEO. 3rd Tank Supply Coy. Awarded M.C.

August 20–21, 1918, west of Ayette. This officer when in com-mand of a sub-section of supply tanks, displayed wonderful coolness, gallantry, determination, and an utter disregard of personal safety, showing a fine example to all those around him. On the approach march he was gassed, and although practically blinded and ordered to hospital, he refused to leave his post. One of his tanks, containing petrol, oil, and grease, received a direct hit and immediately went on fire. He twice entered the flames in an endeavour to save one of the crew, 308617 Pte. Albert Marshall, who was inside. Although he was unsuccessful, and still suffering from the effects of gas and burns, he carried on with his remaining tank until he reached his final objective.

T. 2nd Lieut. PRENTICE, THOMAS EDWARD. 10th Battn. Awarded M.C.

Near Bucquoy, on August 21, 1918, this officer showed conspicuous gallantry and disregard of danger when leading tanks into action through a heavy barrage. Though the mist was very thick and tanks were under heavy fire from close range, this officer led all the tanks of his company forward and showed each one its jumping-off point. It was almost entirely due to this officer's very gallant behaviour that all tanks reached their jumping-off points up to time.

A/Capt. WEBER, CHARLES FREDERICK, M.C. 3rd Battn. Awarded Bar to M.C.

During the action near Achiet-le-Petit on August 21, 1918, this officer commanded his section with splendid gallantry and initiative in most difficult circumstances. During the greater part of the action he was walking about on foot under intense fire in order to keep in touch with the infantry, and by so doing was enabled to render them the greatest assistance. His personal example throughout the day inspired not only his men but the infantry with whom he was working.

This officer has fought with the utmost gallantry in every action since the battalion was formed.

(Military Cross awarded for action at Arras, May 9, 1917.)

Lieut. (A/Capt.) BOWER, IAN. 3rd Battn. Awarded M.C.

Near Achiet-le-Petit on August 21, 1918. This officer displayed great gallantry and resource. The tank section in front of his ran into enemy artillery at point-blank range. Owing to the state of the ground all tanks were confined to the roads. Seeing the danger to the leading section, he got out of his tank under heavy artillery and machine-gun fire, and managed to get his own tanks out of the way and so allowed the leading section to back down the road away from their dangerous position. Whilst performing this act of self-sacrifice his tank was hit, and he and one of his crew wounded and the third member of the crew killed.

T. Lieut. SAUNDERS, CHARLES ARTHUR CONWAY. 12th Battn. Awarded M.C.

This officer was in command of a section of tanks during the operations near Moyenneville on August 21, Gomiecourt on August 23, and Morchies on September 2. He has led his section into action three times, and in every case has shown the greatest coolness and bravery under most trying conditions, his own tank having been put out of action on all three occasions, twice by direct hits and once by fire. During the approach march on the night of September 1-2 he led his tanks to the starting-point under a good deal of harassing fire. He was very cheery throughout and kept his men in good spirits. Finally, on the morning of September 2, he fought his tank with great gallantry, inflicting heavy casualties on the enemy. Five of the crew were put out of action by anti-tank rifle bullets, and all Lewis guns except one rendered useless by machine-gun fire. Lieut. Saunders still continued to fight his tank, acting as brakesman and gunner, until the tank was finally rendered useless by a direct hit on the petrol tank.

Lieut. (A/Capt.) PONSFORD, WILLIAM STEWART. 10th Battn. Awarded M.C.

For conspicuous gallantry and devotion to duty near Achiet-le-Grand on August 21, 1918. While in command of a section of tanks he showed great initiative and resource at a difficult period in the fight and had a complete grasp of the situation as far as it affected his command. The tanks of his section had proceeded into action when Captain Ponsford was informed by an infantry officer that the infantry were held up by heavy fire from the cemetery. At great personal risk he reconnoitred the area and collected some whippet tanks, and with these and the last tank of his section, which had not been into action, launched an attack on the enemy strong point at the cemetery, dislodging the enemy and enabling the infantry to gain their objective. His total disregard of personal danger and coolness throughout were an example to all ranks.

T. 2nd Lieut. HEATH, JOHN EDGAR. 4th Battn. Awarded M.C.

This officer showed great courage and determination when commanding his tank in action on August 22, 1918, between Vivier Mill and Méaulte.

Hearing a battery of hostile field guns in action behind a slight rise on the route, and realising that if his tank went on its course it would be knocked out before it could get its guns into action, he stopped his tank and personally reconnoitred, under heavy fire, the exact location of this battery.

Returning to his tank he manœuvred it to the flank of the battery, and by prompt action with his Hotchkiss guns silenced the battery by dispersing the personnel.

T. Lieut. (A/Capt.) SARTIN, EDWARD LENDEL. 4th Battn. Awarded M.C.

For most conspicuous gallantry and devotion to duty in action on August 22, 1918, near Albert.

He showed the clearest judgment and great initiative in leading his section of tanks.

During the approach march, which was rendered extremely difficult owing to hostile gas shelling, he urged his men on and launched his section into action at the scheduled time.

In action he showed total disregard for his own safety. Under heavy machine-gun fire he moved from one tank to another, leading them most gallantly to their final objective and rendering most useful assistance to the infantry.

T. 2nd Lieut. HAYWARD, WILLIAM HERBERT. 12th Battn. Awarded M.C.

This officer took his tank into action in the attack on Gomiecourt on August 23. He displayed great bravery and initiative, silencing machine-gun nests and paving the way for the infantry to advance. Having fired most of his ammunition he kept advancing with the intention of destroying machine-guns by running over them. Before he had gone very far his tank was put out of action by three direct hits. He gave the order to evacuate the tank and take up Lewis gun positions. An infantry officer came and asked him for tank assistance as his men were held up by machine-gun fire. 2nd Lieut. Hayward seeing a tank on his right made his way to it under heavy fire ; but before reaching it he was wounded and the tank received a direct hit, killing its commander and driver and wounding the crew. He was then joined by a sergeant from the tank which had just been disabled, and with his help he endeavoured to form a Lewis gun post. By crawling along the ground and dragging the gun and ammunition they managed to get within thirty yards of a party of Germans, but here found that the Lewis gun had been damaged by shell splinters and rendered useless. They emptied their revolvers into the enemy, wounding several and dispersing the rest. They then made their way to the nearest body of infantry. On the way they came across two men of 2nd Lieut. Hayward's crew, one of whom was severely wounded and unable to walk. 2nd Lieut. Hayward and the sergeant carried him in turn over ground swept by machine-gun fire to the shelter of a trench. 2nd Lieut. Hayward then reported to the infantry officer in command, and on being told that his services were no longer required he made his way back to the rallying point. His conduct throughout the operations was magnificent.

T. Lieut. (A/Capt.) CLARKE, JOHN PEARD. 12th Battn. Awarded M.C.

For conspicuous gallantry and devotion to duty near Hamelincourt on August 23. This officer was in command of a section of tanks in addition to commanding a tank himself. During the early hours of the attack there was a good deal of mist, and Captain Clarke realised that there was a great danger of his tanks losing direction. He therefore led them on foot, walking in the open under machine-gun and shell fire. In doing this he was twice wounded, once in the arm and once in the leg, but he refused to leave his section and guided them safely to the starting-point. He then entered his tank and led his section into action, advancing through the village of Hamelincourt and clearing it of enemy machine-guns, thus enabling the infantry to advance with few casualties. Throughout the action he showed a complete disregard of personal safety and was a splendid example to all ranks in his section.

T. Lieut. (A/Capt.) DUNN, FRED. 12th Battn. Awarded M.C.

During the capture of Gomiecourt on August 23 Captain Dunn was in command of a section of four tanks. Three tanks of his section were knocked out by direct hits before crossing the Arras-Albert railway. Captain Dunn, who was in charge of the fourth tank, managed by great skill and judgment to get his tank across the railway. He captured more than 100 prisoners and handed them over to the infantry. He destroyed many enemy machine-gun nests, killing the personnel, before his tank was finally put out of action owing to breaking a track. At this moment a heavy fire was brought to bear upon the tank, and Captain Dunn was wounded and one of his crew killed by an anti-tank rifle bullet. With great coolness he evacuated the tank and joined on to the nearest infantry, forming Lewis gun posts. He and his crew did remarkably good work and were especially mentioned by Lieut.-Colonel Henderson, commanding the 2nd Battalion of the Royal Scots, with whom Captain Dunn was operating.

2nd Lieut. FRERE, FRANK. 10th Battn. Awarded M.C.

At Achiet-le-Grand on August 23, 1918, this officer showed conspicuous gallantry and initiative when commanding his tank under very difficult conditions. Although the infantry following him lost touch, this officer realised that it was necessary to clear the enemy from the right flank of the attack. He succeeded in clearing the southern edges of both Achiet-le-Grand and Bihucourt in spite of very heavy enemy fire, and there is no doubt that it was largely due to his prompt appreciation of the situation that our infantry were able to reach their final objective.

Capt. LOLE, GEOFFREY. 11th Battn. Awarded M.C.

For conspicuous gallantry and devotion to duty north of Croisilles from 9.30 P.M. on August 23 to 11 P.M. on August 24, while commanding a section of tanks. During this time Capt. Lole covered 35,000 yards on his feet, followed by his tanks, fought two actions, and brought all his tanks back. He was dead-beat after the first fight and so were his crews, but, largely owing to his cheerfulness and energy, his crews were off again into the second fight four hours after returning from the first. During the second fight he led his tanks into the fight under heavy gun and machine-gun fire, keeping touch with the infantry and with his tanks on foot all the time, 200 yards in front of the infantry. The gallantry shown by this officer and the wonderful energy he displayed when dead beat were so largely the cause of his section doing so well as to deserve the highest praise.

T. Capt. THEOPHILUS, STANLEY CECIL. 11th Battn. Awarded M.C.

Conspicuous gallantry on August 23 during attack on Boyelles in command of a section of tanks. On the previous afternoon he reconnoitred his routes up to the front line in full view and under machine-gun fire in the open. During the attack he led his tanks through heavy gas-shelling into the fight on foot, and directed them during the fight 300 yards ahead of the infantry on foot.

2nd Lieut. KARN, RAYMOND EDWARD. 11th Battn. Awarded M.C.

Conspicuous gallantry on August 23 during attack on Boyelles in command of a tank. His tank got momentarily ditched while he was going for an enemy machine-gun. Leaving his drivers to get the tank out, he rushed the enemy machine-gun with his three gunners, fifty yards off, and put it out of action. This enemy machine-gun was holding up our infantry 100 yards behind the tank. Lieut. Karn then returned to his tank, got it going, and carried on the fight in it.

T. 2nd Lieut. BROMLEY, FREDERICK FARRAR. 6th Battn. Awarded M.C.

On August 23, 1918, near Bihucourt, for conspicuous gallantry in action. When advancing between the infantry and the barrage he saw the enemy escaping beyond the barrage ; without hesitation he drove his tank through the barrage, thereby losing the smoke protection, and inflicted severe loss on the enemy. Later on, in co-operation with another tank, he attacked a field gun battery in the open, causing it to surrender, capturing 150 to 200 prisoners who were subsequently taken over by the infantry.

T. Capt. BAILEY, KENNETH HOLT. 10th Battn. Awarded M.C.

On August 23, 1918, at Achiet-le-Grand, this officer showed exceptional gallantry and initiative in assisting in clearing enemy dug-outs during one hour's halt of the barrage.

Accompanied by only one officer he captured a German battalion headquarters, and captured six officers and forty-three other

THE TANK CORPS BOOK OF HONOUR

ranks. Owing to his prompt action the battalion commander was prevented from destroying his papers and maps, which were captured intact.

T. Lieut. (A/Capt.) HARCOURT, ALEXANDER CLARENCE, D.S.O. 2nd Battn. Awarded M.C.

For skill and courage in action near Chuignolles on August 23, 1918. Although receiving the briefest notice of the coming action, his arrangements were complete and thorough, enabling the tanks under his command to get into action at the proper hour and lead to their objective the infantry, to whom they rendered invaluable assistance.

He followed his tanks into action on foot, and on more than one occasion directed a tank to a point where the infantry required assistance.

For several hours he moved about the field in the open under heavy fire, maintaining touch with section commanders and assisting in removing wounded from tanks which had been disabled by enemy gunfire.

He set an example throughout of gallantry and disregard of his personal safety.

2nd Lieut. HEGGS, JAMES REGINALD. 2nd Battn. Awarded M.C.

In action on August 23, near Chuignolles, this officer, when in command of a tank, was fired on by a battery of field guns, which for some time he could not locate owing to smoke. He drove in among the guns, knocking out the crews with machine-gun fire. He then went through Chuignolles village, where he destroyed twelve machine-guns. Later his tank was hit direct by a shell that broke a track. He repaired the track under heavy artillery and machine-gun fire, and brought his tank back to the rallying point. His coolness and devotion to duty were magnificent.

Lieut. CRAIG, WILLIAM ANDREW, M.C. 2nd Battn. Awarded Bar to M.C.

For skill and gallantry when in command of a tank in action near Chuignolles on August 23. Our infantry were held up by machine-gun fire from a wood beyond the first objective. He took his tank forward, knocked out the machine-gun, and established the infantry beyond the wood. Later, he dealt with very strong resistance north-east of Chuignolles, where he continued in action for an hour on the most difficult sort of ground under heavy fire from an anti-tank gun and numerous machine-guns.

These had stopped the advance of our infantry, who during part of the time were as much as 2000 yards behind.

He did great execution with 6-pndrs. and machine-gun fire. On the way back his tank received a hit in the petrol tank, and the

192

tank was set on fire. All attempts to extinguish the flames having failed, he brought his crew back under heavy fire.

This officer has been previously recommended for gallantry in the action of August 8.

Lieut. WALSH, RUPERT SHARP, M.M. 11th Battn. Awarded D.S.O.

For gallantry and devotion to duty on August 24 when commanding a tank in the fight at Boyelles and Croisilles. After an approach march of 12,000 yards and an attack on Summit Trench on the morning of the 24th, he returned to the rallying point deadbeat after having covered 22,000 yards. Four hours after his return he was ordered to fight again in the evening. His energy and cheerfulness when dead-beat were a fine example to his crew, who were in the same state. He covered his approach march of 2000 yards in one and a half hours and caught up the infantry after they had gone 200 yards. Although he wiped out several machine-gun nests, at dusk the infantry were unable to proceed further owing to the strong resistance.

While crossing a sunken road at dusk his engine gave out and he stuck. Some 200 yards in advance of our own infantry he was surrounded by enemy, very many of whom were killed by fire from the tank. Enemy then shot phosphorous bombs at the tank, which made it impossible for crew to stay in it owing to fumes and all kit inside catching fire.

Lieut. Walsh ordered his crew to evacuate tank and remained behind with Gnr. Perry to put out the fire.

He then got the engine started, put it into bottom speed, and turned the tank for home. He and Gnr. Perry then got out, the fumes being too bad for them, and walked away between the front horns of the tank. All this time they were surrounded by the enemy and were firing at them with their revolvers. After some time Lieut. Walsh got inside the tank again and found the fumes had cleared sufficiently. He and Gnr. Perry then drove the tank home, having covered a total distance that day of 35,000 yards and fought two actions.

Lieut. JONES, CHARLES KEPPEL. 11th Battn. Awarded M.C.

Gallantry and devotion to duty on August 24 during the attack on the Hindenburg Line east of Croisilles. At 8 P.M. his tank got a direct hit from anti-tank gun on the roof which knocked him out. On coming to some time later he went on fighting his tank. Finding he had got ahead of the infantry, he went back and brought them on.

This was his second fight that day and, although dead-beat after having covered 30,000 yards during the day and badly shaken, after recovering consciousness the example he set to his crew was very fine.

THE TANK CORPS BOOK OF HONOUR

A/Capt. LE CLAIR, CHARLES MILWARD, M.C. 3rd Battn.
Awarded Bar to M.C.

Near Biefvillers, on August 24, 1918, this officer handled his tank with gallantry and skill of the highest order. Though subjected to very heavy artillery and machine-gun fire the assistance he gave the infantry was invaluable. Eventually his tank was hit by a shell and stopped about fifty yards from enemy machine-guns; he continued to fight it to the last. He then joined the infantry with one of his guns, until his assistance was no longer required. Later he manned another tank whose crew had become casualties, and took it into action until it, too, was knocked out by a shell. The determination and great gallantry of this officer throughout the whole action were beyond praise.

(Military Cross awarded for action at Battle of Arras, May 23, 1917.)

2nd Lieut. THOMAS, TREVOR. 3rd Battn. Awarded M.C.

During the action of August 25, near Favreuil, he displayed the highest gallantry and devotion to duty in command of his tank. When his tank came under very heavy machine-gun fire, one of his revolver porthole covers was shot away by an enemy machine-gun. An enemy machine-gunner perceiving this, immediately commenced to pour bullets into the tank at very close range. Everyone in the tank, including 2nd Lieut. Thomas, was wounded in several places either by splash or by bullets. On realising what had happened, 2nd Lieut. Thomas rushed to the porthole and held a steel helmet over the aperture, at the same time ordering the crew to evacuate the tank, which they could do, as the enemy were only on one side of it. 2nd Lieut. Thomas, although he received six bullets in his arm and has since had it amputated, continued to hold the helmet over the hole until his crew were safely out. He then attempted to join them, but fell unconscious under his tank and was later brought in by the infantry.

T. Lieut. STEEPLE, JOHN. 9th Battn. Awarded M.C.

During the action near Mory on August 25, 1918, Lieut. Steeple directed his tank with great skill and coolness, although under very heavy hostile artillery fire, and by his skilful manœuvring not only enabled Mory Copse and a sunken road to be captured by the infantry with few casualties, but was able to inflict heavy casualties on the Jager Battalion which was defending them.

After his tank received two direct hits he evacuated it, and established himself in a shell-hole with his guns, firing on machine-gun positions in front, thereby keeping down their fire, enabling the infantry to come up and capture them.

He set a very fine example to his crew.

IMMEDIATE AWARDS—OFFICERS

A/Capt. MONK, ALBERT VICTOR. 3rd Battn. Awarded M.C.

Near Biefvillers, on August 25, 1918, this officer whilst in command of his tank company displayed the greatest bravery and resource. He personally led his tanks into action on foot through an extremely heavy artillery barrage, and although blown into the air by a shell which burst within a few yards of him, continued to carry on. He has previously been brought to notice for gallantry in action, notably at Cambrai in November 1917, and again during the enemy offensive in March 1918.

Capt. PEMBERTON, ALFRED GROSSHOLTZ. 14th Battn. Awarded M.C.

For gallantry and devotion to duty in the period from August 25 to September 4, during which this officer commanded a composite company and took part in the operations near the Bois de Sart on August 27 and the piercing of the Queant-Drocourt line, near Cagnicourt, on September 2. During the approach march on the 1st his tank column was subjected to heavy shell fire, bombing by enemy aircraft, gas, and, finally, machine-gun fire. By the magnificent example that he set, and by his energy and determination, he was mainly responsible for getting his tanks into action in spite of these exceptional difficulties and the fact that many of his men were partially incapacitated by gas. He has set a high standard and shown a fine example throughout the operations.

T. Lieut. WARREN, OLIVER QUIN. 9th Battn. Awarded M.C.

During the action near Monchy-le-Preux on August 26, 1918, Lieut. Warren, although exposed to heavy artillery and machine-gun fire, led his section of tanks on foot, it being too dark to see from the tanks. He successfully guided them to their objectives, pointing out machine-gun nests, and thus materially helping the attack. Seeing that a tank of another section had lost its direction owing to the darkness, he went over to it and guided it to its final objective.

Throughout the action Lieut. Warren showed an utter disregard for his own personal safety, and the success of the tanks was in a large measure due to his gallantry in going ahead on foot and guiding them to their objectives.

Lieut. COLLINS, JAMES. 10th Battn. Awarded M.C.

This officer was in charge of a tank ordered to attack Fremicourt on August 30, 1918. Early in the fight his petrol tank was pierced ; he nevertheless succeeded in keeping it in action, mopping up Fremicourt and taking 150 prisoners. When the infantry were held up south of Fremicourt, Lieut. Collins went ahead on foot to make a personal reconnaissance, bringing back valuable information as to the enemy's dispositions. He then directed his tank against the machine-guns holding up the advance, silencing them, and enabling the infantry to proceed. During the entire action his courage and determination were an inspiration to all.

Lieut. GATTIE, ANTHONY HOWARD. 10th Battn. Awarded M.C.

For most conspicuous gallantry and devotion to duty on August 30, 1918 at Bancourt. He was ordered to attack Bancourt, and as the morning was misty and the air full of dust, making it very difficult to keep direction, he walked in front between his two tanks, guiding them and running from one to the other pointing out targets.

He successfully mopped up Bancourt and silenced the battery of guns south of this place which knocked out one of his tanks. The other tank caught fire, and Lieut. Gattie helped to extinguish the flames and then proceeded to mop up a machine-gun nest which was pointed out to him by the infantry. This he accomplished. During the entire action his coolness, courage, and leadership were a fine example to all ranks.

2nd Lieut. FRERE, FRANK. 10th Battn. Awarded Bar to M.C.

For conspicuous gallantry and devotion to duty on August 30, 1918, near Haplincourt. This officer fought his tank with great skill and determination. His orders were to assist in mopping up Bancourt and to exploit any success in the direction of Haplincourt. This he did, penetrating more than a mile into the enemy's lines entirely unsupported. He inflicted heavy casualties on the enemy and entered the outskirts of Haplincourt. His tank having caught fire, he immediately left the tank and helped to extinguish the flames under heavy machine-gun fire. On the way back he was asked by the infantry to go forward again and engage the machine-guns. This he did succeeding in silencing them although his Hotchkiss guns were all out of action and he had only six rounds of 6-pndr. ammunition left. His determination and fine example inspired all ranks.

T. Lieut. STAUB, THEODORE VIVIAN. 12th Battn. Awarded M.C.

For conspicuous gallantry during the operations near Vaulx Vraucourt on August 31. His tank was put out of action by anti-tank rifle fire and armour-piercing machine-gun bullets, and four of the crew were wounded. The tank was at this time well in advance of the nearest infantry, and Lieut. Staub ordered the crew to evacuate the tank and form Lewis gun posts. One man who was very seriously wounded was left behind. It was found that all Lewis guns had been pierced by machine-gun fire and rendered useless. Lieut. Staub then went back to the tank and brought out the seriously wounded man. The whole time the tank was subjected to heavy machine-gun fire, and armour-piercing bullets were penetrating the sides. He then crawled back to the nearest trench, some 150 yards away, and found a party of the Gordon Highlanders, who promised to hold on until he had got his men safely back. On his return to the tank he ordered the unwounded and slightly wounded to crawl back to the trench. The badly wounded man he bound up and then proceeded to drag him into the trench. The ground was devoid of cover, and he was exposed to heavy fire during the whole journey, which lasted more than two hours. From start to finish Lieut. Staub kept remarkably cool and took command of a situation at all times extremely critical.

T. 2nd Lieut. PATON, SIDNEY. 15th Battn. Awarded M.C.

For conspicuous gallantry on August 31, 1918, during the attack on Vaulx-Vraucourt. 2nd Lieut. Paton was in command of a tank. While ahead of other tanks, and without infantry support, he attacked a number of enemy machine-gun posts. Having silenced the machine-guns and killed several of the crews, he observed the remainder taking to the dug-outs. 2nd Lieut. Paton without hesitation got out of his tank and, accompanied by his corporal, entered all the dug-outs and, armed only with his revolver, took the remaining enemy machine-gunners and some infantry prisoners. These he handed over to our infantry, who came up soon after.

Later, during the same action, while again some considerable distance in front of our infantry, one of the tracks of his tank became loose and needed adjustment. This had to be done from outside the tank under fire. 2nd Lieut. Paton therefore drove up to another machine-gun post and, having silenced the gun, again got out of his tank and took the crew prisoners. He then placed these prisoners close to the tank while the crew made the necessary adjustments to the track.

Having sent these prisoners back to the infantry, 2nd Lieut. Paton carried on into action and eventually rallied. He was in action for over seven hours, and his disregard for personal safety set a splendid fighting example to his crew.

Lieut. UZIELLI, CLIVE FREDERICK. K.O. Royal Lancs. (attached Tank Corps, 15th Battn.). Awarded M.C.

On August 31, 1918, during the attack on Vaulx-Vraucourt, Lieut. Uzielli led his tank into action, proceeding on foot. He was wounded whilst passing through the village, but carried on, fighting his tank until reaching his final objective, where he fought against great odds. Here he himself received a second wound in the chest, penetrating his lungs, and also had five of his crew wounded. He nevertheless brought his tank out of action before being taken to a dressing station. He also fought on August 21, 1918, during the attack on the Arras-Albert railway, and on August 30, 1918, during a previous attack on Vaulx-Vraucourt, and on each occasion he has displayed great gallantry and disregard for personal safety.

T. 2nd Lieut. EDWARDS, ERIC NORMAN. 6th Battn. Awarded M.C.

Near Ecoust, on August 31, 1918, he was in charge of a section of whippets which attacked the Noreuil switch. Although a very junior officer, he showed the greatest initiative and powers of leadership. The operation was entirely successful ; he stood on the back of his tank giving orders to the others to deploy in the required direction, as the undulating ground rendered the targets difficult to pick out.

T. 2nd Lieut. AVINS, HARRY EDGAR. 6th Battn. Awarded M.C.

Near Vraucourt, on September 1, 1918, this officer commanded a whippet which was sent forward to attack Vaulx trench. He successfully engaged two machine-gun emplacements, but when attacking a third was hit by splinters in both eyes. He gallantly continued fighting till all his crew were wounded, when he was forced to withdraw. He showed the greatest pluck and bravery, and his tank was riddled with armour-piercing bullets.

T. Lieut. PRESCOTT, GEORGE AYLWARD. 9th Battn. Awarded M.C.

During the night previous to the action near Dury on September 2, 1918, Lieut. G. A. Prescott, the company reconnaissance officer, laid a line of tape from the starting-point to the front line. This was done under heavy machine-gun fire, artillery fire, and gas, due to the fact that an operation was being carried out in the sector that night. The tape line proved of inestimable value, enabling the tanks to get into their correct positions in the dark. Throughout the operation Lieut. Prescott showed an utter disregard for his own personal safety, exposing himself in order to obtain information which was of great value to his company commander.

Lieut. Prescott set a fine example of devotion to duty under particularly trying circumstances.

Lieut. (A/Capt.) ABBOTS, RICHARD WILLIAM. 11th Battn. Awarded M.C.

For conspicuous gallantry and leadership on September 2, 1918, at Dury. He led his section into action at zero on foot. One of his tanks got hit by a gun and some of the crew were wounded. He found the tank and ordered the crew, who had evacuated it, to go on. This tank was then called for by infantry to knock out a machine-gun in Dury, which it did, thereby enabling the infantry to advance.

When this tank eventually was hit again and completely knocked out, Capt. Abbots went to try and find another tank of his section. All this time he was on foot in advance of the infantry. His leadership and action in ordering the knocked-out tank to carry on undoubtedly saved many casualties to the infantry.

T. 2nd Lieut. PAVEY, SAMUEL. 14th Battn. Awarded M.C.

Near Villers-lez-Cagnicourt, on September 2, this officer displayed very conspicuous gallantry and devotion to duty. While mopping up the Queant-Drocourt line this tank was knocked out by a direct hit. Shortly afterwards, finding another tank which was still mobile, though all its crew except two men had become casualties, he raised a fresh crew and took it over. Proceeding towards his second objective, he cleared up the above village and rallied. On being again called on for help by the infantry, although he had been very badly shaken by his first direct hit and was now much exhausted, he took his tank into action for the third time, and approached a factory which had held up the infantry for some time. Another direct hit knocked out this second tank, but he established a strong point, and by his fire drove a large number of German machine-gunners out of the factory. At this period he was quite unsupported by the infantry and alone.

THE HINDENBURG SYSTEM, SEPT.-OCT. 1918

T. 2nd Lieut. SKIPPON, DAVID LESLIE. 14th Battn. Awarded M.C.

For most conspicuous gallantry and initiative during an attack near Villers-lez-Cagnicourt on September 2, 1918.

His tank proceeded well ahead of the infantry, and in spite of several of his crew being hit he showed great determination, in the face of direct and accurate enemy field-gun fire, in overcoming enemy resistance.

He continued fighting his tank until it received several direct hits—himself and all his crew being badly wounded. He attempted to form a Lewis gun post with the remnants of his crew, but owing to being incapacitated through wounds they fell temporarily into enemy hands.

Our infantry succeeded in advancing and released 2nd Lieut. Skippon and some of his crew. Our infantry report that the action of this officer's tank was particularly gallant and useful. The coolness and devotion to duty displayed by this officer were a magnificent example to all who came into contact with him.

T. 2nd Lieut. SMALLWOOD, GEORGE FREDERICK. 2nd Battn. Awarded M.C.

For conspicuous gallantry and devotion to duty as tank commander near Holnon village on September 18, 1918.

When the infantry were unable to advance owing to very heavy machine-gun fire he cleverly steered his tank through smoke, darkness, and heavy rain to the objective, a distance of over 3000 yards.

Though subjected to an intense fire from close range, which affected all the crew with splash, by his splendid example he kept all his guns going, including the front gun, which he handled himself.

His tank became ditched when crossing a sunken road. In spite of gallant efforts on the part of himself and his first driver it could not be extricated. Another tank caught fire, and all the crew were captured except the tank commander. 2nd Lieut. Smallwood got out of his tank and rescued this officer. During this time the infantry were about 300 yards behind and were unable to advance. He kept the enemy at a distance with his machine-guns, meanwhile sending back a message to the infantry that the situation was in hand, and asked them to advance.

His coolness and grasp of a difficult situation were splendid. He set a fine example which inspired all ranks.

T. 2nd Lieut. HARRISON, HERBERT DEACON. 2nd Battn. Awarded M.C.

During operations east of St. Emilie on September 18, 1918, 2nd Lieut. Harrison commanded tank No. B. 7.9314. The task of getting to the tape line was very difficult owing to the weather and the extreme darkness of the morning. He managed, however, to get his tank off soon after the barrage. He pursued the course ordered for him into Ronssoy, and did invaluable work in mopping up there. During the mopping up the tank became ditched and was surrounded by the enemy. 2nd Lieut. Harrison drove them off with his revolver (as his guns were temporarily out of action owing to the tank being on its side) until our infantry came up. He then went to another part of the village and brought another tank, whose crew were all wounded, to pull his tank out, and continued the work. This work was done under very heavy shell and machine-gun fire.

T. 2nd Lieut. STAMMERS, ALFRED ERNEST. 2nd Battn. Awarded M.C.

During the operations east of St. Emilie on the morning of September 18, 1918, 2nd Lieut. Stammers was commanding tank No. B. 12.9509. The task of getting to the tape line was very difficult owing to the weather and extreme darkness of the morning. He managed, however, to get off soon after the barrage, and did excellent work. Lieut. Stammers and his crew were all wounded, and the tank was damaged by anti-tank gun fire, so that it could not be moved. It is now in the main street of Ronssoy.

T. Lieut. KERR, RODNEY WATSON. 2nd Battn.   Awarded M.C.

For great gallantry and endurance in action near Lempire on September 21, 1918.

This officer took his tank to the first objective and successfully cleared it, inflicting heavy casualties on the enemy. He then proceeded to his final objective, and in spite of shell, machine-gun, and anti-tank rifle fire, continued to pour a withering fire on the large numbers of enemy troops who were defending this place.

During this period his tank N.C.O. was killed, and he himself was severely wounded in the shoulder by anti-tank rifle fire. Despite his wound he took his tank back to the infantry, who were held up by flanking fire, and endeavoured to bring them forward. His untiring efforts to keep in action his tank, which had been punctured in the radiator some time previously, finally proved impossible owing to the engine seizing.

The skill and determined bravery of this officer in carrying on an unequal fight against odds, even though badly wounded, provided a magnificent example to his crew.

T. 2nd Lieut. (A/Capt.) MAITLAND, VICTOR KENNARD. 13th Battn. Awarded M.C.

For conspicuous gallantry and devotion to duty near Pontruet, on September 24, 1918.

Captain Maitland acted as a section commander in an attack, and since the tank commanders in his section had no opportunity of making a reconnaissance of the area in which they were operating, he led his tanks into action on foot, although under heavy artillery and machine-gun fire.

Later on in the operations, seeing that the infantry on the left flank were held up by a nest of machine-guns, he walked across the open under heavy machine-gun fire, and directed a tank so that it succeeded in clearing the enemy machine-guns and enabled the infantry to proceed.

This officer exhibited exceptional courage and powers of leadership under difficult circumstances.

T. 2nd Lieut. WHYTE, DONALD. 13th Battn.   Awarded M.C.

For conspicuous gallantry and devotion to duty as a tank commander near Pontruet on September 24, 1918.

Although enemy resistance was exceptionally strong and his tank was under heavy artillery and machine-gun fire, this officer brought back his tank three times to assist infantry who were being held up, and thus enabled them to advance.

Later the tank received a direct hit from an enemy field gun, which blew away part of the petrol pipe. In spite of heavy enemy fire brought to bear on the tank, 2nd Lieut. Whyte and his crew succeeded in bringing the tank out of action by hand-feeding it.

Throughout the action this officer gave a splendid example of courage and determination.

T. 2nd Lieut. BARKER, CHARLES ROBERT. 13th Battn. Awarded M.C.

For conspicuous gallantry and devotion to duty as a tank commander near Fresnoy on September 24, 1918.

The tank commanded by this officer rendered great assistance to the infantry in overcoming strong resistance. While infantry in his sector were engaged in consolidating their objective he patrolled ahead and engaged enemy machine-guns which were harassing the infantry.

Later the tank received a direct hit from an anti-tank gun, setting the tank on fire. At great personal risk 2nd Lieut. Barker endeavoured to extinguish the flames, but seeing that this was impossible, he removed the machine-guns from the tank, and with his crew engaged the anti-tank gun, silencing it. He assisted the infantry with his machine-guns until they had consolidated.

2nd Lieut. Barker showed throughout the action remarkable courage and a determination that was an example to all.

Lieut. BROWN, JOHN. 7th Battn. Awarded M.C.

For conspicuous gallantry and devotion to duty.

On September 27, 1918, at Inchy, he reconnoitred the ground, and started off the tanks on their correct courses for their respective crossings of the Canal du Nord, thus ensuring the initial success.

On September 29, 1918, at Tilloy, he guided the tanks over an exceedingly difficult part of the country in the dark. The approach march was 4000 yards without any previous reconnaissance. The country was intersected with deep trenches and heavy wire, also a considerable amount of hostile shelling was met with.

He set a splendid example of courage and cheerfulness throughout the operation which gave complete confidence to the crews.

Lieut. BROWNE, DOUGLAS GORDON. 17th Battn. Awarded M.C.

For conspicuous gallantry and devotion to duty.

He showed great skill and ability as company reconnaissance officer in operations on September 27, near Inchy-en-Artois, and on September 30 at Sancourt.

In the first case the success of the operation was mainly due to his reconnaissance of the Canal du Nord and of the route up to it. He led the company tanks right up to the front line and set each one off in the right direction at zero.

In the second case there was no time to make a previous reconnaissance of the ground leading up to the starting-point, but Lieut. Browne led the tanks on an extremely dark night up to the jumping-off point under heavy shell fire.

This officer's hard work and ability had a very material effect on the operations.

2nd Lieut. DOUGLAS, ROBERT BRUCE. 11th Battn. Awarded M.C.

For conspicuous gallantry and devotion to duty in action at Chapel Wood switch on September 27, 1918.

Throughout the action he did excellent work and rendered great assistance to the infantry by putting out machine-gun nests. After reaching the objective he encountered a battery of anti-tank guns and received three direct hits on his tank, wounding him and his first driver. Notwithstanding this he manœuvred his tank and succeeded in knocking out one of these guns. His tank then received another direct hit, causing a fire. He made gallant but ineffectual efforts to extinguish this, and it was mainly owing to his efforts that his crew was rescued from the tank.

2nd Lieut. WILSON, THOMAS CHEENEY. 11th Battn. Awarded M.C.

For conspicuous gallantry and devotion to duty in action at Villers Plouich on September 27, 1918. He cleared the way for the infantry up to the final objective. Then, although wounded and with mechanical trouble in his tank, he pursued the enemy for half a mile beyond his objective, killing a great number and enabling the infantry to consolidate. On his return he took the place of a tank which had been put out of action in another part of the line and enabled the infantry to advance. After having done far more than the task allotted to him, he volunteered to stay with the infantry in case the enemy counter-attacked. Throughout the action he manœuvred his tank with the greatest skill and judgment.

2nd Lieut. BRANDLE, SAMUEL, M.C. 15th Battn. Awarded Bar to M.C.

On the occasion of the attack on the Canal du Nord, near Moeuvres, on September 27, 1918, this officer, regardless of personal risk, supervised the unditching of his tank under heavy machine-gun fire. Although twice wounded, he continued to fight his tank with great determination until it was completely knocked out by a second direct hit. He then established machine-gun posts, and, by covering fire, assisted the infantry in crossing the Canal du Nord. All his crew were wounded, but it was not until he had got them into safety and made his reports at the company rallying point that he himself went to a dressing station. His gallantry and determination in action, during which he personally carried ammunition to the infantry under heavy machine-gun fire, materially assisted operations and were a source of inspiration to all under his command.

Lieut. (A/Capt.) FORSTER, RALPH PERRIN. 15th Battn. Awarded M.C.

On September 27, 1918, at Moeuvres, this officer led his section with conspicuous gallantry. Both his runners were wounded, but he continued to accompany his tanks under heavy hostile fire until they were all knocked out by direct hits. Regardless of personal safety, he supervised the removal of the wounded under heavy fire, and subsequently manning an infantry machine-gun, covered the advance of the infantry. This officer's coolness and gallantry in difficult circumstances were a source of inspiration to all. He displayed qualities of leadership and initiative of a very high order.

Lieut. (A/Capt.) CLAYTON, SYDNEY ARNOLD. 15th Battn. Awarded M.C.

On the approach march preceding the attack on Flesquieres on September 27, 1918, this officer displayed conspicuous courage and initiative in getting into position. On finding that the tank commander and three of the crew of his leading tank had been killed, he himself drove the tank over the newly-selected route, afterwards returning and guiding over each of his tanks in turn. On the development of the attack on Flesquieres, in spite of heavy shelling and machine-gun fire, he led his section through the village, clearing the way for the infantry. Subsequently the infantry were held up by hostile machine-guns in front of Flesquieres ; Captain Clayton led his tanks forward and directed their movements so that the machine-guns were silenced, and the infantry were enabled to advance and capture their objective. The initiative and contempt of danger shown by this officer set a splendid example to his men and greatly contributed to the success of the operations.

2nd Lieut. HEPWORTH, ALBERT. 15th Battn. Awarded M.C.

For conspicuous gallantry and devotion to duty in action near Moeuvres on September 27, 1918. This officer, although he and all his crew were wounded, fought his tank until it was knocked out by a third direct hit. Only when he had got all his men to an aid-post and sent off reports did he himself go to a dressing station. By this time he was completely exhausted from loss of blood. His gallantry and determination in action materially assisted the operations and were a source of inspiration to all under his command.

IMMEDIATE AWARDS—OFFICERS

2nd Lieut. ROBERTS, ALFORD LIONEL. 15th Battn. Awarded M.C.

For conspicuous gallantry and devotion to duty on the occasion of the attack on the Hindenburg front line, near Moeuvres, on September 27, 1918. This officer, although gassed shortly before zero, with great determination took his tank into action. Shortly afterwards he was wounded in fourteen places, but continued to fight his tank until it was knocked out by a direct hit 3¾ hours later. During the course of the action he rendered valuable assistance to the infantry, and throughout the day set a splendid example to all ranks under his command.

Lieut. THOROGOOD, WILLIAM JESSE. 15th Battn. Awarded M.C.

On September 27, 1918, on the occasion of the attack on the Canal du Nord, near Moeuvres, this officer displayed conspicuous gallantry and initiative in organising an attack on an enemy strong point after his tank had become ditched. Having first engaged the enemy with rifles and revolvers and a machine-gun obtained from the tank, Lieut. Thorogood, accompanied by two of his crew and two infantrymen, rushed the strong point and was instrumental in the capture of thirty-five prisoners.

2nd Lieut. WALTERS, EDWIN CECIL. 15th Battn. Awarded M.C.

On September 27, 1918, on the occasion of the attack on the Canal du Nord, the tank in which 2nd Lieut. Walters had been detailed to proceed for the purpose of making technical notes came under heavy machine-gun fire and experienced considerable difficulty in crossing a sunken road. Regardless of personal risk, this officer left the tank and led it across. In addition to making valuable technical notes, he served a gun to great advantage. On the approach march he had assisted in the repair of two tanks which had badly broken tracks, and on the conclusion of the operation of his tank he assisted in the repair of tanks. It was largely due to his gallantry and untiring efforts that his company maintained a high standard of mechanical efficiency.

2nd Lieut. RIDDEL, J. A. 15th Battn. Awarded M.C.

On September 27, 1918, on the occasion of the attack on Flesquieres, this officer, his section commander having become a casualty, and the next senior officer being away reconnoitring forward, assumed command of the section, and led it across a stretch of country exposed to the direct fire of hostile field guns, heavy trench mortars, and the aimed fire of a battery of howitzers. This movement covered the advance of the infantry and enabled the fire of several hostile machine-guns, which had been causing heavy casualties, to be silenced, and field guns, which had been harassing our infantry, to be engaged at close range. All the tanks of this section except one were knocked out by direct hits, and although this officer was himself wounded and taken prisoner, he effected his escape. He set a splendid example of resolution and gallantry throughout the action.

2nd Lieut. TOLMIE, CHARLES. 15th Battn. Awarded M.C.

On September 27, 1918, on the occasion of the attack on Flesquieres, this officer's tank was the only surviving tank of the section. In the face of strong opposition from enemy artillery, he continued to fight his tank, engaging enemy field and machine-guns until almost all his 6-pndr. ammunition was expended. When his tank received a direct hit he then occupied a trench, and with his machine-guns covered the advance of the infantry. It was largely due to this officer's gallantry, initiative, and powers of leadership that a successful advance was achieved.

Lieut. (A/Capt.) KILNER, HENRY ARNOLD. 11th Battn. Awarded M.C.

On September 27, 1918, at Havrincourt Wood. This section commander personally led his tank on foot under a hot machine-gun fire. Seeing that the infantry did not come on, he got into touch with them in person and co-ordinated the attack, passing through an enemy barrage to effect liaison. His conduct and gallantry were directly responsible for the success of that attack, while his conspicuous gallantry and devotion to duty set an example and inspired, not only the tank crew under his personal command, but also the infantry co-operating. The officer commanding 1/5th Manchester Regiment wrote, dated September 27, 1918:

' On behalf of my battalion and myself I wish to thank Capt. Kilner and the whole of your company of tanks for the splendid work you did for us to-day, which I can assure you is fully appreciated by all the men.'

Again on October 8, 1918, this officer displayed coolness and leadership in the attack on Villers-Outreaux. He personally led his tanks and the infantry to their objectives, ofttimes under intense machine-gun, rifle, and shell fire.

2nd Lieut. PARKES, WILLIAM TAYLOR. 7th Battn. Awarded M.C.

For conspicuous gallantry and ability.

On September 28, 1918, near Cambrai, he overcame very heavy enemy resistance at the Marcoing Line, thereby enabling the infantry to capture the position.

During this fighting 2nd Lieut. Parkes was wounded in several places and all his guns were put out of action by the terrific machine-gun fire that was concentrated on him.

His conduct in this and in any other battle, as for instance the action of August 21 at Achiet-le-Petit, has always been a splendid example to his men.

Lieut. NEADELE, THEODORE CHARLES. 301st American Battn. Awarded M.C.

About 8 P.M. on the evening of September 28, 1918, while laying tape for the approach march of his company near Ronssoy, a shell killed one member of his party and wounded Lieut. Neadele and Lieut. McCloskey, the other members of the party. Lieut. Neadele and Lieut. McCloskey assisted each other back to the dressing station at St. Emilie, and after having his wound dressed Lieut. Neadele was instructed to wait for an ambulance to take him to the rear. Instead of doing this Lieut. Neadele returned to the front and finished laying his tape under heavy shell fire and gas. Throughout the action Lieut. Neadele completely disregarded personal danger, and it was due to his work that all the tanks of his company were able to cross the start line at zero.

T. Lieut. (A/Capt.) RAE, SIDNEY CARSON. 9th Battn. Awarded M.C.

During the operations near Bellenglise on September 29, 1918, this officer led his section with splendid judgment and exposed himself freely under heavy machine-gun fire in order to clear enemy machine-gun posts in Riqueval. He then guided his tanks into action near Bellenglise and set his crews a splendid example of personal bravery and devotion to duty.

T. Lieut. WILD, BASIL WARREN. 9th Battn. Awarded M.C.

During the operations near Bellicourt on September 29, Lieut. Wild located a party of the enemy on the western bank of the canal. He at once collected a few infantry and rushed the post, capturing about forty of the enemy. Throughout the day, as company reconnaissance officer, he showed an utter disregard for his own personal safety and procured valuable information for his company commander.

T. Lieut. (A/Capt.) RONEY, HERBERT LESLIE, M.C. 9th Battn. Awarded Bar to M.C.

During the operations on September 29, near Bellicourt, Capt. Roney located a nest of machine-guns on the western bank of the canal, which had not been mopped up and which was holding up the infantry. He immediately collected a party of infantry and personally led them against the machine-guns. By his skilful handling of the party he rounded up about sixty of the enemy.

It was owing to his resourcefulness and courage in leading this attack that the way was cleared for the infantry advance.

T. Capt. (A/Major) HARRISON, HAROLD BURCHMORE. 9th Battn. Awarded M.C.

During the operations near Bellicourt on September 29, 1918, when the tanks approached the canal, Major Harrison found the Americans held up west of the canal. They were prevented from advancing by numerous machine-guns which had not been mopped up in the first advance. Major Harrison at once sent on some tanks to clear the way, and as no officers could be seen at the time, owing to the mist, although under intense machine-gun fire, he organised the Americans in platoons and personally led them forward in rear of the tanks. It was largely owing to his skill and leadership that the Americans were able to reach and cross the canal at that point.

Lieut. (T. Major) HOTBLACK, FREDERICK ELLIOTT, D.S.O., M.C. Headquarters. Awarded Bar to M.C.

For conspicuous gallantry, initiative, and devotion to duty near Quennemont Farm on the morning of September 29, 1918.

This officer, who is G.S.O. 2, Intelligence, was following up the operations when the mist lifted and disclosed a strongly held enemy position dominating the advance to the south. He at once ran across to two tanks and directed them on to this strong point, himself going into action in one of the tanks to make certain of success.

The position was later found to be the actual German front line, and was strongly held with machine-guns and field guns in close support. The tanks met with strong opposition, and the heavy machine-gun fire made it impossible for the gunners in the tanks to work their guns, though the enemy were at close quarters and were exposing themselves freely. Major Hotblack then opened the revolver loopholes and fired his revolver into the enemy repeatedly, driving them off.

He was wounded in the eyes and temporarily blinded. The two tanks of which he was in charge were knocked out by shell fire and his crews almost all wounded. When the position had been cleared of the enemy Major Hotblack, in spite of his wounds, at once got the wounded into safety and organised a hurried defence with a few infantry against a possible counter-attack.

The very prompt and gallant action of this officer overcame a situation which would in all probability have held up our advance to the south of Quennemont Farm.

Major (Bt. Lieut.-Col.) WOODS, HUGH KENNEDY. 9th Battn. Awarded D.S.O.

Conspicuous gallantry and devotion to duty in operation north of St. Quentin on September 29, 1918.

This officer personally deployed his tanks and directed them on to their objectives.

It was largely due to his personal gallantry and efforts that the tank attack was successfully launched and obtained such excellent results.

Lieutenant-Colonel Woods has fought his battalion in actions at Cambrai (November, 1917), Montdidier (July, 1918), Arras (September, 1918), and during the operations in question, in each case with conspicuous success.

He has been cited in orders by General Petain for the Montdidier operations.

T. Major CLOUGH, JOHN, M.C. 16th Battn. Awarded D.S.O.

Firstly. For conspicuous gallantry and excellent leadership on September 29, 1918, near Guillemont Farm. When the attack had obviously miscarried and it was found necessary to organise a fresh attack, this officer went forward in face of heavy machine-gun and shell fire to do this. His section commanders had all been wounded, and regardless of danger or personal safety he showed the tanks where to go and gave his orders. All his section *and* tank commanders were either killed or wounded during this operation.

Secondly. For conspicuous gallantry and cool leadership on the night of October 4–5, 1918, when in action at Montbrehain. Owing to the scheme being very hurriedly arranged, and owing to a very long approach march of 14,000 yards, the latter part through heavy shell fire, both H.E. and gas, this officer led his tanks throughout. As it was imperative for at least eight tanks to reach the start line, he had continually to reorganise the sections as one tank or another broke down. By his strenuous efforts and splendid example all through the night under shell fire he got all his tanks up to the start line, and thereby materially assisted in the capture of Montbrehain. Whilst carrying out his duties he was wounded, but remained in action the whole time, and did not leave until all his tanks that were able to had rallied.

T. Capt. (A/Major) CLIVELY, RICHARD CONSTANTINE. 16th Battn. Awarded M.C.

For conspicuous gallantry and excellent leadership on September 29, 1918, near Quennemont Copse. When the situation was obscure, and it was obvious that the attack which should have preceded had miscarried, and the enemy were holding the line in strength only 500 yards in front, this officer held a conference with the infantry company commanders, and under heavy shell and machine-gun fire organised a fresh attack to endeavour to reach the start line. Regardless of danger and personal safety, he distributed his tanks amongst the infantry, and by his coolness set a splendid example to all ranks.

T. 2nd Lieut. WINCER, GEORGE LESLIE. 16th Battn. Awarded M.C.

Whilst in action on September 29, 1918, north of Guillemont Farm, his tank received a direct hit, killing one of his gunners and severely wounding himself. In spite of this he kept his tank in action, reorganising his crew as they got wounded one after the other, until finally, having received three more direct hits, and all but one of his crew wounded, the tank caught fire, and he was forced to evacuate it. His courage and determination and personal example and gallantry were of the highest order.

T. 2nd Lieut. HUGHES, JOHN OWEN. 16th Battn. Awarded M.C.

Whilst in action in front of the infantry north of Guillemont Farm on September 29, 1918, his tank received three direct hits, wounding himself and his entire crew. Despite this he attempted to get his tank going again, but finding that impossible, he manned the 6-pndr. gun himself, though severely wounded, and kept on firing until he received another direct hit, which set the tank on fire, forcing him to evacuate. His gallantry and splendid example of determination were of the highest order.

Capt. REILLEY, JOHN EDWIN. 8th Battn. Awarded M.C.

For conspicuous skill and devotion to duty on September 29, 1918, at Bellicourt and Nauroy.

Owing to the fact that the primary advance did not materialise, the rôle of the second wave had to be modified. During the approach march the infantry were held up owing to thick fog and heavy machine-gun fire in front of Bellicourt. Captain Reilley, realising the situation, immediately organised an attack against the village, which was successful, thus enabling the infantry to advance.

At a later period of the attack the advance of the infantry was a second time held up by strong hostile opposition from Nauroy. Capt. Reilley again, by his prompt action in directing an attack by his remaining tanks, enabled the infantry to establish themselves east of this village.

Capt. Reilley, under heavy machine-gun and shell fire, with utter disregard for his personal safety, directed his tanks to their objectives and throughout the day inspired all ranks by his initiative, coolness, and leadership

Lieut. KENNEDY, JOHN DAVIES. 8th Battn. Awarded M.C.

At Bellicourt, on September 29, 1918, conspicuous skill and devotion to duty.

Lieut. Kennedy, in the capacity of company reconnaissance officer, showed the greatest zeal and keenness. During the advance he reconnoitred the best route for his company of tanks over the

Hindenburg system, going on ahead many times under heavy machine-gun fire, returning and personally directing the column. His performance, under the most unfavourable tank conditions, of guiding the company over unknown and difficult trench systems, in thick fog and under heavy fire, was an outstanding feature of the day, and was worthy of the highest commendation.

Lieut. Kennedy worked with unceasing energy, and under all circumstances has shown a total disregard for his own safety and the keenest devotion to duty.

Lieut. MICKLE, LEONARD. 8th Battn. Awarded M.C.

At Bellicourt, on September 29, 1918, Lieut. Mickle, as section commander, showed great determination and courage.

On entering Bellicourt heavy machine-gun fire was met from the direction of Nauroy, which held up the infantry advance. In spite of thick mist Lieut. Mickle skilfully led two tanks forward and silenced the machine-guns, thereby allowing the infantry to seize their objective. Later, after the mist rose, he again proceeded on foot, leading his tanks against the ridge to the south of Nauroy, whence heavy machine-gun fire was coming. He successfully enabled the infantry to advance, and was indefatigable until wounded.

Lieut. Mickle's example of determination, initiative, and bravery was beyond praise and inspired all ranks under his command.

T. Lieut. (A/Major) MISKIN, MAURICE JAMES, M.C. 1st Battn. Awarded Bar to M.C.

For conspicuous bravery and initiative in leading his company of tanks in action on September 29, at Bellicourt, and again on October 8, at Beaurevoir : in both instances he rallied a number of tanks and directed them to enemy machine-guns which were holding up the infantry, and by his skilful leading and complete disregard of danger he contributed largely to the success attending those operations.

2nd Lieut. KUSENER, ERNEST. 301st American Battn. Awarded M.C.

On September 29, 1918, in the attack on the Hindenburg Line in front of Ronssoy, after his tank had been put out of action and set on fire by a direct hit which killed four of the crew, Lieut. Kusener entered the blazing tank, which was still being fired on, and dragged the remainder of the crew to safety. He then carried two members of this crew, who had been seriously wounded, to a dressing station, the two trips being made over ground swept by heavy machine-gun fire. Throughout the action Lieut. Kusener conspicuously disregarded personal danger.

2nd Lieut. FROST, ELLIOTT PICKMAN. 301st American Battn. Awarded M.C.

On September 29, 1918, in the attack on Bony, Lieut. Frost's tank was ditched and put out of action. Lieut. Frost, while under heavy artillery and machine-gun fire, attempted to dig his tank out but was unsuccessful. Another tank which had been put out of action near by was started up, but did not have enough men to man the guns. Lieut. Frost went into this tank as a machine-gunner. Shortly after his tank was started it received a direct hit, killing several members of the crew. Lieut. Frost remained with his gun and did excellent work until the tank was ditched. He then returned to his own tank and remained with it for two days, until he was finally able to get it out and bring it in to the rallying point.

2nd Lieut. DUNNING, EARL. 301st American Battn. Awarded M.C.

On September 29, 1918, in the attack on the Hindenburg Line near Le Catelet, Lieut. Dunning pushed his tank through to his objective (a point north of Le Catelet) and was the only tank commander who reached his objective on this sector. Shortly after crossing the Escaut River his tank was put out of action and set on fire by three direct hits. Lieut. Dunning successfully evacuated his tank with his crew, and remained concealed in shell-holes in the midst of German machine-gun nests. At dusk he started to conduct his crew back to our lines, and by great perseverance and coolness, although badly burned about the hands and face, succeeded in crawling through the enemy lines and wire with one sergeant, the remainder of the crew being captured. He reported to his unit, bringing valuable information concerning the German positions.

Major SASSE, RALPH IRVINE. A.E.F. (attached 2nd Tank Bde.). Awarded D.S.O.

For gallantry and devotion to duty whilst attached to this brigade since September 23. On September 29 and October 8 he went in a wireless tank, following close up to the battle with the 301st American Tank Battalion, and getting back the most valuable information regarding the progress of the tanks. He carried out several reconnaissances and obtained exceedingly valuable information before the battle. On October 8, at Brancourt, he left his tank to go and reconnoitre the eastern edge of the village, which was the limit of the first objective. He found our infantry hard pressed, reported it by wireless, assisted in repelling a counterattack, and was able to locate two hostile guns (which were shelling the village) to our gunners, who successfully silenced them. He has displayed the most remarkable energy and initiative.

IMMEDIATE AWARDS—OFFICERS

T. Lieut. (A/Capt.) GLANVILLE, IVAN CECIL ABBOTT, M.C. 8th Battn. Awarded Bar to M.C.

During the operations at Bellicourt and Nauroy on September 29, 1918, this officer displayed great gallantry and devotion to duty.

He was in charge of four tanks attached to the brigade, and on pushing through Bellicourt to the eastern side came under direct heavy shell and machine-gun fire. Notwithstanding this, he continued to move about in the open and directed the tanks under direct enemy observation. Shortly afterwards three of the tanks received direct hits and were put out of action. Capt. Glanville at this stage organised from the survivors of the four crews a party, and pushed on the only remaining tank through the enemy, held the village of Nauroy, and, although wounded, carried on until the advance was complete and the tank no longer required.

By his keenness to assist the infantry at every stage he materially assisted in the success of the whole operations, and by his skilful leadership and conspicuous bravery set a very high example to all.

T. 2nd Lieut. HOLLOWAY, JOHN ARTHUR HAMILTON. 6th Battn. Awarded M.C.

On September 30, 1918, this officer commanded the leading tank that advanced to the attack of Joncourt.

He engaged numerous enemy machine-guns at close range. When his tank was hit by a shell and set on fire he withdrew the crew and took cover near the tank. The enemy, seeing no movement, came forward to surround the tank. 2nd Lieut. Holloway drew his revolver and fired point-blank at them ; he continued firing until severely hit in three places, when he fell in a shell-hole. The enemy then retired with one of the crew as prisoner, leaving 2nd Lieut. Holloway as dead. He was carried into our lines at dusk. The commanding officer of the 15th Lancashire Fusiliers (96th Brigade) said it was a very gallant action, and although regretting the loss of the tank, considered that the fight put up tremendously inspired the infantry.

Lieut. WADESON, ROY AYLMER. 7th Battn. Awarded M.C.

For conspicuous gallantry and devotion to duty.

On September 30, 1918, near Sancourt, he met one of his tank commanders, who informed him that his tank was ditched 500 yards in front of the infantry. He went to try and release them, as there were machine-guns firing from all directions and the men could not get out. Two men were known to be already wounded. He reached the tank (crawling) and found no men inside, but outside found Sergt. Duddridge and Pte. Hilton killed. Lieut. Wadeson had to pass through a machine-gun and gas barrage, being gassed by a shell which burst in his face. This did not deter him from going to the rescue of the crew.

T. 2nd Lieut. BOULT, PERCY. 9th Battn. Awarded M.C.

During the operations near Joncourt on October 1, 1918, when his tank was stopped and under heavy shell fire, 2nd Lieut. Boult put out a smoke bomb to cover the tank. The bomb, however, stuck, and burst partly inside the tank. Thinking that the tank was on fire, 2nd Lieut. Boult ordered his crew to evacuate it. This he was able to do, but not seeing his crew, who were in a shell-hole close by, he drove on into the fight. He was stopped by the infantry, who asked for his support. He explained he was alone and asked for a volunteer crew. An officer and two privates of the 2nd Manchester Regt. volunteered to go with him ; he then drove the tank on into action. As the infantry did not understand the Hotchkiss gun, he continually had to leave the driver's seat and help to load and explain it. During the fight he noticed a signal from another tank (I. 29) which had been hit and was under heavy fire, so drove his tank alongside and took off three gunners. As the infantry had retired, he drove back to their line, when the three infantry volunteers rejoined their unit.

I cannot speak too highly of this officer's resourcefulness and courage.

T. 2nd Lieut. CLEGG, CARLOS. 9th Battn. Awarded M.C.

During the operations near Joncourt on October 1, 2nd Lieut. Clegg fought his tank with great skill, doing great execution amongst the enemy. After his tank had received a direct hit, breaking the track, he evacuated the tank and sent his crew back, and although the tank was in front of our advanced infantry and under heavy shell fire and machine-gun fire he himself remained out in the vicinity of the tank for thirty-six hours. 2nd Lieut. Clegg showed great devotion to duty under very trying circumstances and set a fine example to the remainder of his company.

T. Lieut. (A/Major) PADFIELD, LEONARD. 9th Battn. Awarded M.C.

During the operations near Joncourt on October 1 Major Padfield commanded a composite company of tanks with great skill.

Although under heavy artillery and intense machine-gun fire, he led the tanks on foot and directed them to their objectives.

It was in a great measure owing to his utter disregard of his own personal safety in thus leading them that all his tanks were enabled to reach and secure their objectives.

T. 2nd Lieut. NEEDHAM, ROBERT. 16th Battn. Awarded M.C.

For gallant conduct and devotion to duty on October 1, in action at the sugar factory and Estrees. Just after starting he found that his entire crew had collapsed from fainting and sickness.

He lifted his driver from his seat, and drove the tank himself. At the same time he manned the front gun to useful purpose, alternating firing, loading, and driving. He took the infantry not only on to their objective, but also beyond, assisting to capture Estrees, and finally drove his tank back to the rallying point. During the whole of this period he was totally unassisted by any one member of his crew. A very severe test of endurance, and a splendid example of determination.

' *A very fine performance.*'—(Sgd.) H. J. ELLES, M.-G.

T. Lieut. (A/Capt.) WALTERS, JAMES BENTLEY. 12th Battn. Awarded M.C.

For most conspicuous gallantry and devotion to duty during operations at Seranvillers on October 1, 1918.

Capt. Walters rendered very great services to 2nd Battalion Suffolk Regiment by his fearless conduct. But for the gallantry and initiative displayed by him, our line on the final objective would have been driven back, as there was no anti-tank defence.

Seeing an enemy tank advancing, Capt. Walters engaged it with his own tank and put it out of action. He also did very good work in mopping up the village.

Lieut. (A/Capt.) BAKER, WILFRED ERNEST, M.C. 13th Battn. Awarded Bar to M.C.

For conspicuous gallantry and devotion to duty near Estrees on October 3, 1918.

Captain Baker was acting as a section commander during an attack when some machine-gun fire opened from the rear on the tanks and infantry from hidden positions presumed to be held by us. This officer went forward over heavily swept ground in the open at great personal risk and directed one of the tanks in his section to turn back to deal with the enemy machine-guns. This was successfully accomplished and the infantry enabled to proceed. The gallant conduct and powers of leadership exhibited by Captain Baker throughout a difficult operation were of the utmost value.

2nd Lieut. SMITH, ALBERT ERNEST. 13th Battn. Awarded M.C.

For conspicuous gallantry and devotion to duty as a tank commander near Wiancourt on October 3, 1918.

When the infantry were held up by machine-gun fire from a village this officer brought his tank forward to silence the enemy. The enemy opened fire on his tank with anti-tank rifles, killing two of the crew and wounding a third. In spite of this 2nd Lieut. Smith pushed forward, and continued to fire on the enemy until all opposition ceased and the infantry were established in the village.

Throughout the operation this officer set a most gallant and inspiring example to his crew.

2nd Lieut. MARTIN, REGINALD THOMAS. 13th Battn. Awarded M.C.

For conspicuous gallantry and devotion to duty as a tank commander near Estrees on October 3, 1918.

This officer fought his tank in action, disposing of a large number of machine-gun nests. Later, when his crew had all become unconscious from petrol fumes, he called for, and obtained, volunteers from the infantry to man the tank. With this volunteer crew he again attacked, and driving the tank himself disposed of further enemy opposition in this sector.

Throughout the action 2nd Lieut. Martin showed great gallantry and resource and contributed materially to the success of the operation.

T. 2nd Lieut. HUTCHINSON, WILLIAM SWANN, D.C.M. 8th Battn. Awarded M.C.

For conspicuous devotion to duty and gallantry in the action of October 3, 1918, against the Beaurevoir Line.

2nd Lieut. Hutchinson with great determination brought his tank into action after experiencing severe engine trouble on the approach march. His engine again became disabled through lack of oil at the objective, and 2nd. Lieut. Hutchinson, ascertaining the position, skilfully disposed his machine-guns as posts, forming a defensive flank to the infantry until relieved six hours later. His driver meanwhile had been working on the engine and 2nd Lieut. Hutchinson personally returned under heavy machine-gun fire to a derelict tank to obtain the necessary oil, which enabled him successfully to withdraw his tank under very heavy shell fire on the following morning.

Throughout the action 2nd Lieut. Hutchinson showed the greatest gallantry and determination, and by his initiative and resource saved the infantry many casualties. He brought back his tank under the most adverse circumstances, saving it from certain destruction.

2nd Lieut. FINNSBERG, GEORGE MONTE. 3rd Battn. Awarded M.C.

For conspicuous gallantry and devotion to duty near Estrees during the attack on the Masnières-Beaurevoir line on October 3, 1918. When the infantry were held up by two German strong points this officer showed remarkable skill, initiative, and endurance. Although he was himself wounded in five places, he continued to drive his whippet tank, after his gunner and driver had become casualties, in the van of the attack on those strong points.

At about fifty yards range enemy machine-guns were brought to play on the front of the cab, which necessitated the closing of the flap ; but he continued to manœuvre his car, and in doing so became ditched. He then evacuated his car, and during the process was again wounded and taken prisoner. After three hours in enemy hands he got back to our lines, having been wounded altogether in seventeen places.

It was largely due to this officer's disregard for his own personal safety that his crew were got back and the enemy forced to evacuate the strong points, after which the attack proceeded according to plan.

T. 2nd Lieut. BOULTER, STANLEY. 4th Battn. Awarded M.C.

This officer displayed great courage in action at Beaurevoir on October 5, 1918. In the face of heavy machine-gun fire he proceeded with his tank into the village and silenced several hostile machine-guns. He then returned to the infantry, who had been held up, and led them on. On two occasions before reaching the village the infantry displayed a tendency to stop, and each time this officer got out of his tank and personally urged them forward at great personal risk.

Capt. HAMILTON, ARTHUR PLUMTRE FAUNCE. 16th Battn. Awarded M.C.

For most gallant conduct on the night (October 4–5) prior to the action at Montbrehain. This officer reconnoitred and laid the tape for the tanks from their start line up to near the infantry jumping-off tape, a distance of 1000 yards, under very heavy artillery fire, both H.E. and gas. In addition to other obstacles, the tape had to be laid over four belts of barbed wire. Having completed his task, which took until 6 A.M., he then personally conducted the tanks on foot, pointing out to each one its route and objective. All this was done under heavy artillery and machine-gun fire with a total disregard of danger or personal safety. By his gallant conduct he was undoubtedly responsible for getting the tanks into action, and thus largely making the battle a success. He was accompanied throughout by Captain A. V. Rhodes.

T. Capt. RHODES, ALFRED VIOTTO. 16th Battn. Awarded M.C.

For most gallant conduct on the night of October 4–5, when in command of a section of tanks at the action at Montbrehain. This officer reconnoitred and laid the tape for the tanks from their start line up to near the infantry jumping-off tape, a distance of 1000 yards, under very heavy artillery fire, both H.E. and gas. In addition to other obstacles, the tape had to be laid over four belts of barbed wire. Having completed his task, which took until 6 A.M., he then personally conducted the tanks on foot, pointing out to each one its-route and objective. All this was done under heavy artillery and machine-gun fire with a total disregard of danger or personal safety. By his gallant conduct he was undoubtedly responsible for getting the tanks into action, and thus largely making the battle a success. He was accompanied throughout by Captain A. P. F. Hamilton.

Lieut. (A/Capt.) KELSON, GERALD MILES. 11th Battn. Awarded M.C.

For gallantry, devotion to duty, and good leadership. This officer commanded his company during the action of October 8, at Villers-Outreaux, with great ability. All his tanks were in the enemy line far in front of the infantry, and Captain Kelson went forward alone with total disregard for his personal safety under heavy fire to try and get going again a tank that had been knocked out.

Lieut. MINCHIN, LEONARD EDWARD. 3rd Battn. Awarded M.C.

For conspicuous gallantry and devotion to duty in action on October 8, 1918, at Serain. He showed great courage and resolution when fighting his whippet tank. Upon reaching his objective, the infantry having failed to follow, he repeatedly returned to help them forward. He on several occasions got out of his tank under heavy fire to go and confer with infantry commanders. When his tank had been knocked out and his crew killed he joined the infantry and assisted them in consolidating a position under heavy fire.

Lieut. (A/Capt.) FERRARIO, JOHN ERNEST, M.C. 16th Battn. Awarded Bar to M.C.

For conspicuous gallantry and devotion to duty at Mortho Wood, Villers-Outreaux, on October 8, 1918, when he assisted his company reconnaissance officer in successfully laying tape under heavy shell fire through German posts to German main line. Later he tried to get into a burning tank to rescue some of the crew ; the tank was being heavily shelled. Again, later, he went forward under heavy shell and machine-gun fire to make sure that the last tank of his section had got into action. During the whole action he displayed total disregard to his personal safety.

Lieut. LEDGER, RICHARD HILDRETH. 11th Battn. Awarded M.C.

For most conspicuous gallantry and devotion to duty at Mortho Wood, Villers-Outreaux, on October 8, 1918. As company reconnaissance officer, he went forward in front of the tanks of his company under very heavy shell fire, putting down tape—actually through German posts to the main German line. This was done at night and during an infantry action, but by this officer's skill and energy he enabled the tanks to follow his tape and to get into position without the enemy being aware.

T. 2nd Lieut. WILSON, ARCHIBALD. 1st Battn.   Awarded M.C.

For conspicuous bravery and devotion to duty on October 8, when in command of a tank in the attack in front of Beaurevoir. This officer was selected for the special mission of dealing with Les Folies beyond the Red Line : before reaching it he rendered great assistance to the infantry in assisting to clear Hamage Farm and the trench east of it : from there he went at the request of the South African Infantry to Petite Folie Farm and safely conducted them to it, subsequently engaging and putting out of action two enemy field guns.

While temporarily ditched near Les Folies, his tank was attacked by a party of about fifteen Germans with bombs ; this attack he beat off, killing or wounding most of the enemy.

His coolness and example undoubtedly contributed largely to the success of the operation.

T. 2nd Lieut. BROMLEY, FREDERICK FARRAR, M.C.   6th Battn.
Awarded Bar to M.C.

For his excellent services in front of Premont on October 8, 1918.

As he was leading his section of tanks towards the village he found the infantry were held up by enemy field guns. Showing great initiative, he manœuvred his tanks in such a manner that the batteries were encircled, and coming in at the rear of them he did excellent work, killing the gunners. It was largely owing to this that the guns were captured.

A little later he came upon another battery, from which the gunners fled on the approach of the tanks. He then went forward, and made certain that the village was cleared of the enemy, and then remained on the eastern side in case of counter-attacks.

2nd Lieut. CLARKE, FRANK. 12th Battn.   Awarded M.C.

For conspicuous gallantry and devotion to duty in the operations on October 8, 1918, east of the La Targette-Esnes road.

Immediately after the assault and capture of the objective of the 2nd Battalion, New Zealand Rifle Brigade, at about 07.30, the enemy delivered a counter-attack with two tanks, assisted by two 77mm. field guns. The position was serious, as the tanks advanced to within 150 yards of our men, who had not had time to consolidate. This officer moved his tank into position behind the road, and, with the assistance of another tank, bombarded the two enemy tanks at a distance of about 300 yards, completely disabling the latter.

The enemy crews, while attempting to escape, were shot down by our Lewis gunners.

This splendid action was full of daring and saved a difficult situation.

2nd Lieut. SHERRATT, HAROLD HOWE. 12th Battn. Awarded M.C.

For conspicuous gallantry and devotion to duty in the operations on October 8, 1918, east of the La Targette-Esnes road.

Immediately after the assault and capture of the objective of the 2nd Battalion, New Zealand Rifle Brigade, at about 07.30 the enemy delivered a counter-attack with two tanks, assisted by two 77-mm. field guns. The position was serious, as the tanks advanced to within 150 yards of our men, who had not had time to consolidate. This officer moved his tank into position behind the road, and, with the assistance of another tank, bombarded the two enemy tanks at a distance of about 300 yards, completely disabling the latter. The enemy crews, while attempting to escape, were shot down by our Lewis gunners.

This splendid action was full of daring and saved a difficult situation.

T. Major CAMPBELL, RONALD. 12th Battn. Awarded D.S.O.

During the operations against Niergnies, on October 8, 1918, Major Campbell was in command of a company of tanks. Previous to the operations he personally reconnoitred the ground, and on the evening of October 7 he led his tanks to their start points under an intense enemy barrage. His conduct was at all times magnificent, and his coolness under fire a fine example to all ranks. I cannot speak too highly of the able manner in which he led his company. The G.O.C. 63rd (R.N.) Division has placed on record his appreciation of the gallant manner in which the tanks of Major Campbell's company assisted the infantry, and the B.-G.C. 188th Infantry Brigade reports that ' the tanks were invaluable, and all ranks are enthusiastic regarding the splendid way in which they carried out their tasks.'

2nd Lieut. (A/Capt.) BROWN, HAROLD FREDERICK. 11th Battn. Awarded M.C.

On October 8, at Villers-Outreaux, this officer, who was acting as company engineer at the time, followed up his company's tanks on foot. When tank K. 42 stopped, he made his way through heavy machine-gun fire which was directed at the tank and playing on it and around. After twenty minutes' work he succeeded in starting the tank, when it was enabled to catch up its company. Throughout the entire action, though his specific duty is to advise his company commander on matters technical, he was here, there and everywhere about the battlefield, personally assisting stopped tanks and encouraging the crews. He was untiring in his endeavours both before, during, and after the action. It was entirely owing to his almost superhuman efforts that the tanks of the composite company got into action and remained in action and rallied. Again he acted with similar courage and devotion to duty in the operation of October 10 at Neuvilly, October 20 at the crossing of the Selle River, October 25 at Ovillers. He seemed tireless in his work, which was extremely heavy between the various actions, personally working and directing the refitting of tanks that had been in action and trekking since August 11. From October 26 to November 6 he was continually working on derelict tanks and succeeded in bringing back to Marcoing twelve Mark V* and Mark IV tanks as well as four supply tanks. His gallantry on all occasions, his untiring energy, cheerfulness, and devotion to duty inspired all crews to their utmost limits. It is not overstating the facts to say that it was due to his personal courage, ability, and energy that the company tanks were able to co-operate so successfully with the infantry in these repeated actions. The relentless pressure was kept up on the retreating enemy.

Capt. BURNETT, EDWARD PERCIVAL SEVIER. 11th Battn. Awarded M.C.

October 8, Villers-Outreaux. This section commander effected liaison with the infantry when they seemed hesitating to follow the ,tanks. By his personal direction on that occasion the formidable series of trenches and defences were captured at small cost to the infantry. His powers of courage, leadership, and cheerfulness inspired all the crews of his section, and were the means of bringing the infantry on to their correct objectives at a minimum of cost. He was continually passing from tanks to infantry and infantry to tanks, often under intense machine-gun and shell fire, with the utmost unconcern. He performed his duties in the same fearless and untiring, cheerful manner in the actions of October 21 at Selle River and October 23 near Forest, and by his example inspired his section, who were much exhausted by the prolonged fighting and continual repairs of the much worn tanks.

Lieut. RIDLINGTON, ALFRED CHARLES. 17th Battn. Awarded M.C.

On the Le Cateau-Maretz road on October 9, 1918, this officer displayed great gallantry, skill, and devotion to duty, when in charge of a section of armoured cars. He first attacked, at the request of an infantry platoon, a machine-gun post of ten machine-guns which was holding up our advance, and in conjunction with the infantry successfully cleared it and captured the guns. In proceeding forward with two cars a bridge was blown up behind him by the enemy, separating him from the second car and from our troops. In spite of this, with one car he went forward through the villages of Maurois and Honnechy, which were both strongly held by the enemy, of whom he killed five in one spot in the latter village. By prompt action he prevented the railway bridge from being blow up by the enemy, and then returned by a fresh route to the point where his second car had been left, and brought it safely back to our lines.

T. Lieut. (A/Capt.) CHICK, HERBERT ROBERT. 16th Battn. Awarded M.C.

For gallantry and devotion to duty on October 17, 1918, at Vaux-Andigny. This officer was in command of a section of tanks, and owing to the fog and other reasons which made the situation obscure, found himself in action earlier than expected. He personally led his tanks into action under heavy shell and machine-gun fire, and at great personal risk, and regardless of danger, kept them on their proper course and indicated to each one what points to attack. He at the same time took charge of the infantry in his particular area of operations, showing them where to go and generally assisted them in a marked degree. His fine conduct and example, without regard of personal safety, are well worthy of recognition.

Lieut. JERRAM, ROY MARTIN. 16th Battn. Awarded M.C.

For gallantry and devotion to duty on October 17, 1918, at Vaux-Andigny. This officer drove his tank with marked skill during the first phase of the attack, traversing practically the whole of the first objective, inflicting many casualties on the enemy.

He again went into action the same day, attacking the village of Vallée Mulatre unsupported, and continued in action until knocked out by an enemy battery. He evacuated his wounded and salved the equipment from his tank under heavy fire, his tank being hit thrice more during this period. His courage, coolness, and fine example are well worthy of recognition.

T. 2nd Lieut. LAIDLAW, WILLIAM. 16th Battn. Awarded M.C.

For gallantry and devotion to duty on October 17, 1918, at Vaux-Andigny. This officer was in command of a tank and went into action with the infantry at 5.20 A.M. Having assisted them to their objective, he then went into action again for the second phase, taking them to their furthest point of advance. During this, though his crew was ' gassed,' and he himself was wounded, he nevertheless carried on, driving the tank himself, and finally brought it out of action to the rallying point. His courage, skill, and fine example are well worthy of recognition.

IMMEDIATE AWARDS—OFFICERS

T. 2nd Lieut. NEEDHAM, ROBERT, M.C. 16th Battn. Awarded Bar to M.C.

For gallantry and devotion to duty on October 17, 1918, at Vaux-Andigny. This officer was in command of a tank. By his skilful handling and intrepid daring he attacked various enemy strong points, including a battery of artillery ; he then pushed through 3000 yards beyond our furthest infantry and attacked Wassigny. He inflicted heavy casualties on the enemy and caused great demoralisation on his sector of the front. He returned and visited en route the same localities and found our infantry in possession, finally rallying late in the evening. He was in action continuously without rest for twelve hours. His gallant conduct is well worthy of reward.

Note.—This officer had already been recommended for the Military Cross for the operations on October 1.

T. Lieut. THORNBACK, CHARLES RODNEY. 1st Battn. Awarded M.C.

This officer carried out a highly important and difficult reconnaissance of the River Selle, in close proximity to the enemy, prior to the attack with the 50th Division on October 17, and on the morning of the attack at dawn, in thick mist and under heavy shell fire, after his company commander had been killed, he led his company's tanks across the river, and then, finding another company of tanks lost in the mist, he guided them in turn. It was largely due to this officer's courage and initiative at a critical time that the passage of the river was successfully effected by every tank.

T. 2nd Lieut. HEYWOOD, TOM AUBREY. 1st Battn. Awarded M.C.

This officer has worked indefatigably in getting tanks into fighting fitness for all the recent actions in which they have been engaged, and particularly on October 17, south of Le Cateau, this officer distinguished himself by going under heavy fire to meet tanks rallying. Seeing most of the crew of a tank killed or wounded by a shell, he at once took charge and drove the tank back across the River Selle to the rallying point.

T. Capt. LOWE, ARTHUR STANLEY. 16th Battn. Awarded M.C.

For gallantry and devotion to duty on October 17, 1918, at Vaux-Andigny, when in command of a section of tanks.

He not only accompanied his tanks into action, directing them without regard for his own safety, but also personally assisted the infantry in capturing an enemy post.

His section did fine work during the day and very materially assisted the infantry, which was in the main due to his courageous example and excellent leadership.

T. 2nd Lieut. (A/Capt.) GARROD, EDWARD SAMUEL, M.C., D.C.M. 10th Battn. Awarded D.S.O.

For conspicuous gallantry and devotion to duty in action near Bousies on October 23 and 24, 1918. Captain Garrod was in charge of a section of four tanks. He personally led his tanks, on foot, into the village of Bousies and directed their fire on various strong points and machine-gun nests in houses. Later in the day he went forward and personally reconnoitred strong points that were holding up the infantry advance, returning and directing his tanks against them and giving valuable information to the infantry who were attacking. On October 24, north-east of Bousies, Captain Garrod again displayed the utmost gallantry and initiative, running from tank to tank and directing their fire. He and his tanks were in action continuously from 06.00 hours to 18.00 hours. Throughout the two days' operations Capt. Garrod had no rest and was constantly exposed to very heavy machine-gun, rifle, and shell fire. His utter contempt for his own personal safety, power of command, and initiative were an example to all ranks, and materially assisted the operations being carried through to a successful issue.

T. 2nd Lieut. PULLEY, LEONARD JOHN. 10th Battn. Awarded M.C.

For conspicuous gallantry and devotion to duty on October 23, 1918, in the neighbourhood of Forest and Bousies. Owing to the early hour of the attack, it was difficult to locate the position of the enemy in the darkness. He immediately got out of the tank and directed it on foot, pointing out targets to his gunners, although exposed to heavy shell and machine-gun fire. Later, he found the remains of a company of infantry, who were digging in under heavy machine-gun fire short of their objective. He cleared the machine-guns and personally led the company to their final objective. Throughout the action this officer showed great coolness and gallantry and his conduct was an example to all ranks.

T. 2nd Lieut. HUDDLESTON, LEONARD DAVID. 10th Battn. Awarded M.C.

For conspicuous gallantry and devotion to duty on October 23, 1918. This officer rendered great service to the infantry in the initial stages of the attack in the neighbourhood of Pommereuil, overcoming considerable enemy resistance and taking the infantry with whom he was working to their final objective. He then rallied his tank, and shortly afterwards went into action again to break up an enemy counter-attack which had developed from the east of Eveque Wood. Although he and his crew were exhausted, he did excellent work in destroying enemy machine-gun nests and conducted the infantry, who had been held up, to the third objective, where his tank received three direct hits. Lieut. Huddleston was severely wounded in the right shoulder and neck; he nevertheless succeeded in getting his crew out of the burning tank and conducted them back to the rallying point, where he furnished a clear and concise account of the action and was able to give valuable information although in great pain.

T. Lieut. (A/Capt.) SNEWING, RICHARD CHARLES. 10th Battn. Awarded M.C.

For conspicuous gallantry and devotion to duty in Basuel on October 23, 1918. He led his tanks up to their starting-point under very heavy shell fire, later leading them into action and starting them on their various routes. His tanks having got ahead of the infantry, who were held up, Captain Snewing walked out into ' No Man's Land ' under heavy machine-gun and shell fire, to ascertain their whereabouts. Throughout the action he showed the greatest courage and determination and set a fine example to all ranks.

T. Lieut. GRAY, JAMES ROY. 10th Battn. Awarded M.C.

For conspicuous bravery and devotion to duty on the morning of October 24, 1918, north-east of Bousies. This officer went into action with his tank on the morning in question, and rendered valuable assistance to the infantry by locating and knocking-out machine-gun posts, thus enabling them to advance without casualties. Later, he ran into a nest of machine-guns ; his tank was riddled with armour-piercing bullets, wounding four of his gunners and his driver. Being short-handed, Lieut. Gray took charge of the tank himself and sat in the driver's seat in spite of the fact that bullets were coming through. Although his guns were out of action, he succeeded in putting out the nest of machine-guns by running over them and dispersing their crews. He brought his tank back to the rallying point and, although himself wounded, immediately volunteered to go into action again with a fresh crew. This officer had also been in action the previous day in the neighbourhood of Bousies, and had rendered considerable service.

THE LAST PHASE, NOVEMBER 1918

T. Capt. EDMOND, CECIL HARLOW. 9th Battn. Awarded M.C.

For conspicuous gallantry during the attack on Mormal Forest on November 1, 1918.

I cannot speak too highly of this officer's determination and courage. One tank of his section had its sponson burst in near the front line. He improvised an iron plate and sent it into action.

Another tank had its crew gassed, and he immediately got together a crew of infantry and led them into action. Owing to his splendid example and total disregard for his personal safety, he brought his section into action under a very heavy barrage and at a critical time.

T. Lieut. (A/Capt.) LAMBERT, FREDERICK JOHN. 18th Battn. Awarded M.C.

For conspicuous gallantry and devotion to duty on November 2–4, 1918, during two attacks just west of Landrecies. This officer was in charge of a section of tanks which had been ordered to co-operate with the infantry in an attack on November 2, to clear the high ground in front of Landrecies prior to the main big attack of the Fourth Army on November 4. Capt. Lambert was untiring in his efforts and showed great initiative in making all the preliminary arrangements with the infantry. He then led his tanks up to the starting-point, gave all the tank commanders very concise instructions, and saw them well started on their way after zero. The operation was a success, but one tank was ditched in Happegarbes, and later in the day, when the infantry were forced to retire owing to a very strong counter-attack by the enemy, this tank was in No Man's Land. Notwithstanding this fact, Capt. Lambert, showing great coolness and presence of mind, went forward alone to see in what state the tank was and what prospects there were of getting it out and into running order quickly. He carried out this reconnaissance under sniping and machine-gun fire, but showed utter contempt of the risk he was running. When he returned he was able not only to give concise information about the tank, which enabled us to make arrangements to get it out quickly and into action again after the next infantry advance on November 4, but also gave valuable and useful information of the positions held by the enemy.

He was on the go the whole of the day and night of November 3, keeping in touch with the infantry arrangements for the attack on November 4, and then very successfully led his tanks again into action on the morning of November 4, and remained with them until they had completed their task and the infantry were definitely established on their final objective.

I consider Capt. Lambert's wonderful endurance, coolness, and contempt for danger during the operations from November 2 to 4 were a great incentive to all ranks.

T. 2nd Lieut. STEWART, WILLIAM. 10th Battn. Awarded M.C.

For conspicuous gallantry and devotion to duty west of Landrecies on November 2–4, 1918. This officer was attached to a composite section moving off for an attack on Happegarbes on the morning of November 2. During the approach march one tank broke down. After an hour's hard work 2nd Lieut. Stewart remedied the trouble, and himself guided the tank to the starting-

226

point. On attempting to restart the engine—a few minutes before zero—another fault was detected, and although by this time the enemy barrage had come down all round the tank, this officer again remedied the fault and guided the tank, under heavy fire, to our front line, where he launched it into battle. It was solely due to this officer's coolness and strenuous personal efforts that this tank was enabled to take part in the battle.

Again, on the morning of November 4, 2nd Lieut. Stewart did extraordinarily good work in personally escorting his tanks into action under severe conditions and enemy shell fire.

I consider 2nd Lieut. Stewart's work on both these occasions was a great incentive to all ranks, and very materially influenced the crews of the tanks to putting their best endeavours into the attacks they had to carry out.

T. Lieut. (A/Capt.) NORTH, CYRIL. 6th Battn. Awarded M.C.

During the operations of November 4 to 8, 1918, near Bavai, he showed the greatest initiative and daring as reconnaissance officer to a company of whippet tanks.

He twice worked his way forward under heavy fire beyond our front line to ascertain the nature of the crossings of two rivers.

This enabled the tanks to be moved forward quickly and take advantage of the situation.

T. Capt. (A/Major) COOPER, RICHARD FRANCIS, M.C. 14th Battn. Awarded Bar to M.C.

For conspicuous gallantry and devotion to duty.

To this officer is due almost entirely the successful operation of his tanks in action near Le Quesnoy on November 4.

Rushed into operations with a twenty-five mile approach march and with little or no time for reconnaissance and preparation, it was absolutely due to his *savoir-faire*, quick judgment, command and intense energy that his tanks all left their final lying-up place in complete fighting order and the crews with a full knowledge of their tasks.

During action, he closely followed with his tanks to the final objective, being under very heavy shell fire in the approach march as well as in the earlier part of the attack. By his energy, knowledge, and initiative he was able to get a tank mobile which had broken down, and personally directed the same tank to dispose of a hostile machine-gun which had been holding up the infantry for three hours, and so enabling the latter to advance.

Later on, this tank did most invaluable work in clearing Jolimetz, all of which was due to Major Cooper's exceptional initiative and energy.

He set a magnificent example throughout of the highest soldierly qualifications.

T. Lieut. (A/Capt.) CLEGG, CARLOS, M.C. Awarded Bar to M.C.

During the action near Mormal Forest on November 4, 1918, Capt. Clegg advanced under very heavy machine-gun fire behind his section of tanks and sent back most valuable information. Throughout the action he behaved with the utmost gallantry and was congratulated by the G.O.C. 150th Brigade. He displayed an utter disregard of personal danger and volunteered, when all his tank commanders were exhausted, to take a tank into action if required.

T. 2nd Lieut. BOULT, PERCY, M.C. 9th Battn. Awarded Bar to M.C.

During the action near Mormal Forest on November 4, 1918, 2nd Lieut. Boult's tank broke a track near the front line before zero.

By determination and energy he got it into action up to time. He directed his tank on foot during the greater part of the action, showing the greatest gallantry and disregard of danger, and in a thick fog thus kept direction to an important objective. He fought his tank with four guns out of action later in the day and with two of his crew wounded, and undoubtedly by his devotion to duty saved the infantry many casualties.

T. 2nd Lieut. MURPHY, WILLIAM SYLVESTER. 9th Battn. Awarded M.C.

During the action near Mormal Forest on November 4, 1918, 2nd Lieut. W. S. Murphy set a splendid example to all ranks by his determination and skill. He and all his crew were almost overcome by gas poisoning, yet by his undaunted courage he led the attack through most difficult country, under very heavy machine-gun fire, and destroyed several machine-gun nests that would have held up the infantry. By disregard for his own personal safety he kept the closest liaison with his infantry and overcame all obstacles for them.

T. 2nd Lieut. CROWTHER, PERCY. 9th Battn. Awarded M.C.

During the action near Mormal Forest on November 4, 1918, under heavy shell fire, in the night, 2nd Lieut. Crowther taped a route for tanks that could not be done until Y/Z night. He then led them up to their jumping-off positions, although the machine-gun fire was so severe that all crews were inside their tanks, and by his devotion to duty and determination he ensured that all his tanks were up to time, without which the progress of the operation in question would have been impeded.

IMMEDIATE AWARDS—OFFICERS

T. 2nd Lieut. WALTERS, SYDNEY EVELYN. 9th Battn. Awarded M.C.

During the action near Mormal Forest on November 4, 1918, 2nd Lieut. Walters reconnoitred and taped routes through most difficult country prior to the attack of November 4, 1918, under fire. On the morning of November 4, 1918, he led his tanks with great coolness and judgment through heavy shelling, both H.E. and gas, and machine-gun fire, right up to their jumping-off place; and ensured their starting at zero in complete touch with their infantry. Throughout a very arduous period he displayed a complete disregard of personal danger and devotion to duty.

T. Lieut. SEMPLE, JAMES. 9th Battn. Awarded M.C.

During the action near Mormal Forest on November 4, 1918, Lieut. Semple, as company engineer, displayed great devotion to duty and utter disregard of his own personal safety, repairing tanks under heavy shell fire during the action.

Previous to the action he worked day and night for a week, and it was largely due to his efforts that several tanks of ' A ' Company reached their starting-point at scheduled time.

T. 2nd Lieut. GRAVELLE, HENRY LUTHER. 9th Battn. Awarded M.C.

During the action near Mormal Forest on November 4, 1918, although suffering from the effects of gas and only one of his crew left, 2nd Lieut. Gravelle brought his tank into action. Under a heavy barrage he taught a crew of infantrymen, whom he collected, to man the guns, and went forward and caught up his infantry. He beat down all opposition, and by his determination and skill placed the infantry on their objective.

T. Lieut. WOOLF, BERNARD MONTAGUE. 9th Battn. Awarded M.C.

During the action near Mormal Forest on November 4, 1918, Lieut. Woolf showed great skill and judgment in reconnoitring a most difficult approach march. Under a very heavy enemy barrage he led the tanks of his company forward on foot, showing a complete disregard for personal safety. He then followed up the tanks in action, collecting and sending back most valuable information, and set a splendid example throughout of devotion to duty.

T. Lieut. LOCKWOOD, CROSBY MARSTON. 14th Battn. Awarded M.C.

For conspicuous gallantry on November 4, near Preux.

This officer, as a section commander, after starting his tanks, seeing that the mist was coming down, very fearlessly personally led them through a very heavy enemy barrage, until he was certain that they would not miss their direction. He then advanced with the infantry front line, and finding serious opposition in Hecq, he proceeded, regardless of heavy machine-gun fire, until he found a tank, which he led to the spot, and which, under his supervision, cleared up the situation. Later on, finding one of his tanks with the crew gassed, he borrowed a driver from another tank, and getting four German prisoners to crank up the engine, endeavoured to get into action. He then, on foot, proceeded on to the farthest tank objective with the Royal West Kents, keeping a close liaison between the tanks and infantry. In general, throughout the day, in spite of intense machine-gun fire and heavy shelling, he continually directed his tanks to enemy strong points. His personal leadership and the coolness he displayed contributed materially to the success of the day's operations.

T. 2nd Lieut. CHITTENDEN, PHILLIP STEPHEN. 14th Battn. Awarded M.C.

For very conspicuous gallantry and devotion to duty near Preux on November 4.

His tank received a direct hit and became immobile. He went forward with all his guns and the remainder of his crew to fight with the infantry. He assisted 2nd Lieut. Atley (7th Royal West Kents) to capture a formidable machine-gun position which was still holding out. One of his guns having been disabled, he replaced it with one of the captured enemy machine-guns, and continued at the head of the infantry, later personally capturing eight prisoners in a house. Held up by several enemy strong points he got into touch with 2nd Lieut. R. U. Robinson's tank, with the assistance of which these strong points and twenty-five prisoners were taken. Having left the Royal West Kents on their objective, he moved forward, with his crew now reduced to two; venturing into positions still held by the enemy, he continued fighting in the forefront of the advance entirely without support. He only withdrew when the last of his guns had been put out of action by enemy fire. His initiative, courage, fighting spirit, and cool grasp of situations reflect the utmost credit on this young officer.

T. 2nd Lieut. ROBINSON, RICHARD UNWIN. 14th Battn. Awarded M.C.

For conspicuous gallantry and devotion to duty near Preux on November 4.

To this officer I consider a very material part of the success attained by the Royal West Kents was due. Having knocked out several machine-guns in the orchards west of Hecq, which he systematically traversed, he completely mopped up the village of Hecq, causing by his fire the surrender of many prisoners and enabling the infantry to advance. He then very successfully complied with a request from the O.C. Royal Fusiliers to obliterate a machine-gun nest south of Englefontaine, mopping two more machine-guns *en route*. He found the infantry held up north of Hecq by strong points, consisting of two machine-guns and two trench mortars. One of these he knocked out and the others bolted into wooded country impassable for tanks. At this point the tank was under an intense fire from machine-guns and trench mortars and was rendered immobile by one shot entering the radiator. 2nd Lieut. Robinson evacuated his crew and guns and continued to fight with the infantry, assisting in the capture, about 15.00 hours, of the machine-guns and trench mortars in this area. An appreciation of the work of this officer is evidenced by enquiries as to his name which have already been made by Brigade-Majors of the 53rd and 55th Brigades and O's. C. Royal West Kents and R. W. Fusiliers, all of whom expressed themselves as very highly appreciative of the work he had done.

T. 2nd Lieut. BLAKER, HENRY ROBERT. 14th Battn. Awarded M.C.

For conspicuous gallantry and coolness in action near Preux on November 4.

This tank commander led his infantry into action through heavy shell fire. At one point, finding them unable to get forward, and starting to dig in, he pressed forward with his tank under direct fire from two field guns, killed a large number of the enemy, and finally caused all opposition to cease. He then returned and brought on the infantry and successfully cleared the whole of the eastern portion of Preux and established the infantry in this place. During the day he was wounded in the head, but carried on. On the following day a tank was required for further operations. He immediately volunteered for this duty and proceeded to the action. Throughout he showed a fine example to his crew and to the infantry, and very materially assisted in the success of the operations.

T. 2nd Lieut. BORROW, JOHN THOMAS. 14th Battn. Awarded M.C.

For conspicuous gallantry and devotion to duty.

In the forest of Mormal, on November 4, this officer, in command of a tank, whilst leading his infantry into action, was, owing to the very thick mist, completely cut off from the infantry and his tank surrounded by the enemy. Hostile fire having put out of action his 6-pndr. and three of his machine-guns, he continued to fight with revolvers, and eventually compelled a large enemy strong point to surrender. He then handed over prisoners to the infantry and brought the latter on, and successfully completed all the tasks assigned to him. Later, being informed that a company of infantry was very much in the air near Star Corner and rapidly running out of ammunition, he, on his own initiative, collected all available S.A.A. and proceeded to join this company, although by this time only armed with revolvers. Though right out of his own area, and in very difficult country, he successfully found his way to the desired spot, where he found the infantry in the condition stated. Having handed over the ammunition and obtained a receipt, and finding that he was no longer required, he brought his tank home, itself a highly creditable performance, the country being unknown to him.

T. 2nd Lieut. CROSBIE, DONALD FRASER. No. 2 Tank Supply Coy. Awarded M.C.

For conspicuous gallantry and resource at Landrecies on November 4, 1918. This officer was in charge of three tanks carrying bridging material to the lock at Landrecies. On arrival at the railway station, Lieut. Crosbie, realising that the infantry were held up by a machine-gun nest on the bank of the canal, went forward alone, and hastily reconnoitring the situation, decided that no good purpose could be served by leaving the tanks where they were, as one tank had already received a direct hit. He accordingly transferred the load from the derelict tank to a fit tank, and, under heavy shell and machine-gun fire, led his two tanks to the lock, under direct observation from the enemy.

Through his action he was instrumental in causing the machine-gunners to surrender and enabled the infantry to gain the eastern bank of the Sambre Canal.

He set a fine example of initiative and resource.

T. 2nd Lieut. HARRIS, ARTHUR. 14th Battn. Awarded M.C.

For conspicuous courage at Jolimetz on November 4, 1918, when in charge of a tank.

Seeing that the infantry had been held up, he led his tank forward under very heavy fire, and, by his personal reconnaissance, was able to direct the destruction of many enemy machine-gun posts. Although wounded early in the operations and nearly blind, this officer kept his tank in action and gave most valuable support to the infantry.

T. Lieut. HODGENS, CHARLES JOSEPH. 6th Battn. Awarded M.C.

On November 5, 1918, he was in command of a whippet tank near Bavai. He showed great daring and unusual appreciation of the tactical situation.

He went behind the enemy lines three times, each time returning to bring up parties of infantry to consolidate the positions he had cleared.

All the time he was under heavy fire from armour-piercing ammunition.

T. 2nd Lieut. JONES, H. F. 6th Light Battn., Tank Coy. Awarded M.C.

On November 5, 1918, near Bavai, when leading an infantry advance his whippet tank was put out of action by a field gun. He, together with his crew of two men, were severely wounded. He crawled out into a pit and withstood the enemy, who were entrenched 20 yards away, for an hour, until he was again hit and the party captured. He showed most gallant leadership, and when hit his tank was some two miles ahead of the advanced infantry and had caused the enemy to retire a considerable distance.

T. Lieut. MAY, JOSEPH ALFRED EDWARD. 17th Battn. (A.C.) Awarded M.C.

For exceptional gallantry, determination, and devotion to duty during the advance from Favril to Avesnes on November 7, 1918, while commanding a section of armoured cars. During the whole day his cars were constantly engaging the enemy in closely inter-sected country along roads that were full of obstacles and were being blown up in numerous places by the enemy. His skill and determination in overcoming all difficulties were a fine example to his men.

T. Lieut. DUGUID, WILLIAM. 17th Battn. Awarded M.C.

For exceptional gallantry, skill, and devotion to duty as battalion engineer during the advance to Avesnes on November 7, 1918, and previous days.

The mechanical maintenance of the cars of the battalion re-quired exceptional skill and had to be constantly carried out under fire under his personal supervision. On several occasions he made valuable reconnaissances of roads in the forward areas which had been much damaged by the enemy, and gave an untiring example to all ranks of energy, initiative, and courage.

T. 2nd Lieut. BRYSON, HUGH PATTERSON. 9th Battn. Awarded M.C.

For conspicuous gallantry and devotion to duty during the action near Mormal Forest on November 11, 1918. 2nd Lieut. Bryson led the tanks of his section forward to the attack, thus being able to send valuable information back. He displayed splendid courage and determination, and rallied his tanks after they had reached their objectives. Under heavy machine-gun fire he went from tank to tank during the action collecting and disseminating information.

2nd Lieut. FOWLES, M. E. L. D. 5th Battn. Awarded Croix de Guerre avec Palme.

He volunteered to take part with his tank in a French attack. Went forward without hesitation under a heavy barrage. His progress was held up by enemy bombardment and by his tank taking fire. In these circumstances he displayed courage and resolution altogether admirable. He was seriously wounded during this action.

2nd Lieut. VAISSIERE, H. J. 5th Battn. Awarded Croix de Guerre avec Palme.

He volunteered to take part with his tank in a French attack. Went forward without hesitation under a heavy barrage. His progress was held up by the enemy bombardment and by his tank taking fire. In these circumstances he displayed courage and resolution altogether admirable. He was seriously wounded during this action.

305636 Pte W. G. King. 13th Tank Battalion.

The Tank Corps.

I have read with great pleasure the
Report of your Commanding Officer
on your gallant conduct hear
HALLU on August 10, 1918

This reflects credit on yourself and
on the whole Tank Corps.

H. J. Elles
M.G.

Card of Honour, forwarded to all N.C.O's and men of the Tank Corps who
were awarded or recommended for decorations, together with a distinctive
whistle-cord of the Tank Corps colours (Red, Green and Brown).

CHAPTER VI

IMMEDIATE AWARDS—OTHER RANKS

ST. PIERRE DIVION, 1916

40429 Cpl. TAFFS, A. 'A' Battn. Awarded M.M.
106388 L/Cpl. BEVAN, R. 'A' Battn. Awarded M.M.
32098 L/Cpl. MOSS, S. A. 'A' Battn. Awarded M.M.
32175 Gnr. AINLEY, F. 'A' Battn. Awarded M.M.
32046 Gnr. TOLLEY, A. 'A' Battn. Awarded M.M.

These men formed the crew of a tank operating against St. Pierre Divion on November 13, 1916. Brought up under very difficult conditions, theirs was the only tank to start, and penetrated to the second enemy support line. Here for more than an hour they maintained their position without assistance, their infantry having lost touch owing to the heavy mist. The officer in charge was killed while endeavouring to establish touch. Cpl. Taffs then took command and L/Cpl. Bevan drove on another 200 yards, when the tank was ditched in a German dug-out. The crew worked under fire for over two hours, endeavouring to extricate it. Finding this impossible, they attached themselves to a battalion of the Black Watch and assisted them in mopping up the position.

BEAUCOURT, 1916

200770 Pte. SMITH, A. 4th Battn. Awarded M.M.

For good work during operations on the right of Delville Wood on September 15, 1916, when serving with ' D ' Company.

40051 Sergt. DAVIES, D. 'A' Battn. Awarded Italian Bronze Medal.

Displayed great courage and coolness when in action in a tank on November 18, 1916. He continued to work his gun after being hit by a bullet.

THE TANK CORPS BOOK OF HONOUR

2791 Gnr. THOMAS, H. ' A ' Battn. Awarded Italian Bronze Medal.

Displayed great courage and coolness when in action in a tank on November 18, 1916. He continued to work his gun after being wounded in the head.

75001 Sergt. GIBSON, W. A ' Battn. Awarded M.S.M.

For excellent work with workshop party on the Ancre. He never spared himself and was, by his pluck and devotion to duty, an example to his men.

75086 L/Cpl. FENTON, W. ' A ' Battn. Awarded M.M.

During operations on the Ancre this N.C.O. was constantly engaged under shell fire in repairing tanks. He worked throughout with untiring zeal and devotion to duty and did exceptionally good work.

BATTLE OF ARRAS, APRIL 1917

2678 Pte. MALLIN, J. W. ' C ' Battn. Awarded M.M.

For conspicuous gallantry and devotion to duty. During the Battle of Arras, on April 9, 1917, this man displayed the greatest gallantry in climbing out on top of his tank to remove a burning tarpaulin, although the tank was being subjected to heavy fire at the time at close range. Later, when his tank was put out of action, he displayed great coolness in removing the Lewis guns to a place of safety. Throughout the action he displayed the greatest courage and resource.

75661 Pte. BYRNE, E. O. ' C ' Battn. Awarded M.M.

For conspicuous gallantry and devotion to duty. During the Battle of Arras, on April 9, 1917, this man displayed the greatest gallantry in climbing out on top of his tank to remove a burning tarpaulin, although the tank was being subjected to heavy fire at close range at the time. Later, when his tank was put out of action, he displayed great coolness in removing the Lewis guns to a place of safety. Throughout the action he displayed the greatest courage and resource.

75290 Gnr. LINCOLN, A. H. ' C ' Battn. Awarded M.M.

For conspicuous gallantry and devotion to duty during the attack on the Harp on April 9, 1917. He always volunteered for any dangerous work, which he carried out with the greatest coolness. He was frequently at work outside or on top of the tank exposed to heavy sniping, machine-gun, and artillery fire.

IMMEDIATE AWARDS—OTHER RANKS

2726 Cpl. SPURGEON, C. E. ' C ' Battn. Awarded M.M.

For conspicuous gallantry and devotion to duty. During the Battle of Arras, on April 9, 1917, this N.C.O. showed great devotion to duty in extricating wounded comrades from a wrecked tank, attending to their wounds under heavy fire.

2749 Cpl. VYVYAN, F. ' C ' Battn. Awarded D.C.M.

For conspicuous gallantry and devotion to duty. During the opening of the offensive on April 9, 1917, when the officer had been killed, he took charge of his tank and continued to fight it with the greatest boldness and skill. When he found he could not reach the enemy with his Lewis guns inside the tank, although under heavy fire, he fixed up a Lewis gun on top of the tank, and fired it from there. He thereby greatly assisted the infantry to advance.

76167 Cpl. DUFFIN, R., M.M. ' C ' Battn. Awarded Bar to M.M.

For conspicuous gallantry and devotion to duty. Throughout the action on April 9, 1917, the coolness and devotion to duty displayed by this man was worthy of the highest praise. He was responsible for the silencing of at least two enemy machine-guns, and accounted for many snipers.

2353 Cpl. SMITH, A. E. ' D ' Battn. Awarded M.M.

On April 9, 1917, guided four tanks across the lines to Neuville Vitasse under heavy shell and machine-gun fire. He did the same thing on the 11th instant, and it was due to him that the section succeeded in gaining Heninel and the neighbouring trenches.

75608 Cpl. SMITH, H. W. ' C ' Battn. Awarded M.M.

For conspicuous gallantry and devotion to duty. After the action on April 9, 1917, this N.C.O. was left in charge of two tanks. When one of them was set on fire by a direct hit from hostile artillery he displayed the greatest pluck in entering the burning tank, which contained petrol and ammunition, and saving much valuable equipment. He afterwards drove away the other tank into a place of safety, under heavy artillery fire, thereby showing great devotion to duty and initiative.

10558 Sergt. HATCHER, H. W. ' D ' Battn. Awarded M.M.

On April 9, when his tank was ' bellied ' in a tank trap near Neuville Vitasse, he got out and ran back under heavy machine-gun fire, and warned other tanks advancing to the same point. By this action he was the means of enabling two or three other tanks to proceed without trouble.

76641 Sergt. LATHAN, F. 'C' Battn. Awarded M.M.

For conspicuous gallantry and devotion to duty. During the Battle of Arras, on April 9, 1917, whilst passing through a severe enemy barrage, lengths of barbed wire were caught up by the 'tracks' of his tank which pulled the camouflage cover over the exhaust openings, and caused the whole mass to catch fire. Without waiting for orders, Sergt. Lathan climbed on top of the tank and removed the burning material. Later on this N.C.O. displayed the greatest courage whilst attempting to dig out his tank under heavy fire.

2939 Sergt. PROCTOR, F. 'D' Battn. Awarded M.M.

Set a fine example of coolness and courage under heavy fire and indicating targets on April 9, 1917, during the attack on Neuville Vitasse.

75121 A/Cpl. KERRISON, R. J. 'D' Battn. Awarded M.M.

During the attack on the Hindenburg Line, on the night of April 10–11, this N.C.O. worked unceasingly and cheerfully in assisting to dig out two tanks, under machine-gun fire, which had been 'bellied' in Nepal Trench, and was mainly responsible for having them ready for action before dawn on the 11th.

2527 Sergt. SAKER, F. J. 'C' Battn. Awarded M.M.

For conspicuous gallantry and devotion to duty. During the capture of Monchy-le-Preux, on April 11, 1917, this N.C.O. served his gun with the greatest coolness and effect. When his tank broke down under a very severe artillery barrage, he remained with it, using every effort to get it moving again. When the tank had to be abandoned, he showed great courage and resource in consolidating a trench under heavy fire.

469 Sergt. HAUGH, A. 'C' Battn. Awarded M.M.

For conspicuous gallantry and devotion to duty. During the capture of Monchy-le-Preux on April 11, 1917, this N.C.O. displayed the greatest coolness and courage. Although wounded, he continued to direct the fire of his Lewis guns. He set a magnificent example to his men.

5362 Pte. SAVAGE, A. 'D' Battn. Awarded Croix de Guerre.

Carrying an important message, he went from his tank in search of his section commander under heavy shell and machine-gun fire. Failing to find his section commander, who had moved, he took the message to another tank commander. This second journey was made under very heavy fire, as the tank was in the German wire and a target for all the machine-guns in the neighbourhood. He displayed both gallantry and initiative. The entire crew volunteered for the message and Savage was chosen for the task. (Bullecourt, April 11.)

76563 A/L/Cpl. FLEMING, J. ' C ' Battn. Awarded M.M.

For gallantry and devotion to duty. During the recent operations, especially at Feuchy Chapel on April 13, 1917, during a heavy gas-shell bombardment, this N.C.O. showed great fearlessness and devotion to duty in the repair of tanks. On two occasions he has worked unceasingly for forty-eight hours in most difficult circumstances. His devotion to duty has greatly inspired the other men of his section.

75158 A/Sergt. WATSON, W. ' C ' Battn. Awarded M.M.

For gallantry and devotion to duty. During the recent operations, especially at Feuchy Chapel, on April 13, 1917, during a heavy gas-shell bombardment, this N.C.O. showed great fearlessness and devotion to duty in the repair of tanks. On two occasions he has worked unceasingly for forty-eight hours in most difficult circumstances. His devotion to duty has greatly inspired the other men in his section.

444 Cpl. WILLIAMS, R. J., M.M. ' C ' Battn. Awarded Bar to M.M.

For conspicuous gallantry and devotion to duty. This N.C.O. has always displayed great gallantry. On April 22, 1917, under intense shell fire, he went to the assistance of a wounded despatch rider, who died in his arms. During the action on April 23, as tank driver, he displayed great courage and coolness, and although wounded refused to give up his place.

76267 L/Cpl. LARDNER, E. ' D ' Battn. Awarded M.M.

During the action on the Hindenburg Line on April 23 drove tank D. 4 with great skill under severe shell fire and gave the greatest assistance in locating the enemy when observation was most difficult owing to a heavy mist. Previously brought to notice for gallantry on April 9.

32149 Sergt. LUCK, C. W. ' D ' Battn. Awarded M.M.

During the action on the Hindenburg Line on April 23 drove his tank with great skill and judgment from 4.45 A.M. until 12 noon under severe shell and machine-gun fire, thereby setting a fine example of gallantry and devotion to duty.

1955 Pte. RENNIE, J. ' C ' Battn. Awarded M.M.

For conspicuous gallantry and devotion to duty. During the action on April 23, 1917, this man displayed conspicuous coolness and courage in action under intense fire. This man was also brought to notice for his gallantry in action on April 9, 1917, and the coolness and skill with which he handled his Lewis gun.

45084 Pte. GILFORD, W. ' C ' Battn. Awarded M.M.

For conspicuous gallantry and devotion to duty. During the attack on April 23, 1917, this man displayed conspicuous coolness and courage in action under intense fire. This man was also brought to notice for his gallantry in action on April 9, 1917, and the coolness and skill with which he handled his Lewis gun.

24088 Pte. DOWNING, A. ' C ' Battn. Awarded M.M.

For conspicuous gallantry and devotion to duty. During the action on April 23, 1917, this man displayed conspicuous coolness and courage under intense fire. This man was also brought to notice for his gallantry in action on April 9, 1917, and the coolness and skill with which he handled his Lewis gun.

32505 Gnr. BARNARD, J. W. ' C ' Battn. Awarded M.M.

For conspicuous gallantry and devotion to duty. During the action on April 23, 1917, this man with the utmost gallantry led his tank from the outside across difficult country under intense shell fire. Although seriously wounded during the action he continued to work his gun.

32083 Gnr. DODD, J. H. ' C ' Battn. Awarded M.M.

For conspicuous gallantry and devotion to duty. During the action on April 23, 1917, he did great execution with his Lewis gun. When his tank came under very heavy hostile machine-gun and artillery fire, although wounded, he continued to carry on and fire his gun with great effect.

75290 Gnr. LINCOLN, A. H., M.M. ' C ' Battn. Awarded Bar to M.M.

For conspicuous gallantry and devotion to duty. During the Battle of Arras, on April 23, 1917, this man guided his tank from outside across difficult country under intense shell fire. After being wounded he continued at his work until his tank had reached its destination, without reporting that he had been wounded.

2176 Cpl. KENNEDY, G. ' C ' Battn. Awarded M.M.

For conspicuous gallantry and devotion to duty. During the Battle of Arras, on April 23, 1917, after his tank had received two direct hits and several of the crew wounded, this N.C.O., although wounded himself in the face, insisted on looking after the other wounded men and dressing their wounds under intense shell fire, before being attended to himself. Whilst he was attending to one of the men he was again wounded in the leg.

IMMEDIATE AWARDS—OTHER RANKS

2301 Cpl. LOWE, C. T. ' C ' Battn.   Awarded M.M.

For conspicuous gallantry and devotion to duty. During the action on April 23, 1917, when his officer had been temporarily blinded by splinters, and several of the crew wounded, and the Lewis guns disabled, this N.C.O. displayed conspicuous courage and coolness, and managed to drive his tank back to its starting-point.

2681 Sergt. MILLIKEN, A. J. ' C ' Battn.   Awarded M.M.

For conspicuous gallantry and devotion to duty. This N.C.O. has shown great coolness and gallantry in action, notably during the attack on Gavrelle on April 23, 1917. Owing to his skill and coolness he drove his tank through a heavy barrage to his objective, where it was of the greatest assistance to the infantry, until put out of action by armour-piercing bullets.

2714 Sergt. NOEL, J. ' C ' Battn.   Awarded D.C.M.

For conspicuous gallantry and devotion to duty. During the Battle of Arras, on April 23, 1917, this N.C.O. took command of his tank after his officer had been wounded. He fought his tank with the greatest gallantry and skill, putting out of action many machine-guns, and killing numbers of the enemy besides taking fifty prisoners. His action enabled the infantry to gain possession of the chemical works. He then brought his tank safely back to its starting-point. His skill and gallantry were beyond praise. He was continually in action for nine hours.

2674 Gnr. ILLINGWORTH, W. ' C ' Battn.   Awarded M.M.

For conspicuous gallantry and devotion to duty. During the capture of Monchy-le-Preux, although badly wounded, this gunner carried out his duties by supplying ammunition to Lewis guns, and thus enabling a continuous fire to be maintained from his tank. He showed a fine example to the rest of his crew.

75901 Sergt. HARVEY, C. ' D ' Battn.   Awarded M.M.

During the attack on Bullecourt-Riencourt and Hendecourt gallantly seconded his officers in fighting his tank when all the crew were wounded and the tank had been twice hit.

553 Cpl. HAYWARD, E. W. ' D ' Battn.   Awarded D.C.M.

After the attack on the Hindenburg Line, near Bullecourt, he displayed great gallantry in collecting a crew and bringing in his tank under heavy shell fire after it had been abandoned.

677 Cpl. SMITH, H. ' C ' Battn.   Awarded D.C.M.

For conspicuous gallantry and devotion to duty. He guided his tank from outside across difficult country under very heavy shell fire. When his tank had been abandoned, owing to a direct hit, he carried the wounded to a place of safety. After being partially buried by a shell himself, he continued to search for stretcher-bearers, under a severe barrage, to bring in another wounded man. He displayed a magnificent example of courage and devotion to duty.

466 Cpl. LEVY, W. E. H. 'D' Battn. Awarded M.M.

Bullecourt, May 1, 1917. This N.C.O. showed great coolness and excellent example to his men when in action. Although wounded in the head, he kept his side of the tank clear of the enemy, who were rushing the tank with bombs. He was at this time the only man able to fight on his side of the tank.

75071 L/Cpl. WATERIDGE, A. S. 'D' Battn. Awarded M.M.

Bullecourt, May 3, 1917. When this driver's tank was in a deep crater in Bullecourt, his skilful driving under heavy fire from armour-piercing bullets enabled the tank commander to extricate himself and continue in action. The tank, owing to casualties in personnel, was brought back to starting-point and the wounded crew were replaced. This driver, however, continued at his post during the succeeding operations and was in action seven hours.

2242 Pte. ANDERSON, J. 'D' Battn. Awarded D.C.M.

At Bullecourt, May 3, 1917. Although wounded and blinded in one eye he continued to work his gun with great determination and kept up a steady fire on the enemy. He asked not to be evacuated until the action was over, and made a second journey into Bullecourt.

76860 Sergt. WEEKS, J. 'D' Battn. Awarded M.M.

At Bullecourt, May 3, 1917. When his officer was wounded he took his place in the brakesman's seat and was responsible for getting the car as far back as it did. When he left the car he looked after the wounded by placing them in safety in shell-holes and getting them water. He also got a Lewis gun and ammunition out of the tank and helped to man a shell-hole. All this was done under very heavy machine-gun fire.

203 Pte. HEWLETT, N. 'D' Battn. Awarded M.M.

At Bullecourt, May 3, 1917. He did very good work in the tank after most of the crew were wounded, and he performed the work of three men though badly handicapped by the wounded in the car. It was due to his good work that all the wounded were taken out of the car in safety under machine-gun fire. He then held a shell-hole with a Lewis gun and covered the retirement of the wounded.

IMMEDIATE AWARDS—OTHER RANKS

241 L/Cpl. JAGGER, E. ' D ' Battn. Awarded M.M.

At Bullecourt, May 3, 1917. He showed great gallantry ·and devotion to duty, in that he, after being wounded in the eye, carried on driving although partially blinded. On leaving the tank he also showed great gallantry by bringing back Pte. Whitehall, who was severely wounded, under heavy machine-gun fire.

32393 Pte. LOADES, A. ' D ' Battn. Awarded M.M.

At Bullecourt, May 3, 1917. When under intense machine-gun fire at point-blank range the tank got into a critical position, he without hesitation opened the shield to obtain a better view and enable him to right the tank. This he succeeded in doing, but was shot through the eye, yet, with extreme pluck and determination, he managed to swing the tank before he became unconscious.

242 Sergt. GULLY, J. ' D ' Battn. Awarded M.M.

At Bullecourt, May 3, 1917. When his tank was set on fire by a direct hit and had to be abandoned, he, though wounded, returned with his officer and two of the crew (all wounded), and assisted in putting out the fire and driving the tank back to the starting-point. During the whole of the time the car was subjected to heavy shell and machine-gun fire.

76266 Pte. ASHDOWN, A. E. ' D ' Battn. Awarded M.M.

At Bullecourt, May 3, 1917. He showed great devotion to duty and did excellent work, and though four of the crew were wounded he cheerfully volunteered and went into action a second time.

76209 Pte. ROBERTS, W. ' D ' Battn. Awarded M.M.

At Bullecourt, May 3, 1917. Though wounded early in the action he remained at his post and did good work. Later, when the tank took fire from a direct hit, he assisted in putting out the flames and was of great assistance in bringing in the tank.

75548 Sergt. DAVIDSON, A. ' D ' Battn. Awarded M.M.

Bullecourt, May 3, 1917. When his tank had fallen into a cellar, and under intense machine-gun fire, he, although blinded in one eye at the time, gallantly got out and assisted to unditch the tank, thus enabling it to proceed farther into the enemy lines.

BATTLE OF MESSINES, JUNE 1917

76174 Pte. HOUSLEY, T. G. ' A ' Battn. Awarded M.M.

For conspicuous gallantry and sustained good work displayed on the morning of June 7, 1917, under heavy shell fire. During the difficult crossing of the Dam Strasse by No. 3 Company's tanks, this man gallantly worked on unditching and guided several tanks across the ground. Even though he was knocked over by a shell he still continued to work.

38105 A/Cpl. CLEMENTS, C. H. 'A' Battn. Awarded M.M.

This N.C.O., when Pte. Bryant was wounded in No Man's Land, near Joye, on June 7, 1917, volunteered to leave the tank and dress his wound. He remained with him in a shell-hole for five hours until stretcher-bearers were obtained. During all the time he was under heavy fire from our own and enemy machine-guns. Prior to this he had been twelve hours directing his tank and doing exceptionally hard work, particularly when his tank was ditched. Throughout, under most exhausting conditions, he set an excellent example of keenness and hard work to the men.

75721 Sergt. BRASH, F. 'A' Battn. Awarded M.M.

When his tank was ditched near Joye Farm on June 7, 1917, he went to and fro under heavy fire for ammunition, and dressed a wounded man and assisted to carry him to safety in the Oosttaverne Line. He also displayed great courage and coolness under very trying and dangerous circumstances.

76008 Pte. ROBSON, J. H. 'A' Battn. Awarded M.M.

On June 7, 1917, near Wytschaete, he was wounded in the knee whilst firing at an enemy machine-gun. But, although nearly fainting, he carried on and eventually put the machine-gun out of action, and also killed or wounded about twenty of the enemy who were near the gun.

75026 Pte. GREEN, W. 'G' Battn. Awarded M.M.

On June 7, 1917, although suffering from the effects of gas-shell and starting practically in darkness, this man drove tank No. 2679 with great coolness and judgment, and it was greatly due to his fine work that the tank was enabled to assist in the capture of Fanny's Farm.

75877 L/Cpl. HILL, L. C. Awarded M.M.

On June 7, 1917, during the action, his tank commander was severely wounded. This N.C.O. immediately took charge of the tank and carried on in action. Eventually the tank became ditched, and he did everything possible under shell fire to get it out. Finding that he could not manage this with the small personnel at his disposal, he sent a pigeon message giving full details of the position and location of tank. He showed great coolness and initiative throughout.

76953 Cpl. TAIT, R. A., M.M. 'B' Battn. Awarded Bar to M.M.

On June 7, this N.C.O., without orders, got out of his tank on to the roof under heavy machine-gun and rifle fire in order to put out a fire. Prompt action and courage prevented the fire causing damage to the tank or drawing the enemy's shell fire on to it.

1786 Pte. DONALDSON, L. ' B ' Battn. Awarded M.M.

This man, on June 7, was first driver of tank No. 2682, which reached all its objectives. He showed great coolness and judgment throughout the action, and it was largely due to him that the tank was able to get into action at Wytschaete ahead of the infantry. He drove over very heavily crumped ground practically in darkness.

75016 Pte. BROKENSHA, L. H. ' A ' Battn. Awarded M.M.

Whilst in action near Wytschaete on June 7, 1917, he drove his tank for thirteen hours over badly crumped ground. On the return journey the tank was heavily shelled, and through his keeping perfectly calm and collected the tank arrived back safely in spite of it being hit. I consider that if it had not been for Pte. Brokensha's good driving and coolness, the tank would have been put out of action.

38091 Pte. FRANCOMBE, R. F. ' A ' Battn. Awarded M.M.

In the attack on June 7, 1917, this man drove his tank for seven hours after it had received a direct hit from enemy artillery, which wounded two of the crew and destroyed part of the water-cooling apparatus. His great coolness and skill enabled the tank to reach its objective—the White Château. During the attack the tank used fifty-two gallons of extra water. This was obtained from shell-holes and the pond at the White Château. Latterly the tank could only proceed at about 100 yards at a burst owing to the danger of the engine seizing, and the temperature inside was about 140 degrees. Before the tank was finally abandoned it became ditched, and this man materially assisted in unditching it under very heavy fire.

102748 Sergt. CLOUGH W. R.E.'s. Awarded M.M.

For conspicuous coolness and devotion to duty. He superintended the digging out of a tank that had been ditched in the enemy front line opposite Wytschaete on June 7 last, in full view of the enemy and under very heavy shell fire. His bravery and good example to his men were especially noticeable.

3226 Pte. MARLAND, J. 2nd Manchesters. Awarded M.M.

At the Battle of Messines on June 7, 1917. For exceptional courage and coolness under trying circumstances. He took control of a working party making a route for tanks across the open during a heavy bombardment, and by his personal direction and example the task allotted to his party was successfully carried out.

102709 Sergt. FARISH, F. R.E's. Awarded M.M.

At the Battle of Messines on June 7, 1917. For great energy and devotion to duty. He was in charge of a working party engaged in making a route for tanks across broken country under enemy observation and heavy and continuous shell fire. His great coolness and resource enabled the work allotted to his men being carried to a successful conclusion.

79053 Cpl. SYKES. R.E.'s. Awarded M.M.

At the Battle of Messines on June 7, 1917. For conspicuous coolness and disregard of danger. He supervised the work of a party of men making a route for tanks under very heavy fire from shells, gas-shells and machine-guns. By his personal example and devotion to duty the work allotted to his party was successfully completed.

179969 L/Cpl. WHITE, F. Salvage Co. Awarded M.M.

Conspicuous good work and devotion to duty in repairing and driving out tank No. 2679 under heavy shell fire near Messines on June 16, 1917. For six days he was working at unditching this tank on the ridge near Messines in view of the enemy and exposed to shell fire. On night of June 6, 1917, he drove his tank back with six other men. On the way back he came under heavy shell fire, in the course of which four of his men were gassed, two of whom had to be evacuated. In spite of this he kept on and brought the tank safely back.

BATTLE OF YPRES, JULY 1917

155591 Spr. McWHINNIE, T. 184th Tunn. Coy. Awarded M.M.

While engaged in night operations of exceptional importance near Verbranden Molen on the night July 21–22, 1917, Spr. McWhinnie very ably and gallantly assisted his officers in searching for lost transport. Spr. McWhinnie twice accompanied his officer through an intense barrage of gas-shells. His example of courage and devotion to duty undoubtedly greatly helped in the completion of the work for which the transport was bringing up the material.

68518 Bomb. HUTCHINSON, J. R. Res. D.A.C. Awarded M.M.

For conspicuous gallantry and devotion to duty during the preparation for the Battle of Ypres. From July 24 to 31, 1917, this N.C.O. continuously set a fine example of coolness and devotion to duty under fire to the men under his orders. He successfully made a large dump of petrol and ammunition in spite of being heavily shelled, in particular with gas-shells, night after night. By his courage and skill many casualties to the men under him and much loss of material were avoided.

193317 Cpl. PAPE, W. 184th Tunn. Coy. Awarded M.M.

Cpl. Pape throughout the recent preparations for the offensive has shown great gallantry and resource, and especially on July 26, 1917, near the Yser Canal, when, by his efforts and consummate bravery, he carried on continually important work connected with tank tracks and causeways until completed in spite of very heavy hostile shelling.

3999 Pte. PORTER, H. R.A.M.C. (attached ' B ' Battn.). Awarded M.M.

On the night of July 28–29, 1917, this man showed great gallantry and devotion to duty in attending to wounded under a heavy barrage of gas and other shells south of Zillebeke. On July 31 he attended his company commander with four other orderlies, all of whom were wounded. These he dressed, in addition to several infantry, between Hooge Gap and Jackdaw Reserve, under heavy fire. At the Battle of Messines the cool behaviour of this orderly under fire was reported by his company commander.

69606 Gnr. DOWSETT, J. ' G ' Battn. Awarded M.M.

Operations in the Ypres Salient, July 31, 1917. For conspicuous gallantry and devotion to duty. On two occasions he was responsible for guiding his crew commander by getting out of the tank under heavy shell fire and taking bearings with a prismatic compass.

2788 Gnr. THOMPSON, G. ' G ' Battn. Awarded M.M.

Operations in the Ypres Salient, July 31, 1917. For conspicuous gallantry and devotion to duty. When his tank approached the Steenebeek he volunteered to reconnoitre the ground in front of the infantry, and was able to guide his tank under very heavy rifle and machine-gun fire.

40246 Gnr. COOKE, C. R. ' G ' Battn. Awarded M.M.

Operations in the Ypres Salient, July 31, 1917. For conspicuous gallantry and devotion to duty. He was acting as runner to his section commander (Capt. Powell) throughout the day, and got some valuable messages through under heavy fire.

95453 Gnr. HIGGINS, J. ' G ' Battn. Awarded M.M.

Operations in the Ypres Salient, July 31, 1917. For conspicuous gallantry and devotion to duty. He fought his gun with great gallantry. After his tank was hopelessly ditched east of the Steenebeek he helped to form a post with the rest of his crew, and when the infantry withdrew he remained in action with the infantry until relieved by the Sussex Regiment at dawn, when he rejoined his company after twenty-eight hours' continuous work.

95449 Gnr. COULTAS, B. G. ' G ' Battn. Awarded M.M.

Operations in the Ypres Salient, July 31, 1917. For conspicuous gallantry and devotion to duty. He fought his gun with great gallantry. After the tank was hopelessly ditched east of the Steenebeek he helped to form a post with the rest of his crew, and when the infantry withdrew he remained in action with the infantry until relieved by the Sussex Regiment at dawn, when he rejoined his company after twenty-eight hours' continuous work.

38010 Sergt. STOCKDALE, E. ' G ' Battn. Awarded M.M.

Operations in the Ypres Salient, July 31, 1917. For conspicuous gallantry and devotion to duty. He set a splendid example all day of keenness and cheerfulness, and was always first out of the tank, under heavy fire, when required to unditch. His tank was in front of the infantry at Springfield and able to give valuable assistance.

38180 Cpl. CRAWSHAW, S. ' G ' Battn. Awarded M.M.

Operations in the Ypres Salient, July 31, ' 1917. For conspicuous gallantry and devotion to duty. After his crew commander was wounded, Cpl. Crawshaw took charge of the strong post which had been formed and held it for over three hours, till ordered to withdraw, giving very valuable assistance to the infantry.

72755 Pte. UTTING, H. ' A ' Battn. Awarded D.C.M.

For conspicuous gallantry and devotion to duty during the operations of July 31, 1917. When near Hooge his tank received a direct hit, killing the officer and wounding most of the crew and the section commander's orderly. When the crew were sent back he volunteered to remain and act as orderly. About half an hour afterwards, when guiding a tank on foot over a very difficult piece of ground, he was hit in the leg, but continued for about two hours, under very heavy shell and machine-gun fire, to take messages between tanks. He was of much assistance to his section commander and displayed a cool disregard of personal danger. He set a fine example to the other men.

75234 Cpl. HARTLEY, J. ' B ' Battn. Awarded M.M.

This N.C.O. set a fine example to his men throughout the action of July 31, 1917. When his tank got ditched near Bodmin Copse, as the unditching gear was broken he made several journeys across the open under heavy machine-gun fire to obtain legs.' By this means the tank was unditched and proceeded into action. Later on, after his tank had been put out of action by shell fire, and the crew were ordered to withdraw, he returned under heavy fire to ascertain if there was any chance of saving L/Cpl. Powell (killed), as one of the crew stated that he thought he had not been killed. The tank commander was wounded.

24 L/Cpl. MURDOCH, T. ' A ' Battn. Awarded D.C.M.

On July 31, 1917, when operating in front of the infantry near Westhoek, the tank received two direct hits and his officer and sergeant were wounded. This N.C.O. took charge of the remainder of the crew, two of whom were wounded, and brought them back to a place of safety. Afterwards, under heavy shell and machine-gun fire, he returned to the derelict tank and fetched the pigeons, by means of which a message regarding the position of the infantry was sent off. He then, under heavy shell fire, assisted the two wounded men to the dressing station.

1582 Pte. PRESTON, J. ' B ' Battn. Awarded M.M.

Great courage and devotion to duty near Bodmin Copse on July 31, 1917. He got on top of the tank under rifle and machine-gun fire to get water to refill the radiator. When in action, after the first gunner and several of the crew had been wounded by bullets entering through the sighting slits, he continued to work the gun. This tank was running continuously for more than ten hours.

75769 L/Cpl. McGUIRE, M. ' B ' Battn. Awarded D.C.M.

For conspicuous gallantry during action on July 31, 1917. After his tank had been put out of action by shell fire near Glencorse Wood he volunteered to reconnoitre dug-outs on the slope of the wood, from which machine-gun fire had been directed on the tank. He proceeded alone on foot in front of the advanced infantry and found the dug-outs unoccupied but the enemy still in the wood. He set a fine example to his crew throughout the action, when a post was held for two hours in front of the advanced infantry.

1031 Pte. BIRNIE, E. ' A ' Battn. Awarded M.M.

During the operations of July 31, 1917, his tank received two direct hits whilst operating in advance of the infantry near Westhoek. The tank had to be abandoned, and this man voluntarily remained with his section sergeant, who was badly wounded. He subsequently made his way back under intense machine-gun fire and heavy shelling, and succeeded in getting help to convey his section sergeant to a dressing station, and undoubtedly saved this N.C.O.'s life.

96 Cpl. LUXFORD, W. ' B ' Battn. Awarded M.M.

Coolness and bravery under shell fire, putting on the unditching gear near Clapham Junction on July 31, 1917. After the tank had been ditched and the sponson door blown away, he shouted to the men to carry on, which they did until the tank was hit for the third time and put out of action. When the crew were withdrawn, he volunteered to remain on guard, and did so until relieved about twelve hours later.

76420 Cpl. HILTON, W. ' B ' Battn. Awarded M.M.

On July 31, 1917, when his tank commander and first driver were incapacitated by a shell bursting under the front of the tank near

Clonnel Copse, he took command of the tank and kept going towards his objective. Later the tank was ditched and he assisted to get it out under heavy shell fire, enabling the tank to get into action. This N.C.O. set a fine example to the crew.

75728 L/Cpl. SCANLON, T. ' B ' Battn. Awarded M.M.

During the operations on July 31, 1917, he acted as runner to his section commander under incessant artillery and machine-gun fire, communicating his orders to tank commanders in the neighbourhood of Clapham Junction. He also took a message to another tank 200 yards ahead of our infantry, over ground swept by machine-gun fire. Two other orderlies were killed attempting to go over the same ground.

2940 Cpl. MURCH, A. M. ' A ' Battn. Awarded M.M.

For conspicuous gallantry and devotion to duty during the operations on July 31, 1917, in the vicinity of Westhoek. Though wounded, he remained at his post and assisted to drive the tank. Later, when one of the gunners was wounded, he took over the gun and continued to fire, destroying an enemy machine-gun which was holding up the advance of the infantry. He showed great coolness and courage and set a fine example to the remainder of the crew.

75022 Pte. WILKINSON, E. W. ' A ' Battn. Awarded M.M.

On July 31, 1917, in the vicinity of Westhoek, he drove continuously for fourteen hours with great skill and judgment over very badly crumped ground, and it was due to his driving that the tank was enabled to reach its objective and take part in the action. During the whole of the action the tank was subjected to very heavy shell and machine-gun fire, and although wounded he stuck to his post. Afterwards, when the tank had returned to its rallying point, he remained with it for forty-three hours, though it was still under shell and machine-gun fire. This driver showed great coolness and courage and set a fine example to the remainder of the crew.

32130 Pte. DUNCAN, J. ' A ' Battn. Awarded M.M.

On July 31, 1917, he drove his tank under very heavy shell and machine-gun fire continuously for ten hours, with great skill and judgment, over very badly crumped and marshy ground. When the tank became ditched 200 yards in front of our advanced infantry, near Surbiton Villa, he got out of the tank, and under heavy machine-gun fire collected material for unditching it, and eventually succeeded in getting the tank out and driving it back to the rallying point. He set a fine example to the remainder of the crew. At the Battle of Messines this driver succeeded in driving his tank to its farthest objective and brought it out of action.

32198 Cpl. LEE, A. ' A ' Battn.   Awarded M.M.

He showed great gallantry and steadiness under very heavy shell and machine-gun fire during the action on July 31, 1917. When his tank was preceding the infantry it became ditched in the vicinity of Surbiton Villa, and he got out with his officer and opened fire on the enemy from a shell-hole, forcing the enemy to retire.   On several occasions under very heavy shell fire and machine-gun fire he got out of the tank to fix the unditching gear.   This N.C.O. displayed great coolness and courage, and set, a fine example to the remainder of the crew.

2903 Cpl. DEAN, A. ' A ' Battn.   Awarded M.M.

In the operations in the vicinity of Westhoek on July 31, 1917, when advancing with the first wave of the infantry his tank became ditched and his tank commander was killed.   This N.C.O., on foot, crossed a quarter of a mile of ground under intense machine-gun fire and heavy shelling, and reported to his section commander. Afterwards he returned to his tank and spent over an hour trying to unditch it.   Failing to do this he salved all the Lewis guns and brought the crew back to a place of safety.   He showed great coolness and courage and set a fine example to the crew.

20334 Cpl. JENKINS, D. C. ' C ' Battn.   Awarded D.C.M.

For conspicuous gallantry and devotion to duty.   During the Battle of Ypres, on July 31, 1917, when his officer was killed, he continued to fight his tank with the greatest skill and gallantry until it ' bellied.'   He then took out all his crew and Lewis guns, and placing some on top of his tank and some on the ground opened fire on the enemy and prevented them from advancing.   Finding another tank which had been abandoned owing to the crew having become casualties, he took charge of this tank until it also became ' bellied ' and immovable.

427 Cpl. MYLEHAM, W. ' C ' Battn.   Awarded D.C.M.

For conspicuous gallantry and devotion to duty.   During the Battle of Ypres, on July 31, 1917, this N.C.O. drove his tank for thirteen hours, and twice unditched it under heavy fire.   When the tank was eventually put out of action he went to the assistance of the infantry with a Lewis gun and helped them to repel a counter-attack.   He remained with the infantry until wounded.

75385 L/Sergt. BRAY, R. ' C ' Battn.   Awarded M.M.

For conspicuous gallantry and devotion to duty.   During the Battle of Ypres, on July 31, 1917, as tank N.C.O. he rendered most valuable assistance to his officer.   After his tank had become a casualty and his officer and four of the crew were wounded, although himself twice wounded he remained all night with a wounded comrade until the latter died. Next morning he brought back the remainder of the crew to safety.

2256 Gnr. TARRY, A. J. ' F ' Battn. Awarded M.M.

At Ypres, on July 31, 1917, although his tank had broken down over a mile from the position of assembly, on ' Z ' night he reached the position of assembly in time to go over with the other tanks. When his own tank broke down he was transferred to another tank which had sustained casualties, and drove this tank up to the final objective and back to within one mile of the position of assembly. He showed extraordinary endurance, steadiness, and good driving under most adverse circumstances.

32037 Gnr. ACOCK, R. J. ' C ' Battn. Awarded M.M.

For conspicuous gallantry and devotion to duty. During the Battle of Ypres, on July 31, 1917, this man, with a Lewis gun, kept up covering fire from a shell-hole to enable his tank to be unditched. Later, when a 6-pndr. gunner became a casualty, he took his place and put out of action several enemy machine-guns. Finally, when his tank was put out of action, he worked under heavy fire to get his guns up to the infantry.

38746 Gnr. DOWSE, G. ' F ' Battn. Awarded M.M.

At Ypres, on July 31, 1917, by exceedingly clever and cool driving, he got his tank over very wet and crumped ground to Border House, his objective. Later, after his officer was wounded and his N.C.O. was attending to him outside the tank, the Germans advanced to attack the tank. He turned on a Lewis gun at once, and kept on firing until he collapsed ; the enemy were dispersed and later surrendered.

2282 Gnr. WALKER, J. W. ' C ' Battn. Awarded M.M.

For conspicuous gallantry and devotion to duty. During the Battle of Ypres, on July 31, this man continued to drive his tank after one of his arms had been rendered useless by a bullet wound, and only gave in when in a fainting condition.

92565 Cpl. HORNSEY, C. G. ' F ' Battn. Awarded M.M.

At Ypres, on July 31, 1917, when his tank was ditched, he, with the assistance of Gnr. Lee and the tank commander, managed to get it unditched under very heavy shell fire. Later, when the tank was hit and the officer killed and five of the crew wounded, although slightly wounded in the knee, he got the five men out of the tank and carried them to shelter under heavy shell fire. He then got assistance and helped to dress and get the wounded back to a dressing station.

IMMEDIATE AWARDS—OTHER RANKS

92352 Gnr. CORBY, J. ' F ' Battn. Awarded M.M.

At Ypres, on July 31, 1917, this driver, though the tank had been knocked out by a direct hit and the officer killed, continued at his post until the tank caught fire, when he made great efforts to get the guns out, though the tank was hit three times by shells during this time. His coolness and devotion to duty under very heavy shell fire was a very fine example to the remainder of the crew. He was badly burned while endeavouring to rescue the guns.

38894 Gnr. FRANKCOMBE, C. ' F ' Battn. Awarded M.M.

At Ypres, on July 31, 1917, this driver drove with great judgment and coolness, especially through the Pommern Redoubt, when he was forced to open his flap while machine-gun and rifle fire were turned on to the tank in heavy volume. His presence of mind and gallantry set a very fine example to the crew, and were undoubtedly the cause of his tank reaching the objective and returning to the tankodrome, having dispersed four machine-gun crews and captured a machine-gun *en route*.

77483 Gnr. LUCAS, A. E. ' C ' Battn. Awarded M.M.

For conspicuous gallantry and devotion to duty. During the Battle of Ypres, on July 31, 1917, this man, as leading driver, succeeded by his skilful driving in bringing his tank into action over ground of the worst possible description. All his reflectors having been broken by snipers, he observed his route through the open flap. Throughout the action he displayed the greatest skill and courage.

700 Sergt. HARRIS, A. J. ' C ' Battn. Awarded M.M.

For conspicuous gallantry and devotion to duty. During the Battle of Ypres, on July 31, 1917, though wounded in the stomach by bullet splinters, he courageously continued to fire his gun with great effect. He was a magnificent example to the remainder of the crew.

76653 Gnr. MARSHALL, S. ' C ' Battn. Awarded M.M.

For conspicuous gallantry and devotion to duty. During the Battle of Ypres, on July 31, 1917, he drove his tank under the most difficult conditions for eleven and a half hours. When his tank was hit and in flames he assisted, under heavy machine-gun fire, in getting out one of the crew who was mortally wounded, and carried him to a place of safety.

34535 Gnr. BENNETT, A. ' C ' Battn. Awarded M.M.

For conspicuous gallantry and devotion to duty. During the Battle of Ypres, on July 31, 1917, he was wounded in the face early in the action. Although he was blinded in one eye, he stuck to his gun and did most excellent work with it.

95512 Sergt. HARRINGTON, G. ' F ' Battn. Awarded M.M.

At Ypres, on July 31, 1917, this N.C.O., although wounded in the head and leg, assisted in fixing the unditching gear under fire, and carried on his duties with great coolness and energy during the rest of the day. He volunteered at once for all work and kept up the spirits of the crew, though in considerable pain all the time.

92637 Gnr. YOUNG, S. ' F ' Battn. Awarded M.M.

At Ypres, on July 31, 1917, this gunner, under very heavy shell fire in which he was buried, twice carried messages to 16 Coy. tanks to try and get assistance for his tank, which had incurred a broken coventry chain. Throughout the action he displayed great coolness and gallantry and set a fine example to the remainder of the crew.

112588 Cpl. TINSLEY, W. 184th Tunn. Coy. Awarded M.M.

On the night July 30–31, 1917, near Potijze, when in charge of a party constructing tank crossings over three trenches and making corduroy ramps, Cpl. Tinsley, by his utter disregard of personal danger, greatly facilitated the work of his officer and enabled the crossings to be finished in six hours under very heavy machine-gun and shell fire. Throughout Cpl. Tinsley has shown steadfast devotion to duty.

46482 Pte. DRYDEN, A. ' C ' Battn. Awarded M.M.

For conspicuous gallantry and devotion to duty during the Third Battle of Ypres between the actions of July 31 and August 22, 1917. This man has displayed the greatest gallantry and resource in assisting to salve derelict tanks from the vicinity of Wilde Wood under heavy fire. On August 7, 1917, whilst salving tanks, the party were driven to cover by a heavy bombardment. Two men were found to be missing. Pte. Dryden returned through the barrage and found the two men wounded, dressed their wounds, and helped them to a place of safety, all the while being under artillery fire.

76052 L/Cpl. PRINT, S. ' C ' Battn. Awarded M.M.

For conspicuous gallantry and devotion to duty during the whole period of the Third Battle of Ypres, between July 31 and August 22, 1917. This N.C.O. has displayed the greatest courage and resource in assisting to salve derelict tanks from vicinity of Wilde Wood under heavy hostile artillery fire. By his cheerful manner and fearless conduct he has inspired all his comrades in circumstances of difficulty and danger.

156419 A/Sergt. LEITCH, A. 184th Tunn. Coy. Awarded M.M.

Sergt. Leitch displayed great gallantry and exceptional leadership near St. Julien on the morning of August 13, 1917. The party making tank crossings over the Steenebeek, 100 yards north of

St. Julien, became involved in a heavy hostile barrage, killing the officer in charge and the sapper next to the officer at the outset. Sergt. Leitch, although badly shaken by the burst—which was close to him—pulled their bodies out of the Beek and got his men into shell-holes. After the barrage, which lasted over two hours, ceased, Sergt. Leitch temporarily buried the dead, and sending off those who had been wounded, rallied the party of thirty men, and stood to, expecting an enemy attack. He finally withdrew his men before dawn.

2955 Cpl. ROSS, A. ' G ' Battn. Awarded M.M.

Operations in the Ypres Salient, August 19, 1917. For conspicuous gallantry and devotion to duty. He ably assisted his tank commander (2nd Lieut. Coutts) in holding a line of shell-holes after the objective had been reached, and the enemy driven out of the Cockcroft. He took charge while his tank commander went to fetch the infantry up to consolidate the position. He set a fine example all day.

69986 Gnr. SMITH, H. E. ' B ' Battn. Awarded M.M.

Operations in the Ypres Salient, August 19, 1917. For conspicuous gallantry and devotion to duty. When the other gunners of his crew had been knocked out, although himself wounded, he worked their guns in turn, and afterwards helped in driving the tank. He afterwards returned to his gun and fought it on the way home. His conduct was exemplary throughout the day.

76496 Gnr. SPENCER, A. E. ' C ' Battn. Awarded M.M.

For conspicuous gallantry in the vicinity of the Steenebeek River during the Third Battle of Ypres on August 21, 1917. This man displayed the greatest coolness and gallantry in extinguishing a fire inside his tank, in spite of suffocating fumes and chance of immediate explosion. During the whole action he repeatedly volunteered for any dangerous duty.

24672 Sergt. DEAN, H. ' C ' Battn. Awarded M.M.

For conspicuous gallantry in the neighbourhood of Frezenberg Redoubt during the Third Battle of Ypres on August 21–22, 1917. This N.C.O., by his courage and cheerfulness, kept up the spirits of his crew under most trying circumstances. With utter disregard for his own safety he exposed himself to heavy machine-gun fire and snipers in assisting two severely wounded men to safety.

241 L/Cpl. JAGGER, E., M.M. ' D ' Battn. Awarded D.C.M.

At Buelow Farm, near St. Julien, on August 22, 1917, his tank received a direct hit, killing his officer and sergeant. Under very heavy shell and machine-gun fire he transferred a wounded member of his crew to another tank, returned, and evacuated the remaining two wounded to a shell-hole. After handing over his Lewis guns to the infantry he found that the two wounded had been buried by shell fire. He succeeded in digging them out with his hands and in taking them to the dressing station.

136326 Spr. RIDDELL, W. 184th Tunn. Coy. Awarded M.M.

For bravery and complete disregard of personal danger at St. Julien, at dawn on August 22, 1917. During the approach and passage of the attacking tanks over the repaired road bridge, Spr. Riddell was conspicuous for his fine example under the heavy hostile shelling of the Steenebeek Valley, and especially while filling up the repaired portion of the bridge with bricks as it became pressed down by each successive tank, enabling all attacking tanks to cross this bridge successfully.

78690 Sergt. MISSEN, R. ' F ' Battn. Awarded D.C.M.

For conspicuous gallantry. During the attack at Ypres, between St. Julien and Frezenberg, on August 22, 23, and 24, 1917, he volunteered at great personal risk to crawl back from tank F 41 at Gallipoli to stop our infantry firing on the crew. He got through, though almost surrounded by snipers at close range and under heavy artillery and machine-gun fire from both sides.

69575 Gnr. MORREY, W. ' F ' Battn. Awarded D.C.M.

For conspicuous gallantry and devotion to duty between St. Julien and Frezenberg, on August 22, 23, and 24, 1917. When tank F 41 became ditched in advance of our infantry and completely isolated and surrounded by the enemy, he very ably assisted his officers to fight the tank until the night of the 24th. He was twice wounded on the 22nd, but, with the remainder of the crew, inflicted heavy casualties on the enemy and held them up to the east of Hill 35.

1407 Sergt. DUDLEY, T. J. ' F ' Battn. Awarded D.C.M.

For gallantry at Ypres on August 22, 1917. Although badly wounded in the eyes and nearly blind, he took command of the crew of F 43, which was ditched near Somme Farm, when 2nd Lieut. Harding was hit, sent crew on with guns, and stuck to 2nd Lieut. Harding till he saw he was dead.

69629 Gnr. HAYTON, E. W. ' F ' Battn. Awarded M.M.
69463 Gnr. ARTHURS, F. C. ' F ' Battn. Awarded M.M.
69571 Gnr. BUDD, P. E. ' F ' Battn. Awarded M.M.

For conspicuous gallantry and devotion to duty in action between St. Julien and Frezenberg on August 22, 23, and 24. When tank F 41 became ditched in advance of our infantry and completely isolated and surrounded by the enemy, they very ably assisted their officers to fight the tank until the night of the 24th. Though wounded, they helped to inflict heavy casualties on the enemy and to hold them to the east of Hill 35.

69648 Gnr. BENLEY, J. H. ' F ' Battn. Awarded M.M.

For gallantry at Ypres on August 22, 23, and 24, 1917. This gunner stuck to tank F 41, which was ditched at Gallipoli, for seventy-two hours, and carried on cheerfully under Capt. Richardson and 2nd Lieut. Hill. With the rest of the crew he was responsible for killing many Germans and for holding them up to the east of Hill 35.

69726 Cpl. CALTON, E. L. ' F ' Battn. Awarded M.M.

For gallantry near Spree Farm. During the attack at Ypres on August 22, 1917, he was the only member of the crew of tank F 42 not hit. Though very much shaken, he came back through the barrage to report on the condition and position of the tank to his company commander, and volunteered to guide relief crew back through the barrage to bring in his wounded.

472 Cpl. SCOTT, J. ' C ' Battn. Awarded M.M.

For conspicuous gallantry near Hill 35 during the Third Battle of Ypres on August 22, 1917. When his tank was isolated in front of the infantry this N.C.O. volunteered to go through heavy machine-gun and snipers' fire for further orders and for information to the section commander. He successfully accomplished his mission. Throughout the action he displayed courage and initiative in a marked degree.

75934 Sergt. PRICE, W. ' C ' Battn. Awarded M.M.

For conspicuous gallantry during the Third Battle of Ypres on August 21–22, 1917. His tank was in action for twenty-six hours at Hill 35. During all this time this N.C.O., by his cheerful example and courage, inspired all his comrades and prevented them giving way to exhaustion. At the end of this period he assisted with Lewis gun fire in breaking up the right flank of an enemy counter-attack.

2676 Gnr. PICKWORTH, F. R. ' C ' Battn. Awarded M.M.

For conspicuous gallantry during the Third Battle of Ypres on August 22, 1917. When most of the crew of his tank had been severely wounded near Pommern Redoubt this man displayed great courage and self-sacrifice in several times passing through an intense artillery barrage in his efforts to obtain stretcher-bearers.

76103 Cpl. SMITH, C. 'C' Battn. Awarded M.M.

For gallantry and devotion to duty in action on August 22; 1917, between Glencorse Wood and Inverness Copse. During the whole action he set a splendid example to the remainder of the crew, controlled the fire of other gunners in the tank, and inflicted numerous casualties in heavy fighting.

2861 L/Cpl. DAGLISH, A. 'C' Battn. Awarded M.M.

For very fine driving in a tank during action on August 22, 1917, east of Ypres, over very difficult ground and in face of considerable opposition.

By his coolness and presence of mind in very trying conditions he enabled his tank to inflict heavy casualties on the enemy.

95697 Pte. HOWARD, W. H. 'B' Battn. Awarded M.M.

He was orderly to his section commander on August 24, 1917, in the vicinity of Clapham Junction.

At about 4 A.M. the enemy attacked. Pte. Howard and his section commander were then in the support line. When some of our infantry were seen to be retiring, this private went with his section commander and showed great courage and resourcefulness, shouting, ' Fritz is retiring—Come on, boys,' and leading men forward again.

The infantry were rallied and returned to their positions.

The attack was repulsed.

32248 Cpl. SIMMONS, A. G. 'D' Battn. Awarded M.M.

Near Vancouver, in the Ypres Salient, on August 27, 1917, although wounded and suffering considerable pain, continued to drive his tank with great skill over very difficult ground for two and a half hours until it finally reached its objective. He then fired the forward Lewis gun with good effect, accounting for between fifty and sixty of the enemy.

1290 Gnr. KEHOE, L. E. 'D' Battn. Awarded M.M.

At Hillock Farm, near St. Julien, on August 27, 1917, under considerable shell and heavy aimed machine-gun fire, succeeded in fixing the unditching gear to his tank unaided. When the tank became unditched he unfixed the gear again single-handed, still under heavy fire. His utter disregard of personal danger and his devotion to duty are beyond praise.

201665 Sergt. LINDSAY, J. No. 1 Salvage Coy. Awarded M.M.

On the morning of August 27, 1917, a tank was badly ditched and left at Clapham Junction, near Hooge. It was in view of the enemy and at a place which was constantly shelled. By a remarkable display of perseverance, judgment, and devotion to duty, this N.C.O. succeeded in bringing the tank back.

76467 Cpl. MORRELL, W. ' D ' Battn. Awarded M.M.

North-east of Ypres. At Delta House, north of St. Julien, on September 20, 1917, displayed great courage and resource in working outside his tank on four separate occasions under heavy machine-gun and shell fire when the tank was badly ditched. After reaching the objective he carried Lewis guns and S.A.A. to the infantry under direct fire from the enemy, who were only fifty to one hundred yards distant.

Cpl. Morrell has greatly distinguished himself under fire on two former occasions.

75045 Gnr. LEDGER, H. ' D ' Battn. Awarded M.M.

North-east of Ypres. On September 20, 1917, at Delta House, north of St. Julien, he left his tank on four separate occasions under heavy shell fire when it had become ditched, and collected material to make ramps, and enabled his tank to reach firm ground. When his engine finally gave out, within fifty yards of the enemy's line, he worked unceasingly for over two hours, until everything had been tried to rectify it without avail.

75609 L/Cpl. GUIVER, V. J. C ' Battn. (attached 2nd Bde.). Awarded D.C.M.

For gallantry and devotion to duty while chief wireless operator at a wireless station at Glencorse Wood on September 20–21, 1917. After having erected the aerials, this N.C.O. remained at duty for eighteen hours, continuously under heavy shell fire. The aerials and masts were shot away in all ten times, and each time L/Cpl. Guiver went out himself under shell fire and repaired the damage. The distant mast being finally destroyed, L/Cpl. Guiver showed great initiative by making a substitute out of an iron screw picket insulated with rope. By his initiative and devotion to duty the wireless station was kept open during the whole action.

200195 Pte. ALLEN, C. S. ' A ' Battn. Awarded D.C.M.

For conspicuous gallantry and devotion to duty. On the night of October 1, 1917, he volunteered to accompany the commander of another section to assist in taping a route from Observatory Ridge to Polygon Wood. He was blown up by a shell, but, despite his shaken condition, he still carried on. On the night of October 3, 1917, he again volunteered for this duty and assisted in taping a route from Polygon Wood to Black Watch Corner.

A heavy enemy barrage was encountered, but he continued to assist in laying the tape, running from shell-hole to shell-hole with his officer. On October 4, 1917, he remained with the section commander and accompanied, on foot, the tanks into action. His officer was killed while leading the tanks in front of the infantry. In spite of the enemy being within a few yards of him, this man collected all maps and papers from the body of his officer and took them back to his company commander.

40051 Sergt. DAVIES, D. 'A' Battn. Awarded D.C.M.

For conspicuous gallantry and devotion to duty. On October 3, 1917, when his tank commander was wounded, he immediately took charge and guided the tank, with great coolness, through a heavy barrage to its place of assembly. On October 4, 1917, he took the tank into action and inflicted very heavy casualties on the enemy in the vicinity of Reutel. He undoubtedly contributed largely to the success of the operations in that area, as before the arrival of his tank the infantry were held up owing to heavy machine-gun and rifle fire.

75954 Pte. (A/L/Cpl.) JARVIS, F. 'A' Battn. Awarded M.M.

For conspicuous gallantry and determination. On October 4, 1917, in the vicinity of Reutel, he was badly wounded in the hand, but continued to fire his Lewis gun until the tank came out of action. Later, when the crew were forced to evacuate the tank, he volunteered to remain, despite the heavy enemy barrage, until a guard could be sent to relieve him. The guard was unable to reach him for twenty-four hours owing to the heavy hostile shelling.

200800 Gnr. WOOD, A. 'D' Battn. Awarded M.M.

For gallantry and devotion to duty in the Ypres Salient, north-east of Ypres, on October 9, 1917.

When his tank had been set on fire by a direct hit, and the ammunition inside was beginning to explode, Gnr. Wood rushed back into the tank from a shell-hole into which the tank commander had evacuated the crew as the fire was obviously beyond control, and most gallantly tried to extinguish the blaze with a fire-extinguisher until he was dragged back almost overcome by the fumes. Whilst in the tank Gnr. Wood was in imminent danger of his life from the flames and fumes, the exploding ammunition, and the heavy shell fire to which the tank was being subjected at the time.

Later on he showed an excellent example of courage in assisting to carry back wounded members of his crew under shell fire.

IMMEDIATE AWARDS—OTHER RANKS

PALESTINE DETACHMENT

L/Cpl. HATHERALL, V. Awarded D.C.M.
Pte. JANES, P. Awarded D.C.M.
Pte. OLDKNOW, J. Awarded D.C.M.

On April 17, 1917, for conspicuous gallantry in rescuing the officer and four men of a burning tank in operations against Gaza. These three men were all wounded but succeeded in carrying the rescued officer and men to a trench 200 yards behind them under heavy fire. They then went forward again to the burning tank in an endeavour to save the guns.

Pte. RANKIN, A. Awarded D.C.M.

For conspicuous gallantry as a tank driver on April 19, 1917. Although he was himself wounded, and his officer and the rest of the crew were out of action, he managed to extricate his tank under very heavy shell fire and successfully drove it to a place of safety.

Pte. COOPER, J. Awarded M.M.

On November 2, 1917, for conspicuous bravery in bringing in wounded under very heavy shell fire during the 3rd battle of Gaza.

BATTLE OF CAMBRAI, 1917

76066 Pte. LYTLE, S. E. 'A' Battn. Awarded M.M.

For gallantry and devotion to duty in the operations near Marcoing. On November 19, 1917, he assisted the company reconnaissance officer to lay the tapes marking his company's route. On November 20, 1917, when the infantry were held up by a machine-gun, this man crept round to the rear of its position and endeavoured to locate it. When this proved impracticable, he deliberately exposed himself three times to draw its fire and thus expose itself, A tank eventually put the gun out of action.

200846 Pte. (A/L/Cpl.) TOLSON, J. C. 'D' Battn. Awarded M.M.

For conspicuous gallantry near Flesquieres on November 20, 1917. When his tank had been put out of action by two direct hits, and three of his crew were wounded, displayed marked gallantry and initiative in organising parties to bring in wounded from several tanks which had been knocked out. On three separate occasions he went back under extremely heavy and practically point-blank machine-gun fire to dress and carry in the wounded. With utter disregard for personal safety, and entirely on his own initiative, he undoubtedly saved several lives.

78626 Pte. RICHARDSON, W. ' E ' Battn. Awarded M.M.

At Flesquieres, on November 20, 1917, with tank 'Edward II, under 2nd Lieut. Bion. This man, on receiving the order to evacuate the tank, jumped out first under heavy machine-gun fire, and got a Lewis gun into action to cover the evacuation of the remainder of the crew, all of whom had to evacuate on the most exposed side owing to the door of the other side being jammed.

This man displayed great gallantry all through this action, and his tank commander reports his example as magnificent. By this special act he probably saved several lives.

40376 Cpl. STICKLER, W. H. ' A ' Battn. Awarded D.C.M.

For conspicuous gallantry and devotion to duty in the operation near Marcoing on November 20, 1917. When his tank came under the fire of an enemy field battery at a range of 100 yards this N.C.O. continued to fire his 6-pndr. gun, despite the fact that the tank had received a direct hit and was in flames. He himself silenced one enemy gun with a direct hit.

Throughout the whole operations he set a splendid example to his crew.

75704 Pte. SUMMERS, A. D. ' A ' Battn. Awarded D.C.M.

For conspicuous gallantry in the operations near Marcoing on November 20, 1917. When his tank, owing to its inability to swing at the moment, could not be brought to bear on three enemy machine-guns, this man got out of the tank with a Lewis gun and engaged the machine-guns at a range of about fifty yards. He put the enemy machine-guns out of action, killing the crews as they ran. Throughout the whole time he was exposed to heavy machine-gun fire.

75634 Cpl. MAYGLOTHLING, A. ' A ' Battn. Awarded D.C.M.

For conspicuous gallantry and devotion to duty in the operations near Noyelles on November 20, 1917. Within half an hour of going into action the whole of his crew were wounded, but although he himself was severely wounded he kept the guns in action. His tank was unable to move for nearly an hour, but he still kept the guns going. On four occasions fires broke out in the tank but each time it was put out, and the tank was kept in action until all the ammunition had been expended. When the tank finally came out of action, all four Lewis guns had been hit. This N.C.O., throughout the whole time his tank was in action, set a very fine example to the remainder of his crew.

91302 Gnr. HOULT, J. ' H ' Battn. Awarded D.C.M.

Near Ribecourt, on November 20, 1917. The tank of which he was gearsman got on fire ; he assisted to put this out. Later, between Ribecourt and Marcoing, on November 20, 1917, this gunner showed conspicuous gallantry; after his tank had been knocked out by a direct hit from a shell, which killed his section commander and wounded his tank commander, Gnr. Hoult got out of his tank and advanced on foot at once towards the enemy with his revolver, the infantry being still 300 yards in rear of his position. By this action he stopped the enemy from advancing. This gunner showed great determination and a total disregard for his personal safety.

76687 L/Cpl. BUDD, A. 'C' Battn. Awarded D.C.M.

During the action on the Gonnelieu Ridge on November 20, 1917, this man was first driver of his tank, which received a direct hit, which wounded all the crew except L/Cpl. Budd and another man. The tank was on an enemy trench when hit. This N.C.O., without a moment's hesitation, collected bombs and bombed the enemy away from his tank. He then assisted to get all his wounded crew to a place of safety, and prevented them falling into the hands of the enemy. This N.C.O. has been previously brought to notice for conspicuous gallantry at Arras in April, 1917.

200601 Gnr. GREEN, C. W. 'C' Battn. Awarded D.C.M.

For conspicuous gallantry in action on November 20, 21, and 23, 1917. On the last occasion, during the action at La Fontaine, every member of his crew was wounded. In spite of this he assisted in rescuing the whole crew of another tank which had received a direct hit. He drove his tank out of action with sixteen people on board, eleven of whom were wounded and one killed, all by armour-piercing bullets, inside the tank. The tank was suffering from mechanical defects and was full of steam from a boiling radiator, and eventually received a direct hit when behind our lines. Before returning this tank had expended every round of 6-pndr. ammunition on the enemy in the village. The determination and gallantry shown by this man in extricating his tank under the greatest difficulties was most praiseworthy.

92530 Gnr. MOODIE, R. K. 'F' Battn. Awarded M.M.

For conspicuous gallantry and devotion to duty. During the tank operations on November 20, 1917, this gunner did continuous excellent work under fire. When his tank became ditched he got out and fixed the unditching gear in face of a heavy machine-gun fire. He then deliberately walked round to the exposed side of the tank to direct the driver in getting the tank out. Later in the day, at Masnières bridgehead, he continually passed from tank to tank with messages under machine-gun and snipers' fire.

He displayed great bravery and coolness.

75540 A/Sergt. TAYLOR, G. H. ' D ' Battn. Awarded M.M.

For gallantry and devotion to duty near Flesquieres on November 20, 1917. When his tank had become ditched, mounted his Lewis gun on the parapet of a trench under heavy machine-gun fire, and silenced the enemy, who were preventing our infantry from advancing. Later, though heavily sniped, he ran out to another tank and directed it so that the infantry could advance behind it without being exposed to fire. Again he gave valuable assistance in carrying back wounded under fire. This N.C.O. has been brought to notice for gallantry on a previous occasion.

200695 Pte. FORTUNE, T. ' D ' Battn. Awarded M.M.

For gallantry and devotion to duty near Flesquieres on November 20, 1917.

On his tank being set on fire by direct hits and evacuated, a volunteer was called for to proceed to other tanks and to the infantry, who by this time were well in the rear, and warn them of the position of an active enemy battery.

Although wounded, Pte. Fortune immediately came forward, and in spite of very heavy machine-gun and snipers' fire gallantly carried out his instructions.

78731 L/Cpl. LAYCOCK, H. ' E ' Battn. Awarded M.M.

While performing the duties of driver in his tank in action near Flesquieres on November 20, 1917, he was wounded in the face by splinters from a bullet ; he continued to drive his tank until it was put out of action by a direct hit some hours later. He then volunteered as an orderly to keep his officer in touch with the company commander, and was wounded in the leg by a bullet while doing this. He refused to go to the dressing station, and remained with his crew until they were brought back.

91686 Pte. FRANCIS, W. M. ' E ' Battn. Awarded M.M.

During the Cambrai operations on November 20, 1917. After evacuating the tank, which had received a direct hit, he joined a small advance party of the infantry and assisted in forming a strong point. When a German two-seater aeroplane flew low and fired a machine-gun on the infantry, he retaliated with his Lewis gun, wounding the pilot and forcing the machine to land.

Throughout the whole action he behaved in a most excellent manner and displayed marked coolness.

201444 Gnr. PHILIP, D. T. ' G ' Battn. Awarded M.M.

For conspicuous gallantry and devotion to duty. On November 20, 1917, west of Graincourt, though wounded, he served his 6-pndr. gun in a most cool and gallant manner.

He knocked out an enemy field gun at about 600 yards range which had already knocked out several tanks close by, and which was at the time firing at his own tank.

69737 Gnr. DOE, W. V. ' G ' Battn. Awarded M.M.

For conspicuous gallantry and devotion to duty. He was orderly to his section commander on November 20 and 21, 1917. His conduct was splendid throughout, and he was constantly volunteering to guide tanks forward under heavy shell fire.

201385 Cpl. OWEN, F. ' G ' Battn. Awarded M.M.

For conspicuous gallantry and devotion to duty. On November 20, 1917, he drove his tank with consummate coolness and skill under very great difficulties. At the final objective he had to work untiringly for two hours to get his engine running, while the tank was surrounded by the enemy, who were firing at it very heavily with machine-guns.

2778 Gnr. HUDSON, C. ' G ' Battn. Awarded M.M.

For conspicuous gallantry and devotion to duty. On November 20, 1917, although badly wounded in the head, he continued to use his guns with great coolness and courage after the crew had been forced to evacuate the tank.

Although surrounded by the enemy and wounded a second and third time he remained at his post, showing the greatest bravery.

69954 L/Cpl. HUGO, E. R. ' G ' Battn. Awarded M.M.

For conspicuous gallantry and devotion to duty. His tank was in action on November 20 and 21, 1917. His gallant conduct was particularly noticeable on November 21. He stuck to his gun and worked it with splendid results, although wounded three times. After the third time he acted as gearsman for the remainder of the time the tank was in action. He set a splendid example of grit.

200052 Pte. (L./Cpl.) MURDOCK, T. ' A ' Battn. Awarded M.M.

For conspicuous gallantry and devotion to duty in the operations near Marcoing on November 20, 1917. When his officer was killed this N.C.O. immediately took charge of the tank and directed it to its objective, the crossings over the Marcoing Canal. When his tank was put out of action by a direct hit from a field gun he remained with it awaiting orders. He also assisted in knocking out an enemy 77-cm. gun, killing or scattering the crew with his Lewis guns. Throughout the whole of the operation he set a fine example to the remainder of the crew.

200147 Pte. **SPRINGHAM, P. D.** 'A' Battn. Awarded M.M.

For conspicuous gallantry and devotion to duty in the attack on Marcoing on November 20, 1917. His tank, when a long way in front of the infantry, received a direct hit which killed the tank commander and wounded all the crew and set the tank on fire. Although he was wounded, he got out of the tank and assisted in dressing the wounds of the remainder of the crew, and although under heavy machine-gun fire the whole time, he remained by the tank until the infantry came up half an hour later. He set a fine example to the remainder of the crew, and showed a complete disregard for his personal safety.

75012 Pte. **SMITH, W.** 'A' Battn. Awarded M.M.

For conspicuous gallantry and devotion to duty in the attack at Marcoing on November 20, 1917. This man was the first driver of his tank, and drove with great skill and determination. When blinded by shell fire he insisted on continuing to drive the tank, and when forced to give up he took over the duties of brakesman until the tank was finally put out of action, near its objective, by a direct hit from a field gun. He set a very fine example to the other members of the crew, and on several previous occasions he has acquitted himself in a most courageous manner.

40298 Pte. **MURRAY, R. J.** 'A' Battn. Awarded M.M.

For gallantry and devotion to duty in the operations near Marcoing and Noyelles on November 20 and 21, 1917. During the two days this man, who was the first driver of his tank, drove the tank into action four times. On each occasion it was almost entirely due to the skill and determination of this man that the crew of the tank were enabled to inflict heavy casualties on the enemy.

Throughout the whole time he set a fine example to the remainder of the crew.

200089 Sergt. **LOSE, L. C.** 'A' Battn. Awarded M.M.

This N.C.O. was in charge of a tank in the operations near Marcoing on November 20, 1917. He skilfully got his tank to its final objective, showing great courage and determination, and attacked an enemy field battery at close range. His tank received a direct hit which killed the first driver and wounded Sergt. Lose and four others of the crew. Sergt. Lose got his crew out of the tank and took the wounded back to a place of safety. He then returned to the tank and salved the guns, and with the remnants of his crew stood by the tank until ordered to withdraw.

75417 Sergt. **SAYERS, C. G.** 'A' Battn. Awarded M.M.

For gallantry in the operations near Noyelles on November 20, 1917. Four times a fire broke out in the tank, and each time this

N.C.O. was instrumental in its being put out. Although wounded, he kept the guns in his tank in action and inflicted heavy casualties on the enemy. His coolness set a fine example to the crew during the whole of the operations.

200049 Pte. (L/Cpl.) CHANDLER, L. ' A ' Battn. Awarded M.M.

For gallantry in the operations near Marcoing and Noyelles on November 20 and 21, 1917. He was the first driver in his tank, and throughout the operations on both days he drove with great skill. He was wounded in two places on the second day at about 1.30 P.M., but continued to drive the tank until it was brought out of action in the evening.

77426 Sergt. GARDNER, J. E. ' A ' Battn. Awarded M.M.

For gallantry in the operations near Noyelles on November 20, 1917. This N.C.O. showed great coolness in dealing with an enemy field gun which was firing at his tank at 200 yards range. He knocked out one field gun and silenced another, besides putting several enemy machine-guns out of action and inflicting heavy casualties.

76492 Cpl. EIDMANS, H. P. ' B ' Battn. Awarded M.M.

This N.C.O. carried out his duties as tank N.C.O. most efficiently in action on November 20 and 21, 1917, at the attack on Cantaing. He volunteered to join a crew for which a N.C.O. was required, for the attack on Fontaine on November 23. On this day he continued at duty in action and did very good work after being wounded in the leg.

He has consistently shown fine leadership and great devotion to duty, and set a splendid example which has inspired the crews with confidence.

76487 Cpl. STILLIWELL, H. ' B ' Battn. Awarded M.M.

This N.C.O. showed great gallantry in action on November 20 and 21, 1917. On the latter day, at the attack on Cantaing, when his tank was ditched in a sunken road in front of the village and the Lewis guns could not be used, he fired from the manhole with his revolver on the enemy, who were firing on the tank at close range, and was greatly instrumental in keeping the enemy off for over an hour until arrival of the infantry. The whole time he was using his revolver it was necessary to expose himself to the fire of the enemy.

77457 L/Cpl. STRACHAN, J. ' B ' Battn. Awarded M.M.

This N.C.O. drove a tank in action on November 20, 1917, over the Hindenburg Support Line, and was wounded in the leg. He said nothing about his wound, and went into action again next day at Cantaing. He showed great skill in driving and a determination and devotion to duty that set a splendid example to the crew.

He volunteered to drive his tank in action again on November 23, but was ordered to hospital by the medical officer.

78311 Sergt. HENDON, G. A. 'H' Battn. Awarded M.M.

For conspicuous gallantry in the attack at Ribecourt on November 20, 1917. Although seriously wounded early in the attack he continued for several hours to serve his gunners and to load magazines, passing them to the Lewis gunners of his tank. He remained at his post throughout the whole action.

78480 Sergt. NASH, E. M. 'H' Battn. Awarded M.M.

For conspicuous gallantry north-east of Ribecourt on November 20, 1917.

His tank had received a direct hit, killing his tank commander and seriously wounding all but one of the crew. This N.C.O., although the tank was still under direct fire and only 200 yards from the enemy's battery, took his wounded men to a place of safety. He remained with his tank until it was impossible for him to do any more, and he was ordered to leave it. The tank was several hundred yards ahead of our infantry, who did not come up till over half an hour afterwards.

This N.C.O. throughout showed a total disregard for his personal safety and great coolness under fire, setting a fine example.

200433 Sergt. RADCLIFFE, F. 'C' Battn. Awarded M.M.

During the action on the Gonnelieu Spur, on November 20, 1917, he showed a splendid example of pluck and endurance to the rest of his crew. For a long time after he had been almost blinded by splinters he continued to drive his tank into action.

76444 L/Cpl. PATEMAN, C. R. 'C' Battn. Awarded M.M.

During the action on the Gonnelieu Ridge, on November 20, 1917, his tank received a direct hit which wounded his officer. This N.C.O. collected the remainder of his crew, which he transferred to another tank, and continued the action till its conclusion.

76449 L/Cpl. DAY, B. T. 'C' Battn. Awarded M.M.

During the action on the Gonnelieu Ridge, on November 20, 1917, in the absence of his tank officer, this N.C.O. led his tank into action and fought it with conspicuous gallantry and success. He has previously been brought to notice for gallant conduct, notably during the Battle of Arras in April, 1917.

200560 Gnr. RIDOUT, C. C. 'C' Battn. Awarded M.M.

On November 20, 1917, during the attack on the Gonnelieu Ridge, this man displayed the greatest gallantry. Although severely wounded he insisted on driving his tank to its final objective, which he reached before collapsing from loss of blood.

IMMEDIATE AWARDS—OTHER RANKS

77447 Sergt. GOWARD, W., M.M. ' C ' Battn. Awarded Bar to M.M.

Both on November 20 and 23, 1917, in the attack on the Gonnelieu and Bourlon Ridges, this N.C.O. displayed conspicuous gallantry and set a fine example to the rest of his crew. Although wounded in the face he continued to fire his 6-pndr. with great success, knocking out many enemy machine-guns.
(M.M. awarded for action on July 31, 1917.)

76667 Cpl. GILLIE, C. ' C ' Battn. Awarded M.M.

For conspicuous gallantry in action on November 20 and 23, 1917. On the latter occasion he did splendid work with his gun until wounded in the head, hands, and leg. Until the tank was set on fire he worked the secondary gears with his uninjured hand. In spite of his wounds he showed a fine example of cheerfulness and courage.

200636 Gnr. BARDILL, H. ' C ' Battn. Awarded M.M.

Throughout the action on November 20, 1917, at the Gonnelieu Ridge this man always volunteered for any dangerous duty. He twice left his tank, under heavy machine-gun and snipers' fire, to fetch water for the radiator and fix the fascine. Although wounded in the hand he insisted on going into action again on November 23, and drove his tank with the greatest skill and gallantry in action at Bourlon Wood.

76053 Gnr. BARRON, R. ' C ' Battn. Awarded M.M.

During the attack on Latteau Wood, on November 20, 1917, this man drove his tank with conspicuous gallantry and success. Again, on November 23, he drove his tank with the greatest bravery and coolness through a hail of armour-piercing bullets in the attack on La Fontaine, until dangerously wounded by a bullet in the throat. The excellent work done by this tank was very greatly due to this man's skill and courage.

77480 L/Cpl. CRONIN, D. ' C.' Battn. Awarded M.M.

During the attack on Lateau Wood and Pam Pam Farm, on November 20, 1917, this N.C.O. displayed the greatest gallantry in firing on the enemy with his Lewis gun, although his tank had been pierced by armour-piercing bullets. Throughout the action he showed a magnificent example of courage and cheerfulness. This N.C.O. has been previously brought to notice for conspicuous gallantry both at Arras in April, 1917, and again at Ypres on July 31, 1917.

201078 L/Cpl. SILVESTER, G. ' F ' Battn. Awarded M.M.

For conspicuous gallantry and determination in the operations on November 20, 1917. When his tank commander had been wounded in the head this N.C.O. took command of the tank until his recovery, and on the whole fought a most determined action. His spirit of pluck and cheerfulness was most marked throughout the day and inspired his tired crew.

Again, in the operations against Bourlon village on November 27, when the tank became ditched and was surrounded on three sides by the enemy, this N.C.O. went out several times, under very heavy machine-gun and rifle fire, and bandaged several wounded men and carried them to a place of safety. Had it not been for his courage and self-sacrifice, it is almost certain these men would have fallen into the hands of the enemy.

69540 Sergt. ARNELL, F. ' F ' Battn. Awarded M.M.

On two occasions during the recent operations on November 20 and subsequent days this N.C.O. has been in a tank which has received a direct hit, and on both occasions has shown the greatest courage and resource, and by his splendid example has inspired the survivors under the worst possible conditions. His conduct in action has been of the highest order and of the greatest value to the officers of his company.

92716 Sergt. ABEL, C. ' F ' Battn. Awarded M.M.

For conspicuous gallantry and skill in action. On November 20, 1917, south-east of La Vacquerie, his tank was fired on by a field gun which he at once engaged with his 6-pndr. and silenced, the gun being afterwards reported as destroyed by his tank. Later in the day he did splendid work at Pam Pam Farm. Again in action on November 21 at Marcoing and Roumilly, he accounted for large numbers of the enemy on the railway embankment. He also went into action on the 27th at Fontaine, where he again did most valuable work in face of very heavy machine-gun fire with armour-piercing bullets. He has displayed the greatest courage and disregard of danger throughout the operations, and the success of his tank is largely due to his example.

201212 Cpl. HUNTER, B. ' F ' Battn. Awarded M.M.

On November 20, 1917, in the tank operations, this N.C.O. drove his tank with flaps open, although many splinters were coming through. He saw infantry signalling for assistance, and drove his tank very skilfully to their aid, enabling the officer to capture a machine-gun as well as a strong point and eighty prisoners, who were holding out on the Blue Line.

Again, on November 27, at Fontaine, when his tank had received a direct hit, Cpl. Hunter was wounded in the shoulder and hand and taken by the Germans, who dressed him and told him to walk to the Cambrai road. After proceeding a short way, he turned round and came back into our lines through heavy machine-gun and rifle fire of both sides. He displayed great determination and pluck all through the operations.

IMMEDIATE AWARDS—OTHER RANKS

69619 Gnr. DOLLEY, W. T. ' F ' Battn.   Awarded M.M.

For conspicuous gallantry and devotion to duty. While in action on November 20, 1917, at a critical moment the fascine fell from his tank, wedging the nose of the tank and stopping it. Though well in advance of infantry and under heavy machine-gun fire, he got out and cut it clear with an axe. He was again in action at Crevecourt on the 21st, where he behaved with the greatest gallantry, and did not return until the 24th. On the 27th he again went into action at Fontaine, and was with the leading tank in the fighting in the main street. Here again he showed the greatest courage and devotion. He has at all times during the operations been the mainstay of his crew, and his courage and determination have been very marked.

69432 Gnr. PASCOE, A. ' F ' Battn.   Awarded M.M.

For conspicuous gallantry and devotion to duty. In action on November 20, 1917, his tank having been knocked out by a direct hit, he volunteered to fill up a place in a crew of another tank going into action at Crevecourt. Here he was wounded, and although suffering from great pain and exhaustion he stuck to the tank, which was engaged continuously till morning of 24th, when tank returned to rallying point.

92354 Gnr. BARRETT, W. ' F ' Battn.   Awarded M.M.

For conspicuous gallantry and devotion to duty. He drove through the first day, November 20, 1917, to the Brown Line, where the tank broke a sleeve. He worked at the tank through the remainder of that day and all next night repairing it for action. At Fontaine, on 27th, his tank was blown in by a field gun at ten yards range. He got out and directed his officer from outside in getting clear of the gun and out of the way of the tank following. He was standing in the open street during this time under short-range fire. He displayed great gallantry and coolness throughout.

201747 Gnr. TEBAULT, W. ' F ' Battn.   Awarded M.M.

For conspicuous courage and endurance. He drove his tank through the whole of the operations of November 20, 1917, and reached all his objectives. On the 21st he drove to Crevecourt, and was in action day and night till the morning of the 24th. It is largely due to this man that his tank did such valuable and gallant work. He stuck to his post in spite of the very heavy machine-gun, armour-piercing, and direct shell fire. This man, to my knowledge, has been in the line since March, 1915, and although his nerves entirely broke down in October, 1916, he has pulled himself together and stuck to it in the most creditable manner.

271

THE TANK CORPS BOOK OF HONOUR

78437 Cpl. THOMSON, F. ' I ' Battn. Awarded M.M.

For conspicuous gallantry and devotion to duty. On the morning of November 20, 1917, near La Vacquerie, the tank fought by this N.C.O. crossed the Hindenburg Second Line with three other tanks. The latter were hit in quick succession by field guns at short range. These guns then concentrated on this tank, and the only possible course was to attempt to move behind the crest line of the hill. To effect this a very difficult trench had to be crossed. Three approaches were made under heavy fire, and only at the fourth attempt was a practicable crossing found. It was undoubtedly owing to the courage and discrimination shown by this N.C.O., under the most trying circumstances, that this tank and crew were ultimately saved from destruction.

91944 Gnr. WRIGHT, R. ' I ' Battn. Awarded M.M.
91791 Gnr. BLURTON A. ' I ' Battn. Awarded M.M.

For conspicuous gallantry and devotion to duty. At the action near La Vacquerie, on November 20, 1917, these men acted as orderlies to the company commander. They were continuously taking messages to tanks which were under heavy fire, and were in all cases successful.

78545 L/Cpl. MILLERSON, A. T. ' I ' Battn. Awarded M.M.

For conspicuous gallantry. When his tank was out of action with a broken sprocket, near La Vacquerie, on November 20, 1917, he went to several tanks in the neighbourhood and successfully guided them over some very bad trenches at the Corner Work. This was done under heavy machine-gun and shrapnel fire.

92981 Sergt. FARLEY, A. C. ' I ' Battn. Awarded M.M.

For conspicuous gallantry and devotion to duty. Though wounded in the shoulder and wrist early in the action near La Vacquerie, on November 20, 1917, he continued to fight his guns throughout the day and did not report his wounds until the tank had rallied.

201608 Cpl. TRENDALE, F. G. ' I ' Battn. Awarded M.M.
95759 Gnr. KELLY, J. P. ' I ' Battn. Awarded M.M.

For conspicuous gallantry and devotion to duty. When the tank was ditched near La Vacquerie on November 20, 1917, both these men showed great coolness and gallantry in unditching the tank under heavy shell fire, two other men having been wounded previously when attempting to do the same.

78355 Gnr. HEARSLEY, A. C. ' I ' Battn. Awarded M.M.

For conspicuous gallantry. On the morning of November 20, 1917, near La Vacquerie, the advance tank of No. 9 Section ditched owing to the fascine falling across the front of the turret and obscuring the driver's view. The tank was then under heavy machine-gun and shell fire. This man volunteered to get out and cut away the fascine, also to fix the unditching gear. This he successfully accomplished.

92266 Gnr. BEST, R. ' I ' Battn. Awarded M.M.

For conspicuous gallantry. On November 20, 1917, in La Vacquerie Valley, this man, while his tank was subjected to heavy artillery and machine-gun fire, got on top of the tank in order to release the fascine, which had dropped over the tracks, the releasing gear having failed to act.

201265 Sergt. MAYRICK, C. J. ' G ' Battn. Awarded M.M.

For conspicuous gallantry and devotion to duty. In the operations of November 20 to 23, 1917, this N.C.O. was appointed a tank commander and took part in five tank assaults, each time reaching his objective and handing over the captured position to the infantry. Throughout the action he worked with untiring energy and displayed cool and sound judgment.

Finally he brought his tank successfully to the rallying point.

40311 Pte. SARGENT, J. J. ' G ' Battn. Awarded M.M.

For conspicuous gallantry and devotion to duty. On November 20, 1917, he twice drove his tank through the village of Graincourt with great skill, in the face of the fire of a light field gun which had already knocked out six tanks. His steady courage and good driving assured the capture of the village and enabled the infantry to take possession.

201333 Pte. SYKES, E. ' G ' Battn. Awarded M.M.

For conspicuous gallantry and devotion to duty. On November 20, 1917, when his tank was ditched, and after two men had been killed while endeavouring to fix the fascine in position, he got out under very heavy machine-gun fire and succeeded in fastening it properly, thereby enabling the tank to unditch and resume the fight.

75204 L/Cpl. OWERS, L. ' B ' Battn. Awarded M.M.

This N.C.O. drove a tank on November 21, 1917, in Noyelles, and he showed great courage and skill in driving. A house in the village had been set on fire, and the way of the tank seemed blocked as the flames of the fire reached nearly across the street, the heat and smoke being intense.

L/Cpl. Owers, however, by skilful and daring driving, and at great personal risk, managed to successfully pass the house, although he was obliged to keep the large driver's flap fully open to obtain a sufficient view. The tank carried on in action and was instrumental in clearing the village of the enemy and allowing the infantry to occupy the village with very few casualties.

300366 Pte. HAWGOOD, A. A. ' B ' Battn. Awarded M.M.

This soldier on November 21, 1917, in the village of Cantaing, after fighting his gun with great determination, was wounded in six places and was laid down on the floor of the tank, and while in this position the tank stopped through mechanical trouble. Although badly wounded and suffering great pain, he managed to reach the magneto, which was the cause of the trouble, and this enabled the tank to proceed to its objective and inflict further casualties on the enemy.

The gallantry and devotion to duty of this man set a splendid example to the rest of the crew.

78036 L/Cpl. WINTER, G. ' I ' Battn. Awarded M.M.

For conspicuous gallantry. On the night of November 22, 1917, at Ribecourt, the tank park was heavily shelled, and one tank (2824) received a direct hit on the petrol tank which set it on fire. This N.C.O. as driver, with No. 78549 Cpl. H. G. Brooker and No. 78580 Gnr. A. Speight as gearsmen, entered the burning tank and drove it away from the other tanks. They afterwards extinguished the fire. The courage and prompt action of these men undoubtedly prevented the fire from spreading to other tanks in the vicinity.

78549 Cpl. BROOKER, H. G. ' I ' Battn. Awarded M.M.
78580 Gnr. SPEIGHT, A. ' I ' Battn. Awarded M.M.

For conspicuous gallantry. On the night of November 22, 1917, at Ribecourt, the tank park was heavily shelled, and one tank (2824) received a direct hit on the petrol tank which set it on fire. 78549 Cpl. H. G. Brooker, together with 78036 L/Cpl. G. Winter as driver, and 78580 Gnr. A. Speight as gearsman, entered the burning tank and drove it away from the other tanks. They afterwards extinguished the fire. The courage and prompt action of these men undoubtedly prevented the fire from spreading to other tanks in the vicinity.

92365 Pte. SMITH, T. ' E ' Battn. Awarded M.M.

During the action near Moeuvres, on November 23, 1917, this man was wounded inside his tank, but still remained at his post firing his gun. He was half an hour later again severely wounded through his tank receiving a direct hit. He evacuated with the remainder of the crew, and lay with them in shell-holes for a period of five and a half hours. All this time he suffered extreme pain from his wounds, but refrained from making any noise which might attract the enemy to his and his crew's position. His conduct throughout showed that he had more consideration for the safety of his crew than for his own personal suffering.

40412 Pte. IRVING, R. 'B' Battn. Awarded D.C.M.

On November 23, 1917, during the attack on Fontaine, this man showed great initiative and courage. After his tank had received a direct hit in the front from a shell, which exposed the driving position and wounded the officer and driver, without the slightest hesitation Pte. Irving jumped into the driver's seat and drove the tank out of the village. During the whole of this time the tank was subjected to machine-gun fire. He was wounded in the arm by this fire, but he remained in his position in the driving seat. On its way back the tank received two direct hits from shells, the first of which set the engine on fire. This was put out and the engine restarted, and was got to within about fifty yards of our front line. The tank then became immobile, and the order was given for its evacuation. This man got out two Lewis guns and handed them over to the infantry, and stayed behind with his wounded officer until he got him into a passing tank.

This man's devotion to duty throughout the whole of the action was beyond all praise, and his resourcefulness and fine fighting spirit undoubtedly saved the tank from falling into the enemy's hands.

100629 Pte. YOUNG, W. R.A.M.C. (attached 'B' Battn.). Awarded D.C.M.

This man has been medical orderly to No. 4 Company, 'B' Battn., in all recent operations.

On November 23, 1917, in order to follow up the company tanks closely, he went in front of the infantry into Fontaine. He was blown up by a shell and wounded, but in spite of this he continued to do his duty, attending to infantry wounded as well as those of the tanks. On November 23 he did excellent work in helping to extinguish the burning clothing of two men who were on fire from a burning tank.

Throughout he has displayed the utmost devotion to duty and entire disregard of his personal safety.

75978 Gnr. TODD, A. 'C' Battn. Awarded M.M.

On November 23, 1917, during the attack on La Fontaine, when his tank was set on fire by a direct hit, this man showed the greatest pluck and coolness in helping to extinguish the fire. When he himself and five more of his crew were wounded, he ran 400 yards under intense machine-gun and artillery fire to obtain assistance from another tank, thereby saving the lives of his comrades.

91658 Pte. DOVE, F. S. ' E ' Battn. Awarded M.M.

While performing the duties of first driver in his tank in action east of Moeuvres on November 23, 1917, the tank received a direct hit, killing four of the crew and wounding three of the remainder. Being the only unwounded man, he remained with his tank assisting the wounded, two of whom he eventually sent back after dressing them.

He then remained with his tank for two hours until he saw a tank, commanded by 2nd Lieut. Carter, approaching, when he took the remaining wounded men to this tank and went to his own, refusing to leave it and saying he might be able to get it away. 2nd Lieut. Fairbank, passing in his tank some two and a half hours later, found Pt. Dove alone trying to move his tank back. He ordered him to return. At this time 2nd Lieut. Fairbank's tank received a direct hit and Pte. Dove was wounded.

76099 Sergt. HADLOW, E. ' B ' Battn. Awarded M.M.

During the attack on Fontaine on November 23, 1917, this N.C.O.'s conduct throughout was exemplary and inspiring to his tank crew.

When a heavy fusillade of armour-piercing bullets was opened on the tank, he stuck to his gun and replied vigorously. On one gun being knocked out he immediately manned another gun and effectively silenced the hostile machine-gun, which was causing severe damage to guns and crew. Eventually, when his tank was put out of action by armour-piercing bullets in the radiator, he manned his Lewis gun in the open and fired upon the Germans as they were advancing, inflicting casualties upon them and greatly assisting the infantry, who were unable to advance.

75914 A/Cpl. JUPP, E. J. ' B ' Battn. Awarded M.M.

This soldier on November 23, 1917, approaching the village of Fontaine, was wounded in the right arm, rendering it almost useless. In spite of great opposition by the enemy, this N.C.O. managed to keep his gun firing for several hours, and also helped the other gunners in the tank to remedy stoppages.

By his action and devotion to duty the tank was enabled to inflict heavy casualties on the enemy.

75951 Pte. MOON, H. C. ' B ' Battn. Awarded M.M.

On November 23, 1917, in the successful attack on Cantaing, there was an enemy field gun in action in Cantaing. Pte. Moon drove his tank with great judgment and skill, enabling the gunners in the tank to dispose of the enemy gun crew. He then drove the tank over the trail of the gun, effectually completing its destruction. Pte. Moon drove his tank for about three hours after being wounded, and though much exhausted he managed to bring it successfully out of action, where he collapsed.

In Cantaing there was very severe fighting, and the tank was there for about an hour before the arrival of the infantry.

75233 Cpl. BENNETT, H. ' B ' Battn. Awarded M.M.

On November 23, 1917, in the village of Fontaine, after his officer and driver were both disabled by a direct hit from an anti-tank gun, he at once assumed command, and showed great initiative in extricating his tank from enemy hands under great difficulty and heavy machine-gun fire. He succeeded in bringing his tank to within fifty yards of our own front line, although it received two more direct hits.

This N.C.O. set a fine example and showed a total disregard for his personal safety.

75919 L/Cpl. GILDER, F. C. ' B ' Battn. Awarded M.M.

This N.C.O. showed great determination and coolness as a tank driver during the attack on Fontaine on November 23, 1917.

Although much bruised and suffering from concussion due to a bomb exploding on the top of the tank above his head, he drove his tank with great skill and judgment. The front of the tank was subjected to a hail of machine-gun bullets, but this N.C.O. opened the shutters and used his revolver to good effect, in spite of the fact that he exposed himself in so doing.

The successful withdrawal of the tank from the village, when all guns were hit and out of action, was due to his gallant conduct, determination, and coolness under fire.

78303 Gnr. HUGHES, C. ' H ' Battn. Awarded M.M.

For conspicuous gallantry at Fontaine on November 23, 1917. When his tank was stationary through mechanical trouble and surrounded by the enemy, who bombed and fired at point-blank range and called upon the crew to surrender, he kept up his Lewis gun fire, although he only had the use of one arm, as he had been wounded. His gallant action enabled the tank to successfully withdraw. He showed great devotion to duty under very trying circumstances.

78592 Cpl. BROWNE, E. L. ' H ' Battn. Awarded M.M.

For conspicuous gallantry at Fontaine on November 23, 1917. When his tank was stationary through mechanical trouble and surrounded by the enemy, who bombed and fired at point-blank range and called upon the crew to surrender, he kept up his Lewis-gun fire, although he only had the use of one arm, as he had been wounded. His gallant action enabled the tank to successfully withdraw. He showed great devotion to duty under very trying circumstances.

78661 Gnr. LOCK, C. E. ' H ' Battn. Awarded M.M.

For conspicuous gallantry and devotion to duty at Fontaine on November 23, 1917.

This man was a Lewis gunner in a tank, and entered Fontaine, where there was great opposition. Early in the action Gnr. Lock was wounded in the hand, but in spite of the wound, which was causing him great pain, this soldier stood to his Lewis gun and kept firing during the whole action, which lasted three hours, inflicting many casualties. Gnr. Lock showed great courage and endurance, and his determination had a great moral effect on the remainder of the crew.

78296 Gnr. TOMPKINS, W. H. ' H ' Battn. Awarded M.M.

For conspicuous gallantry at Fontaine on November 23, 1917. When his tank was stationary through mechanical trouble and surrounded by the enemy, who bombed and fired at point-blank range and called upon him to surrender, he kept up his Lewis-gun fire, although he only had the use of one arm, as he had been previously wounded. His gallant action enabled the crew to successfully withdraw. He showed great devotion to duty under very trying circumstances.

91736 L/Cpl. PAVELEY, W. C. ' H ' Battn. Awarded M.M.

For conspicuous gallantry and devotion to duty in the attack on Fontaine on November 23, 1917.

He drove his tank with the driver's flap open in spite of the enemy, who tried to bomb the tank at seven yards distance, and emptied his revolver six times in their midst with good effect.

He skilfully handled his tank to enable the gunners to bring fire upon targets which he pointed out. It would have been impossible for him to have seen the targets with the driver's flap closed. By his gallantry he was the means of inflicting very heavy casualties on the enemy.

92094 Gnr. LEFTWICH, W. ' H ' Battn. Awarded M.M.

For conspicuous gallantry at Fontaine on November 23, 1917. His tank was short of petrol in the village ; although under close and heavy machine-gun fire he voluntarily got out of his tank and filled the petrol tank, which is on the outside. This prompt action enabled the tank to proceed into action and inflict further casualties upon the enemy. This gunner showed a total disregard for his personal safety.

200493 L/Cpl. SMITH, J. ' C ' Battn. Awarded M.M.

At Fontaine, on November 23, 1917, this N.C.O. handled his 6-pndr. with the greatest skill and efficiency in spite of being wounded by splinters from armour-piercing bullets. He silenced five enemy machine-guns, which were holding up the infantry, thereby enabling the advance to be continued. This N.C.O. has been previously brought to notice for gallant conduct during the Battle of Arras on April 23, 1917.

200515 Gnr. RAFFEL, J. ' C ' Battn. Awarded M.M.

On November 23, 1917, during the attack on La Fontaine, 2nd Lieut. Moore was lying in the street severely wounded. Without the slightest hesitation this man got outside his tank and, in spite of a hail of machine-gun and snipers' fire from the houses on either side, carried the officer to a place of safety.

95394 Sergt. HUNT, J. W. ' C ' Battn. Awarded M.M.

During the attack on La Fontaine, on November 23, 1917, although wounded by armour-piercing bullets he continued to fire his 6-pndr. gun, inflicting heavy casualties on the enemy. When wounded a second time, and unable to fire, he did invaluable service by picking up targets for other gunners. His fine example of pluck and endurance undoubtedly assisted in saving his tank from a very critical situation.

201464 Pte. HUNT, S. C. ' G ' Battn. Awarded M.M.

For conspicuous gallantry and devotion to duty on November 23, 1917. Owing to heavy shell fire his tank had been evacuated. Pte. Hunt on his own initiative returned to the tank and, single-handed, drove it into shelter of a sunken road. Owing to his gallant conduct the tank was saved and later successfully rallied.

201283 Pte. RAYNER, T. ' G ' Battn. Awarded M.M.

For gallantry and marked devotion to duty in the action of November 23, 1917. In the absence of a N.C.O. he took charge of the gunners in his tank, directing their fire with great coolness and success.

Later he got out of his tank under heavy shell fire and guided it out of Bourlon Wood in the dark. His action undoubtedly enabled the tank to be withdrawn successfully.

69415 Cpl. PHILLIPS, G. W. ' F ' Battn. Awarded M.M.

For conspicuous gallantry and determination on November 26, 1917, at Masnières. He behaved with the greatest gallantry, holding the bridge with his tank under heavy and accurate shell fire for many hours.

In action at Fontaine on November 27 his tank was ditched, and no unditching gear being available he got out and fixed a wire to a passing tank under close range musketry firing. Later, in the village, while heavy machine-gun fire was in progress, when a tin of oil on the roof got punctured and took fire, he extinguished the flames five or six times till he was exhausted. Throughout the operations he behaved in a most gallant manner.

201185 Pte. ALWAY, A. 'F' Battn. Awarded M.M.

For conspicuous gallantry and initiative at Bourlon on November 27, 1917. After his tank had been hit and the officer wounded, he took command and established a post with a Lewis gun at the cross-roads in front of Bourlon village, thus enabling the infantry to advance. He returned twice to his tank under heavy fire to get ammunition. Later, when the infantry had gone forward and his object achieved, he bound up his officer and got him down to the dressing station. He set a fine example to the rest of the crew, and brought them and his guns into headquarters in the afternoon.

94884 Sergt. BEES, H. 'I' Battn. Awarded M.M.

For conspicuous gallantry and devotion to duty. At Ribecourt, on November 29, 1917, this N.C.O. volunteered to retrieve a tank which had been already derelict. He worked for three and a half hours under heavy shell fire, and finally brought the tank out of the shelled area.

93120 Pte. PELL, G. R. 'E' Battn. Awarded M.M.

At Flesquieres, on November 29, 1917, although twice hit by bullets in the arm and leg, he persisted in remaining with his tank commander (2nd Lieut. Bion) throughout a dangerous and trying period.

92397 Pte. DAHN, J. 'E' Battn. Awarded M.M.

During the action of November 30, 1917, near Flesquieres, Pte. Dahn was wounded in the back by shrapnel, while crossing to the enemy first system; after being dressed he insisted on returning to the driver's seat, and drove his tank for a further two and a half hours, until he became so stiff and exhausted from his wound that he was unable to carry on. His pluck and determination set a splendid example to the whole crew.

M2/053433 Pte. WARE, G. H. A.S.C., M.T. (attached 'B' Battn.). Awarded M.M.

Pte. Ware was the driver of a motor-car on November 30, 1917. He brought an officer from Fins to Gouzeaucourt, and the officer had just left the car as the enemy were entering Gouzeaucourt on the east side. Pte. Ware, hearing that our infantry were short of S.A.A., returned to Fins on his own initiative and loaded up his car with boxes of S.A.A., which he took forward to Gouzeaucourt and delivered to our infantry in the front line. He made several journeys between Fins and Gouzeaucourt, each time bringing forward a load of S.A.A. When in Gouzeaucourt on each occasion he was subjected to machine-gun and rifle fire, but this did not deter him from delivering the ammunition.

His prompt action and total disregard for his personal safety materially helped to save a critical situation.

200061 Cpl. EDWARDS, H. J. ' A ' Battn. Awarded M.M.

For gallantry and devotion to duty in the operations of November 30, 1917, near Gouzeaucourt. His tank received a direct hit which severely damaged the petrol tank. The tank was just in front of our line, and would undoubtedly have proved a good ranging object for the enemy. This N.C.O. realised this, and although under extremely heavy hostile fire he hand-fed the engine and brought the tank back to its rallying point, a distance of three miles.

201827 Pte. STEPHENS, J. E. ' B ' Battn. Awarded M.M.

This man was first driver in a tank, on November 30, 1917, which was in action for about seven hours near Gouzeaucourt. The tank was subjected during the whole time to an intense hostile machine-gun fire and hostile artillery fire. Great difficulty was experienced by the gunners in picking up the exact location of the enemy machine-guns, which were causing considerable casualties to our infantry.

Pte. Stephens opened the flap in front of his tank, thereby exposing himself, in order to obtain better observation and successfully direct his tank towards the hostile machine-guns.

This man showed a total disregard for his personal safety, and enabled the gunners of his crew to inflict severe casualties on the enemy.

91955 Sergt. WHITEHEAD, A. ' H ' Battn. Awarded D.C.M.

At the attack east of Gouzeaucourt on December 1, 1917, assumed command of his tank, the officer being severely wounded and evacuated under the orders of his section commander. Early in the action this N.C.O. was himself wounded, but continued in command of the tank for over five hours and succeeded in penetrating into the enemy's lines and inflicting heavy casualties.

In spite of the heavy fire that was brought to bear upon the tank Sergt. Whitehead patrolled in front of our line, keeping the enemy back till our infantry had consolidated. On one occasion, by good judgment and skilful manœuvring of his tank, he was responsible for the rounding up of a large number of prisoners and fifteen machine-guns, in conjunction with a bombing party of the infantry. Throughout the whole action this N.C.O. showed the greatest gallantry and devotion to duty and set a splendid example to the men of his crew.

200230 Sergt. MORGAN, C. F. 'B' Battn. Awarded M.M.

For coolness and bravery in action on December 1, 1917. He destroyed two enemy machine-guns south-east of Gouzeaucourt which were inflicting heavy casualties on our infantry, maintaining his position at his gun under heavy machine-gun fire, during which his No. 2 gunner was wounded. By his steadiness during the whole action, which lasted six hours, he ably directed the fire of his gunners under very trying circumstances.

Throughout this N.C.O. showed the greatest cheerfulness and determination, inspiring his whole crew and setting a fine example. The tank was completely isolated at the time.

75215 Pte. KINNIS, J. 'B' Battn. Awarded M.M.

On December 1, 1917, this man was gunner in a tank which inflicted severe casualties on the enemy at Gauche Wood. The tank was subjected to intense machine-gun fire during the seven hours that it was in action. Pte. Kinnis set a fine example to his crew by his cheerfulness under trying circumstances.

On November 21 this man was in action for four hours in the village of Cantaing, where the tank was isolated for about one hour until the arrival of the infantry. During this action Pte. Kinnis showed great determination to bring his guns to bear against the enemy and inflicted severe casualties.

91382 L/Cpl. HORSMAN, G. D. 'H' Battn. Awarded M.M.

This N.C.O. was the driver of a tank in action east of Gouzeaucourt on December 1, 1917.

During the action L/Cpl. Horsman was wounded in the face and back, but continued to drive the tank for ten minutes until he collapsed.

A new driver was then put on the driver's seat and L/Cpl. Horsman, being resuscitated, at once took over the duties of gearsman, carrying on until the tank was put out of action.

This N.C.O. showed the greatest gallantry and devotion to duty.

This N.C.O. likewise showed gallantry in the attack on Fontaine on November 21, 1917, his tank on that occasion receiving a direct hit, killing and wounding five of the crew.

78500 Gnr. WINGROVE, F. 'H' Battn. Awarded M.M.

Gnr. Wingrove was a 6-pndr. gunner in a tank in action east of Gouzeaucourt on December 1, 1917. Early in the action this man was wounded in the face and groin, but showed great courage and devotion to duty by continuing to man his gun for over five hours, inflicting heavy casualties on the enemy. He was responsible for knocking out six enemy machine-guns in six successive shots

IMMEDIATE AWARDS—OTHER RANKS

110147 Gnr. WHATNALL, H. 10th Battn. Awarded M.M.

On March 25, 1918, near Achiet-le-Grand, this man was a gunner in a tank in action. He showed the greatest coolness and courage when his tank received a direct hit which wounded the officer and the whole crew. Although wounded himself, he took charge of the tank, and eventually brought it successfully out of action, thus preventing the tank from falling into the hands of the enemy, who were then advancing in large numbers.

76384 L/Cpl. MAILES, A. 10th Battn. Awarded M.M.

Whilst in action near Achiet-le-Grand on March 25, 1918, although badly wounded in the shoulder, this N.C.O. refused to leave the driver's seat, and continued to carry on in action until the tank was disabled by a direct hit. He also remedied two stoppages under heavy fire. It was entirely due to this N.C.O.'s courage and devotion to duty that the tank was able to continue into action and thus delay the advance of the enemy.

203612 Gnr. DWYER, J. 10th Battn. Awarded M.M.

This gunner, together with No. 111353 Gnr. E. Baggott, did very good work with a Lewis gun in assisting to hold up the enemy on March 25, 1918, near Aveluy. They took up a position in a shell-hole in front of our infantry, and fired seventy drums of S.A.A., covering the withdrawal of a battalion of infantry, this battalion having no machine-guns left. They rendered every possible assistance, and undoubtedly saved what was a most critical situation. They were very strongly commended for their great bravery by the officer commanding the infantry battalion.

111353 Gnr. BAGGOTT, E. 10th Battn. Awarded M.M.

This gunner, together with No. 203612 Gnr. J. Dwyer, did very good work with a Lewis gun in assisting to hold up the enemy on March 25, 1918, near Aveluy. They took up a position in a shell-hole in front of our infantry and fired seventy drums of S.A.A., covering the withdrawal of a battalion of infantry, this battalion having no machine-guns left. They rendered every possible assistance and undoubtedly saved what was a most critical situation. They were very strongly commended for their great bravery by the officer commanding the infantry battalion.

10986 Gnr. BRADBURY, E. 10th Battn. Awarded M.M.

This gunner acted as orderly in the action near Achiet-le-Petit on March 25, 1918. During a period of five hours he continually carried messages under heavy shell fire across the open between the company commander and the tank commanders. Throughout the day he displayed the greatest gallantry, and never failed to deliver his messages in spite of the intensity of shell fire.

77268 Gnr. EDWARDS, T. T. 10th Battn. Awarded M.M.

This gunner acted as orderly in the action near Achiet-le-Petit on March 25, 1918. During a period of five hours he continually carried messages under heavy shell fire across the open between the company commander and the tank commanders. Throughout the day he displayed the greatest gallantry, and never failed to deliver his messages in spite of the intensity of shell fire.

95177 Pte. FORD, W. J. 1st Tank Battn. Awarded D.C.M.

For most conspicuous gallantry and devotion to duty on March 26, 1918, at the Bois de Tailles. When his company was fighting a rearguard action covering the withdrawal of the infantry from Bray it became partially surrounded, and, running short of ammunition, a withdrawal was necessary. This man volunteered to remain behind with Capt. F. S. Hunnikin and cover the withdrawal of the remainder of the company with two Lewis guns. He remained with Capt. Hunnikin until the withdrawal of the company was completed, and afterwards until the post was entirely surrounded. Throughout the day his coolness and courage was of the greatest assistance, and he set a splendid example to all ranks. He worked his gun continually throughout the day, and assisted Capt. F. S. Hunnikin to cut his way out with the last drum of ammunition, and carrying a gun.

75804 Pte. (L/Cpl.) SCOTT, R. 1st Battn. Awarded D.C.M.

For most conspicuous gallantry and devotion to duty on March 26, 1918, at the Bois de Tailles. When his company was fighting a rearguard action covering the withdrawal of the infantry from Bray it became partially surrounded, and, running short of ammunition, a withdrawal was necessary. This N.C.O. volunteered to remain behind with Capt. F. S. Hunnikin and cover the withdrawal of the remainder of the company with two Lewis guns. He remained with Capt. F. S. Hunnikin until the withdrawal of the company was completed, and afterwards until the post was entirely surrounded. Throughout the day his coolness and courage was of the greatest assistance, and he set a splendid example to all ranks. He worked his gun continually throughout the day, and assisted Capt. F. S. Hunnikin to cut his way out with the last drum of ammunition, and carrying a gun.

77055 Cpl. HURBY, W. G. 1st Battn. Awarded D.C.M.

For most conspicuous gallantry and devotion to duty while in charge of a Lewis gun team on ridge north-west of Bray on March 26, 1918.

On above date this N.C.O. was one of the Lewis gun company detailed to check the enemy and cover the infantry withdrawal at above-mentioned place. On the infantry withdrawal being completed, O.C. company found both flanks were enveloped, and ordered an immediate withdrawal. Cpl. Hurby volunteered to cover the withdrawal with his gun. He remained firing at either flank until his ammunition was exhausted and the withdrawal of the company was complete. He was subjected to very heavy rifle, machine-gun, and shell fire. He withdrew his gun intact, and rejoined his company later in the day. Throughout the day this N.C.O.'s courage and coolness were of the greatest value.

75346 Cpl. EBSWORTH, A. F. 3rd Battn. Awarded M.M.

During the action at Colincamps on March 26, 1918, this N.C.O., although in bad health and in a very exhausted condition, drove his tank with the greatest fearlessness and skill. It was mainly due to his skilful driving that his tank was enabled to account for so many of the enemy. Cpl. Ebsworth has previously fought as a first driver in the battles of the Somme, Arras, Third Ypres, and Cambrai, in every one of which actions his tank has received a direct hit from enemy artillery, yet he has always driven with the same skill and courage.

92100 Cpl. ROWBERRY, E. C. 4th Battn. Awarded M.M.

For gallantry and devotion to duty on March 26, 1918, near Bray. When firing a Lewis gun in the open he was continually attacked by large numbers of the enemy, who advanced to within a few yards of him. Through skilful manœuvring of his gun he inflicted heavy casualties and prevented the enemy from turning the flank, which was exposed. It was largely due to this N.C.O. that our infantry were able to maintain their position.

93501 Pte. WRIGHT, S. R.A.M.C. (attached 10th Battn.). Awarded M.M.

For great coolness and devotion to duty. At Achiet-le-Petit on March 26, 1918, he made his way through heavy machine-gun and shell fire to tend the wounded, afterwards forming a dressing station and evacuating wounded under heavy fire. He thus prevented many of our wounded from falling into the hands of the enemy.

112970 Cpl. (A/Sergt.) SMITH, E. W. 10th Battn. Awarded M.M.

On March 26, 1918, near Achiet-le-Petit, this N.C.O. was in command of a supply tank. Capt. Davy was in command of the supply section of which this tank was one. The tank in question stopped from engine trouble near a large ammunition dump of 6-inch shells. The officer in charge informed Capt. Davy that he was about to blow it up. Capt. Davy ordered the crew to leave the tank and retire, for two reasons, firstly, because the ammunition dump, which was only twenty-five yards away, was about to be blown up; secondly, because the enemy were within 500 yards and the tank, being a supply tank, was defenceless. Capt. Davy decided to stay near the tank to see if, after the dump had been exploded, there might still be a chance of getting the tank away. Sergt. Smith volunteered to stay with him. They took cover in separate shell-holes, Sergt. Smith being nearer to the tank than Capt. Davy. After the dump had been blown up, Capt. Davy saw Sergt. Smith run to the tank, the gear on the top of which was on fire caused by the flames from the burning dump, saw him enter the tank and shortly reappear; the enemy were then beginning to surround Capt. Davy, Sergt. Smith, and the tank, being about 100 yards from the tank, and firing at it with machine-guns. Sergt. Smith ran back to Capt. Davy, using his revolver as he ran, rejoined him, and together they retired, being shot at from front and flanks. Sergt. Smith reported he had fired the tank from inside, and the last Capt. Davy saw of it was a mass of flames. They both got away untouched and rejoined their section.

Sergt. Smith, by his dash and courage, undoubtedly prevented the tank from falling intact into the enemy's hands.

76408 Gnr. McMASTER, D. 10th Battn. Awarded M.M.

On March 26, 1918, in action near Achiet-le-Petit, this gunner was driving a tank which became unavoidably ditched. In spite of the great danger from a burning shell dump close by, he worked for a considerable time out in the open, and eventually succeeded in getting his tank away and ready for subsequent attacks.

110003 Cpl. ANDERSON, W. 10th Battn. Awarded M.M.

During the action near Gommecourt on the night of March 27, 1918, this N.C.O., although suffering from shock at the time, volunteered to serve as gunner in another tank, his own having been put out of action. During the action he was twice wounded, but he acted as gearsman until the conclusion of the operations, and saw his tank safely back to the rallying point before he himself went to have his wounds dressed.

70019 Cpl. ARCHBOLD, S. 5th Battn. Awarded D.C.M.

For conspicuous gallantry, March 29–30, near Warfusée-Abancourt, when a member of a Lewis gun detachment under 2nd Lieut. H. W. Whyte. This N.C.O. worked a Lewis gun single-handed during the period March 29–30.

He carried the gun and ammunition to a new position; fired the gun and loaded his magazines without assistance for twenty-four hours, during which period he assisted in breaking up two attacks.

On March 30 this N.C.O. was wounded in the head by a sniper, but he continued to work his gun all day, until ordered by his officer to the dressing station.

IMMEDIATE AWARDS—OTHER RANKS

70037 Pte. LYON, W. 5th Battn. Awarded M.M.

For conspicuous gallantry, March 29–30, near Warfusée-Abancourt, when one of a Lewis gun detachment under 2nd Lieut. H. W. Whyte.

This man on several occasions, in broad daylight, carried important messages across the open, under heavy machine-gun and rifle fire at 200 yards range. By his gallantry during this period he rendered himself of the utmost service to his officer.

91907 Sergt. CLEGG, W. 9th Battn. Awarded M.M.

For devotion to duty and the excellent example he set to the men under his command whilst holding an isolated Lewis gun post in Aveluy Wood on April 3. The post was under direct observation and constant fire, and Sergt. Clegg held his men together, and by his example and handling of the situation inspired them to carry out their duty under trying circumstances.

431756 Spr. BROWNBILL, F. 2nd Bde. Sig. Coy. Awarded M.M.

For conspicuous gallantry and devotion to duty at Pigeon Wood and Hannescamp on April 5, 1918.

Spr. Brownbill was a linesman. It was his duty to keep telephone communication through from the forward company to the battalion headquarters. The enemy put down a very heavy barrage which continually cut the cable. In spite of this Spr. Brownbill worked continuously in the open, under heavy shell fire, from 4 A.M. till afternoon, repairing the line. It was entirely due to this man's untiring efforts that communication was kept up. Spr. Brownbill also showed the keenest devotion to duty and total disregard for danger under similar circumstances at Vélu Wood on March 21 and 22.

69844 Pte. BENZIE, W. 7th Battn. Awarded M.M.

Conspicuous gallantry and devotion to duty during the action in and round Merville on April 12, 1918. In spite of a very heavy flank fire, against which he had no cover, he fought his Lewis gun until the last round was fired, and succeeded in wiping out two enemy machine-gun crews, who were causing considerable casualties to the infantry. He then withdrew, and resumed fighting as soon as more ammunition came up.

69893 Sergt. BANNISTER, G. W. 7th Battn. Awarded M.M.

For conspicuous gallantry and devotion to duty during the heavy fighting in and round Merville on April 12, 1918. It was due to this N.C.O.'s initiative and gallantry in getting up ammunition under heavy fire that the guns were enabled to remain in action at a critical time.

91676 Pte. GRIFFITHS, F. T. 5th Battn. Awarded D.C.M.

For conspicuous gallantry near Meteren, April 15-18, 1918.

This man was acting as a runner and carried messages unceasingly, day and night, from his section in the line to his company headquarters. These messages had to be carried across the open under close-range rifle and machine-gun fire. During the attacks by the enemy on April 16 and 17 this man carried several messages across the open through a heavy artillery barrage. He remained on duty for seventy-two hours, until he finally collapsed and had to be carried to the dressing station on a stretcher. His gallantry enabled his company commander to keep in touch with the situation at a most critical time, and to make necessary arrangements to meet it.

78737 Pte. ALLEN, G. 5th Battn. Awarded M.M.

For gallantry near Meteren, April 16 and 17, 1918. This man showed the utmost coolness in handling his Lewis gun under heavy fire. His accurate shooting inflicted very heavy casualties on the enemy, who attacked twice during this period. He engaged and put out of action a German machine-gun, and after all the other members of his crew had become casualties he loaded and fired his gun single-handed, until it was finally put out of action by shell fire.

305184 Pte. THOMPSON, J. 5th Battn. Awarded M.M.
77892 Pte. SMITH, J. W. 5th Tank Battn. Awarded M.M.

For gallantry near Meteren, April 16-18, 1918. These two men were members of four crews under 2nd Lieuts. Dawson and Bayliss which formed a defensive flank when the enemy penetrated our line on the right flank. For two days Ptes. Thompson and Smith kept their guns in action. Their coolness and accurate shooting, under very heavy direct and enfilade fire, enabled them to knock out two German machine-guns and to break up an impending attack which, had it been pushed home, would have endangered the whole line.

72603 Pte. JONES, A. H. 5th Battn. Awarded M.M.
72616 Pte. BRADLEY, F. 5th Battn. Awarded M.M.

For gallantry and devotion to duty near Meteren, April 16-17, 1918, when acting as runners. These two men carried messages, by day and night, across the open between their company headquarters and section headquarters in the front line. The enemy made two attacks during the period in question, and all these messages were carried under heavy machine-gun and rifle fire and through the enemy barrage across the open. The courage which these men displayed was directly the means of enabling their company commander to keep in touch with the situation at a most critical time.

IMMEDIATE AWARDS—OTHER RANKS

200455 Sergt. PARROTT, C. 3rd Battn. Awarded M.M.

For conspicuous gallantry during actions of April 24 and 25, 1918, near Villers-Bretonneux. This N.C.O. commanded his tank in both actions with the greatest skill and bravery under heavy machine-gun and artillery fire. He caused very heavy casualties amongst the enemy, who were formed up ready to attack. When another tank received a direct hit he at once went to the rescue, and managed to save one of the crew and the guns, during which he exposed himself to intense machine-gun and artillery fire, with entire disregard for his own safety.

200459 Cpl. TILL, E. 3rd Tank Battn. Awarded M.M.

During the action on April 24, 1918, near Villers-Bretonneux, his tank was hit by a shell when 1000 yards within the enemy lines. In spite of damaged mechanism, he managed to drive his tank, with the greatest perseverance and skill, to within a few yards of our own lines, salving all the Hotchkiss guns under a heavy artillery barrage. Two days later, although surprised and almost surrounded by the enemy, he drove his tank with the greatest bravery and resource when the remainder of his crew were wounded.

77483 Cpl. LUCAS, A. E., M.M. 3rd Battn. Awarded Bar to M.M.

For exceptionally skilful and daring driving during the actions near Villers-Bretonneux on April 24 and 25, 1918, when he drove his tank right into the middle of a crowd of the enemy, running them down and causing very heavy casualties just as they were forming up to attack. Under intense enemy machine-gun fire he rescued the officer and one other rank and two guns from another tank that had received a direct hit and was out of action. On the following day he again displayed the greatest skill and initiative in running down enemy machine-guns.

75669 Sergt. McKENZIE, J. R. 1st Battn. Awarded M.M.

For conspicuous gallantry and devotion to duty when in action in tank No. 4066 at Cachy Switch Line on April 24, 1918. Although his eyes were affected by enemy gas and his face badly cut by splinters from armour-piercing bullets, in spite of his suffering this N.C.O. continued to serve his quick-firing gun for four hours while his own tank was engaged with two large enemy tanks, one of which was eventually put out of action. Throughout this N.C.O., by his conduct and coolness, set a splendid example to all the men in his crew.

28787 Dvr. BARSBY, H. 17th Battn. Sherwood Foresters (attached 1st Battn.). Awarded M.M.

For conspicuous gallantry and devotion to duty during the fighting near Villers-Bretonneux on April 24–26, 1918.

This man was in charge of a limber attached to the tank company, and part of his duty was to carry up rations and supplies regularly to tanks in forward positions. This duty he carried out without a single failure, in many cases having to go up under heavy shell fire and into areas where heavy gas bombardments were taking place. He always did his duty in a most courageous and fearless manner, and it was largely due to his reliable work, often undertaken at much personal risk, that the fighting efficiency of the company was maintained.

77423 Pte. BOYSON, G. T. 1st Battn. Awarded M.M.

For conspicuous courage and devotion to duty in action on April 24, 1918, near the Bois L'Abbe.

This man was orderly to the officer commanding the section of tanks in action near the Bois L'Abbe. His respirator became damaged and he was badly affected by gas, but most gallantly carried out his duties, carrying messages backwards and forwards under heavy shell and machine-gun fire with utter disregard for personal danger, until eventually he became so ill, as a result of the gas, that he had to be sent for treatment at the casualty clearing station.

On several previous occasions in action he has shown the same fearless devotion to duty and entire disregard for personal risk.

205019 Sergt. BEVERIDGE, R., M.M. 13th Battn. Awarded Bar to M.M.

For conspicuous gallantry and devotion to duty near Millekreisse on April 25, 1918.

This N.C.O. assisted his section commander to lead the section forward under heavy shell fire. Though severely wounded, he refused to leave the section until it had reached its objective.

On a previous occasion, at St. Jans Cappel on April 18, 1918, this N.C.O. showed conspicuous courage and disregard of danger in rescuing three wounded men, who were lying out in the open under heavy shell fire, and conveying them to a place of safety.

304423 Gnr. DREVER, J. W. C. 13th Battn. Awarded M.M.

For conspicuous gallantry and devotion to duty at St. Jans Cappel on April 20, 1918, and near Millekreisse on April 25 and 26, 1918.

Acting as runner for his company, he displayed great courage and resource in carrying messages across open ground through very heavy shell and rifle fire, both in the daytime and at night, between his company headquarters and the advanced posts, thereby rendering very valuable assistance to his company commander. He always showed conspicuous courage and utter disregard of danger.

110247 Pte. GARDNER, T. 1st Battn. Awarded M.M.

For conspicuous devotion to duty and example of coolness and courage in action at the Bois de Hangard on April 26, 1918. This man was acting crew N.C.O. owing to shortage of crew caused by casualties, and although wounded in the head and left arm immediately upon going into action, he carried out his duties in a most thorough manner and set an example of steadiness and resource at a critical time which was invaluable, and doubtless was largely responsible for the success of his tank, which was manned almost entirely by men who had not previously been in action.

75300 Pte. BAIRD, G. 1st Battn. Awarded M.M.

For conspicuous gallantry and devotion to duty in action at Bois de Hangard on April 26, 1918. His tank was hit by a shell and one of his fingers broken in two places, but he still continued to serve his gun with very good results, destroying a number of enemy machine-guns and their crews with shells from his 6-pndr. At the end of the action he made light of his wounds and refused to go to the dressing station as long as there was any useful work he could do. This man's pluck and coolness gave great confidence to the remainder of the crew at a critical time, his behaviour throughout deserving the greatest praise.

200010 Pte. VALLANCE, J. 1st Battn. Awarded M.M.

For most conspicuous gallantry and devotion to duty in action at the Bois de Hangard on April 26, 1918. He was the driver of his tank and was wounded at the beginning of the action. In spite of his wounds he insisted upon carrying on his work, driving in a most skilful manner and making possible the successful use of the tank. By his courage and determination he set an invaluable and excellent example to the remainder of the crew, one only of whom had ever been in action before.

40519 Pte. DINWOODIE, J. 1st Battn. Awarded M.M.

For conspicuous gallantry and devotion to duty. On April 26, 1918, in an attack near the Monument, south of Villers-Bretonneux, this man drove his tank with skill and determination in such a manner that the gunners were able to obtain the most effective fire on the enemy, causing many casualties.

During the action mechanical trouble in the tank occurred ; he gave very great assistance in repairing same, although the tank at the time was under a heavy barrage, being the only tank in action.

By his great determination and perseverance he set a fine example to the remainder of the crew, and it was due to this man's efforts that this tank was brought safely out of action after a successful day's fighting.

75825 Pte. SPENCER, V. 1st Battn. Awarded M.M.

For conspicuous gallantry and devotion to duty. On April 26, 1918, in an attack on the Monument, south of Villers-Bretonneux, this gunner displayed great courage, and although wounded in his left eye early in the action he continued to fire his gun at enemy machine-guns with excellent results, inflicting many casualties on the enemy.

This man's pluck and coolness gave great confidence to the remainder of the crew at a critical time, his behaviour throughout deserving the highest praise.

40102 Pte. WALLACE, N. 1st Battn. Awarded D.C.M.

For conspicuous gallantry and devotion to duty. On April 28, 1918, during an attack made by the Moroccan Division on Hangard Wood, this man, although badly wounded in the early part of the attack, continued to drive his tank with skill and determination in such a manner that the gunners were able to obtain the most effective fire on the enemy, causing many casualties.

He would not leave his tank until he had successfully carried out his orders and brought it back to the rallying point, where, after getting out of his tank, he collapsed as the result of his wounds.

By his great determination and perseverance he set a very fine example to the remainder of the crew, and it was due to this man's gallant work that the operation with this tank was successful.

76425 Cpl. OAKEY, E. C. 5th Battn. Awarded M.M.

For conspicuous gallantry near Vierstraat April 29, 1918.

This N.C.O. was in charge of a Lewis gun crew. On the date in question the enemy bombarded the gun position heavily. This N.C.O. set a splendid example to his men. He was twice buried with his gun, but remained at his post, extricated the men of his team who were buried, and got his gun into action in time to disperse a party of fifty of the enemy who were attempting to advance, and inflicted heavy casualties on them. His gallantry and the example he set his men were undoubtedly responsible for the repulse of the enemy in his sector of trench.

IMMEDIATE AWARDS—OTHER RANKS

75215 Cpl. KINNIS, J., M.M.   2nd Battn.   Awarded Bar to M.M.

For great gallantry and coolness.

At 2 A.M. on May 23, 1918, six tanks were situated in a quarry near Mericourt. Owing to the heavy shelling the camouflage nets and tarpaulins surrounding two of the tanks had caught fire. Cpl. Kinnis collected a party of men from various crews and, utterly disregarding the heavy shell fire and the presence of gas, drove one tank away from the other, and eventually caused both fires to be extinguished.

His spontaneous action and complete disregard of danger undoubtedly resulted in preventing the complete loss of these tanks by fire, and afforded a great example to his men.

The quarry is about twenty-five feet deep, and formed a natural pocket for gas.

75232 Pte. REDMILL, I.   10th Battn.   Awarded M.M.

At Bucquoy, on the night June 22–23, 1918, this man showed conspicuous gallantry when employed as second driver in a tank taking part in a raid. On the return journey his tank broke down when in the middle of the hostile trench-mortar barrage. Though all the Lewis guns had been put out of action and the tank was surrounded by the enemy, this man worked with conspicuous coolness and skill, and after thirty minutes succeeded in repairing the breakdown. By his coolness and determination this man set a fine example to the crew under extremely trying circumstances.

109984 Cpl. FLETCHER, D.   10th Battn.   Awarded M.M.

At Bucquoy, on the night June 22–23, 1918, this N.C.O. showed the greatest gallantry and skill when employed as first driver of a tank taking part in a raid. His tank was detailed to start twenty minutes after zero, and though the enemy barrage had started at that time this N.C.O. showed conspicuous determination in driving his tank to its objective. He was detailed to cover the withdrawal of two other tanks, and though without infantry assistance and heavily fired on by machine-guns at close range this N.C.O. succeeded in dealing with all the enemy posts, and the other tanks withdrew unmolested.

76013 Pte. HARDING, C. V.   10th Battn.   Awarded M.M.

At Bucquoy, on the night June 22–23, 1918, this man showed the greatest gallantry and initiative when a gunner in a tank crew taking part in a raid. While passing through the enemy barrage the first driver of his tank was temporarily blinded by the explosion of a shell. Pte. Harding, whose gun was out of action, at once got into the driver's seat, and though he had not been trained to drive in the dark succeeded in driving the tank along a very complicated route. By his prompt action and fearless driving he prevented the column being checked at a critical period.

HAMEL

111721 Gnr. VIVASH, NAYLASS JAMES. 8th Battn. Awarded M.M.

On July 4, 1918, in attack on Hamel and Vaire-Wood, this driver showed exceptional skill and gallantry when acting as first driver to 2nd Lieut. Prentice. Though slightly wounded early in the action he drove his tank, which was suffering from mechanical trouble, with great skill and in such a way as to clearly carry out his tank commander's orders (2nd Lieut. Prentice). He directed his tank through our protective barrage in order to subdue hostile machine-guns beyond, which were harassing our infantry, and went to Accroche Wood, thereby causing considerable damage and demoralising the enemy.

By his good judgment, skill, and pluck he was able to get his tank out of action, although it was suffering from mechanical trouble caused by a hit from an anti-tank rifle. His performance was all the more commendable as it was his first tank action.

77465 Gnr. FILBY, JAMES ARTHUR. 8th Battn. Awarded M.M.

In the attack on Hamel on July 4, 1918, this driver showed exceptional skill and resource.

Early in the action his tank was heavily bombed on the roof by enemy infantry ; splinters penetrated behind the cab and gave the driver slight concussion. Gnr. Filby refused to be relieved from driving and later, when the enemy got up behind his tank, he reversed the engine and crushed the enemy by driving backwards over them. Throughout the action this man drove with the utmost skill and pluck.

70176 Gnr. REED, WILLIAM SMITH. 8th Battn. Awarded M.M.

On July 4, in the attack on Hamel, this gunner was in 2nd Lieut. Prentice's tank.

After an enemy machine-gun had been silenced, the tank commander got out to make certain that the machine-gun was out of action. Gnr. Reed immediately followed his officer to help, though under heavy machine-gun fire at the time.

By this action he displayed great devotion to duty and gallantry, and assisted his officer in capturing several of the enemy.

IMMEDIATE AWARDS—OTHER RANKS

91622 Cpl. DRAPER, WILLIAM. 8th Battn. Awarded M.M.

In the attack on Hamel on July 4 this N.C.O. handled his tank with the greatest skill and daring. His conduct was of a most exemplary nature, and all the more commendable as at the time he was suffering from severe influenza, but refused to be relieved and insisted on driving his tank throughout the action.

74149 Sergt. (T.M.S.) GREEN, ROBERT MOTTRAM. 13th Battn. Awarded M.M.

For conspicuous gallantry and devotion to duty near Hamel on July 4, 1918.

While the tanks were *en route* to their starting-point one developed serious mechanical trouble, and although there was heavy gas-shelling, which eventually compelled this N.C.O. and the tank engineer to put on and work in their respirators, he assisted the company tank engineer in repairing the damage and getting the tank up in time to take part in the operations. Later in the day he also accompanied the company tank engineer, under heavy shell fire, to a tank that had broken down in an exposed position near our new front line, and although several attempts had been made to get it away without success stayed working at it under very heavy shell, rifle, and machine-gun fire, and rendered great assistance in eventually getting it back to safety. This N.C.O. showed great coolness and disregard of danger.

301422 Sergt. LYNN, CHARLES. 13th Battn. Awarded M.M.

For conspicuous gallantry and devotion to duty near Hamel on July 4, 1918.

Shortly after going into action the driver of Sergt. Lynn's tank fainted from exhaustion, and the tank commander was wounded at the same time. Sergt. Lynn, who was himself wounded in the arm, took the driver's place, and while his tank commander's wound was being dressed continued to drive, and in addition observed and directed the fire of the tank gunners. He drove the tank to its objective and, after the infantry had consolidated, back to our lines.

This N.C.O. showed exceptional courage and set a fine example to the remainder of the crew.

301627 Gnr. BENNS, JOSEPH. 13th Battn. Awarded M.M.

For conspicuous gallantry and devotion to duty near Hamel on July 4, 1918.

He followed his tank commander from his tank and attacked dug-outs which could not be reached by the tank. He killed five of the enemy with his revolver, and with his officer caused the remainder to surrender. While he was attacking the dug-outs he was wounded in the legs, and although unable to stand continued to assist in observing from the tank and directing fire. Throughout the entire action his coolness and courage had a great influence on the crew, especially when the tank was in difficulties.

300434 Gnr. WAITE, WILLIAM THOMAS. 13th Battn. Awarded M.M.

For conspicuous gallantry and devotion to duty near Hamel on July 4, 1918.

His tank was ditched near a dug-out full of the enemy. Seeing that they were coming out, he got out of his tank and shot the first two, driving the others back into the dug-out. He called on the enemy in the dug-out to surrender, but on receiving no reply he fetched bombs from some infantry near by and bombed the dug-out, and eventually secured some thirty prisoners. Throughout the whole action he set a fine example to the remainder of the crew.

308699 Gnr. ROBERTS, FRANK. 13th Battn. Awarded M.M.

For conspicuous gallantry and devotion to duty near Hamel on July 4, 1918.

His tank having broken down and the supply of petrol for priming having failed, Gnr. Roberts went across, under heavy shell and machine-gun fire, to another tank, fetching some and enabling his tank to proceed. After the N.C.O. of his crew had been wounded he showed great coolness and capacity, acting as observer to the tank gunners.

304227 Cpl. RYAN, JOHN. 13th Battn. Awarded M.M.

For conspicuous gallantry and devotion to duty near Hamel on July 4, 1918.

This N.C.O. was acting as observer in the tank when a shell burst near it and splinters penetrated the side plates, wounding him in the arm. Despite the fact that this N.C.O. was in considerable pain and feeling weak and faint, he carried on with his duties, doing splendid work in pointing out targets for the gunners in the tank right up to the final objective and until the tank was on its way back to the rallying point.

301625 Cpl. METTAM, ERNEST AUGUSTUS. 13th Battn. Awarded M.M.

For conspicuous bravery and devotion to duty whilst acting as N.C.O. of a tank near Hamel on July 4, 1918.

Throughout the action he observed and controlled the fire with great skill so that the tank gunners succeeded in knocking out several enemy machine-gun posts, and in consequence saved the infantry many casualties. Two of the machine-guns knocked out by this tank were subsequently brought back. His coolness and courage under trying circumstances had a great influence on the crew.

301950 Gnr. HURST, FRANK HAROLD. 13th Battn. Awarded M.M.

For conspicuous bravery and coolness in driving his tank in action near Hamel on July 4, 1918.

In spite of the fact that his tank was under heavy fire his excellent driving enabled the tank gunners to destroy many enemy machine-gun posts. This tank afterwards brought back to our lines under heavy shell fire a tank disabled on the enemy front line, and it was greatly due to Gnr. Hurst's excellent driving that this was accomplished successfully.

Throughout the whole of the action Gnr. Hurst's coolness and resourcefulness had a great effect on the remainder of the crew.

310903 A/Cpl. WATSON, ARTHUR ANTONY, M.M. 13th Battn. Awarded Bar to M.M.

For conspicuous gallantry and devotion to duty near Hamel on July 4, 1918.

During the attack this N.C.O. showed great ability and courage in driving his tank. While on his final objective, and in full view of the enemy, his tank was badly ditched. It was greatly due to his exceptional skill and resourcefulness as a driver that the tank was finally unditched. His coolness and bravery under difficult circumstances were a splendid example to the remainder of his crew, who eventually succeeded in getting the tank out of danger.

301601 A/Sergt. SCRIVENER, ALBERT CHARLES. 13th Battn. Awarded M.M.

For conspicuous gallantry and devotion to duty as a tank N.C.O. near Hamel on July 4, 1918.

He was an invaluable assistant to his officer as observer to the tank gunners, although early in the action observation was very difficult. In spite of the heavy machine-gun fire brought to bear on his tank, he continued to observe through the open flaps of the observation turret and to indicate targets.

The resolution and total disregard of danger on the part of this N.C.O. undoubtedly caused the enemy serious losses.

201659 M.S./Sergt.-Major SYKES, FRANK. No. 1 Tank Field Coy. Awarded D.C.M.

This warrant officer took up a position in our front line opposite Hamel village, near Corbie, just before zero hour on July 4, 1918, in order to assist any tanks requiring expert mechanical assistance.

He carried out his duties in a very gallant manner and worked continuously, with practically no rest, until all machines were brought back into safety by the night of July 6, 1918.

His expert knowledge of tank repairs, combined with his utter disregard of personal safety during heavy shelling and gassing, contributed very materially to the success of the salvage operations.

I saw this warrant officer on several occasions at work under the most trying circumstances. The utter disregard of his personal safety, together with his promptitude and resourcefulness, set a splendid example and were the admiration of all who came in contact with him.

201658 Sergt. FALVEY, HARRY EDWARD. No. 1 Tank Field Coy. Awarded D.C.M.

On Thursday, July 4, 1918, Sergt. Falvey was ordered, together with his section, consisting of one officer and ten other ranks, to endeavour to salve a tank which had been hit in Hamel village, near Corbie, the same morning. The village was heavily shelled and gassed the whole time during the attempt to get the machine away, necessitating heavy work being carried out in gas-masks.

On the morning of July 5 this officer and two men had to leave for treatment of the effects from gas, followed afterwards by six more of the men, leaving Sergt. Falvey with one assistant only to carry on the repairs, which he completed, thereby enabling the tank to be brought back out of Hamel village on the 6th instant. This N.C.O. throughout the whole time showed great initiative, gallantry, and devotion to duty under extremely trying circumstances.

40284 Sergt. DYER, W. H. No. 1 Field Coy. Awarded M.M.

He went over the top with 2nd Lieut. A. H. Baker and discovered a tank had fallen into the quarry in Hamel village. He searched around under heavy hostile machine-gun fire, and brought another tank, directed it into position, fixed the tow-rope and guided the machine on to level ground. The tank commander and crew then took over. Sergt. Dyer then proceeded to Hamel village, rounded up fifteen German prisoners, and handed them over to another N.C.O. of this company, who was in difficulties owing to shortage of labour.

76378 Pte. GRIMLEY, D. No. 1 Tank Field Coy. Awarded M.M.

For marked devotion to duty under the most difficult circumstances and his high courage during the whole of the salvage operations on July 4, 5, and 6, during which time he performed most excellent work and set a fine example to the other men of his section.

95237 Cpl. TERRINGTON, E. No. 1 Tank Field Coy. Awarded M.M.

He was informed that a tank was lying 200 yards east of Hamel village with the track blown off. He proceeded to the tank immediately, accompanied by two fitters, and commenced the repair under great difficulties owing to the absence of necessary tools and the lack of labour. He rounded up a number of prisoners and repaired the damage, then marched the prisoners back to the infantry position and finally drove the tank safely back. The whole of the work was performed under intermittent machine-gun fire, and the courage and devotion of this N.C.O. cannot be too highly praised.

MOREUIL, JULY 1918

201523 Sergt. TAYLOR, HERBERT WILLIAM. 9th Battn. Awarded D.C.M.

During the operations south of Moreuil on July 23, in the absence of the tank commander, Sergt. Taylor commanded the tank throughout the action with conspicuous success. He fought his tank with great skill and gallantry, destroying upwards of a dozen machine-gun nests, and brought in several guns complete with spare parts. On his own initiative Sergt. Taylor advanced through our protective barrage and patrolled far in advance of the infantry, thereby rendering great assistance. By his cheerfulness, personal control, and gallantry Sergt. Taylor set a splendid example to his crew.

91922 L/Cpl. POLLARD, ARTHUR. 9th Battn. Awarded D.C.M.

During the operations south of Moreuil on July 23 L/Cpl· Pollard was in charge of a 6-pndr. gun, and although the tank was under heavy machine-gun fire he handled his gun with great effect and put out several machine-guns.

When his tank was put out of action by a direct hit and filled with fumes from gas-shells, L/Cpl. Pollard, assisted by Pte. Walker, carried his tank commander, who had been gassed, for 800 yards over ground swept by machine-gun fire to a place of safety. In spite of heavy shelling and machine-gun fire L/Cpl. Pollard returned to his tank; seeing that the infantry were not advancing he blew up the tank, an action which prevented it falling intact into the enemy's hands.

L/Cpl. Pollard showed great gallantry and devotion to duty, and set a splendid example to his crew.

95079 L/Cpl. DUNCAN, JAMES. 9th Battn. Awarded M.M.

During the operations south of Moreuil on July 23 L/Cpl. Duncan fought with the utmost gallantry throughout the action.

Although his tank was under heavy machine-gun fire directed at his gun, he continued to man his gun, and by his skilful shooting he accounted for a very large number of the enemy. When the tank was in front of our infantry and had to be withdrawn under heavy artillery and machine-gun fire, L/Cpl. Duncan got out of the tank and led it on foot, guiding it past some obstacles and through heavily crumped area.

A second time when under heavy machine-gun fire L/Cpl. Duncan got out of the tank to fill up the radiator as the water was running dangerously low. L/Cpl. Duncan showed an utter disregard for his personal safety and set a fine example to the remainder of his crew.

91967 Sergt. CLEGG, WILLIAM, M.M. 9th Battn. Awarded Bar to M.M.

During the operations south of Moreuil on July 23, when his tank had been put out of action by a direct hit, in spite of the heavy shelling and machine-gun fire, Sergt. Clegg at once ran back to another tank which was following and warned the commander of the danger and guided it away from the hostile gun. Segt. Clegg showed an utter disregard for his personal safety and displayed great coolness under very trying circumstances.

92467 Sergt. GOWER, FRANCIS. 9th Battn. Awarded M.M.

During the operations south of Moreuil on July 23, when his section commander was wounded and the tank knocked out by a direct hit, in spite of the heavy artillery and machine-gun fire, Sergt. Gower succeeded in carrying his wounded officer to a place of safety.

92471 Pte. PHILPOT, ARTHUR. 9th Battn. Awarded M.M.

During the operations south of Moreuil on July 23 Pte. Philpot showed great devotion to duty under particularly trying circumstances. After his tank had received two direct hits and he was suffering from the concussion, Pte. Philpot continued to fire his gun and engage several targets until his tank was withdrawn from the action.

94990 Pte. FLETCHER, CHARLES. 9th Battn. Awarded M.M.

During the operations south of Moreuil on July 23 Pte. Fletcher collapsed, after the capture of Sauvillers village, from the effects of fumes in the tank.

After a short rest while the tanks rallied he recovered, and insisted on manning his gun, which he handled with conspicuous success and great skill. Pte. Fletcher undoubtedly accounted for a large number of the enemy. This man showed great determination and a fine fighting spirit under particularly trying circumstances.

91791 Pte. BLURTON, ARTHUR, M.M. 9th Battn. Awarded Bar to M.M.

91944 Pte. WRIGHT, REGINALD, M.M. 9th Battn. Awarded Bar to M.M.

During the operations south of Moreuil on July 23 Ptes. Blurton and Wright acted as runners to Major Johnson, the company commander. Throughout the action, though exposed to heavy artillery and intense machine-gun fire, they continually ran with messages to the tanks. Ptes. Blurton and Wright were utterly regardless of their personal safety and performed very valuable work, especially in collecting tanks for the second attack.

78007 Sergt. PALMER, ALBERT EDWARD. 9th Battn. Awarded M.M.

During the operations south of Moreuil on July 23 Sergt. Palmer was in command of a tank. He showed great initiative and judgment in destroying several enemy machine-gun nests. Sergt. Palmer set a splendid example to his crew.

92186 A/Cpl. MORGAN, LEWIS LAWRENCE. 9th Battn. Awarded M.M.

During the operations south of Moreuil on July 23 when his tank had got rather far ahead of the infantry, and the tank commander did not wish to turn about and go back, as the infantry did not appear to be coming on, in spite of heavy shelling and machine-gun fire Cpl. Morgan volunteered to go back on foot and lead them on. This he successfully accomplished and the advance continued. Cpl. Morgan showed an utter disregard of his personal safety and set a very fine example to the remainder of the crew.

92348 L/Cpl. COLTON, JOHN CHRISTOPHER. 9th Battn. Awarded M.M.

During the action south of Moreuil on July 23, although under heavy hostile shelling and machine-gun fire, L/Cpl. Colton drove the tank with fearlessness and judgment. When his tank was knocked out by a direct hit and had to be evacuated, although wounded himself and under machine-gun fire, L/Cpl. Colton bandaged up the wounded and helped them back. By his cheerfulness under particularly trying circumstances L/Cpl. Colton set a splendid example to his crew.

78552 Pte. OGDEN, L. 9th Battn. Awarded Médaille Militaire.

505844 Pte. TAYLOR, T. 9th Battn. Awarded Médaille Militaire

91967 Sergt. CLEGG, WILLIAM. 9th Battn. Awarded Médaille Militaire.

92737 MARSH, SAMUEL. 9th Battn. Awarded Médaille Militaire.

201523 TAYLOR, HERBERT WILLIAM. 9th Battn. Awarded Médaille Militaire.

78705 Cpl. HOWLETT, CHARLES JOHN WILLIAM. 9th Battn. Awarded Médaille Militaire.

201524 Cpl. LANE, THOMAS. 9th Battn. Awarded Médaille Militaire.

92348 Cpl. COLTON, JOHN CHRISTOPHER. 9th Battn. Awarded Médaille Militaire.

91286 Cpl. MORGAN, LEWIS LAWRENCE. 9th Battn. Awarded Médaille Militaire.

305425 Pte. DRIFFIELD, CLARENCE BELL. 9th Battn. Awarded Médaille Militaire.

91439 SPINDLER, JAMES GEORGE. 9th Battn. Awarded Médaille Militaire,

78014 Pte. TODD, JOHN WILLIAM. 9th Battn. Awarded Médaille Militaire.

Pour leur grande bravoure pendant le combat du 23 juillet 1918.

For great gallantry in action, July 23, 1918.

THE GREAT BRITISH ADVANCE, 1918

93160 Sergt. TAYLOR, GEORGE MIDDLETON. 7th Battn. Awarded M.M.

For continuous good work from February to September, 1918, and for great gallantry on one special occasion when he worked on his tank under heavy shell fire, to get his tank fit and take it away to safety. This was on May 17, near Annequin.

He always sets a splendid example to his crew under fire, and can be relied on for any duty.

40074 L/Cpl. SNEATH, ERNEST. 2nd Battn. Awarded D.C.M.

For conspicuous gallantry and skill as first driver of a tank during operations extending from March to September 16, 1918.

Near Beugny, on March 22, 1918, he displayed exceptional courage and coolness in action, which inspired his crew with confidence.

During the August 1918 operations, near Villers-Bretonneux, he set a splendid example of gallantry and devotion to duty, his skill and initiative being very marked.

During the period he has on three occasions reached his objective and has proved himself to be a determined and resourceful driver. His conduct throughout all engagements is deserving of the highest praise.

76888 Pte. WADDINGTON, GEORGE. 2nd Battn. Awarded M.M.

For conspicuous gallantry and devotion to duty as first driver from March 21 to September 16.

On March 22, near Beugny, he showed great courage and resource in restarting, under heavy fire, his tank, which had stopped owing to mechanical trouble.

Again, on August 8, near Warfusée, his tank had temporarily lost direction owing to the smoke and fog. He voluntarily got out under heavy machine-gun and artillery fire, and was able to take correct compass bearings and redirect the tank on to its correct objective.

It was largely due to his patient driving and great coolness. throughout that his tank fought a successful action and reached its objective.

200325 Sergt. COPSEY, WALLACE. 2nd Battn. Awarded D.C.M.

For outstanding gallantry and devotion to duty in action as tank N.C.O. during operations August 8 to September 16, 1918.

Especially near Beugny, in March 1918, he displayed the greatest coolness and initiative. His tank caught fire on three separate occasions, on the last of which he ran across a stretch of 300 yards of ground under very heavy machine-gun fire to the nearest tank, brought back some Pyrene extinguishers, and was successful in quelling the fire in his tank, thereby saving the lives of his crew.

Since March, he has rendered most valuable services to his company by his ability and keenness, and has earned the reputation of being a N.C.O. who can be relied upon in any emergency.

92836 Sergt. STRANG, JOHN, D.C.M. No. 1 Gun Carrier Coy. Awarded Bar to D.C.M.

During the fire caused by enemy shell fire amongst seventeen gun-carrier tanks at O. 29 b. (Villers-Bretonneux) on the evening of August 7, 1918, Sergt. Strang showed the utmost bravery and coolness in rescuing a tank out of the blaze. The tanks were loaded with explosives for the infantry—gun-cotton, bombs, trench mortars, &c.—besides two fills of petrol each. Although subjected to violent explosions every moment, one of which blew the door off the cabin he was seated in, this gallant N.C.O. continued to drive the tank through intense shell fire to a position of security. It was through his coolness and total disregard for his own personal safety and fine example to his crew that this tank was saved from certain destruction.

92870 Sergt. BREWER, JAMES VICTOR. 6th Battn. Awarded D.C.M.

For gallantry and untiring zeal and work. On August 8 he worked a gun throughout the day, his tank reaching Vauxvillers, eleven miles from the starting-point. On August 9 he again worked a gun throughout the day, running over two machine-guns and killing the crews, under heavy shell fire. On August 10, at Parvillers, whilst in command of a tank, it received a direct hit, and although badly shaken he extricated his crew and guns under very heavy machine-gun fire, and continued to fire outside, causing losses amongst the enemy.

69635 Pte. THOMAS, CHARLES. 6th Battn. Awarded M.M.

During the advance on August 8, near Guillaucourt, he displayed great coolness and devotion to duty. Under intense machine-gun fire on three occasions he rectified engine trouble, having to get out of the tank, which enabled his tank to reach its objective. Later on, when taking his turn at the gun, he did valuable work in silencing three machine-guns.

111481 Pte. IRELAND, DAVID MENZIES. 6th Battn. Awarded M.M.

For exceptional coolness and daring on August 8, near Harbonnières. The transmission seized up; he got out of his tank and for ten minutes, under very heavy machine-gun fire, applied grease to the transmission; the tank then continued forward. When returning, the tank developed trouble in the petrol lead, which he three times mended under heavy shell fire whilst stationary.

165259 Pte. VOWLES, PERCY JOHN. 6th Battn. Awarded M.M.

On August 8, at Guillaucourt, he acted as mounted orderly to a light tank company commander. Throughout the day he carried many messages under heavy machine-gun and shell fire, having his horse eventually shot under him. On one occasion he alone on horseback, with his company commander, charged a large party of the enemy, killing two and capturing the remainder.

201806 Pte. SMETHURST, JOHN. 6th Battn. Awarded M.M.

This N.C.O. displayed great coolness and ability throughout the advance from Villers-Bretonneux on August 8. He was wounded during the action, but continued to drive his tank with the greatest pluck and determination till the end of the action, when he collapsed.

75276 Sergt. HIBBERT, HERBERT. 3rd Battn. Awarded D.C.M.

Near Beaucourt, on August 8, 1918, this N.C.O. commanded his tank with the greatest gallantry. Although wounded in the neck by a bullet, and by splinters in face, thighs, arms, and groin, he continued to command his tank, inflicting heavy casualties on the enemy. He refused to leave his tank until ordered to do so by his section commander. His conduct was a splendid example to the remainder of his crew.

77402 Pte. VEALL, GEORGE FREDERICK. 3rd Battn. Awarded M.M.

Near Le Quesnel, on August 8, 1918, when the driver of his tank became a casualty, the tank was running at full speed and became involved in a maze of trenches.

Although under heavy machine-gun fire, this man volunteered to get out of the tank and guide it out of difficulty. Owing to his coolness and bravery the tank was safely got clear. He has on previous occasions shown conspicuous coolness and bravery in action.

200487 Cpl. THORNTON, ERNEST. 3rd Battn. Awarded M.M.

Near Beaucourt, on August 8, he commanded his tank with conspicuous gallantry and skill, rendering the greatest assistance to the infantry, and accounting for many enemy. When his section commander's tank was hit by shell fire, he screened the crew while they evacuated it, regardless of the danger to his own tank from enemy shells, which were falling all around.

He has on three previous occasions been recommended for gallantry in action.

76399 Sergt. PERKINS, FREDERICK ARCHIBALD. 3rd Battn. Awarded M.M.

Near Beaucourt, on August 8, 1918, as a tank commander, he displayed conspicuous gallantry and initiative, and inflicted many casualties on the enemy. When his tank was damaged by shell fire he got outside, and repaired the damage under heavy fire.

This N.C.O. has fought with distinction and gallantry in every action in which the battalion has taken part since Arras.

75339 Sergt. ALLSOPP, JOHN. 3rd Battn. Awarded M.M.
76687 Cpl. BUDD, ALEXANDER, D.C.M. 3rd Battn. Awarded M.M.

Near Beaucourt, on August 8, 1918, these N.C.O.'s commanded their tanks with conspicuous gallantry and success. Locating two 6-inch naval guns by their flashes, they worked round to a flank and drove the gunners away, inflicting heavy casualties on them as they ran. Later, they drove large numbers of the enemy out of a wood, thus enabling the cavalry to advance. Both these N.C.O.'s have previously been brought to notice for conspicuous gallantry in action.

75868 Sergt. GORDON, JOHN. 4th Battn. Awarded D.C.M.

On August 8, 1918, this N.C.O. led his tank into action on foot under heavy machine-gun fire, as, owing to the heavy mist, there was the possibility of losing direction. He continued to lead it on foot until the mist had cleared.

During the second day's operations, on August 9, when at Beaufort Wood, the infantry informed him that they were held up by machine-gun fire coming from Vrely ; on his own initiative, he altered the course of his tank and went to the village to deal with the machine-guns. On nearing the village his tank was engaged by a battery of light field guns, but he manœuvred his tank so skilfully that he succeeded in capturing the whole battery.

He then dealt with the machine-guns,and after having expended all his ammunition was able to return to the infantry and report all clear.

During these operations he displayed courage and initiative of a very high order.

200870 Pte. BOND, ALBERT JAMES. 4th Battn. Awarded M.M.

At Hangard (near Amiens). After having driven during the night without relief, he drove his tank into action on August 8, 1918, showing conspicuous ability and indifference to danger. He maintained his direction in action in spite of the fact that his tank was full of sparks and flaking from the armour, caused by heavy machine-gun fire. On coming out of action at the end of the day he fainted from exhaustion, but he again drove his tank in battle on the following morning against Warvillers. After it had received two direct hits he still manœuvred his tank so as to avoid further damage. When the wounded were safely removed he brought his tank, which was severely crippled, to its rallying point. In spite of his exhaustion he continued to show absolute devotion to duty.

200921 Pte. LETTS, JOHN FRANK, M.M. 4th Battn. Awarded Bar to M.M.

This man behaved in a most cool and collected manner when in action on the morning of August 8, 1918. After several casualties had occurred and the officer was firing the gun himself, this man (under the directions of his officer) continued to act as first driver and crew N.C.O., maintaining most accurate direction. After the tank was knocked out near Lemaire Wood he rendered great assistance to his officer, though himself wounded by being blown in the air by the explosion of a second shell.

200886 Pte. COX, WILLIAM ROBERT. 4th Battn. Awarded M.M.

Drove his tank in action on August 8 and 9, displaying great skill, courage, and endurance. He was hit in the eye by a shell splinter on August 9, when in action at Warvillers, but continued to drive his tank until the evening, when he brought it to its rallying point, although wounded and in a state of exhaustion.

306209 Pte. KAY, ALFRED. 4th Battn. Awarded M.M.

When in action on the morning of August 8, 1918, near Morgemont Wood, he displayed great presence of mind, in that when his tank caught fire from a direct hit, and though badly wounded in the leg, he promptly rendered great assistance in extinguishing the flames. He then took up a covering position in a shell-hole with a Hotchkiss gun, firing on enemy machine-guns until the infantry came up.

76907 Pte. MORGAN, ARCHIBALD. 4th Battn. Awarded M.M.

For gallantry and devotion to duty throughout the operations August 8–10. On August 8 he drove continuously for nineteen hours until the final objective was reached north of Caix. On August 9 and 10, owing to the sickness of the spare drivers through gas fumes, he again drove continuously throughout operations near Beaufort, Warvillers, and Rouvroy. On two occasions, whilst unditching, he carried on his work on top of the tank under heavy machine-gun and rifle fire. He has always displayed exceptional keenness, and set a splendid example to the remainder of the crew.

76284 Cpl. LAKE, EDWARD WALTON. 4th Battn. Awarded M.M.

Throughout the action on August 8, 1918, he displayed great courage and determination.

When his tank became immobile on Croates trench (Hangard sector) he immediately manned a machine-gun in the open and harassed the enemy until the infantry came up and the trench was taken over by them.

Later, at great personal risk, he entered a burning tank to get spare parts for his own tank, and only came out when quite overcome by smoke and fumes.

200848 Pte. YATES, HARRY IRION. 4th Battn. Awarded M.M.

For gallantry and devotion to duty on August 8 and 9. On August 8 he drove his tank continuously with exceptional skill for fifteen hours over difficult ground, until the final objective was reached. On August 9 he again drove his tank into action, and when the tank developed mechanical trouble in full view of the enemy he repaired it on two occasions, though subjected to heavy machine-gun and rifle fire.

He has always kept his tank ready for any emergency, and has displayed the utmost keenness and coolness at all times.

200900 L/Cpl. BARTON, LEONARD. 4th Battn. Awarded M.M·

This N.C.O. displayed great gallantry during the action near Hangard Wood on August 8, 1918.

His tank received a direct hit which badly wounded his officer and killed three members of his crew.

He immediately took command of his tank and ordered the

remaining unwounded gunners to continue firing at the enemy battery (which continued to fire on the tank), whilst he manœuvred it against the battery. Unfortunately, before he was able to silence the enemy's guns, his tank received another two direct hits, wounding the remainder of the crew; nevertheless he remained by his disabled tank and assisted the wounded to a place of safety.

92275 Pte. COOK, ALBERT EDWARD. 5th Battn. Awarded M.M.

For gallantry and initiative near Domart, August 8, 1918. After the officer and N.C.O. had been wounded, Pte. Cook took command of the tank, and continued to command it throughout the day. He reached all his objectives, and by his initiative and courage rendered most valuable assistance to the infantry.

111527 L/Cpl. BUCHANAN, JOHN. 5th Battn. Awarded M.M.

Near Dodo Wood, August 8, 1918, L/Cpl. J. Buchanan displayed the greatest gallantry. His tank received a direct hit which set it on fire, wounded the tank commander, and killed three of the crew. L/Cpl. Buchanan and Pte. Hall (both members of the crew) entered the blazing tank and succeeded in rescuing the tank commander and the remaining member of the crew, both of whom were wounded. They then got both officer and man safely away. In addition to the danger they incurred through ammunition exploding inside the tank, they were exposed to the enemy's fire throughout.

304851 Pte. HALL, ROBERT. 5th Battn. Awarded M.M.

Near Dodo Wood, August 8, 1918, Pte. R. Hall displayed the greatest gallantry. His tank received a direct hit which set it on fire, wounded the tank commander and killed three of the crew.

Assisted by L/Cpl. Buchanan (another member of the crew), Pte. Hall entered the blazing tank and succeeded in rescuing the tank commander and the remaining member of the crew, both of whom were wounded. They then got both officer and man safely away. In addition to the danger they incurred through ammunition exploding inside the tank, they were exposed to the enemy's fire throughout.

305543 Pte. GLYDE, GEORGE. 5th Battn. Awarded M.M.

For gallantry near Domart and Le Quesnoy, August 8 and 10, 1918. Pte. Glyde was acting as section runner. He showed the greatest gallantry in crossing open ground under heavy artillery and machine-gun fire to deliver messages to the tanks which were operating in front of our infantry.

His quick delivery of these messages contributed in no small degree to the success of the operations.

By his courage he rendered himself invaluable to his section commander.

IMMEDIATE AWARDS—OTHER RANKS

306334 Pte. CULLAM, WILLIAM. 5th Battn. Awarded M.M.

For consistent gallantry during operations August 8, 10 and 11, 1918, between Domart and Le Quesnoy. Pte. Cullam was acting as section runner. During the period in question he carried messages continuously from his section commander to the tanks which were operating in front of our infantry. He was exposed throughout to heavy artillery and machine-gun fire in the open. His courage and devotion to duty enabled his section commander to maintain complete control of his tanks.

95534 Cpl. HILL, ROBERT. 5th Battn. Awarded M.M.

For gallantry near Hamon Wood, August 8, 1918.

After his tank had received several direct hits and he himself had been wounded, he continued to fire his gun until the tank was finally put out of action. He then helped to get away the wounded members of the crew under machine-gun fire. He set a fine example throughout to the men under his command.

91643 Pte. DICKSON, JAMES. 5th Battn. Awarded M.M.

Near Demuin, August 8, 1918, this man was acting as first driver of the tank commanded by 2nd Lieut. Birch. This tank engaged a hostile field battery at close range. Pte. Dickson was wounded early in the engagement, but continued to drive his tank, which he manœuvred with such skill that one gun of the battery was knocked out and many of the gunners killed or wounded before the tank received two direct hits which put it out of action. His courage and coolness on this occasion were worthy of the highest praise.

305568 Pte. ROBERTS, GUY. 5th Battn. Awarded M.M.

For gallantry near Dodo Wood, August 8, 1918. Pte. Roberts was a member of the crew of a tank which had been put out of action by a direct hit. A Hotchkiss gun post was formed about 100 yards from the tank, which the enemy continued to shell persistently.

Pte. Roberts repeatedly crossed this hundred yards of open ground to fetch ammunition from the tank, although he was exposed throughout to heavy machine-gun fire at 300 yards range.

200158 Pte. SMITH, JOHN ARTHUR. 1st Battn. Awarded M.M.

For conspicuous courage and devotion to duty during our attack on August 8, 1918, in the vicinity of Beaucourt-en-Santerre. This man was the driver of tank 9842, which did invaluable work in locating and destroying machine-gun nests. He drove his machine through an inferno of anti-tank fire, and when his officer descended in order to better direct him, he followed out the directions given with the utmost coolness and exactitude, though bullets were penetrating his tank in all directions.

301528 Pte. COOPER, FREDERICK. 14th Battn. Awarded M.M.

For conspicuous gallantry and very conspicuous devotion to duty during the action of August 8 and 9, in the advance from Villers-Bretonneux to Meharicourt. This man did consistently good work as first driver throughout these days. He showed great skill in repairing an engine breakdown, during which time the tank was under heavy shell fire. On both days he showed great skill in driving so as to enable the best use to be made of the fire power of the tank. After driving during these two long and exhausting days he volunteered for action again on the 10th inst. He has throughout set a consistent and splendid example of coolness and determination.

112584 Pte. (A/Cpl.) SMITH, RICHARD EDWARD. 14th Battn. Awarded M.M.

For gallantry and devotion to duty in the advance near Marcelcave on August 8. This N.C.O. whilst commanding a tank, although wounded, got out of his tank and fixed the unditching gear under heavy fire, and remained in action for five hours in exceptionally trying circumstances, only returning when he had severe engine trouble.

112296 Pte. MALARKIE, JAMES WILLIAM. 14th Battn. Awarded M.M.

For gallantry, determination, and devotion to duty during the advance from Villers-Bretonneux to Meharicourt on August 8 and 9. This man drove with great coolness and skill throughout these days.

Though suffering severely from cramp he refused to be relieved. In the action of the 9th he showed much skill and judgment in manœuvring his tank so as to enable the crew to fire at the different targets. He also kept the crew informed of the position of our infantry, and set a splendid example of determination and devotion to duty.

301808 Sergt. CAUNT, WILLIAM HENRY. 14th Battn. Awarded M.M.

For gallantry and devotion to duty on August 8, in the operations near Marcelcave.

When wire, which had become entangled in the tracks of the tank, interfered with the work of the guns, he immediately mounted to the top of the tank and cut it away.

Also, when the tank commander was uncertain of his direction in the mist, he made a reconnaissance of the ground—both these deeds being done when under very heavy shell fire.

Throughout the action, his fearlessness, intrepidity, and cheerful example were invaluable as incentives to good work by the remainder of the crew.

IMMEDIATE AWARDS—OTHER RANKS

93108 Cpl. (A/Sergt.) BALLINGER, GEORGE. 14th Battn. Awarded M.M.

For gallantry and devotion to duty during the advance on August 8, near Wiencourt.

Throughout the action this N.C.O. showed great determination and coolness, especially when the two left-hand 6-pndr. gunners were knocked out. He continued to fire the gun although half-fainting from fumes and under very heavy machine-gun fire which caused many splashes inside the tank. His firing was of great material assistance in clearing the ridge and assisting the infantry to advance.

301290 L/Cpl. FLECK, HARRY. 10th Battn. Awarded D.C.M.

Near Mallard Wood, on August 8 and 9, 1918, this N.C.O. showed conspicuous gallantry and endurance when employed as first driver. Although wounded on the 8th, he continued to drive his tank throughout the action. Again, on the 9th, though suffering severely from his wounds and from petrol fumes, this N.C.O. volunteered to again drive his tank into action, and he continued to drive until he fell unconscious on his way back to his rallying point. Throughout the operations this N.C.O. set a magnificent example of gallantry and devotion to duty.

111364 Cpl. BAYLEY, WILLIAM. 10th Battn. Awarded M.M.

Near Morlancourt, on August 8 and 9, 1918, this N.C.O. was employed as second driver. Although separated from his company and without assistance from technical staff, this N.C.O. kept his engine running throughout the period. This tank was in action three times during the two days, and for a long time was in Morlancourt without any accompanying infantry. It was largely due to this N.C.O.'s gallantry and skill that this tank was enabled to perform such good work. (Second driver to Lieut. McGuire.)

110014 L/Cpl. CURRIE, CHRISTOPHER. 10th Battn. Awarded M.M.

Near Morlancourt he drove his tank continuously for nine hours on August 8 and seven hours on August 9, 1918. He set a magnificent example of coolness and endurance to the remainder of the crew, and it was undoubtedly due to his example that the tank was enabled to reach its objective on both days.

77371 Pte. HILL, JOSEPH. 10th Battn. Awarded M.M.

Near Mallard Wood, on August 8, 1918, this man was wounded while employed as first driver of his tank. He refused to leave his seat, and continued to drive his tank with great coolness and gallantry until the end of the action, when he successfully brought the tank back to the rallying point.

76162 Sergt. HANSON, ALBERT. 10th Battn. Awarded M.M.

Near Morlancourt, on August 8 and 9, 1918, this N.C.O. commanded a tank with conspicuous gallantry and skill. His tank went into action on three occasions on the two days, and on each occasion, owing to this N.C.O.'s clever handling, it succeeded in dealing with a large number of hostile machine-guns. Throughout both days this N.C.O. set a magnificent example to his crew.

301293 Pte. McEUNE, STANLEY CHRISTOPHER. 10th Battn. Awarded M.M.

Near Morlancourt, on August 8, 1918, this man showed conspicuous gallantry and disregard of danger while unditching his tank under heavy shell and machine-gun fire. It was largely due to this man's gallantry that the tank was unditched and was able to go into action again. Again, on the 9th, this man showed conspicuous gallantry in leading his tank into action under fire over unreconnoitred ground.

96647 L/Cpl. SUTTERBY, DANIEL EDWIN. 10th Battn. Awarded M.M.

Near Morlancourt, on August 8, 9, and 10, 1918, this N.C.O. showed conspicuous gallantry and endurance in driving his tank into action each day. When immobile through mechanical trouble, and under very heavy fire in front of our infantry line, he successfully executed necessary repairs and carried on to his objective although suffering from petrol fumes.

94871 Pte. LANE, CHARLES ROBERT. 10th Battn. Awarded M.M.

Near Morlancourt, on August 8, 1918, this man showed conspicuous gallantry and determination when employed as 6-pndr. gunner. Though wounded early in the action, this man refused to leave his post, and continued to work his gun with conspicuous coolness until the tank returned to the rallying point.

95074 L/Cpl. WINSTON, HARRY PHILLIP. 10th Battn. Awarded M.M.

Near Morlancourt, on August 8, 9, and 10, 1918, this N.C.O. drove his tank into action each day. He showed conspicuous endurance, and by skilful handling of his tank succeeded in destroy‑ ing the garrisons of several strong points, in one case bringing in 100 prisoners.

308256 Cpl. (A/Sergt.) COTTERILL, GEORGE BENJAMIN. 5th Tank Supply Coy. Awarded M.M.

Near Morlancourt, on August 8, 1918, this sergeant was in charge of a supply tank loaded with bombs. His tank received a direct hit which started the bombs exploding. He successfully got his crew out of the tank and ordered them back to the rallying point. He then stayed for two hours in the neighbourhood of the tank, though it was being heavily shelled all the time, in the hope of salving some equipment. This N.C.O. set a magnificent example of gallantry and devotion to duty in remaining close to this exploding tank under heavy shell fire, until he was certain nothing could be salved.

200279 L/Cpl. McQUILLAN, THOMAS. 2nd Battn. Awarded D.C.M.

On August 8 and 9 this N.C.O. showed the most extraordinary courage, skill, and devotion to duty as tank driver under the most trying and exhausting conditions.

On August 8, in action east of Villers-Bretonneux, L/Cpl. Mcquillan was instrumental in destroying four machine-guns and a trench mortar by driving his tank over them. His skilful driving allowed the gunners to engage successfully many other important targets.

After having been fighting, trekking, or working on the tank for thirty-six hours consecutively, L/Cpl. Mcquillan again went into action on August 9, east of Harbonnières. In this action the tank at various times received seven direct hits, one of which disabled the left epicyclic gear, making it impossible to turn to the left; also the tank would not run straight, but kept working off to the right. The tank, nevertheless, continued in action, searching the ground for enemy machine-guns, getting forward by describing alternately a wide curve and a circle to the right.

In spite of the tank being almost completely crippled, L/Cpl. Mcquillan successfully brought it back a distance of about three miles to the rallying point.

The conduct of this N.C.O. in thus continuing in action after receiving several direct hits and the determination he displayed in bringing his tank back in its crippled condition are beyond all praise.

200386 L/Cpl. BREESE, HENRY STEPHEN. 2nd Battn. Awarded D.C.M.

On the morning of August 8, when in action near Marcelcave, this N.C.O. showed absolute disregard for his personal safety in driving with all his flaps open through most difficult country, over gun emplacements, big shell-holes, and across broad-gauge railways, to ensure his tank not getting ditched, although heavy machine-gun fire was being directed at all angles on to his tank.

Later, south-west of Bayonvillers, this driver showed the greatest coolness and skill under direct fire from a group of two light field guns which had already disabled several tanks. He skilfully manœuvred his tank close up to the guns without being hit, and enabled one of his gunners to take careful and steady aim at the hostile gun-crews. These fled as soon as correct fire was brought to bear on them, and he then ran over one of the guns before proceeding to his objective.

On the 9th inst. this N.C.O. again showed most admirable qualities in action near Harbonnières, although he was greatly fatigued, having been trekking, fighting, or working on his tank for the previous thirty-six hours.

76488 Pte. MALONEY, CHARLES. 2nd Battn. Awarded M.M.

On August 8, during action east of Villers-Bretonneux and south-west of Bayonvillers, this gunner showed the greatest courage and coolness under heavy machine-gun and shell fire. When approaching Bayonvillers, and his tank was being fired on by two light field guns, he kept his gun in action, and by careful and skilful co-operation with his driver he was eventually able to bring accurate fire to bear on the hostile gunners, thereby disposing of them.

Later, when in the village, he got out of his tank and personally rounded up from cellars and houses at least forty prisoners, and gave chase to one who was endeavouring to escape on a bicycle. He caught him up, shot him, and then, returning, handed over the others to the infantry.

He set a magnificent example during that day and the operations on August 9 to the remainder of the crew.

92419 Cpl. KNIGHT, FRANK NORMAN. 2nd Battn. Awarded M.M.

This N.C.O. was very badly gassed by fumes and rendered almost unconscious during the first stage of the attack on August 8, near Warfusée. His company commander gave orders that the tank need not go into action in the second phase as the whole crew were incapacitated by the fumes.

This N.C.O., however, insisted to his tank commander that they should go into action again. This they did, remaining in action for several hours.

It was greatly due to his extraordinary pluck and splendid example that the crew so readily volunteered to carry on when they were all overcome by the fumes.

This N.C.O. himself continued to serve his gun after the turret had been smashed by enemy bombs.

307426 Sergt. DILLON, MICHAEL. 2nd Battn. Awarded M.M.

In action on August 8, at Harbonnières, although wounded early in the operation, this N.C.O. continued at his post as observer and gunner, showing great skill and initiative throughout the action, and by his coolness and devotion to duty setting a fine example to the crew.

IMMEDIATE AWARDS—OTHER RANKS

306367 Pte. HOLBROOK, JAMES. 2nd Battn. Awarded M.M.

On August 8, at Harbonnières, although suffering from the effects of gas fumes from the engine, and also from wounds, this man refused to quit his post as driver, and continued to drive the tank with great skill and gallantry during the whole action—a period of twelve hours.

200259 Pte. WEATHERLEY, EDWARD WILLIAM SPROT. 2nd Battn. Awarded M.M.

On August 8, while acting as a gunner, this man showed himself to be full of determination at critical moments near Bayonvillers. When a battery of small field guns were firing at close range and shells were bursting around the tank he turned his 6-pndr. on them, and kept the gunners down so effectively that the infantry captured them without a casualty. In this action and in previous ones he has always shown himself to possess a splendid fighting spirit.

50406 L/Cpl. RIVERS, GEORGE. 2nd Battn. Awarded M.M.

In action on August 8, near Bayonvillers, this N.C.O. drove his tank with great skill, manœuvring it to give his gunners good targets. When his tank received a direct hit he showed great gallantry in attending to the wounded under heavy fire, and evacuating them from the tank.

He put out two fires which had broken out in the tank, the fumes inside the tank being so bad that he had to wear his gas respirator when working inside.

Although the steering gear of his tank had been damaged by the shell, he volunteered to try to get the tank back. He was successful in bringing the tank back with no other assistance and under very difficult conditions, a distance of about eight miles. He was then very exhausted, but parked the tank in the company tankodrome.

He has on several previous occasions displayed outstanding qualities in action.

76426 Pte. REEVES, JOHN. 2nd Battn. Awarded M.M.

On August 8 and 9 this man showed great devotion to duty, and by his skilful handling of his Hotchkiss gun accounted for many enemy machine-guns.

On August 9, near Rosieres, after his tank was hit and unable to move, he showed great courage in bringing his gun into action in the open against an enemy battery whilst under heavy shell fire.

His cheerfulness and intrepidity were an example throughout to the crew.

76481 Pte. DEASON, HENRY RICHARD. 2nd Battn. Awarded M.M.

This man acted as orderly to his commanding officer during the attack on Harbonnières on August 8. At one point our infantry were held up by a machine-gun post and he was sent to fetch a tank, which successfully dealt with the opposition. Later, he placed the Australian flag in Harbonnières before either tanks or infantry had entered that part of the village.

Throughout the action he displayed great bravery and cheerfulness.

75237 L/Cpl. McCLURG, MATTHEW. 2nd Battn. Awarded M.M.

In action on August 8, near Warfusée, although wounded and badly gassed by fumes at an early stage in the action, this N.C.O. continued to drive his tank with the utmost skill and coolness.

After rallying, he insisted on going on into the second phase of the attack without waiting for medical attendance, although he was losing a lot of blood.

It was greatly due to his courage and dogged determination that the tank was able to rally at the end of the day's fighting, after doing very useful work in assisting the advance.

75300 Sergt. JESSOP, ROBERT WILLIAM, M.M. 2nd Battn. Awarded Bar to M.M.

In action on August 8, near Lamotte, when his tank had been set on fire by two direct hits and all but the officer and himself were killed and wounded, he assisted in carrying the wounded to places of safety under very heavy fire from an enemy battery firing over open sights.

He then ran for about a mile for a stretcher, and brought it back in time to save the life of one of the crew who was very severely wounded.

38080 Pte. BURFOOT, WILLIAM. 2nd Battn. Awarded M.M.

On August 8 this driver displayed the greatest courage and devotion to duty under trying circumstances in action near Villers-Bretonneux. Owing to the heavy mist and consequent difficulty of seeing, he kept all his flaps open in spite of the fact that on one occasion an enemy machine-gun was firing directly at him, and continued to do so until he ran over both it and its crew.

During the operations on August 8 and 9, east of Harbonnières, he drove with considerable skill, enabling the gunners to take steady aim, thus inflicting many casualties on the enemy.

On August 9, east of Harbonnières, when his tank became ditched through no fault of his own, he rendered very great assistance in fixing the unditching gear under heavy machine-gun fire and bombs from aeroplanes.

This man set a splendid example to his crew.

IMMEDIATE AWARDS—OTHER RANKS

91587 Sergt. MITCHELL, ALFRED JAMES. 8th Battn. Awarded D.C.M.

For conspicuous gallantry and devotion to duty during the attack against Morcourt on August 8, 1918. Sergt. Mitchell commanded tank No. H. 21, and throughout the whole advance he displayed great courage, initiative, and exceptional skill in the handling of his tank and in overcoming all strong points on ' A ' Company, 14th A.I. Battn., frontage. On entering Morcourt his tactics completely demoralised the enemy. He opened rapid fire with both his 6-pndr. guns, the result being that the enemy surrendered almost to a man.

Evidence of his good work is that the infantry company reached its final objective without one casualty.

This N.C.O. only came out of hospital in time to take his tank into action.

78510 Sergt. BROWN, WILLIAM. 8th Battn. Awarded D.C.M.

During the action of August 8, 1918, against Morcourt, Sergt. Brown was in command of the only tank of his section left to assist the infantry. Throughout the whole action he behaved with the greatest coolness, and showed marked ability and rendered maximum help to the infantry. His route was over extremely difficult country ; notwithstanding this, he reached his objective, leading the infantry.

He engaged and silenced a whole enemy battery of three guns.

When near his objective, this N.C.O. entered a dug-out and captured fifty of the enemy single-handed. He set a high standard of courage and determination, with a total disregard of personal fatigue or danger.

305406 L/Cpl. CUNLIFFE, FRANK. 8th Battn. Awarded M.M.

For conspicuous gallantry and devotion to duty, north of Morcourt, on August 8, 1918. His tank had received five direct hits. While the tank was on fire and was under direct artillery fire from the Chipilly Ridge, L/Cpl. Cunliffe returned and salved three Hotchkiss guns, and then remained with his tank until it was impossible for him to do any more, and he was ordered to leave it, whereupon he advanced with the infantry and did considerable execution amongst the enemy. L/Cpl. Cunliffe throughout showed a total disregard for his personal safety and great coolness, setting a fine example though severely shaken from the direct hits on his tank.

205022 Sergt. CHILD, DAVID WILLIAM. 13th Battn. Awarded D.C.M.

For conspicuous gallantry and devotion to duty near Bayon-villers on August 8, 1918.

This N.C.O. acted as a tank commander throughout an attack. Owing to casualties to other tanks operating in his sector, Sergt. Child, with one other tank, attacked, and destroyed enemy machine-gun positions along a tank half-company front. In order to accomplish this, it was necessary to proceed through burning tanks and heavy fire from anti-tank guns.

It was largely due to the skill and initiative with which Sergt. Child handled his tank and overcame enemy machine-gun nests that the casualties to the infantry in the area in which he was operating were exceptionally slight. After reaching the final objective and patrolling during consolidation, this N.C.O. again took his tank forward and, in company with one other tank, successfully attacked a village (Harbonnières).

Sergt. Child displayed remarkable courage and powers of leadership throughout the action.

305570 L/Cpl. WHILES, THOMAS. 13th Battn. Awarded D.C.M.

For conspicuous gallantry and devotion to duty near Bayonvillers on August 8, 1918.

During an attack, the tank in which this N.C.O. was acting as gunner received two direct hits, killing the driver and tank commander and causing the tank to catch fire. Repeated efforts were made to extinguish the flames, but exploding ammunition made this impossible. In spite of the fact that the tank was filled with flames and smoke, this N.C.O. made heroic efforts to get out the bodies of the driver and tank commander until, seeing that life was extinct and being completely exhausted, he left the tank. Later, he rescued a man from a tank of another battalion which had received a direct hit, killing four of the crew. This tank was also on fire, causing ammunition to explode.

Throughout the action the conduct of this N.C.O. was a splendid example of resolution and contempt of danger.

301937 Cpl. OLDROYD, ALFRED. 13th Battn. Awarded M.M.

For conspicuous bravery and devotion to duty near Cerisy-Gailly on August 8, 1918.

This N.C.O. acted as driver of his tank in action. When the tank received a direct hit he showed great coolness and presence of mind and continued to drive toward the enemy positions. The tank subsequently received a second direct hit, which put it temporarily out of action. It was necessary to work outside the tank to effect repairs, and although heavily fired at by enemy machine-guns, Cpl. Oldroyd got out of the tank and assisted his tank commander to make the tank fit for action again.

This N.C.O. throughout exhibited exceptional courage and ability and inspired the remainder of the crew with the greatest confidence.

300219 Sergt. **WILKINSON, ALBERT.** 13th Battn. Awarded M.M.

For conspicuous bravery and devotion to duty near Cerisy-Gailly on August 8, 1918.

During the early part of the action, which occurred during thick mist, he led his tank on foot so as to indicate enemy machine-gun nests which were harassing the advance of the infantry. Later, the tank received a direct hit, wounding the tank commander and setting fire to the tank. Although heavily fired on, Sergt. Wilkinson got out of the tank and helped the tank commander back to a place of safety.

This N.C.O. showed throughout the greatest disregard for personal safety, and by his coolness and ability gave a fine example to the crew of the tank.

305591 Pte. **BALL, NORBETT.** 13th Battn. Awarded M.M.

For conspicuous gallantry and devotion to duty near Cerisy-Gailly on August 8, 1918.

During an attack the tank in which Pte. Ball acted as gunner was temporarily put out of action in a nest of enemy machine-guns. The tank was fired on from all sides at point-blank range and pierced many times by armour-piercing bullets. Although wounded, this man, while repairs were being effected, continued to fire his guns and did great execution among the enemy until the tank was able to proceed.

Throughout the action Pte. Ball showed exceptional coolness and worked his gun with the greatest skill.

305593 Pte. **ROSE, THOMAS FREDERICK.** 13th Battn. Awarded M.M.

For conspicuous gallantry and devotion to duty near Bayonvillers on August 8, 1918.

This man acted as tank observer in an attack. After his tank had been twice hit and a gunner was occupied in putting out the flames, he jumped down from the observer's seat and took the gunner's place. Although the tank was again hit, he carried on firing and put the enemy gun out of action, thus enabling other tanks and infantry to continue the advance.

Pte. Rose showed exceptional skill and resource under difficult circumstances.

304241 L/Cpl. **WASHINGTON, EDWARD.** 13th Battn. Awarded M.M.

For conspicuous gallantry and devotion to duty near Bayonvillers on August 8, 1918.

This N.C.O. acted as driver of a tank during an attack, and although, when the tank received a direct hit, he was wounded on the knee, he continued to drive on until a second hit blew him and the tank commander backward off their seats, causing the tank to run down a ravine out of control and overturn., The tank was on fire, but this N.C.O., after putting out the flames, subsequently, in spite of his wound and severe enemy fire directed on the tank, assisted in righting the tank and getting it safely back to the rallying point.

The coolness and courage shown by this N.C.O. under very trying circumstances had a great influence on the remainder of the crew.

301934 Pte. HOLLAND, FRANK. 13th Battn. Awarded M.M.

For conspicuous bravery and devotion to duty near Cerisy-Gailly on August 8, 1918. During an attack the tank in which Pte. Holland acted as gunner was put out of action in the midst of an enemy strong point. Immediately machine-gun fire was concentrated on the tank from all sides. Although wounded, this man rendered valuable aid in effecting repairs to the tank, which shortly afterwards was able to proceed.

Throughout the action Pte. Holland behaved with great courage and resource, and his coolness and ability were an example to the rest of the crew.

304253 L/Cpl. WHYBROW, FREDERICK. 13th Battn. Awarded M.M.

For conspicuous gallantry and devotion to duty near Cerisy-Gailly on August 8, 1918.

This N.C.O. acted as driver of a tank in action. Although suffering severely from the effects of petrol fumes, he continued to drive throughout the action. The tank was temporarily put out of action in a nest of enemy machine-guns, and fire was concentrated on it from all sides. L/Cpl. Whybrow, although wounded, assisted in effecting the necessary repairs and drove the tank until the objectives had been carried and our new line consolidated. On returning to the rallying point he fainted from exhaustion.

This N.C.O. showed remarkable courage and powers of endurance and a determination that was an example to all.

300391 L/Cpl. HARRIS, CHARLES. 13th Battn. Awarded M.M.

For conspicuous gallantry and devotion to duty near Bayon-villers on August 8, 1918.

This N.C.O. acted as gunner in a tank crew, and during an attack the tank received two direct hits, putting it out of action. The crew were ordered out by the tank commander. Seeing that the tank had caught fire, this N.C.O. volunteered to go back across open ground under heavy rifle and machine-gun fire to try and put the fire out. He reached the tank safely and eventually succeeded, single-handed, in spite of exploding ammunition, in putting out the flames.

Owing to the courage and bravery displayed by this N.C.O. the tank could again be made fit for action.

301419 Pte BARBER, BERTRAM ERNEST. 13th Battn. Awarded M.M.

For conspicuous gallantry and devotion to duty near Bayonvillers, on August 8, 1918.

The tank in which this man was acting as gunner received two direct hits, causing it to catch fire and wounding the tank commander and three men of the crew. Pte. Barber continued to engage the enemy until his machine-gun was put out of action. Although under heavy enemy machine-gun fire, he then carried the wounded out of the tank and assisted them one by one to a place of safety.

The prompt and courageous conduct of this man saved the lives of the wounded and gave a splendid example to all ranks.

206188 Pte. BRIGGS, PERCY. 15th Battn. Awarded D.C.M.

On August 8, 1918, near Morcourt, this driver drove tank O 34 with great skill, fearlessness, and determination throughout the entire operation ; he showed great initiative in handling his tank when under heavy artillery fire from a light battery on the north bank of the River Somme, where the attack had been held up. After the tank had received direct hits on the final objective, and was on fire, he continued to drive it until he had got it back well behind our own lines. His pluck and determination to save his tank from capture or becoming derelict under these conditions, he himself being in a very exhausted condition from his long period of driving and the fumes from his burning tank, were a magnificent example to his crew and the Australian machine-gun personnel.

305102 Pte. ABSON, CHARLES. 15th Battn. Awarded M.M.

On August 8, 1918, during the attack on Harbonnières, this gunner acted as runner to his section commander. He was indefatigable in his efforts to keep up communication between the tanks, section, and company commanders, over a very broad front. He was on the move in the open, under fire, for over three hours, and showed great devotion to duty throughout. On August 9, at Framerville, this gunner acted in a similar capacity to his section commander, who was also on that day commanding tank O 12, the crew commander having become a casualty through exhaustion. Pte. Abson was inside the tank, which was about to rally and suddenly received three direct hits from an anti-tank gun and was set on fire, two of the crew being killed and two others wounded. The remainder were ordered to evacuate, but Pte. Abson remained with his officer and assisted in salving papers and maps, which was successfully done, together with two guns. Further salvage was attempted by him, but he was prevented by the heat and fumes of the tank, which was then burning furiously. He was overcome by these fumes. On reviving, he volunteered to take a message to the company commander. Though much shaken, he passed through a machine-gun and artillery barrage, and succeeded in delivering the message to the company commander, then four miles to the rear at Bayon-villers. This message was of great importance, containing the news of the three left tanks, which had been knocked out. His great endurance, courage, and initiative were of incalculable value to his section commander, and set a fine example to all.

307976 Pte. BOWDLER, FRED. 15th Battn. Awarded M.M.

This driver, on August 8, 1918, near Mericourt, stuck to his seat and continued driving his tank after all the crew had collapsed through fumes and gas, as well as the Australian machine-gun personnel. Later, he drove his tank through field-gun fire from the north bank of the River Somme, and by skilful manœuvring reached his objective east of Mericourt, where the Australian machine-gun personnel and guns were deposited. It was entirely owing to his great endurance and devotion to duty under exceptionally diffi-cult circumstances, that the tank reached the objective. He was continuously in the driver's seat for seven hours.

307774 L/Cpl. GRUNEWALD, HENRY ADOLPH. 15th Battn. Awarded M.M.

For continuous good work and devotion to duty during the operations of August 8 and 9, 1918.

He drove his tank for seven hours in action on the first day, and for three and a half hours in action on the second, and set a fine example of courage and endurance to his crew.

On August 9, during the attack on the village of Framerville, his fine driving was undoubtedly the means of bringing exceptionally good targets to his gunners, and enabling them to knock out enemy observation posts in the village, and especially of securing the infantry from the heavy fire from the south-west corner of the village of Rainecourt. He was under heavy shell fire the whole time, and his coolness and courage were great factors in capturing a very troublesome corner with very little loss to the infantry. This tank inflicted many casualties on the enemy. Though much exhausted he remained at his post throughout, and drove his tank at entire disregard of his own personal safety.

307762 L/Cpl. JEFFCOCK, CLIFFORD. 15th Battn. Awarded M.M.

On August 8, 1918, during the attack on Harbonnières, he drove his tank with the highest skill during the entire action. On

August 9, during the attack on Framerville, by particularly skilful manœuvring, he gave his gunners excellent targets, and was the means of inflicting heavy casualties on the enemy. On being relieved from patrol duty during consolidation by the infantry, he assisted his tank commander to get a disabled tank into tow under heavy machine-gun fire and at the same time replenished his tank with petrol, and was able to tow the other tank to the rallying point, thus preventing the tank which was then in No Man's Land from becoming derelict. The tank was under heavy shell and machine-gun fire during the entire action, and it was this driver's courage and endurance which set a very fine example to his much-exhausted crew. He showed a total disregard of personal danger when fixing the tow-rope to the disabled tank under machine-gun fire which undoubtedly was the means of salving the tank.

76266 Sergt. DRINKWATER, GEORGE. 4th Battn. Awarded D.C.M.

Acting as Hotchkiss gunner during August 8 and 9, he destroyed several machine-gun crews and kept his gun going incessantly, picking up targets with great skill. He maintained fire against a nest of six hostile machine-guns which were firing armour-piercing bullets at his tank. When in action at Beaufort Wood, on August 9, a shell struck his tank on one side, breaking his arm ; he managed to fire from the other side of the tank until the roof of the tank was smashed in by another shell, disabling the rest of his crew. Wounded for the second time, he still continued to assist his tank commander and, with indomitable spirit, he continued to rally his wounded comrades until their tank had been placed out of further danger.

200867 L/Cpl. LAWRENCE, JOSEPH BARRON. 4th Battn. Awarded D.C.M.

Acting as Hotchkiss gunner during August 8 and 9, he destroyed several machine-gun crews and kept his gun going incessantly, picking up targets with great skill. He maintained fire against a nest of six hostile machine-guns which were firing armour-piercing bullets at his tank. When in action at Beaufort Wood, on August 9, a shell struck his tank on one side, breaking his arm ; he managed to fire from the other side of the tank until the roof of the tank was smashed in by another shell, disabling the rest of his crew. Wounded for the second time, he still continued to assist his tank commander and, with indomitable spirit, he continued to rally his wounded comrades until their tank had been placed out of further danger.

200781 Sergt. McNICOLL, WILLIAM. 4th Battn. Awarded D.C.M.

For conspicuous gallantry and devotion to duty when near Cayeux on August 8, 1918.

He successfully commanded his tank and fought it for five miles into hostile territory; but when nearing Cayeux it was put out of action by two direct hits, seriously wounding him and all his crew except one gunner.

He immediately ordered the crew to evacuate the tank, but he himself remained behind and covered the withdrawal of his wounded crew with machine-gun fire, during which time the enemy opened heavy machine-gun fire upon his derelict tank. Eventually, when the infantry arrived, he himself was able to withdraw and was taken to the dressing station.

304356 L/Cpl. RHODES, CECIL. 17th Battn. Awarded M.M.

On the Villers-Bretonneux road during the attack of August 8, 1918, this N.C.O. was in charge of the second car of a section. He displayed the greatest skill and gallantry during a raid into a village which was strongly held by the enemy. He showed great initiative in directing his car generally, and in supporting his officer throughout the operation, the effective fire from his guns killing numbers of the enemy.

78670 Pte. SHEARD, WILLIAM DUNCAN. 17th Battn. Awarded M.M.

For gallantry and devotion to duty on the Villers-Bretonneux road during the attack of August 8, 1918. This soldier, by his coolness and accurate fire of his machine-gun, drove the crew from an enemy field gun which had disabled two armoured cars. He kept down the enemy's fire and thus enabled the crews to get clear of the damaged cars.

309298 Pte. EDMONDS, FREDERICK. 17th Battn. Awarded M.M.

On the Villers-Bretonneux road, during the attack of August 8, 1918, this soldier displayed conspicuous gallantry and devotion to duty. The armoured car he was driving, when in the enemy's territory, received a direct hit from an enemy field gun at short range. While the enemy's gunners were kept off by another car, he worked outside his car regardless of danger until his car was ultimately salved.

302335 Pte. (L/Cpl., A/Cpl.) COX, ALBERT STANLEY VICTOR. 1st Battn. Awarded D.C.M.

For gallantry and devotion to duty in the operations near Beaucourt-en-Santerre on August 8, 1918, as tank N.C.O. At the beginning of the battle his officer was killed, and this N.C.O. at once took over command of the tank, and with great skill brought it to its objective. Throughout the day he worked his tank with extreme skill and judgment. This was Cpl. Cox's first time in action with a tank, and his conduct throughout was magnificent.

IMMEDIATE AWARDS—OTHER RANKS

40098 Pte. MARR, JACK. 1st Battn. Awarded M.M.

For gallantry and devotion to duty in the actions near Beaucourt-en-Santerre on August 8, 9, and 10, 1918. This man was the first driver in his crew and showed wonderful skill and judgment in driving the tank, although most of the time the heat was almost unbearable. On three occasions he drove his car right into machineguns, crushing the gun and its crew, and always manœuvred his tank to the best advantage to enable his gunners to make full use of their guns. As a driver he showed the greatest devotion to duty, and at all times exhibited a wonderful endurance.

75671 M.S/Sergt. REED, THOMAS. 1st Battn. Awarded M.M.

For gallant conduct and devotion to duty in the operations near Beaucourt-en-Santerre from August 8–11, 1918. This N.C.O. worked unceasingly for seventy-two hours on the tanks under his charge, and on every occasion he accompanied the tanks up to the moment of engaging the enemy. He carried out repairs on many occasions under extremely heavy fire, and his untiring zeal contributed largely to the success of his company's operations. His great devotion to duty was a striking example to all.

201804 Pte. HIRST, THOMAS. 1st Battn. Awarded M.M.

For great endurance and devotion to duty on August 8, 1918, near Beaucourt-en-Santerre. As first driver of his tank, although badly wounded in the face, he continued to drive right through the action. His skilful driving throughout the day enabled the gunners to use their guns to the best advantage. His endurance and courage were an example to the remainder of the crew.

76072 Cpl. MOORE, CHARLES. 1st Battn. Awarded M.M.

For gallantry and devotion to duty in the operations near Beaucourt-en-Santerre on August 8, 1918. This N.C.O. was in charge of the 6-pndr. gun, and although the tank was subjected to the most intense machine-gun fire and received a direct hit from a field gun, Cpl. Moore never faltered, and with his gun knocked out the gun which had previously made a direct hit on his tank. Throughout the action he set a most excellent example to his crew.

305827 Pte. JARVIS, HENRY GEORGE. 1st Battn. Awarded M.M.

For great devotion to duty on August 8, 1918, near Beaucourt-en-Santerre. His tank received a direct hit and he was severely wounded, but he stuck to his gun and continued to fire until utter exhaustion compelled him to stop. His courage and endurance were remarkable.

200193 Pte. DAY, ALBERT VICTOR. 1st Battn. Awarded M.M.

For conspicuous gallantry and devotion to duty near Beaucourt-en-Santerre on August 8, 1918. He was first driver of his tank, which received four direct hits from an anti-tank gun, and although machine-gun bullets were penetrating the tank he remained in his seat. His coolness and disregard of danger were a fine example to the remainder of his crew.

77383 Pte. (L/Cpl.) REDSHAW, WILLIAM. 1st Battn. Awarded M.M.

For conspicuous gallantry in action on August 8 and 10, 1918, near Beaucourt-en-Santerre. This N.C.O., although almost overcome by fumes, continued to fight his gun with great effect. His skill and remarkable coolness under heavy fire resulted in many machine-guns being destroyed. He set a wonderful example to his crew, and has always shown exceptional gallantry.

307227 Pte. PARFITT, FREDERICK. 15th Battn. Awarded M.M.

During the attack of the 31st Battalion, A.I.F., from Warfusée-Abancourt, east of Villers-Bretonneux, on August 8, 1918, this man was the driver of one of the Blue Tanks (No. O 49). He drove his tank with great skill, and showed great coolness at times of danger from enemy shelling. On one occasion, when his tank had temporarily broken down, he displayed great skill in repairing the damage, then continuing his journey. His courage and devotion to duty throughout the operation were most marked.

201044 Sergt. SMITH, WILLIAM ERNEST. 2nd Battn. Awarded D.C.M.

On August 8 and 9, when in action, this N.C.O. showed the most extraordinary courage and initiative as tank commander, under the most nerve-trying and exhausting conditions.

On August 8, in action east of Villers-Bretonneux, Sergt. Smith was unable, owing to the heavy mist, to locate enemy machine-guns and trench mortars. He arranged with the infantry that they should indicate the direction from which the sound of firing was coming. He then overcame the resistance and waited until the infantry arrived. In this way he destroyed five machine-guns and two trench mortars. Of these, four machine-guns and one trench mortar were destroyed by the tank being driven over them. Near Harbonnières he found two trains, one on fire, the other, which carried a 6-in. gun, moving away. This train he fired upon and stopped.

After having been fighting, trekking, or working on the tank for thirty-six hours consecutively, Sergt. Smith again went into action on August 9, east of Harbonnières.

When nearing Rosieres the tank received a direct hit on the left sponson. The N.C.O. and one gunner was wounded and one gun disabled. The wounded men having been evacuated, Sergt. Smith was moving forward when he noticed a whippet tank ditched some distance west of Rosieres Station. As the infantry were then advancing without any difficulty he helped to unditch it. He then heard machine-gun fire coming from the station yard. He silenced the gun, and while clearing the station of the enemy he observed a gun of large calibre (believed 9·2 in.) on a ramp in the station, with some of the enemy around it. He made for the gun and the enemy fled.

Seeing no tanks on his left, and presuming that they were all out of action, he began to patrol the whole brigade front. As he was nearing an abandoned German hospital the tank received four more direct hits, one of which disabled the left epicyclic gear, making it impossible to turn to the left, also the tank would not run straight but kept working off to the right. The tank, nevertheless, continued in action, searching the ground for enemy machine-guns, getting forward by describing alternately a wide curve and a circle to the right. After some time the infantry passed the tank, and, as he could not keep up with them he started to come back to the rallying point. Just after turning, the right track was hit, and the shoe and one of the links blown off. The track, however, still held together. A few moments later, another shell hit the left rear horn nearing the driving sprocket without materially damaging the transmission. The tank reached the rallying point, having received seven direct hits.

The conduct of the tank commander in thus continuing in action after receiving several direct hits, and the determination he displayed in bringing his tank back in its crippled condition, are beyond all praise.

201166 Pte. MATTOCKS, BERTRAM STUART. 6th Battn. Awarded M.M.

For extreme bravery at Meharicourt on August 9. After he had shot down two machine-gun teams his tank was hit by a shell and evacuated at 7.30 P.M. Although under very heavy fire from machine-guns, he carried ammunition continually from the tank to his officer, who had taken the guns some distance away.

92337 L/Cpl. SIME, THOMAS. 3rd Battn. Awarded M.M.

Near Rouvroy, on August 9, 1918, he drove his tank with the greatest courage and skill. When engine trouble developed, he got out and sat on the bonnet under heavy machine-gun fire to try and rectify it. He stayed out all night close to the enemy and brought back his tank next day, a distance of ten miles, hand-feeding the carburetter the whole journey, the first part of which was under heavy shell fire.

200607 Pte. OWENS, JOHN TIMOTHY. 3rd Battn. Awarded M.M.

Near Beaufort, on August 9, 1918, as a tank driver, though wounded and quite incapable of doing so, he begged to be allowed to continue driving his tank in order to assist the infantry. Throughout the action he displayed gallantry and resource of the highest order and was a fine example to the remainder of his crew. In all actions in which the battalion has been engaged since third Ypres this man has proved himself a valuable and courageous driver.

200545 Pte. ROBERTS, NOR. 3rd Battn. Awarded M.M.

On August 9, 1918, near Rouvroy, this man drove his tank with the greatest determination and skill. He got out of his tank under heavy machine-gun fire, and successfully fastened a tow-rope to another tank to unditch his tank, and stood out in the open to direct operations.

200540 L/Cpl. BLOODWORTH, WALTER. 3rd Battn. Awarded M.M.

On August 9, 1918, near Rouvroy, this N.C.O. drove his tank with the greatest gallantry and skill. Throughout the action he displayed initiative and endurance in a marked degree. When the engine stopped he got outside and restarted it under very heavy machine-gun and artillery fire. Although this N.C.O. has in three different actions had his tank put out of action by a direct hit from artillery, he has driven a tank with gallantry and resource in nearly every action since the Somme.

76304 Cpl. CLARK, WILLIAM. 4th Battn. Awarded D.C.M.

For conspicuous gallantry in action on August 9, 1918, near Beaufort. Leaving his tank, he ran across the open under heavy machine-gun and rifle fire, and drove away the crew of an anti-tank gun which was preparing to fire on a section of tanks, thereby saving several of them direct hits. He brought back over twenty prisoners from rifle pits near the gun.

308747 Pte. CAULDRON, GEORGE. 4th Battn. Awarded M.M.

For gallantry in action, August 9, 1918, near Beaufort. Though wounded early in the action he continued to serve his gun continuously. He sighted an anti-tank gun and, single-handed, put it out of action, undoubtedly saving other tanks from becoming casualties. He refused to report sick so long as there was a possibility of further fighting, and has always displayed exceptional coolness, devotion to duty, and efficiency.

301496 Sergt. WILDMAN, ARTHUR FRANK. 14th Battn. Awarded D.C.M.

On August 9, near Rosieres, this N.C.O. as a tank commander rendered invaluable assistance to the infantry in the capture of the village. He worked his tank in rear of a battery of two field guns which had been holding up the tanks and had already accounted for one tank. He opened fire on this battery and accounted for most of the crews, putting both guns out of action. He then proceeded to Rosieres village, where he cleared a considerable portion of the village of machine-gun nests. Though severely wounded he brought his tank out of action, reporting to his section commander before proceeding to the dressing station.

301991 Sergt. KERWOOD, GEORGE WALTER. 14th Battn. Awarded D.C.M.

On August 9, near Rosieres, this N.C.O. as a tank commander fought his tank with the greatest dash, being responsible for the capture of a considerable portion of Rosieres village. He knocked out a considerable number of machine-guns with Hotchkiss and 6-pndr. gunfire, and when he had exhausted all his ammunition he used his tank as a battering ram, knocking down portions of houses and walls and causing the enemy to fly in disorder. Three of his crew were wounded, but he kept his tank in action for over two and a half hours.

310867 Pte. McDONALD, ALEXANDER. 14th Battn. Awarded M.M.

For conspicuous gallantry and devotion to duty near Rosieres on August 9. This man, when his officer and N.C.O. had been killed, took command and fought his tank until it was hit by shell fire and caught fire. He then evacuated the two remaining members of his crew, all of whom were wounded, helping them back to our lines under heavy and close range machine-gun fire.

110135 Pte. SUDDABY, TOM. 10th Battn. Awarded D.C.M.

Near Chipilly, on August 9, 1918, this man showed conspicuous gallantry when employed as a gunner. Although he had been wounded on the 8th, he continuously worked his gun for two hours under very heavy machine-gun fire from close range.

He was again wounded on the 9th, but continued to fire his gun until he fell unconscious.

Throughout the action this man showed a magnificent example of gallantry and devotion to duty.

110075 Pte. DICKENSON, GEORGE WILLIAM. 10th Battn. Awarded D.C.M.

In Gressaire Wood, on August 9, 1918, this man showed conspicuous gallantry and skill in repairing his tank after it had been set on fire. His officer had been killed and his first driver wounded. This man put out the fire and repaired the leads, although closely surrounded by the enemy all the time. He then drove his tank through the enemy and brought in fifty of them as prisoners.

112970 Sergt. SMITH, EGERTON WARREN, M.M. 10th Battn. Awarded Bar to M.M.

Near Gressaire Wood, on August 9, 1918, this N.C.O. showed conspicuous gallantry and skill when in command of a tank. This tank caught fire in the enemy lines, and all the crew were seriously affected by the fumes. This N.C.O., single-handed, put out the fire and repaired the engine, although surrounded by the enemy the whole time. It was largely due to this N.C.O.'s gallantry that the tank was able to continue the action.

110156 L/Cpl. REED, JOHN. 10th Battn. Awarded M.M.

Near Morlancourt, on August 9, 1918, this N.C.O. drove his tank with conspicuous gallantry and skill, although severely wounded early in the operation. By his coolness and determination under fire this N.C.O. set a magnificent example to the remainder of his crew.

95680 Pte. PRINGLE, GEORGE. 10th Battn. Awarded M.M.

Near Morlancourt, on August 9, 1918, this man was employed as 6-pndr. gunner. Although his sponson door was blown off early in the action, this man continued to work his gun with conspicuous coolness and gallantry.

111827 Pte. FRANKLIN, ALBERT CHARLES. 10th Battn. Awarded M.M.

Near Chipilly, on August 9, 1918, this man showed conspicuous gallantry when protecting his tank after it had been set on fire. He (with three other men) held off the enemy for three hours with their Hotchkiss guns. When the infantry arrived in a very disorganised state this man helped to reorganise them, and led them on until they reached the final objectives.

302757 Pte. MOATE, JOHN ALBERT GEORGE. 10th Battn. Awarded M.M.

Near Chipilly, on August 9, 1918, this man showed conspicuous gallantry when employed as an orderly. The tank to which he was attached came out of action through broken gear lever. This man volunteered to return to company tank park and fetch a spare part to replace it. Notwithstanding a very heavy barrage, he fetched the part and returned with it, thus enabling the tank to continue the action. Throughout the whole of the operations this man showed conspicuous gallantry in carrying messages under very heavy fire.

111597 Pte. LESTER, RICHARD. 10th Battn. Awarded M.M.

In Gressaire Wood, on August 9, 1918, this man showed conspicuous gallantry and skill in working his gun after his tank had

been set on fire. He successfully held off large pa/
for an hour, thereby allowing the tank to be re
back to its rallying point.

200515 Sergt. RAFFEL, JOHN, M.M. 10th Ba
to M.M.

Near Morlancourt, on August 9, 1918, this N.C.O. showea ᴜᴜ-
spicuous coolness and gallantry. When the 6-pndr. charges in
his tank caught fire he succeeded in putting them out although the
tank was under heavy fire at the time. Throughout the action
this N.C.O. set a magnificent example of coolness and determination.

76996 Pte. PINNOCK, ERNEST JOHN. 2nd Battn. Awarded
M.M.

76431 Pte. SMITH, JOHN FREDERICK. 2nd Battn. Awarded
M.M.

On August 9 these men were gunners in the tank commanded
by Sergeant Smith in the action near Rosieres. In the course of
the action the tank received seven direct hits. Throughout the
operation they displayed dauntless courage, keeping their machine-
guns in action all the while and inflicting heavy casualties on the
enemy under the most trying conditions.

Their devotion to duty and contempt of danger were magnificent.

76981 L/Cpl. NEEDS, HERBERT. 2nd Battn. Awarded M.M.

On August 9, in action near Rosieres, this N.C.O. showed great
courage and devotion to duty under heavy shell and machine-gun
fire. He located an enemy battery at about 800 yards range and fired
on it, causing confusion amongst the gunners, thereby temporarily
stopping their fire, which had been causing casualties to tanks and
infantry.

His tank was then directly hit and rendered immobile, so he took
his Hotchkiss gun out of the tank and advanced with the infantry
as far as their objective. As soon as they were established he
returned to his tank commander for further orders.

Throughout the whole of the operations of August 8 and 9
this N.C.O. set a wonderful example of determination and courage
under heavy fire. .

305527 Sergt. EATON, EDWARD. 8th Battn. Awarded M.M.

For conspicuous gallantry and devotion to duty when in action
at Vauvillers on August 9, 1918. During the operation his tank
was badly ditched and the tank commander gave the order to
evacuate the tank ; while so doing the tank commander was wounded
and Sergt. Eaton took command. He took his crew and guns out
and formed a strong point by the side of his tank, engaged a party
of the enemy who were forming up on the road, and dispersed them.

held this post under very heavy machine-gun fire for some time until the infantry came up. Sergt. Eaton then reported to an Australian officer, who told him to take his guns to the left flank and so cover their advance, which he did. Afterwards he made several unsuccessful attempts to unditch his tank, but when the unditching gear broke, he withdrew his crew and guns to the rallying point. By this N.C.O.'s initiative and quick grasp of the situation he undoubtedly saved the infantry many casualties and enabled the advance to proceed.

91527 Pte. MIDDLETON, CHARLES ERNEST. 8th Battn. Awarded M.M.

For conspicuous gallantry during the operation against Vauvillers on August 9, 1918. When his tank was hopelessly ditched, Pte. Middleton immediately got out on top and endeavoured to fix the unditching gear. Owing to the heavy fire directed on him he was forced to descend. He mounted the tank a second time, and on this occasion placed the gear in position, although his efforts proved unsuccessful in freeing the tank.

He was subjected to heavy fire from the enemy at close range the whole time.

Pte. Middleton throughout the operation displayed a complete disregard of personal danger and maintained a high standard of courage.

306807 Pte. DENT, ALBERT HUDSON. 8th Battn. Awarded M.M.

For gallantry during the attack on Vauvillers on August 9, 1918.

Pte. Dent was a gunner in a tank, and showed the greatest coolness and courage when his tank received a direct hit, which wounded the officer and other members of the crew.

Pte. Dent, finding it impossible further to fight the tank, rescued his wounded officer and, under heavy machine-gun fire, carried him for a considerable distance until he himself received a severe shell wound whilst so doing.

His conduct throughout the day showed the same high standard of morale and self-sacrifice, which set an excellent example to the crew.

18099 Pte. REED, JOHN. 7th Northants Regt. (attached Tank Corps). Awarded M.M.

On August 9, 1918, at Vauvillers, Pte. Reed showed conspicuous courage and disregard of danger in rescuing an Australian officer who had been badly wounded.

The infantry in the attack had been repulsed by heavy machine-gun and rifle fire, and this officer was left wounded in front of their position, when Pte. Reed, at great personal risk and with utter disregard of self, went out under very heavy fire and brought the officer into our lines.

IMMEDIATE AWARDS—OTHER RANKS

304882 L/Cpl. LAWTON, WILLIAM. 15th Battn. Awarded M.M.

On August 9, 1918, 1000 yards east of Vauvillers, when his tank was nearing its objective, a shell exploded a dump of gas shells, in consequence of which the crew, including the officer, were gassed. L/Cpl. Lawton was not entirely overcome by the gas, and straightway took charge of the tank, managed to remove the driver from his seat, and then drove the tank out of the gassed area. He then dragged the crew out of the tank and restored them with drugs. In the meantime, he mounted a Hotchkiss gun in a good position for the purposes of defence. As soon as the crew were in a state fit enough to carry on, L/Cpl. Lawton himself fainted from exhaustion. On recovering he took up his place again in the tank and carried on in the fight, doing deadly work with his gun. During all this time the tank was subjected to heavy shell fire. It was undoubtedly due to the quick action of this N.C.O. that the tank was able to carry on in the fight and do the useful work it did.

304363 Pte. WILSON, ERNEST. 15th Battn. Awarded M.M.

On August 9, 1918, 1000 yards east of Vauvillers, when his tank was nearing its objective, a shell exploded a dump of gas shells, causing the crew to be gassed. Pte. Wilson, together with L/Cpl. Lawton, were not entirely overcome by the gas, and between them managed to remove the driver from his seat and drive the tank out of the gassed area. Pte. Wilson then assisted in getting the crew out of the tank and restoring them with drugs. When the crew had recovered sufficiently to carry on, Pte. Wilson himself fainted from exhaustion. On recovering he took up his place in the tank and carried on firing his gun, doing deadly work amongst the enemy. During all this time his tank was subjected to heavy shell fire. It was undoubtedly due to the quick action of Pte. Wilson, as well as L/Cpl. Lawton, that his tank was able to carry on in the fight and do the useful work it did.

307057 L/Cpl. MELLA, FREDERICK. 15th Battn. Awarded M.M.

On August 9, 1918, 1000 yards east of Vauvillers, when the tank of which L/Cpl. Mella was the driver was nearing a trench strongly held by enemy machine-guns, the gunner who was sitting beside him firing the fore Hotchkiss machine-gun fainted. L/Cpl. Mella immediately carried on with firing this gun as well as driving the tank. When this gun jammed, he immediately drew up the flap over the driver's loophole, and shot three of the enemy with his revolver.

His behaviour throughout this action instilled the whole crew with the utmost confidence.

305135 Pte. HARRISON, NORMAN. 15th Battn. Awarded M.M.

On August 9, 1918, during the attack on Framerville, this gunner, when his tank had received direct hits and was knocked out by an anti-tank gun near the road junction at Flaque, his officer, N.C.O., and three men wounded, he himself much shaken, took out a Hotchkiss gun into the open and maintained an effective fire on the enemy. His quick action, under field-gun and machine-gun fire, enabled the infantry near by to withdraw. He prevented the enemy from approaching the tank and enabled the infantry to consolidate in rear, protecting them from casualties. He then withdrew with his gun and joined the infantry, remaining with them until released. He then brought in his gun and handed it over to the salvage dump. His quick action, coolness, initiative, and good gunnery under fire, at a critical time, were of great assistance to the infantry, who otherwise would have suffered many casualties.

305103 Pte. EVANS, GEORGE WILLIAM. 15th Battn. Awarded M.M.

On August 9, 1918, during the attack on Framerville, when his tank had been knocked out by direct hits from an anti-tank gun, near La Flaque road junction, and his officer and three of the crew wounded, this gunner, on his own initiative, though himself much shaken, quickly got a Hotchkiss gun out of the tank and occupied a small shell-hole in front. He kept up a continuous fire on the enemy, with excellent effect, until the gun was knocked out by a piece of shell and he himself wounded. His prompt action enabled wounded infantry and members of the crew to be withdrawn in safety and the position in rear consolidated. When his gun was out of action he withdrew and joined the infantry, with whom he stayed for some hours till relieved.

His presence of mind, courage, and devotion to duty undoubtedly saved the infantry many casualties during their temporary withdrawal and subsequent consolidation.

201106 Pte. KERR, THOMAS DRUMMOND. 6th Battn. Awarded M.M.

When, on August 10, at Parvillers, his tank commander was mortally wounded, he assisted him to a trench and bound him up. He then, with the gunner, took the tank on into action until it became ditched in No Man's Land. The fumes from the petrol, which began escaping, rendered him unconscious, but during the night he came round and, though burned himself, carried back the gunner, who was also wounded, to safety.

92353 Pte. RENNIE, JOHN. 6th Battn. Awarded M.M.

On August 10, in the attack from Villers-Bretonneux, he drove his section commander's tank into action from 4.20 A.M. till noon, though badly gassed by the petrol fumes. This tank reached its objective and caused many casualties both to the infantry, machine-gunners, and field gunners. He showed initiative under the most trying circumstances.

IMMEDIATE AWARDS—OTHER RANKS

75383 Sergt. BARRETT, PERCY. 4th Battn. Awarded M.M.

For conspicuous gallantry in action near Bois Sud, north-west of Damery, August 10, 1918. This N.C.O. was in command of his tank, and observing an enemy battery position which was holding up the advance of the tanks he engaged it at close quarters.

His tank received a direct hit and was set on fire, but at great personal risk he got out and extinguished the flames, though subjected to very heavy machine-gun fire.

He then, with his crew, manned his guns in the open and gallantly held the position until the arrival of the infantry.

200868 Pte. PERKINS, WILLIAM ALFRED. 4th Battn. Awarded M.M.

For coolness and devotion to duty near Bois Sud, north-west of Damery, when in action, August 10, 1918. This man was a first driver, and when his tank received a direct hit and set on fire, continued to drive until under cover, and he then assisted in putting out the flames. Had it not been for his initiative, probably neither tank nor crew would have been saved, as they were under direct observation and heavy anti-tank and machine-gun fire.

309029 Pte. WILSON, JAMES. 5th Battn. Awarded M.M.

Near Bouchoir, August 10, 1918, this man displayed the greatest gallantry. Although severely wounded and suffering great pain, he continued to fire his 6-pndr. gun for one-and-three-quarter hours, inflicting heavy casualties on the enemy. He refused to leave his post until he had expended all his ammunition.

305636 Pte. KING, WILLIAM GEORGE. 13th Battn. Awarded D.C.M.

For conspicuous gallantry and devotion to duty near Hallu on August 10, 1918.

During an attack the tank in which this man was acting as gunner became ditched in one of the old Somme trenches. The tank at this time was about 600 yards ahead of our infantry. Some twenty machine-guns were immediately concentrated on the tank, which was riddled with armour-piercing bullets, wounding the whole of the crew. Pte. King, although wounded, continued to fire until all ammunition had been expended. When the enemy called upon the tank commander to surrender, this man assisted his officer to defend the tank with revolvers. The enemy were at length forced to retire by our infantry coming up three-quarters of an hour later.

Pte. King had previously done exceptionally well during an attack on August 8, when, with his tank commander, he guided the tank in a thick mist among enemy strong points.

305647 Pte. REILLY, MATTHEW RICHARD. 13th Battn. Awarded M.M.

For conspicuous bravery and devotion to duty near Hallu on August 10, 1918. When the tank in which this man was a gunner was put out of action, he jumped out of the tank, taking a Hotchkiss gun with him, and although under heavy fire engaged an enemy machine-gun at close range, silencing it and killing the crew. Later, when it was found that the tank could not be moved, he volunteered to replace a casualty in another tank. Pte. Reilly behaved with the greatest coolness and courage and showed a complete disregard of danger throughout.

301578 Cpl. BERRY, ERNEST. 13th Battn. Awarded M.M.

For conspicuous bravery and devotion to duty near Hallu on August 10, 1918. Early in the attack this N.C.O.'s tank commander was wounded, and carried away by infantry stretcher-bearers. Cpl. Berry then took command of the tank and engaged enemy machine-gun positions in the area in which his tank had to operate. Seeing that infantry on his flank were being held up, he attacked enemy machine-gunners there and destroyed them. Later, although heavily shelled, he patrolled in front of the objective until the infantry had consolidated. This action was fought over unknown ground and there was no opportunity for previous reconnaissance, but in spite of this the tank did all that was required of it.

By his determination and initiative Cpl. Berry contributed greatly to the success of the operations.

307830 Cpl. RAFFAN, ANDREW. 13th Battn. Awarded M.M.

For conspicuous gallantry and devotion to duty near Hallu on August 10, 1918. After his tank commander had been wounded and the tank had been brought to a standstill, this N.C.O. continued to fight his guns, although under artillery and heavy machine-gun fire at close range. During the period the tank was stationary, Cpl. Raffan fought until his entire crew, with the exception of himself, were wounded, and put out of action seven machine-guns. His determined engagement of the enemy enabled the infantry to continue their advance. Later in the day this N.C.O. volunteered and succeeded in taking over heavily shelled ground. Throughout the action Cpl. Raffan behaved with great gallantry and disregard for personal safety.

75165 T.M.S/Sergt. DOBSON, JOHN RIDLEY. 13th Battn. Awarded M.M.

For conspicuous bravery and devotion to duty near Hallu on August 10, 1918. During an attack T.M.S/S. Dobson heard that one of the tanks of his company had broken down. In spite of heavy artillery and machine-gun fire concentrated on the tank, this N.C.O. walked out to it and succeeded in effecting the necessary repairs so that the tank was able to proceed to its objective. Later on, T.M.S/S. Dobson, although under heavy fire, walked across the open to another tank which had been brought to a standstill, and made sufficient temporary repairs to enable it to get to the rallying point. This N.C.O. showed great coolness and disregard of personal danger.

300223 L/Cpl. GUNTER, FREDERICK. 13th Battn. Awarded M.M.

For conspicuous gallantry and devotion to duty near Hallu on August 10, 1918. When the objective was almost gained, the tank which L/Cpl. Gunter was driving received a direct hit, wounding the tank commander and all the crew except L/Cpl. Gunter and one man.

This N.C.O. took charge of the tank, and having ascertained that all the objectives had been gained, drove the tank back to the rallying point. The action took place over very difficult and unfamiliar country and no previous reconnaissance was possible.

During the day of the action L/Cpl. Gunter drove his tank a distance of 35,000 yards and exhibited exceptional skill throughout.

96657 Pte. VERNON, ALFRED EVERALL. 14th Battn. Awarded M.M.

On August 10, at Fouquescourt, this man's tank received some direct hits and was captured by the enemy. He and another two wounded men were stripped of their clothes, water and food, and left by the Germans. The tank was in the enemy lines, which were at that time very undefined, consisting mostly of outposts and shell-holes. This man was only slightly wounded in the arm, and could have made his escape under cover of darkness, but chose to remain to attend his more seriously wounded comrades. By night he scoured the surrounding ground to obtain water, food, and covering. Forty-eight hours later, a further advance of our infantry rescued this party. The M.O. of the 42nd Canadian Battalion, who dressed these men when they were brought back, stated that both of the others would have died from exhaustion and lack of food had not Pte. Vernon remained with them and cared for them.

305539 Pte. NEAL, HAROLD LESLIE. 8th Battn. Awarded D.C.M.

For conspicuous gallantry and devotion to duty on the night of August 10–11, during an attack after dark near Proyart.

Pte. Neal took charge of a tank after his officer had been killed. Owing to heavy machine-gun fire the infantry had to withdraw, and although his tank was being repeatedly pierced by armour-piercing bullets and all the crew except one other thereby wounded, he served his guns with good effect, remaining out in front for one and a half hours covering the infantry, and finally performed a splendid feat by bringing his tank out with the assistance of the only other remaining member of the crew, after being in action five and a half hours. He himself received several wounds from splinters.

Throughout the action Pte. Neal showed great initiative and set a splendid example to all.

200162 Pte. NEEDHAM, GEORGE. 1st Battn. Awarded M.M.

For conspicuous gallantry and devotion to duty in the operations near Beaucourt-en-Santerre on August 10, 1918. This driver, throughout the eight hours his tank was in action, displayed the greatest skill and judgment in manœuvring over the bad ground. At intervals he used a rifle with good effect. When nearing the objective the tank engaged a battery of machine-guns which succeeded in hitting and putting out of action all the Hotchkiss guns on the tank. The concentrated enemy fire, added to the intense heat, caused the collapse of the remainder of the crew. This man, although nearly fainting, changed into fourth gear and charged the enemy position, thereby enabling the 6-pndr. gun to put the hostile guns out of action. He had also earlier in the action displayed great courage and coolness when the tank engaged an enemy field gun battery at close range. He set a very fine example to the remainder of his crew.

76297 Pte. FIRTH, JOHN. 4th Battn. Awarded M.M.

For conspicuous gallantry in action on August 11, 1918, near Parvillers. When his tank had to be hastily evacuated owing to intense shell and other fire whilst ditched in the British front line, this gunner served the remaining gun in action to the last, and helped to remove machine-guns afterwards. When the enemy appeared to be counter-attacking, and there was danger of the tank falling into enemy hands, this man went back to the tank under intense fire and removed the wedges and firing mechanism of the 6–pndr. guns, although he was twice knocked down by the explosion of shells on the way. This man has on all occasions set a splendid example of coolness under fire and devotion to duty.

75075 L/Cpl. EDWARDS, FREDERICK JAMES. 4th Battn. Awarded M.M.

For gallantry in action on August 11, 1918, at Parvillers. When his tank became ditched in full view of the enemy this N.C.O. made repeated efforts to fix his unditching beam, remaining on the roof to do so, under heavy machine-gun fire from close range. He did not give up until ordered to do so by his officer.

IMMEDIATE AWARDS—OTHER RANKS

200107 Pte. HOLT, GEORGE. 5th Battn. Awarded M.M.

For gallantry near Damery, August 11, 1918. Pte. Holt was one of the crew of a tank which received a direct hit and had to be evacuated. As the tank commander was getting out of the tank he was attacked by several of the enemy. Pte. Holt opened fire on them with his Hotchkiss gun, firing from his shoulder at a range of about five yards, and killed one of the enemy who was about to bayonet the tank commander. He then continued to fire until the crew got safely away. His pluck and presence of mind undoubtedly saved the tank commander's life.

308605 Pte. CUNNINGHAM, PETER ALEXANDER. 3rd Tank Supply Coy. Awarded M.M.

August 11 and 12, 1918, near Le Quesnel.

His supply tank was filling at a petrol dump, which was in close proximity to a shell dump. While in this position they were bombed by enemy aircraft, which caused a fire in each of the dumps. The sergeant and one other member of the crew were wounded. Pte. Cunningham at once took command and ordered the remaining members of the crew to start up the engine and get the supply tank away, while he endeavoured to extinguish the fire in the shell dump. Although he was unsuccessful in his attempt, he did not desist until the supply tank had moved to a safe distance. His devotion to duty saved the supply tank, its supplies, and the remainder of the crew from injury.

306902 Sergt. FORTUNE, WILLIAM HENRY. 2nd Tank Supply Coy. Awarded M.M.

Conspicuous gallantry and devotion to duty.

While being heavily bombed at Le Quesnel, at dusk on August 11, this N.C.O. refused to leave his tank, which he was repairing, and take cover, although the remainder of the crew had been ordered to an adjacent dug-out.

The bombing at this point was so heavy that a large number of men and horses were killed, and it was entirely due to Sergt. Fortune that the tank was able to carry up supplies urgently required that night.

Again, at Meaulte, on August 22, his tank received a direct hit from a shell, wounding two of the crew. Although under intense shell fire, he and the remaining members of the crew effected temporary repairs and succeeded in bringing his tank to safety, a distance of nearly four miles. He undoubtedly saved the tank from being completely destroyed and set a magnificent example of devotion to duty.

307230 Sergt. GIBSON, WALTER R. 15th Battn. Awarded M.M.

At Moyenneville, on August 21, 1918, Sergt. Gibson was N.C.O. of tank O 48. Early in the attack the officer in command of the tank was wounded. Sergt. Gibson then took command, and after having placed his officer in a place of safety, carried on into action with the tank. In spite of the fact that the whole crew were suffering from the effects of petrol fumes, Sergt. Gibson, by his personal example and powers of leadership, reached the final objective, and was able to put at least five enemy machine-guns out of action. He eventually brought the tank back to rallying point. He showed remarkable powers of leadership, and it was entirely owing to his gallantry that the tank was finally rallied from a dangerous position. This N.C.O. has previously been brought to notice for his ability to command a section.

307730 Pte. BERRY, MICHAEL JAMES. 15th Battn. Awarded M.M.

This gunner showed conspicuous gallantry and devotion to duty during the operations of August 21, 1918, in the neighbourhood of Courcelles, Arras-Albert railway.

In spite of exceedingly heavy shell, anti-tank, and machine-gun fire, he dealt with hostile guns quickly and effectively, silencing three and knocking out one. He was wounded early in the action, but, though suffering great pain, he carried on with his gun with great effect. He set a very high example of personal bravery to the remainder of the crew. It was only when his tank became totally disabled that he gave up the fight and had his wound dressed. He carried on as long as any enemy were within his range and vision.

307362 Pte. MURRAY, SYLVESTER. 15th Battn. Awarded M.M.

Near Courcelles, on August 21, 1918, during the attack on the Arras-Albert railway, Pte. Murray acted as runner to his section commander. He displayed conspicuous gallantry and devotion to duty, carrying messages from tank to tank in action. On one occasion it was necessary for the section commander to send an important message to one tank that was considerably in front of the others. Pte. Murray volunteered to go, and in spite of machine-gun fire ran across the open to the tank and delivered the message.

On all occasions Pte. Murray placed the execution of his duty before his personal feelings.

307980 L/Cpl. FRIEND, HARRY. 15th Battn. Awarded M.M.

On August 21, 1918, this N.C.O. showed the greatest courage and devotion to duty on the Arras-Albert railway embankment. He drove his tank the whole morning with the front window open to obtain a better view in the mist, in spite of fire from machine-guns directed on the front of his tank.

Later, when his tank was knocked out by direct hits, and had to be evacuated, he personally extricated a wounded man from the interior, and, though under direct observation of the enemy from both sides and under heavy machine-gun fire, he personally bound up and attended to the wounded man. His skill in driving and disregard of personal danger by keeping his window up were the means of inflicting heavy casualties on the enemy, while his devotion to his wounded comrade under heavy fire was probably the means of saving his life. He set a great example to all ranks in the tank.

304295 Pte. LE BESQUE, THEOBALD FRANCIS MOREY. 15th Battn. Awarded M.M.

On August 21, 1918, during the attack on the Arras-Albert railway, in the neighbourhood of Courcelles, and on August 30–31, 1918, during the attack on the village of Vaulx-Vraucourt, Pte. Le Besque was my runner. On all three occasions he displayed great bravery and disregard for personal safety in carrying and delivering messages under very heavy shell and machine-gun fire. He also rendered very valuable assistance during an occasion upon which a number of tanks had to be withdrawn to the rallying point under very trying circumstances. He also proved to be very reliable on all occasions during operations.

307949 Pte. WADDELL, JOHN BROUGH. 15th Battn. Awarded M.M.

For conspicuous gallantry and devotion to duty during the operations of August 21, 1918, during the attack on Arras-Albert railway. He drove his tank in action through a thick fog for seven hours with the front window open under continuous heavy shell and machine-gun fire. During the capture and clearing of Courcelles, although he was already in a state of great exhaustion from fumes, his coolness and judgment were undoubtedly the means of enabling his gunners to engage and silence machine-guns. After his tank had attained its allotted objective, his tank commander was asked to assist in the capture of the Arras-Albert railway. Here again Pte. Waddell, by excellent driving under heavy machine-gun fire, enabled his tank to destroy at least three hostile machine-guns, silence many more, and capture many prisoners. He patrolled the railway embankment under heavy fire until his tank received a direct hit on each sponson door ; the engine had been struck several times by anti-tank rifle fire, and five of the crew were wounded. He still continued to drive, and eventually managed to get his tank back out of direct observation by the enemy. His complete disregard of personal danger and his courage and endurance materially assisted in the capture of part of the railway embankment, and his coolness after the tank had been hit and the crew wounded undoubtedly saved the tank from absolute destruction and becoming derelict.

304599 Cpl. POLLEY, FREDERICK. 12th Battn. Awarded M.M.

For gallantry and devotion to duty. This N.C.O. set a very fine example to the remainder of his crew by his good work, both before and during the action against Moyenneville on August 21, 1918. The morning of August 21 was very misty. Cpl. Polley volunteered to go forward on foot to reconnoitre the enemy positions. This he did under shell fire, and the information that he brought back enabled the tank to reach its objective and destroy all the machine-guns holding up the infantry. Throughout the whole action this N.C.O. displayed great coolness and bravery.

302746 Pte. BANKS, ERNEST WILLIAM. 10th Battn. Awarded M.M.

Near Achiet-le-Grand, on August 21, 1918, this man showed conspicuous gallantry and initiative when his tank received a direct hit. He took his gun out of the tank and, though under very heavy fire from close range, engaged the enemy, thereby enabling the remainder of the crew to evacuate the tank and take up positions to protect it. He remained protecting the tank, which was just in front of the infantry front line, for thirty hours, and throughout this period showed conspicuous coolness and endurance and set a splendid example to the remainder of the crew.

92134 T.M.S/Sergt. TOWLER, THOMAS GEORGE. 10th Battn. Awarded M.M.

Near Achiet-le-Petit, on August 21, 1918, this N.C.O. showed conspicuous gallantry when repairing tanks under heavy shell fire.

It was largely due to his efforts, and to the fine example which he set to the crews, that two tanks, which were broken down and still under very heavy fire from short range, were repaired and brought back to the rallying point.

92745 L/Cpl. FERNLEY, JAMES. 10th Battn. Awarded M.M.

Near Logeast Wood, on August 21, 1918, this N.C.O. showed conspicuous gallantry and coolness while under very heavy fire. The mist was very thick, and although under heavy fire from close range this man was continually outside the tank, guiding it and assisting to collect parties of infantry who had lost their way. It was largely due to his very gallant conduct that the tank reached its jumping-off point with a party of infantry to follow it.

75962 Sergt. HOWELLS, FREDERICK. 3rd Battn. Awarded D.C.M.

Near Achiet-le-Petit, on August 21, 1918, this N.C.O. commanded his tank with the greatest gallantry and skill. Owing to a heavy mist, conditions were most difficult. In spite of this, the assistance he rendered the infantry was incalculable. At the outset of the day he silenced a nest of a dozen machine-guns and handed them over to the infantry. Later, although under intense artillery fire at almost point-blank range, he engaged parties of enemy infantry and accounted for many of them. After our infantry had been forced to retire, he withdrew his tank with great judgment. Finally, his tank was hit, and although in close proximity to the enemy he blew it up to prevent it falling into their hands.

76455 Gnr. YOUNG, HARRY. 3rd Battn. Awarded M.M.

Near Achiet-le-Grand, on August 21, 1918, after his tank had been knocked out by a direct hit from enemy artillery and he had been wounded in the leg by a bullet, displayed gallantry of the highest order.

The infantry having been driven back a short distance owing to very intense machine-gun and artillery fire, many wounded were lying out exposed to fire. Although wounded himself, this man went backwards and forwards repeatedly, under intense fire, tending to the wounded and helping them to a place of safety across open ground swept by bullets and shells.

200592 Cpl. EDWARDS, CLARENCE WILFRED. 3rd Battn. Awarded M.M.

112399 Gnr. CLARKE, SYDNEY LLEWELLYN. 3rd Battn. Awarded M.M.

Near Achiet-le-Grand, on August 21, 1918, these two men, after their tank had been knocked out by a direct hit from enemy artillery, displayed most conspicuous gallantry by rescuing many wounded infantry who were lying out in the open exposed to intense machine-gun and artillery fire. They carried many to a place of safety, and showed the greatest contempt of danger.

77667 Cpl. GILLIE, CHARLES, M.M. 3rd Battn. Awarded Bar to M.M.

During the action near Achiet-le-Petit, on August 21, 1918, this N.C.O. fought his tank with gallantry and resource of the highest order, inflicting many casualties on the enemy.

After his tank had been put out of action by a direct hit from enemy artillery, he took his guns and formed a strong point well in advance of the infantry. Later, when chiefly owing to his fire the infantry were enabled to advance, he pointed out to them where enemy fire was coming from, and personally led several rushes against the enemy machine-guns. His fine example was most inspiring to all with whom he came in contact.

(M.M. awarded for action at Cambrai, November, 1917.)

200637 Gnr. WITTY, JOHN ALFRED. 3rd Battn. Awarded M.M.

During the action near Achiet-le-Petit, on August 21, 1918, this man as driver of his tank displayed the greatest skill and daring under extremely heavy artillery and machine-gun fire.

Owing to his skill in manœuvring his tank he enabled his gunners to inflict heavy casualties on the enemy. This man has driven a tank in every action of his company or battalion since the formation of the Tank Corps with the greatest gallantry and skill, and was especially brought to notice for gallantry in action on August 8, 1918.

40289 Cpl. BARRETT, FRANK. 12th Battn. Awarded M.M.

For conspicuous devotion to duty and skill. This N.C.O. has done consistent good work both whilst preparing his tank for action and in fighting it. Throughout the attacks on Moyenneville and Hamelincourt on August 21 and 23, 1918, he displayed great skill in driving over the most difficult ground in such a way as to allow his gunners to continue shooting with accuracy. On August 23, when attacking a hostile machine-gun post, the forward Lewis gun jammed. He immediately opened the front window and emptied his revolver into the machine-gun crew, all of whom were killed. His conduct throughout both actions was an example to the crew, and the success of his tank was largely due to his skilful driving and initiative.

76509 Pte. BETTS, JAMES. 12th Battn. Awarded M.M.

For bravery and determination and skilful driving during the actions of August 21 and 23, on Courcelles and Gomiecourt. Whilst passing through a heavy enemy barrage the tank was hit and partially disabled. It was entirely owing to his skill that the tank was brought safely out. After returning from action he again went forward on foot under machine-gun and shell fire and salved the guns of another tank which had been hit and brought them back into our lines. Throughout the two days' action he displayed great skill and gallantry.

201502 Sergt. ROSS, HENRY ERNEST. 7th Battn. Awarded M.M.

At Loupart Wood and Grevillers.

For great gallantry and coolness in action and devotion to duty.

This N.C.O. commanded a tank in action on August 21 and 24, 1918, at Loupart Wood and Grevillers, and, despite thick mist on each day, gained his objective, inflicting severe casualties on the enemy and assisting the advance of our infantry by destroying machine-gun nests. He led his tank throughout with great skill and determination, though wounded, setting a splendid example to his crew.

205035 Sergt. WILLS, ARTHUR. No. 2 Gun Carrier Coy. Awarded M.M.

For services in action during the operations with the IV Corps, August 21 to September 16–17. This N.C.O. has worked incessantly in assisting crews in the repair of tanks which had broken down under enemy shell fire, thus ensuring the prompt delivery of stores and supplies carried by the tanks to the infantry in the front line.

305960 Pte. HOUSTON, GEORGE RAWER. 4th Battn. Awarded D.C.M.

When in action, on August 22, 1918, south of Méaulte. Between the first and second objectives the infantry were being held up by very heavy machine-gun fire on the left, from ground which was unobservable from the tank in that sector.

Pte. Houston volunteered and crossed 400 yards of open ground, under heavy machine-gun fire, to another tank, and explained the situation to the commander, thereby enabling him to knock out several machine-guns. It was a most courageous act, as his own tank was heavily engaged at the time in his own sector.

76588 Pte. WOODSIDE, WILLIAM MILLER. 4th Battn. Awarded D.C.M.

On August 22, 1918, when in action south of Méaulte. When his tank was approaching the first objective, this man, noticing that the infantry in rear were being held up by a machine-gun which the tank had passed without observing, left his tank and attacked the two machine-gunners from behind, killing one with his revolver ; the other at once surrendered. He then returned to the tank and informed the tank commander, who signalled to the infantry to come on. The tank at the time was under machine-gun fire from the front.

111640 Pte. COGGER, CHARLES FRANK. 4th Battn. Awarded M.M.

On August 22, 1918, when in action near Méaulte, he displayed conspicuous gallantry.

He volunteered to accompany his officer, under heavy fire, to locate the exact position of an enemy field battery.

Ater locating the battery he returned to his tank, and when it had been manœuvred into a position to deal with the battery his skilled marksmanship was instrumental in silencing the battery.

75533 Cpl. WEBB, JOHN PERCIVAL. 4th Battn. Awarded M.M.

This N.C.O. was in command of a tank in action south of Méaulte on August 22, 1918.

When, owing to the heavy mist, direction was lost, this N.C.O. guided his tank from outside, although the tank was in action at the time at close range against many machine-guns. It was due to his courage and resource that not only his own tank, but at least two others, were able to keep direction in the mist.

325511 L/Cpl. HOSE, JOHN HORNBY. 4th Bde. Sig. Coy., R.E. (attached 5th Battn.). Awarded M.M.

For conspicuous gallantry near Tailles Wood on August 22, 1918. This N.C.O. was in charge of a wireless apparatus in a tank. The tank came under a very heavy artillery barrage, received a direct hit, and was put out of action. L/Cpl. Hose salved his wireless apparatus, carried it through the barrage to a trench close by and set it up there. He continued to send messages throughout the operations under very heavy fire.

His gallantry enabled communication to be kept up during a very critical period.

308323 Cpl. (A/Sergt.) BELL, WILLIAM. 4th Tank Supply Coy. Awarded D.C.M.

For most conspicuous gallantry and devotion to duty in the Happy Valley, near Morlancourt, on August 22, 1918. After his sub-section commander had been killed, this N.C.O. led his tank on foot through an extremely heavy barrage. Arriving at our front line, he collected an unloading party from the infantry, but under the heavy machine-gun and shell fire all the party became casualties and three of his own crew. By his energy and coolness he collected a second unloading party from the infantry. When the infantry began to withdraw under the devastating barrage, Sergt. Bell and the last member of his crew remained and endeavoured to start up the tank, but could not reach the engine because of the half-unloaded supplies. He remained with his tank until all the infantry had retired, and did not withdraw until the enemy were within fifty yards of him. Later in the day he made several attempts with volunteers to reach his tank, which was now in No Man's Land, but failed owing to heavy machine-gun fire. His conduct throughout was in accordance with the highest traditions of the Tank Corps.

308435 Pte. WALLACE, HERBERT. 4th Tank Supply Coy. Awarded M.M.

For most conspicuous gallantry and utter disregard of personal safety in the Happy Valley, near Morlancourt, on August 22, 1918. One of the tanks in his section was knocked out and set on fire. It was presumed that an officer and a man who were inside the tank had been killed, but, owing to the withdrawal of our infantry, the tank was left well in advance of our own front line and practically in the enemy line. Entirely on his own initiative, Pte. Wallace made four successive attempts to reach the tank, in order to rescue the officer and put out the fire. On the fourth attempt he succeeded in reaching the tank, but the tank was then well ablaze and the ammunition inside it was exploding. No Man's Land at the time was swept by machine-gun fire and shelled by our own and the enemy artillery. Pte. Wallace displayed magnificent gallantry and utter lack of fear.

302805 Gnr. CREIGHTON, BERTRAM. 11th Battn. Awarded M.M.

Devotion to duty at Boyelles on August 22, 1918. Just before starting for the fight he sprained his ankle and could only hobble along. Although warned to go sick, he asked leave to go. His tank was ditched in the fight and the tank commander ordered the crew out to charge a machine-gun which was holding up the infantry, telling Creighton to remain in the tank. Creighton, however, went forward with a Hotchkiss gun over 300 yards of broken country and helped in knocking out and capturing this machine-gun.

His keenness to fight with his crew on foot, although he could scarcely walk, showed a fine example to his crew.

302826 Gnr. CROSS, JAMES. 11th Battn. Awarded M.M.

Devotion to duty when wounded at Boyelles on August 22, 1918. He was wounded in the back whilst driving, but refused to give up his job to anyone else. During two and a half hours in the fight he drove with great judgment and coolness, and only after the fight was over would he give his driving to anyone else, when he was pulled out of the driving seat in a fainting condition.

302781 L/Cpl. SYME, WILLIAM. 11th Battn. Awarded M.M.

Conspicuous gallantry at Boiry Becquerelle on August 23, 1918. His tank having broken down, the tank commander ordered the crew out to carry on the fight on foot. An enemy machine-gun, fifty yards off, was firing at the tank. L/Cpl. Syme on his own initiative rushed the machine-gun single-handed, killed the machine-gun crew, and captured the gun. L/Cpl. Syme was armed with a revolver only.

His gallant act undoubtedly saved casualties amongst the rest of his own crew, and since the machine-gun was also firing at our advancing infantry, this act saved many casualties amongst them too.

95459 Sergt. ROBERTS, JOHN HUGH. 12th Battn. Awarded D.C.M.

During the action at Gomiecourt on August 23 this N.C.O.'s tank received a direct hit which killed both officer and driver and wounded the remainder of the crew. Sergt. Roberts then evacuated the tank, carrying out the badly wounded. He saw to the bandaging of all the wounded, going back to the tank for the surgical haversack and shell dressings. All the time the tank was under rifle and machine-gun fire. At this moment he was joined by an officer from another tank which had also been put out of action. Together they formed a Lewis gun post, and by crawling and dragging the gun and ammunition along the ground they got to within thirty yards of a party of Germans. On trying to get the gun into action, Sergt. Roberts found that a shell splinter had rendered it useless. He thereupon stood up and emptied his revolver into the enemy, wounding several and causing the remainder to retire. In company with the officer he then crawled back to the nearest infantry unit. On the way they came across two badly wounded men of this battalion, one of whom was unable to move, having a wounded arm and fractured thigh. Sergt. Roberts helped to carry them back to the shelter of a trench.

At all times he showed an utter disregard for his own safety and did not hesitate to expose himself, if such was necessary, to help the others.

93106 Sergt. DUNCAN, JOHN. 12th Battn. Awarded M.M.

For conspicuous bravery and devotion to duty. On August 23, 1918, near Gomiecourt. During action the tank of which this sergeant was the N.C.O. ran short of water, and it was only possible to fill the radiator with water from outside the tank. Sergt. Duncan volunteered to climb on top of the tank and fill the radiator, in spite of the fact that he would be exposed to machine-gun fire for over five minutes. He was slightly wounded in the back while doing this, but carried on into action. Later he got out of the tank again, under fire, and fastened the tow-rope on to another tank that had broken down and towed it back. His cheerfulness and disregard for his own safety set a splendid example to the crew.

302814 Sergt. SCOTT, HARRY JAMES. 11th Battn. Awarded M.M.

Conspicuous gallantry at Boyelles on August 23, 1918, when commanding a tank. He fought his tank with great initiative and coolness, and by his fire control enabled his gunners to knock out five machine-guns and a large number of enemy infantry. He fought his tank through Boyelles, which was full of enemy machine-guns, the bad state of the roads necessitating his leading his tank on foot. He then took his tank to the assistance of another tank, and pulled it out, all the time on foot himself.

301309 Cpl. ALLEN, HARRY. 11th Battn. Awarded M.M.

Conspicuous gallantry and devotion to duty at Boyelles on August 23, 1918. His tank was knocked out by gun fire and all his crew wounded. While helping the crew to a safe place outside the tank, he was wounded himself. His officer, Lieut. Kingwell, was too badly wounded to be moved far from the tank, which was still being shelled and fired at by machine-guns. Cpl. Allen, neglecting his own wounds, went back to Lieut. Kingwell and stayed with him till he (Lieut. Kingwell) died some hours later.

For over one hour the tank was in advance of the infantry and so was Cpl. Allen and his dying officer.

94997 Sergt. SHILSTON, PERCY. 11th Battn. Awarded M.M.

Gallantry and devotion to duty on August 23, during the attack on Boisleux St. Marc when in command of a tank. The ground he was fighting over was very difficult and the shelling made it impossible to see properly out of the tank. He led his tank into the fight on foot under heavy machine-gun fire. After patrolling his objective and being no longer required by the infantry, he sent his tank home and tried to salve another tank, which was being heavily shelled, before going back himself.

92995 Pte. BUSSEY, BERTIE FREDERICK. 6th Battn. Awarded D.C.M.

For conspicuous gallantry and devotion to duty in action on August 23, 1918, near Bihucourt. At the commencement of the action his officer and sergeant were both wounded, leaving him the only unwounded man in the tank. After placing the wounded in a safe place outside the tank, Pte. Bussey carried on through the action by himself. He directed the tank towards the enemy, and locking the steering he left the tank to steer itself while he served both guns. This he continued to do for four hours, eventually bringing his tank safely out of action.

Pte. Bussey showed a fine example of determination and resource.

77635 Cpl. PREST, WALTER. 6th Battn. Awarded D.C.M.

On August 23, 1918, at Bihucourt, this N.C.O. commanded a tank with great skill. On several occasions he led his tank on foot under heavy machine-gun fire to ensure crossing over difficult places. When, advancing between the infantry and the barrage, he saw the enemy escaping beyond the barrage, he drove through the barrage, thereby losing the smoke protection, and inflicted heavy casualties on the enemy. Later on, in co-operation with another tank, he attacked and captured a battery of field guns in the open and caused about 150 to 200 to surrender.

309077 L/Cpl. BALL, THOMAS HENRY. 6th Battn. Awarded M.M.

Near Ervillers, on August 23, 1918, L/Cpl. Ball was the driver of a tank in action. He drove his tank with exceptional daring and courage. In spite of heavy shell fire, which was directed at the tank from an enemy battery in the open, this N.C.O. drove his tank straight for the guns and right in among the gun crews, enabling the gunners in the tank to deal very effectively with the enemy gun crews, who abandoned their guns and retired, leaving a number of dead.

69537 Pte. PETERSON, MONTAGUE. 6th Battn. Awarded M.M.

On August 23,1918, near Bihucourt, Pte. Peterson drove his tank under very difficult conditions among enemy field gun batteries firing at short range. This man drove his tank with great bravery, dash, and skill, enabling the gunners to take advantage of all targets. Several times he fired a gun, driving his tank at the same time. It was due to his dash and skill that the tank was enabled to do invaluable work and then return to our lines in safety.

200680 Pte. SHAND, JAMES. 2nd Battn. Awarded M.M.

In action near Chuignolles on August 23. After his tank had received a direct hit, breaking the track, he worked for a period of over an hour in the open repairing the track, the tank being under heavy shell fire all the time.

His calmness and disregard of danger were the means of enabling the tank to be re-started and ultimately brought back.

308194 Pte. ROGERS, OCTAVIUS. 4th Tank Supply Coy. Awarded M.M.

For conspicuous gallantry and devotion to duty near Proyart on August 23, 1918. When his tank, making a second trip with stores in daylight, was unloading immediately behind our final objective, it was observed by the enemy, who concentrated heavy shell fire upon it. All the unloading party became casualties and three members of the crew. The fourth member of the crew was stunned. Although the tank contained trench mortar bombs and detonated grenades and was in momentary danger of being hit, Pte. Rogers jumped on to the tank with his officer, and by great efforts started the engine, thus enabling the rest of the load to be saved.

301455 Pte. KEYLOCK, WILLIAM. 13th Battn. Awarded M.M.

For conspicuous gallantry and devotion to duty as gunner in a tank near Herleville on August 23, 1918.

This private handled his gun with marked skill and courage in face of heavy machine-gun and anti-tank fire.

Owing to his sticking to his gun, in spite of the intense heat and fumes in the tank, severe casualties were inflicted on the enemy and anti-tank gunners driven from their guns. When the tank was put out of action by a direct hit, he advanced with a Hotchkiss gun with the infantry to their objective, when he put out of action at least two enemy machine-guns.

When all his ammunition was expended he helped, under intense machine-gun and rifle fire, to carry two wounded men to a place of safety.

Throughout the day his conduct was beyond all praise and a splendid inspiration to all ranks.

IMMEDIATE AWARDS—OTHER RANKS

305563 Cpl. BOOTH, WILLIAM. 13th Battn. Awarded M.M.

For most conspicuous gallantry and devotion to duty as observer in a tank, near Herleville, on August 23, 1918.

This N.C.O. was wounded early in the action, but in spite of this, with courage and determination, he remained at his post doing most valuable work in directing the fire of the gunners on to machine-gun nests with excellent results.

Later, when the tank became ditched, despite his wound he got out of the tank and assisted in the fitting of spuds and digging, although under very heavy machine-gun and rifle fire, until he was utterly exhausted.

Throughout the action Cpl. Booth showed a splendid example of courage, devotion to duty, and disregard for personal safety.

300283 Cpl. GRIFFITHS, JOHN. 13th Battn. Awarded M.M.

For conspicuous gallantry and devotion to duty as a tank driver, near Herleville, on August 23, 1918.

He drove his tank with the greatest skill and gallantry in spite of very heavy machine-gun, rifle, and anti-tank gun fire, advancing against enemy machine-gun nests and enabling the gunners to put them out of action.

Later he was wounded three times in the head, arm, and leg, but despite this, with great determination he continued to drive his tank until the fumes and heat, added to his wounds, overcame him and he became delirious.

This N.C.O. throughout the action showed great courage and determination, and set a splendid example of gallantry and devotion to duty.

301442 Pte. RINGROSE, WORLEY. 13th Battn. Awarded M.M.

For conspicuous courage and devotion to duty as driver of a tank, near Herleville, on August 23, 1918.

He showed exceptional determination and initiative when driving his tank against a very stubborn resistance of machine-gun and anti-tank fire.

Nearly blinded by ' splash,' he carried on until he was overcome by fumes and heat. He then took his place as gunner, and continued firing until all the ammunition in the tank was expended, by which time the whole of the crew were overcome with the heat.

Owing to his gallantry and determination heavy casualties were inflicted upon the enemy and their resistance broken.

Pte. Ringrose showed exceptional skill and resource under very difficult circumstances.

306306 Cpl. YOUNG, JOHN. 13th Battn. Awarded M.M.

For conspicuous gallantry and devotion to duty as an observer in a tank, near Herleville, on August 23, 1918.

This N.C.O. did most valuable work in observing enemy targets and directing the fire of the gunners on to them. When the driver was wounded he at once took over the forward gun, and continued firing until all opposition was overcome. Altogether he accounted for at least eight enemy machine-guns and put to flight the crews of several others.

Later, when the tank broke a track, although he was wounded in the foot and the tank was under very heavy machine-gun and shell fire, he got out and assisted in repairing the track, refusing to go to a dressing station until the tank went back out of action.

Cpl. Young gave a magnificent example of courage and devotion to duty to all ranks.

301411 L/Cpl. BACKHOUSE, WILLIAM GEORGE. 13th Battn. Awarded M.M.

For conspicuous bravery and devotion to duty as a tank driver, near Herleville, on August 23, 1918.

This N.C.O. showed considerable skill in driving his tank throughout the action, driving over numerous machine-gun nests and at least two anti-tank guns.

In spite of the fact that he was in a fainting condition due to heat and petrol fumes, he continued with great determination to drive his tank. When the tank broke down he got outside and, although under heavy machine-gun and rifle fire, repaired the damage, enabling the tank to proceed to its objective.

L/Cpl. Backhouse's courage and determination were a splendid example to the rest of the crew.

301908 L/Cpl. DICKENSON, ROBERT. 13th Battn. Awarded M.M.

For conspicuous gallantry and devotion to duty as a gunner in a tank, near Herleville, on August 23, 1918.

Although under very trying circumstances, due to heat and petrol fumes and the fact that the tank was under very heavy machine-gun and shell fire, this N.C.O. showed marked coolness and courage in firing his 6-pndr. gun with very effective results against the enemy, being responsible for putting a number of enemy machine-guns out of action. He also knocked out at least one anti-tank gun.

When his tank received a direct hit, putting it out of action, in spite of heavy machine-gun and rifle fire, he showed great disregard for personal danger while assisting in getting the machine-guns out of the tank into action.

Throughout the action L/Cpl. Dickenson's coolness and courage were an invaluable example to the rest of the crew.

IMMEDIATE AWARDS—OTHER RANKS

305379 Gnr. PERRY, PATRICK JOSEPH. 11th Battn. Awarded D.C.M.

Conspicuous gallantry and devotion to duty on August 24, 1918, in the attack on Hindenburg Line, east of Croisilles. His tank was ditched in a sunken road and on fire from phosphorous bombs fired by the enemy. Gnr. Perry stayed in the tank with his officer, Lieut. Walsh, and put out the fire. The fumes being too bad to stay in the tank, Gnr. Perry and Lieut. Walsh turned the tank for home in bottom speed and walked home just in front of it. All this time the tank was surrounded by enemy. Lieut. Walsh was exhausted, and would undoubtedly have collapsed if it had not been for Gnr. Perry forcibly keeping him going. When not getting his officer along, he was firing his revolver at the enemy all round the tank. The tank and Gnr. Perry and Lieut. Walsh all got home.

77447 Sergt. GOWARD, WILLIAM, M.M. and Bar. 3rd Battn. Awarded Second Bar to M.M.

During the action near Bapaume, on August 25, 1918, this N.C.O., whilst in command of a whippet got it badly ditched within 250 yards of the enemy. He immediately took out his guns and formed a strong point 100 yards in front of his tank and about 350 yards in front of our infantry, keeping up an incessant fire on the enemy, informed the infantry of the position, and by this means enabled them to advance. By his coolness and quick appreciation of the situation he not only prevented the infantry from being held up, but inspired both them and his own crew.

(Military Medal won at Ypres on July 31, 1917, and Bar to M.M. at Cambrai, November 20, 1917.)

200445 Gnr. MANHIRE, JOHN RICHARD. 3rd Battn. Awarded M.M.

During the action near Bapaume, on August 25, 1918, although wounded in the eye, this gunner took a message back to the infantry from his tank commander through an intense machine-gun and artillery barrage. After delivering his message he returned again under heavy fire and assisted his tank commander to maintain a strong point 150 yards from the enemy. Although in considerable pain from his wound, he showed pluck and endurance of the highest order. He has previously behaved with great gallantry in other actions.

112006 Sergt. HATTON, PERCY EDWARD. 11th Battn. Awarded D.C.M.

Conspicuous gallantry and devotion to duty at Monchy on August 26, 1918.

After an approach march of 20,000 yards his tank was called on by the infantry to go forward and attack some strong points.

Having cleared these strong points, his tank got ditched and, although standing nearly on its side, he went on covering the advance with his 6-pndr., and knocked out an anti-tank gun which was shooting at his tank. When the tank was at such an angle that he could no longer use his gun, he and his crew left the tank and formed a strong point outside it, still in advance of the infantry. Meanwhile the infantry had reached their final objective for the day, 100 yards behind the tank. Some hours later the enemy counter-attacked and got into Sergt. Hatton's tank. He promptly charged with his crew and turned them out of the tank, killing one German.

He had formed the strong point some little way from the tank, and on several occasions went back to the tank for more ammunition and rations for his crew, quite regardless of enemy machine-gun fire. He stayed out in this strong point in advance of the infantry for twenty-four hours at the request of the infantry, and all this time showed a magnificent example to his crew, who, after driving and fighting for twenty-four hours continuously, were exhausted. On his return Sergt. Hatton asked to be allowed to go and try again to get his tank out.

Sergt. Hatton is forty-eight years of age.

96533 Cpl. WILSON, HENRY CHARLES. 10th Battn. Awarded D.C.M.

For conspicuous gallantry and devotion to duty near Bancourt on August 30, 1918. His tank engaged a German field battery south of Bancourt, and was eventually put out of action by a direct hit, which wounded the officer (2nd Lieut. C. G. Oddy) and rendered the tank useless. There was very heavy machine-gun fire directed at the tank at the time and, realising that it was no longer tenable, Cpl. Wilson gave the order, ' Evacuate the tank,' himself remaining behind and engaging the machine-gun nests with a 6-pndr., and thus keeping down their fire, although himself exposed to the fire of the field battery. It was greatly owing to his gallant conduct that the crew managed to regain our own lines with but two more casualties, and get their wounded officer to comparative safety. Cpl. Wilson continued to work his 6-pndr. until his tank received two more hits, the last of which set it on fire. He then made good his escape and took charge of the crew.

302763 Pte. MANNING, PERCY DONALD. 10th Battn. Awarded M.M.

For conspicuous gallantry and devotion to duty near Bancourt on August 30, 1918. He was badly wounded in the left arm, but although weak from loss of blood continued to serve his Hotchkiss gun with good effect for a period of two hours, when he collapsed. His coolness, courage, and cheerfulness throughout the action were an example to all ranks.

201385 Cpl. OWEN, FREDERICK, M.M. 7th Battn. Awarded Bar to M.M.

For conspicuous gallantry and devotion to duty. On August 30, 1918, he took over command of his tank when his officer was wounded, and successfully cleared his first objective, trenches west of Beugny village. These were thick with enemy machine-guns, which he knocked out, thus enabling the infantry to go forward. He then proceeded to his second objective, Beugny village, receiving a direct hit which carried away his right track at I.20.b.3.9. He at once evacuated his tank and formed four Lewis-gun groups and went forward with the infantry, to whom he rendered most valuable assistance, as they were few and mostly wounded at this point. He remained with the infantry until they consolidated in a trench at I.20.b.6.7., when he returned under orders from his neighbouring officer tank commander to headquarters.

201379 Sergt. DUDDRIDGE, HENRY. 7th Battn. Awarded D.C.M.

For conspicuous gallantry and devotion to duty from August 21 to September 2, 1918. On August 30, 1918, north-west of Beugny, his tank successfully cleared the first objective, putting out of action several machine-gun nests which held up the infantry till he cleared them. He then proceeded to the second objective. By his skilful manipulation of his tank he was enabled to put out of action one enemy field gun (verified the next day) before his tank was hit and set on fire by other enemy field guns in the neighbourhood. His tank was hit seven times. He then evacuated the tank, one man at a time, under heavy shell and machine-gun fire. He took up Lewis-gun posts in a trench about twenty yards in front (at I. 14.d.8.8.), where he was able to render valuable assistance to the infantry, who were very few at that point, most of whom were wounded. He remained there until dusk, when infantry reinforcements arrived, and then returned.

Sergt. Duddridge himself went back to the burning tank under heavy machine-gun fire for extra ammunition. Two of his men had been previously wounded.

Note.—This N.C.O. was also awarded the Belgian Croix de Guerre.

75054 L/Cpl. DOUGLAS, EDWARD JAMES. 12th Battn. Awarded M.M.

For exceptional skill and gallant conduct in the attack on Longatte on August 31, 1918. This N.C.O., by his keenness and untiring energy, got his tank fit for action after coming out of action only twelve hours previously, having worked on his tank for nearly the whole of that twelve hours. In the final stages of the approach march, although suffering from the effects of gas, he went forward on foot with his officer and reconnoitred the line under machine-gun fire. During the action he displayed great skill and courage, driving his tank over extremely bad ground and in a heavy mist, which necessitated the front window of the tank being open for the greater part of the time. He remained perfectly cool, despite the heavy machine-gun fire on the front of the tank. It was undoubtedly owing to his skilful driving and the great assistance he gave to his officer that the tank started promptly at zero hour and reached its objective, enabling the infantry to advance and capture it. On previous occasions, on August 21, during the attack on Moyenneville, and on August 23, during the attack on Hamelincourt, this N.C.O. has showed the utmost devotion to duty, and the success of his tank has been very largely due to his skill and determination.

112224 Pte. BROWN, CHARLES BRADSHAW. 12th Battn. Awarded M.M.

Pte. Brown has on all occasions shown great gallantry and complete disregard of personal safety under fire. On August 31, 1918, during the attack on Noreuil, he rendered great assistance in withdrawing to the shelter of a trench men of a crew who had been wounded by anti-tank rifle bullets. He was subject the whole time to fire from snipers. On all occasions since that date his behaviour under fire has been magnificent.

307422 Pte. POULSON, OWEN. 15th Battn. Awarded M.M.

This man showed great devotion to duty and determination when in action north-east of Vaulx-Vraucourt on the morning of August 31, 1918. Though he received a bullet in the chest he continued to fire his 6-pndr. until, through exhaustion, he collapsed. At all times he showed great coolness and determination when dealing with targets.

307799 Cpl. CAMPBELL, JOHN. 15th Battn. Awarded M.M.

On August 31, 1918, during the attack on Vaulx-Vraucourt, Cpl. J. Campbell displayed great gallantry and disregard for personal safety. On one occasion whilst passing through the village, the tracks of his tank became loose, and therefore needed immediate adjustment to prevent them coming off. On discovering this situation, Cpl. Campbell immediately left his tank under very heavy machine-gun fire and anti-tank rifle fire, and proceeded to adjust the tracks. His behaviour during the whole of the attack set a splendid example to the remainder of the crew.

305933 Pte. (A/Cpl.) SHOOTER, WILLIAM HENRY. 6th Battn. Awarded M.M.

This N.C.O. was a runner in whippet which attacked Vaulx trench on September 1, 1918. He was wounded early on in the action by an armour-piercing bullet, but continued throughout the action showing the utmost gallantry; he assisted his officer to evacuate the tank, which caught on fire in the enemy lines, and made his way back to our lines.

93000 Pte. SIDELL, WALTER. 6th Battn. Awarded D.C.M.

For conspicuous gallantry and devotion to duty on September 1, 1918, near Vaulx-Vraucourt. This man was a gunner in a whippet tank in action. While running over an enemy machine-gun emplacement the tank became ditched on the enemy front line, about 400 yards from our front line. It was almost immediately hit by a shell and set on fire, wounding the officer, driver, and the second gunner. Pte. Sidell pulled out the second gunner, who was hit in two places, and dressed his wounds, and assisted his officer to carry him back as far as one of our forward machine-gun posts. Pte. Sidell then returned alone to attend the driver, Pte. Tacchi, who was severely hit in the body.

He dressed his wounds under very heavy fire and, yard by yard, dragged him back in daylight across the open to our forward post. This journey took Pte. Sidell over two hours, as the enemy, who had apparently seen the previous movement, had machine-guns fired on him from three sides.

By his amazing gallantry and utter disregard for his own safety, Pte. Sidell undoubtedly saved the life of Pte. Tacchi.

93011 Pte. BROWN, FREDERICK ARTHUR. 6th Battn. Awarded M.M.

He drove a whippet in the attack on September 1, on Vaulx trench, when he was wounded twice by armour-piercing bullets. When the tank commander withdrew to reorganise before going in again, he never mentioned he was wounded, but took his tank in again and drove it, displaying the greatest courage and gallantry, and finally, when his officer was hit in both eyes, he drove it out of action and brought it back to safety.

201460 Sergt. PENNY, ALBERT CHARLES. 7th Battn. Awarded M.M.

For conspicuous gallantry and ability.

On September 2, 1918, he took a tank into action at Villers-au-Flos, reaching his objective in the face of heavy shell fire and fire from anti-tank guns and rifles, knocking out several enemy machine-guns. The tank next to his being out of action, he covered the ground allotted to two tanks and did a great deal of valuable work.

Note.—The infantry of 42nd Division have brought this action to the notice of their divisional commander, who has asked for Sergt. Penny's name.

201524 L/Cpl. LANE, THOMAS. 9th Battn. Awarded D.C.M.

During the action near Dury on September 2, 1918, after his tank had received a direct hit and three of the crew, including the tank commander, severely wounded, L/Cpl. Lane and the remainder of the crew carried them to a trench.

L/Cpl. Lane, although exposed to heavy shell and machine-gun fire, crept back and procured a stretcher and succeeded in getting the officer back to a dressing station.

The following day he went out with S/Sergt. Kilburn to the tank, which was exposed to heavy shell fire, and after it had been mended drove it back.

Throughout the action he showed an utter disregard for his own personal safety and set a fine example to the rest of his crew.

92739 Sergt. MARCH, SAMUEL. 9th Battn. Awarded D.C.M.

During the action near Dury on September 2, 1918, Sergt. March noticed that another tank was badly ditched. He manœuvred his tank close to the other, and although under heavy hostile artillery and machine-gun fire, he got out of his tank and, assisted by L/Cpl. Potter, fixed his steel hawser to the tank and successfully unditched it.

It was undoubtedly owing to his gallant conduct that the tank was saved from being knocked out.

Sergt. March showed an utter disregard for his own personal safety and set a fine example to his crew.

91237 L/Cpl. TERZZA, WILLIAM ALFRED. 9th Battn. Awarded M.M.

201537 Pte. BATT, WILLIAM FREDERICK. 9th Battn. Awarded M.M.

201555 Pte. JONES, JAMES. 9th Battn. Awarded M.M.

During the action near Dury on September 2, 1918, when their tank had received a direct hit and the tank commander and two of the crew wounded, although exposed to heavy shell and intense machine-gun fire, L/Cpl. Terzza, Pte. Ball, and Pte. Jones succeeded in carrying them to a trench which was in No Man's Land about 100 yards in front of our infantry. They remained with them for over three hours, and then crept back one by one and brought stretchers and succeeded in getting the three wounded men away to a dressing station.

By their gallant conduct they undoubtedly saved the lives of their officer and two comrades. Throughout they displayed an utter disregard for their own personal safety and set a fine example to all.

306244 Pte. ELLISON, THOMAS. 9th Battn. Awarded M.M.

78030 Pte. SUTTON, FRANK. 9th Battn. Awarded M.M.

During the action near Dury on September 2, 1918, when the unditching beam of their tank had been hit by a shell and freed from the shackles, although exposed to heavy shell and intense machine-gun fire, Ptes. Ellison and Sutton climbed on to the top of the tank and succeeded in re-fixing it. Ptes. Ellison and Sutton set a fine example of devotion to duty under particularly trying circumstances.

91953 Pte. MITCHELL, CHARLES. 9th Battn. Awarded M.M.

During the action near Dury on September 2, 1918, Pte. Mitchell, the company runner, behaved throughout with the greatest gallantry, continually taking messages under heavy fire, although knocked out by debris thrown up by a shell and rendered unconscious for a time. As soon as he recovered he refused to go back, but continued with his company commander.

Pte. Mitchell showed an utter disregard for his own personal safety and behaved throughout with the greatest gallantry.

77190 Cpl. BELL, JAMES. 12th Battn. Awarded D.C.M.

For exceptional gallantry near Noreuil on September 2. His tank was ahead of our infantry engaged in the task of silencing hostile machine-guns when it became badly ditched and shortly afterwards hit by direct shell fire. The tank commander was badly wounded. Cpl. Bell at once took charge of the situation, evacuated the tank, and assisted to carry his officer back to the front line, a distance of 300 yards, through machine-gun and shell fire. He then returned to the tank and stood by for two hours in an endeavour to render it fit for action. During this time the tank was subjected to particularly heavy machine-gun fire. It was not until our infantry had passed through that he finally withdrew. On a previous occasion, during the attack on Gomiecourt on August 23, this N.C.O. had previously shown great gallantry and initiative. On this occasion, when his tank commander had become a casualty and his tank put out of action by a direct hit, Cpl. Bell, who was first driver, took charge of the tank. The tank was at this time some 100 yards in advance of our infantry. Cpl. Bell manned a 6-pndr. gun and kept down the enemy machine-gun fire which was being directed at the tank, thus enabling the crew to evacuate the tank. He then directed the formation of Lewis-gun posts, afterwards returning to the tank under machine-gun fire to get more guns and ammunition.

He carried on firing until the infantry moved forward and no longer required his services. He then returned with his crew and guns to company headquarters. On both occasions he displayed exceptional coolness, initiative, and gallantry, and by taking charge on tank commanders becoming casualties was able to render the greatest assistance to the infantry.

69638 Cpl. COSSUM, FRANCIS HENRY. 6th Battn. Awarded M.M.

Owing to heavy officer casualties, this N.C.O. has, as a tank commander, taken his whippet into action six times in three weeks, showing the greatest daring and initiative. On September 2, near Lagnicourt, he volunteered to go out with his tank in the afternoon to subdue enemy machine-gun fire whilst the infantry advanced their line. This operation was completely successful and resulted in some fifty prisoners being taken without casualties, as the tank worked its way behind the enemy front line. All the time he was heavily shelled and in view of enemy guns. He was wounded later in the day.

93009 Pte. STANNARD, HERBERT VICTOR. 6th Battn. Awarded M.M.

This man, as a whippet driver, has taken a tank into action six times in three weeks, standing the heat and strain inside a whippet with remarkable endurance.

On September 2, 1918, near Lagnicourt, he volunteered to take a tank into action with Cpl. F. H. Cossum, after having worked on his tank all night. He drove the whippet at high speed over difficult ground with remarkable skill and coolness, always under intense machine-gun fire and heavy shelling.

97310 Pte. (L/Cpl.) NORTON, REGINALD GUY. 14th Battn. Awarded D.C.M.

On September 2 this N.C.O. drove his tank with skill and determination in piercing the Queant-Drocourt Line and mopping it up until it was completely knocked out by a direct hit. When his tank commander found another tank, of which most of the crew had been wounded, although suffering from severe shock and fatigue, he persisted in volunteering to drive this tank to the second objective. Again, after having rallied, and help being demanded by the infantry, he drove into action for the third time. In attacking a factory which had prevented the infantry from advancing for some hours, this tank was also knocked out by a direct hit, and this N.C.O. was conspicuous in helping his tank commander to establish a strong point, by fire from which a large body of enemy machine-gunners were forced to abandon the building. At this period, this tank crew were quite unsupported by the infantry. Throughout the day this N.C.O. showed marked courage, determination, cheerfulness and devotion to duty.

97219 Pte. BEELEY, PHILLIP ALBERT. 14th Battn. Awarded M.M.

In the attack on the Queant-Drocourt Line on September 2 this man showed very conspicuous gallantry, determination, and devotion to duty. Although wounded in the forehead early in the action, he continued to drive with great coolness. During the halt at the first objective, although much exhausted, he refused to get out and rest, and insisted on remaining in the tank to adjust the epicyclic brakes. His tank commander, thinking he was too much exhausted to go on, endeavoured to induce him to go back; however, he insisted on driving his tank towards the second objective until he eventually collapsed in the driver's seat.

92069 M/S/Sergt. KILBURN, ROBERT. 9th Battn. Awarded M.M.

During the action near Dury on September 3, 1918, M/S/Sgt. Kilburn, accompanied by L/Cpl. Lane, went out to a tank which had received a direct hit on the day previous; although the tank was under direct observation of the enemy and was being heavily shelled, he succeeded in reaching the tank and repaired the engine.

They then drove the tank back to the company. By his gallant conduct the tank was in all probability saved from receiving further direct hits.

M/S/Sergt. Kilburn showed an utter disregard for his own personal safety and set a fine example of devotion to duty under very trying circumstances.

112321 Pte. BRAY, HORACE PERCIVAL. 1st Gun Carrier Coy. Awarded M.M.

For great initiative and devotion to duty near Havrincourt on September 12, 1918.

Pte. Bray was brakesman on a carrier tank. When returning to refill after having taken up supplies to the line, the tank was hit by a shell which severely wounded the officer and the sergeant, and also wounded Pte. Bray in a lesser degree. Pte. Bray was now the only one of the crew left who was at all capable of carrying on. The tank had been hit while on the sky-line and was now in full view of the enemy and was being shelled. Pte. Bray showed great initiative; he lifted the wounded officer and sergeant out of the tank, and although himself wounded, drove the tank down the reverse slope and out of observation. He then returned and dressed the wounds of the officer and sergeant. The officer was unable to walk and the sergeant could only limp with assistance, nevertheless Pte. Bray, by great determination, carried the officer and at the same time assisted the sergeant to the aid post about 800 yards away. To get to the aid post it was necessary to pass through a valley which was being shelled with gas. Having handed over the officer and sergeant to the R.A.M.C., Pte. Bray reported himself and was sent on to the dressing station, where his wounds were dressed, and he was told that he would be detained. He begged to be allowed to return to duty at once, and eventually was allowed to do so. Pte. Bray's initiative in getting the tank out of observation and his devotion to the wounded are deserving of the highest praise. This man has been brought to notice on a previous occasion for gallantry and devotion to duty.

96986 Pte. PHIPPS, WILLIAM. 2nd Battn. Awarded M.M.

For most conspicuous gallantry and devotion to duty as first driver of a tank near Holnon on September 18, 1918.

In spite of heavy machine-gun fire directed at the tank, he continued to drive with his flap open to gain better observation in the fog and smoke. When the tank became ditched, well ahead of our line, he at once got out of the tank and attempted to fix the beam under heavy shell fire. He desisted only when ordered to do so by his tank commander.

Later, he volunteered to carry a message back to the infantry over ground swept by machine-gun fire and across which the infantry could not advance. He successfully carried the message and was instrumental in our line being advanced 300 yards.

Throughout the action he set a splendid example of bravery and devotion to duty.

91431 Pte. THOMAS, JOSEPH. No. 2 Tank Field Coy. Awarded M.M.

For gallantry and devotion to duty in action at Ronssoy on September 18, 1918.

Tank No. 9509 came under very heavy shell fire and was put out of action by a direct hit, the track being damaged.

Although the enemy were counter-attacking within 1000 yards, near Lempire, and the tank was under heavy fire, Pte. Thomas at once set to work at repairing the track in the open.

He showed the greatest coolness and disregard for his personal safety, and eventually effected the repair, rendering the tank mobile again.

It was owing to his gallant work that this tank was not lost.

76902 Pte. FOSTER, JOHN BERNARD. 2nd Battn. Awarded D.C.M.

For exceptional courage and ability in driving his tank near Lempire on September 21, 1918.

On reaching the final objective his tank commander was severely wounded and the N.C.O. who was driving the tank killed. Without hesitation, he sprang into the driving seat and, in spite of the very heavy anti-tank rifle fire, drove the tank with such skill and tenacity that it enabled the gunners to bring a hail of fire on the enemy machine-gun nests, which had only to deal with this one tank at the time. When the engine seized, owing to the radiator having been pierced by rifle fire, he voluntarily ran across the open under very heavy machine-gun fire, and gained the assistance of another tank to clear up the situation. Eventually he managed to assist his tank commander to reach the shelter of this other tank.

By his remarkable coolness and courage, under most strenuous conditions, he set a very fine example.

IMMEDIATE AWARDS—OTHER RANKS

40406 L/Cpl. RIVERS, GEORGE, M.M. 2nd Battn. Awarded D.C.M.

For marked courage and determination as first driver of a tank near Lempire on September 21, 1918.

He was of invaluable assistance to his tank commander, his skill proving greatly instrumental in repairing his tank under heavy fire and eventually being able to continue again in action. When the tank had been hit a second time, he remained inside and kept up a most successful covering fire, under which part of his crew were able to leave the tank and the infantry to advance still further. He afterwards displayed the greatest gallantry in assisting the remainder of his crew to evacuate the tank under an intense hostile machine-gun barrage.

The consummate daring and continued bravery of this N.C.O. resulted in inflicting great casualties on the enemy, and his example has provided a lasting impression on the minds of his crew.

307340 Cpl. HARPER, JAMES ERIC. 15th Battn. Awarded M.M.

For conspicuous gallantry and devotion to duty in action on the occasion of the attack on the Canal du Nord, near Moeuvres, on September 22, 1918. Although wounded and suffering from fumes, he drove his tank with great determination, in the face of strong opposition, throughout the action until it was knocked out by a third direct hit. When one direct hit rendered one of the epicyclics useless, he manœuvred his tank so that the 6-pndr. gunner was able to knock out an anti-tank battery. This N.C.O.'s coolness and gallantry in difficult circumstances largely contributed to the success of the operations in which his tank was engaged.

307207 Pte. HICKMAN, SAMUEL. 13th Battn. Awarded M.M.

For conspicuous gallantry and devotion to duty at Pontruet on September 24, 1918.

Pte. Hickman acted as gunner of a tank in action and, although wounded and slightly gassed, he refused to be relieved and kept his gun in action, inflicting severe casualties upon the enemy.

Later, when the tank received a direct hit which blew away a portion of the petrol piping, although heavy artillery and machine-gun fire was concentrated on the tank, Pte. Hickman, with another man, volunteered to get out and fill a petrol tin from the petrol tank by means of a hand-pump. This gallant act enabled the tank commander to get the tank back to the rallying point.

Pte. Hickman showed exceptional courage and coolness throughout the action.

305647 Pte. REILLY, MATTHEW RICHARD, M.M. 13th Battn. Awarded Bar to M.M.

For conspicuous gallantry and devotion to duty near Pontruet on September 24, 1918.

371

When the tank in which this man acted as gunner had reached the objective, it received a direct hit, which blew away a portion of the petrol piping.

Although heavy artillery and machine-gun fire was concentrated on the tank, Pte. Reilly, with another man, volunteered to get outside the tank and fill an empty petrol tin from the petrol tank by means of a hand-pump.

This gallant act enabled the tank commander to get the tank back to the rallying point.

Throughout the action Pte. Reilly showed the greatest disregard for personal safety, and by his coolness and confidence gave a fine example to the crew of the tank.

300391 L/Cpl. HARRIS, CHARLES, M.M. 13th Battn. Awarded Bar to M.M.

For conspicuous gallantry and devotion to duty near Fresnoy on September 24, 1918.

L/Cpl. Harris acted as gunner during an attack, and silenced two nests of machine-guns.

When his tank received a direct hit and was set on fire, he, with his tank commander, at great personal risk endeavoured to extinguish the flames, but without success. Although the tank was under heavy artillery and machine-gun fire, he assisted his officer to recover the machine-guns from the blazing tank, and with them engaged the enemy, eventually overcoming resistance at this point.

Throughout the action L/Cpl. Harris showed exceptional coolness and determination.

300380 Pte DRACUP, CHARLES. 13th Battn. Awarded M.M.

For conspicuous gallantry and devotion to duty near Fresnoy on September 24, 1918.

Pte. Dracup was the driver of a tank during an attack on September 24, 1918, and drove with exceptional skill during the early part of the operation.

Later, when the tank received a direct hit from an anti-tank gun and was set on fire, he made repeated efforts to extinguish the flames, but without success. He then removed large quantities of ammunition from the blazing tank, which was under heavy enemy fire, and with his officer engaged the enemy with machine-guns recovered from the tank.

The courage and determination shown by Pte. Dracup under very trying circumstances had a great influence on the remainder of the crew.

308185 Sgt. BROUGHTON, GILBERT. 4th Tank Supply Coy. Awarded M.M.

For gallantry and skill when acting as tank commander on September 27, 1918, near Ronssoy. Although guides and an unloading party detailed from the infantry did not arrive, this N.C.O. found his way in the dark from his final lying-up place to the infantry start-line, which he crossed just after zero. He proceeded through a heavy barrage to his destination immediately in rear of the final objective. On arrival, he discovered that the line had not advanced according to plan. His tank was subjected to violent machine-gun fire, and he could see the enemy who were firing at him. A forward field gun opened on his tank. By clever and determined handling of his tank and crew he unloaded his tank on the blind side. Immediately afterwards his tank was hit and set on fire, he and all the crew being wounded. Showing the utmost coolness and gallantry, he got all the crew out of the tank and brought them all back without further casualties, including one man who was severely wounded. It was entirely owing to this N.C.O.'s skill, initiative, and gallantry that invaluable supplies were correctly delivered and further casualties to his crew prevented. His tank was carrying engineer supplies, ammunition, and water, without which our new position could scarcely have been consolidated.

201482 Sergt. HARRIS, THOMAS HAROLD. 7th Battn. Awarded D.C.M.

For conspicuous gallantry and devotion to duty.

On September 27, 1918, near Inchy-en-Artois, he commanded his tank with bravery, skill, and initiative throughout the operation. The crossing of the Canal du Nord was so difficult, and needed such careful judgment, that Sergt. Harris got out of his tank to make careful reconnaissance and lead it over. After dealing most effectively with all the trenches in his sector and Quarry Wood, he went on to attack Bourlon village. He showed great skill in the way he used his smoke screen by moving up and down in front of the village so that the smoke drifted all over the village. He then went right through the infantry, breaking down the wire and crushing all opposition there.

201299 Pte. POTTINGER, MAURICE WILLIAM. 7th Battn. Awarded M.M.

For conspicuous gallantry and devotion to duty.

On the morning of September 27, 1918, he drove his tank across the Canal du Nord, south-east of Inchy. At this point the banks were extremely steep and considered by some an insuperable obstacle to a Mark IV tank. He reached the wire with the infantry and led them to Quarry Wood. As the tank was not supplied with prisms or periscopes, he drove throughout with his flap open although under very heavy machine-gun fire.

When clearing up trenches on the Red Line the tank, while under a barrage, developed mechanical trouble. Pte. Pottinger showed great resource and skill in rectifying this. He has driven skilfully throughout the whole of five actions since August 21.

95378 Pte. SAVAGE, FREDERICK. 7th Battn. Awarded M.M.

For conspicuous gallantry and devotion to duty.

On September 27, 1918, north of Bourlon; on September 29, 1918, near Cambrai. On the latter occasion his first driver had been wounded; he took his place and drove skilfully through a heavy barrage to his objective. At one time he gallantly assisted in the evacuation of the wounded under hostile machine-gun fire.

He has done consistent good work throughout the operations.

40382 L/Cpl. PARKINSON, ALBERT EDWARD. 7th Battn. Awarded M.M.

For conspicuous gallantry and devotion to duty.

On September 27, 1918, near Inchy-en-Artois. When first driver he had to cross the Canal du Nord to reach his second objective. The canal was considered impossible to cross with a Mark IV tank by many competent judges, and it was only by his wonderful driving and judgment that this formidable obstacle was overcome.

He displayed remarkable initiative and resource throughout the whole action, which lasted six hours. Had it not been for this, the canal would not have been crossed, which would have had a material effect upon the operations, since the tank's final objective was Bourlon village, which it reached, leading the infantry and crushing all opposition.

201270 Pte. BEARDMORE, THOMAS GEORGE. 7th Battn. Awarded M.M.

For conspicuous gallantry and devotion to duty.

On September 27, 1918, near Inchy, he drove his tank with splendid judgment and coolness over the Canal du Nord. After his tank commander was wounded he succeeded in reaching his objective.

On September 29, 1918, after his tank had received a direct hit near Tilloy, he and his tank commander succeeded in getting the wounded away, under heavy shell fire, to a place of safety.

He has shown a complete disregard of personal danger and a willing and cheerful spirit throughout all the operations.

200848 Pte. YATES, HARRY IRION, M.M. 4th Battn. Awarded D.C.M.

During the attack upon the Hindenburg outpost positions, east of Ronssoy, on September 27, 1918, this man drove his tank with great skill and determination, showing great initiative.

Notwithstanding the fact that all his crew were wounded by the fire from anti-tank rifles, which pierced the tank, and were incapable of rendering any assistance, he carried out the orders which had been issued to his officer, and it was solely due to his magnificent courage, devotion to duty, and initiative that his tank reached its objective and was brought back to its rallying point.

200750 Pte. YOUNG, JAMES. 4th Battn. Awarded M.M.

This man succeeded in driving his tank into action against the Hindenburg outpost positions, east of Ronssoy, on September 27, 1918, under exceptionally difficult circumstances, showing great determination. He succeeded in reaching his objective, running down two hostile machine-guns. Again, on September 29, he went into action near the same place and, although wounded, showed the greatest courage in remaining at his post.

He has been in at least ten operations with his company, and has always shown the same determination and devotion to duty.

308252 Sergt. DEW, JAMES. 4th Tank Supply Coy. Awarded M.M.

For continuous gallantry and resource during the period of active operations August 8, 1918, to September 27, 1918.

First, on August 8, 1918, north of Warfusée, this N.C.O., by his cheerfulness and coolness, greatly encouraged the remainder of his section when it came under a burst of heavy shelling.

Second, on August 29, 1918, east of Proyart, he twice in one morning delivered supplies to the infantry when his tank was under direct observation and fire. This was only made possible by his clever choice of ground and gallant leading.

Third, on September 27, 1918, north of Hagicourt, when his tank, with the remaining tanks of the section, while unloading supplies in a forward position, came under heavy and accurate shell fire directed by enemy aircraft, this N.C.O. greatly assisted his section commander by his cheerfulness and courage in keeping the men cool and in preventing confusion in unloading. Throughout the period Sergt. Dew's tank has been a model to the rest of the company. Owing to his unremitting industry it has never once failed to complete a journey to time.

304634 Sergt. MEGREGOR, ARCHIBALD. 15th Battn. Awarded D.C.M.

For conspicuous gallantry and devotion to duty in action on the occasion of the attack on Flesquieres on September 27, 1918. During the final approach march, when practically a complete crew—including the tank commander—became casualties, this N.C.O., who was a spare man, volunteered to take the tank into action with a mixed crew. Although he went into action at short notice, he fought his tank with great determination. He greatly assisted the infantry on the first and second objectives, and finally brought his tank to rallying point without a casualty. This N C.O.'s gallantry and initiative, displayed at a critical moment, largely contributed to the success of the operations in which his tank co-operated.

304940 Pte. WILLIAMS, HORACE. 15th Battn. Awarded M.M.

On September 27, on the occasion of the attack on Flesquieres, Pte. Williams served his gun with conspicuous gallantry and determination in the face of the concentrated fire of field guns and howitzers. When his tank had been knocked out and the majority of the crew had become casualties, he established a strong point, with conspicuous gallantry and regardless of danger, making several journeys for guns and ammunition under heavy hostile machine-gun fire and within 400 yards of the enemy.

304512 SPIERS, WILLIAM. 15th Battn. Awarded M.M.

For conspicuous gallantry and devotion to duty on the occasion of the attack on the Canal du Nord on September 27, 1918. In spite of heavy hostile machine-gun fire he drove his tank with the flap open, thus enabling the tank to be guided over exceptionally difficult ground, and to be driven clear of anti-tank mines. When his tank had received two direct hits and had been rendered useless he assisted, on the canal bank, under intense hostile machine-gun fire, to remove the wounded to a place of safety. His gallantry, initiative, and devotion to duty throughout the operations are worthy of the highest praise.

304667 Pte. SMALL, WILFRID JOHN. 15th Battn. Awarded M.M.

On September 27, 1918, on the occasion of the attack on the Canal du Nord, near Moeuvres, Pte. Small, on the evacuation of his tank, displayed conspicuous gallantry, under heavy hostile fire, in establishing a machine-gun post and covering the advance of the infantry.

Subsequently, although badly gassed, he went to the assistance of a wounded comrade, and in doing so was himself wounded and blinded.

307282 Pte. ORKNEY, THOMAS BELL. 15th Battn. Awarded M.M.

At Flesquieres, on September 27, 1918, although his position in the tank was subjected to heavy shell and anti-tank gun fire, he served his gun with conspicuous gallantry, coolness, and ability, inflicting heavy casualties on the enemy. He was seriously affected by fumes towards the end of the operation, but continued to serve his gun with great courage and determination until the conclusion of the attack.

IMMEDIATE AWARDS—OTHER RANKS

304520 Pte. REGAN, OWEN. 15th Battn. Awarded M.M.

On September 27, 1918, on the occasion of the attack on the Canal du Nord, near Moeuvres, Pte. Regan, although badly wounded in three places, carried one of his wounded officers under heavy shell fire to a shell-hole, which he barricaded with great difficulty. Failing to find any stretcher-bearers, for whom he went in search, he procured a stretcher and placed his officer on it. He remained with him until assistance arrived four hours later, when they were both taken to the dressing station. His gallantry and devotion to duty are worthy of the highest praise.

304657 L/Cpl. BARKER, FRANCIS J. 15th Battn. Awarded M.M.

For conspicuous gallantry and devotion to duty in action on the occasion of the attack on Flesquieres on September 27, 1918. He was wounded in the face whilst placing unditching gear in position under shell fire. In spite of his wound he remained at his task until he was again wounded in the neck. He volunteered to remain with the tank, but his officer handed him over to infantry stretcher-bearers.

304521 Pte. WALKER, HARRY. 15th Battn. Awarded M.M.

On September 27, 1918, on the occasion of the attack on Flesquieres, when Pte. Walker's tank had received two direct hits, and the drivers had become casualties, Pte. Walker, with conspicuous gallantry and determination, attempted to drive, and made progress under the greatest mechanical difficulties, until the tank was completely knocked out by a third direct hit which broke the track. Throughout the action he displayed courage, initiative, and determination of the highest order.

307685 L/Cpl. JENKINS, JOHN. 15th Battn. Awarded M.M.

For conspicuous gallantry and devotion to duty on the occasion of the attack on the Canal du Nord on September 27, 1918. This N.C.O., although seriously wounded, continued to serve his gun, inflicting severe casualties on the enemy and materially assisting operations. When his tank had been knocked out by a direct hit he carried the most severely wounded of his comrades, under heavy machine-gun fire, to a place of safety. His devotion to duty was of the utmost assistance to his officer.

307814 Cpl. SHAMBROOK, WALTER. 15th Battn. Awarded M.M.

For conspicuous gallantry and devotion to duty in action in the attack on Flesquieres on September 27, 1918. This N.C.O., who was in charge of a tank, fought his tank with conspicuous gallantry and determination in engaging hostile field and machine-guns whilst under concentrated artillery and trench mortar fire on the northern

THE TANK CORPS BOOK OF HONOUR

and exposed side of Flesquieres. When his tank received two direct hits he successfully rallied his men. This N.C.O.'s powers of leadership, displayed in difficult circumstances, largely contributed to the success of the operations in which his tank was engaged.

304655 Pte. HALLETT, CHARLES GORDON. 15th Battn. Awarded M.M.

On the occasion of the attack on Flesquieres on September 27, 1918, when the driver of his tank collapsed (on the approach march) this man drove the tank through heavy shell fire to the starting-point, although wounded in the face and partially blinded. In spite of his wounds he volunteered to drive the tank into action, and drove throughout the action until the tank was ditched. He then volunteered to take a message to headquarters, which he did under heavy shell fire. He afterwards returned and worked on his tank until it was unditched. Throughout the action he displayed conspicuous gallantry and initiative.

304897 Pte. BROWN, GEORGE HENRY. 15th Battn. Awarded M.M.

On September 27, 1918, on the occasion of the attack on Flesquieres, Pte. Brown drove his tank, in the face of heavy shell fire, with conspicuous gallantry and determination, until, after reaching the objective, his tank was knocked out by a direct hit. Pte. Brown then established a machine-gun post, regardless of danger making several journeys, under heavy hostile machine-gun fire at close range, for guns and ammunition. Throughout the action he displayed conspicuous courage and initiative.

305135 Pte. HARRISON, NORMAN, M.M. 15th Battn. Awarded Bar to M.M.

For conspicuous gallantry and devotion to duty in action on September 27, 1918, between Moeuvres and Bourlon Wood. Pte. Harrison, although under heavy hostile machine-gun fire, and bleeding freely from a face wound, drove his tank with flaps open so as to secure better vision. With the utmost gallantry and determination he succeeded in running his tank over a machine-gun post, crushing two machine-guns and six of the crew.

305202 Cpl. WYLLIE, MARCUS. 15th Battn. Awarded M.M.

For conspicuous gallantry and devotion to duty on September 27, 1918, on the occasion of the attack on the Canal du Nord, near Moeuvres. This N.C.O., although seriously wounded (his wound resulted in the loss of an eye), continued to pick up targets and encourage his men until his tank was knocked out by a direct hit.

His gallantry, determination, and spirit of leadership were a source of inspiration to all.

IMMEDIATE AWARDS—OTHER RANKS

95735 Pte. WHITEHOUSE, JOHN. 15th Battn. Awarded M.M·

On September 27, 1918, on the occasion of the attack on the Canal du Nord and at Graincourt and Cantaing, this man drove his tank continuously for eleven hours. Throughout the action he showed great initiative and devotion to duty, although during the latter stages he was on the verge of collapse. It was largely due to his gallantry and determination that the tank reached the final objective and returned, having performed most valuable service in the assistance of the infantry.

308132 Pte. HALL, HAROLD. 15th Battn. Awarded M.M.

For conspicuous gallantry and devotion to duty in action on September 27, 1918, on the occasion of the attack on the Canal du Nord and at Graincourt and Cantaing. Pte. Hall drove his tank for eleven hours, and later totally collapsed through exhaustion. It was largely due to his gallantry and determination that the tank reached the final objective and returned, having performed most valuable service in the assistance of the infantry.

307129 Pte. KAIGH, GEORGE. 15th Battn. Awarded M.M.

For conspicuous gallantry in action on the occasion of the attack on the Canal du Nord, near Moeuvres, on September 27, 1918. Pte. Kaigh, although severely wounded at the commencement of the action, continued to serve his 6-pndr. gun against enemy strong points until his tank was knocked out by a direct hit. His determination and devotion to duty, in spite of his wounds, materially assisted in the advance of the infantry and in the success of the operations in which his tank was engaged.

96868 S/Sergt. WOOD, JOHN ROBERT. 11th Battn. Awarded M.M.

This staff-sergeant in the action of September 27, at Havrincourt Wood, seeing a tank stop, made his way in front of the infantry through an enemy barrage of machine-gun and shell fire to the tank, and materially assisted the crew to get it going once more, so that it joined up once more in the attack. He worked on his own initiative, his officers being detained at a tank that had broken down before reaching the starting-point. During the actions of October 8 at Villers-Outreaux; October 10, Caudry; October 20, Selle River; and October 25 at Ovillers, this staff-sergeant followed up the tanks into action, in company with and materially assisted his officer, A/Capt. H. F. Brown, in keeping the tanks in action. He displayed untiring energy, ability, courage, and devotion to duty throughout these prolonged operations, inspiring the crews both in action and between actions to do their very utmost. It was greatly owing to his continual efforts that tanks were able to carry on the battle, some tanks having been in action or on the move since August 11, near Amiens. His work was beyond praise.

95502 Sergt. HENRY, WILLIAM. 11th Battn. Awarded M.M.

For conspicuous courage and devotion to duty at Gouzeaucourt, September 27, 1918. After the officer and all the crew, except for one man, had been seriously wounded, and the tank, K 4, received a direct hit which blew off the sponson doors and stopped the engine, the enemy turned machine-guns on to the tank, penetrating the tank through the open door. This N.C.O. and the one man, keeping their guns in action, silenced the enemy fire and drove back hostile infantry that endeavoured to approach. He then evacuated the wounded officer and men, handing them over to the infantry.

97110 Pte. ECCLESHILL, CHARLES WILLIAM. 11th Battn. Awarded M.M.

This driver, on September 27, at Havrincourt Wood, drove his tank, K 42, with utmost skill and endurance, after a long approach march, being for ten hours in the driver's seat at a stretch. His skilful driving and conning of the tank was responsible to a material extent for the excellent work done by the tank, whose whole crew were thanked in writing by the officer commanding the 6th Manchester Regiment. His endurance and courage in driving the tank with flaps open over very difficult ground inspired the whole crew, whose work on that day was beyond all praise. His continual cheerfulness when others were exhausted materially contributed to the success of the tank in the most important action.

97084 S/Sergt. CRIDLAND, GEORGE WILLIAM. 11th Battn. Awarded M.M.

At Gouzeaucourt Wood, on September 28, 1918, when tank No. K 12 was knocked out, Staff-Sergt. Cridland proceeded at once to the tank in daylight, though it was in full view of the enemy, who were consistently shelling it. He reached the tank, after passing through heavy hostile shell fire, and proceeded to make the necessary repairs. Having been engaged on the work for some hours, the enemy delivered a counter-attack, driving the infantry back into line with the tank, which eventually become practically a strong point. Staff-Sergt. Cridland carried on with his work of repairs in cold blood and despite these stirring events, the tank all the time being a target for machine-gun fire. The enemy were eventually beaten off, and this N.C.O. succeeded in salving the tank, entirely by his own efforts, and driving it back to the rallying point at dawn, September 29, 1918.

91434 Pte. WESTON, ROBERT. 9th Battn. Awarded M.M.

During the operations near Bellenglise on September 29, after his tank had received a direct hit, wounding Pte. Weston, the driver, in the face and blinding him in one eye, he stuck to his post and endeavoured to drive the tank out of action until a second direct hit broke the track. The tank was then evacuated. Pte. Weston set a fine example of devotion to duty to the remainder of the crew.

95429 Pte. BEARDSLEY, AMOS. 9th Battn. Awarded M.M.

During the operations near Bellenglise on September 29, 1918. When the tank had received a direct hit, killing three of the crew, Pte. Beardsley remained in the tank until a second direct hit seriously wounded another man and killed the N.C.O. Pte. Beardsley assisted the wounded gunner to a trench, where, however, he died in a few moments. Pte. Beardsley at once went back to the tank, which was under heavy shell fire and machine-gun fire, and helped the driver, who was also severely wounded, to a trench. He then remained close to the tank watching it until he was relieved by a guard.

He displayed great devotion to duty under particularly trying circumstances.

308803 Pte. BRUCE, ALEXANDER MASON. 9th Battn. Awarded M.M.

During the operations near Bellenglise on September 29, after a shell had hit the front of the tank, killing the tank commander, Pte. Bruce, although severely wounded in the hand and eye, continued to drive the tank, swinging her to avoid the shell fire. A few minutes later the tank received a second hit, stopping the engine. Pte. Bruce remained in the tank endeavouring to repair the damage ; the tank however had to be left, but Pte. Bruce remained in the vicinity for some time afterwards, when he was found by his section commander, who ordered him back.

Pte. Bruce gave a fine example of devotion to duty under very trying circumstances.

307335 Cpl. RATCLIFFE, WILFRED. 9th Battn. Awarded M.M.

This N.C.O., being in charge of a tank during the action at Bellenglise on September 29, 1918, noticed that a tank had been put out of action by a gun concealed in a copse. He manœuvred his tank in order to outflank the gun, but was hit almost immediately afterwards, one of his crew being killed and others wounded. He removed four wounded men from the tank under heavy machine-gun and shell fire, and remained with the fourth, who was very badly hit, all night, getting him away to the dressing station the following morning. He behaved very coolly and with the utmost bravery in very difficult circumstances.

THE TANK CORPS BOOK OF HONOUR

78550 Pte. BOYEK, WILLIAM. 9th Battn. Awarded M.M.

After his tank had received a direct hit whilst in action near Bellenglise, on September 29, 1918, he continued to drive, endeavouring to take his tank out of the enemy's fire. Whilst doing this his tank was again hit, breaking a track. He then helped to carry the wounded out of danger under heavy artillery fire, and set a splendid example of bravery and coolness to the crew.

78969 Pte. SHERGOLD, WILLIAM. 9th Battn. Awarded M.M.

This runner showed splendid bravery and coolness in action near Riqueval on September 29, 1918, taking messages from tank to tank under heavy machine-gun fire.

78096 Pte. HARWOOD, HAROLD CHANNING. 9th Battn. Awarded M.M.

This runner showed splendid bravery and coolness in carrying messages under heavy machine-gun fire and artillery fire near Riqueval on September 29, 1918. On every occasion the message was delivered.

78024 Pte. KEYWORTH, FREDERICK LEOPOLD. 9th Battn. Awarded M.M.

Pte. Keyworth showed great skill in driving his tank in action at Bellenglise on September 29, 1918, under heavy shell fire, enabling the crew to use their guns successfully against enemy machine-gun posts. After seeing the infantry to their objective his tank was hit. The crew evacuated their tank and, taking their guns, assisted the infantry. Running short of ammunition, Pte. Keyworth twice obtained more from his tank under heavy shell fire. Throughout the action Pte. Keyworth showed great bravery and devotion to duty.

567942 L/Cpl. WICKS, PERCIVAL. R.E. (T.) (3rd Bde. Signals.) Awarded M.M.

For conspicuous gallantry and devotion to duty near Bellicourt on September 29, 1918, when N.C.O. in charge of a wireless station on a tank. During a dense mist the tank ran into the enemy, and it was largely due to this N.C.O. that the station was successfully withdrawn. Later on in the day he entered his station and kept it working under heavy shell fire, constantly repairing the aerial.

75897 Cpl. SHARP, ARTHUR WILLIAM. 4th Battn. Awarded M.M.

For conspicuous gallantry and devotion to duty during an attack upon the Hindenburg Line at Bellicourt, on September 29, 1918. Before zero the driver of his tank became a casualty and, although

382

himself only a gunner, he immediately took over the driving of the tank and took it into action over the Hindenburg Line under most difficult weather conditions.

When his tank became under direct artillery fire, it was largely due to his coolness that it was skilfully manœuvred behind a smoke screen which was produced from the tank.

He drove his tank further into the enemy's positions than any other tank in his company.

305392 Pte. (A/Sergt.) DIBBEN, FRANK CHARLES. 16th Battn. Awarded D.C.M.

As tank commander, on September 29, 1918, near Quennemont Copse, he fought his tank with great skill and determination until it got ditched by falling through into a dug-out. Under very heavy shell and machine-gun fire he repeatedly tried to unditch his tank. He continued to do this until he was so pressed by the enemy that he had to desist. He then withdrew his Hotchkiss guns and crew to a trench and established a strong point. Under cover of their fire he then went to his tank again and removed magnetos and 6-pndr. hammers complete, though the enemy were within a few feet of him. He remained and fought with the infantry all day and until far into the night, and did not return to the tankodrome until the following morning. His extreme gallantry and devotion to duty, with total disregard of personal safety, are worthy of the highest praise.

307891 Cpl. (A/Sergt.) BROWNING, PERCY. 16th Battn. Awarded M.M.

Whilst in action on September 29, 1918, near Guillemont Farm, his officer was wounded by an armour-piercing bullet. He thereupon assumed command of the tank and fought it until it received several direct hits and burst into flames. He evacuated all his Hotchkiss guns and then formed a strong point with the infantry, fighting with them for the remainder of the day until dark, when they told him on inquiry that he could be of no more assistance.

75517 Pte. (A/Cpl.) HAMER, CHARLES DENTON. 16th Battn. Awarded M.M.

This N.C.O. was first driver to Sergt. Dibben on September 29, 1918, near Quennemont Copse.

He ably supported his tank commander throughout the day, assisting in the attempts to dig out the tank when ditched, under heavy shell and machine-gun fire, and also in removing magnetos and 6-pndr. hammers when the enemy were within a few feet of them. He formed the strong point with Sergt. Dibben and fought there with him until far into the night. His loyal assistance and devotion to duty are worthy of the highest praise.

305528 Cpl. POWELL, SIDNEY ELLIS. 8th Battn. Awarded D.C.M.

During the action against Nauroy, on September 29, 1918, this N.C.O. assumed command of his tank after his officer had been wounded, and under difficult conditions successfully fought the enemy, rendering great assistance to the infantry.

When returning to the rallying point the tank received a direct hit which set it on fire. Cpl. Powell, at great personal risk, entered the burning tank and made a very determined but unsuccessful attempt to extinguish the flames and save the tank.

By his coolness, courage, and devotion to duty he set a splendid example to the remainder of the crew.

91955 Sergt. WHITEHEAD, ALFRED, D.C.M. 8th Battn. Awarded M.M.

In the action against Nauroy, on September 29, Sergt. Whitehead, D.C.M., commanded a tank with very great ability.

Owing to thick mist operations were delayed, and this gallant N.C.O. showed great initiative in leading his tank, in the face of heavy machine-gun fire, towards the village, where he rendered invaluable assistance to the infantry. He maintained close touch with the infantry, getting out of the tank for this purpose constantly, and was wounded whilst so doing. Throughout the day he showed great determination, initiative, and personal bravery.

91466 Cpl. PURCELL, SIDNEY. 8th Battn. Awarded M.M.

For conspicuous devotion to duty.

During the action on September 29, 1918, whilst waiting at the starting-point near Bellicourt, this N.C.O. was wounded in the leg while attending to his officer, who had just been hit.

In spite of the wound and a stiffening limb, he determinedly carried on when orders to advance were received, and drove his tank throughout the action splendidly until it received a direct hit.

The conduct of this N.C.O., in fighting spirit and high courage, was most marked, and the example he set to his crew cannot be too highly commended.

306341 Pte. GRALEY, JOHN. 8th Battn. Awarded M.M.

On September 29, 1918, whilst in action at Nouroy, Pte. Graley showed conspicuous courage and disregard of danger. His tank received five direct hits ; the tank commander and all the remaining members of the crew were killed, and Graley was wounded and burned. With complete disregard of his injuries, however, he made repeated valiant attempts to rescue his comrades from the burning tank, but without avail.

305703 Pte. JUDSON, BROOKS. 8th Battn. Awarded M.M.

For conspicuous devotion to duty near Bellicourt on September 29, 1918.

An anti-tank gun had already put tanks out of action, and was engaging the tank of which Pte. Judson was a gunner. He volunteered to go forward under cover of the prevailing mist and locate the gun. Notwithstanding heavy machine-gun fire, he was successful and, returning to his tank, knocked out the anti-tank gun by skilful shooting. The courage and initiative of this gunner are worthy of the highest praise.

T3/024937 Sergt. FRENCH, RUPERT. 5th Cav. Res. Park (attached 5th Tank Bde.). Awarded M.M.

On September 29, 1918, about 1 P.M., this N.C.O. showed determination and disregard of personal safety in attempting to deliver supplies of petrol, oil, and grease with a convoy of G.S. limbers. He twice attempted to enter Bellicourt, which was then still in German hands and under machine-gun fire, but was driven back each time. He held on until receiving orders from 2nd Lieut. Bennett, 16th Tank Battalion, to retire.

1803585 Sergt. ROSENHAGEN, CARL. 301st American Tank Battn. Awarded D.C.M.

In the attack on the Hindenburg Line on September 29, 1918, Sergt. Rosenhagen's good judgment and coolness enabled his tank to reach its objective, where it was knocked out by three direct hits. Sergt. Rosenhagen accompanied his tank commander through the German lines, being the only enlisted member of the crew to escape, and bringing back valuable information.

1803587 Sergt. RUHS, HENRY. 301st American Tank Battn. Awarded M.M.

In the attack on the Hindenburg Line on September 29, 1918, Sergt. Ruhs was badly wounded when his tank received a direct hit. He assisted in removing the wounded members of the crew from the burning tank and then joined the infantry and carried on.

1776335 Pte. DAVIES, RUSSELL C. 301st American Tank Battn. Awarded M.M.

In the attack on Bony, September 29, 1918, his tank was ditched. Pte. Davies got out of the tank and, under heavy machine-gun fire, dug the tank out. While digging, Pte. Davies was wounded, but entered the tank and drove it after the driver became a casualty.

112232 Sergt. DICKINSON, GEORGE. 11th Battn. Awarded M.M.

For conspicuous gallantry and devotion to duty when in command of a tank in action at Gauche Wood on September 29, 1918. Shortly after zero his tank had mechanical trouble. He continued to repair it under direct observation and heavy shell fire until he was ordered out of it by his company commander. After dusk the tank was repaired, and Sergt. Dickinson himself drove it out of action through a dangerous minefield after ordering his crew to get outside the tank.

200172 Pte. HUTCHINSON, ROBERT LEONARD. 1st Battn. Awarded M.M.

In the action on September 29, 1918, in the taking of the tunnel crossing near Bellicourt, this soldier was first driver of his tank, and throughout the action displayed great courage and devotion to duty, and drove his tank with great skill and coolness.

When his tank was evacuated owing to being on fire, he re-entered on two occasions—once to help another member of the crew and again to get the medical bag. At the time the ammunition inside was exploding and he was exposed to great danger.

92313 Pte. COWLEY, JOSEPH. 6th Battn. Awarded M.M.

On September 30, 1918, in the attack on Joncourt, when his tank, commanded by Cpl. Bridges, was knocked out, Pte. Cowley remained with Cpl. Bridges near the tank, and when it grew dusk Pte. Cowley very gallantly assisted in getting four wounded infantry back to dressing station. These men had been lying in the front of our lines since 4 A.M. and could not possibly have got back without assistance.

92991 Cpl. BRIDGES, GEORGE. 6th Battn. Awarded M.M.

On September 30, 1918, during the attack on Joncourt, Cpl. Bridges, in command of tank No. 385, engaged a large number of enemy machine-guns and materially assisted the infantry into the western outskirts of the village. His tank was heavily shelled and he threw out a smoke screen, but received a direct hit on the carburetter and immediately burst into flames. He then attempted to get his guns out, but was driven back by the flames.

On learning from some infantry that the officer of the leading tank was lying wounded in the open some distance in front of our lines, in spite of the very heavy machine-gun fire, Cpl. Bridges crawled out and found 2nd Lieut. J. A. H. Holloway, who was severely hit. The only way to get him back to our lines was to carry him over the ridge, which was being continually swept with machine-gun fire at close range and in full view of the enemy. Cpl. Bridges decided to wait until dusk. Lieut. Holloway was by this time delirious, and this N.C.O. had the greatest difficulty in keeping him quiet, as the enemy were continually patrolling the sunken road, which was only fifteen yards distant. When dusk came, Cpl. Bridges carried the officer over the ridge and down to the dressing station, two miles away, being under fire most of the journey.

91932 Cpl. GRAYSON, FRANK. 9th Battn. Awarded M.M.

This N.C.O. commanded a tank throughout the action near Joncourt on October 1, 1918, and fought his tank in a most gallant manner, doing great execution amongst the enemy and assisting the infantry to all their objectives.

On previous occasions he has always shown gallantry and devotion to duty in action, and always sets a splendid example to his men.

305537 Pte. PERRINS, WILFRED. 9th Battn. Awarded M.M.

Before the action on October 1, at Joncourt, he carried out a reconnaissance under heavy machine-gun and shell fire, and behaved in a very gallant manner as runner during the action, carrying messages which were all delivered.

On other occasions he has shown great devotion to duty in action.

78582 Pte. SUNDERLAND, JAMES. 9th Battn. Awarded M.M.

This private showed splendid bravery and devotion to duty whilst in action at Joncourt on October 1, 1918, under heavy armour-piercing machine-gun fire, which came through the sponson. He carried on firing until severely wounded in the arm, putting out several machine-guns.

200761 Pte. (A/Sergt.) BLACK, ARTHUR JOSEPH. 16th Battn. Awarded M.M.

For great gallantry and devotion to duty in action on October 1, at Estrees. This N.C.O. drove his tank during the whole of the approach march, during the action, and back to rallying point, a period of twelve hours, refusing to be relieved. Near the rallying point his tank was put out of action and the enemy commenced shelling it heavily. Despite this, and at great personal risk, he salved his guns and as much equipment as possible. By his total disregard of danger and fine sense of duty he set a splendid example to the rest of the crew.

200560 Pte. GARDEN, ALEXANDER. 3rd Battn. Awarded M.M.

On October 3, 1918, near Estrees, when his tank was hit by anti-tank rifle fire and the crew wounded, this gunner, although wounded himself, brought the whippet out of action and conveyed the badly-wounded personnel to a dressing station. After having his own wound dressed he remained at duty, and endeavoured to drive his whippet to rallying point through a heavily shelled area. His great coolness and presence of mind showed a high sense of duty, and he remained with his whippet until relieved by his company commander.

205021 T.M.S/Sergt. HAYES, HERBERT. 13th Battn. Awarded M.M.

For conspicuous gallantry and devotion to duty near Estrees on October 3, 1918.

During an attack T.M.S/S. Hayes heard that one of the tanks of his company had broken down. In spite of heavy artillery and machine-gun fire brought to bear on the tank, this N.C.O. walked across the open to it and succeeded in effecting the necessary repairs, so that the tank was able to again attack and reach its objective.

This N.C.O. showed great coolness and disregard of danger.

300407 Sergt. ROGERS, FREDERICK CHARLES. 13th Battn. Awarded M.M.

For conspicuous gallantry and devotion to duty near Estrees on October 3, 1918.

This N.C.O. acted as a tank commander during an attack and engaged an enemy strong point held by machine-guns and an anti-tank gun. His tank received four direct hits from the anti-tank gun, killing two of the crew and wounding all of the others. Sergt. Rogers, although the only unwounded member of the crew, continued to engage the strong point until all his guns were put out of action.

The gallant conduct and determination shown by Sergt. Rogers under difficult circumstances are worthy of the highest praise.

305567 Pte. FIANDER, GEORGE. 13th Battn. Awarded M.M.

For conspicuous gallantry and devotion to duty near Wiancourt on October 3, 1918.

Pte. Fiander acted as gunner of a tank during an attack. This tank met with strong opposition and several anti-tank rifle bullets pierced the tank, killing two of the crew and severely wounding another. In spite of the fact that the tank was being riddled with anti-tank rifle bullets and armour-piercing bullets, Pte. Fiander continued to fire upon the enemy, and destroyed nests of enemy machine-guns until all opposition in this sector had been overcome. Pte. Fiander showed remarkable courage and a determination that was an example to all.

IMMEDIATE AWARDS—OTHER RANKS

301428 Pte. BLACKMAN, ALBERT EDWARD. 13th Battn. Awarded M.M.

For conspicuous gallantry and devotion to duty near Wiancourt on October 3rd, 1918.

Pte. Blackman was driver of a tank in an attack. This tank met with strong opposition and was pierced many times by bullets from anti-tank rifles, killing two of the crew and severely wounding a third. Despite the fact that the tank was being riddled with anti-tank rifle bullets and armour-piercing machine-gun bullets, Pte. Blackman continued to drive in a most brilliant manner, enabling the gunners to bring their fire to bear most advantageously on the enemy, so that enemy opposition at this point was eventually overcome.

Throughout the action Pte. Blackman drove with great skill and showed exceptional courage and coolness.

308741 Pte. WILLMERS, HARRY. 13th Battn. Awarded M.M.

For conspicuous gallantry and devotion to duty near Estrees on October 3, 1918.

This man acted as gunner in a tank during an attack. The tank received a direct hit, killing the driver and wounding Pte. Willmers in the back and head. In spite of his wounds Pte. Willmers continued to fire, and succeeded in putting an enemy machine-gun post out of action. Pte. Willmers gave a splendid example of courage and determination.

76742 Pte. WESTWATER, WILLIAM. 16th Battn. Awarded M.M.

Whilst in command of a tank on October 3, 1918, in the attack on Prospect Hill, he showed the greatest skill and judgment, at all times keeping in close touch with the infantry and assisting them whenever held up. His handling of his tank was such that he surmounted all obstacles which proved fatal to the others, and was the only tank to reach the final objective on that part of the front. This was exceptionally praiseworthy as it was his first experience in action in command of a tank, which he brought safely back to the rallying point.

201029 Sergt. SMITH, ALFRED WILLIAM. 5th Battn. Awarded D.C.M.

This N.C.O. accompanied and assisted 2nd Lieut. T. Farrell in the attack on Ramicourt on October 3, 1918.

When their tank had been set on fire by hostile guns, he brought in two wounded comrades and the body of a third (killed) at the risk of his own life. He then went into Ramicourt, which was being

attacked by the infantry, and single-handed captured twenty of
the enemy by routing them out of their dug-outs with his revolver.
These he handed over to the 8th Sherwood Foresters.
This N.C.O. showed exceptional valour and ability throughout
the action.

92659 Sergt. CLEMENTS, ALBERT EDWARD. 5th Battn. Awarded
M.M.

This N.C.O. took a tank into action at Ramicourt on October 3,
1918, and in going through an intense hostile barrage received
several direct hits.

In spite of the heavy shelling and machine-gun fire this N.C.O.
made very gallant attempts to rally his crew and save his guns,
until he was seriously wounded by enemy machine-gun fire.

Throughout the action he showed the greatest gallantry and
disregard for his personal safety.

305227 Pte. ADAMS, CHARLES. 5th Battn. Awarded M.M.

When this man's tank had been put out of action at Ramicourt,
on October 3, 1918, by hostile shell fire in the enemy lines, and the
Hotchkiss guns also out of action, the enemy had closed in on three
sides and had demanded surrender ; he fired smoke bombs with
such skill and rapidity that it was entirely due to his action that
the remainder of the tank crew were able to regain our lines with
only one casualty.

Throughout the action he exhibited exceptional gallantry.

92880 L/Cpl. WILLIAMS, GARFIELD. 8th Battn. Awarded M.M.

During the action of October 3, 1918, against the Beaurevoir Line,
L/Cpl. Williams distinguished himself by his coolness, courage,
and devotion to duty.

His tank was put out of action through mechanical trouble at
the objective, and his officer withdrew the gunners to take up a
strong point on the infantry flank. L/Cpl. Williams remained
inside the tank with his second driver, repairing it, for six hours, the
whole time being subject to heavy artillery shelling. It was due to his
coolness and perseverance that the tank was eventually put in order
and brought back to the rallying point.

305216 Pte. HAMILTON, BERNARD. 1st Battn. Awarded M.M.

This gunner was in action in a tank on October 8, in front of
Beaurevoir, and knocked out a field gun north of Sonia Wood. Later,
when both drivers were overcome by fumes, he drove the tank.
During this time the tank received a direct hit which killed the

N.C.O. and wounded one man; he, however, continued to drive on and dealt with hostile machine-guns.

Finally, the tank was knocked out by a further hit which wounded two other men, but Pte. Hamilton remained on guard alone until relieved next day. He showed splendid spirit and determination and a fine example to all.

40319 Pte. DINWOODIE, JOHN, M. M. 1st Battn. Awarded M.M.

It was mainly due to his excellent driving and coolness under trying conditions on October 8, in front of Beaurevoir, that his tank was enabled to pick up several important targets. He showed a complete disregard of danger, and exposed himself in order to find targets. His splendid spirit and determination were a fine example to the crew and materially assisted the operations in which they took part.

200164 Cpl. HIX, GEORGE JOE. 1st Battn. Awarded M.M.

In action on October 8, at Beaurevoir, this N.C.O. commanded a tank, and when both his drivers were incapacitated from effects of gas and fumes, although suffering himself from the same cause, he drove the tank throughout the action with the greatest courage and commanded it with skill and determination.

200167 Cpl. (A/Sergt.) MARTIN, PERCIVAL WILLIAM. 1st Battn. Awarded M.M.

He commanded a tank on October 8 in the attack from Beaurevoir, displaying the greatest determination and courage. He helped to knock out an enemy field gun and to clean up Sonia Wood. Receiving a direct hit, he got out, investigated the damage, and decided to go on and reached his objective. Then he went across to the tank on his right and assisted to knock out some machine-guns which were holding up the infantry, finally rallying with two of his crew wounded. He set a fine example to N.C.O. tank commanders.

308429 Pte. QUINN, FRANCIS. 6th Battn. Awarded D.C.M.

In action near Fraicourt Wood, on October 8, 1918, with Capt. Allen, this gunner succeeded in effectively silencing a nest of machine-guns which were holding up the advance.

He then put out of action an anti-tank gun, and, finally, came upon a battery of field guns, the crews of which attempted to turn two guns on the tank, but these were knocked out.

The tank then received a direct hit, which burst the door open, blew in the roof, and wounded Pte. Quinn in the shoulder and arm, throwing him on the floor. In spite of this, he took it in turns with his commander, who was also wounded, to keep the door closed—the fastenings had been broken by the concussion—and to keep a gun in action with his remaining sound arm.

201212 Cpl. HUNTER, BENJAMIN, M.M. 6th Battn. Awarded Bar to M.M.

When in action near Fraicourt Wood on October 8, 1918, the tank of which this N.C.O. was in charge received a direct hit, which set it on fire. On evacuating the tank, he and Pte. Lewis found they were surrounded by the enemy and cut off from our own infantry. Grasping the situation, with great presence of mind they rushed the nearest enemy post and captured the entire garrison, about twelve in number, whom they brought back and handed over to the infantry.

201236 Pte. LEWIS, ERNEST. 6th Battn. Awarded M.M.

In the action near Fraicourt Wood, on October 8, 1918, the tank received a direct hit and caught fire. The tank was evacuated, when Cpl. Hunter, who was in charge of the tank, found they were cut off from our infantry. Without hesitation they rushed the nearest enemy post and captured the whole of its garrison, about twelve in number, whom they brought in and handed over to our infantry.

69720 Cpl. HOWLETT, GEORGE FREEMAN. 6th Battn. Awarded M.M.

During the action before Premont, on October 8, 1918, he commanded and fought his tank for three and a half hours in a very gallant manner. In spite of the fact that he got slightly wounded, he continued to fight his tank until he had finally established the infantry on their objective, after having cleared numerous enemy machine-gun nests in sunken roads, etc., which were holding up the advance, and securing many prisoners.

201813 Pte. BISHOP, CHARLES. 6th Battn. Awarded M.M.

Whilst in the action before Premont, on October 8, 1918, the officer in charge of the tank of which this man was the driver became a casualty early in the fight. Pte. Bishop immediately took command of the tank, and fought it throughout the whole action in a most commendable manner, only returning to the rallying point after five hours' continuous driving.

"*Officer's job excellently and gallantly performed.*"—(Sgd.) H. J. ELLES.

306252 Pte. RICHARDSON, ERNEST HIDDON. 6th Battn. Awarded M.M.

On October 8, 1918, before Fresnoy, the tank of which he was gunner came under very heavy machine-gun fire, which damaged the engines and also slightly wounded this man. In spite of his wound he continued to fight his guns, two of which were damaged by hits whilst he was firing them. He remained in the tank for two hours, working with the driver in an endeavour to repair the engines, during which time the tank was very heavily shelled.

This man has behaved very gallantly and done excellent work in action during the present operations.

95248 Pte. CRONIE, THOMAS CALDWELL. 3rd Battn. Awarded M.M.

On October 8, 1918, at Serain, he drove a whippet tank entirely new to him with the greatest gallantry and coolness for seven hours. At one time his tank developed mechanical trouble which he successfully mended under shell fire. Later, his skill undoubtedly saved his machine whilst it was under heavy shell fire, and his courage and devotion to duty were an example to the rest of the crew. He succeeded in bringing his tank to its objective in spite of great difficulties, such as railways and sunken roads, and enabled the gunners to do considerable execution amongst the enemy.

1803492 Sergt. MONAHAN, PATRICK. 301st American Tank Battn. Awarded D.C.M.

On October 8, 1918, in the vicinity of Ponchaux, Sergt. Monahan exhibited great coolness and judgment in handling his tank, alternately driving and firing 6-pndrs. and machine-guns after the remainder of the crew had been gassed. When the tank was ditched, Sergt. Monahan got out of the tank and attached the unditching gear under heavy machine-gun fire. By his own efforts Sergt. Monahan kept his tank in action, and did good work by putting out machine-guns and aiding the infantry to advance.

1803594 Sergt. PARKER, LEON. 301st American Tank Battn. Awarded D.C.M.

On October 8, 1918, in the vicinity of Ponchaux, Sergt. Parker displayed exceptional coolness and judgment in the handling of his tank after the tank commander and all but one other member of the crew had been gassed. Sergt. Parker took his tank to its objective and rallied.

109754 Pte. HUTCHINSON, THOMAS WILLIAM. 12th Battn. Awarded M.M.

For gallantry and devotion to duty in the attack on Niergnies on October 8, 1918. Although wounded in the head and hand soon after zero he continued to drive his tank with the utmost courage and skill, and succeeded in reaching the final objective in spite of the fact that the tank was pierced by armour-piercing bullets, which wounded three of the crew.

309845 Sergt. SHARP, BASIL CONNEL, M.M. 11th Battn. Awarded Bar to M.M.

307591 Sergt. KNOWLES, W. A. 11th Battn. Awarded M.M.

During the operations near Walincourt on October 8, 1918, these two N.C.O.'s, each in command of a tank, displayed conspicuous gallantry and courage and a fine sense of the tactical situation when taking forward their tanks. Keeping up a continuous machine-gun and 6-pndr. fire, they went forward on the exposed right flank of the battalion and cleared out a quarry holding several of the enemy, enabling the battalion to continue the advance. On one occasion Sergt. Sharp got out of his tank under heavy machine-gun fire so as to be able to control the movements of the tanks from a more favourable position and to keep up liaison with the battalion.

Throughout these tanks were of the greatest assistance to my battalion, due entirely to the able and gallant handling of the N.C.O.'s in command.

200186 Pte. (L/Cpl.) BOCOCK, WILLIAM EDWARD. 1st Battn. Awarded M.M.

This N.C.O. has consistently done excellent work in every action with the battalion since August 8.

On October 8, at Beaurevoir, when suffering severely from the effects of gas and fumes, he continued to stick to his driver's seat throughout the action, setting a fine example to the crew.

309328 Pte. (L/Cpl.) NICHOLLS, FRANK. 17th Battn. Awarded M.M.

On the Le Cateau-Maretz road on October 9, 1918, this N.C.O. displayed great gallantry, skill, and devotion to duty. He drove his armoured car with great skill and determination against a strong point containing ten hostile machine-guns, and his action was largely instrumental in clearing it and capturing the guns. When, later, his car was the only remaining one out of three, and his rear was cut off by the enemy blowing up a bridge behind him, he proceeded forward through two villages strongly held by the enemy and successfully brought his car through them, and finally back to our lines by another route. The safe return of the car and whole crew was largely due to his gallant and skilful driving.

307071 Sergt. HARRIS, HELSER CLARKE. 3rd Tank Supply Coy. Awarded M.M.

October 10, 1918. Preselles. This N.C.O. was in charge of a supply tank, No. 2537, which was carrying infantry stores. The stores contained S.A.A., detonated Stokes mortars, and ground flares. The tank caught fire on top, where these stores were being carried. The S.A.A. was exploding, the boxes containing the Stokes were burning, and the ground flares were going off. Sergt. Harris and No. 307502 L/Cpl. H. Pike, with complete disregard of their own personal safety, got on top of the tank and removed all the stores, and extinguished the fire with ' Pyrenes.' By his coolness and great presence of mind he undoubtedly saved the tank from destruction and prevented almost certain casualties among troops in the neighbourhood.

307502 L/Cpl. PIKE, HENRY. 3rd Tank Supply Co. Awarded M.M.

October 10, 1918. Preselles. This N.C.O. was a member of the crew of supply tank No. 2537, which was carrying infantry stores. The stores contained S.A.A., detonated Stokes mortars, and ground flares. The tank caught fire on top, where these stores were being carried. The S.A.A. was exploding, the boxes containing the Stokes were burning, and the ground flares were going off. L/Cpl. Pike and No. 307071 Sergt. H. C. Harris, with complete disregard of their own personal safety, got on top of the tank and removed all stores, and extinguished the fire with ' Pyrenes.' By his coolness and great presence of mind he undoubtedly saved the tank from destruction and prevented almost certain casualties among troops in the neighbourhood.

307506 Pte. UMPLEBY, JAMES DALTON. 3rd Tank Supply Coy. Awarded M.M.

October 10, 1918. Preselles. This man was a member of the crew of supply tank No. 2537, which was carrying infantry stores. The stores contained S.A.A., detonated Stokes mortars, and ground flares. The tank caught fire on top, where these stores were being carried. The S.A.A. was exploding, the boxes containing the Stokes were burning, and the ground flares were going off. Pte. Umpleby, with 307071 Sergt. H. C. Harris and 307502 L/Cpl. H. Pike, with complete disregard of their own personal safety, got on top of the tank and removed all the stores, and extinguished the fire with ' Pyrenes.' By his coolness and great presence of mind he undoubtedly saved the tank from destruction and prevented almost certain casualties among troops in the neighbourhood.

308110 Pte. (A/L/Cpl.) BALL, ROBERT. 16th Battn. Awarded M.M.

For conspicuous gallantry and devotion to duty on October 17, 1918, at Vaux-Andigny. When his officer became a casualty early in the morning, he assumed command of the tank, and fought it with great skill up to the objective, where it was put out of action. He only vacated his tank after it had received seven direct hits and was set on fire and he himself was wounded. All the rest of his crew except one were killed, and that one wounded.

95160 Cpl. BODY, WILLIAM. 1st Battn. Awarded M.M.

For great gallantry and devotion to duty on October 17, in the crossing of the Selle, south of Le Cateau. This N.C.O. was in command of a tank which he fought with the utmost coolness and determination, and although shot through the arm he continued to clear the roads, woods, and hedges, refusing to proceed to a dressing station until he had brought his tank back to our own lines.

40078 Pte. BROWN, PERCY VICTOR. 1st Battn. Awarded M.M.

For conspicuous gallantry and devotion to duty on October 17, in the crossing of the Selle, south of Le Cateau. Though suffering from the effects of enemy gas shelling in the early morning, he drove his tank continuously for nine hours, and although it received three direct hits from shells he succeeded in manœuvring it safely out of action after his objective had been gained.

He displayed a fine spirit of resolute endurance and devotion to duty.

305236 Pte. DUNCAN, GEORGE. 1st Battn. Awarded M.M.

In the action on October 17, in the crossing of the Selle, south of Le Cateau, this man rendered great service to his section commander. After the other runners had become casualties he reconnoitred the ground under heavy hostile machine-gun fire to find routes for the tanks, which were delayed by heavy mist and smoke, thus enabling them to reach their objectives with the minimum loss of time.

200106 Cpl. COLLINS, SIDNEY. 1st Battn. Awarded M.M.

For conspicuous gallantry and devotion to duty in action south of Le Cateau on October 17, when in command of a tank.

This N.C.O. showed great coolness and initiative throughout the day and rendered valuable assistance to the infantry.

He engaged and silenced an enemy field gun and also knocked out an enemy trench mortar battery and two machine-guns.

His coolness and courage throughout the action was a great example to his crew.

30845 Sergt. SHARP, BASIL CONNELL. 11th Battn. Awarded M.M.

On October 20, on the left of Amerval, his tank having been put out of action by anti-tank guns, this N.C.O. displayed great disregard of danger, sent his crew to rear, and with one man helped to repel a counter-attack, attaching himself to the nearest infantry. Previous to his tank being put out of action this N.C.O. walked ahead of his tank under direct enemy machine-gun fire, trying to locate enemy machine-guns. He refused to leave the front line until he received a direct order, notwithstanding the fact that his tank was out of action.

305236 Pte. DOWNIE, ROBERT. 12th Battn. Awarded M.M.

For gallantry and devotion to duty under heavy machine-gun fire. This private, during the operation against Beaurain, on October 23, on his own initiative left his tank and, under heavy enemy machine-gun fire, went forward in order to establish contact with the infantry, as he was unable to use his guns until he knew their position owing to darkness. He found the position of the infantry and obtained from an officer information regarding the direction of the hostile machine-gun fire. He returned to his tank and reported to his tank commander, with the result that the enemy was engaged and a large number surrendered. Owing to this man's determination and utter disregard of his own personal safety at a time when our infantry were held up, his tank was able to clear a ridge which was strongly held by the enemy and allow our infantry to go forward. Pte. Downie has in previous actions shown an utter disregard of his own personal safety in the execution of his duties, and by his general behaviour has materially assisted in keeping up the morale of the crew.

110036 Sergt. WIGHT, PETER CONNELLY. 10th Battn. Awarded M.M.

For conspicuous gallantry and devotion to duty on October 23, 1918, in the neighbourhood of Basuel and Pommereuil. The nature of the tank operations were such that his tank was to proceed and co-operate with his sub-section commander's male tank. Finding that the male tank was unable to overcome a preliminary obstacle in the shape of a railway arch, this N.C.O. promptly took his own tank through the arch, and although he had only a slight knowledge of objectives and the ground, he picked out his route and got to his objective, breaking down very considerable enemy resistance to our infantry advance, knocking out many enemy machine-guns and crews. The ground was difficult, and the darkness and early morning mist were a great obstacle. On reaching the village of Pommereuil his tank broke down, and although harassed by enemy snipers and shell fire, he continually exposed himself and succeeded eventually in repairing the tank. He then regained touch with the infantry and assisted them to their final objective, when he returned to the rallying point and furnished a very clear and concise report as to the situation, which proved of the utmost value. His courage, determination, and coolness were an example to all ranks.

308394 Sergt. FENWICK, THOMAS. 4th Tank Supply Coy. Awarded M.M.

For gallantry, coolness, and enterprise when in command of a supply tank north of Le Cateau on October 23, 1918. His tank was used for the purpose of carrying up signal stores and laying two main telephone lines up the 18th Divisional Front, thus keeping the brigade, and at times battalions in the line, in touch with Divisional Headquarters. This N.C.O. skilfully led his tank through the village of Montay under heavy shell fire and in the dark by a difficult route to the tank bridge over the river. His tank was always up to time when required. This N.C.O. carried on his work for ten hours over difficult and unreconnoitred country. On several occasions his tank came under heavy bursts of shell fire. On one occasion he pushed his tank so far forward in order to lay the cable to time that he was ordered back by an infantry officer. It was mainly owing to this N.C.O.'s gallantry, enterprise, and determination that Divisional Headquarters were able to keep in touch with brigades and battalions through a difficult and successful operation.

307543 Pte. HEARN, EDWARD. 10th Battn. Awarded M.M.

For conspicuous gallantry and devotion to duty on October 24, 1918, north-east of Bousies. Pte. Hearn was wounded early in the action and suffering slightly from gas, but he managed to keep his 6-pndr. in action throughout the engagement. It was owing to his devotion to duty, in spite of his wound, that the tank was enabled to maintain its fighting efficiency, as the remainder of the crew, with the exception of himself and the driver, were badly gassed. He had been in action on the previous day and done very good work. His conduct throughout was an example to all ranks.

111637 Pte. CARR, WILFRED JAMES. 10th Battn. Awarded M.M.

For conspicuous gallantry and devotion to duty west of Landrecies on November 2, 1918. This man was a gunner in a tank assisting the infantry in the attack on that date. He showed great endurance in keeping his gun in action during the whole of the attack, and at one time, under heavy shrapnel and machine-gun fire, got out of the tank and cleared away a quantity of barbed wire which was obstructing his fire. Pte. Carr showed utter contempt for danger in this action, and his conduct was a wonderful incentive to all ranks.

309395 Pte. PAGE, JUSTIN. 14th Battn. Awarded M.M.

For gallantry and devotion to duty.

At Jolimetz, on November 4, 1918, while acting as first driver to 2nd Lieut. A. Harris, he showed a splendid example of coolness and determination. Though slightly wounded early in the engagement he continued to drive for four hours with the greatest skill. On several occasions when the front Hotchkiss gun jammed he dispersed parties of the enemy by opening one of the front flaps and firing his revolver. It was entirely due to his skilful driving that the tank reached its final objective and captured the village of Jolimetz.

309305 Cpl. GLAYSHER, ALFRED. 14th Battn. Awarded M.M.
309150 Pte. (L/Cpl.) KINGSBURY, WILSON FRASER. 14th Battn. Awarded M.M.

For gallantry and devotion to duty.

This N.C.O. and man, near Preux, on November 4, formed part of the crew of the tank commanded by 2nd Lieut. R. O. Robinson. To this tank is largely attributed the successful advance of the infantry on the left of the attack to their objective, wiping out numerous machine-gun nests in the advance west of Hecq, and finally taking the village It then cleared the south of Englefontaine at the request of the division on our left, and next, a strong position north of Hecq; in both cases enabling the infantry, hitherto held up, to advance. When finally knocked out by a direct hit, the crew went on fighting with the Hotchkiss guns on foot until it had assisted the infantry to clear the whole area of machine-guns and trench mortars. The tank commander reports that the courage, coolness, and morale of the whole crew were, without exception, uniformly very high indeed. The work of the tank and its crew has been the subject of special mention by the 53rd and 55th Brigades, the Royal West Kents, and the R. W. Fusiliers.

92575 Pte. COSTA, RUSSELL. 9th Battn. Awarded M.M.

For exceptional skill and devotion to duty during the action near Mormal Forest on November 4, 1918. Pte. Costa's foot-brake and clutch were seized together and no other driver could swing the tank. He drove continuously for nine hours, through heavy shelling, part of the time with gas-mask on. At one critical period, with heavy machine-gun fire on the front of his tank, he could not keep direction in the fog and opened the port-holes, regardless of the danger, and destroyed five enemy machine-gun nests by driving over them.

78957 Pte. WHEELER, FREDERICK ALFRED. 9th Battn. Awarded M.M.

During the action near Mormal Forest on November 4, 1918, Pte. Wheeler showed the greatest devotion to duty during five hours' heavy fighting in his tank. All the crew were suffering from gas and petrol fumes, and it was mainly owing to this man's cheerfulness and example that the crew were kept together and fought their tank so well.

In a thick fog the tank lost direction, and this man volunteered to find the sister tank. Under very heavy machine-gun fire he left the tank, found the other tank, obtained touch with the infantry, and enabled his tank commander to do most valuable work.

201543 Pte. HUNTER, ARTHUR. 9th Battn. Awarded M.M.

During the action near Mormal Forest on November 4, 1918, although suffering from gas poisoning, Pte. Hunter continued to drive his tank continuously for nine hours, no one else being available. Driving in a gas mask, in a thick fog, although under very heavy machine-gun fire, he kept his front windows open and exposed himself all the time in order to pick up targets for his gunners, showing great devotion to duty.

78065 Sergt. SNARY, THOMAS HENRY. 9th Battn. Awarded M.M.

For initiative and devotion to duty while in command of a tank.

During the action near Mormal Forest on November 4, 1918, while on the approach march, Sergeant Snary's tank had the sponson door knocked in, leaving a large gap in the side. He filled it up with a track plate, encouraging his crew, and going into action fought his tank with the greatest gallantry. In spite of considerable engine trouble, thick fog, and gas this N.C.O. reached his objective and destroyed several enemy machine-guns.

No officer was available to command this tank, and Sergt. Snary more than justified the trust reposed in him.

78103 Pte. JEFFRIES, JOHN. 9th Battn. Awarded M.M.

During the action near Mormal Forest on November 4, 1918, for devotion to duty and great gallantry. Although twice wounded, Pte. Jeffries continued to serve his gun and accounted for several enemy machine-guns. His skill, coolness, and courage were a very fine example to his crew.

95087 Pte. HODGE, ALEXANDER. 9th Battn. Awarded M.M.

During the action near Mormal Forest on November 4, 1918, this driver, by his coolness and very skilful driving, took his tank through thick woods and destroyed several machine-gun posts that were holding up the infantry. For three hours, in a thick mist and under heavy machine-gun and artillery fire, he drove with open front windows, displaying an absolute disregard of personal danger.

308773 Pte. ALLEN, ARTHUR. 9th Battn. Awarded M.M.

For conspicuous gallantry and devotion to duty during the action near Mormal Forest on November 4, 1918. The whole of his crew had become casualties and his tank knocked out by a direct hit. On recovering his senses he immediately tried to get the tank out by himself. He succeeded in moving it some distance when it received another direct hit and he was again wounded. Pte. Allen set a splendid example of devotion to duty.

91456 Cpl. WOODWARD, JAMES HENRY. 9th Battn. Awarded M.M.

During the action near Mormal Forest on November 4, 1918, by his coolness, skill, and initiative, Cpl. Woodward, in command of a tank, kept all his crew, who were badly gassed, cheerfully at their posts during a very trying action. His observation of fire and handling of his men resulted in the destruction of fourteen enemy machine-gun positions and the killing or capturing of their personnel. His devotion to duty while suffering himself from gas poisoning was a fine example to his men.

301878 Pte. BUCKMASTER, GEORGE ARTHUR. 14th Battn. Awarded M.M.

Near Preux, on November 4, this first driver's tank received a direct hit and became immobile early in the battle. He accompanied his officer, who went on fighting with the infantry on foot, with his Hotchkiss guns. Always in the forefront of the infantry, this man displayed exceptional coolness in every situation in which his party found themselves. Besides capturing several of the enemy on his own initiative, and using a captured enemy machine-gun with great effect, he immediately volunteered to go through very heavy machine-gun fire and take a message to a tank which was seen moving off in the distance. This he successfully accomplished, and personally led the tank back across the enemy's front to the village of Hecq, where the infantry were held up, with the result that this tank cleared the village and enabled the infantry to advance.

301517 Pte. HINKS, ALBERT EDWARD. 14th Battn. Awarded M.M.

Near Preux, on November 4, when this man's tank was ditched, he climbed out on to the roof with a Hotchkiss gun, though the tank was under heavy machine-gun fire from two machine-gun posts within fifty yards. He put down and silenced their fire and fixed the unditching beam. He resumed fire whenever the enemy attempted to reopen it. Owing to the position of the tank no other guns could be brought to bear on the enemy. At this period the tank was completely 'in the air.' The very heavy enemy fire had caused the infantry to temporarily withdraw.

Their subsequent advance was in a great measure due to the action of this gunner.

309807 Pte. WEBBER, HARRY. 14th Battn. Awarded M.M.

For conspicuous gallantry near Preux on November 4. This man's tank having been knocked out early in the action, he accompanied his officer throughout the day, fighting with and in advance of the infantry, carrying and using a Hotchkiss gun. Throughout the day this man displayed considerable gallantry, and the work he did with his Hotchkiss gun throughout was most effective. His officer states that his conduct was at all times a very high and an inspiring example to the rest of the party and to the infantry in the neighbourhood. This party was subjected frequently to intense machine-gun and trench mortar fire, and during the operations had four Hotchkiss guns and the captured machine-guns which they had been using knocked out by enemy fire. Together with his officer, this man, as one of two of the crew left, only withdrew when the final tank's objective had been reached and all the guns of the party had been knocked out.

304376 Pte. MORRIS, ARTHUR VINCENT. 17th Battn. (A.C.). Awarded D.C.M.

On the Landrecies road, in the Mormal Forest, on November 4, this soldier displayed most conspicuous gallantry and devotion to duty. His armoured car was hit, overturned, and two of the crew wounded, a considerable distance in front of our troops. The car was evacuated with a party of the enemy firing at close range. In getting the wounded back to our lines they were met by another party of the enemy who attempted to stop them. Pte. Morris killed two of the enemy and, by covering the retirement of the party, succeeded in getting them back to our lines in safety. On September 29, at Bony, his car was hit and took fire. In making his way back to our lines he heard that Pte. Sheard (whose car had also been knocked out by a direct hit) had been left badly wounded. He immediately went back under very heavy fire and brought Pte. Sheard to a place of safety. He said nothing about it at the time and the details were only ascertained at a later date.

309255 Pte. SUMMERSBY, STANLEY. 17th Battn. (A.C.). Awarded M.M.

In the Forêt de Mormal, near Landrecies, on November 4, 1918, this soldier displayed great gallantry and devotion to duty. The armoured car he was driving was hit and ran into the ditch when about 800 yards in front of our leading infantry. Although the car was continually fired at by the enemy, Pte. Summersby, knowing that the car was urgently required to protect our infantry, worked with greatest gallantry and skill until he succeeded in getting his car into action again.

309106 Pte. MAY, ARTHUR. 17th Battn. (A.C.). Awarded M.M.

For great gallantry and devotion to duty during the advance from Catillon to Liessies from November 4 to 11, 1918. As driver of an armoured car, which continued fighting by itself after the other car of his section had been disabled, he showed a gallant spirit during a trying time, particularly at Haut Lieu, when his car got ditched within 150 yards of the enemy, who opened fire with machine-gun and shell. He worked under fire with great gallantry to get his car back on the road so that it could again assist our infantry.

305531 Pte. PAYNE, FREDERICK GEORGE. 6th Battn. Awarded M.M.

During an attack by a light tank company near Bavai, on November 5, 1918, he showed the greatest bravery and disregard of danger. Although behind the enemy front line, he got out to rectify mechanical trouble.

When his driver was hit he bound him up, and then endeavoured to bring forward the infantry to take advantage of the situation. He displayed rare initiative and powers of leadership for a private soldier.

304850 Pte. SHIELDS, WILLIAM. 17th Battn. (A.C.). Awarded M.M.

At Taisnieres, on November 6, this soldier displayed great gallantry and devotion to duty. When his armoured car was hit by enemy's machine-guns and ran into the ditch in such a way that his guns could not fire, he displayed great initiative in getting his gun out of the car and mounting it on a bank to fire at the enemy, who were trying to reach the car. He remained there and protected his crew while they worked to get the car on the road again. Pte. Shields has on many occasions shown a fine example of courage and resource.

78500 A.M.S. Sergt. DANIEL, REGINALD. 17th Battn. (A.C.). Awarded M.M.

During the advance from Landrecies to Avesnes, on November 7, this N.C.O. displayed gallantry, skill, and devotion to duty, and rendered most valuable services at a critical time in maintaining the mechanical efficiency of, and in salving under fire, armoured cars which had been temporarily put out of action by the enemy. To his resource and technical skill this battalion is indebted for armoured cars which were kept in action at a time when they were most valuable. On many occasions this N.C.O. has carried out repairs to armoured cars under fire.

92124 Pte. BALL, GEORGE. 17th Battn. (A.C.). Awarded M.M.

At Taisnieres, on November 7 and 8, this soldier displayed great gallantry, resource, and devotion to duty in salving armoured cars which were disabled by the enemy's fire. He has frequently rendered valuable service in repairing armoured cars under fire in the most difficult situations.

304341 Pte. THOMSON, CHARLES. 17th Battn. (A.C.). Awarded M.M.

At Taisnieres, on November 6, this soldier displayed great gallantry and devotion to duty, when his armoured car was hit by enemy's machine-guns and ran into the ditch in such a way that his guns could not fire. Without the slightest hesitation he got out of the car and mounted his gun on a bank, and engaged a party of the enemy who were firing a machine-gun at the car. Pte. Thomson has on many occasions shown a fine example of courage and resource.

304860 Pte. MOORHEAD, ROBERT ANDREW. 17th Battn. (A.C.). Awarded M.M.

For gallantry and devotion to duty during the advance from Catillon to Liessies, and particularly on November 9 at Haut Lieu, when his car was ditched within 150 yards of the enemy's position and was fired on by both machine-gun and shell fire. Although the car was under direct observation, this soldier, knowing that the armoured car was urgently wanted to protect our infantry, set a fine example and showed great gallantry in working under fire to get the car back into action.

205225 Pte. BEESLEY, ROBERT PERCY. 17th Battn. (A.C.). Awarded M.M.

For great gallantry and devotion to duty during continuous fighting from June 10 up to cessation of hostilities, November 11. This soldier has acted as despatch rider to the armoured cars. Without the protection which the armoured cars possess, he has taken despatches to them in the most exposed positions, having on one occasion, August 9, been wounded and still carried on. His determination in getting to his objective is most marked. He has never failed to deliver his despatch under any circumstances.

305018 Pte. (L/Cpl.) YOUNG, GEORGE. 14th Battn. Awarded M.M.

For conspicuous gallantry and marked determination and devotion to duty.

Although gassed, this N.C.O. fought his 6-pndr. gun with marked skill, and after it had been put out of action by hostile fire he calmly continued to repair it, though the tank was being subjected to very heavy machine-gun fire at very close range, one machine-gun being only from some ten to twenty yards away, causing a continuous shower of splinters to enter the tank from all sides, and during which time one Bosche was actually on top of the tank.

78354 Cpl. BARRETT, BERT. 8th Battn. Awarded M.M.

This N.C.O. has been in many tank engagements. Throughout each action he has set a fine example to the remainder of his crew by his great coolness and devotion to duty under most trying circumstances.

91892 L/Cpl. WELHAM, ARTHUR GEORGE. 8th Battn. Awarded M.M.

For exceptionally good and meritorious service. This N.C.O. has been in many tank actions, both as a gunner and driver, and has at all times, by his coolness under fire and his devotion to duty, set a really fine example to the remainder of his crew.

FOREIGN DECORATIONS

75540 Cpl. TAYLOR, GEORGE HOSBURGH, D.C.M., M.M. 4th Battn. Awarded Médaille Militaire.

For marked gallantry and devotion to duty. At Chapel Hill, south of Gouzeaucourt, on March 21, 1918, after his officer and all his crew, with the exception of one, had become casualties, he collected three infantrymen to work the Lewis guns and drove his tank into action on two occasions, in spite of extremely heavy shell fire directed against the tank. On each occasion he drove back the enemy's infantry and inflicted heavy casualties. It was only after three of his guns had been put out of action and two of the infantry Lewis gunners had become casualties that he brought his tank out of action. His courage, initiative, and devotion to duty were beyond all praise.

77055 Cpl. MURLSY, WILLIAM GEORGE, D.C.M. 1st Battn. Awarded Croix de Guerre.

For most conspicuous gallantry and devotion to duty while in charge of a Lewis gun team on ridge north-west of Bray on March 26, 1918.

On above date this N.C.O. was one of the Lewis gun company detailed to check the enemy and cover the infantry withdrawal at the above-mentioned place. On the infantry withdrawal being completed, O.C. company found both flanks were enveloped, and ordered an immediate withdrawal. Cpl. Murlsy volunteered to cover the withdrawal with his gun. He remained firing at either flank until his ammunition was exhausted and the withdrawal of to the company was complete. He was subjected to very heavy rifle, machine-gun, and shell fire. He withdrew his gun intact and rejoined his company later in the day. Throughout the day this N.C.O.'s courage and coolness were of the greatest value.

IMMEDIATE AWARDS—OTHER RANKS

70019 Cpl. ARCHBOLD, SIDNEY, D.C.M. 5th Battn. Awarded Médaille Militaire.

For conspicuous gallantry, March 29 and 30, near Warfusée-Abancourt, when a member of a Lewis gun detachment under 2nd Lieut. H. W. Whyte. This N.C.O. worked a Lewis gun single-handed during the period of March 29–30.

He carried the gun and ammunition to a new position, fired the gun, and loaded his magazines without assistance for twenty-four hours, during which period he assisted in breaking up two attacks.

On March 30 this N.C.O. was wounded in the head by a sniper, but he continued to work his gun all day until ordered by his officer to the dressing station.

7618 Pte. DRISSE, PETER HENRY. Central Workshops. Awarded Médaille d'Honneur avec Glaives en Bronze.

In the absence of an official interpreter, Pte. Drisse rendered valuable assistance in liaison work between French and British subjects, thus amicably settling local disputes to the satisfaction of both parties.

He further rendered much help during the months of March and April of this year, when some 9000 French refugees were accommodated at Central Workshops, sparing neither time nor trouble in attending to their many wants and replying to their numerous inquiries.

200043 C.S.M. ROBERTSON, DONALD, D.C.M. 1st Battn. Awarded Médaille d'Honneur avec Glaives en Argent.

For conspicuous good service and devotion to duty throughout the operations in which his company has been engaged during the past seven months.

During the fighting in March and April 1918 he carried on his duties with great self-sacrifice and regardless of personal risk, supervising the carrying up of rations and supplies for the crews and making provisions for the relief and comfort of the men who had been in action.

In the same way during the recent operations he followed up closely with the reserve men and made all possible provision for the tank personnel.

On numerous occasions he has asked to go into action in tanks and has always acted in the most gallant and devoted way.

302654 Pte. THOMPSON, HERBERT. Central Workshops. Awarded Médaille d'Honneur avec Glaives en Bronze.

During March and April, when some 9000 French refugees from the Nœux-les-Mines sector were accommodated at Central

Workshops, Pte. Thompson, in addition to his regular duties, did all in his power to cater for the feeding and comfort of these unfortunate people. He showed throughout the utmost interest, and cheerfulness in carrying out his duties.

201659 M/S/Sergt. SYKES, FRANK, D.C.M. 1st Field Coy. Awarded Médaille d'Honneur avec Glaives en Argent.

During the action near Mailly-Raineval on July 23, 1918, whilst 9th Tank Battalion were operating with the IX French Corps, M/S/S. Sykes showed the greatest gallantry in proceeding under heavy hostile shell fire to a tank which had been temporarily put out of action by a direct hit; he, after investigating the damage, returned on foot, still under heavy enemy fire, and obtained assistance of mechanics and led them to the disabled tank, and through the efforts of this party the tank was again put into fighting condition. During the whole time this warrant officer showed an excellent example of courage and devotion to duty, with an utter disregard for his personal safety.

76177 Sergt. EVANS, ARTHUR. 1st Field Coy. Awarded Croix de Guerre avec Etoile Vermeil.

During the operations with the IX French Corps, between Morueil and Mailly-Raineval, on July 23, 1918, Sergt. Evans proceeded under heavy hostile shell and machine-gun fire to a tank which was flying the distress flag.

He personally remedied the break-down, and owing to his untiring efforts the tank was enabled to again proceed into action. Sergt. Evans throughout the action showed splendid initiative and was of the greatest assistance to his unit; the whole time he showed an utter contempt of danger and worked most gallantly under very trying circumstances, having been wounded in the arm early in the action.

92836 Sergt. STRANG, JOHN, D.C.M. and Bar. 1st Gun Carrier Coy. Awarded Chevalier de L'Ordre de Leopold II.

During the fire caused by enemy shell fire amongst seventeen gun carrier tanks at O.29.b. (Villers-Bretonneux) on the evening of August 7, 1918, Sergt. Strang showed the utmost bravery and coolness in rescuing a tank out of the blaze. The tanks were loaded with explosives for the infantry—gun-cotton, bombs, trench mortars, &c., besides two fills of petrol each. Although subjected to violent explosions every moment, one of which blew the door off the cabin he was seated in, this gallant N.C.O. continued to drive the tank through intense shell fire to a position of security. It was through his coolness and total disregard for his own personal safety and fine example to his crew that this tank was saved from certain destruction.

308950 Pte. MURRAY, JAMES. 4th Battn. Awarded Médaille d'Honneur avec Glaives en Bronze.

For conspicuous gallantry and devotion to duty on August 8, 1918, when in action at Hangard.

Although partially overcome by fumes inside the tank, and his second gunner being wounded, he single-handed continued to serve his 6-pdr. gun, handling it so skilfully that he inflicted severe losses upon the enemy machine-gunners.

Subsequently, although wounded himself and suffering much pain and being almost exhausted, he still insisted upon continuing to serve his gun until the final objective was reached.

111527 L/Cpl. BUCHANAN, JOHN, M.M. 5th Battn. Awarded Médaille d'Honneur avec Glaives en Bronze.

Displayed great gallantry near Villiers-aux-Erables on August 8, 1918, when a member of the crew of a tank working with 42nd French Division. When the tank finally received two direct hits and was set on fire, this N.C.O. at great personal risk rescued his tank commander from the blazing tank under heavy fire.

40079 Pte. BROWN, PERCIVAL VICTOR. 1st Battn. Awarded Médaille d'Honneur avec Glaives en Bronze.

For conspicuous bravery in action on August 8, and for great skill in driving his tank.

Although having to negotiate a thick wood under heavy fire he showed remarkable coolness and bravery. It was entirely due to his driving that the tank was enabled to reach and wipe out several enemy machine-gun posts, and inflict heavy casualties on him.

In previous actions he has always displayed the same skill and gallantry, and set a splendid example to his crew.

76226 Sergt. DRINKWATER, GEORGE, D.C.M. 4th Battn. Awarded Médaille Militaire.

Acting as Hotchkiss gunner during August 8 and 9, he destroyed several machine-gun crews and kept his gun going incessantly, picking up targets with great skill. He maintained fire against a nest of six hostile machine-guns which were firing armour-piercing bullets at his tank. When in action at Beaufort Wood on August 9 a shell struck his tank on one side, breaking his arm ; he managed to fire from the other side of the tank until the roof of the tank was smashed in by another shell, disabling the rest of the crew.

Wounded for the second time he still continued to assist his tank commander, and with indomitable spirit he continued to rally his wounded comrades until their tank had been placed out of further danger.

92791 Pte. WALKER, ALBERT. 6th Battn. Awarded Médaille Militaire.

During the fighting on August 8 he displayed unusual initiative. He drove his tank with the observing flap open for an hour under intense fire, refusing to close it. Later, when his officer was killed, he took command of the tank and controlled the guns with marked success during very difficult fighting.

M1/09251 L/Cpl. CARRESS, EDWARD. 4th Bde. M.T. Coy. Awarded Médaille d'Honneur avec Glaives en Argent.

During a period covering over three days from August 8, 1918 this N.C.O., who was in charge of the lorry carrying maintenance stores and tools for the 5th Tank Battalion, performed extremely good work in finding and then bringing up supplies and spares to disabled tanks. He managed to bring his lorry up to several broken-down tanks under heavy fire, and worked continuously, driving and assisting in repairs to tanks, for over three days without a break.

110075 Pte. DICKENSON, GEORGE WILLIAM, D.C.M. 10th Battn. Awarded Belgian Decoration Militaire.

In Gressaire Wood, on August 9, 1918, this man showed conspicuous gallantry and skill in repairing his tank after it had been set on fire. His officer had been killed and his first driver wounded. This man put out the fire and repaired the leads although closely surrounded by the enemy all the time. He then drove his tank through the enemy and brought in fifty of them as prisoners.

76304 Cpl. CLARK, WILLIAM, D.C.M. 4th Battn. Awarded Decoration Militaire.

For conspicuous gallantry in action on August 9, 1918, near Beaufort. Leaving his tank he ran across the open under heavy machine-gun and rifle fire, and drove away the crew of an anti-tank gun which was preparing to fire on a section of tanks, thereby saving several of them direct hits. He brought back over twenty prisoners from rifle pits near the gun.

305636 Pte. KING, WILLIAM GEORGE, D.C.M. 13th Battn. Awarded Decoration Militaire.

For conspicuous gallantry and devotion to duty near Hallu on August 10, 1918.

During an attack the tank in which this man was acting as

gunner became ditched in one of the old Somme trenches. The tank at this time was about 600 yards ahead of our infantry. Some twenty machine-guns were immediately concentrated on the tank, which was riddled with armour-piercing bullets, wounding the whole of the crew. Pte. King, although wounded, continued to fire until all ammunition had been expended. When the enemy called upon the tank commander to surrender, this man assisted his officer to defend the tank with revolvers. The enemy were at length forced to retire by our infantry coming up three-quarters of an hour later.

Pte. King had previously done exceptionally well during an attack on August 8, when, with his tank commander, he guided the tank in a thick mist among enemy strong points.

200867 L/Cpl. LAWRENCE, JOSEPH BARRON, D.C.M. 4th Battn. Awarded Croix de Guerre.

For most conspicuous gallantry and devotion to duty when in action near Bois Sud, north-west of Damery, on August 10, 1918. This N.C.O., although seriously wounded (his tank being hit by a hostile shell, which wounded the whole of the crew), with the greatest determination continued to drive his tank against an enemy machine-gun position until it was again hit and set on fire. Even then he continued to remain at his post, and although in great danger assisted in extinguishing the flames until he became exhausted through loss of blood.

76906 Cpl. DAVIS, WILLIAM JOHN. 4th Battn. Awarded Médaille Militaire.

This N.C.O. displayed conspicuous gallantry when in command of a tank in action in the vicinity of Méaulte, on August 22, 1918. When, owing to the heavy mist and smoke from the shells, it became almost impossible to keep direction, this N.C.O. immediately got out of his tank and guided from in front, although under heavy hostile machine-gun fire from almost point-blank range.

He showed total disregard of danger, frequently going across to the infantry and supplying them with information as to what obstacles were in front of them.

Unfortunately, his tank received a direct hit from hostile gunfire before it reached its objective, but he succeeded in getting the infantry to which he was attached in touch with another tank on their flank.

92995 Pte. BUSSEY, BERTIE FREDERICK, D.C.M. 6th Battn. Awarded Decoration Militaire.

For conspicuous gallantry and devotion to duty in action on August 23, 1918, near Bihucourt. At the commencement of the action his officer and sergeant were both wounded, leaving him the only unwounded man in the tank. After placing the wounded in a safe place outside the tank, Pte. Bussey carried on through the action by himself. He directed the tank towards the enemy, and locking the steering he left the tank to steer itself while he served both guns. This he continued to do for four hours, eventually bringing his tank safely out of action.

Pte. Bussey showed a fine example of determination and resource.

95459 Sergt. ROBERTS, JOHN HUGH, D.C.M. 12th Battn.
Awarded Decoration Militaire.

During the action on Gomiecourt, on August 23, this N.C.O.'s tank received a direct hit which killed both officer and driver and wounded the remainder of the crew. Sergt. Roberts then evacuated the tank, carrying out the badly wounded. He saw to the bandaging of all the wounded, going back to the tank for the surgical haversack and shell dressings. All the time the tank was under rifle and machine-gun fire. At this moment he was joined by an officer from another tank which had also been put out of action. Together they formed a Lewis-gun post, and by crawling and dragging the gun and ammunition along the ground they got to within thirty yards of a party of Germans. On trying to get the gun into action, Sergt. Roberts found that a shell splinter had rendered it useless. He thereupon stood up and emptied his revolver into the enemy, wounding several and causing the remainder to retire. In company with the officer he then crawled back to the nearest infantry unit. On the way they came across two badly wounded men of this battalion, one of whom was unable to move, having a wounded arm and fractured thigh. Sergt. Roberts helped to carry them back to the shelter of a trench.

At all times he showed an utter disregard for his own safety and did not hesitate to expose himself if such was necessary to help the others.

305379 Gnr. PERRY, PATRICK JOSEPH, D.C.M. 11th Battn.
Awarded Decoration Militaire.

Conspicuous gallantry and devotion to duty on August 24, 1918, in the attack on Hindenburg Line east of Croisilles. His tank was ditched in a sunken road and on fire from phosphorous bombs fired by the enemy. Gnr. Perry stayed in the tank with his officer (Lieut. Walsh) and put out the fire. The fumes being too bad to stay in the tank, Gnr. Perry and Lieut. Walsh turned the tank for home in bottom speed and walked home just in front of it. All this time the tank was surrounded by enemy. Lieut. Walsh was exhausted and would undoubtedly have collapsed if it had not been for Gnr. Perry forcibly keeping him going. When not getting his officer along he was firing his revolver at the enemy all round the tank. The tank and Gnr. Perry and Lieut. Walsh all got home.

112006 Sergt. HATTON, PERCY EDWARD, D.C.M. 11th Battn. Awarded Chevalier de L'Ordre de Leopold II.

Conspicuous gallantry and devotion to duty at Monchy on August 26, 1918.

After an approach march of 20,000 yards his tank was called on by the infantry to go forward and attack some strong points. Having cleared these strong points, his tank got ditched, and although standing nearly on its side he went on covering the advance with his 6-pndr. and knocked out an anti-tank gun which was shooting at his tank. When the tank was at such an angle that he could no longer use his gun, he and his crew left the tank and formed a strong point outside it, still in advance of the infantry. Meanwhile the infantry had reached their final objective for the day—100 yards behind the tank. Some hours later the enemy counter-attacked and got into Sergt. Hatton's tank. He promptly charged with his crew and turned them out of the tank, killing one German.

He had formed the strong point some little way from the tank, and on several occasions went back to the tank for more ammunition and rations for his crew, quite regardless of enemy machine-gun fire. He stayed out in this strong point in advance of the infantry for twenty-four hours at the request of the infantry, and all this time showed a magnificent example to his crew who, after driving and fighting for twenty-four hours continuously, were exhausted. On his return Sergt. Hatton asked to be allowed to go and try again to get his tank out.

Sergt. Hatton is forty-eight years of age.

200045 Cpl. SPICER, MALCOLM DOUGLAS. 1st Battn. Awarded Médaille d'Honneur avec Glaives en Argent.

As a driver in the corps, Cpl. Spicer has always shown a wonderful example for gallantry and devotion to duty. He has taken part in all the tank actions since the formation of the corps.

In every action he has worked with untiring energy to get his tank in perfect fighting condition.

Cpl. Spicer has always shown the greatest coolness under fire and inspired the utmost confidence in the rest of his crew.

76055 Pte. (D/R.) HOLT, REGINALD. 1st Battn. Awarded Croix de Guerre.

For gallantry and great devotion to duty as a temporary despatch-rider in actions ranging over two years. Pte. Holt has always delivered his despatches, frequently under heavy artillery and

413

machine-gun fire. On two occasions he delivered them to tanks when on the point of engaging the enemy.

On many occasions he has collected and brought back, on his own initiative, valuable information at times when other means of communication were not available.

His never-failing cheerfulness and his great devotion to duty have always been exhibited in the highest degree.

201769 Sergt. HARRISON, CHARLES NORMAN. D. and M. School. Awarded Médaille d'Honneur avec Glaives en Argent.

This N.C.O. has been with the Mechanical School since its formation and has done exceptionally good work as assistant instructor throughout.

110302 Cook Sergt. COHEN, SAMUEL. T. and R. Depôt. Awarded Médaille d'Honneur avec Glaives en Argent.

A fine example of generous work productive of high results.

His work has showed considerable economies, and from his cookery instruction his corps has received distinct benefits.

200439 B.Q.M.S. PHILLIPS, ALBERT HENRY. 3rd Battn. Awarded Médaille d'Honneur avec Glaives en Vermeil.

This warrant officer during the recent operations near Amiens rendered valuable services in keeping up the supply of tank spares and equipment which were urgently required to keep the tanks of the battalion in action.

Throughout the operations he displayed most exceptional ability and zeal, and it was greatly due to his efforts that so many tanks were kept fit for action.

75200 Sergt. CROSS, ERNEST MARK. 1st Battn. Awarded Médaille d'Honneur avec Glaives en Argent.

For conspicuous devotion to duty throughout the last four years in France. Sergt. Cross has been with the battalion since its formation and has never been absent from duty. His untiring energy and his wonderful grasp of official routine have been of the utmost value. His unfailing capability and his knowledge have never been so exemplified as in the recent operations, and are deserving of the utmost praise.

200599 C.Q.M.S. GALT, HECTOR JAMES. 3rd Battn. Awarded Médaille d'Honneur avec Glaives en Bronze.

Throughout the recent operations near Amiens this N.C.O. showed remarkable organising ability and did extremely valuable work in keeping his company supplied with rations during the fighting.

During the absence of the regimental sergeant-major through sickness he performed the duties with ability and zeal.

200860 Pte. EMSLEY, ALBERT EDWARD. 4th Battn. Awarded Médaille d'Honneur avec Glaives en Bronze.

For devotion to duty while acting as orderly to the battalion reconnaissance officer.

For the past two years this man has invariably accompanied the battalion reconnaissance officer when the latter has been reconnoitring ground previous to an operation.

During this period he has always shown great ability and conducted himself with great coolness in situations involving considerable personal danger. His work has been of an unusually high order.

201917 B.S.M. BIRD, RICHARD. School of Gunnery. Awarded Médaille d'Honneur avec Glaives en Vermeil.

This warrant officer has been the sergeant-major in charge of the 6-pndr. School, and has done notably meritorious work in organising the instruction of the large classes that have passed through the school.

ROLL OF HONOUR

OFFICERS AND OTHER RANKS OF THE TANK CORPS
KILLED IN ACTION OR DIED OF WOUNDS

'For their name endureth for evermore.'

OFFICERS

Name.	Substantive Rank.	Town.
ADNEY. . . .	Lieut.	Sonwen, Lancs.
ALLAN, J . . .	Lieut.	Aberdeen
ASSER, L. E. . .	2nd Lieut.	Herne Bay
ATKINSON, M. L. .	2nd Lieut.	Leamington Spa
ATKINSON, W. E. .	2nd Lieut.	Southport
BALL, J. . . .	2nd Lieut.	Mapperley
BATES, L. G.. . .	Lieut.	Cork Hill
BAYLISS, P. B. . .	2nd Lieut.	Sparkhill
BELL, H. R. . .	2nd Lieut.	Bickley
BERRY, J. L. . .	T. Lieut.	Carnoustie
BIGARD, M. . . .	2nd Lieut.	Glasgow
BIRNIE, W. J. G. . .	Lieut.	—
BLACK, G. . . .	Lieut.	London
BLACK, J. . . .	Lieut.	Wigtown
BLACKWOOD, W. L. .	Lieut.	—
BOAG, H. E. . . .	2nd Lieut.	West Ealing
BONE, C. J. . .	2nd Lieut.	Westcliff-on-Sea
BOWN, C. W. . .	Lieut.	Yeovil
BRADBURY, A. . .	Lieut.	Manchester
BRASSINGTON, W. H. .	Lieut.	Settle
BROWN, E. M. . .	Lieut.	Isleworth
BROWN, J. C. . .	Lieut.	Dundalk
BROWN, W. A. R.. .	2nd Lieut.	Edinburgh
CAESAR, G. T. . .	2nd Lieut.	Streatham
CARR, F. C. . . .	2nd Lieut.	Birmingham
CARROLL, J. C. . .	Lieut.	Blackheath
CARTWRIGHT, E. M. .	2nd Lieut.	Bromley (Kent)
CASSELS, H. L. . .	2nd Lieut.	London
CHAMBERS, P. C. . .	2nd Lieut.	Finchley
CHARLTON, B. . .	2nd Lieut.	Streatham
CHRISTIAN, A. . .	2nd Lieut.	Brockley

Name.	Substantive Rank.	Town.
CHRISTOPHER, R.	T. Lieut.	Monkseaton
CLEGG, L.	Lieut.	London
COE, H. J.	2nd Lieut.	Kenley
COLEMAN, E.	2nd Lieut.	Wakefield
COLLEY, E. V.	Lieut.	Hove
CORDNER, J. H.	Lieut.	Belfast
COTTLE, S. J.	Lieut.	—
COURT, G. F.	Lieut.	Herne Bay
CURTIS, W. C.	2nd Lieut.	Wallop
DALE, H.	2nd Lieut.	Petworth
DAVENPORT, A.	2nd Lieut.	Oxford
DAVIDSON, W. M.	Lieut.	Aberdeen
DAVIES, D. J.	Lieut.	—
DAVIES, H. P.	2nd Lieut.	—
DAWES, W. H. G.	2nd Lieut.	Manchester
DE FAYE, E. F.	2nd Lieut.	Jersey
DESPARD, E. R.	2nd Lieut.	Queen's Co
DUCKETT, H. A.	2nd Lieut.	—
DUNCAN, C. W.	Lieut.	—
DUNMAN, C. N. I.	Lieut.	Chelsea
ECKLEY, F. G.	2nd Lieut.	Bristol
EDWARDES, Hon. C.	Lieut.	London
EHRHARDT, J. A.	2nd Lieut.	Birmingham
ELLIS, J. C.	2nd Lieut.	Leicester
EMERY, G. W.	2nd Lieut.	London
EVANS, L. A.	2nd Lieut.	London
FERGUSON, T. J.	2nd Lieut.	Glasgow
FLANEGAN, L. C.	Lieut.	Clacton-on-Sea
FOSSETT, R. G.	2nd Lieut.	Streatham
FRANKENSTEIN, G. J.	2nd Lieut.	Broughton
FRASER, E. L.	2nd Lieut.	London
GALSWORTHY, E.	2nd Lieut.	Appledore
GATFIELD, R. A.	Lieut.	—
GATWARD, F. J.	2nd Lieut.	Cambridge
GIBSON, J. W.	2nd Lieut.	Mansfield
GLAISTER, G. F.	Lieut.	Preston
GLASSCOCK, S. F.	Lieut.	Forest Hill
GODFREY, N. C.	2nd Lieut.	Weston-super-Mare
GOODWIN, J. S.	2nd Lieut.	—
GOWER, F. J. H.	2nd Lieut.	Layfield

ROLL OF HONOUR

Name.	Substantive Rank.	Town.
GRATWICK, P. C. . .	Lieut.	—
GREEN, J. G. A. . .	2nd Lieut.	North Kensington
GREEN, T. W. . .	2nd Lieut.	Liverpool
GREGSON, W. . .	2nd Lieut.	Preston (Lancs.)
GREY, J. . . .	2nd Lieut.	Dundee .
GROVE, C. F. S. . .	Lieut.	New Malden
GUMMER, F. . .	2nd Lieut.	Cardiff
HAINING, W. S. . .	2nd Lieut.	Prestwick
HANNAN, J. M. A. .	2nd Lieut.	—
HARDING, S. C. . .	2nd Lieut.	Leicester
HASELER, W. H. . .	Lieut.	Birmingham
HAWKINS, K. J. . .	2nd Lieut.	Sutton (Surrey)
HENDERSON, T. . .	2nd Lieut.	Cork
HEYWOOD, H. . .	Lieut.	West Hampstead
HILL, B. E. . . .	T. Capt.	Bournemouth
HOLT, F. H. . . .	2nd Lieut.	London
HOPKINS, H. G. B. .	Lieut.	—
HOWARD, E. S. . .	2nd Lieut.	Woodhouse (Yorks)
HOWELLS, J. E. . .	2nd Lieut.	Mountain Ash
HULTON, B. W. . .	2nd Lieut.	Oldham
HUME, A. J. . . .	2nd Lieut.	London
HUMPHREYS, N. F. ·	T. Capt.	Tow Law (Durham)
JAMIESON, W. O. . .	Lieut.	Darvel
JEFFERIES, R. O. G.	Lieut.	Guildford
JENKINS, K. G. . .	Lieut.	—
JONES, H. P. M. . .	Lieut.	—
JONES, R. A. . .	2nd Lieut.	Pontardulais
KEOGH, F. B. . .	Lieut.	Baldoyle
KEPPEL-PALMER, S. L.	Lieut.	Johnstone
KINGWELL, H. R. .	Lieut.	London
KLEE, A. M. . .	2nd Lieut.	Old Charlton
KNIGHT, G. ST. J. . .	Lieut.	London
LARKINS, L. H. . .	T. Capt.	London
LAWRIE, A. R. . .	Lieut.	Kirkintilloch
LAZONBY, J. C. . .	2nd Lieut.	Manchester
LEACH, S. . . .	2nd Lieut.	Wavertree
LEEK, M. F. W. . .	Lieut.	Alsager (Cheshire)
LEES, J. L. . . .	Lieut.	Belfast
LEGGE, R. C. . .	Lieut.	Lindfield
LETHEBE, H. T. . .	Lieut.	Hammersmith

Name.	Substantive Rank.	Town.
LEY, G. A. H.	2nd Lieut.	— .
LINDEN, N. E.	2nd Lieut.	Waterval, Boden, S. Africa
LONGTHORPE, F..	2nd Lieut.	Bradford
LORD, E. J.	2nd Lieut.	Leicester
LYNCH, J. W.	2nd Lieut.	Liscard (Cheshire)
MACARTNEY, T. H.	2nd Lieut.	—
McCOULL, W. S.	Lieut.	—
MACFADYEN, J. D.	Lieut.	Letchworth
McLEAN, G. D.	Lieut.	Ottawa
MANN, G. W.	T. Major	Wimbledon
MANSFIELD, H. J..	A/Capt.	London, N.
MARCH-PHILLIPS, S. L.	2nd Lieut.	Exeter
MARCHANT, F. S.	Lieut.	Newcastle-on-Tyne
MARSHALL, H. G. H.	2nd Lieut.	Glasgow
MARSHALL, J. A..	2nd Lieut.	—
MARTIN, R. .	2nd Lieut.	Edinburgh
MATHESON, M. A..	A/Capt.	Dufftown
MAY, F. H. .	2nd Lieut.	Clevedon (Somerset)
MEUGENS, G. E.	Major	Kensington, W.
MILLAR, W..	2nd Lieut.	Dumfries
MISKIN, M. J.	Lieut.	—
MONAGHAN, D. L.	T. Capt.	West Ealing
MORGAN, C. J.	2nd Lieut.	Belfast
MUIRHEAD, J. L..	T. Capt.	Glasgow
MUMBY, H. C.	2nd Lieut.	Sale (Cheshire)
MURRAY MENZIES,D.L.	Lieut.	—
NELSON, T. A.	Capt.	—
NEWSOM, H. B.	2nd Lieut.	Andover
NORWOOD, R. H..	2nd Lieut.	Fulham
OGDEN, W. F.	2nd Lieut.	Harrogate
O'SHEA, D. T.	2nd Lieut.	London
PALMER, D. A.	Lieut.	—
PAYNE, J. R. S.	Lieut.	Kirkoswald
PHILLIPS, W.	2nd Lieut.	Bristol
PILGRIM, S. A. F..	2nd Lieut.	Colne (Lancs)
POQUE, R. T.	2nd Lieut.	Salisbury
PORTEOUS, T. W..	2nd Lieut.	Middlesbrough
PORTER, J. C.	2nd Lieut.	London
PORTER, J. W.	2nd Lieut.	Tooting

Name.	Substantive Rank.	Town.
POWER, L. H.	2nd Lieut.	London
PURVES, T. H.	2nd Lieut.	Edinburgh
RANKIN, F. A.	2nd Lieut.	—
READY, N. H. A.	2nd Lieut.	Long Stratton
RILEY, J. S.	Lieut.	Accrington
ROBERTS, C. A.	2nd Lieut.	Huddersfield
ROBERTSON, C.	T. Lieut.	—
ROBINSON, F. A.	T. Capt.	Seven Kings
ROBINSON, W.	2nd Lieut.	Hull
RODDAN, R.	2nd Lieut.	Crewe
RODGERS, J. R.	Lieut.	—
RUSSELL, W.	2nd Lieut.	Nottingham
RUTHERFORD, M.	2nd Lieut.	Leeds
RYRIE, A.	Lieut.	Glasgow
SAILEARD, P.	Lieut.	—
SANES, G. F.	2nd Lieut.	Blackburn
SCOTT, E. E.	Lieut.	Nottingham
SEDDON, H.	2nd Lieut.	Leigh (Lancs)
SEWELL, C. H.	Lieut.	—
SEYMOUR, B.	2nd Lieut.	York
SHACKLETON, H.	Lieut.	Halifax
SHARP, A. A. C.	2nd Lieut.	Parkstone (Dorset)
SLADE, S. H.	T. Lieut.	Bristol
SMITH, F. H.	2nd Lieut.	Abersychan (Mon.)
SMITH, H. T. B.	2nd Lieut.	—
SMITH, S. H.	2nd Lieut.	Donaghmore
SPENCER, H. B.	T. Lieut.	—
SPRAY, A.	T. Capt.	Cheetham, Manchester
STAINSBY, T. C.	2nd Lieut.	Darlington
STEVENS, G. G.	Lieut.	Glasgow
STOCKLEY, W. E.	Lieut.	London, N.
STOKES, H.	2nd Lieut.	Boscombe
STORM, J. N.	2nd Lieut.	Doncaster
SWEARS, H. M.	Lieut.	Totnes (Devon)
TALBOT, F. C.	2nd Lieut.	London
TARBOT, W. D.	2nd Lieut.	—
TESTI, G.	2nd Lieut.	Rotherham
TRAFFORD, G. T.	Lieut.	Rosetta (Natal)
TRIPE, A. K.	Lieut.	Plymouth
TUCKER, L. A.	2nd Lieut.	Alton (Hants)
TUITE, M. A. W.	2nd Lieut.	Dulwich
TURNER, J.	2nd Lieut.	Glasgow

Name.	Substantive Rank.	Town.
VARDY, M.	2nd Lieut.	London
VIVEASH, W. H.	Lieut.	Lower Slaughter (Glos)
WAIN, R. W. L.	2nd Lieut.	—
WAKEFIELD, S. C.	2nd Lieut.	London, N.W.
WALSER, G. P.	2nd Lieut.	York
WALKER, T. P. P.	2nd Lieut.	Blackheath
WARD, R. O. C.	T. Major	London
WARD, S. R.	Lieut.	Bermuda
WEIGHTS, J. H.	2nd Lieut.	Chester
WEST, R. A.	Capt. (A/Lt.-Col.)	London
WHITE, W. C.	Lieut.	Romsey (Hants)
WILD, B. W.	Lieut.	London
WILDE, H.	Lieut.	Broughton (Lancs)
WILSON, A. S.	2nd Lieut.	—
WILSON, T. R.	2nd Lieut.	Shifnal (Shropshire)
WITTER, H.	2nd Lieut.	Southport
WOOD, N. C.	T. Lieut.	Kamloops, B.C., Canada
WOOD, R. B.	A. Major	London
WRIGHT, W. T. C.	2nd Lieut.	Plumstead
WYLLIE, A. T.	Lieut.	Kilmarnock

Total of Officers killed or died of wounds, 212.

OTHER RANKS

Number.	Name and Initials.	Rank.	Town of Residence.
305102	ABSON, C.	Pte.	Chelsea
307679	ADAMS, J.	,,	Aldershot
110296	ADAMS, J. A.	,,	Longford
309966	ADAMS, W. B.	,,	Virginia, U.S.A.
201054	ADAMSON, E. C.	Cpl.	Sunderland
76386	ADSATT, A. H.	,,	Burford, Oxon.
200019	AFFLICK, R.	L/Cpl.	Stow, Midlothian
301902	AINSWORTH, H.	Cpl.	Horwich
307712	AIRSY, J.	Pte.	Oldham
78870	ALDER, W. G.	,,	Swindon
78918	ALDERMAN, T.	,,	Melton Mowbray
206125	ALLAN, A.	,,	Perth
75747	ALLAN, W.	,,	Dundee
200864	ALLEBONE, H. A.	,,	Rushden
200195	ALLEN, C. S.	,,	Doncaster

ROLL OF HONOUR

Number.	Name and Initials.		Rank.	Town of Residence.
200125	ALLEN, F. A.	.	L/Cpl.	Hampton
75377	ALLINGHAM, W.	.	Sergt.	Fay Gate
301626	ALLISON, W. .	.	Pte.	Stoneycroft
111430	ALSTON, R. .	.	,,	Oldham
95653	ALTY, T. .	.	,,	Southport
107696	ALTY, T. .	.	A/Cpl.	Wigan
77327	AMBROSE, A.	.	Pte.	Islington
305173	ANDERSON, W.	.	,,	Glasgow
307443	ANDREWS, D.	.	,,	Ayr
95434	ANDREWS, H.	.	Cpl.	Braintree
305934	ANNEAR, R. .	.	Pte.	Plymouth
307160	ANTHONY, A. S.	.	,,	Crossford, Fife
75807	ANTHONY, T. .	.	,,	Uphall
94875	ARCHER, F. .	.	,,	Billingborough
76054	ARGYLE, A. .	.	,,	Long Eaton
75044	ARNOLD, H. E.	.	,,	Horns Cross
75930	ARSCOTT, F. .	.	,,	Holloway
92457	ASHPLANT, W.	.	,,	Liverpool
202053	ASQUITH, N. .	.	Cpl.	Morley, Leeds
206186	ATKINSON, T.	.	Pte.	Barnoldswick ;
305777	ATLEY, W. .	.	,,	Sunderland
305878	BAILEY, A. W.	.	Pte.	Southsea
305770	BAILEY, F. F.	.	Cpl.	Swindon, Wilts
76037	BAILEY, F. W.	.	Sergt.	Tottenham
200030	BAIN, A. .	.	Pte.	Aberdeen
206147	BAINES, J. R. .	.	,,	Kettering
96641	BAKER, W. .	.	,,	London, N.
206133	BALDCOCK, J.	.	A/Cpl.	Coventry
301775	BALLOCK, F.	.	Pte.	Leeds
75217	BAMFORD, H.	.	Cpl.	Rochdale
92740	BAMWELL, W. S.	.	,,	Somerset
77007	BARBER, F. M.	.	Pte.	Sandown
201484	BARKER, C. M.	.	Cpl.	Hitchin
40245	BARLOW, A. S.	.	Pte.	Botton
206120	BARLOW, H. .	.	L/Cpl.	Chesterfield
200923	BARNARD, C. E.	.	Cpl.	Tuffley
97222	BARNETT, P. B.	.	Pte.	Mansfield
206145	BARNETT, T. J.	.	,,	Edenbridge
306446	BARNETT, W.	.	,,	Blackheath
92966	BARR, E. A. .	.	,,	Forest Gate
76203	BARRATT, A. E.	.	,,	Walthamstow
76375	BARRETT, C. .	.	,,	Glamorgan
78849	BARRETT, J. P.	.	,,	Tonbridge
307828	BARRIE, G. F.	.	,,	Kirkcaldy

Number.	Name and Initials.	Rank.	Town of Residence.
307848	BARROW, A. D. .	Pte.	Belhelvie
111222	BARTLE, J. H. .	Sergt.	Camborne
109859	BARTLETT, E. .	Pte.	Hereford
40094	BARTLETT, J. B. .	A/Cpl.	Pontypridd
76048	BARTON, F. . .	Pte.	Woodford Bridge
306998	BARTY, G. . .	,,	Dundee
78602	BASHFORD, J. T. .	,,	Middlesbrough
77328	BASSON, F. W. R. .	,,	Poplar, E.
95772	BATCHELOR, F. .	Cpl.	Gomshall
75401	BAXTER, W. . .	Pte.	Westcliffe
305364	BAYLISS, T. . .	,,	West Bromwich
307445	BAYNTON, H. E. .	,,	Leytonstone
300368	BEALES, A. . .	,,	Hounslow
300368	BEALES, A. N. .	,,	Marylebone
78763	BEAVES, E. V. .	,,	Watford
95593	BECK, J. . .	L/Cpl.	Springburn
78093	BECKETT, W. C. .	Pte.	Cricklewood
305625	BELL, A. E. . .	,,	Birkenhead
111729	BELL, C. . .	L/Cpl.	Runcorn
75584	BELL, J. R. M. .	Pte.	Durham
308323	BELL, W. . .	,,	Darlington
92692	BELLUS, W. . .	,,	Manchester
109575	BENNETT, J. . .	,,	Aberdeen
91332	BENNETT, J. . .	Cpl.	Heckmondwike
92373	BENSTEAD, J. .	Pte.	Hull
91863	BERROW, W. R. .	,,	Shearham
69735	BERRY, J. R. . .	,,	Birmingham
92686	BEVAN, T. . .	,,	Swinton
69514	BEWS, W. E. . .	,,	Leith
302800	BEYNON, W. . .	,,	Poplar, E.
302784	BILL, K. . .	,,	Ealing
304427	BILLINGTON, A. .	,,	Lancaster
75977	BING, F. W. . .	,,	Ramsgate
94921	BLACKIE, H. . .	,,	Bristol
305772	BLACKLER, A. .	Cpl.	Southsea
201609	BLACKWELL, A. .	Pte.	Southport
69515	BLACKWELL, C. A..	,,	Caversham
77374	BLAIN, J. . .	,,	Larkhall
205174	BLAKEBOROUGH, G.	,,	Middlesbrough
201708	BLANCHARD, H. G.	Cpl.	Portsmouth
91784	BLEANEY, E. . .	Pte.	Burton Latimer
711706	BLENT, J. . .	,,	Shrewsbury
201089	BLOOR, G. . .	,,	Drayton
200069	BLUNN, E. . .	,,	Glenluce
200552	BOLINGBROKE, W.	,,	Brookwood
304410	BOLTON, R. E. .	,,	Lancaster

ROLL OF HONOUR

Number.	Name and Initials.	Rank.	Town of Residence.
307882	BONCHER, H.	Pte.	Sheffield
302859	BONCHER, M. G.	L/Cpl.	Charmouth
69865	BONSFIELD, E.	Pte.	Middleton-in-Teesdale
302030	BOSWELL, I. T. C.	,,	Banchory
200284	BOUCHER, T. W. G.	,,	Northfleet
75572	BOURNE, E.	,,	Durham
92868	BOWERMAN, R. V.	,,	Starcross
206100	BOWN, B.	,,	Nuneaton
76663	BRABENDER, P.	,,	Glasgow
109856	BRADBURY, E.	,,	Glossop
302736	BRADFORD, A. G.	,,	Bermondsey
206144	BRADLEY, G.	Sergt.	Carrickfergus
69524	BRAEDY, E. H.	Pte.	Stepney
69600	BREWER, S.	,,	Fraddon
305065	BRIMS, J.	,,	Glasgow
200842	BRITT, L. C. W.	,,	St. Leonards-on-Sea
308073	BRITTON, W. M.	,,	Glasgow
305362	BROOK, T. W.	,,	Huddersfield
69773	BROOKS, P. T.	,,	Sheffield
69254	BROWN, A.	,,	Doncaster
77299	BROWN, F. A.	A/Cpl.	Camberwell
96907	BROWN, H. G.	Pte.	Harrow
304827	BROWN, J.	L/Cpl.	Newcastle-on-Tyne
92276	BROWN, J.	Pte.	Reading
92503	BROWN, R. P.	,,	Chester
305084	BROWN, S.	,,	Dumfries
202048	BROWN, S. T.	,,	Clapham, S.W.
77449	BROWN, W.	,,	Linlithgow
40060	BROWNING, J. A.	,,	Foots Cray
95072	BUCHANAN, J.	,,	Glasgow
305560	BUCKLEY, W.	,,	Wigan
69571	BUDD, P. E.	,,	Birmingham
76110	BUFFIN, E.	,,	Bargoed
91593	BULLOCK, F.	,,	Manchester
109683	BULMAN, G.	,,	Aspatria
69568	BURCH, J.	,,	Birmingham
109861	BURLAND, A.	,,	Cardiff
200118	BURNETT, W. G.	,,	Chichester
307286	BURNS, H.	,,	Manchester
91350	BURRARS, W.	,,	Cardiff
200020	BURRELL, A.	L/Cpl.	Midlothian
75057	BURROWS, F.	Pte.	Liverpool
201234	BURSFORD, A.	,,	Newmarket

Number.	Name and Initials.	Rank.	Town of Residence.
92860	BURT, J.	Pte.	Old Kent Rd., S.E.
205774	BURT, L. H.	Cpl.	Hornsey
78722	BUSH, G. C.	Pte.	Nottingham
76137	BUTCHER, G.	,,	Wood Green, N.
205202	BUTCHER, P. E.	,,	Pewsey
301846	BUTLER, —	,,	Clonmel
201314	BUTTERWORTH, W.	,,	Manchester
304518	BYGATE, S.	,,	Newcastle-on-Tyne
201266	CAFFREY, G. A.	,,	Machynlleth
109583	CAIRNEY, E.	,,	Greenock
78343	CALDAINE, W. L.	,,	London, W.
75613	CALDHAEM, S.	,,	Strand, W.C.
308039	CALDWELL, C.	,,	Kilmarnock
94892	CAMERON, A.	,,	Argyle
69788	CAMERON, W. E.	,,	Barnsbury
307799	CAMPBELL, J.	,,	Montrose
305291	CAMPBELL, J. S.	Cpl.	South Shields
75210	CAMPBELL, W. S.	,,	Markinch, Fife
77285	CANTLE, R. G.	Pte.	Pontnewydd
75228	CARLSON, W. R.	Cpl.	Dublin
201966	CARNIE, W. J.	Sergt.	Kintore
75950	CARTER, E.	Pte.	Durham
95180	CARTER, H. H.	,,	Devonport
206150	CARTMAN, F.	,,	Bury
110235	CATHERALL, T. H.	,,	Ashton-in-Lyne
75328	CAVE, T.	,,	Hove
91859	CAYGILL, H.	,,	Northallerton
206114	CHADWICK, J.	Cpl.	Leeds
96976	CHALLICE, H. J.	Pte.	Newmarket
201449	CHANDLER, A. T.	L/Cpl.	Birmingham
307238	CHANDLER, J. W.	Pte.	Cheadle
200049	CHANDLER, L.	Cpl.	Woking
76614	CHAPMAN, G. A.	Pte.	Cambridge
76389	CHAPPLE, W.	,,	Fowey
306895	CHARLES, J.	,,	Llanelly
76972	CHAVE, S.	Sergt.	Hounslow
92640	CHESHIRE, S. A.	Pte.	Finsbury
92960	CHEVERTON, J.	,,	Cambridge
76083	CHIAZZARE, J. A.	,,	Natal, S. Africa
91638	CHIDGY, D.	,,	Bristol
304901	CHILDS, F.	,,	Hampstead
200084	CHITTY, H. P.	,,	Clapham, S.W.
91883	CHIVERS, E.	,,	Lowestoft
302744	CHIVERS, R. S.	Cpl.	Plaistow
95049	CHYMIST, F.	Sergt.	Stafford

Number.	Name and Initials.	Rank.	Town of Residence.
301561	CISSELL, G.	Pte.	Paddington
302868	CLAREY, J. C.	Sergt.	Barnsdale, Australia
201049	CLARK, A.	Pte.	Dundee
205006	CLARKE, G.	,,	Rugby
112703	CLARKE, J.	Cpl.	Tipton
206156	CLAYTON, O.	Pte.	Great Harwood
202072	CLAYTON, T.	,,	Preston
301999	CLEAL, W.	,,	Tredegar
206121	CLEGG, W.	A/Sergt.	Burnley
92659	CLEMENTS, A. E.	Sergt.	Walworth
111718	CLEWES, C.	Pte.	Middlewich
76643	CLOUGH, P.	,,	Blackburn
301773	COATES, H. J.	,,	Selby
206109	COCKER, H. H.	,,	King's Norton
70079	COLE, J. H.	,,	London, N.W.
75867	COLLINS, C.	L/Cpl.	Stirling
305283	COLLINS, F. S.	Sergt.	Bletchley
76465	COLLINS, J. B. J.	Pte.	Dartford
305106	COLLINSON, A. R.	,,	Scarborough
308011	COLQUHOUN, A.	L/Cpl.	Rutherglen
301618	COMLEY, C. H.	,,	Burton-on-Trent
69922	COMMINS, V.	Pte.	Manchester
305945	COMMON, R. V.	Cpl.	Fratton
109905	CONNAH, A.	Pte.	Chester
307935	CONNELLY, H. P.	,,	Glasgow
302850	CONRICK, R. L.	,,	Victoria, Australia
200311	COOK, A. W.	,,	Worplesdon
202043	COOK, J. B.	,,	Downham Market
77238	COOK, L.	,,	Newport
305849	COOK, W. C.	,,	Swindon
201828	COOPER, H. C.	Cpl.	Hendon
305378	COOPER, W.	Pte.	Stockport
92356	COOPER, W. J.	,,	Edinburgh
200385	COPESTAKE, A. E.	L/Cpl.	Marlow
40322	COPPACK, J. C.	Pte.	Chester
307860	CORNEY, J. F.	Cpl.	Greenock
40413	CORRIE, J.	Pte.	Langholm
307105	CORRIS, E.	,,	Liverpool
78116	COTTON, T.	,,	Tamworth
92698	COUSINS, P.	,,	Manchester
92671	COUTTS, R.	,,	Shepherd's Bush
200014	CRADDOCK, V. E.	,,	E. Wolverhampton
75370	CRANE, A. R.	Sergt.	Kennington, S.E.
200686	CRANE, G. E.	Pte.	Homerton
95626	CRAWFORD, J.	,,	Falkirk

Number.	Name and Initials.	Rank.	Town of Residence.
94869	CREASEY, C. E.	Pte.	Boston
76476	CRESSHALL, F.	,,	Islington
95412	CREWE, M. T.	,,	Tonbridge
107684	CRICHTON, J. G.	,,	Manchester
91354	CRIMMER, H. C.	L/Cpl.	Leyton
308919	CRIPPS, E. C.	,,	Gloucester
95156	CROCKER, F. .	,,	Stonehouse
78300	CROFT, R.	Cpl.	Belfast
91702	CROLEY, W. C.	Pte.	Wood Green
305702	CROME, R.	,,	Wigan
308213	CRONE, D.	,,	London, N.1
300378	CROSSLEY, E. G.	,,	Bradford
75285	CROWE, F.	Cpl.	Barking
69617	CROXTON, J. A.	Pte.	Streatham
112364	CROZIER, H. .	,,	Preston
206138	CROZIER, H. .	,,	Preston
304773	CRUTCHFIELD, W.	Sergt.	Harlington
308920	CUDSWORTH, W. M.	Pte.	Manchester
305678	CULL, H. L. .	,,	Southsea
306334	CULLUM, W. .	,,	Liverpool
305406	CUNCLIFFE, F.	L/Cpl.	Nelson
110014	CURRIE, C. .	,,	Glasgow
376824	CUSHIN, E.	Pte.	Pudsey
202543	CUTLER, H. .	,,	Barnsley
200080	CUTTING, E. W.	Sergt.	Ilford
95586	DANDS, A. .	Pte.	Bristol
307041	DANIELS, E. .	,,	Horsham
95192	DASH, P.	,,	Exeter
368831	DAVENHILL, H.	,,	Walsall
77450	DAVIDSON, W.	,,	Lancaster
111758	DAVIES, A. .	,,	Aberdeen
91918	DAVIES, T. .	,,	Ferryhill
306366	DAVIES, T. R..	,,	Toronto, Canada
201064	DAVIS, L. J. .	,,	Bow, London
306173	DAVIS, W. .	Sergt.	Bristol
301946	DAVISON, W. S.	Pte.	Sunderland
200922	DAWSON, C. .	,,	Stroud Green
78257	DAY, A. E.	,,	Somerset
308954	DAY, T. W. .	,,	Deptford
75451	DEAN, T.	Sergt.	Liverpool
95750	DEAN, W.	Pte.	Brierfield
300382	DEIGHTON, W.	,,	Selby
91641	DENISON, H.	,,	Keighley
302803	DENMAN, W. .	,,	London, W.
78565	DENNARD, C. T.	,,	Liverpool

Number.	Name and Initials:	Rank.	Town of Residence.
306807	DENT, A. H.	Pte.	Norwich
112182	DIAS, S.	„	Jamaica
305049	DICK, A.	„	Troon
202070	DICKENS, W.	„	Salford
78367	DICKSON, W.	„	Sunderland
112880	DOBBIE, A. S.	„	Clyde Bank
307829	DOBBIE, J. S.	„	Blackpool
308059	DOIG, J.	„	Invergowrie
200780	DOODSON, E.	„	York
302807	DORGAN, J.	Cpl.	Glanmire (Cork)
201621	DORONING, J. G. W.	Pte.	Ilford
76715	DOUGAN, A.	„	Paisley
93048	DOUGLAS, G.	„	Edinburgh
301832	DOUGLAS, H.	„	Glasgow
206113	DOW, R. B.	Sergt.	Glasgow
96425	DOWN, A.	Pte.	Devon
301986	DOWNEND, A.	„	Barnsley
77497	DOWNING, B.	„	Wangford
76978	DOWSE, T. R.	„	Fulham
307433	DREWETT, C. G.	Cpl.	Kingston-on-- Thames
305425	DRIFFIELD, C. B.	Pte.	Wood Green
75921	DRUMMOND, A. M. K.	„	Oban
92562	DRURY, C.	„	Putney
201379	DUDDRIDGE, H.	Sergt.	Somerset
304595	DUDDRIDGE, T. G.	Pte.	Lambeth
69536	DUDLEY, S. R.	„	London, S.E.
305098	DUFF, J.	„	Dufftown
304904	DUKE, C.	„	Lambeth
111819	DUKE, C. S.	„	Walworth
78559	DUNCAN, J.	„	Tillicoultry
307985	DUNKERLEY, H.	„	Burnley
306339	DUNN, A.	„	Jesmond
92521	DUNN, D.	„	Grangemouth
206112	DUNN, J.	„	Glasgow
301613	DYER, H. T.	Cpl.	Burnley
201089	EASTHAM, W. H.	Pte.	Accrington
76649	EASTON, D.	A/Cpl.	Burnside
70026	EDWARDS, C.	Pte.	Stratford
307787	EGLINTON, D.	„	Uddingstone
95539	ELLIOTT, D.	„	Glasgow
201859	ELLIOTT, W. J.	„	Norwich
76933	ELLIS, A. W.	„	Limehouse
307080	ELLIS, F. J. J.	„	London, N.E.
306430	ELMS, A. J.	„	Bristol

Number.	Name and Initials.	Rank.	Town of Residence.
309242	EMERSON, S. G.	Pte.	Brixton
91768	EMPSON, G. A.	L/Cpl.	Clapham, S.W.
301542	ENGLAND, T. .	Pte.	Pontefract
307619	ENGLAND, W.	,,	Sheffield
206184	ENTWISTLE, J. S.	,,	Darwen
91334	ESAU, C. E. E.	,,	Brighton
92665	ETHERINGTON, T. .	,,	West Hartlepool
302937	EVANS, H.	,,	Pontypridd
75281	EVANS, L.	L/Cpl.	Morley
206127	EVANS, P. J. .	Cpl.	Blackheath
201247	EVENDEN, H. E.	Pte.	Gravesend
76214	EVERTON, W. H.	.,,	Isle of Wight
306111	EWAN, W. M.	,,	Clyde Bank
91706	EYLES, T. C. N.	,,	Wimbledon
96734	FAIRLEY, A. D.	Pte.	Edinburgh
111767	FEAR, D. J. .	,,	Pengam
76858	FEARN, G. .	,,	Derby
109584	FEARN, W. M.	,,	Dundee
308309	FENSOM, F. A. W. .	:,	Woodhouse
307015	FENSOME, W..	,,	Luton
95478	FENTON, L. .	Sergt.	Jersey
308573	FERGUSON, A.	Pte.	Paisley
206180	FERGUSON, R. E.	,,	Stoke-on-Trent
305367	FIDLER, J. H..	,,	Conisborough
206161	FISHER, G. C.	Cpl.	Nottingham
40070	FITZJOHN, C. H.	Pte.	Southampton
205113	FLEMING, C. .	Sergt.	Derby
309128	FLEMING, W. A.	Pte.	Liverpool
305275	FLETCHER, T. H.	,,	Walsall
201123	FLETCHER, W. H. .	,,	Manchester
40342	FOOT, G.	,,	Great Missenden
109688	FORBES, M.	,,	Aberdeen
96411	FORBES, R. L.	,,	Greenock
308642	FORD, A.	,,	Derby
301839	FORD, J. J.	,,	Newcastle-on-Tyne
302791	FORDE, J.	,,	Cork
201147	FORMAN, T. R.	,,	Newcastle-on-Tyne
307797	FORSEYTH, R.	,,	Lanark
91934	FORSTER, T. .	,,	Durham
91645	FOSKETT, A. E.	,,	Halesowen
76753	FOWLER, M. C.	L/Cpl.	Edinburgh
95583	FOX, G. E.	Pte.	Pudsey
77394	FRANCE, A.	Cpl.	Sheffield
76671	FRASER, J. .	Pte.	Dundee
302452	FRASER, F. B.	,,	Aberdeen

Number.	Name and Initials.	Rank.	Town of Residence.
69977	FRAYER, C.	Pte.	Bournemouth
78710	FRENCH, H. J.	Sergt.	London, S.E.
96962	FULLER, O. C.	Pte.	Trunch
91616	FURLONGER, A. F.	Cpl.	Haslemere
202068	GAEN, F.	Pte.	Emlym
201872	GAGE, J. C.	,,	Leyton
201932	GALES-WISE, J. J. .	,,	Marsh-by-Sea
308000	GALLAGHER, E.	,,	Glasgow
75257	GALWAY, W. .	,,	Holywood
200815	GAMMON, W. P.	,,	Exeter
301630	GANNON, F.	,,	New York
206105	GARDNER, B. R. L..	,,	Wycombe
78122	GARNER, H. .	,,	Wellingborough
309145	GARNER, T. R. H.	,,	Liverpool
76427	GATES, A. J. .	,,	Brockenhurst
305897	GEAR, R. C.	,,	Southampton
302607	GEE, A. W.	,,	East Dereham
95111	GEMMELL, R. J.	,,	Camelon
40097	GEORGE, H. G.	Cpl.	Swansea
110393	GEORGE, S.	Pte.	Leeds
112916	GIBBONS, J.	,,	Thelfield
307389	GIBSON, F.	Cpl.	Warrington
306070	GIBSON, G.	Pte.	Durham
304957	GIBSON, J.	,,	Glasgow
76175	GILBERT, A. .	,,	Hocton
95388	GILL, E. T.	Cpl.	London, S.E.
109637	GILLARD, F.	Pte.	Somerset
76766	GLASGOW, S. .	L/Cpl.	Haddington
78455	GLASSBROOK, J.	Pte.	Wimbledon
109957	GLEN, E. T.	,,	Greenock
77416	GLOVER, S.	,,	Beeston
305543	GLYDER, G. S.	,,	Ilfracombe
69624	GODFREY, E. .	,,	Oxford
91766	GODLEY, R.	,,	Brighton
77304	GOODALL, F. .	,,	Congleton
201999	GOODALL, R. .	,,	Newburgh
96565	GOODE, C.	,,	Kettering
307020	GOODWIN, C. .	,,	Woodstock
202049	GOODWIN, H. C.	,,	Norbury
76672	GORDON, A. .	,,	Huntley
308137	GORDON, K. M.	,,	Dingwall
42196	GORDON, W. .	,,	Galway
200953	GOSLING, S. C.	,,	Framlingham
110044	GRAHAM, J. G.	,,	Edinburgh
307703	GRAHAM, V. K.	,,	Liverpool

2 F

Number.	Name and Initials.	Rank.	Town of Residence.
75779	GRAINGER, F.	Pte.	Hanley
96599	GRAINGER, J. J.	,,	St. Pancras
304214	GRAVES, A.	,,	London, N.
92975	GRAY, E. G.	,,	Harrow
301475	GRAY, G.	Cpl.	Brora
92519	GREEG, J.	Pte.	Paisley
76797	GREEN, F.	,,	Bishops Castle
92776	GREEN, F.	,,	Alverford
200601	GREEN, S. W.	Sergt.	Croydon
305807	GREENTREE, G. H..	Pte.	Emsworth
91687	GREGORY, E.	,,	Bath
96251	GREIG, E.	Cpl.	Perth
40178	GRIFFEN, L. I.	Pte.	Dundee
111677	GRIFFITHS, F.	,,	Haverford
200968	GRIFFITHS, J.	L/Cpl.	Glynceiriog
201221	GRIFFITHS, J. W.	Cpl.	Chester
201148	GRIFFITHS, R. L.	Pte.	Dundee
75812	GRINDLEY, R.	,,	Edinburgh
70181	GRUNDY, R.	,,	Darlington
205674	GUILFORD, W.	,,	Ross
305222	GUNN, R. W.	,,	Nottingham
308758	GUYTE, W.	,,	Plumstead
110359	HAIGH, C.	Pte.	Dewsbury
92752	HAINES, W. J.	,,	Swindon
96923	HALES, E. J.	,,	Leyton
95547	HALL, E. J.	,,	Birmingham
75351	HALLIDAY, J.	,,	Glasgow
75351	HALLIDAY, J.	,,	Glasgow
92987	HALLS, L.	,,	Brandon
305224	HAMILTON, W.	,,	Glasgow
112233	HAMMOND, J. W.	,,	Yarmouth
201348	HAMMOND, H. C.	Cpl.	Blackpool
305326	HAMON, F. J.	Pte.	Jersey
110487	HAMPTON, C. D. G.	,,	Cardiff
307623	HANDLEY, J. C. C.	,,	Middleham
95272	HANDLEY, R.	,,	Mitcham
304639	HANDS, W.	Cpl.	Birmingham
78600	HANRY, R.	Pte.	Tyne Docks
200123	HANSFORD, J. S.	,,	Maidenhead
76713	HANTON, D.	,,	Arbroath
91969	HARDMAN, F.	Cpl.	Rhodes
91636	HARGREAVES, —	Pte.	Skipton
306216	HARLAND, W.	,,	Filey
96688	HARMAN, W. E.	,,	Poplar, E.
76278	HARNESS, F.	,,	Wainfleet

Number.	Name and Initials.	Rank.	Town of Residence.
69282	HARRIES, C. A. .	Pte.	Sandown
75944	HARRIES, G. . .	,,	Burwell
91457	HARRIS, A. A. .	,,	Bedford
109640	HARRIS, J. W. .	,,	Acton
75445	HARRISON, T. R. S.	,,	Rufforth
201160	HARRISON, W. .	,,	Ryton-on-Tyne
302869	HARWOOD, C. J. .	L/Cpl.	E. Dulwich
95075	HATCH, A. . .	Pte.	Uxbridge
201226	HATCHARD, W. E. .	,,	Ross
75590	HATCHER, H. W. .	,,	Balham
95342	HATHRILL, F. .	,,	Ogbourne
112006	HATTON, P. G. .	,,	Acton
91506	HAWES, A. H. .	,,	Bromley
91598	HAY, G. H. . .	,,	Plymouth
300425	HAYDEN, A. .	,,	Leyton
300208	HAYDOCK, E. .	,,	Whalley
200377	HAYNES, L. . .	,,	Stafford
75369	HEBENTON, T. W. .	,,	Chiswick
304889	HELLENS, A. J. .	,,	Swansea
91961	HELLEWELL, W. .	Cpl.	Salford
206115	HERCUS, J. . .	Pte.	Midlothian
206191	HEWSON, A. W. .	,,	Coventry
95722	HICKS, H. . .	,,	Bristol
76176	HIGGS, W. . .	,,	Edmonton
206096	HILLHOUSE, R. .	A/Sergt.	Stirling
69830	HILTON, M. . .	Pte.	Hull
76420	HILTON, W. . .	Cpl.	Oldham
70175	HINDMARCH, E. .	Pte.	Sunderland
200931	HISCOTT, H. . .	,,	Paddington
201844	HODKINSON, L. .	,,	Beeston
78590	HOGG, R. . .	Sergt.	Tynemouth
201115	HOLLAND, D. .	Pte.	Guildford
70044	HOLLY, G. A. . .	,,	Plaistow
200876	HOLMAN, A. W. .	,,	Uffculme
75330	HOLMAN, F. C. .	,,	Pagnell
78301	HOLME, W. . .	,,	Durham
75443	HOLMES, E. E. .	,,	Chingford
201962	HOLMES, T. . .	,,	Longfield
77541	HOLMES, W. . .	,,	Darlaston
76169	HOLWILL, E. J. .	,,	Neath
95497	HONEYBALL, H. .	,,	Ardleigh
200092	HOPE, H. R. . .	Sergt.	Hull
92775	HOPKINS, A. . .	Pte.	Fareham
206116	HOPKINS, G. S. .	,,	Chichester
91881	HOPKINSON, B. W. .	,,	Ruddington
78568	HOPPER, C. C. .	,,	Leeds

Number.	Name and Initials.		Rank.	Town of Residence.
300427	HOPPER, J. H.	.	Pte.	Blaydon
95689	HORTON, E. .	.	,,	Lincoln
109664	HOUSTON, J. F.	.	L/Cpl.	Glasgow
301790	HOWARTH, S.	.	Pte.	Newton Heath
78357	HOWIE, L. L. .	.	,,	Aberdeen
308723	HOWSATH, D.	.	,,	Clare
205778	HUDSON, W. W.	.	,,	Birmingham
75862	HULLITT, L. J.	.	,,	Gloucester
307330	HULSMEIER, A.	.	,,	Sunderland
200086	HUNT, A. G. .	.	,,	Somerset
96749	HUNT, D.	.	,,	King's Lynn
110250	HUNT, F.	.	,,	Frome
301328	HUNT, F. G. .	.	,,	Melbourne, Aust.
69979	HUNT, H.	.	,,	Leek
91385	HUNT, H. W. .	.	,,	Bedminster
109783	HUNT, J. A. .	.	,,	Bow, London
206128	HUNTER, D. L.	.	,,	Glasgow
95498	HUNTER, F. M.	.	,,	Edinburgh
304419	HUXLEY, E. J.	.	,,	Shrewsbury
307660	HUXLEY, H. .	.	,,	Manchester
109913	INCE, G. E.	.	Pte.	Glamorgan
76835	INGHAM, F. G.	.	,,	Doncaster
302961	INGLEBY, G. E.	.	,,	Sheffield
304742	IRELAND, W.	.	,,	Preston
300397	IRWIN, W. .	.	,,	Maryport
206143	JACKSON, G. .	.	Pte.	Birmingham
78003	JACQUES, R. .	.	,,	Accrington
201718	JACQUES, W. .	.	,,	Cirencester
302765	JAMESON, P. J.	.	Cpl.	Catford
91508	JARVIS, A. .	.	Pte.	Newcastle-on-Tyne
306357	JARVIS, R. E. .	.	,,	Stock
307762	JEFFCOCK, C. .	.	Cpl.	Leeds
305801	JEFFERY, E. .	.	Pte.	Redruth
307631	JEFFERY, H. .	.	,,	Uckfield
97281	JENKISON, C. E.	.	,,	Salisbury
77199	JESS, L. R.	.	,,	Cricklewood
205607	JOHN, H. P. .	.	,,	Swansea
69522	JOHNSON, F. .	.	,,	Kettering
75617	JOHNSON, G. H.	.	Sergt.	Westminster
78783	JOHNSON, H. .	.	Pte.	Grimsby
69609	JOHNSON, W. T.	.	,,	Kingston
76749	JONES, A. F. .	.	,,	Brixton
200957	JONES, T. J. .	.	,,	Wrexham

Number.	Name and Initials.	Rank.	Town of Residence.
206177	JONES, W.	Pte.	Sutton
91294	JONES, W. J.	L/Cpl.	Flint
69668	JOYCE, A.	Pte.	Wolverhampton
302818	KANE, D.	Pte.	Dublin
92304	KEATING, J. B.	,,	Redcar
95759	KELLEY, J.	,,	Liverpool
300321	KENNEDY, R.	L/Cpl.	Houghton-le-Spring
109703	KENNERLEY, E. J.	Pte.	Newport
75215	KENNIS, J.	,,	St. Leonards
76855	KENT, H.	L/Cpl.	Mansfield
305819	KERRISON, A. F.	Pte.	Portsmouth
92859	KERSLAKE, S. E.	,,	Greenwich
301593	KETLEY, T. E.	,,	London, N.
301455	KEYLOCK, W. T.	,,	Blaina
200406	KILMINSTER, W. J.	L/Cpl.	Walthamstow
206134	KILMINSTER, C.	Pte.	Ellesmere Port
305636	KING, W. J.	,,	Eastham
206187	KIRELUS, B. B.	,,	London, S.E.
69384	KIRK, W.	,,	Long Eaton
92119	KITCHING, G.	,,	Hull
78729	KITCHING, H. R.	,,	Bradford
76568	KNIGHT, F. J.	L/Cpl.	Uckfield
205622	KNIGHTING, G. T.	Cpl.	Fulham
205140	KNOWLES, L.	Pte.	Macclesfield
91494	KNOX, S.	,,	Belfast
95674	KNOX, W.	,,	Balerno
201254	LANCASTER, H. S.	Pte.	Stockport
306960	LANDLES, W.	,,	Blackpool
92871	LANDREY, W. W.	,,	Lancaster
77533	LARCOMBE, J.	,,	Newport
75714	LAST, A.	,,	Bury St. Edmunds
306674	LAWRENCE, O.	,,	St. Blyth
78657	LAWS, R.	,,	Whatfield
308222	LAWTON, W.	,,	Liverpool
305115	LEACH, H.	L/Cpl.	Manchester
76692	LEADBEATER, J. H.	Sergt.	Oldham
75019	LEADER, E. J.	Pte.	Holloway
201343	LEAROYD, G.	,,	Tow Law
206131	LEAT, H.	,,	Aldershot
75205	LEATHERLAND, H.	,,	Northampton
305007	LECKIE, J. H.	,,	Barrhead
308078	LEE, A. H.	L/Cpl.	Manchester
75348	LEESE, R.	Pte.	Burslem
92094	LEFTWICH, W.	,,	Knightsbridge

Number.	Name and Initials.	Rank.	Town of Residence.
78932	LEGGETT, W. H.	L/Cpl.	Halifax
307909	LEVY, J.	Pte.	Windsor
110363	LEWIS, C.	,,	Cowbridge
200966	LEWIS, J. C.	,,	Aberdeen
76984	LEWIS, P. H.	,,	Oxford
69472	LEWIS, N.	,,	Smethwick
69816	LIDDELL, W.	,,	Tweedmouth
394674	LIND, J. A. T.	,,	Charlton
96763	LING, S. G.	,,	Attleborough
69883	LINTON, F. H.	,,	Canterbury
95276	LITTLEJOHNS, F. W. H.	,,	Holwill
75605	LODGE, E. G.	,,	Ramsgate
76782	LORD, H.	,,	Cleckheaton
91495	LORD, J.	,,	Cramshawbooth
70008	LORLEY, T.	,,	Hereford
200839	LOWE, F. W.	,,	Warwick
200829	LOWSON, A.	,,	Dundee
310904	LUNN, A. E.	,,	Hull
200225	LUXFORD, W.	Sergt.	London, S.W.
200315	McBLAIN, W.	Pte.	Edinburgh
69583	McBRIDE, J.	,,	Glasgow
304234	McCABE, J.	,,	Liverpool
306113	McCASKIE, M. L. J.	,,	Skelmorlie
77175	McCLOY, H.	,,	Belfast
75902	McCONNACHIE, E.	,,	Wallasey
76075	McCOY, C.	,,	Liverpool
206111	McCRAW, W.	,,	Kelso
77524	McCULLOCK, D.	,,	Edinburgh
75220	McDONALD, J.	L/Cpl.	Fraserburgh
93076	MACE, F.	Pte.	Stevenage
306111	McEWAN, E. M.	L/Cpl.	Clydebank
78138	MACFIE, J. R.	Cpl.	Glasgow
305180	McGHIE, T. K.	Pte.	Uddington
76679	McGILLIVRAY, J.	,,	Linlithgow
304896	McGILP, J. M.	,,	Glasgow
304895	MACHIN, C.	,,	Glasgow
91525	McINTOSH, F.	,,	Craigston
201206	MacKAE, R. J.	,,	Conon Bridge
206169	McKENZIE, J.	,,	Birkenhead
111866	McLACHLAN, J.	,,	Greenock
305705	McLENNAN, M.	,,	Luss
76557	McNAMEE, E. C.	,,	Portsmouth
92554	McNAUGHTON, S.	Pte.	Kintells
309255	McNICOLL, W.	Cpl.	Hythe
111578	MAIN, W.	,,	Aberdeen

Number.	Name and Initials.	Rank.	Town of Residence.
78077	MALE, F. C.	Pte.	Cardiff
111773	MALE, A.	,,	Barnet
306161	MALLETT, J. H.	,,	Penryn, Cornwall
308026	MALONE, M.	,,	Linlithgow
76680	MALTMAN, J.	,,	Glasgow
91528	MANSELL, J. B.	,,	Walworth
301896	MARKHAM, A. E.	,,	Fulham
200310	MARQUIS, P.	L/Cpl.	Glasgow
75737	MARR, F.	Pte.	Cambuslang
92392	MARR, J.	,,	Gateshead
201097	MARSDEN, A.	,,	Darwen
308617	MARSHALL, A.	,,	Birmingham
96932	MARSHALL, R.	,,	Farnham
75843	MARTUM, F.	L/Cpl.	Glamorgan
69481	MARTUN, A.	Pte.	Brockley, S.E.
40336	MASON, R. G.	,,	Farnham
201188	MATHEWS, D.	,,	Chesham
306869	MATHIESON, R.	,,	Jersey
92751	MATHISON, C. M.	,,	Preston
78457	MEAD, F. E.	,,	Westcliffe-on-Sea
76979	MEARS, R. D.	,,	Goodmayes
76078	MEECH, A. L.	L/Cpl.	Clapham, S.W.
307058	MERCER, C.	Pte.	St. Helens
75395	MERRITT, F. R.	,,	Charshalton
306997	METHVEN, M.	,,	Crieff
301625	METTAM, E. A.	,,	Nottingham
96740	MILES, A.	,,	Harefield
95127	MILLARD, A.	,,	Stratford-on-Avon
304301	MILLER, A. D.	,,	Buxted
75559	MILLER, J.	,,	Newcastle-on-Tyne
93025	MILLER, J.	,,	Glasgow
95197	MILLS, W. B.	,,	Woolwich
95619	MILNE, F. J.	,,	Ilford
307032	MITCHELL, A.	,,	Dunsfold
91815	MITCHELL, A. H.	Cpl.	Scunthorpe
78662	MOCKETT, L. C.	Pte.	Harpenden
308547	MOISE, E.	,,	St. Louis, U.S.A.
200758	MONKS, H.	,,	Transvaal, S.A.
305086	MOONIE, J.	,,	Glasgow
110367	MOORE, J.	,,	Chorley
308563	MORELAND, A.	,,	Greenwich
201346	MORGAM, J. C.	Sergt.	Wigmore
307231	MORRIS, E.	,,	Bantry
91948	MORRIS, H.	Pte.	Leyland
302834	MORRIS, J.	,,	Lewisham
307437	MORRIS, J.	Cpl.	Wolverhampton

Number.	Name and Initials.	Rank.	Town of Residence.
94936	MORRISON, K.	Pte.	Nuneaton
307055	MOSCATE, S. E.	,,	Chester
200897	MOSS, W.	Cpl.	Poulton-le-Fylde
97295	MOTT, S.	Pte.	Hertford
40236	MOULDING, W.	,,	Erith
206170	MOURYER, F..	,,	Birmingham
202052	MUIR, J.	Cpl.	Galston
77475	MULLEN, W. .	Pte.	Sunderland
307801	MULLOLLAND, J. .	Cpl.	Glasgow
200254	MURIE, D.	Pte.	Alexandria, N.B.
304617	MURPHY, F. .	L/Cpl.	Newton-le-Willows
75463	MURPHY, J. .	Pte.	Leeds
306300	MURPHY, J. J.	,,	Alloa
95535	MURRAY, A. .	Cpl.	Edinburgh
201053	MURRAY, J. .	Sergt.	Edinburgh
75336	MURRAY, R. .	Pte.	Grimsby
95214	MYERS, A.	,,	Manchester
200328	MYERS, J.	Sergt.	Thornton Heath
201294	NASH, C. J.	Pte.	Bristol
201198	NASH, R. H.	,,	Nottingham
76277	NAVEN, T.	,,	Stockport
95332	NEAL, D. G.	,,	Powick
96412	NELSON, J. R..	,,	Greenock
201322	NEWELL, C. .	,,	Birmingham
205475	NEWELL, J. H.	,,	Morecambe
78470	NEWTON, E. .	,,	Pendleton
200523	NEWTON, J. .	L/Cpl.	Fife
201462	NICHOLLS, J.	Pte.	Nantwich
95039	NICHOLSON, S.	,,	Teignmouth
78781	NOKE, E. P. .	,,	Worcester
92272	NORGATE, G. P.	,,	Alton
91731	NORMAN, W..	Sergt.	South Watton
304641	NUTH, J. S.	Pte.	Viewsley
92261	OATES, R. L. .	Pte.	Mirfield
95647	OLIVER, J.	,,	Scunthorpe
40352	O'MAHONEY, V. L..	,,	Farnborough
77375	OMER, A.	,,	Hull
75556	ORKNEY, A. .	,,	Bedlington
111458	ORMEROD, T..	,,	Oswaldthistle
69930	ORTON, J.	,,	Oldham
201614	OSBORNE, S. W.	,,	Brighton
78424	O'TOOLE, B. .	Sergt.	Malden
200926	OUSELEY, J. C.	L/Cpl.	Bermondsey
75642	OVER, W. T. E.	Pte.	Portsmouth

Number.	Name and Initials.	Rank.	Town of Residence.
304810	OWEN, W. H.	Pte.	Derby
77477	OX, C.	,,	Canning Town
309107	PAMPHILON, J. A.	Pte.	Acton
305066	PARIS, J.	,,	Midlothian
305533	PARKER, W.	,,	Redwarf
40380	PARKIN, C.	,,	Rotherham.
206135	PARKINSON, A.	,,	Preston
76630	PARRETT, W.	,,	Liverpool
91559	PARTINGTON, J.	,,	Freshfield
95185	PATCHETT, I.	,,	Newtown-
308947	PATTEMORE, J.	,,	Malden
92176	PATTERSON, E. V.	A/Cpl.	Kilworth
98246	PATTINSON, J.	Pte.	Stanhope
95015	PAYNE, A. E.	,,	Keston
200567	PEACE, A. R.	,,	Grantham
307334	PEACOCK, J.	,,	Leeds
304855	PEARSON, R.	,,	Chesterfield
77009	PEARSON, V. A.	,,	Kensington
92342	PEATTIE, D.	,,	Edinburgh
95533	PEATTIE, W.	Sergt.	Haddington
92830	PECK, P. M.	Pte.	Cambridge
300405	PECKETT, H.	,,	Huddersfield
112344	PEERS, E. C.	,,	Buxton
78325	PELLING, L.	,,	Croydon
112864	PERKIN, W. M.	,,	Newbridge Hill
96408	PERRIN, J.	,,	Liverpool
306268	PETTIGAN, D.	,,	Edinburgh
78349	PETTY, D.	,,	Kingston-on-Thames
201549	PHIBBS, R. Q.	,,	Northenden
307210	PHILBURN, J. H.	,,	Keighley
69415	PHILLIPS, G. W.	Sergt.	Fairborough
75107	PHILLIPS, E. J.	Pte.	St. John's Wood
91467	PHILLIPS, W. C.	A/Cpl.	Gillingham
306970	PHILLIPS, S. R.	Pte.	Swinton
78366	PICKEN, R. H.	L/Cpl.	W. Hartlepool
305925	PICKERING, W.	Pte.	Durham
206172	PIGG, A. G.	,,	Royston
308808	PILCHER, L. C.	Sergt.	Camberwell
202002	PINDER, P. A.	Pte.	New Basford
69445	POLKINGHORNE, W. W.	,,	Plymouth
95357	POMFRET, J.	,,	Blackburn
301745	PONNTAIN, J. W.	,,	Liverpool
76366	POOLE, W. H.	Sergt.	Bradford
205772	POORE, P. A.	L/Cpl.	Worthing

Number.	Name and Initials.	Rank.	Town of Residence.
308479	POSENER, A.	Pte.	Shoreditch
75918	POWELL, G. H.	,,	Merstham
109613	POWELL, W. A.	,,	Swansea
301560	POWELL, W. H.	,,	Cambridge
70006	PRESCOTT, H.	,,	Leigh
205780	PRESTON, A. .	,,	Beckenham
201143	PRESTON, J. E.	,,	Nelson
96427	PRICE, A.	,,	Gloucester
301312	PRICE, F.	,,	Brierley Hill
75883	PRIDMORE, J.	,,	Peterborough
206168	PRIMMER, O. G.	,,	Lancaster
200822	PROCTOR, F. .	Sergt.	Thornton Heath
200665	PRYCE, H. C.	Pte.	Kings Langley
308147	PULMAN, J. H.	,,	Devon
309182	PURKISS, A. .	,,	Bow, E.
78482	QUANTRILL, F. W. .	Pte.	Bungay
201019	QUARTERMAN, G. .	Cpl.	Northampton
96856	QUINN, J.	Pte.	Poulton-le-Fylde
302835	RAINBOW, A.	Pte.	Potters Bar
200736	RAMSELL, G. .	,,	Stafford
109596	RANKINE, R.	,,	Laurieston
200786	RAWORTH, P.	,,	Harrogate
69551	REA, R. H.	,,	London, S.W.
200430	READ, H.	Sergt.	Tunbridge Wells
92258	REDMAN, L. .	Pte.	York
206151	REEVE, L.	,,	Birmingham
306128	REID, T.	,,	Douglas
94599	REID, W.	,,	Kirkintilloch
201452	RELSALL, H.	,,	St. Helens
301467	REYNOLDS, G. W. .	,,	Kilburn
95685	RHODES, W. .	,,	Alford
110386	RHODES, G. H.	Cpl.	Bradford
200862	RICHARDS, A.	Pte.	Callington
307098	RICHARDS, S.	,,	St. Austell
307471	RICHARDSON, T. N.	,,	Montrose
201963	RICHMOND, J. C.	,,	Guildford
309841	RICKABY, F. L.	,,	Newmarket
95413	RIDDROUGH, J. P. .	,,	Salterforth
78807	RIDINGS, C. A.	,,	Manchester
76645	RIMMER, J. .	,,	Blackburn
112012	RITCHIE, . .	Sergt.	Portsmouth
301750	ROBERTS, A. .	Pte.	Manchester
92632	ROBERTS, C. A.	,,	Islington
78530	ROBERTS, H. .	,,	Dolgelly

ROLL OF HONOUR

Number.	Name and Initials.	Rank.	Town of Residence.
110131	ROBERTS, H. . .	Pte.	Sheffield
206146	ROBERTS, J. . .	,,	Manchester
95595	ROBERTSON, G. J. .	L/Cpl.	Glasgow
200947	ROBERTSON, J. J. .	,,	Montrose
206101	ROBERTSON, R. .	Pte.	Hanwell
95419	ROBINS, A. . .	,,	Burnley
304916	ROBINSON, F. .	,,	Tring
206117	ROBINSON, P. N. .	,,	Preston
94838	ROBINSON, W. G. .	,,	Herne Hill
110127	ROBSHAW, G. .	,,	Huddersfield
200502	RODGER, J. . .	L/Cpl.	Kirkcaldy
92481	PEDGERS, R. . .	Pte.	Broughton
94915	ROMANS, S. . .	L/Cpl.	Staines
308843	RUDDOCK, A. J. .	Pte.	Barnsbury
200981	RUMP, J. H. . .	,,	Hackford
96759	RUSHIN, S. . .	,,	Tudsfield
306776	RUSLING, W. .	,,	Scunthorpe
305881	RUSSELL, A. J. .	,,	Weymouth
75236	RUSSELL, E. . .	,,	Sheffield
302282	RUSSELL, H. . .	,,	Glasgow
76686	RUTHERFORD, T. .	,,	Stirling
201445	RUTTER, H. M. .	,,	Cambridge
69808	SAMMOM, W. . .	Pte.	Bradford
109780	SANDFORD. W. J. .	,,	Worcester
304236	SANKEY, E. . .	,,	Warrington
91963	SAPSEAD, H. .	,,	Eccles
301687	SATTERSTAL, W. .	,,	Leeds
206108	SCAIVENER, S. B. .	,,	Nuneaton
91240	SCARLETT, E. H. .	,,	Stoken Church
91256	SCHOLEY, T. E. .	,,	Whitley Bridge
306578	SCOFIELD, W. .	L/Cpl.	Manchester
78684	SCOTHERN, B. .	Pte.	Sheffield
307925	SCOTLEY. H. L. .	,,	Mansfield
76594	SCOTT, H. . .	,,	Rushden
206124	SCOTT, M. C. . .	,,	Paisley
112815	SCOTT, S. H. . .	,,	Cambridge
200026	SCOTT, W. W. .	,,	Dundee
307981	SEAMAN, A. . .	,,	Accrington
305767	SEARLE, S. . .	Sergt.	Lostwithiel
93080	SELVAGE, J. . .	Pte.	Bow, E.
201227	SHAKESPEARE, A.	,,	Redditch
307991	SHANNON, J. . .	,,	Ecclefechan
201457	SHARP, F. G. .	Cpl.	Staverton
200246	SHARP, J. W. .	Pte.	Hambie
96717	SHAVE, A. D. . .	,,	New Béckton, E.

Number.	Name and Initials.	Rank.	Town of Residence.
306136	SHAWYER, C. E. .	Pte.	Isle of Wight
78670	SHEARD, W. D. .	,,	Dewsbury
78515	SHEFFIELD, E. .	L/Cpl.	Cleethorpes
91574	SHELFORD, H. J. .	Pte.	Stevenage
78969	SHERGOLD, W. .	,,	Wimborne
109589	SHREWSBURY, L. D.	,,	St. Albans
205169	SIFFLEET, A. L. .	Sergt.	Eastbourne
307373	SILLITOE, R. . .	Pte.	Wednesbury
200871	SIMMONS, A. J. .	Cpl.	Salisbury
40354	SIMMONS, L. . .	Pte.	Nottingham
92342	SIMPSON, J. P. .	,,	Bellywhiskers, Ireland
111137	SINCLAIR, R. . .	,,	Inverkeithing
305187	SKIRVING, W. R. .	,,	W. Hartlepool
111892	SLATE, W. . .	,,	Hornsey
76748	SLINGER, F. W. .	,,	Manchester
307615	SMEDLEY, H. F. .	,,	Loughborough
76357	SMITH, A. E. . .	Cpl.	Accrington
301437	SMITH, A. E. G. .	Pte.	Croydon
200450	SMITH, A. J. . .	,,	Newbury
308355	SMITH, A. J. . .	,,	Southampton
96578	SMITH, A. T. . .	,,	Hempstead
76103	SMITH, C. W. . .	Sergt.	Primsdown
94815	SMITH, E. S. . .	Pte.	Nottingham
206140	SMITH, F. C. . .	,,	Selsey
76210	SMITH, F. W. . .	,,	London, S.E.
200238	SMITH, G. . .	,,	Tunstan
77433	SMITH, H. . .	,,	Pagnell
301573	SMITH, H. J. . .	,,	Camberwell
201003	SMITH, L. . .	,,	Birmingham
111547	SMITH, N. . .	,,	Leeds
305003	SMITH, R. . .	,,	Cupar
92365	SMITH, T. . .	,,	Glasgow
78635	SMITH, T. R. . .	,,	Canning Town
94933	SMITH, W. . .	,,	Birmingham
95195	SNELL, R. . .	,,	Bradwinch
95163	SNELL, T. W. .	,,	Plymouth
109743	SONSTER, A. G. .	,,	Rugby
78372	SOUTH, J. W. . .	,,	Graffoe
306735	SOWESBY, W. .	,,	Scarborough
76152	SPICE, G. . .	L/Cpl.	Wandsworth
40220	SPREADBOROUGH, A.	Pte.	Bisley
200063	SQUIRE, A. J. .	Cpl.	Lynton
69531	SQUIRE, J. . .	Sergt.	Camberwell
307483	STANIFORD, P. .	Pte.	Rochester
301394	STANTON, W. .	Cpl.	Huddersfield

Number.	Name and Initials.	Rank.	Town of Residence.
205361	STANLEY, T. A.	Pte.	Cardiff
70125	STAPLES, W.	,,	Colchester
201993	STARK, J.	,,	Leith
201073	STARKEY, J. B.	,,	Nottingham
110045	STEEL, D.	,,	Glasgow
92437	STEWART, A..	,,	Glasgow
205282	STEWART, J..	,,	Errol
91925	STEWART, J. B.	,,	South Shields
76446	STICEL, D.	,,	Southsea
304608	STIDDARD, S. G.	,,	Bristol
206159	STIVRING, F. R.	,,	Sheffield
76451	STOBE, B. J. P.	,,	Walthamstow
305070	STODDART, W.	,,	Linlithgow
308709	STODDART, H.	,,	Nelson
301733	STOKES, G.	,,	Derry
306042	STOKOE, W. J. B.	,,	N. Washington
92634	STONE, H. S.	Cpl.	Holloway
78879	STONEBRIDGE, A. V.	Pte.	Colchester
301904	STORER, C. H.	,,	Old Rasford
306194	STRAUGHAN, T.	,,	Hetton-le-Hole
202051	STRUTHERS, G. J..	Cpl.	Hamilton
305525	STURGESS, A..	Pte.	Buckingham
201682	SUATT, C. A..	,,	Kilburn
76298	SUGGET, J. J.	,,	Durham
300450	SULLIVAN, T.	,,	New Kent Road, London
76293	SUMMERHILL, G.	,,	Cramlington
109620	SUMMERS, S..	,,	Aberfan
76915	SUMMOCKS, A. H. W.	,,	Camberwell
201876	SUTHERLAND, J.	,,	Edinburgh
305831	SUTTON, E. P.	,,	Portsmouth
305535	SUTTON, F. C.	,,	Melton
200985	SUTTON, G. W.	,,	Ebury Bridge, S.W
92713	SUTTON, T.	Sergt.	Newton Stewart
76051	SWIFT, A.	Pte.	Birmingham
92268	SYDNEY, E. G.	,,	Charwell
92958	TABON, A. J..	,,	Cherryhinton
307601	TACCHI, W. G.	,,	Hythe
76579	TAMER, W.	,,	Harlesden
77388	TARRY, J.	,,	Northampton
200411	TASSELL, E. W.	,,	Bedford Park
202005	TATE, E.	,,	Warkworth
304626	TATLOW, T.	,,	Haslingden
76610	TATTERSALL, J.	,,	Gateshead
306420	TAYLOR, C. B.	,,	Liverpool

Number.	Name and Initials.	Rank.	Town of Residence.
200970	TAYLOR, G.	Pte.	Oldham
92329	TAYLOR, G. S.	,,	Leith
309335	TAYLOR, H.	,,	Eastbourne
305220	TAYLOR, J.	,,	Glasgow
78777	TAYLOR, T.	,,	Kidderminster
308663	TEBBUTT, A. E.	,,	Kettering
78584	THELWELL, J.	,,	Mold
92937	THOMAS, A. G.	,,	Liverpool
205361	THOMAS, E. B.	,,	Cardiff
73068	THOMAS, G. H.	,,	Royston
201892	THOMAS, M. D.	,,	Glanamman
91745	THOMAS, T. H.	,,	Durham
206123	THOMPSON, J.	,,	Dunfermline
305661	THOMPSON, T. A.	,,	Glasgow
77162	THOMSON, J.	,,	Berwick
97058	THOMSON, L. C.	L/Cpl.	Stowmarket
112738	THORNLEY, A.	Pte.	Macclesfield
94829	THORPS, N. L.	,,	Fulham
200565	TIFFEN, H. J.	,,	Oswald
78250	TILKE, F. H.	,,	Pontypridd
307678	TILLMAN, H. J.	,,	Wandsworth
92398	TIPPER, W. H.	,,	Putney
110380	TIPPING, F. W.	,,	Nottingham
97041	TODD, G. P.	,,	Muswell Hill
78054	TODD, J. W.	,,	Bradford
77401	TOMLINSON, H.	,,	Leeds
75390	TOMSETT, A.	,,	Forest Row
78040	TOPLISS, A. E.	,,	Waltham
200875	TOWNSEND, C. E.	L/Cpl.	Huthwaite
75888	TRACE, E.	Pte.	Wellingborough
96827	TRIPLOW, H. G.	,,	Baldock
304481	TUCK, A. J.	,,	Putney
201594	TUDOR, L. G.	,,	Cardigan
92449	TUNNICLIFFE, C.	,,	Blackburn
75436	TWIGG, G. G.	,,	Tunstall
112819	TYER, J.	,,	Liverpool
91933	TYMAN, H.	,,	Stanley, S. O.
95104	TYRIE, W.	,,	Forfar
201202	TYSON, E.	,,	Barrow-in-Furness
97349	UNDERWOOD, E.	Pte.	Stoke-by-Clare
302728	UPFOLD, L. A.	,,	Redhill
76999	UPPINGTON, T. H. S.	,,	Bristol
308634	UTTON, B. A.	,,	Southend-on-Sea
94979	VAUGHAN, H.	Pte.	Kidderminster
77402	VEALL, G. F. W.	,,	Sheffield

ROLL OF HONOUR

Number.	Name and Initials.	Rank.	Town of Residence.
304488	VENTON, W. R. .	L/Cpl.	Bodmin
301160	VENTRIS, A. . .	Pte.	Southend-on-Sea
215285	VERNON, J. T. .	,,	Bishop's Castle
111721	VIVAST, J. T. . .	,,	Stourbridge
40288	VOICE, A. J. C. .	,,	Haslemere
206181	VOILE, M. C. . .	,,	Southborough
75674	WAINE, J. . .	Pte.	Islington
75274	WAINWRIGHT, J. C.	,,	Alfreton
301708	WAITE, B. . .	,,	Knaresborough
301822	WAKELAM, C. .	,,	Newport
110041	WALKER, D. .	L/Cpl.	Wishaw
75327	WALKER, J. . .	Pte.	Nottingham
200037	WALKER, W. .	L/Cpl.	Brechin
76820	WALKER, W. H. .	Pte.	Sheffield
70036	WALL, J. E. . .	Sergt.	Birmingham
205775	WALLACE, G. .	Pte.	Culsalmond
206183	WALLACE, H. . .	,,	Rugby
95213	WALLIS, G. E. .	,,	Hull
92127	WALLSGROVE, L. . .	C.S.M.	Leamington
308703	WALMSLEY, H. .	Pte.	Burnley
76279	WALTERS, A. .	,,	Walsall
307626	WARBURTON, D. P.	,,	Hyde
304265	WARD, H. V. C. .	,,	East Ham
78033	WARD, R. J. C. .	L/Cpl.	Westcliffe-on-Sea
78594	WARDEN, J. . .	Pte.	Nottingham
78978	WARRINGTON, F. S.	,,	Dudley Hill
76225	WATERS, C. W. .	,,	Kennington
307475	WATERS, E. H. .	,,	Tufnell Park
308733	WATKINS, A. .	,,	Pontypool
301324	WATKINS, A. J. .	L/Cpl.	Walthamstow
308249	WATKINS, J. . .	Pte.	Ipswich
76270	WATSON, L. . .	,,	Clapham, S.W
304649	WATSON, T. H. .	,,	London, N.
111424	WATTS, P. . .	,,	Eastleigh
78253	WEBB, E. W. . .	,,	Bournemouth
200262	WEBSTER, J. . .	,,	Leith
76860	WEEKS, J. . .	Sergt.	Glamorgan
206127	WEIR, J. D. . .	Cpl.	Leith
92589	WELLS, G. D. .	Pte.	Tottenham
40015	WELLS, J. C. . .	,,	Manchester
76015	WELSH, T. H. M. .	,,	Malvern
307734	WELSH, W. . .	,,	Kirkcaldy
76142	WEST, W. S. .	A/Sgt.	Putney
94931	WESTON, H. J. .	L/Cpl.	Upton-on-Severn
206151	WESTON, C. L. .	Pte.	Harrow

Number.	Name and Initials.	Rank.	Town of Residence.
201074	WHALE, H. . .	Pte.	Sheffield
95338	WHALE, W. E. .	,,	West Bromwich
307133	WHARTON, F. .	,,	Liverpool
78809	WHEDDON, A. H. .	,,	Woolwich
201722	WHELAN, J. .	,,	Liverpool
206163	WHITCOMBE, A. H. P.	Cpl.	Somerset
200865	WHITE, D. N. .	,,	Kenilworth
75003	WHITE, J. W. .	Pte.	Elchingham
78683	WHITE, R. A. .	,,	Thrapston
93482	WHITELEY, J. .	,,	Broughton
78583	WHITTARD, A. .	,,	Hackney
76374	WHITTINGHAM, H.	Cpl.	Brixton
91856	WHITTON, F. . .	Pte.	Ripon
112390	WHITWORTH, W. .	,,	Heywood
96841	WHORFE, J. A. .	,,	Brandon
91269	WIGFORD, C. W. .	,,	Kingston-on-Thames
76112	WILCOCKSON, J. K. M.	,,	Eastbourne
69447	WILD, G. F. . .	,,	Brixton
305952	WILDGOOSE, J. A. .	,,	Kingsley
76300	WILKIN, J. . .	,,	Glasgow
305908	WILKINS, E. G. .	,,	Oxford
306565	WILKINSON, A. .	Sergt.	Blackburn
305978	WILKINSON, B. J. .	Pte.	Canterbury
110274	WILKINSON, H. G. .	,,	Stockport
304652	WILKINSON, W. .	,,	London, W.
201211	WILKINSON, W. W.	,,	Leeds
202014	WILLIAMS, A. C. .	Cpl.	Penarth
205638	WILLIAMS, E. A. .	L/Cpl.	Leicester
709887	WILLIAMS, H. C. .	Pte.	Leintwardine
78546	WILLIAMS, R. .	,,	Churchtown
40149	WILLIAMS, W. C. .	,,	Dawlish
200788	WILLIAMS, W. G. .	L/Cpl.	Tylorstown
91250	WILLINGTON, H. .	Pte.	Wolverhampton
201249	WILLIS, B. B. .	,,	Ipswich
92187	WILLS, R. . .	,,	Perth
305798	WILLS, S. S. . .	,,	Portsmouth
306120	WILSON, A. G. .	,,	Ecclefechan
201277	WILSON, H. J. .	Sergt.	Stoke-on-Trent
70043	WILSON, J. . .	Pte.	Dalston
110383	WILSON, J. R. .	,,	Newcastle-on-Tyne
200340	WILSON, W. . .	,,	Leith
78047	WILSON, W. . .	L/Cpl.	Oldham
305526	WILSON, — . .	Sergt.	Beverley
96944	WILTON, J. W. .	Pte.	Biggleswade
304964	WINTER, D. .	A/Cpl.	Glasgow

ROLL OF HONOUR

Number.	Name and Initials.	Rank.	Town of Residence.
202003	WINWOOD, W. C.	Pte.	Pershore
40222	WISE, A. J.	,,	Woking
93103	WISHART, W.	,,	Scone
110336	WOLLAWAY, W.	,,	Doncaster
76059	WOOD, B.	L/Cpl.	Oldburgh
76836	WOOD, S.	Pte.	Knottingley
306591	WOOD, T.	Cpl.	Middlesbrough
206119	WOOD, W.	,,	Paisley
78509	WOODBURN, W.	Pte.	Ayr
301306	WOODS, J. C.	,,	Holloway
200988	WRAY, L. H.	,,	Nocton
201642	WRIGHT, A.	L/Cpl.	Leicester
75917	WRIGHT, A. F.	Cpl.	Clapham, S.W.
76918	WRIGHT, E. J.	Pte.	Worcester
205287	WRIGHT, G. E.	L/Cpl.	Spalding
92708	WRIGHT, W. M.	Pte.	Northampton
200260	WYLIE, D.	,,	Perth
206141	YALLOP, R. R.	,,	Norwich
75073	YOUNG, B. J.	,,	Wimbledon
5971	YARROW, E.	,,	Gateshead

Total of Other Ranks killed or died of wounds, 1107

INDEX TO HONOURS

OFFICERS

454

OTHER RANKS

HONOURS INDEX—OTHER RANKS

458

HONOURS INDEX—OTHER RANKS